W9-CDJ-922

Second Edition

UP AGAINST THE CORPORATE WALL

Modern Corporations and
Social Issues of the Seventies

S. PRAKASH SETHI

School of Business Administration
University of California, Berkeley

PRENTICE-HALL, INC., ENGLEWOOD CLIFFS, NEW JERSEY

Library of Congress Cataloging in Publication Data

Sethi, S. Prakash.
    Up against the corporate wall.

    Bibliography: p.
    1. Industry—Social aspects—United States—Case
studies. I. Title.
HD60.5.U5S47 1974   301.5′1   73-22486
ISBN 0-13-938233-X
ISBN 0-13-938225-9 (pbk.)

© 1974, 1971 by PRENTICE-HALL, INC., Englewood Cliffs, New Jersey

All rights reserved. No part of this book may be
reproduced in any form or by any means without
permission in writing from the publisher.

Printed in the United States of America

10 9 8 7 6 5 4 3 2 1

PRENTICE-HALL INTERNATIONAL, INC., *London*
PRENTICE-HALL OF AUSTRALIA, PTY. LTD., *Sydney*
PRENTICE-HALL OF CANADA, LTD., *Toronto*
PRENTICE-HALL OF INDIA PRIVATE LIMITED, *New Delhi*
PRENTICE-HALL OF JAPAN, INC., *Tokyo*

To
those "haves" and "have-nots" among us
who still have hopes
that when men of reason get together
they will plan the survival
and not the extinction
of the human race and of humanity
this book is affectionately dedicated.

CONTENTS

PREFACE TO THE SECOND EDITION

PREFACE

I
THE QUALITY OF LIFE

A.
CONSERVATION OF THE NATURAL ENVIRONMENT

Georgia-Pacific Corporation, Portland, Oregon

Redwood National Park Controversy   *3*

Pacific Gas & Electric Company, San Francisco

Attempt to Construct a Nuclear Power Plant at Bodega Bay   *23*

II
THE CHANGING NATURE OF GOVERNMENT AND BUSINESS RELATIONSHIPS

A.
POLITICS AND BUSINESS

The ITT Affair (A)

Influence of Big Business in Politics and Government: Antitrust Case Settlement and Campaign Contribution   *55*

B.
CORPORATIONS AND
THE UNITED STATES FOREIGN POLICY CONFLICTS

The ITT Affair (B)

Interference in the Chilean Presidential Elections   *102*

Coca-Cola and the Middle East Crisis   212

C.
INDIRECT/DIRECT USE OF
THE PRESIDENT'S EXECUTIVE AUTHORITY

The Steel Price Controversy

Kennedy-Johnson and the Discretionary Use of Presidential Power   218

D.
GOVERNMENT AND BUSINESS AS PARTNERS

The Supersonic Transport (SST)

A Case Study in Government-Industry Cooperation and the Determination of National Priorities   252

III
CORPORATE INTERESTS AND SOCIAL AND
ECONOMIC NEEDS OF ETHNIC MINORITIES

A.
SOCIAL AND ECONOMIC PRESSURES

Eastman Kodak Company (A), Rochester, New York

Conflict with a Minority Group—FIGHT   279

B.

DISCRIMINATION

Crown Zellerbach Corporation, San Francisco

Conflict with the Equal Employment Opportunity Clause of the Civil Rights Act, 1964   *301*

IV

CORPORATIONS, THEIR DEPENDENCIES, AND OTHER SOCIAL INSTITUTIONS

A.

CORPORATIONS AND THE STOCKHOLDERS

Securities and Exchange Commission
versus Texas Gulf Sulphur Company

Use of Material Information by Corporate Executives and Other "Insiders" in the Sale and Purchase of Company Stock for Personal Gain   *333*

B.

CORPORATIONS AND THE INDIVIDUAL

General Motors' Nadir, Ralph Nader

Corporate Economic Interests and Encroachment on an Individual's Privacy   *373*

Bethlehem Steel Company and the Woodroofe Incident

To What Extent Can a Corporation Control an Employee's Social and Political Activities?   *399*

Motorola v. Fairchild Camera

The Case of C. Lester Hogan et al.   *407*

C.

CORPORATIONS AND THE NEWS MEDIA

A.B.C. + I.T.T. $\underset{=}{?}$ Free Press   424

Eastman Kodak Company (B), Rochester, New York

Conflict with a Minority Group—FIGHT:
The Role of the News Media   452

D.

CORPORATIONS AND THE CHURCH

Eastman Kodak Company (C), Rochester, New York

Conflict with a Minority Group—FIGHT:
The Role of the Church   467

SELECTED BIBLIOGRAPHY   483

PREFACE TO THE SECOND EDITION

The basic nature of social conflict between corporations and certain segments of society has remained unchanged during the past three years. Conflict revolves around the society's changed expectations of business in general and large corporations in particular, on the one hand, and business's willingness and ability to modify its behavior to meet these expectations, on the other hand. Even where there is a meeting of minds between business and social elements on objectives, there are considerable differences of opinion as to who should do the job and how the costs should be shared.

There seems to be a sincere desire on the part of many businesses to attempt to attack various social problems for which they have rightly or wrongly been blamed. These efforts notwithstanding, the pace of the conflict seems to have accelerated recently and is manifested in many more directions—directions that were only vaguely discernible when the first edition was being prepared.

This second edition takes cognizance of these dimensions by including new case studies dealing with the activities of corporations in the areas of United States domestic policy, internal political affairs of foreign countries, ecology, and use of material inside information by corporate management for personal gain. In addition, where relevant, the case studies from the first edition have been brought up to date by incorporating the latest developments. Admittedly, some of the material from the first edition had to be dropped to keep the book to a manageable size. However, the core of the first edition has been retained, and I therefore hope that this edition will be more representative of the spectrum of business-society controversies.

Subsequent to the publication of the first edition, many readers and reviewers questioned the omission not only of success stories in business-society controversies but also of my analysis of the issues and recommended courses of action for business to follow. These exclusions were based on the following considerations:

1. The nature of success in dealing with business and social problems has been sporadic and inconsistent. Therefore, in two apparently similar situations, there is no guarantee that similar policies will be successful. No theoretical framework has yet been developed to understand the total phenomena in a manner that would yield consistent interpretation. Moreover, the nature of the problem is so complex and multifaceted that we are not sure that we have identified all the important variables—a necessary precondition to the development of a theoretical framework.

2. The instances of business failure to handle social controversies have been far greater in number and magnitude than the instances of success. Consequently, although we may not be able to say "what works," we are in a better position to say "what is not likely to work," based on our study of the failures.

3. Since learning is as much a function of the availability of data as it is of their interpretation, I have refrained from prejudicing the reader's mind by imposing my own interpretation. Instead, I have tried to provide the reader with an accurate picture of the particular incident; the sociopolitical environment in which the incident took place, which must be taken into account to understand the *what, how,* and *why* of the incident; and the viewpoints of the parties involved in as objective a manner as possible. The book provides the reader interested in doing further research or seeking the opinions of various experts with ample suggestions for additional reading that will help him to arrive at his own conclusions.

4. Although I have refrained from giving my own analysis and recommendations in the book, I have given considerable thought to the nature of these conflicts and to the precautions that business and other social groups could take to avoid them in the future. Analyses of specific case studies are presented in a teacher's manual, which is available on request from the publisher. My analysis of the general nature of social conflicts and possible approaches to their solution has been presented in various articles, which have since been collected and published (Dow Votaw and S. Prakash Sethi, *The Corporate Dilemma: Traditional Values and Contemporary Problems* [Englewood Cliffs, N.J.: Prentice-Hall, Inc., 1973]).

I am grateful to various educators and business executives who were kind enough to write me about their reaction to the first edition. Their concrete suggestions and constructive criticisms were greatly influential in determining the content of the second edition.

Many friends and associates assisted in the preparation of this book and gave generously of their time and ideas. Among them are Professor John Hogle of Golden Gate University, San Francisco, who coauthored "Securities and Exchange Commission versus Texas Gulf Sulphur Company," and Professors Michael Conant and Robert N. Katz, who clarified some legal points. The assistance of Mr. Hamid Etemad and Ms. Wendy Quinones in researching parts of this book is greatly appreciated.

I also wish to express my thanks to the Institute of Business and Economic Research, University of California, Berkeley, for providing partial financial support for research and secretarial services. In particular, thanks are due to Mrs. Nancy Blumenstock for copyediting and to Mrs. Ellen McGibbon and Mrs. Betty Kendall for their typing of the various drafts of the book.

S. PRAKASH SETHI
University of California
Berkeley, California

PREFACE

As the United States enters the seventies and the decades beyond, it carries a plethora of new problems and social conflicts that have added to the nation's rhetoric. These include the protection of our environment by restricting both the amount of pollution and the amount of destruction, the concern for social justice, the search for relevance in our work and play, the protection of individual rights from abrogation by large institutions—public and private, and the reordering of national priorities.

Most of these problems have been with us for quite some time, but during the past ten years a variety of factors has brought them new importance:

1. The population mix has changed and a large segment is now composed of people born in the postdepression era, who are not haunted by the fear of scarcity, are not motivated by the specter of ever-increasing consumption, and are not willing to accept without question a system whose primary concerns are based on economic rationality.

2. A communications explosion, especially of television, has made millions of people aware of the inequities in social justice, the differences between the "haves" and the "have-nots," and the frustration and anger caused by social and economic deprivation.

3. A benign neglect of the problems of pollution and the exploitation of natural resources without regard to their effect on our environment have brought about a dangerous situation which cannot be ignored. Issues become salient to the public by personal experience, and the deterioration of the environment can no longer be hidden or wished away.

4. Economic, social, and political institutions have increasingly become less responsive to the changing needs of their constituents, leading the dissatisfied members of society to conclude that their grievances

cannot be redressed without a restructuring of social institutions and a reordering of national priorities.

Another remarkable change has been the emergence of large business corporations as the main culprits, in the eyes of the public, for major social ills. In this context, the large business corporation has assumed a place equal to, if not higher than, that of the big government as the villain. The corporations have been accused of creating "values" that are highly materialistic and thus undermine the normative values of the "good life." They have been accused of polluting the environment for their own financial gains, undermining the individual intellectual activity and creativity of the human mind by trivializing its work and achievement; bureaucratizing a large part of human activities and standardizing products, culture, and performance to the lowest common denominator of economic efficiency; exercising considerable authority—along with the Congress and the Pentagon—on the prosperity or decline of various communities and their inhabitants; sapping the political vitality of the middle class; and contributing to the alienation of faceless masses from the democratic processes.

The ills of the society cannot solely be attributed to large business corporations. Those who loudly accuse the corporations of prostituting the physical, social, and political environment cannot escape part of the blame for they also share in the ill-gotten gains of the corporations. However, the corporations are responsible because of their close identity with the economic goals of society. Their loud disclaimers notwithstanding, corporations have not given consumers "what they want," because the selection processes of consumers are determined by the number of alternatives available to them and by their ability to evaluate the alternatives: both these factors are considerably influenced by the corporations. The large size of individual corporations and their control, individually and collectively, of the nation's productive facilities make it difficult to believe that they are passive instrumentalities subject to the control of market mechanisms.

It is therefore understandable that segments of the population have increasingly resorted to confrontation tactics in their efforts to involve corporations in activities that are nonprofit oriented and might very well force these corporations to offer new rationales for their activities, change their manner of operation, and even increase the cost of doing business.

The corporations have to some extent recognized their partial immunity from competition, their increased economic and social power, and their responsibility for contributing to a better community life within which they must exist. However, this recognition has come hesitantly, in insufficiently small doses, invariably as partial cure rather than as preventive measure, and above all, only if it did not hurt the firm's profitability. Thus corporations have insisted on complete independence in determining products and profits, have fought measures of public control in pollution and other areas as economically prohibitive, and have demanded tax and other incentives for going into "nonprofit" activities. The emphasis has been on measuring the effect of these "nonprofit" activities on the profit potential of the corporation rather than on evaluating the effect of their "for profit" activities on the larger social goals. It is like allowing one department of a large company to exploit all the other departments to increase its own profitability.

The results have been predictable and disappointing. During the past few years business corporations have started, jointly and individually, a host of programs in community help—urban renewal, minority hiring, beautification, pollution control, communication with students—but their success, taken in the aggregate and in relation to their capacity, and barring a few isolated instances, has been either negligible or negative.

Conflicts between large corporations and other segments of society are likely to be intensified because neither the corporations nor other ruling members of the establishment seem willing to perceive these changes or willing to take bolder steps to revitalize the system. Their efforts are still directed at putting down brush fires and repairing occasional leaks to make the system work in its present form. As Neil Chamberlain pointed out in "The Life of the Mind in the Firm" (*Daedalus,* Winter 1969):

> It is still considered a high economic virtue that our major corporations behave like somewhat softened, but scrimping Scrooges or modest, but misanthropic misers—whose actions are governed only by the test of whether they are efficient in adding to a revenue stream and whose only purposes are limited dispersal to a limited stockholder clientele and reinvestment to maintain or augment the profit flow.
>
> . . . The argument is concerned with the standards that apply to the conduct of those organizations which give our society its special character. If our corporations were wholly government-owned, but still applied only the profit efficiency test to their operations, the result would be the same. . . . There is much to be said for leaving control over our giant corporations in private hands—diffusion of discretion and power is a value not to be given up lightly—if we can broaden the standard by which we judge their activity, if we can free them from a test of efficiency more relevant to the past than to the present.

The objective of this book is to expose the student, through a series of case studies involving business corporations, to a variety of problems that are increasingly becoming the prime concern of both business and society. It is aimed at developing in the reader a sensitivity to the issues involved, an awareness of the complexity of the motives of various parties, and a familiarity with the success and failure of their strategies and tactics. The areas covered can broadly be divided into: business and the quality of life, business and other social institutions, business and the community, business and the individual, business and government, military industrial complex, and business and foreign policy.

Case studies were selected on the basis of their timeliness and their ability to bring out as many facets of the problem as possible. I have tried to provide equal depth in every topic covered, but because of the difficulty in gathering data I might not have been uniformly successful. I have also tried to make the material as factual and objective as possible so as not to bias the reader with my own opinions and prejudices.

This book is primarily designed for executive development programs and for readers interested in business and society, business and public policy, business and government, and management policy. The issues involved are complex and of broad social import, and the case studies are somewhat long because they cover many facets of the conflicts and parties involved.

This book would not have been possible without the cooperation of many corporations and their executives, who generously contributed their time and information. However, the responsibility for material included in the cases and for errors of omission and commission is strictly my own. Thanks are especially due to Allen-Bradley Company, Bank of America, Crown Zellerbach Corporation, Dow Chemical Company, Eastman Kodak Company, Fairchild Camera and Instrument Corporation, and Motorola, Incorporated. Chandler Publishing Company graciously permitted the use of copyright material from my book, *Business Corporations and the Black Man*. A debt of gratitude is due also to Professor Ivar Berg (Columbia University), Professor Michael Conant (University of California), Professor Rick Pollay (University of British Columbia), Professor Lee E. Preston (State University of New York), and Professor Dow Votaw (University of California) for their valuable comments in the preparation of this book.

In addition to my research assistant, Michael Hawkins, other graduate students contributed in varying degrees, especially Peter Stoppello, Norbert Schaefer, and Rodney Gully. Their assistance is gratefully acknowledged. I also want to thank my editor, Mrs. Jan Seibert, who contributed greatly to the readability of the manuscript, and Patricia Murphy, who typed it in many drafts. Ackowledgments are also due to the School of Business Administration and to the Institute of Business and Economic Research, University of California, Berkeley, for typing and clerical assistance in the preparation of the manuscript.

And finally, I am grateful to my wife, Donna, who in the months immediately preceding and following our marriage encouraged me with affection and helped me with constructive criticism by reading the various drafts of the manuscript.

S. Prakash Sethi
Berkeley, California

I
THE QUALITY
OF LIFE

A.

CONSERVATION OF
THE NATURAL ENVIRONMENT

Georgia-Pacific Corporation,
Portland, Oregon

Redwood National Park Controversy

When you've seen one redwood tree, you've seen them all.

Ronald Reagan,
Governor of California

In September 1964 the National Park Service of the U.S. Department of the Interior completed a survey of the redwood region of Northern California.[1] The survey was made in an attempt to assess the remaining stock of coast redwood *(Sequoia sempervirens),* the need for its further preservation, and the possible establishment of a redwood national park. The Park Service found that 85 percent of the original coast redwood forests had been logged, mostly since 1900. Only 2.5 percent of the original stock was preserved in state parks. The survey estimated that if the remaining old-growth redwoods were not preserved they would, at present logging rates, be completely gone in thirty years. George B. Hertzog, Jr., director of the National Park Service, stated in the foreword that

[1] U.S., Congress, Senate, Report 641, 90th Cong., 1st sess., October 12, 1967.

"on June 25, 1964, a meeting was held with President Johnson to brief him on the progress of the study. The President . . . requested the Secretary of the Interior to formulate recommendations for his consideration." [2] This study proved to be a major catalyst in the reaction that was to result eventually in the formation of a redwood national parkland and in the controversy that surrounded its creation.[3]

A flood of legislation dealing with the establishment of a redwood park was begun. Proposals ranged from the 90,000-acre plan favored by the Sierra Club, and introduced by several senators and congressmen, to the 39,264-acre proposal transmitted to Congress by the secretary of the interior as the administration's recommendation and introduced as S. 2962 by Senator Thomas Kuchel of California. All interested parties were agreed that a park should be established, but the controversy raged over questions of where and how large it should be. The park proposed in S. 2962 was primarily located in the north unit on Mill Creek in Del Norte County, with a small 1,600-acre strip along Redwood Creek in the south unit in Humboldt County. The 90,000-acre proposal consisted of large acquisitions in both the north unit and the south unit. The private lands of the north unit were primarily owned by Miller-Rellim Lumber Company and Simpson Timber Company. The south unit lands were held by Arcata Redwood Company, Simpson Timber Company, and Georgia-Pacific Corporation (G-P).

WHY GEORGIA-PACIFIC OPPOSED THE ESTABLISHMENT OF NATIONAL REDWOOD PARK

The lumber companies wanted as small a park as possible, preferably containing little more land than was already preserved in existing state parks, so that their commercial operations would be unchanged. Georgia-Pacific put forth the following reasons for this position. (1) The "park-like" redwoods had already been saved. More than 100,000 acres were preserved in state parks and the nation did not need to save more. The

---

[2] "The Redwoods: A National Opportunity for Conservation and Alternatives for Action," report prepared by the National Park Service, U.S. Department of the Interior, under a grant provided by the National Geographic Society, September 1964, p. 3.

[3] In a personal communication, a spokesman for G-P stated: "If the Park Service report failed to indicate the true park quality redwoods were almost entirely protected and that the remainder of the redwoods still not harvested were quite ordinary forests, the report was grossly misleading . . ." This was one of the basic issues through the battle. To put it another way, the great redwoods the public really cared about were flatlands along creek beds where the largest and most unique are located. The vast acreage of ordinary commercial redwoods contains specimens that are generally younger and smaller and are situated on slopes.

expenditure of public funds for the acquisition of more redwood land would be a misuse. (2) The redwoods that existed on commercial lands were not of parklike quality. Existing groves of that quality were already in the state parks. (3) In any event, the existence of the redwoods was not threatened because lumber companies were reseeding and converting to sustained-yield practices.

G-P's position is further understood in the light of some of the company's background. Georgia-Pacific as an organization has exhibited fantastic growth. An article in *Dun's Review* cites the company's "seven-fold growth in a scant ten years." [4] Much of the credit, the article says, was due to Owen Cheatham, then G-P's chairman, who had taken it from a company largely dependent upon lumber to a diversified corporation with over 250 products. This transition was made by Cheatham's adroit use of debt leverage and the company's unique circumstances. He first used long-term debt to acquire timberland in an industry that was rapidly consolidating. This debt was also used to diversify the company into manufacturing, thus giving it an outlet for its raw materials.

G-P pioneered several industry trends. It was the first to use technological breakthroughs that made pulp production a major factor in the wood products industry. With this technology in mind, it was the first to buy land in the southern United States for timber production. But neither of these moves could have been made without long-term debt financing, and this debt could not have been possible without the unique advantages of the lumber industry. Some of these advantages are mentioned in the *Dun's Review* article—"tax advantages that accrue to the timber grower, depletion allowances that enable him to deduct the cost of his timber from his sales prices before paying taxes, and the capital gains tax that applies to all profits from timber." The result of these advantages is that while most corporations pay an average 48 percent tax, G-P in 1964, with 20 percent of its operations in lumber, paid a 34.4 percent tax on its profits. Giving further credit for the company's performance, the article states that "it is because of its first rate management team, not because of one man alone, that G-P ranks as one of the most skillfully run companies in the country." The article concludes, "But however expert its management, there is no questioning the fact that timberlands are still the true source of G-P's prosperity. For it is on timber that the company's three great weapons—its high borrowing ability, its low tax rate, and its spectacular cash flow are based."

G-P's unique organizational situation was not the only reason for its position on the redwood park. Resistance to the removal of private lands from commercial timber production for park purposes was strengthened

[4] "Second Growth at Georgia-Pacific," *Dun's Review,* May 1965, p. 48.

by the conditions that prevailed in the timber industry, especially in the redwood industry, which was consolidating and converting to pulp production. The following testimony by C. Davis Weyerhaeuser, retired from the Weyerhaeuser Corporation but still chairman of the board of Arcata Redwood Company, indicates the situation in the redwood region:

> We are opposed to the removal or withdrawal of any further redwood-producing lands from redwood production. . . . We have a selfish reason. Because from a marketing standpoint there is a limited amount of redwood being placed on the market. Our promotional expenses are consequently very high. And when a market is thin, people tend to lose interest in the product. And I am afraid that if a substantial producer of redwood is removed from the market, we might have real difficulty selling our product.[5]

Weyerhaeuser Corporation and U.S. Plywood closed their plants in Humboldt County in 1966. In the ten-year period from 1952 to 1962, 110 mills in Del Norte and Humboldt counties ceased operations. However, G-P recently invested over $50 million in a new redwood pulp plant, and Simpson Timber invested almost $20 million in a similar enterprise.

In addition to conversion to pulp production, the redwood industry was making the transition to sustained-yield operations. According to the National Park Service study, new growth would equal cut growth by 1985.[6] Second-growth redwood grows fast but matures slowly. It is inferior to old growth for lumber, but it is ideally suited to pulp production. To make the transition as easy as possible, the lumber companies needed their old-growth lands. Although G-P had total holdings of several million acres, the loss of several thousand acres in the redwood region jeopardized the profitability of operations in that area. The following testimony by William J. Moshofsky, assistant to the chairman of G-P, indicates what the effect of the park might be on G-P's operations:

> *Mr. Johnson:* Mr. Moshofsky, if the large park in the Sierra Club plan were to be adopted by the Congress of the United States, you stated in your statement you would liquidate . . .
>
> *Mr. Moshofsky:* That is correct. We would not be able . . .
>
> *Mr. Johnson:* (continuing) Humboldt County.

[5] U.S., Congress, Senate, Subcommittee on Parks and Recreation of the Committee on Interior and Insular Affairs, *Hearings on S. 1370, S. 514* and *S. 1526,* 90th Cong., 1st sess., 1967, p. 250.
[6] "The Redwoods," p. 23.

Mr. Moshofsky: That is correct. We would not be able to continue.

Mr. Johnson: How many employees do you have in Humboldt County at the present time?

Mr. Moshofsky: 1,400.

Mr. Johnson: 1,400 people. You operate how many facilities?

Mr. Moshofsky: We operate a relatively new kraft pulpmill, the redwood sawmill in Samoa, that is across the bay from Eureka, another sawmill at Big Lagoon, a plywood plant, a stud mill plus, of course, our woods operations.

Mr. Johnson: If Senate bill 2515 were to be adopted, what effect would that have on your company's operations in Humboldt County?

Mr. Moshofsky: It would have an impact but not nearly as serious as the Sierra Club 90,000 acre proposal. The big problem is that every acre of old-growth mature timber that is taken from our operations will make it more difficult for us to make a transition from old-growth type of operation to a second growth. In other words, we are waiting for these stands of second growth to come up to enough maturity to process effectively in our present operations, and every acre that you remove from this old-growth base makes it more difficult and it is hard to project exactly what would happen.[7]

SUPPORTERS OF A LARGE REDWOOD PARK: CONSERVATION ORGANIZATIONS

The proposals for a large redwood park faced strong opposition from the lumber industry, yet they received strong support from conservation groups and organizations. The establishment of a redwood national park had long been a goal of conservation organizations. In reviewing the history of preservation of the coast redwoods, the National Park Service cited the efforts of the Save-the-Redwoods League, a private conservation organization founded in 1918 and supported primarily by funds from the Rockefeller Foundation. The league's activities are noteworthy not only for their effectiveness but also for the manner in which they achieved their objectives. The league performed the delicate task of reaching conservation goals without alienating, and in fact often by cooperating with, private business interests. The National Park Service study quotes the following statement about the league:

[7] U.S., Congress, House, Subcommittee on Parks and Recreation of the Committee on Interior and Insular Affairs, *Hearings on H.R. 1311 and Related Bills,* 90th Cong., 2d sess., April 16 and 18, 1968, p. 487.

The Save-the-Redwoods League has done excellent work, not alone in the purchase of redwood areas and in the development of the park project in northern California, but in furnishing evidence that an organization of this character can secure the widest cooperation of the agencies of the state and nation, including both the nature lovers and the men of business concerned with lumber operations. I am sure that the Save-the-Redwoods League has the respect and confidence of the people.[8]

As of January 1964, 102,689 acres were preserved in twenty-eight redwood state parks. Of this total 48,383 acres were estimated to be virgin-growth redwood. These lands represented approximately $19 million, of which nearly $10 million was donated through the Save-the-Redwoods League.[9] The only thing that had consistently escaped the league was the establishment of a redwood national park of worthwhile size and stature.

The Sierra Club, however, emerged as the leading park proponent in the redwood national park controversy. In 1963, prior to the National Park Service study, the Sierra Club published *The Last Redwoods,* a book in its Exhibit Format series, which eloquently presented the case for preservation of the coast redwoods. In 1965 the club designated five major conservation issues as prime objectives. Among these was the establishment of a redwood national park. The club's aim was to establish as large a park as possible, preserving and protecting in ecological units as much old-growth acreage as possible. It favored a park consisting of redwood groves in both a north unit along Mill Creek in Del Norte County and a south unit along Redwood Creek in Humboldt County. The Sierra Club considered the park a now-or-never proposition. Repeated efforts over the past century had failed to establish a redwood national park, and National Park Service estimates indicated that the remaining virgin redwoods not already preserved would be completely gone in thirty years. The club repeatedly took the position that what could be rescued today, this hour, this very minute was the most that could ever be saved.

The philosophy and objectives of the Sierra Club are fundamentally preservationist. In the words of David Brower, then the club's executive director:

The Sierra Club owes its beginnings to one of America's most famous naturalists—John Muir. In 1892 he founded the club in order to make certain that wilderness and wildlands would continue to exist in our civilization. . . .

[8] "The Redwoods," p. 28.
[9] *Ibid.*

However, even John Muir could not fully realize the tremendous demands that the 20th century would be making on the remaining wilderness areas. Already many of the most magnificent natural areas have been lost forever—all in the name of "progress.". . . That is why the Sierra Club has adopted . . . "not blind opposition to progress, but opposition to blind progress". . . as its motto.[10]

To achieve its objectives the organization researched the complex issues involved in the establishment of the park, and promulgated information to club members, political figures, and the general public. The club's 90,000-acre proposal was presented to several congressmen and was first introduced in October 1965. In its early attempts to mobilize public opinion in support of the park, the Sierra Club had not singled out any of the lumber companies for criticism. But there was clearly a fight on between the lumber companies and the Sierra Club. The club decried industry practices and the companies' opposition to park proposals, and it saw the lumber industry as the major pressure in the failure of previous efforts to establish a redwood national park. In the October 1965 issue of the *Sierra Club Bulletin,* in an article entitled "The Redwood National Park—a Forest of Stumps?," the club president, Edgar Wayburn, made the following plea for passage of a park bill before Congress adjourned:

Consider what has happened in the past two and one-half years, since the National Park Service and the National Geographic Society started their study of the redwoods. Reliable statistics suggest an increase of 34 percent in logging of virgin redwoods. In recent testimony before the California State Park Commission, it was stated that in Humboldt County, over 50 percent of privately owned virgin timber that was present in 1963 had now been logged off. In boosting its output, the redwood industry has razed some of the last and finest river flats. It has invaded almost the last pristine watersheds. And it has laid bare many partially timbered slopes.

This logging has respected neither the proposed national park boundaries nor the irreplaceable values—both scenic and scientific—that it has destroyed. The consequent loss to park potential is obvious and staggering.

Because of the vast extent of past logging in the redwood region, it has been necessary already to include cutover lands within the boundaries of the proposed national park. But Congress hardly can be expected to appropriate millions of dollars for a forest newly

[10] David Brower, Sierra Club promotional literature.

bereft of its trees. If cutting on the present scale and in the present random pattern continues, it is obvious that chances for an adequate Redwood National Park will become progressively more bleak. As members of the redwood industry have said, in five years there won't be much worth worrying about.

It can still be hoped that the redwood industry will cooperate; failing this, the use of condemnation or of a moratorium on cutting may be essential. Otherwise we may leave to future generations only a memory of another national park—and a forest of stumps! [11]

The club then moved outside its own immediate membership to mobilize public opinion in favor of the park on a larger scale. On December 17, 1965, the Sierra Club took out a full-page ad in five newspapers with the headline "An open letter to President Johnson on the last chance to really save the redwoods."

THE LEGISLATIVE STRUGGLE

On February 23, 1966, Secretary of the Interior Stewart L. Udall transmitted the administration's 39,264-acre, $60 million proposal to Congress. In doing so, he said that he "wanted to pick a park and not a fight." [12] It appeared that Secretary Udall's strong 1963 support of the creation of a redwood national park, expressed when he wrote the foreword to *The Last Redwoods,* had diminished. The Sierra Club, disappointed with the overall size and location of the administration's proposal, speculated that lumber interests were lobbying strongly in Washington and getting results. The club stepped up its efforts.

The first hearings on the park legislation (S. 2962) were held in Crescent City, California, in June 1966 and in Washington, D.C., in August 1966. During these hearings the Sierra Club raised the question of cutting in the prospective park areas. On September 7 a moratorium on cutting in proposed park areas was agreed to by the Senate and five lumber companies. According to Congressman Don H. Clausen, of the First District in California, which includes the redwood region, "the action removes the need

---

[11] Edgar Wayburn, *Sierra Club Bulletin,* October 1965. In a personal communication William J. Moshofsky, assistant to the chairman of G-P, stated: "We strongly disagree with and question the accuracy of the statements attributed to Dr. Wayburn particularly without presenting the material correcting the misstatements. We consider these statements libelous. While they may be privileged in a plea to Congress, we do not think the privilege extends to reprinting. At the least there should be an indication that what they said was considered by others to be most inaccurate."

[12] *Sierra Club Bulletin,* August 1967, p. 8.

for the rather drastic and somewhat punitive bill recently proposed by the President and Secretary Udall." [13] Following is the text of a telegram sent to Senator Kuchel of California by Gray Evans, vice-president of Georgia-Pacific, agreeing to the moratorium:

It has been the long standing policy of Georgia-Pacfic Corporation that the special interests of the Corporation, its employees and their families must be sacrificed if the national interest requires it. We earnestly believe however, that this national interest must be clearly established before such a sacrifice is required. Under pending national park proposals Georgia-Pacific Corporation could lose as much as 75 percent of its timber reserves in the redwood region. This loss would jeopardize our entire industrial complex in Humboldt County representing 1500 jobs and an annual payroll of $8 million.

Our opposition to the further acquisition of privately held lands for redwood park purposes is a matter of record with you and the Congress. All of the park-like groves are already preserved in existing parks or are voluntarily set aside by industry awaiting public acquisition. Existing redwood parks are largely unused and undeveloped. Most of our Redwood Creek holdings are commercial timber lands which are unsuitable for national park purposes.

Nevertheless, we recognize that some people believe it is in the public interest to establish a national redwood park on our land and that they are concerned that our harvesting operations might impair the alleged park-like quality of the land pending Congressional action. We wish to let you know Georgia-Pacific Corporation is and always has been willing to work out any reasonable adjustment in our harvesting program on our redwood lands in order to minimize cutting in proposed redwood park areas. We believe a one-year period would give everyone sufficient time to study carefully the needs for more redwood parks and the suitability or unsuitability of our land for such parks.[14]

The first hearings on redwood park legislation brought out a number of difficult and complex obstacles to the creation of a park. The question of whether any of the lumber companies would be forced to liquidate their operations was of major concern to the congressmen responsible for formulating the park boundaries. As a result, the problems and conditions of the lumber industry in the redwood region were thoroughly aired. In addition

[13] *Humboldt Times-Standard* (California), September 8, 1966.
[14] Gray Evans, vice-president, G-P, telegram to Senator Thomas Kuchel, September 7, 1966.

the impact on the local area was given consideration. The issue was whether the unemployment and loss of tax revenues caused by establishment of the park would be offset by increased tourist trade and in-lieu payments made to the counties. The Sierra Club maintained that the timber economy was unstable and that the area needed the diversification that a park and tourist economy would provide. G-P claimed that the short tourist season made park projections overly optimistic.[15] It pointed to recent investment as a sign of stability and emphasized the impact of the loss of timber-producing lands on its ability to continue operations.

Anticipating these obstacles, the National Park Service asked Arthur D. Little, Inc., to prepare reports on the projected impact of the creation of a park on Del Norte and Humboldt counties.[16] Both reports indicated that both counties were largely dependent on the timber industry, but employment was already declining. This decline was due primarily to three factors: (1) depletion of old-growth timber, (2) reduction of timber cut to sustainable levels, and (3) automation. The reports also indicated, however, that the removal of lands for park use would result in further short-term decline in employment until the early 1970s. In addition to the problem of overall employment was the problem of labor mobility. Some of the people employed in the lumber industry would have to find work in the tourist industry. As one industry employee put it, "When you have to tell a lumberjack that he's out of a job because of the park, it doesn't help much to tell him that in five years he'll be able to get a job selling redwood burls to tourists."

Further complications were brought out in the hearings. The land acquisition procedures posed difficult problems. Congress had recently encountered tremendous problems in the acquisition of land at Point Reyes and wanted to avoid the same situation in the redwood region. Once plans for land acquisition are announced, land prices increase tremendously. The assurance of funding through the use of land-and-water-fund revenues was in doubt. Not only was it not clear how much land could be acquired for a given sum, it was not even clear how much could be allocated for acquisition.

In addition it was not clear whether the state of California was willing to contribute the three state parks in the region for inclusion in a national

[15] According to a G-P spokesman, the company's statement of a short tourist season "had its foundation in Chamber of Commerce figures and an economic study done for the Redwood Park and Recreation Committee by Dr. H. DeWayne Kreager, an independent industrial economist based in Seattle." It was following his study that the National Park Service decided to hire Arthur D. Little, Inc., to do one for them. Kreager and Little were in wide disagreement on a number of points.

[16] A. D. Little, Inc., "The Impact of the Proposed Redwood National Park on the Economy of Del Norte County," Report to the National Park Service, March 1966; and "The Economic Impact of Possible Additions to a Redwood National Park in Humboldt County," April 1967.

park. Governor Edmund G. Brown had strongly supported the establishment of a park but was seeking an exchange of U.S. Forest Service lands in return for the state parks, an arrangement that the Forest Service opposed. Ronald Reagan, in the 1966 California gubernatorial campaign, was reported to have said, "When you've seen one redwood tree, you've seen them all." When he was elected in November, the chances of including the California parks looked even more doubtful.

All the problems in establishing a redwood park seemed to favor those interested in a small park, and after the moratorium on cutting was agreed to, the Sierra Club once again increased its efforts. When the club members realized that Congress was unlikely to appropriate sufficient funds for a 90,000-acre park, they substituted a 72,000-acre, $100 million proposal, although still advocating the desirability of their original plan. They continued to supply information to members of Congress, answers to industry arguments, and solutions to the problems raised.

On January 25, 1967, the Sierra Club resumed its full-page ad campaign in four major newspapers. The ad read in part: "History will think it strange that America could afford the Moon and $4 billion airplanes while a patch of primeval redwoods—not too big for a man to walk through in a day—was considered beyond its means." The ad contained bar charts of the redwoods that once existed, those yet uncut, and the portion that the park would save. The ad also contained coupons to be sent to G-P, Arcata Redwood Company, and Governor Ronald Reagan of California expressing support for the park, and readers were urged to write to their congressmen and the president.

On February 24, and again on July 1, 1967, the club placed an ad with the headline: "Mr. President: There is one great forest of redwoods left on earth; but the one you are trying to save isn't it. . . . Meanwhile they are cutting down both of them." [17]

On April 17 and 18, 1967, the Senate held further hearings on the park bills before it, and in June and July the House held its first hearings on park legislation. William J. Moshofsky of G-P made the following statement to the House Parks and Recreation Subcommittee, reasserting the company's position on the park:

In summation of our position, Mr. Chairman, Georgia-Pacific (1) Does not oppose creation of a Redwood National Park if that should be the decision of the U.S. Congress. (2) Georgia-Pacific does most strongly oppose the taking of privately owned commercial forest land for inclusion in a Redwood National Park. This has been our position

17 *The New York Times*, January 25, 1967.

throughout this controversy. We believe it is a justifiable position and one truly in the national interest.[18]

The company also began to put forth this position in letters responding to letters and coupons it received and in a full-page ad responding to the Sierra Club ad.

On August 10, 1967, the Committee on Interior and Insular Affairs met in executive session and ordered a clean bill, S. 2515, to be reported. S. 2515 authorized a two-unit, 66,384-acre park at an estimated cost of $76 million. The committee stated the following advantages of the new bill:

> The committee, after considering all of the many proposals, accepted S. 2515 introduced by Senators Jackson, Kuchel and Bible. In the judgment of the committee, S. 2515 is superior to S. 1370 [the administration proposal] as introduced. It saves more of the remaining unprotected superlative stands of virgin redwoods. It spreads the impact of land acquisition over four companies, rather than concentrating on only one company's holdings. If enacted, as introduced, S. 1370 probably would have forced the largest employer in Del Norte County out of business. The committee believes that no company which has a genuine interest in staying in the redwood timber business will be obliged to cease operations as a result of the enactment of S. 2515.
>
> The committee believes that any initial adverse impact of the creation of the park on the local economy will be temporary. S. 2515 will shift the bulk of the land acquisition to Humboldt County, which has a much sounder tax base than Del Norte County. Seventy-one percent of the land in Del Norte County is already owned by the State or Federal Government. The bulk of the land acquisition program authorized by S. 2515 is in Humboldt County where only 21 percent of the land is owned by the State and Federal Governments.[19]

On September 5, 1967, the *Humboldt Times-Standard* reported that the moratorium on cutting had been extended. The paper also reported the following comment on the possibility of swift congressional action:

> In asking for extension of the moratorium, [Senators] Jackson and Kuchel told the companies they expected the Senate to act on legisla-

---

[18] U.S., House, *Hearings,* p. 485.
[19] *Ibid.,* p. 1.

tion to authorize a Redwood National Park before adjourning for the year.

However, Chairman Wayne H. Aspinall, D. Colo., of the House Interior Committee has said he has "no desire" to take up redwood national park legislation this year and his committee has not yet acted on the bill.[20]

On November 1, 1967, S. 2515 passed the Senate by a vote of seventy-seven to six. On November 16 the Sierra Club charged in a press release that "the Georgia-Pacific Corporation has begun logging operations in a key part of the Redwood National Park approved recently by the Senate. He [Edgar Wayburn] said the operation was started before the expiration of a moratorium agreement."[21] The *Humboldt Times-Standard* reported on November 24 that Georgia-Pacific claimed that "the boundary line on the map is 600 feet wide when enlarged to ground size. With the knowledge we have now, we've been falsely accused."[22] To try to clarify things further, the paper reported the following events:

June 1967—G-P advised Senator Jackson that "in order to avoid irrevocable damage to our long-range plans it would be necessary to resume operations in some of these areas."

July 1967—Rock was placed on road L-2-2.

August 1967—Cutting started in the L-2-2 area, above MacArthur and Elam Creeks.

September 1, 1967—G-P president R. B. Pamplin wired Senator Jackson, extending the cutting "moratorium" 60 days. "This does not mean that at the end of the period the timber involved would be harvested," Pamplin said. "It simply means that intelligent management calculated to maintain redwood forests forever on all the land would be put back into effect."

October 26, 1967—Hauling logs in the area started, including right-of-way trees cut prior to February 1965.

November 1, 1967—S. 2515 passed the Senate, 77–6.

---

20 *Humboldt Times-Standard,* September 6, 1967.
21 *San Francisco Chronicle* (California), November 16, 1967.
22 *Humboldt Times-Standard,* November 24, 1967. Mr. Moshofsky further comments: "It was proven to the satisfaction of the National Park Supervisor from Crater Lake and others we were not in the park area approved by the Senate, indeed had a minimum safety factor of about 1,500 feet, but they declined to make this public. In any event, a clear detail map never was supplied to us in spite of repeated requests to the National Park Service."

November 9, 1967—G-P forester A. H. Merrill received a copy of the map specified in the park bill (NP-RED-6112). Cutting was halted east of station 38 on the L-2-2 road, some 1,900 feet from where G-P thinks the park boundary is and about 6,200 feet from the center of Redwood Creek.

November 14, 1967—Kuchel and Jackson wired Pamplin, implying that G-P cutting flies in the face of overwhelming public opinion and in a manner calculated to frustrate consideration of the bill by the House. The statements were made on the basis of ground and air surveys by the National Park Service.

November 16, 1967—The Sierra Club and Citizens for a Redwood National Park charged that G-P had cut inside the park boundary.

November 17, 1967—G-P vice-president Harry A. Merlo stated, "from the sketchy park outline we have received some part of this [cutting] may be within it [the park]. We have stopped all cutting in that area and are hopeful a more precise location for park boundaries will be made available to us."

On November 29 Georgia-Pacific rejected a request from thirty-four congressmen to stop cutting timber in a large area adjacent to that in the proposed Senate bill pending House action.

The Sierra Club took another full-page ad in *The New York Times* on January 18, and in *The Wall Street Journal* on January 23, 1968, entitled "Legislation by Chain-saw?" The ad read, in part, as follows:

Georgia-Pacific, in committing these acts, may not be violating any laws. Nor is it violating the wording of promises it has made. To explain: A year ago, after tremendous public pressure, G-P and three other logging concerns agreed to halt logging within redwood areas proposed as parks, until the Senate had acted to define the boundaries. Now the Senate has done so. But the House has not. G-P, therefore (unlike the other three redwood companies) feels it may now quickly cut down everything beyond the Senate lines. Then, you see, there will be no point in having the House, or Secretary Udall add the Emerald Mile or the MacArthur-Elam Creek area, or others. The trees will already have become patio furniture.

On December 4, Rep. Jeffery Cohelan reported, with outrage, his exchange with G-P on this question. (From the *Congressional Record*):

Cohelan: Adjacent to the Senate park boundaries are virgin redwoods lovely enough to grace the best redwood national park. . . .

These trees are now being fed to the sawmills of the Georgia-Pacific Corp., forever blocking the opportunity for us to choose them to dignify a park worthy of its name . . . We thus wrote the following letter to Georgia-Pacific (signed by Cohelan and 34 other congressmen):

"Since the entire question of the precise lines and acreage of the proposed park should be finally determined some time next spring, we hope that this request to suspend further logging (in some 3,000 acres adjacent to the Senate boundary) will be favorably considered."

Georgia-Pacific answered:

". . . it is necessary for us to do some harvesting in this area in order to run our plants on an economically sound basis. For the above reason and in the interest of our employees, our stock holders and good forest management and indeed as a corporate citizen, we respectfully must decline your request."

Mr. Cohelan then said, "The second largest lumbering concern in the world says it cannot accord the House the same concern it voluntarily gave the Senate. . . . I deplore this indifference to the public interest."

The ad also contained five coupons, as some of the earlier ads had, which the reader could clip and send to the president of Georgia-Pacific, the president of the United States, Representative Wayne Aspinall (chairman of the House Interior Committee), his congressman, and the president of the Sierra Club requesting information or membership.

On January 23, 1968, it was reported that the president of G-P had threatened to sue the Sierra Club and had stated that "the Congress of the United States should immediately conduct a full investigation of the Sierra Club and the vendetta tactics being employed by the Club." [23]

Both the Sierra Club and Georgia-Pacific became increasingly impatient as the controversy dragged on. The delay was clearly attributable to political malingering. Nearly five years passed between the completion of the NPS study and the final passage of legislation.

On January 8, 1968, the following statements, which indicate the growing impatience with congressional intransigence, were reported:

A Georgia-Pacific Corporation vice-president has denied a statement released by United Press International, in which he allegedly went on record supporting the Senate Redwood National Park bill.

23 *San Francisco Chronicle,* January 23, 1968.

UPI, in a story distributed on its wire service for release today, quoted Georgia-Pacific executive Robert O. Lee, Portland, as saying, "We are not going to fight this any more. We hope the House will accept the Senate bill."

". . . it has created uncertainty in the local economy," said Fred Laudenberger, the North Coast Timber Association's secretary-manager. "It has held up private investment. People are waiting to see what is going to happen."

Echoing the feelings of most North Coast businessmen and timber operators, a Georgia-Pacific spokesman said: "It's got everybody upset and has got to be resolved. We hope Congressional action will be completed in 1968." [24]

The House held additional hearings on April 16, 1968; and in June, when the park bill was about to be brought to the House for a vote, the most dramatic political maneuvering in the long controversy was performed by the chairman of the House Interior Committee, Representative Wayne Aspinall. Several major conservation bills were before Congress. Included among these was a North Cascades Park in the state of Washington. Washington's Senator Henry Jackson was chairman of the Senate Interior Committee. Other major bills concerned Colorado River water projects, in which Representative Aspinall was extremely interested. These bills were to be worked out in Joint House-Senate conferences, and Aspinall wanted to increase his bargaining power. The Redwood National Park gave him the opportunity.

Representative Aspinall forced an amended version of S. 2515 out of committee on June 25, 1968. This version limited the park to 28,000 acres. When this happened, the Sierra Club's fears grew. Its members redoubled their efforts. A floor fight was threatened by several congressmen, but it never materialized because if a fight developed, Aspinall had the power to kill the park legislation completely. Aspinall brought the bill before the House on July 15, under suspension of the rules. This meant that it could not be amended. He said that a compromise bill would be worked out in a House-Senate conference committee. A vote against the bill under suspension of the rules again ran the risk of losing a park of any size. After a bitter debate, the bill passed 388 to 15. The joint conferences were held in August, and in September the House and Senate passed a 58,000-acre compromise. The compromise included 30,000 acres of old-growth redwoods of state redwood park lands, and 28,000 acres of

[24] *Humboldt Times-Standard,* January 8, 1968.

private timberlands of which 3,450 acres belonged to Georgia-Pacific. In retrospect it seems unlikely that Aspinall ever had any intention of creating a 28,000-acre park.

On September 11, 1968, the following comment appeared in *The New York Times* in an article entitled "Redwood Victory." "However, because of insistent pressures from Georgia-Pacific and other timber companies, the park will be considerably less than ideal in its layout." [25]

On October 2, 1968, the bill was signed into law (PL 90-545) along with three other major pieces of conservation legislation, thus ending the Redwood National Park controversy. President Johnson at the signing made the following statement about the park and its establishment:

> I believe this act of establishing a Redwood National Park in California will stand for all time as a monument to the wisdom of our generation—The Redwoods will stand because men of vision and courage made their stand, refusing to suffer any further exploitation of our natural wealth, or any greater damage to our environment.[26]

POSTSCRIPT

This case was written for inclusion in the first edition of this book. I sent a copy of the case to G-P as a matter of courtesy, and also to check the accuracy of certain statements and facts. A spokesman from G-P responded with clarification as to certain facts and asked that the case be changed in a manner that I felt would have impinged on my prerogative of a fair presentation of material. The G-P communication also carried an implied threat of legal action if all the changes desired by the company were not made. Although I was willing to make changes to clarify various points, I was not willing to make the other type of changes.

Since the case was entirely based on published material, G-P had no ground for legal action. However, rather than risk a long delay in the publication of the book, the G-P case was deleted from the first edition. This case is being included in the current edition with clarifying statements presenting the G-P viewpoints in footnotes wherever pertinent. Following are two communications which have a bearing on the controversy.

[25] *The New York Times,* September 11, 1968. In a communication to the author Mr. Moshofsky retorts: "It should be noted that the Editorial Page editor of The New York Times was a Sierra Club official. In fact, this editor wrote a number of strongly biased editorials during the Redwood Park controversy."

[26] Statement by President Johnson, October 2, 1968.

GEORGIA-PACIFIC CORPORATION

900 S.W. Fifth Avenue
Portland, Oregon 97204

WILLIAM J. MOSHOFSKY
Assistant to the Chairman

January 6, 1971

Mr. S. Prakash Sethi
Assistant Professor of
    Business Administration
School of Business Administration
University of California, Berkeley
Berkeley, California 94720

Dear Mr. Sethi:

I was distressed to receive your December 28 letter and wish to reiterate that we strongly object to your publishing your inaccurate and damaging paper in book or any other form without the corrections included in my letter of December 16. You were certainly aware of this in some detail many weeks ago as a result of our early conversation on the subject.

I would appreciate knowing whether your book is being written and published on university time and at university expense. I also suggest that the document be removed from the presses until appropriate corrections can be made.

While I can understand your desire to proceed and regret the delay in getting our written comments to you, I find it hard to believe any kind of urgency from your standpoint could justify publishing educational material so inaccurate. This strongly suggests academic irresponsibility which cannot be sanctioned in our school system.

It seems to me that institutions of higher education—particularly those schools teaching business administration—should bend over backwards to present objective, accurate material particularly in light of the many, unjustified attacks on business from so many quarters.

Sincerely,

(Signed) William J. Moshofsky

UNIVERSITY OF CALIFORNIA, BERKELEY
School of Business Administration

Berkeley, California 94720

January 25, 1971

Mr. William J. Moshofsky
Georgia-Pacific Corporation
900 Southwest Fifth Avenue
Portland, Oregon 97204

Dear Mr. Moshofsky:

I was quite unhappy to read your letter of January 6, 1971. However, I delayed answering it until today as I wanted to think over its contents. Moreover, I did not wish to respond to you in anger.

Your absurdly amateurish attempt at threatening me would have been comical but for the issue involved and for the air of injured innocence you exuded. Let me say here, unequivocally, that I believe your allegations to be without any merit whatsoever. However, rather than argue with you and risk costly delay in the publication of my book, my publisher (who, it may surprise you to learn, is a commercial publisher) and I have decided to delete the Georgia-Pacific case from the book. You can now believe that the purity and virtue of Georgia-Pacific have been saved from the invading barbarians.

In your letter you accuse me of "academic irresponsibility which cannot be sanctioned in our school system." However, if your letter is an indication of the kind of "business responsibility" that you would like the country to applaud, God save us all. You want business schools "to bend over backwards to present objective, accurate material particularly in light of the many, unjustified attacks on business from so many quarters." I suggest that *you* do some serious soul searching. Obviously, in your view "objective" and "accurate" mean "favorable to" Georgia-Pacific. You do not want independent or objective inquiry. You apparently do want institutions of higher learning to be the public relations arm of the business corporations.

While preparing my book, I had the opportunity of working with top executives from some of the largest and best known American corporations. I found them to be mature and objective enough to accept honest criticism and concede the fallibility of human beings and even of their own organizations. You may be interested to learn that you are the only one

21

of the many corporate officers to whom I talked or corresponded, who threatened, demanded, refused clearance or opposed my comments because they did not show their companies in a completely favorable light. But for my experience with the others, your conduct would really have been a depressing forecast for the future of American business and its important place in our society.

Yours truly,

(Signed) S. Prakash Sethi
Assistant Professor of
Business Administration

Pacific Gas & Electric Company, San Francisco

Attempt to Construct a Nuclear Power Plant at Bodega Bay

To hell with posterity! After all, what have the unborn ever done for us? Nothing. . . .
To hell with posterity! That, too, can be arranged.

> —A statement made facetiously by Lord Richie-Calder, noted newspaperman and author and long concerned with problems of ecology.

BACKGROUND

Bodega Head is a thumblike peninsula jutting out of the California coastline approximately fifty air miles north of San Francisco. The headland, until 1959, was privately owned by three families, and as a result its natural beauty and ecology remained intact. Two of these private holdings, 648 acres owned by Mrs. Rose Gaffney and the tip of the headland owned by Mr. Garry Stroh, could be traced to the original Spanish land grant.

Because the headland had been preserved, the State of California Division of Beaches and Parks became interested in acquiring the land for a recreation area and, independently, the University of California became interested in the area as a site for a Northern California marine facility. The site was also chosen by the Pacific Gas and Electric Company, a private California utility, as being suitable for the location of a generating plant to provide electrical power to the rapidly growing metropolitan San Francisco Bay Area.

In 1953 an informal faculty committee was formed at the University of California (U.C.), Berkeley, to obtain a marine facility in Northern California. Dr. Cadet Hand, a marine biologist at U.C., was a member of the committee and was influential in its organization. Dr. Hand discovered the beauty and richness of the peninsula when he first visited it shortly after World War II. "I was overwhelmed with it," Hand said later. "There were the ocean, the cliffs, the tidepools, and over here those rich mudflats in the harbor. It was a biologist's paradise." [1] The committee was given formal recognition by the university administration in 1955, and in the summers of 1956 and 1957 classes were held in a rented shack at Bodega Bay. Spurred by Dr. Hand and awed by what they saw, the committee began actively pursuing plans for a permanent marine laboratory on the headland.

In this attempt the committee first learned of the state of California's interest in Bodega Head for a recreational park. The State Division of Beaches and Parks had included the headland in its 1955 master plan for park development, and $350,000 was appropriated in the 1956–57 budget for acquisition of the land. However, under California's "home rule" law, which requires local concurrence with state proposals, the Sonoma County Board of Supervisors held absolute veto power over the state's park plan. The board requested that Bodega Head be included in the master plan for the county, but County Planning Director Jack Prather refused. The board upheld this decision and approved the plan without Bodega Head.

In April 1957 the state, still seeking the inclusion of Bodega Head in its park system, agreed to meet with the university to coordinate their plans, and in May a joint committee reached a mutually acceptable plan of action. Three months later, however, in July 1957, the Division of Beaches and Parks reported cryptically that its plans for Bodega Head had "been forestalled by planned purchase of a major portion of the headland by a private utility company."

PG&E STEPS IN

The Pacific Gas and Electric Company moved quickly in the acquisition of the permits and rights necessary for a generating plant on Bodega Head.

---

[1] David Pesonen, "A Visit to Atomic Park," unpublished manuscript. San Francisco, California. Used with permission of the author.

Experience over the years had taught it that this was the best way to handle the delicate task of establishing a generating plant. The first public announcement of PG&E's plans was not made until May 1958. PG&E president M. R. Sutherland issued a brief statement to the effect that "preliminary purchasing negotiations" were underway for a site on which to build a "steam-electric" generating plant.[2]

Although no mention was made of a nuclear facility, there were rumors that the plant would be atomic. These rumors were fueled when in September 1958 Kenneth Diercks, the company's land agent in Sonoma County, told the supervisors: "No decision can be made as to when actual construction of this facility will commence or as to the type of plant to be constructed, whether conventional or nuclear, until the time of installation is much nearer at hand." [3] However, the previous month a PG&E spokesman had told a meeting of the American Institute of Electrical Engineers that PG&E was committed to a course that would lead the utility to large-scale use of economic nuclear power.[4] And only six months later President Sutherland told reporters at a press conference in San Francisco that "an atomic power plant will be built in one of the nine Bay Area counties . . . as soon as it can be done at reasonable cost" and that it was to be in operation "by 1964 or 1965." [5] Although he would not say that he was referring to Bodega Head, no other acquisitions were being made that would have been remotely feasible for an atomic power plant.[6]

PG&E continued to acquire the necessary rights and permits for a conventional generating plant. In September 1958 the county supervisors granted a delay in the improvement of a small airstrip which was in the proposed path of high-power lines from the Head as requested by PG&E, even though the company owned no property in the county at that time.[7] In October 1958 the company filed condemnation proceedings against all of Mrs. Gaffney's property and indicated that the Stroh ranch would also be acquired. It stated that it needed all this land for site access for borings and so on. No mention was made of the AEC requirement for a three-quarter mile radius around a nuclear installation (a reactor at Horseshoe Cove would necessitate owning approximately six hundred acres of headland).[8]

On October 15, 1959, the company announced that the site had been changed to the tip of the headland to get away from the San Andreas Fault

[2] *Santa Rosa Press Dispatch,* May 23, 1958.
[3] Pesonen, "A Visit to Atomic Park."
[4] *San Francisco Chronicle,* August 20, 1958.
[5] *Santa Rosa Press Dispatch,* April 5, 1959.
[6] Pesonen, "A Visit to Atomic Park."
[7] Joel W. Hedgpeth, "Bodega Head—A Partisan View," *Bulletin of the Atomic Scientists,* 3, March 1965, 3.
[8] Pesonen, "A Visit to Atomic Park."

zone, although the type of plant was still unannounced.[9] The suit against Mrs. Gaffney was modified to include only sixty-five acres, and plans were made to purchase the Stroh ranch. This modification of land area coincided with an AEC revision stating that only a one-half mile radius was required around a nuclear installation—the revised property line followed such a radius.[10] Although the ranch had been in Mrs. Stroh's family for over a century and the family repeatedly stated that they did not want to sell, a grant deed to PG&E was filed in the Sonoma County Courthouse less than one month following the announced site change.[11] Allegations that Stroh was intimidated into selling via a party-crashing incident causing "great violence, destruction and bloodshed"[12] were stoutly denied by PG&E, which stated in 1961, in answer to the charge, that "the transaction was concluded in terms satisfactory to Mrs. Stroh."[13]

Then, in November 1959, the Sonoma County Board of Supervisors granted a use permit to PG&E for power lines over Doran Park, a sandspit running northeast from the Head. The supervisors deemed a public hearing unnecessary despite a petition carrying thirteen hundred signatures in opposition.[14]

Gene Marine, writing in *The Nation,* cited this as only one of many instances of flagrant disregard for the public interest:

> Then there's Doran Park, a sandspit which, with Bodega Head, makes Bodega Bay one of the only five safe harbors along 300 miles of tortuous, treacherous Pacific Coast. Doran Park was turned over to Sonoma County by the State of California on condition that it be preserved as a park. At its widest point, it's less than 350 feet wide. PG&E will run power lines down the center of the park; its easement is 180 feet wide. Why don't they put the wires underground? "Uneconomical."[15]

In February 1960 the Sonoma County Board of Supervisors granted the company a use permit to build a steam-electric plant on Bodega Head, again without public hearings and without the submission of plans as this would "impose a hardship on the company."[16]

[9] Hedgpeth, "Bodega Head—A Partisan View," p. 4.
[10] *Ibid.*
[11] Pesonen, "A Visit to Atomic Park."
[12] *Ibid.*
[13] *Ibid.*
[14] *Ibid.*
[15] Gene Marine, "Outrage on Bodega Head," *The Nation,* June 22, 1963, p. 525.
[16] J. B. Neilands, "Industrial Radiation Hazard," unpublished manuscript. University of California, Berkeley, February 1963.

REACTION BY THE UNIVERSITY OF CALIFORNIA, BERKELEY

Meanwhile, neither the state nor the university faculty committee had given up on Bodega Head. The state announced in July 1958, one year after abandoning the Head, that it had been negotiating with PG&E to buy whatever portion was left for the park system.[17] The university's reaction, at the faculty level at least, was less submissive. The faculty committee wanted to fight the company and asked permission to seek the governor's intervention. The administration declined this request and told the committee to find another site for the marine facility.[18]

Since July 1958 the University of California faculty committee had investigated the possibility of acquiring alternate sites for a marine laboratory and had further investigated the impact the PG&E facility would have on the Bodega Bay marine environment. Members of the committee asked two professors from the Scripps Institute of Oceanography to meet with PG&E to assess the impact of the plant on the surrounding environment. They indicated that the discharge from the plant might not disperse as rapidly as originally thought but might displace normal tidal flows for a considerable period of time.[19] Chancellor Seaborg reported in a letter to Philip Flint of the Sierra Club:

> Horseshoe Cove might be expected to be bathed for periods of some hours in the essentially unmixed effluent at near discharge temperatures. . . . The fact that the ecological future of Bodega Head was unpredictable made it undesirable to locate a marine laboratory at Horseshoe Cove, in view of the plans for the power station.[20]

However, on November 29, 1960, the committee told Chancellor Seaborg that, despite the obvious drawbacks, Bodega Head was still the best site available for the marine laboratory.[21] The committee still felt that the university ought to oppose PG&E's proposed plant officially. The committee summed up this negative feeling by concluding:

> Weighing all relevant aspects, we agreed unanimously that there was not a single one of these sites that was equal to Bodega Head as

---

[17] Pesonen, unpublished manuscript.

[18] Hedgpeth, "Bodega Head—A Partisan View," p. 3.

[19] J. D. Frautschy and D. L. Inman, Preliminary Report of Investigation of Bodega Head, made to Professor Roger Y. Stenier, Department of Bacteriology, University of California, Berkeley, June 14, 1960.

[20] Marine, "Outrage on Bodega Head," p. 526.

[21] *Daily Californian* (UCB), December 14, 1962, p. 3.

it now stands. Bluntly stated, a unique Class A site for a marine facility is being exploited for power production.[22]

As a result of this decision, a portion of the headlands was purchased and plans were made to share the peninsula with PG&E. No official position of opposition was taken by the university. The following comment on the report appeared in *The Nation:*

In fact nothing was done about that report at all. It was written twenty-three days after the election of John Kennedy; a short time later the Chancellor [Seaborg] became the chairman of the AEC.[23]

The article also noted that the AEC contributed a sizable sum to the university.

PG&E ANNOUNCES PROPOSED POWER PLANT
TO BE A NUCLEAR FACILITY

In July 1961, after obtaining county permits for a conventional steam-generating plant, PG&E announced its intention to build a nuclear power plant on Bodega Head.[24] Prior to this announcement the controversy centered primarily on the best use of the land—for research and recreation or for power generating—and secondarily on the manner in which the land-use issue was being decided. However, with the formal announcement of a nuclear facility, public safety became a major issue. Three problem areas were associated with establishing this nuclear facility:

1. The geological instability of the Bodega Head and the proximity of the reactor to the San Andreas Fault zone
2. The location of a nuclear reactor near a major population center
3. The problem of radioactive waste discharge

---

[22] *Ibid.*
[23] Marine, "Outrage on Bodega Head," p. 22.
[24] William E. Bennett, "Dissenting Opinion in the Order Denying Reopening of Hearings on the Application for a Certificate of Public Convenience and Necessity for the Bodega Bay Atomic Park," Decision No. 65706.

GEOLOGICAL INSTABILITY OF BODEGA HEAD

PG&E apparently chose the site without much advance consideration of its geologic features.[25] To study it in detail, however, it hired a competent staff of experts, which included Dr. Dan Tocher, a consulting seismologist from U.C.; Dr. William Quaide, a consulting geologist from Claremont; the firm of Dames and Moore, soil mechanics engineers; and Dr. George Housner of Cal Tech, PG&E's principal consultant on structural design.

Drs. Tocher and Quaide filed a report to the company on September 18, 1960. This study showed the reactor site to be approximately one thousand feet from the western edge of the San Andreas Fault [26] and indicated that the headland is "strongly jointed and is faulted on old minor faults. However, there have been no movements in these faults in the past few thousand years . . . [which] strongly implies, but does not guarantee, that there will be no movements throughout the life-expectancy of a power plant." [27] It also revealed that "the intensity of the faulting and jointing in the rock is so great that the formerly massive rock is now broken into a mosaic of blocks with average dimensions of approximately one foot." [28] In June 1960 Dr. Housner wrote to Mr. Worthington, PG&E's civil engineer: "As regards gross ground movement produced by faulting, I would say that if there appeared even a small likelihood of this happening, then the site should not be used. The investigation of Dr. Tocher and Dr. Quaide should be aimed at assessing the likelihood that active movement will occur in the San Andreas Fault zone near the site on Bodega Head. . . ." [29] "No evidence was found in the geologic examination to indicate the existence of a *large fault* beneath the plant or tunnel sites. Chances of disruption of the sites by breakage along a large fault are therefore small." [30]

Dames and Moore filed three reports, with the last the most definitive. From borings at the test site, they found the bedrock to be of poor quality and much deeper than originally thought.[31] As a result they concluded that the reactor pit, designed to be ninety feet deep, could be excavated without blasting, except for the "last twenty to thirty-five feet." [32] Further-

---

[25] Hedgpeth, "Bodega Head—A Partisan View," p. 3.
[26] California Public Utilities Commission, Application 43808, Appendix IV.
[27] *Ibid.,* Sec. 8, p. 12.
[28] *Ibid.,* Sec. 7, p. 5.
[29] *Ibid.*
[30] *Ibid.,* Sec. 8, p. 9. (Emphasis added.)
[31] *Ibid.,* Sec. 17, log of boring shaft 16.
[32] *Ibid.,* Sec. 17, conclusions.

more, the generating plant and other surface installations would be based on approximately sixty-five feet of sands and clays at the point of juncture with the reactor.[33] This despite Tocher and Quaide's earlier admonition:

> It is important from the standpoint of ability to withstand strong ground shaking that the buildings and any other large appurtenances be constructed on foundations resting on the hard quart-diorite bedrock. Should the borings reveal that bedrock will not be reached at practicable depths where it is proposed to erect structures, serious consideration should be given to alternate sites.[34]

PROXIMITY OF PLANT TO URBAN CENTERS: DANGERS OF RADIATION TO THE POPULATION

The location of the plant in an earthquake fault area compounded the ordinary problems of public safety generally associated with the location of a nuclear facility near large population concentrations. The first such problem can arise when an accident caused by seismic activity or other origins results in a major failure of the nuclear safety systems. The company based its safety system on "pressure suppression containment," a novel design used to replace the traditional dome. One of the factors leading to the adoption of this system seems to have been its significantly lower cost.[35] The AEC originally rejected this type of system when it was proposed for the Humboldt County nuclear facility; it reversed itself four months later, however,[36] and called it an improvement over traditional containment systems, even though there was no operational experience upon which to base this opinion.[37] Dr. James E. McDonald questioned the integrity of the safety system on the basis of testimony given by PG&E witnesses to the effect that if an earthquake caused movement of two feet the first two barriers could be punctured, but the critical system would be undamaged; he argued that "the *triple* barrier to escape of volatiles is admitted to be, potentially, reduced to a single barrier [the reactor vessel itself] in event of major seismic displacements. . . . [This] clearly demands that very serious consideration be given to the . . . consequences of fission-product release at Bodega. . . ." [38]

[33] *Ibid.*, Sec. 12.
[34] *Ibid.*, Sec. 8, p. 11.
[35] Neilands, "Industrial Radiation Hazard," p. 8.
[36] Marine, "Outrage on Bodega Head," p. 524.
[37] AEC Docket No. 50-205, p. 12.
[38] Dr. James E. McDonald, "Meteorological Aspects of Nuclear Reactor Hazards at Bodega Bay," published by the Northern California Association to Preserve Bodega Head and Harbor, June 1964, p. 43.

No one knows what would happen if the core melted down. In 1963 the AEC was given $19 million to build a reactor in Idaho and allow it to suffer the maximum credible accident to see what would happen. Until this is done, all assumptions will be mere speculation. However, one recognized study conducted by the AEC in 1957, known as the Brookhaven Report, gives some startling statistics. Based on a 100 to 200 megawatt capacity reactor (much less than the 325 megawatt capacity of PG&E's reactor) located thirty miles from a major city, it theorizes the following results of a major accident: thirty-four hundred deaths, forty-three thousand injuries not including several hundred thousand cases of long-term radiation damage, and property damage of from $2 billion to $4 billion.[39] Dr. McDonald's study of meteorological conditions on the Bodega coast stated that due to the prevailing wind patterns and temperature inversion traps, radioactive gases from the site could easily be funneled into the San Francisco Bay Area without appreciable diffusion.[40] Thus, the conditions surrounding the Bodega reactor were, if anything, more extreme than the hypothetical Brookhaven case. Dr. Samuel Glasstone, in commenting on a boiling water reactor slightly smaller than the one proposed for Bodega, wrote: "Some doubt has been expressed concerning the stability of a boiling water reactor operating at such a high power, but the problem can be resolved only by experience." [41] There have been several major reactor accidents in the past, and seldom has there been a full explanation of the causes: Great Britain's Windscale in 1957; Arco, Idaho's, incident in 1955, in which three people were killed; Chalf River reactor in Canada, in which nine hundred safety devices did not prevent a meltdown which released ten thousand curies of fission products.[42] Of course, design changes have been made which make these particular types of accidents unlikely, but it is presumptuous to assume that no new imperfections will arise.[43]

PROBLEMS OF WASTE DISPOSAL

Another significant hazard of the Bodega reactor was the nuclear wastes which were to be discharged into the water and air. Dr. McDonald outlined some of the problems of radioactive wastes in the air. Included

[39] Adolph J. Ackerman, "Atomic Power, a Failure in Engineering Responsibility," *Journal of Professional Practice, Proceedings of the American Society of Civil Engineers,* October 1961, p. 48.

[40] McDonald, "Meteorological Aspects," p. 51.

[41] Samuel Glasstone, "Sourcebook on Atomic Energy," *AEC,* p. 471.

[42] Lindsay Mattison and Richard Daly, "A Quake at Bodega," *Nuclear Information,* VI, No. 5, April 1964, 3.

[43] David E. Lilienthal, "When the Atom Moves Next Door," *McCall's,* XCI, No. 1, October 1963, 228.

among the hazards were a plume-down wash for the stack directly into the channel traveled by the fishing boats [44] and fog- and drizzle-borne contamination due to shifts in prevailing winds.[45] With regard to this second point, an excerpt from an article by C. Auerbach in *Nature* disclosed that milk samples taken in the Windscale area *"before* the accident contained 44 $\mu\mu$c. of Iodine—131/1, as compared with 5.6 in the United Kingdom as a whole." [46] Dr. Neilands, professor of biochemistry at U.C., calculated that based on the discharge control system at Humboldt Bay, the exhaust valve (which closed automatically if the release rate of radioactive noble and activation gases exceeded two million microcuries per second over a ten-minute period) would not have been activated until after over seventy-eight hundred million microcuries had been discharged.[47]

The other type of waste release, that is, through the cooling system into the ocean, also presented a hazard. While the annual discharge rate was very small, comprising only one-third of the natural radiation in the sea water, the elements produced by the plant were far different from those occurring naturally. More important is the remarkable ability of shellfish, in which the area abounds, to concentrate radioactive ions which can then be ingested by people.[48]

The concern regarding nuclear hazards was also related to the issue of solid waste disposal. David Lilienthal, former chairman of the AEC, stated the problem very clearly in a *McCall's* article in 1963:

> The AEC tells us that in another fifteen years or less a substantial percentage of the electricity of the country will be produced in atomic power plants. Dr. Donald R. Chadwick, Chief of the Division of Radiological Health of the U.S. Public Health Service, estimated in April 1963, that "the accumulated volume of radioactive wastes from nuclear installations . . . will increase from about one and a half million gallons, the estimated 1965 volume, to two billion gallons in 1995." These huge quantities of radioactive wastes *must somehow be removed* from the reactors, must—without mishap—be put into containers that will never rupture; then these vast quantities of poisonous stuff must be moved either to a burial ground or to reprocessing and concentration plants, handled again and disposed of by burial or otherwise, *with a risk of human error at every step.*[49]

[44] McDonald, "Meteorological Aspects," pp. 28–29.
[45] *Ibid.,* pp. 30–31.
[46] C. Auerbach, "Effects of Atomic Radiation," *Nature,* April 27, 1963, p. 343.
[47] Neilands, "Industrial Radiation Hazard," p. 6.
[48] *Ibid.,* p. 6.
[49] Lilienthal, "When the Atom Moves Next Door," p. 52.

He further stated that to continue to project as our goal ten or twelve full-scale power plants in a dozen years, before a safe method of meeting this problem had been demonstrated, was irresponsible financially and revealed a questionable attitude toward public health and safety.[50] Not only did the wastes have to be disposed of, but they had to be kept out of circulation for centuries.[51] This created another problem:

At the present time, these wastes are mainly stored in stainless steel tanks, the life of which is expected to be much less than the duration problem. It is thus possible that we are passing on to future generations a formidable commitment to guard and juggle our atomic garbage.[52]

THE ROLE OF THE ATOMIC ENERGY COMMISSION

The responsibility for insuring the public safety with regard to nuclear power has been vested in a federal agency, the Atomic Energy Commission (AEC). In 1954 the Atomic Energy Act charged the AEC to promote civilian uses of nuclear power as well as to license and regulate privately operated reactors. In 1955 the AEC announced a demonstration program in which it offered to underwrite part of the cost of certain atomic power projects. This program was expanded in 1957 to include all types of projects, as long as (1) they could make significant contributions toward the achievement of commercial atomic power and (2) construction could be completed by June 1962.[53] The requirement for early completion was motivated by the agency's desire to show concrete results in its development program as insurance for its continued funding. Government aid and subsidies to civilian commercial reactors were considered necessary to insure continued development of nuclear power which was not competitive with conventional power.

On January 31, 1961, the AEC optimistically predicted that more than one million kilowatts of nuclear power would be available by the end of 1963, compared with three hundred fifty thousand kilowatts then available. Most of the new generating capacity would be added in 1961–62 when fifteen nuclear power plants were expected to start up.[54]

The AEC's dual role of regulating and promoting civilian reactors car-

---

[50] *Ibid*, p. 228.
[51] Ackerman, "Atomic Power," p. 47.
[52] Neilands, "Industrial Radiation Hazard," p. 5.
[53] Ackerman, "Atomic Power," p. 46.
[54] *The Wall Street Journal*, January 31, 1961, p. 15.

ried an inherent conflict, which the *Wall Street Journal,* on March 20, 1961, reported that the agency recognized and was trying to alleviate:

The AEC announced it is reorganizing in order to separate its regulatory and promotional functions.

The aim is to ensure that the AEC's regulatory responsibilities concerned with such matters as the location and licensing of atomic reactors and licensing of industrial use of radioisotopes, are not jeopardized by the commission's eagerness to promote industrial use of the atom. . . .

The [House-Senate Atomic Energy] committee will also publish the record of a University of Michigan Law School study on A.E.C. organization conducted by two former A.E.C. attorneys, William H. Berman and Lee M. Hydeman. Their report will urge that the preferred step is total separation of the A.E.C.'s regulatory and promotional functions.[55]

The AEC did not totally separate the two functions and even under its reorganization could not eliminate the conflict in responsibilities. At the 1962 hearings pursuant to Section 202 of the Atomic Energy Act, Congressman Chet Holifield, chairman of the Joint Committee on Atomic Energy, read a letter that he had written to AEC Chairman Seaborg earlier that month, in which he expressed concern and disappointment at the pace and extent of the atomic power program. In commenting on budget requests, he said that the AEC had shown a lack of enthusiasm for "our civilian atomic power program" and recommended accelerated development of a number of projects including Bodega Bay.[56] The committee then spent the entire day chiding Seaborg for distorting press releases, emphasizing weapons and space, and delaying programs by "studying them to death." In defending himself, Seaborg mentioned several times that the Bodega Bay plant was one situation in which the commission was moving ahead.[57]

Dr. Seaborg cited another source of pressure in a report to the president in 1962:

It should be recognized that, largely as a result of early optimism, we have, in a short space of time, developed a competitive nuclear equipment industry which is over-capitalized and under-used at the

[55] "A.E.C. Reorganizing in Effort to Separate Its Regulatory, Promotional Functions," *The Wall Street Journal,* March 20, 1961, p. 7.

[56] Marine, "Outrage on Bodega Head," p. 525.

[57] Pesonen, "A Visit to Atomic Park."

present time. . . . Fortunately, it now appears that only relatively moderate additional government help will be necessary to insure the building of a substantial number of large, *water-type* power reactors that will be economically competitive in the high-fuel-cost areas of this country and the world. This would increase public acceptance, keep the nuclear industry healthy and help to furnish the plutonium necessary for a breeder reactor economy as soon as it can be adequately developed.[58]

In response to pressure from Congress and the industry, the AEC granted concessions to PG&E, some of which could adversely affect the public safety:

1. In the interim between PG&E becoming interested in Bodega Head and its filing with the AEC, regulations regarding locating a site near an active earth fault were liberalized three times.[59] Even so, the Bodega site was less than the currently required one-quarter mile distance, and nothing had been said.
2. The pressure suspension containment system used at both PG&E plants, which cost considerably less than the traditonal dome, was approved after having been rejected as unsafe.
3. Shortly after PG&E announced interest in the site, the AEC reduced fuel charges by 34 percent.[60]

It also appeared likely that the AEC had tacitly agreed to license the Bodega Bay reactor before the case ever began. As noted, the commission was using the plant as evidence that it was "moving ahead" long before the application was even submitted; even more persuasive was the fact that PG&E had spent over $4 million before the hearings were even scheduled.

THE CONTROVERSY

In November 1961 PG&E overcame the final hurdle at the county level when the Sonoma County Board of Supervisors approved, again without public hearing, the company's suggested route for the access road, which followed the tidelands around the bay. When the tidelands road was proposed, the university objected.

[58] United States Atomic Energy Commission, *Civilian Nuclear Power,* a report to the president (Washington, D.C.: Government Printing Office, 1962).
[59] Pesonen, "A Visit to Atomic Park."
[60] *Ibid.*

One of the university's basic considerations in acquiring this particular facility was the variety of organisms to be found in the mudflats of the bay. Chancellor Strong wrote a letter of protest outlining the university's position to the Army Corps of Engineers, who had to approve the route since it might affect navigation in the bay.[61] The County Board of Supervisors was apoplectic at this opposition[62] and ordered the Harbor Commission to meet with the chancellor and "explain the facts of life to him."[63] There is no account of this meeting, but it seems to have had an effect on the chancellor's position, for in January 1962 he wrote to Ray Ruebel, secretary-manager of the Bodega Bay Chamber of Commerce, stating that the university was interested only in that portion of the road crossing the university's property and that the remainder was of less importance.[64] The faculty committee did not share this view, however (which was, in fact, contrary to Strong's position less than two months previously): At the public hearings on the road in February, Dr. Cadet Hand opposed the tidelands route in its entirety, stating that any disturbance of the mudflats would affect the ecology of the area so vital for effective research.[65] Dr. J. B. Neilands made the following statement concerning the tidelands road to the northern section of the University Academic Senate:

Not long after a firm decision to locate at Horseshoe Cove had been reached, it was announced that a tidelands access road would be built around the inner rim of the harbor in order to connect the southern tip of Bodega Head to the mainland. This roadway proved to be a convenient arrangement between PG&E and certain Sonoma County officials, the latter now completely dazzled by the prospect of acquiring a giant tax bonanza for the county. The tidelands in question had been leased to the county from the State with the provision that, for final transfer of title, a major improvement must be placed thereon within a certain time period. The lease was running out on the county. PG&E required an access road as well as a convenient place to dump their fill and rip-rock from the excavation. The townspeople were, and still are, much opposed to the roadway and with some difficulty they succeeded in forcing the county to apply to the Army Engineers for the necessary permit.

The hearing was held on February 15; the entire proceedings have been transcribed and the transcription exists as a public document. It

---

[61] Letter to Col. John A. Morrison, Army Corps of Engineers, from Chanc. Edward Strong, University of California, Berkeley, December 1961.

[62] *Santa Rosa Press Democrat,* December 15, 1961.

[63] *Ibid.*

[64] Letter to Mr. Ray Ruebel, Bodega Bay Chamber of Commerce, from Chanc. Edward Strong, University of California, Berkeley, January 31, 1962.

[65] Letter to Chanc. Edward Strong, University of California, Berkeley, from Dr. Cadet Hand, acting director, Bodega Marine Laboratory, February 21, 1962.

describes a bitterly fought contest between Sonoma County officials on one side and the fishermen of Bodega Bay plus certain expert marine biologists on the other side. On this occasion the Acting Director stated that he had the authority of the Chancellor to oppose the roadway "in its entirety" and that a *previous realignment arrangement* with the county did not prevent the destruction of "some of the very values which led us to choose this headland as our site in the first place." In this stand he is strongly supported by the Western Society of Naturalists and by a number of other marine biologists.[66]

Professor Neilands suggested the possibility that a "family relationship" between the university and PG&E may have prevented the university from "fighting to preserve its biological integrity." He pointed out that:

1. PG&E Board Chairman James Black raised $2.4 million for the campus student union in 1958;
2. Walter Haas, who contributed the money to build the Walter Haas Clubhouse at Strawberry Canyon, was on the Board of Directors of PG&E;
3. The senior attorney for the company was John Sproul, son of R. Gordon Sproul, president emeritus of the university; and
4. The university could cut its $2 million annual electric bill in half if it bought power directly from the Central Valley Project, but inexplicably had not.[67]

Dr. Neilands said:

Unfortunately I can find not a shred of evidence that the University has taken advantage of this cordial relationship in order to persuade the company to place the proposed power plant where it would be less destructive to scenic, recreational and possible scientific values.[68]

In October 1961, PG&E filed an application with the California Public Utilities Commission for a "certificate of public convenience and necessity to construct, install, operate and maintain Unit #1, a nuclear power unit, at its Bodega Bay Atomic Park." [69] Hearings were held on March 7, 8, and 9, 1962, with little opposition, and it appeared as if the company had surmounted another major hurdle without encountering any significant opposition.

66 *Daily Californian,* October 29, 1964, p. 3.
67 *Ibid.*
68 *Ibid.*
69 California Public Utilities Commission, Application 43808, Preface, p. 1.

At the Public Utilities Commission hearings, Richard Ramsey, Sonoma County counsel, submitted a booklet containing all twenty-six of the county's resolutions involving the plant, none of which even remotely suggested that it would be atomic.

The company was obviously not eager to delve too deeply into the geology and seismology of the Bodega Bay area at these PUC hearings. When asked if the consultants' reports were to be placed in evidence, PG&E counsel John Morrissey replied:

> Well, we didn't intend to put any of them in. They are quite lengthy, they are quite voluminous. Certainly, they are available for the Commission staff to look at and to study. Indeed, if we can get extra copies, we will give you an extra copy. . . .[70]

PUC counsel Bricca then argued that, without documentation and direct testimony of the consultants, the assurances given by Mr. Worthington constituted hearsay.[71] But this line of inquiry was interrupted by a recess and not raised again until the close of the proceedings, three months later. At that time, Worthington rather reluctantly agreed to submit the reports [72] and subsequently filed the compilation known as Exhibit 48 on July 9, 1962.

At this point, however, public sentiment began to grow in opposition to PG&E's use of Bodega Head. PG&E's repeated refusals to hold public hearings made people more and more critical. Dr. Wayne Olson of Sonoma State College was quoted as saying, "The decision to build was made not by the people, but by a power elite—the AEC, the PG&E and the county supervisors." [73]

In response to an article entitled "Nature vs. the Atom," [74] printed February 11, 1962, Karl Kortum, director of the San Francisco Maritime Museum and a native of Sonoma County, wrote a letter to the editor of the *San Francisco Chronicle,* protesting the process through which engineers were making the decisions on the establishment of social priorities. The letter, which appeared on March 14, 1962, presented the following imaginary dialogue between PG&E officials:

> Conservationists from the State Park Commission and the National Park Service came in the last decade to walk among the lupine and decide that this should be a public preserve.

[70] California PUC Hearings, Application 43808, transcript, pp. 37–38.
[71] *Ibid.,* p. 38.
[72] *Ibid.,* pp. 1402–13.
[73] K. S. Roe, "Bodega, Symbol of a National Crisis," *American Forests,* 69, December 1963, 25.
[74] "This World," *San Francisco Chronicle,* February 11, 1962.

But about the same time came men of a different type. They too walked out on the point and gave it the triumphant glance of demigods.

I am reconstructing. These men are engineers from a public utility and as a member of the public it is my privilege and duty to speculate. The scene shifts to the home office.

"Our engineering boys think we ought to grab Bodega Head."

"They do? (low whistle) That might be a little rough."

"Why? Why more than Moss Landing or Humboldt Bay?"

"Well it's more scenic. There will be more protest. The State Park people and the National Park people are already on record for public acquisition."

"Our engineers say we need it. We'll just buy fast. Get in ahead of them. It's legal."

"Well . . ."

"What we can't buy we'll condemn."

"What about the public protest? This one could get a little noisy."

"Keep it at the county level. Or try to. Every service club in every town has got our people in it rubbing shoulders. In the country, opinion is made at the weekly luncheon . . ."

"How about the newspapers?"

"It's the local businessmen who buy the space. Oh, I don't say we haven't got some work to do. But those guys have got other things on their minds—they're scratching out a living."

"Have you got an angle? I mean apart from the fact that we want it."

"Oh sure. We'll get out some releases and speeches on how the county tax base will be improved. We might even try calling it a tourist attraction."

"And the county officials?"

"They're O.K. We'll set the tone up and they'll respond to it. Just as elected representatives should. Oh you might get some idealist . . ."

What is the matter? Why do these things come to pass?

The answer is simple. Our engineer demigods are obsolete.

The idea of shaking their pedestals to see if they will topple over has only lately come upon us. (A covey bit the dust lately when the Tiburon Bridge was cancelled.)

The engineers of this public utility may find their callousness has crested at Bodega Head. Just as the Toll Bridge Authority engineers crested with the bridge that sags frugally from Richmond to San Rafael. Or the highway engineers with the two deck freeway that spoils the Embarcadero.

An atomic plant doesn't have to be built at Bodega Head. Without any expertise whatsoever, I can make that statement categorically. It is just a matter of whose engineers you listen to.

Engineers have amazing resources. They have been able to prove that it is mechanically impossible for a bee to fly.

"You can't lick the biggest 'city hall' of them all . . ." wrote Ed Mannion in his column in the *Petaluma Argus Courier* on February 17, pointing out that two friends, one a member of the county grand jury and the other a prominent newspaper reporter, had urged him to give up the fight.

Well, Ed, you can lick them. If everyone reading this would take five minutes to write a letter they would be licked. But a licking is not what to ask for; regulation is sufficient—regulation in the full breadth of the public interest. We have a Public Utilities Commission charged with doing just that.[75]

As a result of Mr. Kortum's letter, the Public Utilities Commission received over twenty-five hundred letters protesting the atomic plant at Bodega Head.[76] In response to this public outcry, the hearings were reopened in May and ran into June 1962.

The second set of hearings was very vocal and the "record gives the clear impression that the vast majority of the public does not want this unit at this place at this time." [77] Nevertheless, the company ultimately received a certificate of convenience from the PUC subject to AEC approval of the construction.

AFTERMATH OF HEARINGS

After PUC approval came on November 8, 1962, an *ad hoc* organization quickly entered the fray—the Northern California Association to Preserve Bodega Head and Harbor, headed by David Pesonen. On December 28 PG&E applied to the AEC for a construction permit and with it filed a "Preliminary Hazard Report." This report had the same basic documentation as Exhibit 48, filed with the PUC. Noting some fundamental differences between the two and some major discrepancies in Mr. Worthington's testimony, the Northern California Association to Preserve Bodega Head and Harbor filed a request to reopen the hearings before the PUC. The association pointed out that Mr. Worthington had testified that (1) the San Andreas Fault was "approximately a mile" from the reactor vessel; (2) the foundation would be located "in solid granodiorite";[78] and later, responding to a question concerning his reasons for believing that the Bodega site would be better than the company's site in Humboldt Bay, "Why it's on solid rock." [79] Both statements contradicted the Dames and Moore report, which

[75] *San Francisco Chronicle,* March 14, 1962.
[76] Hedgpeth, "Bodega Head—A Partisan View," p. 4.
[77] Bennett, "Dissenting Opinion," p. 3.
[78] California PUC Hearings, Application 43805, transcript, p. 42.
[79] *Ibid.,* p. 1004.

was omitted from the Preliminary Hazard Report analysis. Some of Tocher and Quaide's conclusions had been significantly changed.[80] The report was finally forwarded to the AEC more than a year after the original analysis had been filed.

In July 1963 the *ad hoc* group's application for a rehearing was denied by a four-to-one vote. William M. Bennett, president of the commission, stated in his dissenting opinion:

We are here dealing so far as seismic activity is concerned with a voluntary exposure to risk. It is obvious that few ventures are entirely risk free, but this is not to say that risk should be courted unneces- sarily . . . only blind compulsion would insist upon placing this plant in the heart of one of nature's choice areas and in frightening proximity to an active fault line.[81]

Following the rehearing denial, the association brought suit in the Su- preme Court of the State of California to force a rehearing. It also sued in Superior Court to have the county permits rescinded on the grounds that no public hearings were held.

As indicated at the second PUC hearings, public opposition to the Bodega Head atomic power plant was widespread. The fact that no local, state, or federal agency or organization had opposed the plant—either in its own interest or in the public interest—created an atmosphere of doubt and suspicion about the degree to which the public safety and interest were being served. The Association to Preserve Bodega Head served as a focal point for the widespread but unorganized opposition to the atomic plant. The association began to document the case for preserving Bodega Head and the dangers involved in establishing a nuclear facility there. It also began to prepare and distribute literature presenting this documentation to the press and the public.

To counter the complex technical reports provided by PG&E on the sta- bility of the Bodega Head area, the association requested further studies. Dr. Pierre Saint-Amand, a consultant seismologist from the Naval Ord- nance Test Station, China Lake, and expert analyst of Chile's 1960 quake, was asked to investigate the site. His conclusion was that "Bodega Head is a very poor location for a reactor. . . ." [82] "Each time the San Andreas

[80] California Public Utilities Commission, Memorandum of Action Concerning Late Filed Exhibit 48 and Related Evidence, May 6, 1963, pp. 39–41.

[81] Bennett, "Dissenting Opinion," p. 7.

[82] Pierre Saint-Amand, "Geologic and Seismologic Study of Bodega Head," pub- lished by the Northern California Association to Preserve Bodega Head and Harbor, 1963, p. 20.

Fault has moved, it has jumped a distance of four to eight meters. Strain is estimated to be accumulating at a rate of about six to seven meters per century across the Fault. Hence one could expect at least one great earthquake per century." [83] He stated that as the reactor site was on the "zone of fling" it would undergo a horizontal movement of some three to four meters [84] and "a worse foundation situation would be difficult to imagine." [85] He concluded:

It is surprising, in view of the expert advice given by Tocher and Quaide, and by Housner, that another site was not chosen and that construction has gone ahead.[86]

At this time another study was undertaken, this one sponsored by the United States Geological Survey. The investigators, Julius Schlocker and Manuel Borilla, first inspected the site in the summer of 1963. Their work was completed in September and they found no evidence of active faulting through the reactor site.[87] However, the company continued its excavation, and the AEC reported in October that a fault through the site itself had been discovered. Schlocker and Borilla returned and conducted a three-month investigation. They reported in January that the fault was comparable to that on Point Reyes, which had had considerable movement in 1906.[88]

PG&E responded to these findings with reports of its "own consultants" who advised them that the plant could still be built safely.[89] It is significant to note that two of the four reports predated the discovery of the new fault and that Dr. Quaide had developed severe doubts as to the advisability of the project:

There is a chance that the fault could break beneath the plant's site in case of an earthquake. I still think the probability is low . . . but it is necessary to face the moral issue: "If there is even a slight chance of danger should we go ahead and build the plant?" [90]

[83] *Ibid.*, p. 14.
[84] *Ibid.*, p. 17.
[85] *Ibid.*, p. 19.
[86] *Ibid.*, p. 20.
[87] USGS TE-884, December 1963. As cited in David Pesonen, unpublished manuscript.
[88] *Ibid.*, p. 14.
[89] *San Francisco Chronicle,* January 28, 1964.
[90] *Ibid.*

On the other hand, Dr. Tocher stated:

We are firmly of the opinion that movements of this nature ["minor vibrations" associated with an earthquake along such "auxiliary faults"] will in no way constitute a hazard to the plant.[91]

As a direct result of the discovery of the shaft fault in January 1964, and possibly because of the full array of geologic and seismologic reports, the company revised its proposed structure in March 1964. To compensate for horizontal movements of from one to two feet, the pit would be packed with a compressible material of a then undetermined type.[92] This decision was a complete reversal of Mr. Worthington's earlier statement: ". . . the one thing that will not change is the fact that we are founding the reactor structure on solid rock and surrounding it with very heavy concrete structures." [93] The approach was novel and could well have been very effective according to the staffs of the AEC Division of Reactor Licensing [94] and the AEC Advisory Committee on Reactor Safeguards.[95] However, the former felt that as "experimental verification and experience background" were lacking, "we do not believe that a large nuclear power reactor should be the subject of a pioneering construction effort based on unverified engineering principles, however sound they may appear to be." [96]

At the same time, the Association to Preserve Bodega Head had published a number of booklets and pamphlets recounting the events and actions that had occurred in PG&E's attempt to establish the plant. This literature was bad publicity for the company, and the public increasingly began to view PG&E and the various public agencies and organizations as irresponsible. The mounting pressure of negative public opinion as mobilized by the association began to influence the AEC.

On October 27, 1964, the AEC issued two reports regarding the Bodega Bay reactor. One, from the commission's Advisory Committee on Reactor Safeguards, stated that, in its opinion, the company's plant could be operated with reasonable assurance that it would not constitute an undue hazard to the health and safety of the public. The other, from the commission's Division of Reactor Licensing, stated that, in its opinion, "Bodega Head

[91] *Ibid.*

[92] U.S. Atomic Energy Commission Application Docket, No. 50-205 by Pacific Gas and Electric Company, Amendment.

[93] California PUC Hearings, Application 43808, transcript, p. 383.

[94] AEC Docket, No. 50-205.

[95] Advisory Committee on Reactor Safeguards, "Report on Bodega Bay Atomic Park, Unit No. 1," October 20, 1964, p. 2.

[96] AEC Docket, No. 50-205, p. 13.

is not a suitable location for the proposed nuclear power plant at the present state of our knowledge." Its reason for this conclusion was the feeling that there was not enough experimental and actual operating data on the proposed design [97] to ensure that it would withstand an earthquake of potential intensity. Immediately following the AEC reports, PG&E announced that it was abandoning the project in which the company had invested several million dollars and which had caused controversy for nearly seven years. PG&E's decision was surprising since under AEC licensing procedures a final decision on the company's $61 million project would not be made until a public hearing had been held by an Atomic Safety and Licensing Board, appointed by the AEC. The initial decision of the three-member board could be protested by the company, the public, or other interested parties before final action was taken.[98]

On November 2, 1964, the following explanation for the company's decision was reported in the *Wall Street Journal:*

> Robert Gerdes, PG&E president, said the doubt raised by the AEC staff "although a minority view, is sufficient to cause us to withdraw our application: We would be the last to desire to build a plant with any substantial doubt existing as to the public safety."
>
> Mr. Gerdes stated that PG&E has made provisions "for adequate electrical generating capacity elsewhere to take care of our customers' needs for the several years immediately ahead."
>
> The company said it has spent $4 million at the site for grading, excavating and road building.[99]

PG&E MAKES A SECOND RETREAT

It seems the problems of PG&E were not over with the cancellation of the Bodega Bay nuclear plant. On January 19, 1973, PG&E announced withdrawal of its applications, without prejudice, to the AEC and the California Public Utilities Commission for authority to construct the $830 million plant at Point Arena on the Mendocino coast. The project included plans for constructing two nuclear generating units of more than one million kilowatts each which were scheduled for completion in 1979 and 1980, respectively.[100]

Among the reasons cited were the "unresolved geological and seismo-

[97] *Ibid.*
[98] *The Wall Street Journal,* October 28, 1964, p. 30.
[99] *Ibid.,* November 2, 1964, p. 7.
[100] Dale Champion, "PG&E Drops Point Arena A-Plant Plan," *San Francisco Chronicle,* January 20, 1973, p. 1.

logical questions recently raised by the U.S. Geological Survey (USGS) and further uncertainties caused by the passage of Proposition 20, the Coastal Initiative." [101] PG&E's John F. Bonner announced that "all work has stopped at the Mendocino site, except for completing geologic and seismic investigations already in progress." [102]

The USGS, which had been serving as a consultant to the AEC, told PG&E in September 1972 that it had "uncovered evidence indicating strong possibility of previously unsuspected active earthquake faulting at or near 586-acre Point Arena plant site." [103] As a result, the AEC expressed serious reservations as to the acceptability of the site and directed PG&E to conduct further studies. The company has since supplied the AEC with progress reports for evaluation by the USGS. On January 8, 1973, USGS sent another report to AEC which concluded that "given the present state of the art of off-shore geophysical techniques and considering the physical characteristics of the Point site it was not now possible to resolve all questions as to suitability of the site." [104]

Another reason for withdrawing the application cited by the company was the passage of the Coastal Initiative in 1972, which was designed to control the development of the California coastline for three years while regional commissions drew up land-use regulations. Popularly known as Proposition 20, the Coastal Initiative was passed in the teeth of strong opposition from many large industrial corporations, land developers, agribusiness and utilities, including PG&E (which contributed in excess of $25,000 to the campaign against its passage).

In a letter to the author a company spokesman stated:

In regards to coastal siting, PG&E is cooperating fully with the Coastal Zone Conservation Act and the newly established Coastal Zone Conservation Commissions. The effect of the Act on utility operations, however, is delaying construction of needed new power plants at coastal sites which already have been acquired and which have been zoned by local authorities for power plants. Because of this, and for the short-term, we will probably have to build alternative plants at yet unselected sites not subject to the Coastal Zone Conservation Act. Unfortunately, the alternatives to coastal nuclear power plants are less desirable environmentally and economically.

Included in the Coastal Zone Conservation Act is the development of a Coastal Plan, including a power plant siting element. We will endeavor to assist the Coastal Zone Conservation Commissions in

---

101 PG&E press release, January 19, 1973.
102 *Ibid.*
103 Champion, "PG&E Drops Point Arena A-Plant Plan."
104 *Ibid.*

identifying coastal sites within our service area which should be considered for inclusion in the Plan.[105]

David E. Pesonen of the Sierra Club, who was one of the leaders in the fight against PG&E on its Bodega Bay nuclear plant construction, commended the company "for acknowledging the inevitable before a bitter fight which would have ended with the same result." However, he severely criticized company officials "for attempting to set Proposition 20 up as any basis for their decision. Proposition 20 is really a smokescreen addressed to the company's stockholders." Pesonen went on to say: "In the light of this new case and Bodega it is clear that no more coastal sitings should be permitted in California. PG&E has a duty to explore the technology of alternate sources of energy and alternate inland siting of thermal plants, fossil and nuclear." [106]

[105] Letter from Christopher C. Newton, Nuclear Information, PG&E, San Francisco, March 28, 1973.
[106] Champion, "PG&E Drops Point Arena A-Plant Plan."

HOW HAZARDOUS ARE
THE NUCLEAR PLANTS?

More than fifteen years of nuclear power plant construction and the experience of more than twenty operating nuclear power plants have not silenced or even diminished the intensity of the controversy associated with their potential hazards. Although some fears about nuclear plant operation have been partially alleviated, new concerns have surfaced in the light of experience: lack of data on the potential hazards associated with increasing the size of individual plants and using untested technologies; and public doubt and apprehension about the Atomic Energy Commission, nuclear equipment manufacturers, and nuclear plant operators and their motives and concern for safety.

A perusal of the available nonclassified material leaves one with the impression that while the proponents of nuclear power have generally underestimated the potential hazards, its critics have frequently used scare tactics by resorting to exaggerated estimates of loss of life and property. The result has been a lack of the serious discussion that must precede any balanced evaluation of risks, benefits, and ways to minimize the hazards of building and operating nuclear power plants.

HAZARDS ASSOCIATED WITH MANUFACTURING
AND OPERATING PROCEDURES

The most frequently occurring hazards in the construction and operation of nuclear power plants are those associated with deficiencies in technology and operating procedures, and these may be the most dangerous hazards.

In a recent article, the *Wall Street Journal* cited numerous examples of plant shutdowns, slowdowns, and delays caused by deficient and shoddily made equipment. "Basically the hardware industry in this country isn't in very good health," according to Milton Shaw, the director of reactor development for the AEC.[1] The big utility companies, lured by the cost advantages of nuclear power plants over fossil fuel and hydroelectric plants and by the availability of nuclear fuel, have been increasing the size of

---

[1] Thomas Ehrich, "Atomic Lemons: Breakdowns and Errors in Operation Plague Nuclear Power Plants," May 3, 1973, p. 1.

their nuclear plants. Equipment manufacturers have further encouraged this expansion by offering "turn-key" projects. However, the larger plants have been achieved by "scaling up former technology instead of developing new technology," causing costly plant slowdowns or shutdowns and increasing the cost of building and operating plants. The problems caused by these "design deficiencies" are augmented and "aggravated" by operating procedures that reflect a "lack of training and an attitude in conflict with good safety practices." [2]

ENVIRONMENTAL HAZARDS

Apart from the problems associated with the operation of nuclear power plants, some environmental problems, such as waste disposal, radiation leaks, and contamination, are caused simply by their very existence.

Waste Disposal

The wastes from nuclear reactors are radioactive and highly toxic substances. They are routinely removed from the reactors and replaced by new nuclear fuel. Removal of the wastes from the reactor sites for ultimate disposal in underground storage tanks is also a routine operation. Although they are no longer usable in the plants, these wastes remain radioactive for a long time. According to AEC Commissioner William O. Doub, "some have half-lives in the decades and are present in amounts that make them potentially dangerous for hundreds of years." [3]

The problems of transportation, storage, and safekeeping of nuclear waste are of grave importance, even to the AEC. Its recent unsuccessful bid to use abandoned Kansas salt mines as a burial ground is one example, as is the realization that a Nagasaki-type bomb can be made in an ordinary laboratory using the available public information and only eleven to twenty-two pounds of one of these wastes—plutonium. Another aspect is highlighted by the fact that a plane carrying a package of plutonium was hijacked to Cuba. Although the AEC has issued very tough standards for the future handling of radioactive materials, the problems associated with waste disposal cannot be considered solved.

Unpredictable Factors

The San Fernando Valley earthquake of 1971 destroyed an "earthquake-proof" concrete hospital, with the loss of a number of lives. Should

[2] *Ibid.*, p. 18.
[3] "Why It's a Good Idea to Break Up the AEC," *Business Week,* June 30, 1973, p. 41.

the "quake-proof" structure of the nuclear power plants fracture in the event of an earthquake, causing a rupture in vital parts of the backup cooling system of the reactor, the consequences could be so staggering that they must be considered—regardless of what we are told about the infinitesimal chances of such an occurrence. Unpredictable natural phenomena in the past caused damage that was, at least to some degree, repairable, but the existence of nuclear power plants radically changes the type, extent, and repairability of damage that may be caused by a natural phenomenon. The question then becomes, How safe are our nuclear power plants? Would they withstand an earthquake? How reliable and trouble-free are our most reliable emergency systems? Finally, is the risk to the environment and to mankind itself worth the benefits gained from nuclear power?

The China Syndrome and Related Safety Issues

Basically, a nuclear reactor is like a firebox for the fossil fuel combustion chamber of conventional electric plants. Instead of the coal or fuel oil used in conventional plants, nuclear plants use a compact maze of fuel rods filled with thimble-sized pellets of nuclear fuel. Each of the seven to nine million tiny pellets contained in the reactor's heart—the reactor vessel—generates power equal to a ton of coal. Once coal is burned, the remains are only ashes; but the remains of nuclear fuel stay hot even after the plant is shut down, resulting in an "after-heat" problem whether the plant is working or not. Should the coolant substance, normally water, be lost to the reactor vessel, a loss-of-coolant-accident known as LOCA, the heat generated by the continuing nuclear reaction would increase the temperature and cause a meltdown. Without proper coolant circulation, some of the fuel cladding would deform, blocking coolant circulation to other claddings and causing an increase in the rate of temperature rise and possibly a total meltdown of the claddings.

In a meltdown situation, the fuel will be exposed to the water. With a temperature increase of a thousand degrees every few seconds, it would not take long to reach 4982°F., the melting point of uranium oxide. The melting of the fuel would cause hot, active nuclear fuel and cladding material to fall to the bottom of the reactor vessel, melt through the foot-thick steel at the bottom, and drop onto the concrete below, shattering the concrete and burning into the ground. Due to the direction of its travel, this phenomenon is known as the *China syndrome*. Under the least favorable conditions, radiation thus released would be dangerous to an exposed population over an area of nearly one hundred miles downwind, resulting in hundreds of human fatalities, thousands of injuries, and billions of dollars in property losses. To be exact, according to the Brookhaven report, thirty-four hundred fatalities, up to forty-three thousand injuries, $7 billion in property damage, and the long-term contamination of an area as large as the state of California could be expected.

The China syndrome is the most serious potential problem with nuclear power plants. To prevent its occurrence, an emergency backup cooling system, technically known as the Emergency Core Cooling System (ECCS), must start operating immediately to avert a temperature rise in the reactor vessel. Any delay or malfunctioning of the ECCS could result in the China syndrome with its disastrous consequences. Thus, the reliability of ECCS becomes the central point in nuclear power plant safety.

At this time there are only twenty-nine commercial nuclear power plants in operation; they account for 4 percent of the nation's total power. However, nuclear power plants are projected to provide 60 percent of the nation's required power by the year 2000, and one thousand power plants might be in operation by the year 2025.[4] Obviously, as the reactors proliferate, the dangers multiply and the chances of accidents rapidly increase.

The ECCS's reliability depends primarily on two things: (a) the design of the system, which is restricted by available technology, and (b) the reliability of quality control in the construction of the system. The frequent shutdowns of the existing twenty-nine power plants due to equipment failures make one doubt the engineering safety of the ECCSs that is claimed by their designers and the AEC.[5] Existing nuclear power plants operate at less than 50 percent of capacity because of immature design technology and the inadequate quality control in their construction. Examples of these problems are valve blowouts, seawater seepage corroding the reactor, and fuel impurities.

Under such circumstances, can or should the nation rely on the AEC's and industry's safety claims? On the one hand, the leading nuclear reactor manufacturers claim that their designs and equipment are foolproof; on the other hand, the buyers of the plants, the utility companies, do not agree. "We think there's a real question about [the quality of the equipment] we're buying," says Donald Allen, president of Yankee Atomic Electric.[6] However, most utility men believe that most atomic plants will deliver on their promise of cheap, abundant electric power once the "learning-curve" stage is over.[7] With no "hard" experimental data, the designs of emergency safety systems are based on computer-simulated data or tests. However, in practice, the reliability of these systems is not supported.

The central question is, Will the ECCS work in a loss-of-coolant acci-

---

[4] "The Uninsurable Risk," *San Francisco Chronicle,* June 18, 1973, p. 17.
[5] Ehrich, "Atomic Lemons," pp. 1, 18.
[6] *Ibid.,* p. 1.
[7] *Ibid.*

dent? The nuclear industry asserts that it will. However, Ralph Nader thinks it will not and has joined Friends of the Earth in a suit seeking to shut down twenty of the twenty-nine nuclear power plants on the grounds that they are unsafe.

BREAKUP OF THE ATOMIC ENERGY COMMISSION

The dual role of the AEC as both promoter and regulator of the use of nuclear energy and the resultant conflict of interests has been one of the major causes of criticism of the AEC from the time it was first established. Over the years this criticism has grown as the commission has been accused by respected, well-informed scientists, by congressmen, and by the general public of sacrificing concern for public safety to the promotion of nuclear power plants for commercial use.

The government has finally heeded this criticism. In June 1973 President Nixon recommended to Congress that it break up the AEC into two separate groups. Under his proposal, AEC's research and development staff would become part of a new agency to be fashioned after the National Aeronautics and Space Administration and to be called the Energy Research and Development Administration. Safety and regulatory functions of the AEC would be handled by a new nuclear energy commission.[8] At the time of this writing, Congress had not acted on the proposal.

REFERENCES

ALEXANDER, TOM, "The Big Blowup over Nuclear Blowdowns," *Fortune,* May 1973, p. 216.

LAPP, RALPH E., "Nuclear Power Safety—1973," *New Republic,* April 28, 1973, pp. 17–19.

"Nuclear Reactor Safety: A Skeleton at the Feast," *Science,* May 28, 1971, p. 918.

People's Lobby, "A Condensation of Nuclear Reactor Safety: An Evaluation of New Evidence," by IAN A. FORBES, DANIEL F. FORD, HENRY W. KENDALL, and JAMES J. MACKENZIE. Washington, D.C., July 1971.

————, "A Critique of the New AEC Design Criteria for Reactor Safety Systems," by DANIEL F. FORD, HENRY W. KENDALL, and JAMES J. MACKENZIE. Washington, D.C., October 1971.

[8] *Business Week,* June 30, 1973, p. 40.

U.S., CONGRESS, SENATE, COMMITTEE ON INTERIOR AND INSULAR AF-FAIRS, *Hearings Pursuant to S.R. 45, A National Fuels and Energy Policy on Environmental Constraints and the Generation of Nuclear Electric Power: The Aftermath of the Court Decision on Calvert Cliffs,* Parts 1 and 2, Serial No. 92–14, 92nd Cong., 1st sess., November 3, 1971.

II
THE CHANGING NATURE
OF GOVERNMENT
AND BUSINESS RELATIONSHIPS

A.

POLITICS AND BUSINESS

The ITT Affair (A)

Influence of Big Business in Politics and Government:
Antitrust Case Settlement and Campaign Contribution

We are not talking here [in the ITT affair] about isolated encounters between the government and a huge corporation from which deals would be likely to emerge. Rather these are on-going relationships in which the Very Rich buy goodwill day in day out, the year around and it cuts both ways.

—Editorial, *Washington Post,* March 14, 1972

As a businessman, fundamental in my mind is the question of "What does a diversified company such as IT&T do that is good for the economy and/or bad for the economy?"

On this basis, knowing the degree of effort that our company has consistently in the last 12 years expended as well as the personal effort of our management and myself to strengthen the company within the domestic economy . . . I am surprised to find a company such as ours, and there are others, without much chance of stating its case, but in the category of nonconstructive and fearsome force within our society.

—Harold S. Geneen, Chairman and Chief Executive of ITT, in a statement before the U.S. Senate Judiciary Committee on March 16, 1972

The ITT affair, as it has since come to be known, involved contributions by a large corporation to a presidential political campaign for the alleged purpose of securing favorable settlement of antitrust cases involving the company. The case raises serious questions about relationships between business and government. It is the recognized right of all citizens, including business corporations, large and small, to argue their side before elected political bodies, government agencies, and high officials. However, it is not clear whether the channels of appeal are equally open to all concerned or whether the degree of "sympathetic consideration" by public officials is based on the relative economic strength and political muscle of the petitioner.

Three other questions transcend the immediate issues of ITT. One, is there something in the processes of government decision making and public policy formulation that makes it possible—laws to the contrary and without an attempt to corrupt—for large corporations and vested interests to secure easy entry into the channels of government attention to make their views known, and also to secure more favorable decisions? Two, is it possible that constant and continuous interaction between government officials and business leaders becomes so pervasive that a different and more lenient set of criteria are applied in the enforcement of laws concerning large corporations? Three, to the extent that modern large corporations are private governments, which to be effective must interact with public governments, do conditions exist in their internal governance that make them behave in a particular manner in their outside dealings? If so, can their internal governance be modified to make their external behavior more acceptable to social standards and expectations?

The ITT affair is not the first case involving a large corporation's attempt to buy political influence and channel it to its own economic advantage. The very nature and diversity of activities pursued by large corporations in general and conglomerates in particular are such that their interests are inevitably linked with and dependent upon the general public policies pursued by the federal government, as well as the specific courses of action determined by various government bodies. However, the timing of the ITT incident was so sensitive, the level of public officials and corporate executives so high, and the nature of the incidents, both before and after the disclosure, so bizarre that it brought into public limelight all the various facets of business-government interaction, which had hitherto been confined to a select few.

Enter Jack Anderson: The Dita Beard Memo

On February 29, 1972, only five days after the Senate Judiciary Committee voted to confirm the nomination of Acting Attorney General Richard J. Kleindienst to succeed John Mitchell as Attorney General,[1] the following appeared in the "Washington Merry-Go-Round," the nationally syndicated column by Jack Anderson:

> We now have evidence that the settlement of the Nixon administration's biggest anti-trust case was privately arranged between Attorney General John Mitchell and the top lobbyist for the company involved.
>
> We have this on the word of the lobbyist herself, crusty, capable Dita Beard of the International Telephone and Telegraph Co. She acknowledged the secret deal after we obtained a highly incriminating memo, written by her, from ITT's files.
>
> The memo, which was intended to be destroyed after it was read, not only indicates that the anti-trust case had been fixed but that the fix was a payoff for ITT's pledge of up to $400,000 for the upcoming Republican convention in San Diego.
>
> Confronted with the memo, Mrs. Beard acknowledged its authenticity. . . .

The memo detailed a meeting between Mrs. Beard, Attorney General John Mitchell, and Republican Governor Louis Nunn at the governor's Kentucky mansion. Mrs. Beard indicated that Mitchell confided to her that

> he was sympathetic to ITT but had been prevented until then from helping the company because of the zeal of the Justice Department's anti-trust chief, Richard McLaren.
>
> After his harangue, Mrs. Beard said, Mitchell agreed to discuss the anti-trust matters and asked bluntly, "What do you want?" meaning what companies did ITT most want to keep if the anti-trust cases were settled.
>
> "We have to have Hartford Fire because of the economy," Mrs. Beard recalled saying. . . .
>
> And, she said, when the Justice Department announced its settlement with ITT on July 31, more than two months later, it conformed to the agreement she had made with Mitchell. . . .
>
> It [the memo] is addressed to W. R. (Bill) Merriam, head of ITT's Washington office. It is marked "Personal and Confidential" and its last line asks, "Please destroy this, huh?"
>
> The memo warns Merriam to keep quiet about the ITT cash pledge for the Republican convention. "John Mitchell has certainly kept it

---

[1] U.S., Congress, Senate, Committee on the Judiciary, *Hearings on Nomination of Richard G. Kleindienst, of Arizona, to be Attorney General,* Part 2, 92nd Cong., 2nd sess., March 1972, pp. 392–93. References to this source will hereinafter be referred to in the text as *Hearings,* following by part and page number.

on the higher level only," the memo says, "we should be able to do the same. . . .

"I am convinced, because of several conversations with Louie (Gov. Nunn) re Mitchell that our noble commitment has gone a long way toward our negotiations on the mergers coming out as Hal (ITT President Harold Geneen) wants them.

"Certainly the President has told Mitchell to see that things are worked out fairly. It is still only McLaren's mickey-mouse that we are suffering. . . .

"If (the convention commitment) gets too much publicity, you can believe our negotiations with Justice will wind up shot down. Mitchell is definitely helping us, but cannot let it be known."

The implications of this memo were explosive, and the timing of its publication left little doubt that its allegations would be fully investigated. The year 1972 was a presidential election year, with the incumbent Republican administration strongly identified as a friend of big business. ITT immediately issued the following statement:

There was no deal of any kind to settle our antitrust cases. It is unfair to the individuals involved to even suggest such a possibility. Agreement was reached with the Justice Department only after hard negotiations between our outside legal counsel and the then-Assistant Attorney General Richard McLaren and his staff.

Neither Mrs. Beard nor anyone else except legal counsel was authorized to carry on such negotiations. The June 25, 1971, memorandum attributed to Mrs. Beard was seen for the first time by the ITT official to whom it was addressed when it was brought in by a member of Mr. Anderson's staff last week.

The San Diego contribution of the Sheraton Hotels was made as a nonpartisan joint effort of the San Diego community and was purely in support of a local situation. . . . There was no tie-in of any kind between this local joint participation and any other aspects of ITT's business. [*Hearings,* Part 2, p. 393]

Kleindienst also denied any wrongdoing during the 1971 settlement and requested that his confirmation hearings be reopened immediately so that he would not take office "with a cloud over my head, so to speak" (*Hearings,* Part 2, p. 96). The Judiciary Committee, with a majority of Democrats, including some very vocal administration critics, was quite willing to oblige.

To keep the facts of the case straight and the sequence of events comprehensible, the narrative that follows has been divided into two sections.

The first section deals with the ITT contribution to the Republican convention and the attempts at its coverup. The second section deals with settlement of the antitrust case involving ITT and the Hartford Insurance Company.

I. GOP CONVENTION PLEDGE

The hearings were reopened on March 2, 1972, with Richard Kleindienst as the lead-off witness. In his testimony Kleindienst admitted to some general discussions about the ITT case with Felix Rohatyn, an ITT director. He emphatically denied putting any pressure on McLaren or having any part in the settlement of the ITT case. He went on to state:

> I would like to conclude my remarks by saying categorically and specifically that at no time, until some time in December 1971, did I have any knowledge of any kind, direct or indirect, that the ITT Corp. was being asked to make any kind of a contribution to the city of San Diego or to the Republican Party with respect to the prospective national convention of the Republican Party in San Diego. I never talked to a person on the face of this earth about any aspect of the San Diego Republican National Convention or the I.T.&T. Corp. I never talked to Mr. Mitchell about any aspect of this case. He never mentioned any aspect of this case, and there is not a person in this world who, if they testify truthfully, can come forward and say either that I had knowledge of anything going on with respect to the San Diego Convention and the I.T.&T. Corp. or that in any way, under any circumstances, I had anything whatsoever to do with anything that the Department of Justice, the Government of the United States, myself, or Judge McLaren, in connection with these matters. [*Hearings,* Part 2, p. 100]

Little did Kleindienst realize that in asking for a reopening of his hearings, he was opening a Pandora's box. Once started, the hearings assumed a life of their own and led into things that if Kleindienst had known earlier would be brought up, he would never have wished anyone to investigate. As the hearings progressed, the personal integrity of many of the principals, including the nominee for attorney general, was called into question. The settlement of the antitrust suits mentioned in the memo had been controversial when it was announced. The suggestion that it had been a political fix negotiated at the highest level of government raised questions that first touched the individuals involved and then went beyond to the very heart of the relationship between business and government, and between government and what the *Washington Post* called the "Dismal Swamp of American politics." [2]

What finally emerged from the hearings was not a clarification or a denial of any specific deal, but revised and "refreshed" testimony, lapses of memory, and conflicting testimony by witnesses, which so obscured the truth about what might or might not have been arranged between ITT and the Nixon administration that little could be determined with any certainty. But what did emerge with great clarity was the picture of a corporation sparing no effort or expense to influence events in its own favor and an administration apparently receptive to such efforts.

The Memo and Its Allegations

The two events around which the memo centered were hardly secret, and each was controversial in its own right. In July 1971 the Antitrust Division of the Justice Department abruptly accepted an out-of-court settlement of three cases aginst ITT. These were suits in which the government sought the divestiture of three of ITT's recently acquired subsidiaries: Canteen Corporation, the leading company in vending machine production; Grinnell Corporation, a leader in production and sales of fire protection devices; and Hartford Fire and Casualty Insurance Company, the nation's sixth largest insurance concern. Richard McLaren, then assistant attorney general in charge of antitrust, repeatedly stressed his intention of taking these cases to the Supreme Court, for they were based on a departure from traditional legal interpretation of the antitrust laws as they applied to conglomerate mergers, and McLaren wanted his theories clarified and vindicated in the Court. ITT's acquisition of Hartford Fire was the largest corporate merger in history, and McLaren had been adamant that any settlement with ITT would have to include complete divestiture of Hartford. Nevertheless, the 1971 consent decree by which all three cases were settled allowed ITT to keep Hartford while divesting itself of approximately $1 billion of other assets. This sudden change in McLaren's position left many wondering if the close ties between ITT and the administration (both President Nixon and Attorney General Mitchell had been attorneys in a firm that had represented an ITT subsidiary) did not have something to do with McLaren's change of mind.

The abandonment of these cases even caused expressions of disappointment in some business circles. *Business Week,* for example, commented, in an editorial entitled "The Antitrusters Cop Out":

[2] Editorial, March 14, 1972.

The sudden settlement last weekend of the government's package of antitrust cases against International Telephone & Telegraph Corp. is a singularly unsatisfying end to an important episode in government-business relations.

The ITT cases were promoted by the Nixon Administration as an attempt to establish a clear judicial definition of the limits on corporate growth in a modern society. By suddenly agreeing to accept the settlement, the government antitrusters have thrown away the chance to do that. They have added another scalp to the Justice Dept.'s belt, but they have not done anything to clarify the vague legal rules under which merger-minded corporations must operate.

Clarification not only of the law but of the economics of mergers is badly needed. Very little serious investigation of the implications of corporate bigness has been undertaken in this country either by the government or by students of business. It will take a major series of legal tests, ending in the Supreme Court, to prompt the rigorous analysis necessary to determine how big and how fast a company can grow without endangering the public interest.[3]

At approximately the same time, in "shining green coincidence,"[4] it was announced that ITT, through its subsidiary Sheraton Hotels, had made a generous contribution to the financing of the Republican National Convention by underwriting a $400,000 cash guarantee to bring the convention to San Diego.[5]

At first San Diego did not want the GOP convention. However, at the urging of the White House and influential national and state Republican leaders, it reluctantly agreed to make a bid. The business community and the San Diego City Council were both reluctant to furnish the cash needed for the bid, but the area's Republican Congressman Bob Wilson's announcement on June 3 that he had received $400,000 in pledges from sources he would not then identify made it possible to begin collecting pledges from other local businesses. The contribution's size, although Sheraton later said the $400,000 figure was "highly exaggerated,"[6] made it extremely conspicuous and legally questionable.

On December 13, 1971, Lawrence F. O'Brien, the Democratic national chairman, raised questions concerning the link between ITT's antitrust settlement and convention pledge in a letter to Attorney General Mitchell, which was passed on to Kleindienst:

[3] *Business Week*, August 7, 1971; also cited in *Hearings*, Part 2, p. 575.
[4] "The ITT Affair: Politics and Justice," *Newsweek*, March 20, 1972, p. 24.
[5] "Sheraton's GOP Parley Aid Affirmed," *San Diego Union*, August 6, 1971.
[6] "San Diego Is Split on Convention Aid," *The New York Times*, September 13, 1971, p. 38.

Continuing public reports about the methods of financing the 1971 Republican National Convention raise a serious cloud over the recent out-of-court settlement by the Department of Justice of three antitrust cases involving International Telephone and Telegraph Corp.

Among other things, O'Brien asked three specific questions:

Before the selection of San Diego as host city, did Chairman Bob Wilson of the House Republican Campaign Committee meet privately in New York with ITT officials and if so, to what purpose?

After the selection of San Diego, did Congressman Wilson (whose district includes San Diego) meet with Deputy Attorney General Kleindienst to discuss resolution of the government's antitrust case against ITT, or any other aspect of that case? If so, why?

Are you able, through a candid exposition of all the facts, to allay any suspicion that there is a connection between ITT's sudden largesse to the Republican Party and the nearly simultaneous out-of-court settlement of one of the biggest merger cases in corporate history—to ITT's benefit? [*Hearings,* Part 3, p. 1662]

In his reply, which was later to haunt him, Kleindienst wrote O'Brien that he had no prior knowledge, direct or indirect, of ITT's subsidiary Sheraton Corporation of America's pledge of $400,000 to San Diego for hosting the GOP convention. He also stated:

The settlement between the Department of Justice and ITT was handled and negotiated exclusively by Assistant Attorney General Richard McLaren. . . . Mr. McLaren kept me generally advised as to the course of negotiations with ITT and with his reasons for endeavoring to work out a settlement with it. Prior to the final conclusion of these settlement negotiations and the effectuation of a settlement between the Department of Justice and ITT, Mr. McLaren made his final recommendation in the matter to me with which I concurred. [Emphasis added]

In a tone of injured innocence, Kleindienst went on to say:

I firmly believe the American people are entitled to know at all times how their public servants arrive at the decision-making process. Assistant Attorney General McLaren will be able to provide that information upon his return. The American people, however, may well begin to question the fairness and responsiveness of the political process when they read of alleged statements of fact, alluded to by you in your letter to the Attorney General which were made without any factual basis or substance whatsoever. [*Hearings,* Part 2, pp. 120–21]

However, as I noted earlier, Kleindienst later admitted before the Judiciary Committee not only to knowing about ITT's antitrust case settlement but also to playing an active part in bringing it about. Nor was his admission voluntary, since it came out only after Jack Anderson had made allegations in his column accusing him of actually lying.

The Repercussions of the Memo: The Justice Department

Denials that there had been any impropriety in the settlement came immediately, first from John Mitchell and then from Kleindienst himself. Attorney General Mitchell issued the following statement:

> I was not involved in any way with the Republican National Committee convention negotiations and had no knowledge of anyone from the Committee or elsewhere dealing with International Telephone and Telegraph. In fact, I do not know as of this date what arrangements, if any, exist between the RNC and ITT.
>
> When the Department of Justice first brought action against ITT, I removed myself from all consideration of such matters. I have not discussed the subject with anyone from ITT or in the Department, with one exception, the exception being that at a reception held in the executive mansion of the State of Kentucky, a Mrs. Beard approached me on the subject. I advised her that I was not familiar with the matter and that the appropriate people representing ITT should take the matter up with the appropriate people in the Department of Justice. That was the only time I have seen Mrs. Beard and the above is the extent of our conversation on the subject.
>
> With respect to the allegations that the President discussed the matter with me, there would be no occasion for him to do so and he did not. [*Hearings,* Part 3, p. 1269]

In the reopened hearings, Kleindienst was accompanied by McLaren, at that time a federal judge in Illinois, and Felix Rohatyn, the director of ITT with whom Kleindienst had had the meetings that Anderson reported. The three men described a chronology in which Rohatyn had contacted Kleindienst in April 1971 to persuade him that the Antitrust Division should hear an ITT presentation that a forced divestiture of

Hartford would be "almost a fatal blow" [7] to the company and would also damage the national economy. As a result of this meeting, a larger meeting was held, with staff members from the Antitrust Division and the Treasury Department, various ITT representatives, Kleindienst, and Rohatyn. McLaren thereafter arranged for an analysis of ITT's presentation by an outside consultant and, chiefly, he said, on the basis of that consultant's report, McLaren decided that divestiture of Hartford should not be required. He then recommended a settlement proposal to Kleindienst, and they made a joint call to Rohatyn to say that if the broad outlines of the proposal were acceptable, negotiations over its smaller details could begin. Negotiations started during the latter part of June 1971 and culminated in the consent decree of July 31, by which ITT retained Hartford.

All three men insisted that there had been no undue pressure on McLaren to change his mind. McLaren himself testified that

> the decision to enter into settlement negotiations with ITT was my own personal decision; I was not pressured to reach this decision. Furthermore, the plan of settlement was devised, and the final terms negotiated, by me with the advice of other members of the Antitrust Division, and by no one else. [*Hearings,* Part 2, p. 113]

But flaws began to appear almost immediately in this categorical testimony, and it rapidly became "one of those maddening exercises in which every loose end seems to unravel itself into half a dozen more." [8] Testimony was revised and refreshed, omissions were corrected, conflicting evidence was presented, and relevant information was refused to the committee without any change in the Justice Department's posture of studied indifference. Indeed, all the witnesses—and Kleindienst in particular—seemed utterly unaware that their credibility was suffering as they "tried to patch up with new facts the inconsistencies that developed as the hearings went on." This naïveté, whether assumed or real, was difficult to believe in these "apparently sophisticated men" [9] and did nothing to enhance their already seriously damaged image. It became easier and easier to believe that witnesses were admitting only what was impossible to hide and resorting to forgetfulness and such drastic measures as "executive privilege" when no other means of preventing the discovery of embarrassing facts could be found. ITT's own actions (discussed in the next section) exhibited an arrogance whose chief characteristic was an apparently "unlimited faith in the gullibility of the public." [10]

[7] "ITT's Arrogance," *New Republic,* April 8, 1972, p. 4.
[8] "The ITT Case: End of the Affair?" *Newsweek,* April 10, 1972, p. 17.
[9] "Know-Nothing Mitchell," *New Republic,* March 25, 1972, p. 5.
[10] Editorial, *St. Louis Post-Dispatch,* March 22, 1972.

When confronted with the conflicting evidence, Kleindienst claimed lapses of memory that became too numerous for comfort. More damaging, however, to his reputation and credibility than the sheer number of the memory lapses he claimed was the pattern of omissions that they caused. The events that Kleindienst did not at first remember significantly enlarged his own role in the events, showed in greater detail the efforts ITT was making to pressure McLaren into a settlement favorable to the company if one could not be obtained on the merits of the case, and, even more importantly, outlined White House involvement in the settlement, through a presidential aide known as "Mr. Fixit" for big business, Peter M. Flanigan.[11] So incredible was the situation that at one point Kleindienst dolefully admitted: "I guess I set in motion a series of events by which Mr. McLaren became persuaded that . . . he ought to come off his position with respect to a divestiture of Hartford by ITT" (*Hearings,* Part 2, p. 156).

Among the more glaring examples of Kleindienst's lapses of memory were the following:

1. He had been approached at a neighborhood social event by one of his neighbors, John Ryan, deputy director of ITT's Washington office, who described himself as the company's antitrust "listening post," or "focal point" (*Hearings,* Part 3, p. 1068). Ryan asked Kleindienst if he would listen to an ITT economic presentation; Kleindienst agreed, and Rohatyn was assigned to make the presentation. Kleindienst did not remember this contact independently, but he had his "recollection refreshed" by Rohatyn (*Hearings,* Part 2, p. 133) and refused to see as significant what he regarded as a chance meeting. Although this meeting may have been a chance occurrence from his point of view, it represented part of a coordinated campaign by ITT to obtain a settlement, as will be noted later.

2. Just before his meeting with Rohatyn, Kleindienst received a plea from an ITT lawyer to delay the case against ITT's acquisition of Grinnell, which was scheduled to be filed before the Supreme Court. Kleindienst requested the solicitor general to apply for the thirty-day delay, which was granted, and during that period, McLaren heard the financial and economic arguments that allegedly changed his mind. Even more important than these bare facts is the identity of the lawyer who requested the delay: Lawrence Walsh was deputy attorney general (the position Kleindienst held) during the Eisenhower administration; he was appointed by President Nixon to be deputy chief negotiator at the Paris peace talks in 1969, and he was chairman of the American Bar Association Committee on the Federal Judiciary, which was responsible for clearing administration nom-

[11] "Is He the White House 'Mr. Fixit'?" *The Wall Street Journal,* March 21, 1972, p. 18.

inees for all federal judgeships. Kleindienst, as deputy attorney general, was in charge of judicial appointments, and through their contact on that matter, he and Walsh were close friends. Kleindienst admitted of Walsh: "He isn't an ordinary attorney, as far as I am concerned" (*Hearings,* Part 2, p. 291). But his role in obtaining the crucial delay in the Grinnell case was only brought out by Kleindienst after pointed questions about this delay.

Further complicating Walsh's relationship with Kleindienst and with these cases, and highlighting the question of the propriety of his contacts with Kleindienst, is the fact that when Richard McLaren was nominated to be a federal judge several months after the settlement of these cases (raising questions of the judgeship's being the carrot that induced McLaren to allow the settlement), it was Walsh's committee that reviewed his candidacy and cleared him in a matter of hours.

3. Kleindienst was repeatedly questioned about any contacts he might have had with the White House over these cases, and he repeatedly answered that there had been none. It later appeared, however, that the role of presidential aide Peter Flanigan was quite important. Flanigan was White House liaison with business and was supposed to help businessmen in their problems with the federal government and Congress. At first the White House refused to allow Flanigan to testify, claiming executive privilege. However, he later appeared before the committee after Senator Sam J. Ervin threatened to filibuster Kleindienst's nomination to death unless Flanigan did testify. His appearance was made under such stringent limitations on the range of questioning that his testimony was virtually worthless. Nevertheless, almost two months later, the committee received a letter from Flanigan, responding to some questions that were not covered in his testimony. In this letter he admitted calling Kleindienst about the Ramsden report. He also acknowledged that Kleindienst was present when he personally delivered the report to McLaren (*Hearings,* Part 3, p. 1639).

Departing Attorney General John Mitchell's testimony showed the same pattern of initial omissions and subsequent corrections as Kleindienst's, although Mitchell's was also characterized by flat statements that were widely disbelieved and by statements that contradicted other witnesses, with no resolution ever advanced. In his first statement, Mitchell stated that he "was not involved in any way with the Republican National Convention negotiations." However, Washington observers believed the situation to be different. As the *Washington Post* pointed out:

> For some time now, the steady hand of Attorney General John N. Mitchell has been in control of national Republican politics, even though President Nixon's 1968 campaign manager may wait a while

before officially severing his connection with the Justice Department. [12]

That this was no wild speculation was later confirmed in the Watergate hearings in June 1973, during the testimony of various officials of the Committee to Re-Elect the President (CREEP). In the spring of 1972 a professed ignorance on Mitchell's part of the exact financial arrangements for the 1972 GOP convention might have been credible, but his categorical denial of knowledge of, and interest in, any convention arrangements was such an unconvincing denial of the obvious that one is almost forced to wonder what it was intended to accomplish.

New fuel was soon added to this flickering suspicion. California's Lieutenant Governor Ed Reinecke and his aide, Edgar Gillenwaters, stated to Jack Anderson's aide, Brit Hume, to several other reporters, and to Senator John V. Tunney that they had briefed Mitchell fully on San Diego's prospects as host for the convention in May 1971, with the briefing including a discussion of the ITT financial commitment. According to Reinecke:

> I discussed it with the Attorney General. . . . Whether I was the first one or not I didn't ask him.
>
> But we did discuss it and he was very pleased to see the progress we'd made, not just with Sheraton but with getting the city and county to come around. . . .
>
> This was strictly a political thing between Sheraton and their desire to help get the convention to San Diego. The fact that I was talking to John Mitchell was not that he was attorney general. He was, you might say, the political arm of the administration.
>
> And so when I went to Washington on space shuttle business I made it a point to go there to see what we could do about bringing this convention to San Diego. . . .[13]

Senator Tunney, a political colleague and friend, called Reinecke to point out to him that his testimony conflicted with what Mitchell had said. An obviously disturbed Tunney recounted the telephone call in the hearings:

> You [Reinecke] said that unless you were subject to a failing memory, there was no question that you had brought up the $400,000 to be given to the city of San Diego to bring the convention to San

[12] "Mitchell Gearing Up to Steer Campaign," *Washington Post*, October 10, 1971.
[13] "Lieutenant Governor Reinecke's Shift on ITT Story," *Sacramento Bee*, March 3, 1972.

Diego. When I pointed out to you that Mr. Mitchell was probably going to testify to the contrary you said, "Well, all a person has is his integrity," and you indicated that you recalled the conversation. You also said that unless you were losing your memory, that unless you were subject to a failing memory, there was no question that these matters had been brought up. [*Hearings*, Part 3, p. 1524]

That call was on Thursday, March 2. On Friday, March 3, Reinecke called a press conference and stated:

On the May 16, 1971, trip to Washington, D.C. we did not meet with Attorney General John Mitchell as I had previously reported. . . . My discussions with Attorney General Mitchell concerning the convention was at 9:30 A.M. on September 17, 1971. . . . This would have been the first time either of us (Reinecke or Gillenwaters) discussed any such offer with the Attorney General.[14]

But this correction, like those of other witnesses, only served to cloud the issue further. Even Reinecke's corrected version of events did not coincide with the version given by Mitchell who, in a great show of indifference to the entire topic, *failed to remember any discussion whatever with Reinecke about the convention* (*Hearings*, Part 2, pp. 547–69).[15]

In June 1973 Reinecke gave yet another version of events to the FBI which, at the request of special Watergate prosecutor Archibald Cox, was investigating the possibility of perjury by either Reinecke or Mitchell. Reinecke now said he had told Mitchell of Sheraton's pledge during a telephone call in May or June 1971 before the settlement of ITT's cases had been reached. (Recall that Reinecke's first version indicated that he had had a *meeting* with Mitchell in May.) Asked whether his statement did not contradict Mitchell's repeated denials of knowledge of this pledge, Reinecke said, "It would appear to be in contradiction, yes." [16]

Another part of Mitchell's earlier denial stated that he had "not dis-

14 *Ibid.*

15 For the reaction of the press on the hazy memories and evasiveness of Mitchell, Kleindienst, and other witnesses, see, for example, the following sources, most of which are contained either in the *Hearings*, in the "Separate Report of Senators Bayh, Kennedy, and Tunney on the Supplementary Hearings Regarding the Nomination of Richard Kleindienst as Attorney General (as Revised and Supplemented)," or in *Editorials on File*, 1972: editorial, *Arkansas Gazette*, April 23, 1972; editorial, *Louisville Times*, April 24, 1972; "Kleindienst: Without a Doubt," *New Republic*, May 13, 1972; editorial, *Arkansas Democrat*, March 24, 1972; editorial, *St. Louis Post-Dispatch*, April 28, 1972; and "Lofty Discussions: How Mitchell Kept His Door Open," *San Francisco Chronicle*, March 16, 1972.

16 "ITT's Offer: I Told Mitchell, Reinecke Insists," *San Francisco Chronicle*, June 28, 1973, p. 11.

cussed the subject [of ITT's antitrust cases] with anyone from ITT" except Mrs. Beard. This was a believable statement, for, despite his claim that "anybody has the right to go into any department and talk to anybody," Mitchell "had the reputation of being as approachable as a medieval cardinal." [17] He admitted in testimony, however, that he had, after all, had a thirty-five-minute meeting with Harold Geneen, ITT's president, on August 4, 1970. Mitchell testified that he "assented to the meeting on the express condition that the pending ITT litigation would not be discussed. Mr. Geneen agreed to this condition. The pending ITT litigation was not discussed at the meeting" (*Hearings,* Part 2, p. 540). Instead, they had discussed the department's antitrust policy with respect to conglomerates. This policy, however, was at that time demonstrated in action by four pending cases, and three of the four were against ITT. Furthermore, ITT Vice-President Edward J. Gerrity told the committee that the purpose of the meeting was to take another try at seeing "if we could move the Justice Department toward some sort of reasonable attitude toward our position" on a settlement involving ITT's antitrust suits (*Hearings,* Part 2, p. 1198). A summary of ITT documents prepared by the SEC was released to the public by another congressional committee almost a year after Kleindienst's hearings supported Gerrity's statement. It contained a summary of a memo from Gerrity to Vice-President Spiro Agnew, dated August 7, 1970. The memo consisted of a thank-you letter concerning an attached memo and a suggestion that Mitchell get the facts relating to ITT's position to McLaren. It indicated that there was a friendly session between Geneen and Mitchell, in which Mitchell told Geneen that Nixon was not opposed to the merger and that Nixon believed that mergers were good. Mitchell apparently said that ITT had not been sued because bigness is bad.

This memo contradicted another part of Mitchell's statement and supported a vigorously disputed remark of Mrs. Beard's. Mitchell had at first stated: "With respect to the allegations that the President discussed the matter with me, there would be no occasion for him to do so and he did not." Gerrity's memo, however, indicates just the opposite, as did Mrs. Beard both in her memo and in her description to Brit Hume of her meeting with Mitchell at the Kentucky Derby party.

See the Rabbits Run: Actions of ITT

ITT officials moved rapidly to cover their tracks following the publication of Dita Beard's memo. The combination of denials, retractions, and other shenanigans was often so outrageous and bizarre that ITT became

[17] Mary McGrory, "Lofty Discussions: How Mitchell Kept His Door Open," *San Francisco Chronicle,* p. 13.

identified to the public as the author of events external to the hearings that "reached the full stance of a comic opera . . . a full grown Amos 'N Andy minstrel with Mrs. Beard in the role of Madam Queen." [18]

For starters, Mrs. Beard immediately disappeared from Washington after publication of her memo and was unavailable when hearings reopened on March 2, 1972. A subpoena was then issued by the committee, and the FBI was assigned the task of locating her. ITT officials denied knowledge of Mrs. Beard's whereabouts; in fact, they said, she was specifically told to keep them informed of where she was and had not done so. Jack Anderson, however, reported that when his office talked to Mrs. Beard a few days previously, she told them, "ITT has told me to get out of town." [19]

On March 4 Mrs. Beard was located in Denver, in the Rocky Mountain Osteopathic Hospital, where she had been admitted on March 3 for treatment of angina pectoris. Her doctors stated that her health would not permit a personal appearance in Washington. However, through an agreement with her doctors, arrangements were made for a select committee of senators to question her in Denver later in the month.

It was later alleged during the Watergate hearings that G. Gordon Liddy, then counsel for CREEP and one of the chief convicted conspirators in the Watergate bugging case, had whisked Mrs. Beard out of Washington.[20] Furthermore, E. Howard Hunt, also convicted in the Watergate case, visited Denver in disguise to talk to Mrs. Beard prior to her testimony before the select panel of senators from the Judiciary Committee.

ITT itself did not long remain in the shadow of Mrs. Beard's dramatic sickbed reappearance. Anderson charged that ITT officials, after being shown the memo, sent security officers from New York to put Mrs. Beard's files through a document shredder "to prevent their being subpoenaed after disclosure of the memo" (*Hearings*, Part 2, p. 392). This reaction of "near panic" [21] and the subsequent efforts by ITT officials were aimed at minimizing both the company's appearance of concealment of facts and restoring ITT's public credibility. On March 15 Geneen testified that although he knew no details about the incident, it was "probably more a reaction to the feeling that our files were suddenly open to the public . . . and certainly not any kind of action to, you might say, prevent a review of our files by any legitimate agency" (*Hearings*, Part 2, p. 666). He promised a full report by the following day. This was of particular interest, since Anderson reported Mrs. Beard as saying that one of the documents

[18] Editorial, *Chicago Daily Defender*, April 25, 1972.
[19] "Kleindienst Says He Set Up Talks on ITT Accord but Denies It Was Tied to GOP Convention Fund," *The New York Times*, March 3, 1972, p. 20.
[20] "Other Break-Ins Reported," *San Francisco Chronicle*, June 4, 1973, p. 8.
[21] "Investigations: 'Fake'?," *Newsweek*, March 27, 1972, p. 28.

shredded contained instructions for her to approach Mitchell at the Kentucky Derby party.

On March 16 Geneen and several ITT lawyers faced the committee to continue their detailed testimony on the memo's allegations and the shredding incident. Howard J. Aibel, vice-president and general counsel for ITT, testified that William Merriam, ITT's Washington office chief, had instructed his staff the day after he saw the memo "to remove any documents that were no longer needed for current operations as well as documents which, if put into Mr. Anderson's possession, could be misused and misconstrued by him. . . ." (*Hearings,* Part 2, p. 704). This was, he stated, in accordance with a long-standing company policy of destruction of noncurrent confidential and other material, which had not been previously complied with in the Washington office.

In later testimony, Merriam indicated that he had merely taken advantage of the situation to have the office comply with this policy. When it became apparent that there would be committee interest in the incident, four outside lawyers had been retained to ascertain that no material pertinent to the investigation had been destroyed. Aibel described the documents as primarily tourist brochures about San Diego, newspaper clippings, copies of speeches, and material relating to past Congresses. These were, he said, the only documents in the files that related to the San Diego convention. He admitted, however, that he could say only in a general way which documents were actually destroyed and that John Ryan from ITT's Washington office had helped Mrs. Beard in deciding which documents from her files were to be destroyed. Geneen and the other ITT witnesses insisted that there had been no intention to impede the committee's investigations and that there had been no documents in the files relevant to the investigation (*Hearings,* Part 2, pp. 713–28). However, as Senator Tunney observed, since all of the witnesses were relying "on the memory of those who would be acting contrary to their self interest" to remember the destruction of relevant material, "it would be quite unexpected to expect that an official of the Washington office would now admit that there was embarrassing document shredding" (*Hearings,* Part 2, p. 728).

Geneen and Aibel had been questioned in detail about Mrs. Beard's memo and its allegations, and three facts about it had been noted: There was no existing file copy of the memo; it lacked certain normal file markings; and Merriam claimed never to have seen it before Hume brought it to the office. In two days of testimony, March 15 and 16, there was never a suggestion of doubt about the memo's authenticity. Suddenly, on March 17, Mrs. Beard issued the following statement:

> Mr. Anderson's memo is a forgery, and not mine. I did not prepare it and could not have since to my knowledge the assertions in it

regarding the antitrust cases and former Atty. Gen. (John N.) Mitchell are untrue. I do not know who did prepare it, who forged my initial on it, how it got into Jack Anderson's hands or why. But, I repeat, I do know it is not my memo and is a hoax.

I did prepare a memo at about the time indicated, at the request of (W. R.) Bill Merriam, to him concerning plans for the Republican convention in San Diego. However, it was not the memo Jack Anderson has put in evidence before the Senate.[22]

Mrs. Beard's lawyer, who later stated that ITT was paying his fees ($15,000 was his initial retainer), hinted that evidence to prove the forgery charge would be forthcoming.

ITT immediately came to Mrs. Beard's support, claiming that the two Washington staff members who had been present when Hume first showed Mrs. Beard the memo would say that she had only recognized it by the initial *D* penciled next to her name. On March 20 ITT turned up what it called the "genuine" memo, carrying the same date as the Anderson memo; but this one, an innocuous job description, was so different from what Mrs. Beard said she had written that the company was forced to admit the next day that they had made an error and that their genuine memo was not the original after all. At that time the FBI produced a report that offered its expert opinion that the Anderson memo had been prepared in the ITT office at the time indicated. ITT countered with its own experts' report that it could *not* have been prepared in June 1971 but was more likely written in January 1972.

On March 26 Mrs. Beard herself finally testified before that "bunch of little bums," [23] as she referred to the senators who had come to interview her. Her testimony did little to dispel the confusion. She continued to deny that she had written the memo or that there was any connection between ITT's campaign pledge and the antitrust settlement. But she admitted to authorship of sections of the memo that linked Mitchell to the convention planning he had denied being part of and that stated that he knew of ITT's pledge. She also claimed to have written the last paragraph of the memo, which *specifically* linked the two events.

But after several hours of testimony, Mrs. Beard collapsed with a sudden recurrence of her heart symptoms. It would be at least six months before she could testify again, said her doctors, and the senators, understandably disturbed at what they had heard, went back to Washington to continue the hearings without her.

Mrs. Beard's illness also became a subject of controversy. Her condi-

[22] "ITT Lobbyist Calls Memo a 'Forgery'; Evidence Promised," *Los Angeles Times,* March 18, 1972.
[23] "Dita Beard on Dita Beard," *Time,* April 3, 1972, p. 16.

tion was attested to by several doctors, including two cardiologists—Dr. Victor Liszka, her long-time personal physician in Washington, and Dr. Leo Radetsky in Denver. Dr. Liszka appeared before the committee on March 6 amid rumors that ITT would be making an all-out effort to discredit Mrs. Beard. His testimony did little to contradict this rumor as he described Mrs. Beard's excessive drinking and heavy use of tranquilizers. He further testified that the side effects normally associated with the particular cardiac and circulatory problems that troubled Mrs. Beard were mental and emotional disturbances. He went on to testify that Mrs. Beard had told him that she was "mad and disturbed" when she wrote the memo (*Hearings,* Part 2, p. 232).

This testimony, which would have provided ITT with a convenient explanation for Mrs. Beard's memo, was seriously questioned. The following day the medical director of the American Heart Association termed Dr. Liszka's testimony about the side effects of cardiac problems "nonsense." [24] But even more damaging, the Justice Department informed the committee the day *after* Dr. Liszka's testimony that they had interviewed him about Mrs. Beard on March 3, and 5, 1972, and, furthermore, that earlier in the year he had been under investigation for alleged fraud in receiving excess Medicare payments. Although Dr. Liszka had been cleared of these allegations, at the time of the hearings a grand jury was considering similar evidence against his wife, also a doctor, with whom he operated a joint practice.

It was subsequently discovered that Dr. Radetsky, Mrs. Beard's Denver cardiologist, was the subject of a similar investigation, still in progress at the time he cared for Mrs. Beard. Inasmuch as Dr. Radetsky was responsible for terminating Mrs. Beard's testimony and for making the decision that she would not be available to testify again for six months (although she would be able to leave the hospital at the end of the week), the discovery that he was under investigation for fraud made his reliability questionable.

The committee also received telegrams from two other doctors caring for Mrs. Beard in Denver—Dr. Joseph Snyder and Dr. Ray Prior—stating in essence that there was no positive finding about Mrs. Beard's illness and that further tests were necessary before any definite diagnosis could be made. A week after her "collapse," Mrs. Beard checked out of the hospital for an evening, during which she was interviewed by CBS newsman Mike Wallace. Although she had left the hospital in a sweater and skirt, she wore a hospital gown for the interview. Nevertheless, according to the *Worcester Evening Gazette* (Mass.), "Those who watched the show saw

---

[24] "Ex-Governor of Kentucky Asserts Mitchell Rebuffed ITT Lobbyist," *The New York Times,* March 8, 1972, p. 21.

a salty, colorful woman who did not look as if she were at death's door." [25] It was too much to accept without a snicker, and newspaper editorials and columns took advantage of the rare opportunity to view what the *St. Louis Post-Dispatch* called the "squirming of this 6.7 billion dollar conglomerate under the light of public scrutiny." [26]

II. THE HARTFORD FIRE COMPANY ACQUISITION

The ITT pledge of financial contributions to the GOP convention was allegedly linked to a favorable settlement of the Justice Department's antitrust suit against ITT involving the Hartford Fire Insurance Company. In this section I shall examine the merits of the case, the circumstances that led up to it, and the real or suspected efforts made by ITT to persuade (read "coerce") various public officials and agencies to act in ways favorable to ITT.

The Consent Order

On July 31, 1971, Assistant Attorney General Richard W. McLaren announced the details of a consent order settling the government's antitrust suit against ITT involving the latter's acquisition of Canteen Corporation, Grinnell Corporation, and Hartford Fire Insurance Company. The consent order settled one of the biggest antitrust cases in the history of the Justice Department. However, by not carrying the case to the Supreme Court, the department lost an important opportunity to test the limits of Section 7 of the Clayton Act and to clarify its application to conglomerate mergers. Under the terms of the consent order, ITT was required:

1. To divest Canteen Corporation and the Fire Protection Division of Grinnell Corporation within two years.
2. To divest (a) Hartford or (b) Avis Rent-A-Car, ITT-Levitt and Sons, Inc., and its subsidiaries, ITT Hamilton Life Insurance Company and ITT Life Insurance Company of New York.
3. To refrain from acquiring any domestic corporation with assets of more than $100 million and to refrain from acquiring leading companies in concentrated U.S. markets without the approval of the department or the court. Under the agreement, a leading company was defined as one with annual sales of more than $25 million and

---

[25] Editorial, *Worcester Evening Gazette,* April 4, 1972.
[26] Editorial, *St. Louis Post-Dispatch,* March 22, 1972.

holding 15 percent of any market in which the top four companies accounted for more than 50 percent of total sales.

4. To refrain from acquiring any substantial interest in any domestic automatic sprinkler company or any domestic insurance company with insurance assets exceeding $10 million.

5. To discontinue the practice of reciprocity—using purchasing power to promote sales—by ITT and all of its subsidiary companies.

McLaren declared it to be a significant victory for the government in that it "obtained very substantial divestiture, the largest ever in an antitrust case, and strong injunctions against ITT's making any more of the giant and leading firm mergers. . . . We thus stopped the clear leader of what we felt was a highly competitive merger movement dead in its tracks, and we required it to back up quite a ways to boot" (*Hearings*, Part 2, p. 254).

A significant number of people, however, were disappointed by the government's willingness to settle and considered it a reversal of the policy that was so forcefully enunciated by the Nixon administration when it first came to power. McLaren had consistently maintained, and so stated at his confirmation hearings before the Senate Judiciary Committee on January 29, 1969, that he believed that "the antitrust laws, more particularly Section 7 of the Clayton Act, are able to reach conglomerate mergers." [27] He propounded similar views in public statements on more than one occasion.[28]

Perhaps the best and most articulate summary of McLaren's views is in his testimony before the House Ways and Means Committee:

Let me state briefly how I conceive the responsibility of the Antitrust Division in the light of current developments.

Our basic antitrust statutes are few in number; their provisions are relatively concise; and they have been the subject of major amendments on but few occasions since the Sherman Act was passed in 1890. . . .

Perhaps the cardinal reason for the achievements of antitrust has been the capacity of the basic law to adapt to changing circumstances.

[27] Quoted in "Separate Report of Senators Bayh, Kennedy, and Tunney on the Supplementary Hearings Regarding the Nomination of Richard Kleindienst as Attorney General (as Revised and Supplemented)," p. 31. Hereinafter referred to as "Separate Report."

[28] See, for example, "Antitrust—Republican Style," *Dun's Review,* October 1969; "Conglomerates Under Attack," *Newsweek,* March 10, 1969; "Antitrust Chief McLaren Promises Suits to Block Large Conglomerate Mergers," *The Wall Street Journal,* March 7, 1969, p. 2; and "McLaren Clarifies Administration Policy in Antitrust War on Conglomerate Mergers," *The Wall Street Journal,* March 28, 1969, p. 5.

. . . In short, antitrust law seeks always to remain equal to the vital task entrusted to it—the protection of a free competitive society.

The evolving nature of antitrust law is, I think, particularly relevant to a discussion of conglomerate mergers, for two principal reasons. First, there is every indication that conglomerate mergers are increasing in both frequency and magnitude at an unparalleled rate and are bound to have a significant impact on business activity. Second, if we define conglomerate mergers to mean those which are neither horizontal nor vertical, it is apparent that different conglomerate mergers may present different kinds of threats to competition and thus may require different kinds of analyses.[29]

McLaren also stated: "we are willing to risk losing some cases to find out how far Section 7 will take us in halting the current accelerated trend toward concentration by merger." [30]

In his oft-quoted speech to the Georgia Bar Association in Savannah, Mitchell, who was then attorney general, strongly backed McLaren's get-tough antitrust policy and claimed that "the future vitality of our free economy may be in danger because of the increasing threat of economic concentration by conglomerate corporate mergers." The merger trends of the mid-1960s "leave us with the unacceptable probability that the nation's manufacturing and financial assets will continue to be concentrated in the hands of fewer and fewer people—the very evil that the antitrust laws were designed to control." [31] In another speech before the American Bar Association, Mitchell asserted: "Never has there been a more urgent need for vigorous enforcement of our antitrust laws." [32]

Therefore, McLaren's announcement of the settlement of the antitrust cases against ITT left many observers puzzled and dissatisfied. *Business Week* called its editorial on the settlement "The Antitrusters Cop Out." [33] In the following months two further events were to take place that cast a grave shadow of doubt on the settlement and the propriety of the actions of the parties involved.

The first event was the announcement by Congressman Bob Wilson, on August 5, that the $400,000 pledge to the San Diego Convention and Tourist Bureau came from the Sheraton Corporation of America, an ITT subsidiary. This confirmed rumors that had been circulating since June 21 when Wilson had announced the pledge without naming the source.[34]

[29] U.S., Congress, House, Hearings before the Committee on Ways and Means on the Subject of Tax Reform, 91st Cong., 1st sess., p. 2389.

[30] *Ibid.*

[31] "News Analysis and Interpretation: ITT Log Book: Names, Dates . . . and Questions," *St. Louis Post-Dispatch,* March 26, 1969, p. 3E.

[32] *The Wall Street Journal,* March 28, 1969, p. 5.

[33] August 7, 1971.

[34] *San Diego Union,* August 6, 1971.

The second event was the nomination by the White House, and the subsequent confirmation "in record time" by the Senate, of McLaren as a federal judge. Although all parties vehemently denied at that time—and still deny—any connection between these two events and McLaren's antitrust policy or the ITT settlement, doubts arose about the strange coincidence of events, doubts that were intensified with the publication of the Dita Beard memo and subsequent events.

The Background of the Antitrust Cases

In early 1969 ITT decided to acquire the Canteen Corporation; with $240 million in assets, Canteen was the leading vending machine producer in the country. The Justice Department considered this merger a violation of antitrust laws. The merger of ITT, the largest pure conglomerate in the United States, with the leader of the vending machine business was obviously more than a "foothold" or "toehold" acquisition and could have anticompetitive implications.

McLaren's policy on such mergers was reflected in the guidelines issued by the department and was repeatedly stressed by Justice Department officials: "The Department of Justice will probably oppose any merger by one of the top 200 manufacturing firms or any leading producer in any concentrated industry" (*Hearings,* Part 2, p. 141). As early as April 7, 1969, ITT was formally informed by McLaren of his intention to bring suit against the merger. The thrust of this suit was apparently the merger's ability to facilitate reciprocity or a reciprocity effect.

ITT, therefore, was very well aware of its antitrust violation. Nevertheless, it went ahead and consummated the merger on April 25, 1969. The Justice Department filed suit, asking for the divestiture of Canteen, on April 28, 1969. Shortly after the announcement of this suit, plans for two more mergers that apparently violated the administration's policy guidelines were made public by ITT. The company announced its intention to acquire (1) the Grinnell Corporation, a leading company in the sales and production of fire protection devices, industrial piping, and sprinkler systems, and (2) the Hartford Fire and Casualty Insurance Company, the nation's sixth largest insurance company and second largest fire insurance company.

As might be expected, the Justice Department opposed both mergers. Its intention to bring suits against ITT was announced on June 23 and 30, 1969, and the suits, seeking preliminary injunctions, were filed on August 1, 1969.

The Justice Department's opposition was again based on the reduction of competition and the threat of reciprocity that might be caused by the mergers. Specifically, in *Grinnell,* the main thrust of the suit was that once acquired by ITT, Grinnell would be entrenched as the dominant company in the manufacture and installation of automatic sprinklers, with ITT's immense resources at its disposal. All other suppliers were small regional companies or contractors. ITT could provide or finance huge contracts to Grinnell through its various subsidiaries, such as ITT-Levitt—the leading real estate developer and home builder; ITT-Hamilton Insurance; and ITT-Hartford. This could make it virtually impossible for the small competitors to survive, much less compete.

In the Hartford case, reciprocity was argued as the basis for suit. It was contended that the immense purchasing power of ITT, spread across every branch of the economy, could not but help Hartford, with a resultant powerful effect on the insurance industry. Furthermore, because of the special nature and structure of the insurance business, most of ITT's suppliers would favor doing business with Hartford even if no pressures to do so were applied. Vertical integration aspects of the merger could trigger other similar mergers.

The government also argued that ITT's three acquisitions of large and leading companies were part of its growth and concentration of economic power, as stated by McLaren:

> . . . we expect to argue that the three acquisitions are not only part of ITT's program of acquiring large leading companies, but are part of a general merger trend which, if continued, will have substantial anticompetitive effects upon the economy as a whole. . . .
>
> It is interesting to note that ITT ended 1969 as Number 9 on FORTUNE's list of 500 Largest Industrial Corporations (up from Number 11 in 1968). It has continued to make acquisitions—albeit smaller ones than those at issue—and it is my opinion that if we lose these cases against ITT, or do not obtain meaningful relief, we will have to seek new legislation which will be effective to stop the resurgence of big-firm mergers which will almost inevitably result. [*Hearings,* Part 2, p. 1245]

Due to the novelty and complexity of these cases, the Justice Department in both the Hartford case and the Grinnell case was denied its request for preliminary injunctions against the mergers, thereby opening the way for a direct government appeal to the Supreme Court. These cases, as well as *Canteen,* which had similarly been initially decided against the government, were brought to trial and appealed very quickly.

In November 1970, while the cases were in progress, ITT proposed an out-of-court settlement involving its retention of Hartford, but divestiture of Canteen, Grinnell, ITT-Levitt, and some other insurance operations of

ITT. This would have, to some extent, eliminated the reciprocity and vertical integration effects of the acquisitions. To be specific, ITT was the major consumer of Canteen's "in-plant feeding program" (15 percent of its sales). Therefore, divestiture of Canteen would eliminate the reciprocity and anticompetitive aspects of this merger. Divestiture of Levitt, ITT's real estate and home builder, along with the fire protection division of Grinnell, would also eliminate some apparent vertical integration and reciprocity. Finally, divestiture of small insurance operations would remove the obvious possibility of horizontal integration in the insurance business. Retention of Hartford, however, would leave untouched ITT's movement toward more economic concentration and a tendency toward vertical integration in the insurance of other ITT subsidiaries.

This settlement was rejected by the Antitrust Division, and the appeals continued. To no one's surprise, the court rejected the government's contentions in *Grinnell* on December 31, 1970, on the grounds that there was no legal precedent. This was the final lower court decision, and the case could now be appealed to the Supreme Court. This procedure was recommended by McLaren to Solicitor General Erwin N. Griswold on February 24, 1971, and although Griswold did not agree with McLaren's theories, he approved the appeal, and preparations for the submission of the jurisdictional statement to the Court were begun.

Canteen, being tried in Chicago, suffered a similar fate. In July 1971 the government's case was rejected by the District Court.

Hartford Fire Insurance Company

Hartford Fire Insurance Company was a leading writer of property and liability insurance. Pertinent financial data for Hartford as of 1969 were as follows:

Consolidated assets:	$ 1.98 billion
Premium receipts:	968.80 million
Net income:	53.30 million
Excess cash over required reserves:	400.00 million

The ITT-Hartford merger was the largest corporate merger in history. The acquisition had to be approved by the Connecticut insurance commissioner. Even before the start of these proceedings, in June 1969, the Justice Department announced its opposition to the merger. In August 1969 the department sought a preliminary injunction against the merger in the Connecticut District Court, but this was denied in November 1969 after lengthy hearings.

The Connecticut insurance commissioner was charged with the responsibility for protecting policyholders from possible risks from such a merger. In December 1969 Commissioner William R. Cotter ruled against the merger, a move that surprised many observers and enraged many Hartford shareholders, as well as financial concerns that had bought Hartford stock on the expectation that the merger would be approved. Although Commissioner Cotter did not give his reasons for rejecting the merger, the *Hartford Times* noted that Cotter "suggested that a tender offer, directly to the stockholders, would have been more appropriate," thus bringing the merger under the provisions of Public Act 444.[35]

Public Act 444 was basically designed to make it as difficult as possible for an outsider, especially a noninsurer, to take over Connecticut's rich insurance companies. This act was presented to the Connecticut legislature early in 1969, after such big Connecticut insurers as Aetna Life and Casualty, Travelers, and Hartford were rumored to be acquisition targets of noninsurance companies. When raids by acquiring companies into the giant surplus funds of some insurance companies were reported, Connecticut felt the need for action. However, ITT had consistently denied that Hartford's huge cash flow and reserves were its reasons for acquiring the company:

> Harold Geneen, Chairman of ITT, said in an exclusive statement to the [Hartford] *Times* last fall *that he had no plans to raid Hartford's $900 million reserves, and that he wanted instead to see Hartford continue growing and become an international company through ITT's connections abroad.* [Emphasis added] [36]

On January 28, 1970, Cotter's decision was appealed to the Connecticut Superior Court, ITT, Hartford, and three of Hartford's stockholders sued the commissioner, seeking an injunction and claiming that the commissioner's decision was unfounded.[37] Cotter's decision had not discouraged ITT's acquisition plans, and it renewed its effort to take over Hartford, this time through a new tender offer that was more generous to Hartford shareholders, thereby forcing the commissioner to reconsider his decision.

Throughout the lengthy hearings, ITT claimed that it was immensely strong financially and economically. ITT stated that it intended to pump money into Hartford for further growth. The soundness of ITT's management team and its intention to improve upon Hartford's management were persistent arguments. There was no indication that ITT wanted to take

---

[35] "Cotter vs. ITT: Strong Image Unfolds," *Hartford Times*, December 18, 1969.
[36] "Hartford Fire, ITT Sue Cotter," *Hartford Times*, January 29, 1970.
[37] "Cotter Sued on Merger," *Hartford Times*, January 29, 1970.

advantage of any of Hartford's assets, excess available cash, or borrowing power. However, as it turned out later, during its negotiations with the Justice Department over an antitrust settlement, ITT argued that a divestiture of Hartford would inflict a severe and crippling financial blow to ITT stockholders in particular and the U.S. economy in general.

During the hearings, ITT promised help with the financing of the proposed Civic Center in Hartford and committed the company to building a Sheraton Hotel there.[38]

On May 23, 1970, the commissioner reversed his earlier decision and approved the merger. Formal steps toward the actual acquisition were soon completed, as was the Justice Department's suit against them.

Settlement Negotiations

With two lower court decisions in hand on February 24, 1971, McLaren urged the solicitor general to push the *Grinnell* case to the Supreme Court. Griswold later testified that he considered it a "difficult case to win." However, "there was no way that we could find out whether the existing statute . . . was adequate to deal with conglomerate mergers except by taking the case to the Supreme Court and seeking their decision" (*Hearings,* Part 2, p. 372).

By April 19, 1971, the case was ready for submission to the Supreme Court. However, on that date, in response to a phone call and letter from ITT attorney and personal friend Lawrence Walsh, Acting Attorney General Richard Kleindienst asked the solicitor general to request an extension of time from the Supreme Court. Although McLaren and the solicitor general did not relish the idea of requesting a delay, for different reasons, the extension was nonetheless requested and granted.

Walsh's letter, which Kleindienst later stated he had never seen, reads in part as follows:

> Looking back at the results of Government antitrust cases in the Supreme Court, one must realize that if the government urges an expanded interpretation of the vague language of the Clayton Act, there is a high probability that it will succeed. Indeed, the Court has at times adopted a position more extreme than that urged by the Department. . . .
>
> It is our hope that after reading the enclosed memorandum, which is merely a preliminary presentation, you and Dick McLaren and the Solicitor General would be willing to delay the submission of the

[38] "ITT Replies to Attack from Nader," *Hartford Courant,* April 29, 1970; "Cotter Denied Hotel Plans Swayed ITT Decision," *Hartford Courant,* March 11, 1972.

jurisdictional statement in the *Grinnell* case long enough to permit us to make a more adequate presentation on this question. [*Hearings, Part 2, pp. 263–64*]

One day later, although Kleindienst "did not associate the two" (*Hearings, Part 2, p. 348*), Kleindienst met for the first time with Felix Rohatyn to discuss the impact that a Hartford divestiture would have upon ITT. Kleindienst was sufficiently impressed, he said, by Rohatyn's presentation to make arrangements for a second, larger meeting. On April 29, 1971, Kleindienst, McLaren, a representative of the Treasury Department, and attorneys and staff of the antitrust division, after a fifty-minute wait for Rohatyn (who was at a simultaneous, although reportedly unrelated, meeting with, among others, Mitchell and Flanigan), met with Rohatyn, two ITT attorneys—Howard J. Aibel and Henry Sailer—and others representing ITT. ITT's argument was not based on the merits of antitrust statutes or their applicability. Its new approach was a financial one with three basic arguments, all dealing with the results of a divestiture of Hartford:

1. The divestiture of Hartford was impractical; a forced spinoff, the only feasible way of divestiture, would have a devastating effect—a reduction by as much as 45 percent—on the liquidity and cash position of ITT.
2. The divestiture of Hartford would also affect ITT's credit rating and therefore its borrowing position abroad. This could have an adverse effect on the U.S. balance of payments, to which ITT was a substantial positive contributor.
3. The divestiture of Hartford would cause an immediate diminution of approximately $1.2 billion in the price of ITT stock. This not only would wreak hardship on the owners of ITT stock but could have a substantial unsettling impact—a "ripple effect"— on the stock market and possibly the economy as a whole.

For the Justice Department's further study, the ITT group left behind a set of documents meant to substantiate their arguments. In addition, Rohatyn forwarded a letter to McLaren acknowledging the meeting and stressing the points he had raised.

Independent Analysis

After the April 29 meeting, McLaren decided to check the merit of ITT's arguments. Bypassing the economists on his own staff, McLaren chose an outside, independent consultant, Richard Ramsden. Ramsden had previously been a White House Fellow and, during that time, had prepared for McLaren an analysis that was used for the settlement of the controversial Ling-Temco-Vought–Jones & Laughlin merger case. In both instances, White House aide Peter Flanigan was involved in securing Ramsden's services. According to McLaren, at the time of the ITT presentation he did not know how to reach Ramsden and therefore asked Flanigan to contact him. For reasons never clarified, Ramsden's sole contact in Washington regarding the preparation of his analysis of ITT's presentation was with Flanigan, labeled by the *Wall Street Journal* as business's "Mr. Fixit."

According to Ramsden's testimony, he met Flanigan in the latter's office at the White House for about twenty minutes. Flanigan informed him that his assignment was to be ITT and that McLaren wanted Ramsden to examine *solely* "the financial consequences of divestiture of Hartford Insurance Company by ITT" (*Hearings,* Part 3, p. 1352). Flanigan also gave Ramsden a document for study entitled "Memorandum on Economic Consequences of a Hartford Divestiture by ITT" (*Hearings,* Part 3, p. 1356). As to the nature of this document, Ramsden stated:

> I can make two comments about the memorandum: First of all, it was obviously written by someone who thought there were some financial consequences that were bad for ITT in the divestiture of Hartford. That was obvious.
>
> The second thing that was very obvious about the memorandum was that it was in no way based on any facts; it was in no way based on any analysis. It was basically unsubstantiated opinion. . . . [*Hearings,* Part 3, p. 1356]

Ramsden testified that he spent a total of five days preparing the report but charged the government for only two days—the time he was actually away from his normal work. Ramsden did not talk to McLaren directly; he analyzed what Flanigan told him McLaren wanted. Ramsden also testified that he was not told what the purpose of the analysis was; nor did Flanigan tell him that the "memo" was prepared by Felix Rohatyn, an ITT director.[39]

Ramsden's report weighed heavily in McLaren's decision, and in his later testimony he repeatedly referred to it as a solid and substantive piece of analysis. In his memorandum to the deputy attorney general dated June 17, 1971, recommending the settlement, McLaren noted:

---

[39] "ITT Report's Author Undercuts Rationale of Justice Agency on Anti-trust Accord," *The Wall Street Journal,* April 18, 1972, p. 4.

We have had a study made by financial experts and they substantially confirm ITT's claims as to the effects of a divestiture order. Such being the case, I gather that we must also anticipate that the impact upon ITT would have a ripple effect—in the stock market and in the economy.

Under the circumstances, I think we are compelled to weigh the need for divestiture in this case. . . . Or, to refine the issue a little more: Is a decree against ITT containing injunctive relief and a divestiture order worth enough more than a decree containing only injunctive relief to justify the projected adverse effects on ITT and its stockholders, and the risk of adverse effects on the stock market and the economy?

I come to the reluctant conclusion that the answer is "no." I say reluctant because ITT's management consummated the Hartford acquisition knowing it violated our antitrust policy; knowing we intended to sue; and in effect representing to the court that he need not issue a preliminary injunction because ITT would hold Hartford separate and thus minimize any divestiture problem if violation were found. [*Hearings*, Part 2, p. 111]

In later testimony, McLaren defended the settlement as being good for the economy. However, Ramsden testified that his report could not be used to draw any such conclusion. A similar conclusion, that a divestiture of Hartford would not be detrimental to the economy, was arrived at independently by some economists and financial experts both within the Justice Department and in academic circles (*Hearings*, Part 3, pp. 1374–95). As to the protection of ITT's stockholders, the Supreme Court, in *United States* v. *E. I. Du Pont de Nemours & Co. et al.* (1961), held that this hardship argument was not admissible:

Those who violate the Act may not reap the benefits of their violations and avoid an undoing of their unlawful project on the plea of hardship or inconvenience.

If the Court concludes that other measures will not be effective to redress a violation, and that complete divestiture is a necessary element of effective relief, the Government cannot be denied the latter remedy because economic hardship, however severe, may result. [*Hearings*, Part 3, p. 1404]

The Aftermath

A final agreement was announced on July 31, 1971, thereby ending three years' hard work by the Antitrust Division in the interests of getting a landmark Supreme Court decision. However, many questions remained unanswered:

Why did the government settle at all?

Why should ITT be allowed to keep Hartford's $1.98 billion by divesting only $796 million in other assets?

What was the effect of the settlement on competition?

Why did McLaren, with his twenty-five years of deep commitment to antitrust, approve the shift so rapidly?

The agreement was in the form of a consent decree and was thus subject to Court approval. On August 23, 1971, the Justice Department announced that the agreement had been filed for the approval of the Court and would become final in thirty days. On September 21, 1971, Reuben B. Robertson, on behalf of Ralph Nader's group, filed a petition with the Justice Department protesting the proposed agreement on the grounds that ITT and Hartford had already begun some policies with clear anticompetitive implications. He also noted that the consent decree, in the form presented to the Court, failed to protect against the problem of entrenchment. He further argued that despite what ITT had presented to the courts, ITT had already been involved in reciprocity.

The response by the Justice Department was a quick one. On September 22, 1971, McLaren rejected Nader's arguments.

Realizing the government's position, Nader's group submitted a "Memorandum of *Amici Curiae*" to the Connecticut District Court. While making many legal and technical points, it opposed the merger on the basis that the consent decree had not provided for the full relief intended by the law. It urged the court to reject the decree and to initiate its own hearing and inquiry into the terms, merit, and reasons for such a decree. The court, however, noting that the merger had never been declared illegal,[40] "summarily rebuffed" (*Hearings,* Part 3, p. 1283) these arguments, and the decree was approved and finalized on September 24.

THE SECURITIES AND EXCHANGE COMMISSION'S ROLE IN THE ITT AFFAIR

It appears that no governmental agency that had dealings with ITT could avoid the long shadow of doubt about decisions favorable to ITT, decisions that were seemingly contrary to the agency's established policies. There seems to be a consistent pattern of hasty decisions, ambiguous explanations, and, more important, "lucky" coincidences to explain an

---

[40] "Approval Is Seen for ITT Merger," *The New York Times,* September 24, 1971, p. 57.

incredibly fortunate chain of events whenever ITT is involved. We have already seen it happen in the case of the Justice Department. In this section I will briefly cover the SEC's involvement in another dimension of the government's antitrust case against ITT.

The SEC Suit

On Friday, June 16, 1972, the Securities and Exchange Commission charged that ITT and two of its top executives had violated federal securities laws in June and July 1971. This occurred, the SEC charged, while the Justice Department and ITT were privately negotiating a settlement of three antitrust cases. The SEC suit, in the federal court for the Southern District of New York, accused ITT of failing to disclose the settlement talks with the Justice Department in a supplement to a prospectus filed with the SEC. The prospectus covered 26,668 shares of ITT stock sold in July 1971 by a unit of Hartford. Two ITT executives, Senior Vice-President Howard J. Aibel and Secretary and Counsel for Corporate Affairs John J. Navin, were also charged with selling stocks on the basis of inside information.

In the same suit, the SEC brought charges against ITT and two investment banking institutions, Lazard Frères & Company of New York and Mediobanca of Milan, Italy. The SEC charged that they had violated securities laws in the unregistered distribution of $1.7 million worth of ITT Series N preferred stock between November 1970 and May 1971, under a fee-splitting arrangement through which Lazard Frères and Mediobanca divided $2.17 million.

The suit against ITT and its executives was a relatively mild one. The SEC did not seek any sanctions other than restraining those charged from future securities law violations. However, according to the agency's Rule 10B-5, the SEC could have brought fraud charges against the company and its officers and required repayment of the profits made by the executives' sales.[41]

Commenting on charges against ITT and its officials, the SEC stated that *they had been filed after two years of investigating ITT's acquisition of Hartford*. It was therefore a matter of some surprise when "two days later, the SEC suit was settled by consent agreement under which the defendants, without conceding past violations, agreed they wouldn't violate securities laws in the future." [42] Once again, two years of effort produced

---

[41] For a detailed explanation of Rule 10B-5, see "Securities and Exchange Commission versus Texas Gulf Sulphur Company," pp. 349-51 of this book.

[42] "Handling of 'Politically Sensitive' ITT Files to Be Reviewed by House Commerce Unit," *The Wall Street Journal*, December 18, 1972, p. 3.

a consent decree on charges to which the company and its officials never admitted any guilt. As *Business Week* cynically pointed out, "People who violate securities laws seldom go to jail; instead they often consent to an injunction—that is, they agree not to do in the future what they neither admit nor deny doing in the past." [43] Thus, it appeared that ITT had again carried the day. Commenting on the settlement, *Business Week* editorialized:

The penalty assessed by the Securities and Exchange Commission . . . is woefully inadequate. What appeared to be a stiff regulatory action when the SEC went into court turned into a painless slap on the wrist after the corporation and the two executives signed consent decrees agreeing not to do it again.

The SEC could have asked the court to order the two executives to pay the corporation back the $7-a-share additional profit that they made by selling their stock before a public announcement that the company had entered into a consent decree with the Justice Dept.— an action that proved bearish for the stock. But the SEC's general policy is not to ask defendants such as these to pay back profits. Instead, the commission feels that its action may trigger civil suits where the real damage will be inflicted.

The commission needs to reevaluate this policy. The SEC should not expect somebody else to do its painful dirty work.[44]

The Background

Between June 18 and July 31, 1971, heavy sale of ITT stock by ITT officers and other associates came to Wall Street's attention. Even one of ITT's subsidiaries sold 41,280 shares of common and 8,500 shares of convertible preferred stock. From the beginning of 1971 through June 18, 1971, ITT executives had been heavy buyers of ITT stock. This trend did not continue, however. Reports filed with the SEC by ITT insiders show that in six weeks, between June 18 and July 31, 1971, ITT executives dumped a total of $3.1 million in ITT stock. SEC regulations require that all major stockholders and officers of a company report their stockholdings every month.

This change in the trend of insider transactions was called a coincidence by company spokesmen. The Senate hearings, however, revealed that a telephone call on June 17, 1971, from the Justice Department to Felix Rohatyn could well have been the turning point for these transactions.

---

[43] "The 34 Boxes of Dynamite," *Business Week,* October 21, 1972, p. 61.
[44] "Make the Penalty Fit," *Business Week,* July 1, 1972, p. 60.

Rohatyn, under intense questioning by Senator Edward M. Kennedy, testified that he had informed Geneen and Aibel within twenty-four to forty-eight hours after the call from Justice. Testimony during the hearings showed that at least a few ITT officials learned by June 18, 1971, or thereabouts that the government had proposed a settlement which was then unacceptable and undesirable to ITT, although it would not require divestiture of Hartford. This settlement eventually caused a $7-per-share drop in the price of ITT stock, from $62 to $55 per share, on the first day of trading after it had been announced. The officers, however, enjoyed prices ranging from $62 to $68 per share by selling before the announcement.

Trading on the basis of inside material information, undisclosed to the public, is prohibited by SEC Rule 10B-5. The ITT officials involved and other corporate spokesmen denied any charges of trading based on inside information. On the contrary, they all claimed that their sales were for different reasons having nothing to do with information about the negotiations with Justice. Aibel, for example, testified that his sell order had been placed on June 17, and it was not until after the order was executed on June 18 that he learned of the call from Justice. On another occasion he testified that he had not learned of the settlement proposal until June 21. Rohatyn, however, was certain he had spoken to Aibel within at most forty-eight hours after the call from Kleindienst and McLaren. Furthermore, on June 18 Aibel had accompanied Geneen to make a court deposition regarding the Hartford acquisition for an SEC inquiry.

Other ITT officials who sold stock during this period claimed selling motives that, like Aibel's, were not dependent on the pending settlement. Bateson said he sold to pay his son's savings account for a withdrawal he had made for the down payment on a house he had decided to buy on June 1. H. V. Williams, a director, said the timing of his own sale was "absolutely a coincidence." [45] Hart Perry, a director and senior vice-president, said his stocks were sold to repay loans incurred to exercise his stock options. He had only learned of the settlement on July 31. Other officers involved similarly explained that they wanted to repay loans and had sold as soon as the law allowed them to do so and keep the proceeds.

A unit of Hartford, Hartford Accident and Indemnity Company, sold 26,666 shares of ITT common stock. It also denied any knowledge of the proposed settlement, although Hartford and ITT share some directors—including Geneen.

It is interesting to note that ITT failed to disclose its settlement negotiations with Justice to the SEC. ITT issued a prospectus on July 22, 1971, with not even a hint about the negotiations that concluded nine days later. In fact, it states, concerning the antitrust cases: "ITT is asserting a vigor-

---

[45] "A Lucky Break," *The Wall Street Journal*, March 16, 1972, pp. 1, 14.

ous defense. Trial on the merits in this case is expected to begin in September, 1971." [46] The prospectus was originally issued on April 19, for registration of certain letter stock, and was updated on July 22 when additional shares were added. In its defense, ITT stated that the reason there was no mention of negotiations was that "the agreement in principle was rejected on July 6," [47] although such a rejection was not mentioned during the Senate hearings.

The Thirty-four Boxes of SEC Files

During its investigation of ITT's possible violation of SEC regulations, the SEC subpoenaed documents and papers from ITT files. However, when the SEC quietly settled its case within a week after filing formal charges, the state of Ohio and Ralph Nader's group demanded that the hearings be made public or SEC might wind up in court. Both groups wanted access to SEC files. Almost simultaneously, Representative Harley Staggers, chairman of the House Interstate and Foreign Commerce Committee, and Representative John Moss decided they wanted to look at the files also in connection with their own investigations.

SEC Chairman William Casey refused to hand over the files to the congressional investigators, claiming that the case was still under investigation. Soon after (October 6, 1972), the SEC packed every scrap of the ITT files into thirty-four boxes and sent them to the Justice Department. Two days later Casey wrote to Staggers that "he couldn't deliver the files because Justice had asked for them—'for possible criminal prosecution.' " Justice, however, told two newspaper reporters "it hadn't asked for the files, Casey had offered them." [48]

In later testimony before Congressman Staggers's committee, Casey stated that he feared that if the ITT material in SEC files were prematurely made public, it might interefere with the possible prosecution of a criminal case against ITT by the Justice Department. In later questioning, however, it was revealed that Casey had discussed with White House Counsel John Dean the possibility of the extension of executive privilege to SEC for its refusal to furnish congressional committees with the ITT files, including the plans for the transfer of the files to the Justice Department. Charles Whitman, Casey's administrative assistant, testified that he kept a few documents out of the thirty-four boxes after informing Casey, because they were "politically sensitive." [49]

[46] "ITT: Emerging Contradictions," *The Wall Street Journal*, March 22, 1972, p. 16.
[47] *Ibid.*
[48] *Business Week*, July 1, 1972, p. 60.
[49] "Casey Says Politics Affected SEC Decision to Keep Files on ITT Case from Congress," *The Wall Street Journal*, December 15, 1972, p. 3.

Staggers's request for the files was made on September 23 and was repeated on September 28, and the discussion between Dean and Casey took place on October 3, 1972; SEC voted for the transfer of the files to Justice on October 4, and the actual transfer took place on October 6.

When he testified, Casey provided the House committee with a summary of ITT papers contained in the thirty-four boxes, as well as with a secret SEC working paper on the case. This paper, later made public by Staggers, indicated that "several key Nixon administration officials were instrumental in helping International Telephone and Telegraph Corp. reach the controversial 1971 antitrust settlement with the Justice Department." The officials named were Vice-President Spiro Agnew, Treasury Secretary John Connally, former Commerce Secretary Maurice Stans, and former Commerce Secretary Peter Peterson.[50] This disclosure thus raised the possibility that Connally and others may have perjured themselves in their earlier testimony concerning their roles in the ITT affair. The paper also mentioned a Mitchell statement to the effect that President Nixon knew of the merger and considered it "good."

Ralph E. Erickson, former deputy attorney general, later testified before the same subcommittee that he had emphasized in conversations with both Dean and Casey that the Justice Department had no need for the files in connection with the investigation it was then conducting into possible perjury of witnesses during the hearings into Kleindienst's testimony. The Justice Department, Erickson said, had not requested the files. His statements so flatly contradicted the version of events that Casey had outlined in his testimony that the House committee was confronted with the possibility of perjury and falsification of records in its own hearings.

And the end was still not in sight. The entire matter seemed to be headed for final unraveling, however, when special Watergate prosecutor Archibald Cox was assigned the task of reopening the case. Attorney General Elliot Richardson instructed Cox to investigate "whether ITT officials obstructed a stock trading investigation . . . and whether any witnesses perjured themselves at last year's Senate hearings on the nomination of Richard Kleindienst for Attorney General." The job was given to Cox, Richardson stated, because "the ITT inquiry has begun to overlap with the Watergate investigation, particularly in the area of subjects for interview." [51]

Casey, now Undersecretary of State for Economic Affairs, testified before the House Commerce Subcommittee in June 1973 that during the

---

[50] "ITT Saga (Cont'd): Agnew, Connally, Stans Linked to ITT Effort in the Hartford Case," *The Wall Street Journal,* March 19, 1973, p. 1.

[51] "ITT Antitrust Accord Still a Political Issue as Possible Link to GOP Pledge Is Studied," *The Wall Street Journal,* June 11, 1973, p. 8.

SEC's probe of ITT, John Erlichmann, then President Nixon's principal domestic affairs assistant, had telephoned to ask whether the SEC's pursuit of ITT documents was necessary. Casey testified that he thought this call was "clearly improper if he was suggesting not to take the evidence." [52]

Internal Revenue Service—Favorable Tax Ruling

For the ITT-Hartford merger to go through, it was important that ITT receive a favorable tax ruling from IRS so that the merger could be tax-free. That is, so that the Hartford stockholders would not be required to pay a capital gains tax on the exchange of their Hartford stock for ITT stock. An unfavorable ruling could have killed the merger.

To gain such a ruling, ITT made an application in "routine fashion" claiming that it had fulfilled all the IRS requirements, and the ruling was granted forthwith. However, it later appeared that ITT may not have fulfilled all the IRS requirements and may have been in technical violation of the regulations, and that in these and "in other aspects of the sale, too, the IRS tended to make things as easy as possible for ITT." [53]

The regulations for a tax-free Type B merger, by which ITT intended to acquire Hartford, required that ITT pay for Hartford stock *only in stock*. However, at that time ITT already owned 1.7 million shares, or about 8 percent, of Hartford's outstanding stock, which it had acquired for cash in the open market. IRS had earlier informed ITT that only if this stock was first disposed of, under conditions acceptable to IRS, could the merger become tax-free.[54] Earlier IRS rulings in such cases had held that such a sale must be an *unconditional divestiture of the stock to unrelated third parties prior to the tender offer by the acquiring corporation or the vote of the shareholders of the acquired corporation* (whichever is appropriate) for a stock-for-stock acquisition (*Hearings,* Part 3, p. 1303 [emphasis added]). ITT was thus required to divest itself of its holdings of 8 percent of Hartford stock.

ITT reached an agreement with Mediobanca through Lazard Frères and presented it to the IRS to satisfy the requirements of Section 368(1) (B). Under the agreement with the bank:

1. Mediobanca was guaranteed against any losses in the transaction if it resold the stock through Lazard Frères at any time during the

[52] "ITT Case Phone Calls Told," *San Francisco Chronicle,* June 28, 1973, p. 11.
[53] "How ITT Maneuvered to Get a Tax Ruling in the Hartford Deal," *San Francisco Chronicle,* October 12, 1972, p. 1.
[54] "ITT Tax Ruling Linked to Complex Maneuvering," *The New York Times,* March 26, 1972, pp. 1, 52.

eighteen months prior to May 31, 1971. (This was the basis of the fee-splitting charge by the SEC.)

2. Mediobanca was guaranteed a profit of 25.5 cents per share if it sold the stock during the second half of 1970, but 51 cents per share if it sold it during the first five months of 1971.

3. As an inducement for Mediobanca to enter into the contract, ITT *paid* a premium of 76.5 cents per share.

4. The price of the stock was not fixed at the time of the agreement but was to be determined by one of three options, from which the bank was to choose one, provided in the contract:

The first option called for the bank to pay $51 a share or the market price for the huge block on the day of closing as determined by Lazard Frères, if that price was higher. . . .

The second option would have set the price at the "fair market value" of the stock during a two-week period in May 1971, more than 18 months after the stock was supposedly to change hands, in November 1969. . . .

The third option . . . provided that the price would be whatever the bank could sell the Hartford shares for, or ITT shares it might receive in a merger, whenever the bank chose to sell up to May 31, 1971.[55]

It was reported that the bank had ruled out the first option on the day it signed the contract. By doing this, the only normal business option was deleted immediately. With this option eliminated, the actual content of the transaction as specified in the contract was as follows:

1. Mediobanca did not have to pay anything to ITT but a credit on its own books, if this was deemed appropriate.

2. ITT would not receive any money because prices were not set, and, in fact, the transaction could not have been completed without the stock prices, which had not been determined at that time.

3. The buyer, Mediobanca, did not have to take *any risk,* even a normal one, associated with the stock transactions. On the contrary, ITT, the seller, accepted all risk in addition to an unreasonably high inducement and an unusual profit guarantee.

It could be argued, therefore, that there was no arm's-length transaction between Mediobanca and ITT and that the bank never bought the stock at all. As the *Wall Street Journal* stated:

[55] Easing a Merger," *The Wall Street Journal,* October 12, 1972, pp. 1, 19.

Even before signing a contract to buy them, Mediobanca got $1.3 million in fees. Later, when Mediobanca got ITT stock in exchange for those Hartford shares, it sold the ITT stock and passed the proceeds (about $100 million plus accumulated dividends) along to ITT as payment for the original Hartford stock. So it could be argued in substance that the bank merely held the Hartford stock for ITT until the tax problem was resolved and there was no longer any possibility that it might fall into unfriendly hands opposed to a merger, pocketing a $1.3 million fee for its trouble. In fact, this is essentially what the SEC has concluded, a reading of its complaint in the now-settled suit makes clear.[56]

Apparently Mediobanca had converted the Hartford stock into ITT's Series N preferred stock after the merger had taken place. In late 1970 Mediobanca sold the stock to the Dreyfus Marine Midland Corporation, a New York mutual fund now known as the Dreyfus Fund. This stock, according to the provisions of the contract, was sold through Lazard Frères. In mid-1970 ITT named Dreyfus to manage an estimated $10 million in ITT pension fund assets. This transaction generated $2.2 million in fees, of which Mediobanca received $1.3 million, thus providing the grounds for the SEC investigation that revealed the details of this transaction.

When pressed by a reporter from the *Wall Street Journal*, IRS refused to discuss the case on the grounds that "its rulings in such cases are private matters between it and the taxpayer." However, it conceded that "private rulings are made strictly on the basis of facts as presented by the taxpayer involved [and] any verification is done when and if the taxpayer's returns are audited." [57]

In another aspect of the case, IRS was proved to be lenient with ITT. It has been IRS policy, in stock-for-stock mergers, to require the company to sell previously acquired stock "before an offer is made" to other shareholders. This could mean "the deadline is when the acquiring company first publicizes the terms of its offer." [58] However, in the case of ITT, the offer was first publicized on December 23, 1968; proxy solicitations were mailed to Hartford stockholders on July 24, 1969; and yet it was not until October 14, 1969, that ITT submitted the Mediobanca contract to IRS for approval. Only a week later it was cleared by IRS. When asked for an explanation, an IRS official responded: "That's a technical point; it isn't the kind of thing I've ever heard discussed." [59]

The IRS ruling was a private one and subject to reversal at the time of

---

[56] *Ibid.*, p. 1.
[57] *Ibid.*, p. 18.
[58] *Ibid.*
[59] *Ibid.*

audit, should the company then prove to be in violation of IRS regulations. In July 1972 a class action suit was filed by a former Hartford stockholder, Hilda Herbst, asking that the merger be set aside because ITT's circular to Hartford stockholders did not mention the risk to them in the event of an unfavorable tax ruling. The suit, which has yet to come to trial, asks for a rescinding of the merger and payment of damages to Hartford stockholders.

If the IRS decides that the tax ruling is not binding, it could cost Hartford stockholders millions of dollars in back taxes. However, looking at the history of all these events, the *Wall Street Journal* gloomily predicted that "little will happen, of course, unless IRS decides to go after ITT. And that seems unlikely." [60]

The contradictions in IRS's handling of ITT were further compounded when, in another case of stock ownership, IRS challenged a woman's claim to ownership as starting *when the stock was delivered to her* rather than four months earlier when she signed an agreement entitling her to stock. IRS argued, and the court agreed, that she *owned* the stock from the earlier date because she carried the risk of ownership and also received dividends. Yet in the case of ITT, the transfer of Hartford stock to Mediobanca had been considered a sale even though ITT carried all the risks of ownership. [61]

However, it appears that the *Wall Street Journal*'s gloomy prediction of October 12, 1972, about the unlikelihood of IRS's punishing ITT was premature, as it did not and could not foresee the Watergate scandal and its ripple effect on every aspect of the ITT-Hartford merger. On April 19, 1973, ITT announced that IRS Washington headquarters was "reconsidering" the favorable tax ruling it made in late 1969, permitting the ITT-Hartford merger. The reconsideration was requested by the New York office of the IRS. There was no comment by the IRS. [62]

---

[60] *Ibid.*

[61] "Attention ITT Fans: Here's Another Curious Wrinkle on That Curious Tax Ruling," *The Wall Street Journal*, April 18, 1973, p. 1.

[62] "IRS Favorable Tax Ruling in ITT Purchase of Hartford Fire Is Being 'Reconsidered,' " *The Wall Street Journal*, April 19, 1973, p. 4.

APPENDIX A

ITT'S PLACE IN THE SUN: THE MANAGEMENT'S VIEW

Any discussion of ITT is incomplete without a reference to the character of its president and chief executive, Harold S. Geneen, his management philosophy, and his views on the role of large corporations in general and ITT in particular in the socioeconomic and political affairs of the world. Born in 1910, he is considered the most dynamic and successful corporate executive in America and is often compared with Alfred P. Sloan, designer of General Motors' management system. His rewards are commensurate with this general opinion; in 1971 he received $812,494 in salary and bonuses, making him the highest-paid executive in the nation.

During his tenure as head of ITT, which began in 1959, Geneen has shaped the company and its executive corps in his own image. His record of success has been achieved by an almost single-minded devotion to his work, which consumes eighteen hours of an average day, and by meticulous attention through regularly scheduled reports and meetings to the details of ITT's multitudinous and varied operations.

Descriptions of ITT under Geneen emphasize the insularity and narrowness of its upper levels of management. *Time* quotes one former ITT executive as saying, "It is a whole way of life to work for ITT, like joining a monastic order. That is part of ITT's special strength—a feeling that you are working for an order and not just a mortal company." [1] The magazine goes on to describe the working life of these executives:

> While at ITT, they live in a cloistered world—partly out of *esprit de corps,* partly because they do not have the time to get outside. Admission to this world comes only after eight hours of psychological testing. . . . Once in, the ITT executive, like Geneen himself, tends to meet and socialize only with other ITTers. A Brussels host who gave a party for ITT European officials from New York last year got them to attend only by promising that he would be the sole non-ITT person there.[2]

Pressures to perform and conform within this confined and rarefied atmosphere are formidable. *Time*'s European economic correspondent Roger Beardwood, the only journalist ever to attend one of ITT's top

---

[1] "Corporations: ITT's Big Conglomerate of Troubles," *Time,* May 1, 1972, p. 75.
[2] *Ibid.,* pp. 75–76.

management meetings, described the atmosphere as "a cross between a self-criticism session in a Soviet factory and question time in the British House of Commons." [3] Those who survive ITT's rigorous demands, often at the expense of their personal lives and outside interests, are fiercely loyal to both the company and Geneen.

According to Geneen, "The best people to run companies are not geniuses . . . they are too difficult to get along with. The best people are well-rounded men with ambition." [4] Writing in *Fortune* about ITT and Geneen, Carol Loomis observed, "Geneen has made I.T.T. a monument in his own image, and there seems no way of knowing whether it is strong enough to be preserved by the next caretaker. Meanwhile, Geneen himself will be working to build the monument a little higher." [5]

Once we understand this inbreeding, we can begin to see some possible reasons for ITT's posture toward other social institutions, both domestic and foreign. Being insulated, the company tends to be suspicious of all outsiders and their motives; unfamiliar with outsiders' goals and motives, it tends to treat them as similar to its own, that is, everyone has a price and everyone can be bought. Since the company's management considers its objectives to be of a higher order, it looks down on everything that appears to be a stumbling block to the achievement of its goals and therefore considers it its duty to crush all opposition ruthlessly. Like all fanatics, it believes that ends justify means. Although its inbreeding provides for a concentrated and directed attention to the pursuit of the company's goals, it also leaves the company ill prepared to meet new outside pressures. Its inward-looking communication system filters out all information that is new and not directly related to current company activities. However, it is this information that is most vital in warning the company of changes in its external sociopolitical environment.[6] "It can easily produce the kind of surprise that all ITT's figures cannot warn against: the shock of discovering that there is an outside world filled with people to whom continuous increases in ITT profits do not necessarily seem the *summum bonum*." [7]

Thus, in Geneen's view, the fortunes of the nation are intimately linked with the fortunes of ITT:

Specifically, 12 years ago when I started with IT&T, we brought back approximately $15 million annually to contribute to the credit

[3] *Ibid.*, p. 75.
[4] Carol J. Loomis, "Harold Geneen's Moneymaking Machine Is Still Humming," *Fortune*, September 1972, p. 220.
[5] *Ibid.*
[6] Dow Votaw and S. Prakash Sethi, *The Corporate Dilemma: Traditional Values versus Contemporary Problems* (Englewood Cliffs, N.J.: Prentice-Hall, Inc., 1973), pp. 167–213.
[7] *Time*, May 1, 1972, p. 75.

side of the balance of payments. This year [1972] we will bring back approximately $300 million from repatriation of earnings, exports, and so forth. . . . In short, any company such as IT&T, which is scheduled during the next 10 years to bring back on the order of $5 billion from abroad, without imports, cannot be said to be working against the national interest in these trying times. . . .

I think that the committee should understand that IT&T has paid a high price for a unique position enabling it to contribute to the U.S. balance of payments, and more importantly that IT&T's interest in growth was not a question of mere aggrandizement, but arose from the necessity of balancing foreign risks and the need for credit abroad to maintain market share and expand our repatriation of dollars, while at the same time keeping a degree of security for our shareholders by leveraging our foreign credit off the strength of our domestic base.

I make these points because I think it should be clear to the members of this committee that we are trying to run a constructive enterprise, an honest enterprise, a hard-working enterprise, one which has enabled us to become one of the top five contributors to the national balance of payments. [*Hearings,* Part 2, p. 644]

The attitude of self-righteousness and disdain for the views of others, when accompanied with a large measure of economic power, can breed insensitivity to public opinion and the blind arrogance so typical of ITT's dealings with the outside world. According to one observer who followed the company's dealings with Washington during and after the Senate Judiciary Committee's hearings, ITT executives regard "the company [as] a sort of nation in itself, unencumbered by democracy's annoying requirement of accountability." [8] According to the *New York Times:*

I.T.T., in fact, often acts and sounds more like a government than a private company. It employs foreign American diplomats and former foreign correspondents, including a recent Pulitzer Prize winner. In recent years it has established its own foreign-policy and foreign intelligence units. . . . ITT has its own international communications network, its own fleet of jetliners and its own counter-espionage operation.[9]

Given his faith in the righteousness of his cause, Geneen is not known for accepting gracefully any setbacks in his grand design or challenge to

[8] "ITT's Arrogance," *New Republic,* April 8, 1972, p. 3.
[9] "I.T.T.: A Private Little Foreign Policy," *The New York Times,* March 26, 1972, Sec. 4, p. 4.

his authority. For example, when it appeared that the Justice Department was not to be deterred from its antitrust policies against conglomerates, Geneen decided to give McLaren a taste of what to expect if he were to take on ITT. In a speech before the stockholders at ITT's annual meeting, he declared that ITT would continue its growth plan—no matter what. Referring to the Justice Department, he stated: "It is clear that whatever the guise, by imaginary or strained legal theories, what we are experiencing is a direct attack on bigness as such." He also indicated that companies like ITT must have strong domestic bases and the support of the U.S. government if they are to continue growing abroad "to be able to compete with full effectiveness in overseas markets [we] cannot be hamstrung at home. It is of the greatest importance that we do not deliberately weaken the international capabilities of American Business which alone must be counted on to improve our balance of payments." [10]

Around the same time, there was growing

an anti-McLaren whispering campaign to smear his policies as partisan and anti-Semitic. The whispers, *of unknown origin,* but circulating widely in New York and Washington are based on the uncertain presumption that most executives of new conglomerates are Democrats and Jews while most old establishment companies are headed by non-Jewish Republicans. [Emphasis added] [11]

To get its message across, ITT spends lavishly on its public relations efforts. For example, each year ITT throws a big bash on the St. Regis roof in Manhattan for "several hundred journalists ranging from financial writers to police-beat hacks." The company's methods for handling the press, however, are not known to be subtle and often border on open arm-twisting. [12]

This attitude, however, carries with it certain dangers. The House Antitrust Subcommittee, in earlier investigations, concluded that "Mr. Geneen is without question a superior individual with many talents. His exceptional drive and ambition, however, have produced an overly enthusiastic program for ITT's growth" (*Hearings,* Part 2, p. 697). The methods by which ITT at times accomplishes its growth are open to similar charges of overenthusiasm. ITT's staff includes former newspapermen and congressional aides who are expert and knowledgeable in dealing with their former colleagues. Its board of directors includes such personages as former CIA director John A. McCone. The late NATO Secretary-General Paul Henri

---

[10] "Is ITT Starting a Long War?" *Magazine of Wall Street,* July 19, 1969.

[11] Louis M. Kohlmeier, "Nixon's Trustbuster Feels the Heat," *The Wall Street Journal,* December 16, 1969.

[12] See "A.B.C. + I.T.T. ? Free Press" in this book.

Spaak and the late UN Secretary-General Trygve Lie (ITT-Norway) were also on its board of directors.[13]

The political influence embodied in this list, as well as ITT's wealth and other resources, is always directed at accomplishing the goals and fostering the image of the company, regardless of the obstacles before it. ITT's enthusiasm for any particular project is seldom dampened by adverse actions of governmental agencies, as in the antitrust cases, or by public opinion, as with the almost unanimous local disenchantment with the idea of the Republican convention in San Diego. On the contrary, the company seems to continue to bring various pressures to bear until resistance is dissipated. "ITT is almost famous for this," one former executive says. "The overall theory of management is that if one approach can do it, seven approaches can do it seven times better." [14] Accusations of pressure, political maneuvering, and lack of candor were present during ITT's attempted acquisition of ABC–TV, described elsewhere in this book, and have recently surfaced in ITT's foreign dealings. Fear of the nationalization of its assets in Chile led the company to attempt to influence the policies not only of other American companies but also of the American government, to change Chile's political and economic outlook. Similar high-level influence was exerted to lower the company's tax liabilities in Japan and (unsuccessfully) to gain the approval of the British government to build an undersea cable linking the United States to the United Kingdom.[15] And, according to *Time,* ITT will often procure favorable governmental decisions by providing "some unrelated economic benefit. In Peru, it agreed to build an $8 million hotel and a factory in order to get a favorable settlement of the government's attempt to take over the ITT-owned telephone subsidiary." [16]

ITT's peculiarly myopic view of the world, it has been rather frequently argued recently, may be its single greatest weakness. And this is, as *Time* suggests,

the sort of naiveté that U.S. business can no longer afford. ITT has clearly been a leader in the consuming drive for higher profits. But Geneen's direction has not yet fitted it to an age in which all corporations must give great weight to broader values.[17]

[13] "Communications: ITT's Public Relations Fiasco," *Business Week,* April 1, 1972, pp. 23–24.
[14] Brit Hume, "Checking Out Dita Beard's Memo," *Harper's Magazine,* August 1972, p. 44.
[15] Stephen M. Aug, "I.T.T. Pushes Its Cases at the Top," *Sunday Star* (Washington), March 5, 1972; also cited in "Separate Report," pp. 226–28.
[16] *Time,* May 1, 1972, p. 78.
[17] *Ibid.*

APPENDIX B

ITT: THE CONGLOMERATE BEHEMOTH

By any standard, ITT is a big company. In 1972 it ranked eighth in terms of assets and ninth in terms of sales among the top 500 industrial corporations. In addition, its finance and insurance subsidiaries' interest and premium income increased to $1.7 billion.

ITT has grown primarily through acquisitions, an incredible 250 of them between 1961 and 1971. During the same period, profits have grown from a meager $36 million to $407 million.[1] In 1972 it employed approximately 428,000 people (making it the third largest U.S. employer) and operated in more than eighty countries.

The company is engaged in a wide variety of activities, such as the following:

a. Telecommunications and electronic equipment
b. Life, fire, and casualty insurance
c. Production and sales of chemical cellulose, wood pulp, lumber, and wood-derived chemicals
d. Mining, beneficiating, and marketing of silica and attapulgite
e. Consumer and business services
f. Processing and distribution of food products
g. Manufacture and distribution of automotive parts
h. Operation of a wide variety of utilities

The domestic manufacturing division alone has the following four principal divisions, which together generated $1.7 billion in sales:

1. The Industrial and Consumer Product Group (56 percent of sales) designs, makes, and sells equipment and accessories for the automotive, construction, and process industries, and components for aviation, computers, and construction industries.
2. The Defense-Space Group (18 percent of sales) engineers, designs, makes, sells, installs, and maintains telecommunication and electronic equipment for the U.S. government and its allies.
3. The Telecommunications Equipment Group (8 percent of sales) provides engineering and makes, sells, installs, and maintains tele-

[1] Carol J. Loomis, "Harold Geneen's Moneymaking Machine Is Still Humming," *Fortune*, September 1972, p. 88.

phone apparatus, switching systems, automatic toll-ticketing, and transmission equipment.

4. The Natural Resources Group (18 percent of sales) provides services such as the production of chemical cellulose, wood pulp, lumber, creosoted wood products, and wood-derived chemicals. It is also involved in mining, beneficiating, and marketing silica ceramics and attapulgite.

However, as a truly multinational company, ITT is the largest producer and supplier of telecommunications and electronics in the world. In that capacity, it generated $2.8 billion of sales, principally selling electronic and telecommunication equipment to national governments.

Consumer and Business Services includes a huge number of companies producing routine life necessities and rendering a broad spectrum of services.

In utility operations, ITT is one of the dominant companies in the world, operating a wide range of services and facilities.

ITT's subsidiaries are often the largest or among the most dominant companies in their areas of operation. For example:

1. Sheraton Hotel Corporation is the largest hotel chain in the United States.
2. Continental Baking Company is the largest producer of bread, cakes, snack foods, frozen food, and related products in the United States.
3. Hartford Fire Insurance is the largest fire insurance company in the United States.

B.

CORPORATIONS AND
THE UNITED STATES
FOREIGN POLICY CONFLICTS

The ITT Affair (B)

Interference in the Chilean Presidential Elections

Let's stop apologizing for America's wealth and power. Instead let's use it aggressively to attack those problems that threaten to explode the world.

We *can* win the race with change. We *can* preserve our leadership. But to do so we have to recapture the faith and trust of a world in ferment. We have to revitalize the American dream, and cast it in terms that the new people of a new world can understand and appreciate and aspire to.

—Richard M. Nixon

All that ITT did was to present its views, concerns, and ideas to various departments of the U.S. government. This is not only its right but also its obligation. The right is a very important constitutional right, and . . . it is not wrong for a citizen to try to approach government officials to discuss with them his problems and concerns.

—Harold S. Geneen, Chairman
and Chief Executive of ITT, in a
statement before the U.S. Senate
Subcommittee on Multinational
Corporations

Jack Anderson Again

It seems that ITT had not heard the last of Jack Anderson with his publication of the Dita Beard memorandum. Three weeks after the first memo appeared, Jack Anderson exploded another bomb in his column, where he accused ITT of attempting to plot against the 1970 election of leftist Chilean President Salvador Allende, to trigger a military coup, and to create economic chaos in Chile. The column read, in part:

Secret documents which escaped shredding by International Telephone and Telegraph show that the company, at the highest levels, maneuvered to stop the 1970 election of leftist Chilean President Salvador Allende.

The papers reveal that ITT dealt regularly with the Central Intelligence Agency and, at one point, considered triggering a military coup to head off Allende's election.

These documents portray ITT as a virtual corporate nation in itself with vast international holdings, access to Washington's highest officials, its own intelligence apparatus and even its own classification system. . . .

They show that ITT officials were in close touch with William V. Broe, who was then director of the Latin American division of the CIA's Clandestine Services. They were plotting together to create economic chaos in Chile, hoping this would cause the Chilean army to pull a coup that would block Allende from coming to power.

ITT Director John McCone, himself a former CIA head, played a role in the bizarre plot. . . .

The plot to bring about a military coup by applying economic pressure is spelled out in a confidential telex, dated September 29, 1970, to ITT's President Harold S. Geneen from one of its vice presidents, E. J. Gerrity. Here is Gerrity's description of the plot:

1. Banks should not renew credits or should delay in doing so.
2. Companies should drag their feet in sending money, in making deliveries, in shipping spare parts, etc.
3. Savings and loan companies there are in trouble. If pressure were applied they would have to shut their doors, thereby creating stronger pressure.
4. We should withdraw all technical help and should not promise any technical help in the future. Companies in a position to do so should close their doors.

5. A list of companies was provided and it was suggested that we approach them as indicated. I was told that of all the companies involved ours alone had been responsive and understood the problem. The visitor (evidently the CIA's William Broe) added that money was not a problem. . . .[1]

ITT's immediate response was that Anderson's allegations had "no foundation in fact."[2] As subsequent columns appeared, quoting more ITT documents, the company had no comment to make.

A State Department spokesman also denied that the U.S. government had tried to prevent Allende's election. The spokesman stated that the Nixon administration had "firmly rejected" any ideas of "thwarting the Chilean constitutional processes"[3] and that the government's actions were firmly in line with the president's stated policy that the United States was willing to live with "a community of diversity in Latin America: we deal with governments as they are. Our relations depend not on their internal structures or social systems, but on acts which affect us in the Inter-American system."[4]

But these denials had little effect on the tide of events that followed Anderson's new revelations. The Senate Foreign Relations Committee voted immediately to investigate the charges and created a subcommittee on multinational corporations, headed by Senator Frank Church (D—Idaho), to study the impact of these corporations on the formulation of American foreign policy. Although hearings were not scheduled to begin until after the 1972 presidential election, the committee immediately asked ITT for all documents relating to Chile during the turbulent period surrounding Allende's accession to power.

And in Chile itself, the accusations were a "political windfall" for Allende,[5] allowing him to divert public attention from the country's severe economic troubles to the ever-present fears in Latin America of American domination and subversion by the CIA (see Appendix A). He was also able to link the alleged plotting by ITT and the CIA to the earlier assassination of the army commander. "The revelations in the United States of the documents should convince every Chilean that the nation's inde-

[1] "The Washington Merry-Go-Round: Memos Bare ITT Try for Chile Coup," *Washington Post*, March 21, 1972, p. B-13.
[2] "ITT Said to Seek Chile Coup in '70," *The New York Times*, March 22, 1972, p. 25.
[3] "Intervention in Chile Is Denied," *San Francisco Chronicle*, March 24, 1972, p. 14.
[4] Richard M. Nixon, *U.S. Foreign Policy for the 1970's, A Report to the Congress*, February 25, 1971, p. 53.
[5] "Allende Finds ITT Story Useful," *San Francisco Chronicle*, March 24, 1972, p. 14.

pendence is at stake today," said one Allende supporter.[6] Furthermore, the negotiations between ITT and the Chileans over compensation for the company's expropriated property were abruptly terminated, and the Chilean government began to consider the possibility of confiscating all of the company's assets in Chile.

Even though ITT's efforts were unsuccessful in preventing Allende's election, the very nature of the involvement, the audacity with which the plans were conceived, the contempt in which ITT held all other parties, and, more important, the extent to which ITT sought and received entrée into the CIA and other governmental agencies to pursue its objectives raise serious issues of far greater import than the particular incident in question. For example:

1. How much direct and indirect influence do large U.S. multinational corporations exercise in the molding of American foreign policy to serve their private needs? To what extent should the foreign policy of a country be guided by the interests of the overseas operations of its business institutions?
2. What role should government play in protecting the interests of its citizens—individuals and corporations—from expropriation by foreign governments?
3. What are the avenues open to multinational corporations to seek redress for expropriation by foreign governments?
4. Is there a need for international control of multinational corporations? If so, how might it be brought about, and what form should it take?

Background History: ITT in Chile

ITT's involvement in Chile began in 1927 when it acquired the Chile Telephone Co., Ltd., an English company founded in 1899. In 1930 ITT was granted a fifty-year concession to operate the company, and under that contract the present Compañía de Teléfonos de Chile was organized. Its 37,607 telephones in operation in 1930 increased to 360,000 by 1971, when the company had a book value of $153 million, almost fifty-nine hundred employees, and a monthly payroll of approximately $3.8 million. Two years of negotiations between ITT and the Chilean government culminated in 1967 in an agreement by which the Corporación de Fomento de la Producción (CORFO, the government development agency) and other

[6] *Ibid.*

Chilean nationals could purchase up to 49 percent of ITT's stock in the company. By 1971 the Chilean government owned approximately 24 percent, the Chilean public 6 percent, and ITT 70 percent of the company's stock.

In support of its telephone system, ITT owned in 1971 a number of related enterprises. Standard Electric-Chile was established in 1942 for the production of telecommunications equipment. The company, a $2.2 million investment on ITT's part, had approximately eight hundred Chilean employees and an annual payroll of over $2 million in 1971. ITT World Directories operated a subsidiary in Chile for four years prior to 1971, Guías y Publicidad, which published telephone directories. It also owned All America Cable and Radio-Chile, an international telegram company with assets of $600,000.

After its 1927 purchase of the Chile Telephone Company, ITT World Communications laid a cable across the Andes in 1928, providing Chile's first international service to Argentina and Uruguay, and linked the country to the rest of the world by radio through its terminus in Buenos Aires. As of 1971, ITT World Communications assets in Chile had a book value of $3 million. In 1968 the Chilean government negotiated a purchasing agreement, this time a total buy-out through ENTEL, the government international communications unit. As of 1971, ENTEL owned about 10 percent of the company.

Finally, in 1968 ITT purchased the Carrera and San Cristóbal hotels, agreeing to integrate them into the Sheraton Hotel system. These hotels represented in 1971 an investment of $8.4 million.

ITT explains, in a public relations brochure that emphasizes its value to the country, that the Chile Telephone Company is a regulated public utility, with three members of its board of directors appointed by the Chilean government, by which the government participates in the formulation of the company's operating and financial policies. The company's books have been audited annually by an independent accounting firm, and these audits have each year been approved not only by the government's representatives on the board but also for more than forty years by the Chilean Ministry of Finance. Thus, ITT states, the Chilean government has "not only certified the value of the Chile Telephone Company but has also thereby in effect confirmed the amount of ITT's investment of approximately $153 million in the company." [7] Between 1961 and 1970, ITT asserts that its reinvestment in the company and payment of withholding taxes amounted to more than $84 million, plus an additional $40 million of supplier financing through the ITT system and foreign bank loans, while it withdrew during the same period only $19 million in net

[7] *ITT History in Chile,* International Telephone and Telegraph Co., p. 3.

remittances. Thus, for every dollar taken out of Chile, ITT reinvested or paid in taxes more than six dollars.[8]

In addition, the company contributed to "no less than 50 cultural, civic and educational organizations throughout the country."[9] These included blood bank efforts; the Red Cross; help for the blind; support for the national symphony, philharmonic orchestra, and other performing arts; on-the-job training programs provided without charge to students of high schools, professional training schools, and colleges; a university-level scholarship program; and support for major sporting events.

This record of public service, however, was not sufficient to counteract the Chileans' resentment over the extent of foreign ownership of capital and industry in their country. During the 1970 presidential campaign only one of the three candidates, Jorge Alessandri Rodríguez, former president and candidate of the right-wing National party, supported the private free enterprise system that made such foreign ownership possible. Radomiro Tomic Romero, supported by the ruling Christian Democratic party, advocated a continuation of then president Eduardo Frei Montalvo's policies of gradual "Chileanization" of important sectors of the economy.[10] Dr. Salvador Allende Gossens, a long-time Socialist and candidate of the Popular Unity party (a coalition of Communists, Socialists, Social Democrats, Radicals, and dissident Christian Democrats), campaigned on a platform that called for extensive land reform and rapid nationalization of monopolies and vital industries, many of which were controlled by foreign capital (see Appendix B, Exhibit 2).

In spring 1970, with the presidential campaign in progress, ITT's political information indicated that Allende would win the popular election in the fall. ITT's total assets in Chile were valued at approximately $160 million, about $100 million of which was insured against expropriation by the Overseas Private Investment Corporation (OPIC). Allende had made clear the probable fate of these assets in any administration he would head, and ITT became understandably concerned over this eventuality (see Appendix A).

ITT Swings into Action

ITT was apparently unwilling to let the situation drift and give up its Chilean assets without a fight. The actions ITT took, the way it went

[8] *Ibid.*
[9] *Ibid.*, p. 4.
[10] U.S., Congress, Senate, Report to the Committee on Foreign Relations by the Subcommittee on Multinational Corporations, *The International Telephone and Telegraph Company and Chile, 1970–71*, June 21, 1973, p. 2. All citations from this source will hereinafter be referred to in the text as *Report*, followed by page number.

about them, and the ultimate outcome are vividly detailed in the ITT interoffice memoranda, cables, and letters, and the company's communications with various government officials and representatives of other businesses. These documents were first made public by Jack Anderson. Some of these were later inserted into the *Congressional Record* by Senator Fred Harris. ITT also furnished copies of these documents to Senator Church's subcommittee, at the latter's request, and these were made public record by the subcommittee. A selected number of these documents are reproduced in Appendix B.

The Senate hearings opened on March 20, 1973, almost a year after the initial disclosure of these documents, and they raised as many questions as they answered. The record shows that ITT executives were particularly prone to loss of memory and vagueness over detail. In cases of apparent contradictions and conflicts in their testimony, ITT executives blandly attributed these to failure of communication within the organization, an incredible admission in view of ITT's reputation of being an extremely tightly run ship with Geneen having a genius for administration. ITT actions, as culled from the documents and testimony of witnesses at the hearings, can be divided into three significant time periods: the pre-election period, the period between the popular election and the congressional election, and the period after Allende came to power.[11]

The Period Preceding the Popular Election of September 4, 1970

During May and June 1970, ITT Director John McCone (see Table 1 for cast of characters) held a series of meetings with his successor at the CIA, Richard Helms. McCone pointed out to Helms the magnitude of both business investments and OPIC guarantees that were at stake if Allende were elected and asked whether the United States would interfere to encourage support for "one of the candidates who stood for the principles that are basic to this country" (*Report*, p. 3). Helms indicated that, although this matter had been considered by the "Forty Committee," the interdepartmental committee that oversees CIA covert activities, the decision had been to do nothing. Although the CIA could still undertake certain minimal actions, Helms was pessimistic about the chances of defeating Allende in the popular election. (It is interesting to note that the U.S. Embassy at this point was predicting that the conservative Alessandri would win a plurality of 40 percent in the popular vote. ITT's information predicted a plurality for Allende, and it was ITT's intelligence that was accurate.)

[11] The format in this section is the same as that followed in the *Report*.

TABLE 1

Cast of Characters

AIBEL, H. J.	ITT's senior vice-president and general counsel.
ALESSANDRI, JORGE	Candidate for the presidency of the republic.
ALLENDE, SALVADOR	Senator, candidate for the presidency of the republic.
BARTLETT, CHARLES	Columnist of conservative tendencies of the *Evening Star* and other North American newspapers.
BENNETT, R. E.	ITT's executive vice-president.
BERRELLEZ, ROBERT	ITT's chief of Latin American public relations, situated in Buenos Aires.
BERTINI, JORGE	Member of the Economic Committee of Unidad Popular.
BRITTENHAM, RAYMOND LEE	ITT's senior vice-president.
BROE, WILLIAM	Director of CIA Latin American Clandestine Services.
DUNLEAVY, F. J.	ITT's vice-president, situated in Brussels.
EDWARDS, AGUSTIN	President of board of *El Mercurio*, an anti-Communist newspaper in Chile.
FISHER, JOHN	U.S. State Department director for the area of Bolivia-Chile.
FREI, EDUARDO	President of the republic until November 3, 1970.
GENEEN, HAROLD S.	ITT'S chairman and chief executive.
GERRITY, EDWARD J.	ITT's senior vice-president, corporate relations and advertising.
GUILFOYLE, JACK	ITT's vice-president in New York, and ITT's president for Latin America.
HENDRIX, HAL	ITT's director of public relations for Latin America.
HERRERA, FELIPE	President of Inter-American Development Bank.
KORRY, EDWARD	U.S. ambassador to Chile.
MATTE LARRAIN, ARTURO	Brother-in-law of Jorge Alessandri and director of his presidential campaign.
McCONE, JOHN	Ex-CIA director and member of ITT's board of directors.
MERRIAM, WILLIAM R.	ITT's vice-president in charge of the Washington office.
NAVIN, J. J.	ITT's secretary.
NEAL, JACK D.	ITT's director of international relations.
PERKINS, KEITH	ITT's director of public relations.
PORTA ANGULO, FERNANDO	Commander in chief of the Chilean navy.
PRATS, CARLOS	Chief of staff of the Chilean army. Commander in chief of the army following the assassination of General Schneider.
SCHNEIDER, RENE	Commander in chief of the Chilean army (assassinated).
THEOFEL, N.	ITT's vice-president.
TOMIC, RADOMIRO	Christian Democratic party candidate for the presidency of the republic.
VAKY, VIRON PETER	Adviser to Henry Kissinger for Latin American affairs.
VALDES, GABRIEL	Minister of foreign affairs in the government of Frei.
VIAUX, ROBERTO	Ex-general of the army.
WALLACE, EDWARD R.	ITT's vice-president and assistant director, corporate relations and advertising.

At one of these meetings, McCone suggested to Helms that someone on his staff should be in contact with Geneen. According to the subcommittee, "it was McCone, through his suggestion to Helms, who set in motion a series of contacts between the ITT and CIA in connection with Chile" (*Report*, p. 3). The *Washington Post* quoted one government official involved with the case as saying, "ITT's relationship with the CIA is no mystery. If you have John McCone on your board it gives you a certain kind of entree." [12]

On July 16, 1970, Geneen met with William V. Broe, director of the Latin American division of the CIA's Clandestine Services, for the first time. At this meeting, Broe testified, Geneen offered to assemble a "substantial" election fund for Alessandri, to be controlled and channeled through the CIA. Broe said he refused the offer and informed Geneen that the CIA was not supporting any candidate in the election. Geneen, who is consistently described as having almost total recall of facts and figures, testified

> that he did not recall having offered a "substantial" sum of money to the CIA. . . .
> But Mr. Geneen told a Senate subcommittee that, since he had "no recollection to the contrary," he would accept the testimony of . . . Broe. . . .
> Mr. Geneen said that, assuming he did make the offer of cash to Mr. Broe, it was probably an "emotional reaction" to learning from their conversation that the United States was planning no action to attempt to defeat Dr. Allende. . . .[13]

Geneen also testified that he had made a similar offer in 1964, and the CIA had also rejected that offer (*Report*, p. 4). And when Broe refused his offer to support Alessandri, Geneen stated, the matter "died right there." [14]

The Period between September 4, 1970 and the Congressional Election of October 24, 1970

As ITT had predicted, Allende won a narrow plurality in the September 4 popular election. The results were as follows:

[12] "Congress, OPIC Probe ITT's Efforts against Chile's Allende," *Washington Post*, February 19, 1973, p. A-4.

[13] "Geneen Concedes ITT Fund Offer to Block Allende," *The New York Times*, April 3, 1972, pp. 1, 17.

[14] "ITT Head Talks about Chile Case," *San Francisco Chronicle*, April 2, 1972, p. 1.

	Votes	Percent
Allende	1,075,616	36.3
Alessandri	1,035,278	35.3
Tomic	824,849	28.4

Source: Report, p. 2.

These results stimulated immediate activity.

Allende's narrow victory did not assure his ultimate election. Since he had not won a majority of votes, the Chilean congress would have to choose between him and Alessandri, who had received the next highest number of votes. This congressional election was set for October 24. On September 9 Alessandri announced that if he were elected by the congress, he would immediately resign. This would enable outgoing President Eduardo Frei, who was constitutionally prohibited from succeeding himself, to run against Allende in a new election. In such a two-way contest, many believed that Frei would win with a clear majority of the popular vote. This plan became known as the "Alessandri formula" (see Appendix B, Exhibits 1, 3, 4).

However, ITT was unwilling to accept Allende's election as a *fait accompli* (Appendix B, Exhibits 6, 7). ITT's Chile office made the following recommendations to promote "stop Allende" activities:

1. We and other U.S. firms in Chile pump some advertising into *Mercurio* [anti-Communist newspaper]. (This has been started.)
2. We help with getting some propagandists working again on radio and television. . . .
3. Assist in support of a "family relocation" center in Mendoza or Baires [Buenos Aires] for wives and children of key persons involved in the fight. This will involve about 50 families for a period of a month to six weeks, maybe two months.
4. Bring what pressures we can on USIS in Washington to instruct the Santiago USIS to start moving the *Mercurio* editorials around Latin America and into Europe. Up until I left they were under orders not to move anything out of Chile.
5. Urge the key European press, through our contacts there, to get the story of what disaster could fall on Chile if Allende & Co. win this country.

These are immediate suggestions and there will be others between now and October 24 as pressure mounts on Frei and the Christian Democrats. [Appendix B, Exhibit 4]

According to McCone's testimony, Geneen again called upon him and told him that

> he [Geneen] was prepared to put up as much as a million dollars *in support of any plan that was adopted by the government for the purpose of bringing about a coalition of the opposition to Allende* so that when confirmation was up, which was some months later, this coalition would be united and deprive Allende of his position. [*Report,* p. 4; emphasis added]

On Geneen's urging, McCone communicated this offer to both Henry Kissinger and Helms.

At roughly the same time, another ITT official, International Relations Director Jack Neal, communicated the same offer to both Viron Peter Vaky, Kissinger's assistant for Latin American Affairs, and Assistant Secretary of State Charles Meyer (Appendix B, Exhibits 3, 5).

Geneen's purpose in offering these funds was the subject of heated controversy in the hearings. Geneen himself testified that "it was intended to be a very open offer," to be used either to finance an anti-Allende coalition in the Chilean congress or for development aid.[15] According to McCone,

> at no time had Mr. Geneen contemplated that the proffered fund . . . would be used to create "economic chaos," despite recommendations to that effect from various people within ITT and others within the CIA.

> "What he had in mind was not chaos," Mr. McCone said, "but what could be done constructively. The money was to be channeled to people who support the principles and programs the United States stands for against the programs of the Allende-Marxists."

> These programs, he said, included the building of needed housing and technical assistance to Chilean agriculture.[16]

E. J. Gerrity, senior vice-president for corporate affairs and advertising, similarly stressed that the funds were for constructive uses.

Other ITT witnesses, however, as well as the documents of the period, make these assertions highly dubious. Despite ITT's highly effective internal communication system, there is no evidence that such constructive intentions were ever communicated to several key individuals. Gerrity ad-

---

[15] "ITT Head on Chile," *San Francisco Chronicle,* April 3, 1973, p. 24.
[16] "McCone Defends ITT Chile Fund Idea," *The New York Times,* March 22, 1973, p. 1.

mitted that he had not included any constructive purposes in his instructions to Merriam, who had subsequently instructed Jack Neal on his contacts with Kissinger's office and the State Department. Neal testified that he had no knowledge of what the money was to be used for, and stated that when he spoke to Meyer at the State Department, "I didn't elaborate" on the potential uses of the funds. "We didn't go into it," he said.[17] Vaky of Kissinger's office said he had understood the offer to be toward helping block Allende's election. Gerrity also admitted that he could not remember having discussed this issue with Geneen *(Report,* p. 5).

Furthermore, Chile had been the recipient of more than $1.5 billion in aid between 1961 and 1971 (Appendix C), and the senators found it impossible to believe that ITT would think $1 million more would have a serious impact on Chile's economic situation. According to Senator Case:

> The whole body of evidence, memoranda, internal communications in the company, communications among all of you shows great disillusionment on the part of ITT with a program of aid to Chile [Appendix B, Exhibit 11] . . . this adds to the difficulty of believing that a relatively small amount of additional aid would be of any value. [*Report,* p. 5]

The subcommittee concluded in its report that Gerrity's assertions had

all the earmarks of an afterthought. As Senator Percy put it, "The implausibility of this story is what bothers us. It just does not hang together. It does not make sense for reasonable, rational men . . . to really feel that this assistance could have an impact. [*Report,* pp. 5–6]

The communications from ITT's observers in Chile during the period following the popular election contain no mention of any constructive aid or the results of such aid. They do, however, contain detailed analyses of the political situation and the possible consequences of ITT's intervention (Appendix B, Exhibits 4, 5, 9, 10, 15, 16, 18, 19).

ITT officials continued their efforts to block Allende's election. Robert Berrellez and Hal Hendrix, two ex-newspapermen responsible for reporting on Chile's political situation, cabled their recommendations to New York on September 17 (Appendix B, Exhibit 4). Merriam showed a copy of this cable to Broe and solicited his assessment of their recommended ac-

---

[17] "ITT Officials Offer Conflicting Views," *The New York Times,* March 23, 1973, p. 8.

tions. According to Merriam, Broe "agreed with the recommendations." [18] A week later, on September 29, Broe met with Gerrity in New York. This was the first in the series of CIA-ITT meetings that were initiated by the CIA; Broe had, in fact, arranged the meeting at the instruction of CIA Director Helms. The content of this meeting raises substantial questions about the *actual* policy the U.S. government might have been following as opposed to its *stated* policy and about its possible use of ITT as an instrument of covert actions, contrary to stated policy. Stated policy, both before and after Allende's election, was that the United States would take no position on the election. Yet at this meeting Broe, *on the instructions of Helms,* presented a plan of action "to accelerate economic chaos in Chile as a means of putting pressure on Christian Democratic Congressmen to vote against Dr. Allende or in any event to weaken Dr. Allende's position in case he was elected" *(Report,* p. 9). The suggested actions included the following:

1. Banks should not renew credits or should delay in doing so.
2. Companies should drag their feet in sending money, in making deliveries, in shipping spare parts, etc.
3. Savings and loan companies there are in trouble. If pressure were applied they would have to shut their doors, thereby creating stronger pressure.
4. We should withdraw all technical help and should not promise any technical assistance in the future. Companies in a position to do so should close their doors.
5. A list of companies was provided and "it was suggested that we approach them as indicated." [*Report,* p. 10]

Gerrity told Geneen after the meeting that he did not think this plan was workable and later wrote to Merriam that Geneen "agrees with me that Broe's suggestions are not workable. However, he suggests that we be very discreet in handling Broe" (Appendix B, Exhibits 8, 10).

Charles Meyer of the State Department later attempted to explain that Broe's suggestions were "merely the exploration of a possible policy option" *(Report,* p. 10) although he later conceded that had these suggestions been carried out, they would have constituted a change in policy that would have needed governmental approval at a higher level than CIA Director Helms. But he would not disclose whether the Forty Committee, which oversees CIA covert activities, had specifically approved the plan and, thus,

---

[18] "CIA–ITT Plans on Chile Reported," *The New York Times,* March 21, 1973, p. 1.

whether it did represent policy or, as Senator Church suggested, whether "ITT did successfully lobby the CIA on behalf of a covert operation, without policy approval." [19]

The question of policy was further confused by the September 17 telegram from Berrellez and Hendrix, which stated: "Late Tuesday night (September 15), Ambassador Edward Korry finally received a message from State Department giving him the green light to move in the name of President Nixon" and gave him authority to do "all possible—short of a Dominican Republic-type action—to keep Allende from taking power" (Appendix B, Exhibit 4). Hendrix later explained that the source of this information was a Chilean who was not connected with the American Embassy and that the source had mentioned neither President Nixon nor the Dominican Republic. Then-Ambassador Korry testified that he had cabled the State Department that an Allende victory would not be in the best interests of the United States (Appendix B, Exhibits 14, 31, 32). The subcommittee stated in its report:

> When Ambassador Korry was questioned about the "green light message" he refused to tell the Subcommittee what his instructions from Washington were. Assistant Secretary of State Meyer also refused to say what the Ambassador's instructions were and the Department refused to furnish copies of the cables it sent to Santiago. In the face of the refusal of the State Department to cooperate, it is impossible for the Subcommittee to determine definitely whether the Ambassador in fact received a cable substantially along the lines described by Hendrix. [*Report,* p. 7]

This, in turn, made it impossible to determine whether ITT and the CIA were acting with or without official approval—in other words, who was using whom for what.

Meetings between Broe and ITT officials continued during October 1970, resulting in a regular exchange of information about the Chilean situation. Cables that ITT received from Santiago were passed along to Broe, and Broe kept Merriam informed of the CIA's assessment of the situation. Other contacts continued as well. Meetings between ITT's Jack Neal and Ambassador Edward Korry led to a letter from Merriam to Kissinger on October 23 (Appendix B, Exhibits 14, 21), the day before the congressional vote, outlining the measures that ITT felt the government should take. (On October 18, Alessandri had withdrawn from the congressional runoff, and Allende's victory was a foregone conclusion by this

[19] "CIA's Action on Chile Unauthorized, Ex-Aide Says," *The New York Times,* March 20, 1973, p. 3.

time [Appendix B, Exhibits 16–20]. The government did not respond to the suggestions (Appendix B, Exhibit 30).

Allende in Power

On October 24 the Chilean congress confirmed Allende as president, and he was sworn in on November 4. ITT now had to face the unpleasant reality it had hoped to avoid (Appendix B, Exhibits 22, 25, 27). Its strategy now changed to attempting to weaken his power (perhaps causing the collapse of his government) and to securing favorable terms in the inevitable Chilean takeover of Chiltelco. The suggestions made earlier by Broe and rejected by both Gerrity and Geneen seemed to take root after Allende was actually in power.

At the suggestion of a representative of the Anaconda Company, ITT's Merriam invited Washington representatives of major companies with interests in Chile to form an Ad Hoc Committee on Chile. This committee began meeting in January 1971 and included representatives of Anaconda, Kennecott, Ralston Purina, Bank of America, Pfizer Chemical, and Grace and Co. (Appendix B, Exhibits 34, 36). The Bank of America representative wrote that

> the thrust of the meeting was toward the application of pressure on the (U.S.) Government, wherever possible, to make it clear that a Chilean take-over would not be tolerated without serious repercussions following. . . . ITT believes the place to apply pressure is through the office of Henry Kissinger. [*Report,* p. 12]

This representative, as well as Ralston Purina's, withdrew from these meetings, feeling that any program such as ITT was advocating would compromise its ability to negotiate successfully on its own properties in Chile *(Report,* p. 13).

Banks interviewed by the subcommittee also indicated their opposition to the kind of policy being pursued by ITT. According to the subcommittee's report:

> Several of the bank witnesses said that, from their perspective, creating economic chaos would have been counterproductive. The banks had large amounts outstanding in loans to the Chilean Government, as well as to Chilean businessmen. Economic chaos might have meant that the loans could not have been repaid.
> A number of bank witnesses said that in order to operate in a large number of countries around the world they have adopted strict

policies of non-involvement in the political affairs of the countries where they do business. . . . Involvement in host country politics would inevitably mean impairment of their ability to function. [*Report,* p. 12]

ITT's own internal memoranda show that other companies were not cooperating with its efforts (Appendix B, Exhibits 1, 13, 16, 34, 36, 37, 38, 39, 40).

It might be noted here that some members of ITT's legal department who were responsible for ITT's Chilean activities did not agree with the company's strategy and tactics, which were then largely directed by the company's public relations department, as they felt these would lessen chances of a settlement with Allende and might also jeopardize their claims with the Overseas Private Investment Corporation (OPIC) (Appendix B, Exhibit 24).

But, characteristically, ITT persevered in its own program, disregarding protests from its own legal department, its observers in Chile, other companies with which it was in contact, and the inaction and disinterest of governmental agencies other than the CIA (Appendix B, Exhibits 23, 26, 27, 33, 37, 38).

Negotiation over Chiltelco's fate began in March 1971, and it is possible to question the good faith of ITT's negotiating stance on two points. First, there is evidence that ITT was negotiating with the attitude that if a satisfactory settlement could be arranged over its own property, these arrangements might be used against other American interests in Chile. Geneen testified during the subcommittee hearings that he hoped "some sort of plan might be developed by our Government that might induce Dr. Allende to proceed with nationalization in a way that would permit orderly recovery of the vast U.S. investments, including ITT's, that were at stake." [20] But the company's internal memoranda indicate that ITT expected to receive a purchase offer similar to one it had earlier negotiated successfully with the Peruvian government. In that settlement, as described by the subcommittee, ITT had persuaded the Peruvian government that

a satisfactory agreement with ITT would demonstrate that it was not inherently hostile to foreign investments. ITT persuaded the Peruvian government that it could then argue that its decision to expropriate, without compensation, the property of the International Petroleum Company (IPC) a wholly owned subsidiary of the Exxon Corporation, was a special case and not an indication of general financial irresponsibility. [*Report,* p. 14]

[20] "No Interference with Chile Elections, Top ITT Official Tells Senate Committee," ITT press release, April 2, 1972, p. 3.

An ITT officer described the company's hopes in Chile:

> When Allende signs the copper legislation and formally expropri-
> ates Anaconda and Kennecott, there must be increased international
> resentment against the Government of Chile, and, as in the case of
> Peru, on their expropriation of IPC, we were able to capitalize on
> this and eventually arrive at a deal which allowed them to announce
> internationally that copper and IPC were special cases and here is an
> arrangement we made in reasonable negotiation with ITT. [*Report*,
> p. 14]

Efforts to Get Other U.S. Companies Involved

An important component of ITT's strategy was to seek the cooperation
of other U.S. businesses operating in Chile in its efforts to slow down and
otherwise damage the Chilean economy. However, as in the earlier periods,
the company was unsuccessful in these efforts (Appendix B, Exhibits 12,
13, 28, 40). Nevertheless, the company continued its plans even after its
meetings with Allende, when it became clear that such a strategy could
backfire.

Geneen later testified that during this period ITT "and other companies"
made

> suggestions and representations to the U.S. Government, including
> Congress, concerning the expected and actual expropriations, and the
> fact that Dr. Allende seemed to be moving in a direction to avoid
> fair payment. These suggestions sought to enlist U.S. Government
> support to make it clear that the U.S. would not lightly accept arbi-
> trary and unlawful action by Dr. Allende, and that the U.S. would
> take *all lawful steps* to protect the property of U.S. nationals in Chile.
> [Emphasis added] [21]

Meetings with President Allende and
Negotiation with the Chilean Government

On March 10 Jack Guilfoyle and Francis Dunleavy of ITT met with
President Allende, at which time Allende said he had not yet decided what
to do about Chiltelco. He further stated that he did not then plan to seize

---

[21] Statement of Harold S. Geneen, chairman and chief executive, ITT, before the
Senate Subcommittee on Multinational Corporations of the Senate Foreign Relations
Committee, April 2, 1972, p. 7.

control of Chiltelco and that he might even be interested in a mixed company (Appendix B, Exhibit 35).

After this meeting, the Chilean press and the government began to attack the company, alleging that it was deliberately allowing service to deteriorate, that equipment was obsolete, that engineers and technicians were not receiving adequate training, that the rate increase requested by the company was exorbitant, and that the company was generally not fulfilling its obligations under the concession originally granted to it (Appendix B, Exhibits 35, 41, 42). ITT naturally denied these charges, pointing out the sharp cash squeeze caused by shortfalls in the previously agreed-upon purchasing plan by CORFO and by the mandatory 35 percent wage increase decreed by the government in early 1971, while at the same time there had been no action on the rate-increase petition that would offset these pressures.

On May 26 another meeting was held between Allende and ITT officials. Allende now said that he had decided to proceed immediately with nationalization. ITT was offered $24 million for its interest in the company, and Allende stated that once agreement in principle was reached over the terms of the sale, the government would expect to take over operation of the company at once. ITT refused the $24 million offer, insisting that the government pay the full book value of $153 million. This was despite the fact that ITT had been fully prepared for an offer based on book value less the total remitted abroad since 1931 (Appendix B, Exhibit 35). ITT also opposed the idea of government control of the company during arbitration, fearing its value would deteriorate during this period.

Negotiations thus ended in an impasse, and the government, stressing its eagerness to take control of the company, charged that ITT was deliberately delaying settlement. Even the anti-Communist newspaper *Mercurio,* while denouncing the government's actions, complained of Chiltelco's inferior service and the distribution of service—telephones were still so expensive in Chile that only middle-class and wealthy families could afford them (Appendix A, Exhibit 42). These attacks continued and increased during the summer while ITT officials continued to meet with the government commission authorized to carry out negotiations. Both sides never wavered: ITT insisted on payment of full book value ($153 million), and the Chileans insisted that book value was not an appropriate criterion on which to base compensation. Finally, in August, the government wrote that it would accept ITT's suggestion of international arbitration over the value of Chiltelco.

No further action was taken until September 1, however, when Chiltelco's bank accounts were frozen by the government for nonpayment of taxes. The company blamed its admitted inability to pay these taxes on the government's inaction on its rate-increase request, and on the falloff in remittances to the company because of Allende's policies and attitudes toward it. The government, however, had earlier charged that ITT had been siphoning off Chiltelco profits through its telephone directory company, Guías y Publicidad (Appendix A, Exhibit 41). On September 25 Benjamin Holmes, the Chilean manager of Chiltelco, and officials from Guías y Publicidad were arrested on fraud charges. Finally, on September 29, the government of Chile officially expropriated the Chile Telephone Company.

Although the Chilean government had given every indication that it intended to pursue negotiation and arbitration over compensation for ITT's interest in the company (in fact, negotiations were resumed in December, only to be terminated again after publication of Jack Anderson's column), ITT had no faith that a settlement could be arrived at that could be considered satisfactory from its viewpoint. Accordingly, the company once more swung into action, and Merriam, through presidential aide John Ehrlichman, obtained a meeting between Geneen and General Haig, Henry Kissinger's deputy, and Secretary of Commerce Peter Peterson. Peterson later testified that at this short luncheon meeting Geneen had given a straightforward presentation of what had happened in Chile. Immediately after this meeting, Geneen instructed Merriam to forward to Peterson ITT's suggested actions. The result was Merriam's October 1 letter to Peterson (Appendix B, Exhibit 43) to which was attached an eighteen-point action plan designed "to see that Allende does not get through the crucial next six months." Among Merriam's specific suggestions:

> Continue loan restrictions in the international banks such as those the Export/Import Bank has already exhibited.
> Quietly have large U.S. private banks do the same.
> Confer with foreign banking sources with the same thing in mind.
> Delay buying from Chile over the next six months. Use U.S. copper stockpile instead of buying from Chile.
> Bring about a scarcity of U.S. dollars in Chile.
> Discuss with CIA how it can assist the six-month squeeze.
> Get to reliable sources within the Chilean Military. Delay fuel delivery to Navy and gasoline to Air Force. (This would have to be carefully handled, otherwise would be dangerous. However, a false delay could build up their planned discontent against Allende, thus, bring about necessity of his removal.)
> Help disrupt Allende's UNCTAD plans.
> It is noted that Chile's annual exports to the U.S. are valued at $154 million (U.S. dollars). As many U.S. markets as possible should be closed to Chile. Likewise, any U.S. exports of special importance to Allende should be delayed or stopped. [*Report,* p. 15]

What's Wrong with Taking Care of No. One?

According to the subcommittee, the company's attitude, motivation, and strategies with regard to its Chilean investment could best be summed up by Gerrity's question: "What's wrong with taking care of No. 1?" (*Report*, p. 17). The subcommittee went on to state:

> This is not to say that there was no reason for concern on the company's part over the fate of its investments in Chile. . . . Whether compensation would be paid, or, if paid, whether such compensation would be adequate was not clear. . . . So the company's concern was perfectly understandable.
>
> So, too, was its desire to communicate that concern to the appropriate officials of the U.S. Government and to seek their judgment as to how the United States would view the possible eventuality of a seizure of company property without adequate compensation. It is also understandable that the company would wish to have the U.S. Government's assessment of the likelihood of an Allende victory, so that it could plan for such an eventuality in terms of negotiations, investment strategy, and corporate profitability targets.
>
> But what is not to be condoned is that the highest officials of the ITT sought to engage the CIA in a plan covertly to manipulate the outcome of the Chilean presidential election. In so doing the company overstepped the line of acceptable corporate behavior. If ITT's actions in seeking to enlist the CIA for its purposes with respect to Chile were to be sanctioned as normal and acceptable, no country would welcome the presence of multinational corporations. Over every dispute or potential dispute between a company and a host government in connection with a corporation's investment interests, there would hang the spectre of foreign intervention. No sovereign nation would be willing to accept that possibility as the price of permitting foreign corporations to invest in its territory. The pressures which the company sought to bring to bear on the U.S. Government for CIA intervention are thus incompatible with the long-term existence of multinational corporations; they are also incompatible with the formulation of U.S. foreign policy in accordance with U.S. national, rather than private interests. [*Report*, pp. 17–18]

THE OPIC GUARANTEE

Another element of ITT's investment in Chile involved the company's claim against the Overseas Private Investment Corporation (OPIC), which had insured ITT's investment in Chile against expropriation.

OPIC was established by Congress in January 1971 to take over the expropriation-guarantee program from the Agency for International Development, which had operated similar programs since 1958. OPIC has the responsibility of "promoting American business investment in less developed countries by insuring investments against expropriation, blocked currencies, and war risks." [22] OPIC has insured business ventures in ninety countries for a total of $2.1 billion, with $400 million of reinsurance with Lloyd's of London. Its staff numbers 133 and its budget is $4 million. OPIC charges a premium rate of 1.5 percent to insure against the three types of risks it covers. It does not insure investments in Indochina, Cuba, China, the Soviet Union, some of the Eastern European countries, Western Europe, Canada, or any other developed country.

OPIC has had rough going since its inception, and in 1972 the House "came within 26 votes of cutting off the OPIC's authority to make new insurance commitments, loans, or loan guarantees. . . . Some members of Congress doubt that the U.S. government should shoulder any of the risk of investment abroad, especially for big corporations," [23] because it will drag the United States into conflicts between private industry and foreign governments where it is frequently not clear who is to blame, and where foreign policy considerations may make it undesirable to meddle at a particular time.

OPIC's chief, Bradford Mills, strongly defends the concept of government insurance to cover such private risks on three grounds:

1. If the United States is to help the poor countries develop, and also maintain its present leadership position in the world markets, it must protect U.S. corporations against unusual non-business-type risks so that they will invest in these countries.
2. Other European countries are providing similar coverage to their businesses and at rates that are about one-third those charged by OPIC. For example, for the three standard risks, Denmark, Germany, and Norway charge only 0.5 percent, Japan 0.55 percent, France and Holland 0.8 percent, and the United Kingdom 1.0 percent.[24] Mills maintains that such low premiums amount to indirect subsidy, and if the U.S. government were to withdraw its guarantees, it would put U.S. business in an unfair competitive position against companies from other countries for a share of trade and investment in less-developed countries.

[22] "Washington Report: Insurance for ITT?," *The New York Times,* April 8, 1973, Sec. 3, p. 6.
[23] *Ibid.*
[24] Richard F. Janssen, "The Problem of Expropriation Risks," *The Wall Street Journal,* May 9, 1973, p. 18.

3. The less-developed countries are less likely to take illegal and confiscatory actions against U.S. companies and will settle claims on a more businesslike basis when such investments are insured by an agency of the U.S. government. Not to do so would lead to a confrontation with the U.S. government where the stake, in terms of cutoff of foreign aid and development loans, is much higher than capital funds from a single company.

Such arguments, however, draw equally strong counterarguments. American labor protests that such assistance is contributing to the export of American jobs and contends that multinationals go to less-developed countries for cheap labor. Some congressmen believe that, given the situation at home, helping poor lands is a luxury that they "can no longer afford." [25]

European authorities also reject the arguments of low premium rates by suggesting that investment risks in less-developed countries may be different for multinationals from different countries. Furthermore, low premiums must be evaluated as part of total assistance provided by governments to multinationals. States one international expert: "All the programs are subsidies in the sense that governments are the final guarantors of private risks." [26]

At the time of Allende's election, OPIC had a total commitment in Chile of approximately $500 million in guarantees against expropriation: $105 million of that commitment was to ITT, with other large policies held by Anaconda, Kennecott, and Cerro de Pasco. ITT's insurance contract, its amount and conditions, became a part of the negotiations with the Chilean government when the government demanded, in August 1971, that it receive copies of the contract for study before further negotiations could take place. ITT refused to allow the contract to be released and forwarded the demand to OPIC.

Following Chile's nationalization of ITT properties, the company filed a claim with OPIC for $92.5 million. The company had every reason to expect sympathetic treatment from OPIC's Mills. When the Senate subcommittee was hearing testimony on ITT's attempt to enlist the CIA's help to block Allende's election, Mills pointedly refused to advise Congress of OPIC's opinion of ITT's claim, saying that a decision would soon be forthcoming.

On April 9, 1973, OPIC rejected ITT's insurance claim on the grounds that ITT "failed to comply with its obligations under the OPIC contracts to disclose material information to OPIC. In addition, ITT increased OPIC's risk of loss by failing to preserve administrative remedies as required by

[25] *The New York Times,* April 8, 1973, Sec. 3, p. 6.
[26] Janssen, "The Problem of Expropriation Risks."

the contracts, and by failing to protect OPIC's interests as a potential successor to ITT's rights." [27] Earlier, OPIC had denied Anaconda's claim for $154 million for its Chilean copper mines. That claim is under arbitration.

Although OPIC's formal announcement was in "obscure language" on which officials refused to elaborate,[28] the agency appeared not to be accusing ITT of provoking the Chilean government into nationalizing Chiltelco, which would have been a legitimate reason for refusing the claim. ITT announced that under the terms of its contract, it would immediately submit the claim to an independent arbitration panel, which could reverse OPIC's decision. It might be noted here that internal company correspondence released by the subcommittee indicates that ITT's legal department was afraid that the company's activities in interfering in Chile's election might prejudice their claim with OPIC (Appendix B, Exhibit 24).

Many congressional observers felt that the decision from OPIC was based on political considerations. At a time when the agency was attempting to obtain an additional appropriation of $72.5 million, the *Wall Street Journal* quoted one Capitol Hill source as saying, "I think there would have been a political storm [in Congress] if they'd have approved the claim." Denying the claim, and allowing it to go to arbitration, "depoliticized" the case, the source stated.[29] OPIC denied that political considerations had affected its decision; "The reasons given for the denial didn't arise out of the [Senate] hearings," an OPIC spokesman said.[30]

The OPIC guarantee was used in another manner that caused the subcommittee some concern. Both McCone and Ambassador Korry had used the OPIC guarantees as a reason for advising U.S. intervention in the election: "If OPIC had to compensate the companies under the guarantees, so the argument went, the cost would ultimately be borne by the U.S. taxpayer, since OPIC lacked adequate reserves to meet these potential liabilities." The report concluded: "Thus, at least in the case of Chile, OPIC insurance became an argument for American intervention 'to protect the taxpayer'" (*Report*, p. 19). This was not, the subcommittee believed, foreseen when OPIC was established, and it promised to consider the matter in later hearings on OPIC.

ITT's at It Again

The April 30, 1973, issue of *Newsweek* carried a short news item to the effect that ITT was "taking an active interest in the re-election cam-

---

[27] "Federal Insurer Bars ITT's Claim for Its Chile Unit," *The Wall Street Journal,* April 11, 1973, p. 2.

[28] "U.S. Won't Pay ITT for Chilean Loss," *The New York Times,* April 10, 1973, p. 2.

[29] *The Wall Street Journal,* April 11, 1973, p. 2.

[30] *Ibid.*

paign of Idaho's Democratic Senator Frank Church." [31] Recall that Senator Church, as chairman of the Subcommittee on Multinational Corporations of the Foreign Relations Committee, had taken part in the investigation of ITT's involvement in Chile's political affairs. And Neil McReynolds, head of ITT's public relations in the Northwest, visited Idaho to collect "what he calls 'background material' on Church." [32]

[31] "The Periscope: ITT in Idaho," p. 15.
[32] *Ibid.*

APPENDIX A

POLITICAL ENVIRONMENT IN CHILE
IMMEDIATELY PRECEDING ALLENDE'S
ELECTION

ITT consistently stated that critics of its actions in Chile took these actions out of the context of the Chilean environment, which was extremely hostile to American investment in general and ITT in particular. This Appendix provides a short glimpse of that environment through renderings (not literal translations) of speeches and newspaper articles from both before and after Allende was inaugurated as president. These quotations show that Allende's coalition had indeed launched an extensive propaganda campaign against foreign investment, or at least foreign control, in Chile.

The coalition that supported Allende, called the Unidad Popular (Popular Unity), consisted of the Communist, Socialist, Radical, and Social Democratic parties, along with the Military Popular Action Movement and Independent Popular Action. Their basic platform was approved on December 17, 1969, and read, in part:

1. Chile is living a profound crisis which manifests itself in social and economic stagnation, generalized poverty, and the delays of all kinds suffered by workers, peasants, and the other exploited classes. It is also seen in the growing difficulties faced by employees, professionals, small and medium-sized businessmen, and in the minimal opportunities available to women and youth.

Chile's problem can be solved. Our country has great resources, such as copper and other minerals, a great hydroelectric potential, vast expanses of forest, a long coastline rich in marine species, more than sufficient agricultural lands, and so forth. It also has the will to work and the desire for all Chileans to progress together in their professional and technical capacity.

What then has failed? What has failed in Chile is a system which does not meet the necessities of our times. Chile is a capitalistic country which depends on imperialism, is dominated by bourgeois sectors that are structurally linked to foreign capital and cannot solve the country's fundamental problems. These are the same problems that derive from class privileges, and which will never be renounced voluntarily. Furthermore, as a consequence of the development of world-wide capitalism, the surrender by the national monopolistic bourgeoisie to imperialism progressively increases and accentuates its dependence in its role as the minor partner of foreign capital.

2. In Chile, the reformist and developmental solutions, that the Alliance for Progress encouraged and the government of Frei made its own, have not succeeded in changing anything important.

3. The development of monopolistic capitalism denies the widening of democracy and exacerbates anti-popular violence.

4. The imperialistic exploitation of backward economies is carried out in many ways. Some are through investments in mining (copper, iron and others) and in industrial banking and commercial activities, through the technological control that obliges us to pay extremely high sums for equipment, licenses, and patents through usurious North American loans, that obliges us to spend in the United States and transport the purchased articles in North American ships, as well as others. Imperialism has snatched away from Chile large resources, equivalent to double the capital invested in our country throughout the whole of its history. The North American monopolies, with the complicity of the bourgeois government, succeeded in taking control of almost all our copper and nitrate. They control foreign trade and dictate economic policy through the International Monetary Fund and other organizations. They dominate important industrial and service sectors. They enjoy privileged laws while they impose monetary devaluation, the reduction of salaries, and distort agricultural activity through agricultural surpluses. They also interfere in education, culture, and the communications media. Taking advantage of military and political agreement, they have tried to penetrate the armed forces.

5. Chile governs and legislates in favor of the few, the big capitalists and their followers, the companies that dominate our economy, and the large landowners whose power remains almost intact. . . .

The only truly popular alternative, and consequently the fundamental chore that the government of the people has before it, is to end the dominion of the imperialists, the monopolists, and the landholding oligarchy, and to begin the construction of socialism in Chile.[1]

Throughout 1971 the leftist partisans and press continued their attacks on foreign ownership in Chile. Peter Vuskovic, director of the University of Chile's Institute of Economics, charged that between 1966 and 1968, foreign penetration in major industrial firms had increased from 38 percent of those firms to more than 50 percent. Of the 160 most important enterprises, he said, 33.8 percent were infiltrated with foreign capital, if not controlled by it, and of the 100 most important, the percentage of foreignization rose to 40. Furthermore, "in the last few years . . . a new means [of foreign penetration] has been devised, and that is technology as the means of colonization." [2]

[1] *El Siglo*, December 23, 1969.
[2] *Ibid.*, August 22, 1970.

Charges against specific companies were also made, both by the press and by the government. In August an Anaconda executive made some disparaging remarks about the Chilean Congress, a criminal suit was brought against him. A government-investigating commission also determined that Anaconda had been supporting Alessandri's candidacy and had contributed to Andalién, a right-wing terrorist group. The outcry against Anaconda's actions was very strong and served further to connect foreign influence and investment in Chile with the right wing in Chilean politics.[3] Ford, too, came under attack during this period, when the Council for the Defense of the State accused the company's Chilean branch of fraud against the government.[4]

As the popular election drew near, attacks on foreign capital increased. A government study, it was reported, showed that foreign investment was concentrated in those sectors of the economy that had shown the greatest growth or the greatest potential for growth, which received special benefits from the government. The study also found that most of the foreign companies were monopolies and that they competed with Chilean enterprises in the same sectors, driving the Chilean companies out of the market. The study further charged that "the payment of royalties, patents, designs, technical assistance, and so on, do not seem to be any remuneration for a technological transfer, but rather an alternate way to take money out of the country." [5]

Allende himself made his position very clear. In a speech at the University of Chile, he stated:

> The Unidad Popular was born to defend Chile from capitalistic exploitation and from foreign intervention. Because Chile, as long as she remains economically dependent, and as long as her natural resources are not controlled by the government, cannot emerge from her present state of underdevelopment.[6]

In a later speech, Allende disclosed the industries that he planned to nationalize, among which was included ITT.[7]

These attacks on foreign capital were not moderated after Allende's victory in the popular election. Oscar Garreton, a member of Allende's government, accused the large corporations in Chile, most of which were foreign controlled, of fixing prices, controlling bank credit, operating arbitrarily during periods of labor fluctuations, and selling poor quality prod-

---

3 *Ibid.*, August 26, 1970.
4 *Ibid.*, August 29, 1970.
5 *Ibid.*, September 2, 1970.
6 *Ibid.*, August 4, 1970.
7 *Ibid.*, September 3, 1970.

ucts, all to the detriment of the smaller Chilean enterprises. Furthermore, he said, the large corporations do not operate at full capacity, and their technology is advanced and automated, both of which contribute to a low employment figure.[8]

Another economist, Orlando Caputto, charged:

In the year 1969, the egress of capital through profits from foreign investments, interest and payments on mortgages came to about $480 million. This figure amounts to almost half of the income for Chilean exports. In other words, Chile uses half the dollars from its exports to cover increasing needs for the importation of goods, especially capital goods, and intermediate products. The egress of capital as profit is explained basically by American investments in copper. However, the new orientation of foreign capital, located increasingly in the industrial sector, has uncovered other alternative ways to remit money. Payments for technology, for overbilling on imports (paying artificially raised prices to leave a greater quantity of dollars abroad) and for short or long-term financial operations. Also, foreign capital operating in national industries imports a large part of its raw materials in the majority of cases. This is one of the main ways of taking out money, since the price of these imports is overbilled.

In Chile, the scandalous loss of $14 million through overbilling was undoubtedly one of the elements considered when the illegal importation of parts being done by Ford Motor was denounced.[9]

That Allende and the UP meant to fulfill these promises was made clear almost immediately after Allende's congressional confirmation, when the government moved in December to nationalize the copper-mining industry.

[8] *Plan,* October 1970.
[9] *Ibid.*

APPENDIX B

The following exhibits are part of the background documents on ITT's involvement in Chile which columnist Jack Anderson used as the basis of his assertions in his column "Washington Merry-go-Round." The documents were submitted by ITT to the Subcommittee on Multinational Corporations of the Committee on Foreign Relations, U.S. Senate, pursuant to the hearings by the subcommittee on ITT and Chile, and were later released to the public by the subcommittee. Many of the documents were also inserted by Senator Fred R. Harris in the *Congressional Record* (April 11, 1972), pp. S 5858–71.

Exhibit 1

INTERNATIONAL TELEPHONE AND TELEGRAPH CORPORATION
INTERNATIONAL HEADQUARTERS

SYSTEM CONFIDENTIAL

TO: H. S. Geneen
FROM: E. J. Gerrity
DATE: September 10, 1970

CONFIDENTIAL

SUBJECT: Chilean Situation

1. Attached is a copy of Ernie Wiener's telex on reaction in Brazilian Government and business circles to the Chilean election. It indicates, as we have reported, that the result in Chile is drawing Brazil close to Argentina. Wiener, of course, is unaware of the Peruvian Government reaction.

The New York Times reports today the first move in Chile toward the plan that *Ambassador Korry* strongly believes is possible of doing, that is, of making Alessandri president with the intention that he resign so new elections may take place, is underway. At the moment we believe chances of that succeeding are *minimal*.

2. Our poll of companies with plants, or activities in Chile continues to show an almost complete lack of interest on their parts. In Washington the Monsanto and RCA reps told Bill Merriam they were unaware of any concern by their managements. Bill asked them to go back and check.

Our polling here and in Washington will continue.

cc: R. E. Bennett
    F. J. Dunleavy
    H. J. Aibel
    R. L. Brittenham
    W. R. Merriam
    E. R. Wallace

Exhibit 2

COMPANIA DE TELEFONOS DE CHILE
SANTIAGO 1

SYSTEM CONFIDENTIAL

TO: Mr. J. W. Guilfoyle
FROM: B. W. Holmes
DATE: September 10, 1970

CONFIDENTIAL

I am attaching hereto translation into English of the Basic Communications Program prepared by the Popular Unity Committee existing in Empresa Nacional de Telecomunicaciones (Entel-Chile), which, as I understand, has served as a basis for the speeches and statements of Mr. Allende as Presidential Candidate.

I am briefly stating hereunder the most important references contained in that program in relation with Compañía de Teléfonos de Chile.

a) Total restructuring of the communications area including the Direction of Post and Telegraph, Compañía de Teléfonos de Chile, Entel-Chile, Superintendency of Electrical Services and other similar companies (page 1, second and last paragraphs).

b) Criticizes most severely the telecommunications systems due to the ineptitude of the bourgeosie and the people who direct them, particularly the system of Compañía de Teléfonos de Chile, with respect to which is indicated that its service is insufficient and of poor quality.

Poor distribution of services, due to the fact that the majority of the work and countrymen areas lack telephones, which is a consequence of the arbitrary management on the Company's part, of the investments it makes, and the high cost of installations and monthly rents (page 2, paragraph 3 and first part of page 3).

c) Strongly criticizes ITT and its subsidiaries, ITTCOM and CSESAC, as well as the concession contract of January 23, 1930; the expansion convenio of January 15, 1958; the memorandum of agreement of February 6, 1965; and the convenio of October 6, 1967 based on the mentioned memorandum of agreement (pages 4, 5 and 6).

d) Lack of fair equivalence in payment of Corfo contributions (page 7, second paragraph).

e) Concealment of profits on the part of Companía de Teléfonos de Chile (page 8).

f) Surreptitious operations on the part of ITT's subsidiaries in Chile (page three first paragraphs).

g) Immediate nationalization of CTC and ITTCOM, prior an exhaustive investigation to be carried out by an Intervention Commission to be appointed in this respect (page 11, last part).

h) Immediate participation of workmen in the Companies' Board of Directors (page 13, paragraph 1).

i) Even before nationalization, the Company will be forced to provide with telephone service the population centers and other parts of the country (page 13, paragraph 2).

cc. Mr. Stimson

Exhibit 3

ITT WASHINGTON OFFICE
Washington, D.C.

SYSTEM CONFIDENTIAL

TO: Mr. W. R. Merriam
FROM: J. D. Neal
DATE: September 14, 1970

CONFIDENTIAL

SUBJECT: Chile—White House; State Department; Attorney General

After you read me Mr. Geneen's suggestions about Chile on Friday, September 11, I took the following action over the weekend:

WHITE HOUSE—KISSINGER'S OFFICE

Late Friday afternoon I telephoned Mr. Kissinger's office and talked with "Pete" Vaky, who is the State Department's Latin American adviser to Kissinger.

I told him of Mr. Geneen's deep concern about the Chile situation, not only from the standpoint of our heavy investment, but also because of the threat to the entire Hemisphere. I explained that $95 million of our holdings are covered by investment guarantees, as are those of other American corporations, but that we are reluctant to see the American taxpayers cover such losses.

I told Mr. Vaky we are aware of Ambassador Corry's position re Alessandri being certified and then resigning in order for Frei to run again. Also, we have heard rumors of moves by the Chilean military.

Mr. Vaky said there has been "lots of thinking" about the Chile situation and that it is a "real tough one" for the U.S. I admitted we understand the difficulty of the U.S. position but we hope the White House, State, etc., will take a neutral position, or not discourage, in the event Chile or others attempt to save the situation.

I told Mr. Vaky to tell Mr. Kissinger Mr. Geneen is willing to come to Washington to discuss ITT's interest and that we are prepared to assist financially in sums up to seven figures. I said Mr. Geneen's concern is not one of "after the barn door has been locked," but that all along we have feared the Allende victory and have been trying unsuccessfully to get other American companies aroused over the fate of their investments, and join us in pre-election efforts. [Emphasis added.]

Mr. Vaky said to thank Mr. Geneen for his interest and that he would pass all of this on to Mr. Kissinger. He offered to keep us informed.

STATE DEPARTMENT—ASST. SECRETARY MEYER

Early Saturday morning I telephoned Assistant Secretary of State for Latin American Affairs, Charles (Chuck) A. Meyer, at his office. I repeated to him the same rundown I gave "Pete" Vaky.

"Chuck" said he could understand Mr. Geneen's concern and appreciated his offer to assist. He said State is watching the situation as closely as possible and awaiting the October 24 date when the Chilean Congress decides the winner.

He said the Chileans themselves are becoming quite concerned; even the labor unions see a disadvantage in Allende. He said "this is a Chile problem" and they have done a good job in "screwing-up their own dessert."

He said the head of Kennecott Copper has been in to report he feels they have lost their big mining area "El Teniente."

Meyer said he would keep me informed and trusts we will advise his office of pertinent news.

ATTORNEY GENERAL

I went to a wedding reception at the Korean Embassy late Saturday. I was in hopes of finding Secretary Rogers and especially Under Secretary of State U. Alex Johnson who is a close friend of the Ambassador's, but they did not attend. Mrs. Rogers was there; so we chatted with her.

I ran into Attorney General Mitchell; so decided to mention Chile just in case the subject reached him in a cabinet meeting or otherwise.

Mr. Mitchell mentioned Mr. Geneen's recent visit with him. He said he could understand Mr. Geneen's concern over ITT's Chile investiment. I told him I had already spoken to the White House and State Department.

Exhibit 4

INTERNATIONAL TELEPHONE AND TELEGRAPH CORPORATION
INTERNATIONAL HEADQUARTERS

SYSTEM CONFIDENTIAL

TO: E. J. Gerrity
FROM: H. Hendrix/R. Berrellez
DATE: September 17, 1970

CONFIDENTIAL

SUBJECT: Chile

The surface odds and foreign news media appear to indicate that Salvador Allende will be inaugurated as President November 4, but there now is a strong possibility that he will not make it.

The big push has begun in Chile to assure a congressional victory for Jorge Alessandri on October 24, as part of what has been dubbed the "Alessandri Formula" to prevent Chile from becoming a Communist state.

By this plan, following Alessandri's election by Congress, he would resign as he has announced. The Senate president (a Christian Democrat) would assume presidential power and a new election would be called for 60 days ahead.

Such an election would most likely match President Eduardo Frei, then eligible to run again, against Allende. In such a contest, Frei is considered to be an easy winner.

Late Tuesday night (September 15) Ambassador Edward Korry finally received a message from State Department giving him the green light to move in the name of President Nixon. The message gave him maximum authority to do all possible—short of a Dominican Republic-type action— to keep Allende from taking power. [Emphasis added.]

At this stage *the key* to whether we have a solution or a disaster is Frei—and how much pressure the U.S. and the anti-Communist movement in Chile can bring to bear upon him in the next couple of weeks.

The Mercurio newspapers are another key factor. Keeping them alive and publishing between now and October 24 is of extreme importance. They are the only remaining outspoken anti-Communist voice in Chile and under severe pressure, especially in Santiago. This may well turn out to be the Achilles heel for the Allende crowd.

Following are some significant points as we see the Chile situation on this date, plus some comment on various factors and a few basic recommendations:

1. Allende and the Marxist-Socialist coalition (Unidad Popular) are acting like he is the elected President. They are pressing hard on all fronts to consolidate his slim September 4 election plurality into a solid victory in the congressional vote. Chile's Communist Party, a part of the UP coalition, is directing the pressure. Strategy is coordinated by the USSR. Party discipline and control thus far is extraordinary

2. *The anti-Communist elements, with Alessandri's supporters in the forefront and Frei in the wings (both prodded by the U.S. government), are maneuvering—now rather efficiently—to capture the congressional vote and set the stage for a new national election. Given the atmosphere in Chile today, the prospect of a new election is looking more and more attractive as the future looks more and more bleak.* [Emphasis added.]

3. Since Allende and the UP won only a bit more than a one-third of the total national vote, it is strongly believed that in a two-man race and "democracy vs. communism" showdown, Frei would get most of the Christian Democratic vote—since this would put the party back in power— and all the rightest [*sic*] vote that supported Alessandri.

4. For the recent campaign the CD leadership was put in the hands of Radimoro [*sic*] Tomic, who has a deep-grained hatred for Frei and the U.S. The CD national committee is slated to meet early next month and it is expected Frei will regain leadership control. (Tomic already has pledged his support to Allende.)

5. Looming ominously over the successful application of the "Alessandri Formula" is the threat of an explosion of violence and civil war if Allende loses the congressional vote. Allende, the UP and the Castroite Revolutionary Movement of the Left (MIR) have made it clear they intend to fight for total victory. Thus, some degree of bloodshed seems inevitable.

6. Is the Chilean military capable of coping with nationwide violence or a civil war? Opinion is divided on this in Santiago. Korry has said he considers the armed forces a "bunch of toy soldiers." Well-informed Chileans and some U.S. advisers believe the army and national police have the capability. There are definite reservations about the air force and navy. We know that the army has been assured full material and financial assistance by the U.S. military establishment.

The Chilean military will not move unilaterally to prevent Allende from taking office. They will act only if it is in the framework of the constitution.

7. President Frei has stated privately to his closest associates, to Alessandri and to a State Department visitor last weekend in Vina del Mar that the country cannot be allowed to go Communist and that Allende must be prevented from taking office. Publicly, however, he is keeping out

of the battle up to this point while feeling steadily increasing pressure from the U.S. and his own camp. Never known for displaying guts in a crunch, he is faced with a dilemma of not wanting to be charged with either turning Chile over to Communist rule or contributing to a possible civil war. A parlay of his highly inflated ego and a chance to occupy the presidency six more years may provide the necessary starch for his decision.

To help strengthen his position, efforts are being made this week to turn this weekend's observance of Chile Independence Day into a pro-Frei demonstration. Main feature of the observance will be a military parade by about 25,000 troops assembled in Santiago.

8. *Ambassador Korry, before getting a go-signal from Foggy Bottom, clearly put his head on the block with his extremely strong messages to State.* [Emphasis added.] He also, to give him due credit, started to maneuver with the CD, the Radical and National parties and other Chileans— without State authorization—immediately after the election results were known. He has never let up on Frei, to the point of telling him to "put his pants on."

By the same token, last week when an emissary of Allende called at his office to pay respects and say that the "Allende government wanted to have good relations with the Ambassador and the United States," Korry responded only that he had been "so busy with consulate affairs helping to get visas for Chileans wanting to leave the country that he had not had time to think of the future." Thus ended the interview.

9. The anti-Allende effort more than likely will require some outside financial support. The degree of this assistance will be known better around October 1. We have pledged our support if needed.

10. There is no doubt among trained professional observers with experience in the U.S., Europe and Latin America that if Allende and the UP take power, Chile will be transformed quickly into a harsh and tightly-controlled Communist state, like Cuba or Czechoslovakia today. The transition would be much more rapid than Cuba's because of the long-standing organization of the Chile Communist Party. This obviously poses a serious threat to the national security of the U.S.—Sol Linowitz, Senator Church and others of the same thought notwithstanding—and several Latin American nations. It also is obvious from Allende's pronouncements that existing business and financial links with the U.S. would be strangled.

*   *   *   *   *

At a meeting with Arturo Matte at his residence Sunday (September 13), he seemed in a more relaxed frame of mind than on the last visit and he made these points:

A. The "Alessandri Formula" through which the way would be opened for new elections had the government's and Frei's personal approval. Once elected by Congress, Alessandri would resign, thus carrying out a pre-election pledge that he would do so unless he received a plurality or majority of the votes in the regular balloting.

B. Alessandri did publicly announce his plans to resign if elected last week. It was subsequently learned Frei saw and approved the text of the announcement before it was released to the public.

C. Frei and his party (at least that wing that he commands) have a deep interest in this for two reasons: it would block the assumption of power by a Marxist and also give the Christian Democrats a new chance to regain power, this time backed by the Alessandri camp. Alessandri's announcement had the effect of alerting the Marxists and Allende that a powerful last-ditch effort was afoot to block them and it also probably may have partially checked a PDC congressional vote swing toward Allende.

D. Matte said the armed forces are agreed on the extreme danger to democracy that Allende's assumption of power involves. They agree he must be stopped. However, the armed forces leadership and Frei prefer a constitutional way out (i.e., congressional election of Alessandri) that doesn't preclude violence—spontaneous or provoked.

E. A constitutional solution, for instance, could result from massive internal disorders, strikes, urban and rural warfare. This would morally justify an armed forces intervention for an indefinite period. But it was apparent from Matte's exposition that there is little hope for this. The Marxists will not be provoked. "You can spit in their face in the street," Matte said, "and they'll say thank you." This means that the far left is aware of and taking every precaution to neutralize provocation.

F. A plan suggested to Frei, said Matte, calls for the creation of a military cabinet. This would be a form of extreme provocation since it would hint at the makings of a coup. It would have a definite psychological effect on the congressional voters who may be undecided about whom they'll vote for in the runoff. But, added Matte, Frei is reluctant to do it without some reason to justify it in the eyes of the public. We inferred from this that Frei will not act on this unless he is confronted with a severe national crisis.

G. The armed forces boss, René Schneider, is fully aware of the danger of Allende moving in. But he will not budge an inch without Frei's okay. *One retired general, Viaux, is all gung-ho about moving immediately, reason or not, but Matte said Schneider has threatened to have Viaux shot if he moves unilaterally. Although Viaux has some following after his abortive rebellion a few months ago, it is doubted he commands strength enough now to carry it off alone.* [Emphasis added.]

H. Frei, said Matte, is highly worried about the damage to his stature in the hemisphere; he is concerned that he may become, as the Brazilians have put it, the Kerensky of Latin America.

But he still refuses to take the reins in his hand without "moral" reasons, Matte said.

I. Could he be persuaded, Matte was asked, by assurances of fullest support from Washington? He thought that over a while and finally said he thought that would help. The distinct impression, however, was he might have felt this would have to be done with consummate skill and tact so as not to offend Chilean national dignity. (Korry's new mandate may serve this purpose.)

J. The military has contingency plans ready for whatever scope operation is necessary, Matte said.

The conclusions from this session were:

The leader we thought was missing is right there in the saddle (Frei), but he won't move unless he is provided with a constitutional threat.

That threat must be provided one way or another through provocation. At the same time, a subtle but firm enough pressure must be brought to bear on Frei so that he'll respond.

Matte did not mention money or any other needs. At the end when it was mentioned we were, as always, ready to contribute with what was necessary, he said we would be advised. [Emphasis added.]

*   *   *   *   *

A Communist party congress was held in Santiago early this week. Among topics discussed was expropriation. The CUT, national labor confederation, was placed in charge of mapping expropriation plans. The CUT is controlled by the Communist party.

According to informants monitoring the party congress, the priority schedule has been put in the hands of a man named Bertini and roughly looks like this:

1. Copper companies.
2. The Mercurio newspaper chain.
3. Two unspecified "attractive" interests.

(These three items would be acted upon quickly. It is assumed in Santiago that Chiltelco probably would fall in item No. 3.)

4. Following the early expropriations, a commission would be named to study which industries should be taken over. The next group of takeovers would be slated for about one year later. Within two years the process would be complete.

*   *   *   *   *

The Mercurio chain is hitting at Allende and the Communist party with effect. Allende this week sent one of his top lieutenants, Alberto Jerez, mentioned as his choice for foreign minister, to see A. Edwards chief representative in Santiago.

Purpose of the post-midnight session was to blackmail Mercurio into stopping its anti-Communist campaign. Jerez stated bluntly that Mercurio and A. Edwards were committing suicide with their attitude. He said Allende had no intention of trying to fool Edwards. He planned to expropriate the newspapers and destroy what they stand for. Jerez added that the other Edwards interests in Chile could be affected more or less by the the attitude taken by the papers in the weeks ahead. He said the papers [*sic*] was "inciting sedition and if this continued we cannot control the MIR, which wants to burn the plant." He also said Edwards could return to the country (he is in the U.S. on business and his family now is in Baires) but if he came back and the paper refused to change "he could be hanged in the Plaza de Armas" after Allende takes power.

The paper in Santiago is in financial trouble. Since election day it is running about 10 to 15 per cent of its normal advertising. They will have a close squeeze meeting this end-of-the-month pay roll.

* * * * *

As you have read in news stories, Chile's economy is sagging badly. But runs on the banks have stopped and the escudo has settled back down to around 25 on the black market.

Unemployment is rising rapidly, especially in the construction sector. About 5000 workers already have been laid off in Santiago construction as projects are being shut down. It is estimated that over-all layoffs will affect about 30,000 in Greater Santiago by the end of this month.

* * * * *

We will be advised what help we can contribute as present activities develop between now and early October.

We have recommended, apart from direct assistance, the following:

1. We and other U.S. firms in Chile pump some advertising into Mercurio. (This has been started.)

2. We help with getting some propagandists working again on radio and television. There are about 20 people that the Matte and Edwards groups were supporting and we should make certain they are revived. [Emphasis added.] Allende now controls two of the three TV stations in Santiago and has launched an intensive radio campaign.

3. Assist in support of a "family relocation" center in Mendoza or Baires for wives and children of key persons involved in the fight. This will involve about 50 families for a period of a month to six weeks, maybe two months.

4. Bring what pressure we can on USIS in Washington to instruct the Santiago USIS to start moving the Mercurio editorials around Latin America and into Europe. Up until I left they were under orders not to move anything out of Chile.

5. Urge the key European press, through our contacts there, to get the story of what disaster could fall on Chile if Allende & Co. win this country.

These are immediate suggestions and there will be others between now and October 24 as pressure mounts on Frei and the Christian Democrats.

cc: E. Dunnett
      K. Perkins
      E. R. Wallace

Exhibit 5

ITT WASHINGTON OFFICE
Washington, D.C.

SYSTEM CONFIDENTIAL

TO: Mr. W. R. Merriam, Vice President
FROM: J. D. Neal
DATE: September 21, 1970

CONFIDENTIAL

SUBJECT: Chile

The excellent Chile report of September 17 to Mr. Gerrity from Hal Hendrix and R. Berrellez is in such depth there is little to add with reference to my call at the State Department on September 16. However, there are a few points of interest.

John Fisher, the new Director of Andean and Pacific Affairs, said Ambassador Korry is fully convinced that if Allende becomes President there will be no half measures—the country will be communist controlled.

Along the lines of the H-B report, State said the Allende-Communist forces moved *very quickly* to take over all possible media, TV, radio, etc.; *El Mercurio* newspaper is about the only source fighting Allende.

State has little or no faith in the Chilean military's willingness or ability to take control.

Should the Christian Democrats make demands of Allende, such as not to change the form of the government, meddle with the military, etc., the State Department said Allende will agree but will not live up to his promises.

I told Fisher we had spoken to the White House and to his boss, Assistant Secretary Meyer, and that we are ready to see anyone or do anything possible. He said he understood our concern, but thought we had covered the water front. [Emphasis added.]

Exhibit 6

SYSTEM CONFIDENTIAL

TO: Mr. T. L. Schmidt
FROM: W. R. Merriam
DATE: September 23, 1970

CONFIDENTIAL

In a conversation with Ned this morning, he feels it's about time to move on getting someone to do something about Chile on the floor of the House and/or Senate.

The attached clippings, together with an editorial from the *Washington Post* of yesterday, and Ralph Dungan's stupid piece this morning of the *Post*, should serve as background.

I suggest you get together with Bernie Goodrich to decide what can be prepared. Incidentally, Bernie leaves on Saturday for Europe so you will have to work fast on that end of it.

cc: Mr. B. Goodrich

Exhibit 7

INTER-OFFICE MEMORANDUM
ITT WASHINGTON OFFICE
1707 L Street, N.W.
Washington, D.C. 20036

SYSTEM CONFIDENTIAL

TO: Mr. W. R. Merriam
FROM: B. A. Goodrich
DATE: September 23, 1970

CONFIDENTIAL

SUBJECT: *U.S.I.S. Visit on Chile*

I visited today with Robert Amerson, assistant director for Latin America, U.S.I.S., and Mike Canning, of the U.S.I.S. Chilean Desk. I first backgrounded them on our information on the Chilean situation. They agreed with our information in most cases except they seem to feel that with each passing day the chance of any successful move by Frei or Alessandri is diminishing.

I told them that I was there for three basic reasons. First, to let them know what we were doing in terms of supporting Mercurio's shaky financial situation; to urge them to circulate widely the Mercurio editorials throughout Latin America, if they were not already doing so; and to ask them if there is anything they can see that we can do as a private company which may not be possible for government to do. On the latter point they stressed that nothing overt should be done that could be interpreted as U.S. intervention. I assured them that our people were well experienced in that field.

They said that they appreciated what we were doing in terms of financial support of the newspaper. In answer to my question about moving the Mercurio editorials around, Amerson said the editorials were appearing every day and U.S.I.S. is circulating them.

cc: J. V. Horner
    J. D. Neal

Exhibit 8

SYSTEM CONFIDENTIAL

TO: Mr. H. S. Geneen—Intel. Brussels
FROM: E. J. Gerrity
DATE: September 29, 1970

CONFIDENTIAL

Subsequent to your call yesterday I heard from Washington and a representative called on me this morning. He was the same man you met with Merriam some weeks ago. We discussed the situation in detail and he made suggestions based on recommendations from our representative on the scene and analysis in Washington. The idea presented, and with which I do not necessarily agree, is to apply economic pressure. The suggestions follow:

1. *Banks should not renew credits or should delay in doing so.*

2. *Companies should drag their feet in sending money, in making deliveries, in shipping spare parts, etc.*

3. *Savings and loan companies there are in trouble. If pressure were applied, they would have to shut their doors, thereby creating stronger pressure.* [Emphasis added.]

4. We should withdraw all technical help and should not promise any technical assistance in the future. Companies in a position to do so should close their doors.

5. A list of companies was provided and it was suggested that we approach them as indicated. I was told that of all the companies involved ours alone had been responsive and understood the problem. The visitor added that money was not a problem.

He indicated that certain steps were being taken but that he was looking for additional help aimed at inducing economic collapse. I discussed the suggestions with Guilfoyle. He contacted a couple of companies who said they had been given advice which is directly contrary to the suggestions I received.

Realistically I do not see how we can induce others involved to follow the plan suggested. We can contact key companies for their reactions and make suggestions in the hope that they might cooperate. Information we received today from other sources indicates that there is a growing economic crisis in any case.

Guilfoyle received a call this afternoon from a representative of the key candidate asking us to do nothing to rock the boat because forces are at work to solve the problem.

I advised the visitor that we would do everything possible to help but I pointed out in detail the problems we would have with the suggestions he had made.

Finally, Bob Berrellez has just sent a report which is pessimistic as to the outcome next week. This report is being delivered to you by Mr. Barr of the technical department who is leaving for Brussels this evening.

cc: F. J. Dunleavy—Intel. Brussels; Guilfoyle—ITT N.Y.; Merriam—ITT Washington.

Exhibit 9

SYSTEM CONFIDENTIAL

TO: Hal Hendrix—ITTHQNY
FROM: Robert Berrellez—ITTLABA
DATE: September 29, 1970

CONFIDENTIAL

SUBJECT: *Chileans*

Capsuled situationer:
It appears almost certain that marxist Salvador Allende will be confirmed by the Congress as Chile's next President. The Congressional runoff vote is scheduled October 24.

There's only a thin tendril of hope of an upset based on a sharp and unlikely switch in voting sentiment among the Christian Democrats who hold the balance of power in the runoff. The prevailing sentiment among the PDC is said to favor Allende.

A more realistic hope among those who want to block Allende is that a swiftly deteriorating economy (bank runs, plant bankruptcies etc.) will touch off a wave of violence resulting in a military coup.

President Eduardo Frei wants to stop Allende and has said so to intimates. But he wants to do it constitutionally—i.e., either through a congressional vote upset or an internal crisis requiring military intervention.

The armed forces are ready to move to block Allende—but only with Frei's consent, which does not appear to be forthcoming. In other words, Frei has passed the ball to the armed forces and the miiltary will not act without Frei's orders unless internal conditions require their intervention.

– 0 –

Details:
1. Chances of thwarting Allende's assumption of power now are pegged mainly to an economic collapse which is being encouraged by some sectors of the business community and by President Frei himself. The next two weeks will be decisive in this respect. Cash is in short supply. But the government is printing more money. There's an active black market with the escudo moving at a 29 to US$ 1.00 rate on Monday. It had gone down to $26.50 to US$ 1.00 on Friday. The pre-election rate was 20 to 21 to US$ 1.00. Undercover efforts are being made to bring about the bankruptcy

of one or two of the major savings and loans associations. This is expected to trigger a run on banks and the closure of some factories, resulting in more unemployment.

2. The pressures resulting from economic chaos could force a major segment of the Christian Democratic party to reconsider their stance in relation to Allende in the Congressional runoff vote. It will become apparent, for instance, that there's no confidence among the business community in Allende's future policies and that the health of the nation is at stake.

3. More important, massive unemployment and unrest might produce enough violence to force the military to move. The success of this maneuver rests in large measure on the reaction of the extreme and violent (Castroite, Maoist) left in Allende's camp. So far he has been able to keep these elements controlled.

4. It's certain that Allende is on to this scheme. He has referred to it in recent public statements. He is also certainly aware of the government's (and Frei's) complicity. Last week the finance minister issued a pessimistic report on the national economy, placing the blame on the results of the September 4 election. The statement was issued with Frei's blessings. Although it reads as an objective and realistic evaluation of economic conditions, the statement aroused the Allende camp which severely criticized it as provocative.

5. All previous evaluations of Frei's weaknesses in a crisis are being confirmed. Worse, it has been established beyond any doubt that he is double-dealing to preserve his own stature and image as the leader of Latin America democracy. For instance: he told some of his ministers he'd be more than willing to be removed by the military. This would absolve him from any involvement in a coup that, in turn, would upset Allende. Then, he turned right around and told the military chiefs he is totally against a coup.

6. A group of respected political and business leaders called on Frei Sunday at Viña del Mar, the beach resort, to call his attention to these lapses. I could not determine the results of this confrontation or its basic purpose. The assumption is that by confronting Frei, the group hoped to press him into a definitive move in the one desired direction.

7. As a result of all this inertia, an aura of defeat has enveloped important and influential sectors of the community. Some businessmen who seemed all gung-ho about stopping Allende are now talking in terms of trying to make some deals with him. Others have given up and are getting ready to leave the country.

8. Some Chilean businessmen have suggested we try to deal in some manner with Allende in an effort to rescue at least a portion of our investment instead of losing it all. At this writing, we have been told Allende's

representatives have asked for a meeting with Sheraton representatives to discuss Allende's future policies concerning the hotels. My personal view is that we should do nothing to encourage or help the Allende team. Every care should also be exercised to insure that we are not identified with any anti-Allende move.

9. No hope should be pegged to conditions the Christian Democrats are demanding from Allende in exchange for their support in the Congressional vote. Some believe that if Allende turns them down the PDC will not vote for him. Allende will promise anything at this stage. Furthermore, many of the conditions the PDC is making are covered by the constitution to which Allende will pay lip service for a while until he is firmly in the saddle and has consolidated his hold so that he can move toward converting Chile into a communist, self-perpetuating state.

10. It is obvious from his latest remarks, however, that Allende fears something is in the wind to deprive him of the presidency in the congressional vote. On Monday he warned that he would bring the nation to civil war if he was not voted into power.

11. Meantime, the Russians are busy helping shore up Allende's defenses. Since the September 4 election, the Russian embassy staff in Santiago added 20 new staffers.

12. An extreme rightist faction launched a series of terrorist acts Sunday (bombings mostly) in what appeared an amateurish attempt to provoke the Castroite-Maoist sector into a violent backlash that would produce the conditions conducive to a military intervention. The bombings failed to arouse anything outside of police action which resulted in the arrest of some of the bombers. This, we are told by the most authoritative sources, is the far right's last effort to provoke the far left in this particular manner.

- 0 -

The sum-up:

1. A Congressional defeat for Allende is unlikely at this stage. The defeated Christian Democratic candidate, Radomiro Tomic, is backing Allende and can take a sizable segment of the PDC vote with him.

2. Despite some pessimism, a high level effort continues toward getting Frei and/or the military to stop Allende.

3. Although its chances of success seem slender, we cannot ignore that a roadblock to Allende's assumption to power through an economic collapse has the brightest possibilities.

cc: Messrs. E. Gerrity, ITTHQNY

        E. Wallace,   "
        K. Perkins,   "
        E. Dunnett,   "

Exhibit 10

SYSTEM CONFIDENTIAL

TO: Messrs. Merriam/Neal/Ryan
FROM: E. J. Gerrity
DATE: September 30, 1970

CONFIDENTIAL

Yesterday, subsequent to my visit from Mr. Broe, Jack Guilfoyle was advised of the following by Enno Hobbing of CIA:

Hobbing was visited yesterday by Gregorio Amunategui, who is an Alessandri representative. Gregorio had come from Santiago and his message to Hobbing from Alessandri was—keep cool, don't rock the boat, we are making progress—.

This is in direct contrast to what Broe recommended.

I will call you later to discuss HSG's reaction to my telex in some detail. He agrees with me that Broe's suggestions are not workable. However, he suggests that we be very discreet in handling Broe.

Allende obviously must be aware of this sort of plotting since his Unidad Popular has penetrated nearly everything in Chile. In one impromptu speech early this week he noted that Chile "was now swarming with C.I.A. agents."

A significant straw in the wind was noted this week while in Chile. The Commander of the Navy, Admiral Fernando Porta, was put on temporary leave of absence. His sudden departure from the scene was attributed unofficially to a meeting of four other admirals with Allende, with the reported consent of Admiral Porta. The meeting allegedly was arranged to pledge the Navy's support to Allende.

It also is significant that in spite of all the gossip and speculation about Viaux, no action has been taken against him. However, the Commander of the Army, General Rene Schneider, still shows no open indication of supporting Viaux.

Meanwhile, Allende and his representative have been ardently romancing the armed forces at various levels and have continued to infiltrate the lower ranks. . . .

While Chile was bubbling with rumors last week, it is completely the opposite this week. The capital is in a bad state of depression, the general public seemingly resigned to the fact that Allende has won and that the next order of business is to determine how to survive and live with a Marxist government. Some anti-Allende spokesmen who show this resignation speak of starting to work toward winning a "second round."

Exhibit 11

ITT WASHINGTON OFFICE
Washington, D.C.

PERSONAL & CONFIDENTIAL

TO: Mr. W. R. Merriam
FROM: J. D. Neal
DATE: September 30, 1970

CONFIDENTIAL

SUBJECT: Chile—A Questionable U.S. Policy

The unfortunately heavy probability that Allende will take office in November is well known to the State Department and Embassy Santiago. Both believe Allende will start early and systematically attack foreign private enterprise. Thus forewarned, we should hope the Nixon Administration will be prepared to move quickly to exert pressure on Allende. However, because of our weak policy in the Hemisphere during the past two years, we cannot count on such immediate and effective action.

I fear the Department of State will convince the White House to again circumvent the Hickenlooper Amendment—as it has done in Peru, Bolivia, and Ecuador, etc. Instead, I look for the silent pressure (?) which will call for a drying-up of aid and instructions to U.S. representatives in the international banks to vote against or abstain from voting on Chilean loans.

For the past several years the State Department has been predicting an upsurge of Marxism in Chile, and foresaw the culmination of the threat in the September, 1970, elections. Knowing this, the U.S. stepped up its AID program in an attempt to help Chile remain democratic. . . .

The foregoing means the U.S. realized the danger of Marxism in Chile; so fought it with grants and loans, but did not have the extra forethought to follow its intuition by taking a more active part during the pre-election period to assure the defeat of Allende. [Emphasis added.]

The State Department and AID admitted in public congressional hearings that, "Chile is a country of major U.S. assistance emphasis because of its important political role in the Hemisphere." They continued the hearing by saying the liberal U.S. loan policy to Chile is justified because they were putting the money in there to fight Marxism. However, now that its program failed to prevent Allende from winning the election, the U.S. says, "This is a Chilean matter, thus, we must not interfere!"

Why should the U.S. try to be so pious and sanctimonious in September and October of 1970 when over the past few years it has been pouring the taxpayers' money into Chile, admittedly to defeat Marxism. Why can't the fight be continued now that the battle is in the homestretch and the enemy is more clearly identifiable?

Exhibit 12

ITT WASHINGTON OFFICE
Washington, D.C.

SYSTEM CONFIDENTIAL

TO: Mr. E. J. Gerrity, Jr.
FROM: W. R. Merriam
DATE: October 7, 1970

CONFIDENTIAL

SUBJECT: Chile

Our man reports nothing new and "picture is not rosy." He says Prewett column exaggerated. Repeated calls to firms such as GM, Ford, and banks in California and New York have drawn no offers of help. All have some sort of excuse. [Emphasis added.] English papers were delivered. His only message is that everyone should keep the pressure on because Allende should not take office with complete support and also for the weakening we might accomplish after he does take office—"there is always a chance something might happen later."

The information we are receiving from Hendrix and Berrellez is up-to-date, factual, and concise as any coming out of Chile. The State Department says it is swamped with rumors and facts; so there is no lack of information there either.

Everyone foresees an Allende victory in Congress unless some last minute miracle takes place. There is no, repeat no, solid news showing even a chance that Allende can be stopped.

The State Department says one factor which has paved the way for Allende is the failure of President Frei to take a strong position against Dr. Allende. They feel he could be stopped if Frei would stand firm for his country and quit trying to play the part of Hamlet, wishing to go down in history as the great democrat. Frei has not rallied the Christian Democrats as is believed possible.

The lack of strong political activity on the part of Chile has hampered outsiders like the U.S. and Argentina in trying to help defeat Allende.

Assistant Secretary of State Meyer leaves tomorrow for a week in Haiti and Santo Domingo (while Santiago burns)! [Emphasis added.]

Exhibit 13

SYSTEM CONFIDENTIAL

TO: Mr. McCone
FROM: W. R. Merriam
DATE: October 9, 1970

CONFIDENTIAL

At Ned Gerrity's suggestion I am attaching a summary of a report which we recently received from our people in Latin America. I think you will find it interesting.

Today I had lunch with our contact at the McLean agency, and I summarize for you the results of our conversation. He is still very, very pessimistic about defeating Allende when the congressional vote takes place on October 24. Approaches continue to be made to select members of the Armed Forces in an attempt to have them lead some sort of uprising—no success to date. . . .

Practically no progress has been made in trying to get American business to cooperate in some way so as to bring on economic chaos. GM and Ford, for example, say that they have too much inventory on hand in Chile to take any chances and that they keep hoping that everything will work out all right. Also, the Bank of America had agreed to close its doors in Santiago but each day keeps postponing the inevitable. According to my source, we must continue to keep the pressure on business.

I was rather surprised to learn that in this man's opinion the Nixon Administration will take a very, very hard line when and if Allende is elected. As soon as expropriations take place, and providing adequate compensation is not forthcoming, he believes that all sources of American monetary help, either through aid or through the lending agencies here in Washington, will be cut off. He assures me that the President has taken at this time (better late than never, I guess) a long, hard look at the situation and is prepared to move after the fact. . . . [Emphasis added.]

Exhibit 14

ITT WASHINGTON OFFICE
Washington, D.C.

SYSTEM CONFIDENTIAL

TO: Mr. W. R. Merriam
FROM: J. D. Neal
DATE: October 15, 1970

CONFIDENTIAL

SUBJECT: Chile—Conversation with Ambassador Korry

This morning, I called on the U.S. Ambassador to Chile, Edward M. Korry, who is in Washington on consultation.

ALLENDE TO PROCEED SLOWLY

The Ambassador believes Allende, upon taking office, will proceed cautiously and slowly. It will not be necessary for him to initiate new legislation because he will already have sufficient authorization to carry out most of his socialistic program.

The Ambassador said that regardless of Allende's many faults and idealistic beliefs, he is known to be a man of his word; so it is quite certain he will carry out his campaign promises. This means nationalization of everything which he thinks should fit into his Marxist scheme.

This action against U.S. private concerns will quickly bring Allende face to face with U.S. policy.

AID STOPPED

Ambassador Korry said he has reduced the amount of U.S. aid "already in the pipe-line" as much as possible. He estimates the amount to be $30,000,000.

Also, there is a much larger amount for which Chile has been given letters of credit, but he didn't say how much.

The Ambassador said he had difficulty in convincing Washington the need to "cut-off" every possible assistance to Chile, but he insisted because he needs this as a bargaining point. This "cut-off" will be denied by State, who will say, as it has in the past, "there has been no shut down of aid to Chile; the program is under review."

MILITARY EQUIPMENT

Ambassador Korry says there is no leverage as regards aid, because Chile will not seek it right away. He feels Allende will quickly need equipment for the military.

I said if we won't furnish that then the Russians will. The Ambassador thinks *not*. Too, he believes it would take too long to convert the Chilean Army from U.S. equipment to Russian.

U.S. HARD LINE

The Ambassador said that if Allende starts to expropriate American businesses, the U.S. will insist on immediate and just compensation in dollars. In the event U.S. mining companies are taken, payment might be arranged in ore.

The Ambassador intimated he plans a hard line with Allende in respect to complying with obligations.

Personally, he feels Allende is going to pay his bills in order to maintain Chile's international prestige.

Ambassador Korry believes the U.S. pressure points with Allende include our source of development fund, market for Chile's products, our world prestige, etc. He seems to think he can insist that Allende restrict himself to internal democratic procedures rather than be the tool of Castro and Russia. . . .

U.S. POLICY RE ALLENDE

The Ambassador said there are several alternatives of action, the main ones being to provoke Allende and cause a rupture in our relations with Chile, thus, lose all without a try.

The second would be to try to live with Allende—not appease him—take a firm line, but attempt to negotiate at every turn.

The second alternative seems to be the one the U.S. will take. The position will have to be taken soon because on the November inauguration of Allende, President Nixon must send a message of congratulation or the world will know of the rebuff.

Ambassador Korry wished to know whether Mr. Geneen would be in New York this weekend at which time he would try to see him. I told

Mr. Korry that Mr. Geneen would be at the Cape or in Maine, but that maybe he could call the Ambassador early next week.

Mr. Korry said if Mr. Geneen had any ideas about U.S. policy toward Allende's government he hoped this would be relayed to the White House immediately. [Emphasis added.] He said other companies with Chilean investments should do the same. He feels any complaints or ideas should be made now rather than after October 24.

Exhibit 15

INTERNATIONAL TELEPHONE AND TELEGRAPH CORP.

SYSTEM CONFIDENTIAL

TO: E. J. Gerrity
FROM: H. Hendrix (dictated by phone from San Juan)
DATE: October 16, 1970

CONFIDENTIAL

SUBJECT: Chile

Unless there is a move by dissident Chilean military elements by this time next midweek, the consensus in Santiago is that Salvador Allende will win the October 24 Congressional run-off easily and be inaugurated as President November 4.

The chance of a military coup is slim but it continues to exist—at least to this date.

A key figure in this posibility is former Brigadier General Roberto Viaux, who last October led an insurrection by members of the First Artillery Regiment in a demand for more pay and improved working conditions. This revolt collapsed quickly. Viaux was summarily dismissed from the Army but overnight his actions made him a hero to a large group of active and retired officers and enlisted personnel.

Clearly, Viaux was gearing up to launch a move last week. Rumors that he would trigger a coup on October 9 or October 10 were rampant in Chile and spilled over into Buenos Aires, Argentina.

It is a fact that word was passed to Viaux from Washington to hold back last week. It was felt that he was not adequately prepared, his timing was off and he should "cool it" for a later, unspecified date. Emissaries pointed out to him that if he moved prematurely and lost, his defeat would be tantamount to a "Bay of Pigs in Chile."

As part of the persuasion to delay, Viaux was given oral assurances he would receive material assistance and support from the U.S. and others for a later maneuver. It must be noted that friends of Viaux subsequently reported Viaux was inclined to be a bit skeptical about only oral assurances. [Emphasis added.]

Meanwhile, Viaux has been conferring with high-ranking and junior officers about taking some action to prevent Allende from becoming President. He has pledges of support from several, but unfortunately not from any key troop commanders, at least to our knowledge.

Whatever resistance starch there was left in many anti-Allende groups was thoroughly dissipated by the Christian Democratic National leadership decision October 5 to support Allende in Congressional balloting. . . .

Allende this week has had a series of meetings with Chilean business leaders, seeking pledges of support. He reportedly made it clear to all visitors that he intended to move as rapidly as possible with his industrial nationalization plans, legally with the aid of a Congress he will be able to control. He has not clearly defined a manner of compensation in his plans to nationalize the basic mining, banking, communications, both national and foreign, enterprises in Chile. . . .

We are also experiencing similar union difficulties. Workers at Chiltelco staged an illegal strike Wednesday morning, October 14, demanding special increases in wages and cost of living bonuses. Their demands represented about 18 million escudos, which translates roughly into $1.5 million. . . . Holmes took the position of ignoring the workers' demands and the company advised both the union and the Frei government that the strike was totally illegal because the union agreement is valid until December 31, 1970.

Workers at ITT COM in Santiago also are pressuring for wage increases and are threatening strike action.

Exhibit 16

PERSONAL AND CONFIDENTIAL

October 20, 1970

CONFIDENTIAL

The withdrawal yesterday in Santiago of Jorge Alessandri from the Congressional run-off election for President of Chile marked the final step in the collapse of political resistance to the election of Salvador Allende.

In a message to his supporters in the right-wing National Party, Alessandri stated he did not wish them to vote for him in the balloting Saturday. The message also carried a personal endorsement of Allende, thus virtually assuring that Alessandri's backers will throw their votes to Allende in a show of national unity.

That Alessandri would take this action was evident last week in Santiago. His top advisers reported that he was very bitter now towards President Frei, feeling that Frei had double-crossed him in the post-election plans to win the Congressional election away from Allende. Frei did just that.

Now there is general resignation that Allende will win easily in Congress, and most likely will be inaugurated November 4.

Except among the Allende supporters, a cloud of depression and worry has settled over Santiago and there is no outward sign of any organized opposition. Once the Christian Democrats swung to Allende at their national convention October 5, hope of stopping Allende and his Marxist-Socialist Unidad Popular evaporated quickly and the gloom took hold firmly.

In this atmosphere, many Chileans have turned to thinking about what they can now do to survive economically and politically under Marxist rule. Thus, future announcements of deals and arrangements with Allende should not be surprising.

In spite of the forementioned, there remains in Chile a faint whisper of hope—or wishful thinking—that a military coup will be staged to prevent Allende from assuming the presidency.

The chance of a coup diminishes with each passing day, but some civilian and military personnel continue to look toward former Brigadier General Roberto Viaux to lead a military action against lame duck President Eduardo Frei before November 4, putting the armed forces in power and thus preventing Allende from taking office.

Viaux has considerable popular following in the lower ranks of the armed forces and some support among officers. But so far he has not won any pledges of support from officers who command troops.

Allende is continuing almost daily meetings with business, industrial and military leaders to explain his programs and seek support. His efforts have paid off. He has made it clear he plans to proceed as soon as possible with nationalization of industries that would allegedly benefit Chile, using legal means and providing compensation—without being specific. He has convinced many military officers that he won't disturb the military structure.

Allende will inherit an economy in critical condition. He also will apparently inherit considerable labor strife and has indicated he will take a hard line with union unrest and demands for increased wages. Thus, organized labor—mostly Communist controlled—is pressuring now for wage and benefit improvements through wildcat strikes. The Anaconda strike and one against the Chile Telephone Company last week are examples.

The rift between Ambassador Ed Korry and his superior at the State Department has reached the point where he deals now directly with the White House and does not always share his input and instructions with State. Korry was in Washington last week for consultations and was supposed to return to Santiago during the past week-end. But he is remaining in the Washington and New York area for a short time. The word among Korry's colleagues is that Charles Meyer and his deputy, John Crimmons, are determined to get Korry out of Chile—and out of the Department, if possible.

In summary, there is little indication now of any remaining resistance to Allende in Chile—apart from the forementioned long-shot military action. There are some Chileans who speak of planning now for a "second round" against Allende, but they also admit that the odds for a second round are rather slim.

Exhibit 17

INTERNATIONAL TELEPHONE AND TELEGRAPH CORP.
INTERNATIONAL HEADQUARTERS

SYSTEM CONFIDENTIAL

TO: Mr. H. S. Geneen
FROM: E. J. Gerrity, Jr.
DATE: October 20, 1970

CONFIDENTIAL

SUBJECT: Chile: the Aftermath

Assuming that Allende will take power on November 4, barring a last-minute coup, the following broad plan of action is recommended both to protect us, as best possible, in Chile and to guard against the inevitable reactions that will occur primarily in Argentina and Brazil. . . .

It is important that we establish the following—on the record as much as possible: What does the State Department estimate will happen to U.S. investment in Chile?

In the event of expropriation, what will the U.S. do? Will it take a hard line or go the "soft route" followed first in Peru and now in Bolivia? Will it press for payment in dollars to the expropriated owners?

Will it invoke the Hickenlooper Amendment, and if it did would it matter? What is at stake? Will AID funds be cut off? (Please see Jack Neal's memo concerning his conversation with Ambassador Korry who, Neal reports, says he has gotten approval to cut off aid if expropriation occurs, and who adds that aid funds in the pipeline will be cut off *where possible*. If the worst occurs I see no reason why aid in any form should be continued.)

What does State estimate the effect of Allende's takeover will be in the rest of Latin America?

We believe that State should be pinned down on the record in a written exchange of views so that, in effect, a formal history is set down. *State has been absolutely wrong on the outcome in Chile, as other Government agencies have, but State has the fundamental responsibility for the U.S. position and it has been wrong consistently. It is our assumption that it will also, based on its record, probably be wrong about the effects of the Allende presidency.* [Emphasis added.]

With a member of the board of directors, we propose that the outlined program above be implemented with: Dr. Kissinger, Mr. Meyer and Mr. Irwin of State, with certain other persons to be determined and, ultimately, with Secretary Rogers and the President. When these visits are carried out, we should demand that U.S. representatives of international banks take a strong stand against any loan to countries expropriating American companies or discriminating against foreign private capital.

As part of the overall action, we should ask our friends in Congress to warn the Administration that continued mistreatment of U.S. private capital will bring about a cutoff of the U.S. taxpayers' funds to international banks.

Allende has already moved to take over communications—the press, radio, TV—in Chile—in emulation of his friend Fidel Castro, of the Chinese Reds, and of the so-called proletarian dictatorships everywhere. Only El Mercurio and Radio Cooperativa Vitalicia hold out against his threats and intimidation, and once he is running the country their fate is sealed.

Freedom is dying in Chile and what it means to Latin America, and to us—to free men everywhere—is not pleasant to contemplate. [Emphasis added.]

We should offer an additional action plan which would involve reduction of American diplomatic representation in such South American capitals as Santiago, Lima, La Paz, Quito, etc. . . .

Because the Chile situation is so interrelated to our overall position in Latin America, and therefore of such importance to our stockholders, I believe that you would want to meet in Washington with the highest officials to personally express our deep concern with developments that have such serious impact.

This program has been discussed with Mr. Aibel, Mr. Brittenham, Mr. Dunleavy, Mr. Guilfoyle and Mr. Merriam, as well as with Mr. Hendrix, Mr. Berrellez, Mr. Perkins and Mr. Wallace, of our Department, and they are aware of the details.

cc: F. J. Dunleavy
     R. E. Bennett
     H. J. Aibel
     R. L. Brittenham
     J. W. Guilfoyle
     W. R. Merriam
     E. R. Wallace

Exhibit 18

INTERNATIONAL TELEPHONE AND TELEGRAPH CORP.
INTERNATIONAL HEADQUARTERS

PERSONAL AND CONFIDENTIAL

TO: E. J. Gerrity
FROM: Hal Hendrix
DATE: October 22, 1970

CONFIDENTIAL

SUBJECT: Chile

Bob Berrellez called this morning from Santiago to report that shortly after 0800 this date an attempt was made on the life of General Rene Schneider, Army commander-in-chief in Chile.

General Schneider was gravely wounded by shots fired by occupants of a car described as a white-grey Falcon. One of the shots reportedly struck him in the neck.

The assassination attempt occurred as the general was leaving his home to go to his office. Three vehicles blocked the path of his car, and machine-gun fire came from one.

An official communique stated that General Schneider's condition was "delicate." He was rushed to a hospital and underwent immediate surgery. President Frei and other government officials are standing by at the hospital.

The assailants escaped and there was no immediate indication who was involved.

In recent days, however, police and army squads have been picking up extreme right-wing terrorists. Thus, the quick assumption in Santiago is that right-wing terrorists are responsible.

Observers speculate that the attempt is (1) revenge against Schneider for his refusal to support plans for a military coup against Frei to block Allende from taking office, or (2) an attempt to arouse violent reaction among the extreme left. The latter is considered unlikely because of the rigid discipline managed by the Communist Party.

Yesterday, authorities arrested a retired police Major, Jose Cabrera, and found a small arsenal in his home. This morning's El Siglo, the Communist party daily in Santiago, said the capture of the Major revealed a plot to kill Allende. The main conspirators, said El Siglo, were the CIA and General Lanusse of Argentina.

Tuesday, a retired army major, Arturo Marshall, was arrested and described as a leader of a right-wing terrorist group.

In mid-morning, General Carlos Prat, chief of staff, was named interim commander in chief.

The army was put on alert and ordered to remain in barracks. All roads leading out of Santiago have been blocked. There were rumors that air line flights were cancelled but Berrellez says that all international carriers are operating. . . .

We will continue to monitor the situation. Whether it will develop into any military action remains to be seen, but at this stage it seems doubtful with General Prat now in command.

Prat supported Schneider in his attitude toward General Roberto Viaux, who had attempted to spark a military coup earlier. Prat does not like Viaux personally. As far as we can determine, Prat will display the same loyalty to Frei as Schneider did in the past.

cc:　E. R. Wallace
　　　K. Perkins
　　　W. R. Merriam, Washington

Exhibit 19

PERSONAL & CONFIDENTIAL

TO: E. F. Gerrity
FROM: Hal Hendrix
DATE: October 22, 1970

CONFIDENTIAL

SUBJECT: Chile

Responding to a telephone call from Allende, B. Holmes met with him yesterday afternoon to discuss the Chiltelco operation.

According to Bob Berrellez, who spoke with Holmes after the meeting, the meeting was very cordial. They wound up speaking on a first name basis.

Holmes told Berrellez that Allende told him "not to worry, be calm." It also developed that apparently Allende is rather ill-informed about Chiltelco and seemed to be unaware of the buy-out program now in effect with CORFO.

As a result of the meeting, Holmes is preparing a paper for Allende on Chiltelco's operations, its relationship to CORFO and the terms of the convenio.

Berrellez noted that from what he has observed, Allende gave Holmes the same kind of soothing massage he has given several other leading business executives in Santiago recently. As Bob put it, he has been through this reassuring kind of romancing before, i.e. Cuba, Dominican Republic, to be specific.

Allende also paid a call yesterday on Alessandri and spent fifty minutes with him. Details of the talks were not disclosed but he hoped to see the Matte brothers later today in hopes of getting a reading on what was said.

cc: E. R. Wallace
K. Perkins

Exhibit 20

ITT WASHINGTON OFFICE
Washington, D.C.

SYSTEM CONFIDENTIAL

TO: Mr. E. J. Gerrity, Jr.
FROM: W. R. Merriam
DATE: October 22, 1970

CONFIDENTIAL

SUBJECT: Chile

I have just met with Dr. Danielion, Tim Stanley, and Jack Neal on the above subject. All of us went over in great detail possible repercussions in Chile if and when it becomes known that we are pushing the State Department along certain lines. I, personally, feel that we don't have much to lose one way or the other, unless, of course, our so-called "pressures" come back to haunt us in other Latin American countries. This I also doubt.

Awaiting Senate floor action is an Inter-American Bank appropriation amounting to $2.9 billion. This appropriation has passed the House, has been reported out of the Senate Foreign Relations Committee, and supposedly will be taken up after the recess.

We are planning, together with some of the other members of IEPA, to approach Senators Scott and Mansfield to see if they will just "forget" to take up the bill. We could prepare statements from them which would get a message to the other Latin American countries that Chile's action is affecting them too, albeit indirectly. . . .

Following is our idea of a white paper to be presented to Assistant Secretary Meyer. Jack and I feel that perhaps it will be more effective if HSG were to talk to Meyer over the telephone rather than deliver a white paper to Meyer's desk. We can do the latter, of course, but the telephone call would be the important thing.

Exhibit 21

INTERNATIONAL TELEPHONE AND TELEGRAPH CORPORATION
Washington Office

SYSTEM CONFIDENTIAL

TO: Dr. Henry A. Kissinger
FROM: William R. Merriam
DATE: October 23, 1970

CONFIDENTIAL

Dear Dr. Kissinger: As a result of recent events in Latin America, foreign private enterprise in that area is facing its most serious exposure.

President Nixon, one year ago, in his speech before the Inter-American Press Association said, "We will not encourage private investment where it is not wanted, or where local political conditions face it with unwarranted risks."

ITT does not wish to go where it is not wanted, but we, too, have President Nixon's "strong belief that properly motivated private enterprise has a vital role to play in social as well as economic development."

Our company knows the peoples of the Americas deserve a better way of life and we believe we have a substantial interest in diminishing their problems. The countries themselves are unable to furnish necessary development funds, the U.S. taxpayers cannot, and U.S. private enterprise can provide only that part which a proper climate affords. Everyone agrees the job will have to be done on a coordinated basis.

ITT has given serious consideration to circumstances now facing Hemisphere development. We are convinced the present moment is a most expedient time to reappraise and strengthen U.S. policy in Latin America.

I attach a paper containing our estimations plus specific reference to the Chilean situation. This is respectfully submitted; I would appreciate your comments.

Sincerely,
William R. Merriam,
Vice President.

Exhibit 22

SYSTEM CONFIDENTIAL

TO: Hal Hendrix, ITT HQ NY
FROM: Robert Berrellez—ITT LA BA—CHILTELCO
DATE: October 25, 1970 (sent by traveler)

CONFIDENTIAL

SUBJECT: Chileans

1. Marxist Salvador Allende has been elected to the Chilean presidency by the congress and the first step toward the total communization of this country has been taken. . . .

3. *Having just recently given Tito a personal presidential blessing, Washington will certainly arouse liberals everywhere if it turns its back on Allende. Such inconsistencies are fodder for the editorial pages.*

4. *However, if Washington just sits there and does nothing to thwart Allende, it will be inviting a sharper turn toward leftist nationalism— which translates into more danger for foreign investments—among other Latin American countries.* [Emphasis added.]

5. Allende does not have the large personal following that President Frei once enjoyed and thus has no real power base from which to move independently as he hopes. He lacks Castro's charisma and in a crunch could not—as Fidel can—bring the crowds out into the street for massive demonstrations of support. At least not without the acquiescence of the Communists and the leftist bloc that put him in power. . . .

Exhibit 23

SYSTEM CONFIDENTIAL

TO: Mr. E. J. Gerrity
FROM: J. W. Guilfoyle
DATE: October 27, 1970

CONFIDENTIAL

I would suggest that we give consideration to having a cable sent to President-elect Allende of Chile from Mr. Geneen. Contents of the cable should not be congratulatory, but along the general lines of "We plan to operate and expand Chiltelco in conformance with the Concession Contract and the Convenio." Reference should also be made to the fact that we will continue to favor Corfo acquiring additional ownership of the shares of Chiltelco in conformance with the Convenio.

While talking with Benny, when I was there two weeks ago, he indicated that it might be possible that Allende would want to see an ITT representative shortly after taking office. I think if we could be on record that we are willing to live by the terms and conditions of the prior Convenio, we might have a basis for some beginning discussions.

What are your thoughts on this? I will discuss it with you on my return.

cc: Messrs. Geneen, Bennett, Dunleavy,
Perry, Aibel

Exhibit 24

SYSTEM CONFIDENTIAL

TO: Mr. H. J. Aibel
FROM: R. R. Dillenbeck
DATE: October 28, 1970

CONFIDENTIAL

SUBJECT: Chile/Memorandum to Geneen and Letter to Kissinger

Thank you for providing me with copies of Mr. Gerrity's memorandum to Mr. Geneen on the subject of Chile and Mr. Merriam's letter to Henry Kissinger with enclosure.

The letter to Kissinger, insofar as I can tell, was not checked with either Legal or Treasury Department representatives who are currently members of the "team" interfacing with the Department of State on the AID/Chiltelco problem. Given the magnitude of our potential problem in Chile and the care with which our relationships with the State Department must be conducted as a result, I find it almost unbelievable that a letter of this nature was delivered to State without any apparent effort to coordinate with the Chile "team."

In my judgment, the letter strikes a note which I believe the State Department will find uncongenial. The forceful approach it argues is contrary to the policy of the "low silhouette" as I understand it which is clearly the current approach of State. Putting aside whether or not the policy is correct, our leverage to effect a change in this policy is minimal. Identifying ourselves as being opposed to well-defined State Department policy at a time when it is imperative that we have the full confidence of our opposite numbers in State and at AID's successor (OPIC) seems to me possibly to jeopardize efforts which will be made to collect on the AID guarantee insurance. The State Department, and OPIC to the extent OPIC is identified with State Department policy, are almost universally opposed to the Hickenlooper Amendment. It is a continuing irritant to them that ITT supports Hickenlooper. Since I believe it highly unlikely that the Hickenlooper Amendment will be formally invoked in the Chilean context, regardless of what happens, we only can hurt ourselves by continually being identified with the Hickenlooper supporters.

I am not primarily concerned with the substance of the material delivered to Kissinger, even though I disagree with the tone of the letter and would take issue with some of the substance as well. What I am concerned with is the lack of corporate coordination which this letter indicates. On October 1, pursuant to top-level corporate instructions, Mr. Goldman, Mr. Meyer of the Treasury Department and I attended a meeting at AID in Washington to review the status of the ITT/AID guarantees in Chile in light of political developments there. Mr. Merriam's office was notified by my secretary of this trip and the date and time and purpose of the meeting were provided. No representative of the Washington office appeared at this meeting. After the meeting, a memorandum was prepared by Mr. Goldman and was sent to you, with copies to Messrs. Gerrity, Hendrix, Merriam and Neal of the Public Relations Department. Even a hasty reading of this memorandum would cause one to realize that ITT must speak with one voice concerning the corporate attitude toward Latin America in general and toward Chile in particular. It is my understanding that it was agreed to by Messrs. Dunleavy et al that there would be coordination on all levels concerning the handling of the Chile situation. Perhaps this message was not conveyed to the Public Relations Department but I believe Mr. Gerrity attended the meeting at which Mr. Geneen was also present where the policy was clearly stated.

In summary, I would be most appreciative if there would be anything that you could do to prevent this kind of "end run" from taking place in the future. I anticipate extremely difficult negotiations in Chile and in Washington concerning ITT's Chilean investments. Failure of the ITT personnel involved to work as a team can only complicate the lives of all of us and, more seriously, possibly jeopardize recovery of the AID insurance.

For your guidance, I have attached a copy of the October 2 memorandum.

Before I had seen the Merriam letter to Kissinger, I had a chance to see Mr. Gerrity's note to Mr. Geneen entitled "Chile: the Aftermath." At my request, Bob Crassweller prepared an analysis of this memorandum and stated his personal views with which I totally associate myself. A copy of Bob's memorandum is attached hereto and I think you will find its balance, judgment and literate nature refreshing when compared to the other effort. Should you think it appropriate, perhaps Mr. Geneen would appreciate having some exposure to an opposite view to that to which he has been exposed already.

I am sure Mr. Gerrity knows that my views differ substantially from his and those of Jack Neal with respect to Latin America and perhaps that is the reason the Legal Department is not given an opportunity to participate in advance of dispatch of material outside of ITT. I think this kind of performance is not up to the best standards of ITT where opposing views are supposedly worked out in-house and then a united front presented. End runs such as this caused by the Public Relations Department are demoralizing and eventually self-defeating to ITT's business goals.

cc: Mr. R. G. Bateson

COMMENTS ON CHILE

The following observations are prompted by the attached memorandum dated October 20, 1970 from E. J. Gerrity, Jr. to Mr. Geneen:

I

Referring first to the broadest question raised by the Gerrity memorandum, I think it is correct to conclude that characteristics and directions of the Allende government are not yet marked out in full detail, although of course the country will swing sharply to the left. The exact nature of the leftist measures that it will take, however, and the speed with which these will be realized, are by no means clear.

A. Certain factors point to a quick movement leftward. The government will have all the usual incentives to produce quick results. The enthusiasm and fanaticism of some of the members of the coalition will naturally create pressure for immediate measures. If the present economic decline continues, and particularly if a mood of panic arises, the Government may be forced into harsh steps at an early moment.

B. Other factors point to the likelihood of a slower leftward movement. Allende has agreed to constitutional guarantees that will have a moderating influence. There are six members of his coalition, and the difficulties of coalition politics often make it necessary to proceed with caution. The government would have little to gain by the adverse internal and foreign reactions that would result from hasty radical action, and Allende may find it easier and more profitable to attain his ends by a gradual process, step by step, without exciting his opposition into a really strong confrontation.

II

The difficulty of appraising internal developments authoritatively at this time makes it likewise impossible to predict with any confidence the impact of the Chilean experience upon the rest of Latin America.

A. There is no reason to believe, however, that a domino effect will be created. Such a reaction has failed to materialize from the Cuban example, in spite of the fact that the Cuban government has maintained a considerably more forthright dedication to Communism and to foreign subversion than is associated with any of Dr. Allende's pronouncements. It is not realistic to say that Chile itself is an exception to this Cuban generalization; Allende is close to Castro on a personal basis, but the long and gradual leftward tendency in Chile appears to have roots that preceded the Cuban experience, and the Chilean self-image would be offended by the suggestion that this major country was dominated and led in its development by a small and remote island.

B. The situations of Chile's neighbors vary considerably from each other, and a uniform reaction is highly improbable. This is fortified by the strength of nationalism everywhere.

1. The most important neighbor is Argentina, which has long been accustomed to asserting its dignity and its stature in opposition to Chile. It is not at all realistic to think that the present state of public opinion, to say nothing of the government, would meekly turn 180 degrees and head to the Communistic left.

2. Peru has its own brand of nationalism and statism, and these are jealously regarded by the government. There is also an 80 year tradition of rivalry with Chile, and bad feelings between the two countries.

3. Bolivia is so volatile that its reaction cannot be generalized. In any event, however, from the point of view of ITT Bolivia is relatively unimportant, and whatever reaction it does show is unlikely to be more stable than previous regimes and reactions have been.

4. The other countries of South America are insulated by distance and by other differences. Brazil is too large to be heavily influenced by Chile. Venezuela and Colombia are far away and nothing that is in prospect in either one of them indicates that they would be vulnerable to the Chilean example.

III

The reaction of the Department of State (D.O.S.) will necessarily depend upon the development of the factors considered in I and II above.

A. As a generalization, however, it is unlikely that D.O.S. will jeopardize hemispheric relations by taking an extremely hostile stance vis a vis Chile, or by making what D.O.S. would consider an overly-strenuous and impolitic intervention on behalf of one or more American companies with confiscated Chilean assets. D.O.S. is likely, in other words, to do whatever can be done in a restrained and realistic manner, as was the case in Peru, but it is unlikely to make an all-out effort in circumstances over which it exerts little control or leverage. The history of the D.O.S. involvement in the oil nationalization programs in Mexico in 1938, in Bolivia in the 1950's and in 1969, and with IPC in Peru, all point in this direction. Aid and other forms of cooperation might well be reduced, but it is not likely that the Hickenlooper Amendment will be invoked, at least publicly and officially. There are at least two reasons for this. First, the Allende government would be likely to make some offer of compensation; this might be inadequate, but it would at least be arguable, and this would undercut application of the Hickenlooper doctrine. Second, in any event D.O.S. will make a determined effort to preserve its flexibility and its options by refusing if at all possible to have recourse to so rigid a sanction.

B. Specifically, with reference to particular recommendations in the Gerrity memorandum:

1. I see no reason to imagine that D.O.S. will allow itself to be "pinned down on the record in a written exchange of views so that, in effect, a formal history is set down." There are innumerable ways of avoiding this, even while maintaining correspondence, and it seems clear enough that D.O.S. will not commit itself in writing to firm policy stances for the sole purpose of satisfying ITT.

2. It is not entirely clear to me why Mr. Gerrity contends, on the one hand, that it is important that ITT establish on the record the estimate of D.O.S. as to what will happen to U.S. investment in Chile; and on the other hand comments a few paragraphs later that D.O.S. has been wrong in Chile so far and is always wrong anyway. In this connection I think it is likely (although I am not certain) that D.O.S. expected a narrow victory by Allesandri [sic], so did ITT, and most other observers. In the event, the Allende margin over Allesandri [sic] was a bit more than 1% and no one purports to be infallible to that degree in any Latin American political situation.

3. In the top paragraph on page two, it seems to me presumptuous to "demand" that the White House require U.S. representatives in international banks to take a "strong stand" against any loan to countries expropriating American companies or discriminating against foreign private capital.

4. I also think that the second paragraph on page two, recommending that ITT request members of Congress to warn the Nixon administration that mistreatment of U.S. private capital will result in terminating U.S. contributions to international lending institutions, is presumputous.

5. The fifth paragraph on page two, suggesting that ITT urge staff reductions in the U.S. diplomatic establishments in Latin America, is naive and unrealistic, and would certainly be resented in Washington.

6. All of the points discussed in paragraphs 3, 4 and 5 above, would, if implemented in the manner indicated, in the Gerrity memorandum, be counter productive rather than helpful. They would be ideally calculated to support leftist assertions about American economic imperialism, and their tendency would be to stimulate a nationalistic backlash against foreign private investment generally.

7. The reappraisal of the ITT position in Latin America referred to in the Gerrity memorandum might be helpful, but this should come after the Chilean situation has been clarified. Although it is impossible to be dogmatic or to read the future, it is likely that a thorough and dispassionate analysis would yield a reasonably optimistic estimate of a program based on increased investment in a broad cross section of industrial and commercial fields, with greater geographical diversification.

Exhibit 25

INTERNATIONAL TELEPHONE AND TELEGRAPH CORP.

SYSTEM CONFIDENTIAL

TO: Mr. W. R. Merriam
FROM: E. J. Gerrity
DATE: October 29, 1970

CONFIDENTIAL

SUBJECT: Chile

On Saturday, Salvador Allende, a Marxist, was elected president of Chile. He did not attain a majority for election when his countrymen balloted last month. He received about 36 per cent of the vote and thus the election was thrown into the Congress. On that basis it is said that a Marxist has for the first time anywhere been freely elected in a democracy.

Three years ago, Allende said:

"The United States is in trouble, everywhere. The wave of the future is Marxist-Leninism."

If that is so, freedom is in danger, everywhere. [Emphasis added.]

Attached is a memorandum describing briefly Allende's background, indicating his thinking. He admires Red China and relies on Fidel Castro for advice. In his hands, Chile's future seems plain.

Exhibit 26

INTERNATIONAL TELEPHONE AND TELEGRAPH CORPORATION
INTERNATIONAL HEADQUARTERS

SYSTEM CONFIDENTIAL

TO: E. J. Gerrity
FROM: Hal Hendrix
DATE: October 30, 1970

CONFIDENTIAL

SUBJECT: Charles Meyer

Per your request for a personal viewpoint sketch of Charles Meyer, following are some of my thoughts:

Meyer came aboard at the Department of State as Assistant Secretary for Inter-American Affairs in March, 1968.

Previously, he was a Sears Roebuck executive in Latin America, with about 14 years residence in Bogota, Colombia, where he performed as an outstanding merchandiser in the Sears Roebuck joint-effort program in Latin America. Sears had been knocked out of business during the 1948 Bogota riots, and, in effect, it was Meyer's mission to restore the company's presence. In that role he performed well. But Meyer's Latin America experience was limited to the north coast of South America and Mexico.

During the last two and one-half years at State, for all his great personal charm, elegance and wit on social occasions, he ranks very high as the weakest Assistant Secretary in recent times—at least during my 22 years of association with the area.

He has only secondary or tertiary relations with the President, for example, who from the beginning has relied on his National Security Council team, Henry Kissinger, and Latin America specialist Viron Vaky for top guidance on the Latin Area. His clout with Secretary Rogers is about as potent.

By the same token, Meyer has suffered—as has his area department within State—because of other pressing administration priorities around the world, and surely in the U.S.

But Meyer clearly has been ineffective in the bureaucratic infighting for attention at State, and, therefore, in the Nixon administration.

He also on numerous occasions has exercised bad judgment in dealing with the press that covers Latin America. His contacts with press are extremely limited as a result.

There has been an enormous lack of imagination prevalent in the Latin Section of State under Meyer's direction, with very few exceptions. With him and his deputy, John Crimmons, the general theme has been don't make any waves; don't rock the boat. Granted, there is the traditional State timidity within the careerist system for this particular attribute of Meyer's administration, but he has failed to encourage either creative or independent thought. This is a complaint heard throughout Latin America in our embassies. He certainly has not fought for his area of his section in the manner of some of his predecessors, notably Tom Mann, Henry Holland, or even Jack Vaughn in his short sit in the slippery Assistant Secretary chair.

In retrospect Meyer may, of course, be the victim of the new Latin area strait jacket called the "low profile of the U.S. in Latin America," which when applied to Chile today could be a salient reason why the United States failed even to head off in 1970 that which it so successfully and energetically aided Chileans to avoid in 1964—the emergence of a Marxist president. Meyer and Crimmons jointly led the effort to make certain that the U.S. this time did nothing with respect to the Chilean election. [Emphasis added.]

Meyer's public statements in Latin America all seem to be flavored with apology, which certainly doesn't reflect U.S. strength.

As stated in the beginning, I consider Meyer one of the weakest yet in the long string of Assistant Secretaries. I also believe it would be better for us if he returned to Sears Roebuck. [Emphasis added.]

cc: E. R. Wallace
      K. Perkins
      E. Dunnett

Exhibit 27

SYSTEM CONFIDENTIAL

TO: H. Hendrix—ITTHQNY
FROM: R. Berrellez—ITTLABA
DATE: November 6, 1970

CONFIDENTIAL

SUBJECT: Chileans

1. Salvador Allende was inaugurated last Nov. 3 as Chile's President (until 1976) without incident. At every public appearance during the two-day inauguration festivities, he was a living, breathing image of political moderation, a perfect vehicle that Moscow will now thoroughly exploit to give their brand of communism a touch of bourgeoise respectability they hope will make it palatable—and even desirable—in other Latin American countries.

2. Evidence that the ploy is working in Chile can be found among Allende's conservative opposition. The very people who were once urging Washington to take firmer action to stop Allende now believe they can co-exist with him. They say that "Washington must do nothing in terms of economic or political reprisal that will force him to turn toward the extreme left."

3. Allende has made a most compelling pitch for moderation and national unity. And it would be altogether believable were it not for a few grim undercover signs that clearly indicate the leftwing extremists (Castroites, Maoists) have already moved in to consolidate power bases from which democracy will be slowly but thoroughly strangled long before Allende's six-year term is up.

4. Most alarming of these signs is the presence in Santiago of Cuban political police personnel, trained in Moscow, and headed by Luis Fernandez Ona, described as one of their best agents. The Cubans and other Iron Curtain "tourists" and delegates to an industrial fair now underway in Santiago, arrived within hours of the September 4 voting which gave Allende a plurality in the voting.

5. A weekly newspaper, PEC, recently published a detailed account of the clandestine movement of the leftwing [extremists] in Chile. The account has been termed "highly accurate" by authoritative sources, persons in a position to know.

6. This version, supplemented by information from other sources, indi-

cates the visitors have taken up residence in homes and apartments in Santiago, suggesting a lengthy stay.

7. Fernandez Ona arrived ostensibly on a romantic mission. He fell in love, a purposely muted public version alleges, with Beatriz Allende, daughter of the President, while she visited in Havana. Beatriz is said to have been the bearer of an alleged special message from Fidel Castro urging Allende to (a) keep copper in the dollar market (b) don't fall into the Soviet clutches, and ad infinitum. Once believable, the message's authenticity becomes more questionable when viewed in the light of what has been going on quietly underfoot.

8. Fernandez Ona's mission is said to be concerned mainly with the shoring up of security for the governing coalition against a military coup or subversion from any other quarter. The Popular Unity front that put Allende in power had organized highly effective security units (commandos) that apparently had infiltrated the police. These are expected to serve as cadres for "committees" in defense of the new regime in the same manner that General Alberto Bayo organized "Committees for the Defense of the Cuban Revolution" in 1959. There was one committee to each block in every key urban community. Thus, when the Bay of Pigs invasion came in April, 1961, the committees were ready to finger—and imprison—anyone suspected of disloyalty.

9. Collaborating with the Cubans are Chilean leftist extremists, the self-styled "revolutionary left" that vigorously opposed—until Castro intervened to quiet them—the "peaceful" quest for power by the Communists and more moderate Socialists. Published statements last week showed the "revolutionary left" is still agitating in schools and universities urging "vigilance committees" to prepare now for any move by the moderates to thwart a total socialization of the country.

10. Numerically the extreme left may be small, but it has been proven in post-war Europe and more recently in Cuba that a militant, disciplined minority can quickly and effectively neutralize and overpower a majority.

11. A grim development that may greatly strengthen Allende's and the Communist position was the assassination of Gen. René Schneider, head of the Armed Forces until he was gunned down in late October (see Oct. 25 report). What initially appeared to be a professional job handled from within the Army turned out to be a poorly organized and bungled kidnap attempt in which at least two ex-military figures are directly involved.

12. Among those arrested in the Schneider killing was General Roberto Viaux, a retired officer who gained national prominence and a measure of lower-rank following last year when he led an abortive pay-hike rebellion against the Frei government. Viaux, a conservative strongly opposed to Allende and around whom coup elements appeared to be rallying after the Sept. 4 election, has a lawyer who has indicated more Army brass may be involved.

13. If it turns out that some top level military chiefs are involved, even indirectly, with Viaux, this will give Allende the moral and political authority to purge the Armed Forces command and move his men into strategic military positions. This would, in effect, neutralize the Armed Forces which so far have displayed nothing but passivity amid the approaching storm.

14. In one of his most revealing press interviews, President Allende told Julio Scherer, a highly respected Mexican journalist (Excelsior of Mexico City) last Nov. 2: (a) He will use the plebiscite (constitutionally correct) wherever necessary to go around Congress if needed reforms were blocked by legislative action. Asked if this would not eventually lead to the disappearance of Congress as an effective legislative body, Allende said emphatically "Never would we make Congress disappear." (b) Describing the flight of investment capital as part of a "climate of terror," imposed on Chile, he said its continuation would force a limitation of individual guarantees under the Constitution. He added: "If reactionary violence comes, we will respond with revolutionary violence." (c) If Chile finds itself isolated and blockaded as did Cuba, "There then is no alternative but armed insurrection. We are disposed to anything."

Our Havana files are not available, but a flashback to the year 1959 brings memories of highly similar remarks by Castro when, like Allende, he was impressing almost everyone within earshot of his moderate political views while his brother Raul and Che Guevara worked quietly behind the scenes for the mousetrap job that followed. For instance, Castro said that elections were not necessary. That the people were the Congress of Cuba, that until the subversives were liquidated and the climate of terror imposed on Cuba from inside and outside was lifted, there would have to be special "precautions" imposed on the citizenry for the defense of the revolution, that counter-revolutionary violence would be met with implacable revolutionary violence.

The Sum-Up:

1. The view by Chilean conservatives, now trying to make deals with Allende, that U.S. economic and political reprisals will force Allende farther to the left is a correct assessment. It ignores a fact, however, that whether or not he likes it, Allende will be forced far to the left eventually regardless of what policy Washington adopts.

2. The view among another sector that U.S. reprisals will force Allende into the leftwing extremist camp and that this will trigger a popular and military reaction against his government has little merit. The military has shown no disposition to act in the clutch. There is little reason to believe their mood has changed. It is even questionable that they have the capacity to handle the kind of massive nationwide reaction the far left can mount: general strikes, urban guerrilla warfare. Time is swiftly eroding the military capacity to move against the Allende coalition, even in defense of the Constitution, if such a moral issue arises.

Exhibit 28

680 PARK AVENUE, NEW YORK, NEW YORK

November 9, 1970

Mr. Jack D. Neal
Director, International Relations
Int'l. Telephone & Telegraph Corporation
1707 L. Street, N.W.
Washington, D.C.

Dear Jack:

The attached letter to President Allende of Chile, signed by Mr. Jose de Cubas, was sent out today.

This letter is being circularized to the CoA Trustees and to the Steering Committee but is not being given wide distribution or released to the press at this time. Further action regarding possible additional distribution is beng held in abeyance pending President Allende's reaction, if any.

We believe that this is a very firm but positive and constructive message and sincerely hope that it will elicit a favorable response for further dialogue between the Chilean Government and Council Members.

Sincerely,
(Signed) Henry R. Geyelin
Executive Vice President

Exhibit 29

COUNCIL OF THE AMERICAS
680 Park Avenue New York, New York

November 5, 1970

His Excellency Dr. Salvador Allende
President of the Republic of Chile
Palacio Presidencial La Moneda
Santiago, Chile

My dear Mr. President: . . .

3. With regard to the past, let me stress that companies operating in Chile with U.S. capital have substantially promoted the human and economic development of the Chilean people and their country. Foreign-capitalized companies have enhanced the personal dignity and self-fulfillment of many thousands of Chileans and their families by providing them with modern skill-training and general education, rapid promotion to positions of high responsibility within these companies, much-increased income and constantly growing opportunities for service to their country. Specifically, U.S.-capitalized companies have opened rich world markets to Chilean exports, and through import-substitution activities they have helped Chile to produce at home much of what it formerly needed to buy from abroad.

4. With regard to the future, and this is what is really important to Chile and to the U.S., I feel that the following statements represent the consensus of thinking in the forward-looking managements of most U.S. companies:

a) Enlightened private enterprise working in close cooperation with an enlightened government is today the best (I am tempted to say the only) method for development. There are many examples around the world today to prove that this cooperative effort of private sector and government will be even more essential in the future.

b) Nationalization of private economic enterprises, with subsequent ownership and management by the state, inevitably exacts a grievous social cost from people and their countries.
Hundreds of thousands of private savers, not only foreign but also Chilean, would be forcibly deprived of their investments in those enterprises slated for nationalization by your platform. There is no evidence that the incoming Chilean government will possess, or can

acquire, the resources to afford these hundreds of thousands of private savers the prompt, adequate and effective compensation for nationalization which is specified under international law.

c) Multinational companies are the most effective element for development today and will be even more so tomorrow, as:

1) The multinational company "goes international" primarily to serve or develop markets. Thus, it will prosper only if the host country prospers. It is committed to the host country's prosperity. It plans for the future.

2) The multinational company is so complex that, to survive, it must be run by an efficient technostructure with a forward-looking philosophy with regard to profits and their distribution. Being basically growth-oriented, it will generally reinvest a large percentage of its earnings.

3) The multinational company has prestige and power in its home country and can be the best ally, where it counts, to "sell" the need for overseas development.

4) The multinational company has the technological, financial and manpower resources and the organization needed for success. It operates by objectives, but it is generally still flexible enough to react with the required speed when considering the all important "time factor of development."

5) The multinational company is outward-looking and export-minded. Though it recognizes the value of intelligent import-substitution programs, it does not consider these as an end in themselves.

6) The multinational company is trying hard to learn to become a good corporate citizen throughout the world. Due to the dynamic competitive society which it supports, it knows that if it fails in this very important task, others are there to take its place. In addition, its fundamental belief in a competitive philosophy results in its accepting pluralistic situations in private/public economies without undue fear of being overwhelmed.

I reiterate, the Council of the Americas is deeply concerned about what may happen to Chilean-U.S. relations. It is concerned that many years of collaboration which, in our view, have been to the overall good of Chile and the U.S., will cease. We are, above all, concerned that—at a time when the private sector in the U.S. has become both a dynamic and innovating force internationally and has acquired the techniques and the will for development—at a time when, due to its responsiveness to what the market wants, it is becoming increasingly involved with the quality of life

—the U.S. private sector may be rejected by Chile in exchange for theories which once were new but which are no longer suitable to the pressing new needs of the year 2000.

The Council of the Americas earnestly desires to maintain the historic Chilean-U.S. cooperation. Council representatives are prepared to meet at any time, in any mutually acceptable place, with representatives of your government to work out ways and means of continuing this cooperation. Indeed, the Council and the forward-looking multinational corporations of which it is composed are eager to work with all who seek to build a peaceful, integrated, world-wide economy, devoted to rapid social development.

Sincerely,
(Signed) JOSE DE CUBAS, President
Council of the Americas

Exhibit 30

THE WHITE HOUSE
Washington, D.C.

TO: Mr. William R. Merriam
FROM: Henry A. Kissinger
DATE: November 9, 1970

CONFIDENTIAL

Dear Mr. Merriam: Thank you very much for your letter of October 23 and the enclosed paper on United States policy toward Latin America. I have read it carefully and I have passed it to those members of my staff who deal with Latin American matters. It is very helpful to have your thoughts and recommendations, and we shall certainly take them into account. I am grateful for your taking the time to give them to me.

With best regards,
HENRY A. KISSINGER

Exhibit 31

LATIN AMERICA, INC.
Buenos Aires, Argentina

PRIVATE AND CONFIDENTIAL

TO: H. Hendrix
FROM: R. Berrellez
DATE: November 13, 1970

CONFIDENTIAL

SUBJECT: Ed Korry

1. There are deep doubts among diplomats and U.S. businessmen in Chile that Ambassador Ed Korry, a Nixon political appointee, will survive under the Salvador Allende administration. Korry alienated Chilean friends antagonized his Chilean critics and embarrassed many Americans with petulance in the final days of the Frei government.
2. Korry estranged himself from the State Department over the Chilean issue and was dealing directly with Nixon on policy and strategy. The source of this information is Korry himself. The Ambassador became a hard liner (economic reprisals, etc., against Chile) after Allende registered a plurality in the Sept. 4 elections while State chose to play it indifferently. Because of this, Korry's diplomatic career certainly seems at an end.
3. Korry also blew his composure with the U.S. news media and became a sort of male Martha Mitchell in off-the-record briefings. . . .
4. From Embassay friends we've learned Korry is fully aware of his position and has put out a few probes into the business community to sample future opportunities. I've not had a chance to verify this personally. . . .
10. Although he was close to Frei, Korry apparently did not get along at all with Foreign Minister Gabriel Valdez. . . .
11. . . . Valdez [has been quoted] as saying:
"With no other Ambassador have I had more problems than with this Mister Korry. We have had problems with Argentina, but never formally with its Ambassadors. I cannot stand or accept this diplomat." He added referring to Korry: "What nature does not endow, diplomacy does not lend." . . .

13. It is certain that Foreign Minister Valdez made his personal views on Korry clear to the diplomatic colony. Diplomats could not escape seeing the press barrage.

14. *For this reason, Korry's usefulness as a diplomat in Latin America has been destroyed. And his usefulness in a business capacity in this same area now becomes, I believe, questionable.* [Emphasis added.]

Exhibit 32

SYSTEM CONFIDENTIAL

TO: Keith Perkins
FROM: Hal Hendrix
DATE: November 18, 1970

CONFIDENTIAL

SUBJECT: Ed Korry

After your inquiry about Ed Korry in Chile, I asked Bob Berrellez to put down his current observations on him since Bob has been spending a lot of time lately in Santiago. His current comments are attached.

Apart from this, I might add my personal view. I did not know Korry until he showed up in Chile and I was working for Scripps-Howard. Since he formerly worked for UPI, which S-H still owns, we had no problem in establishing a good working relationship.

At the outset it was obvious to me that Korry was (and still is) one of the die-hard New Frontier types from the Kennedy administration. He was and is an extremely clever writer and phrase-maker. He also is brash, at times quite arrogant. He is a great name and place-dropper. In many respects he bears a strong resemblance to Peter Jones, which I guess accounted for their former close personal relationship. Like Jones, he has a habit of using people to his advantage until they are of no use to him. He also has a habit, I learned, of saying one thing to one person and a different story to his next visitor. As one good friend, who has worked closely with him, put it to me recently, "Korry is a man that not even the management of the U.S. government or ITT could keep in harness if he didn't like the fit of the harness."

I feel fairly certain from some of his past comments that he is trolling for a position with ITT when he gets bounced by State. If we want two-of-a-kind in the house, that's probably what we would get.

Exhibit 33

PERSONAL AND CONFIDENTIAL

TO: E. J. Gerrity
FROM: Hal Hendrix
DATE: November 20, 1970

CONFIDENTIAL

SUBJECT: Chile-Latin America-HSG

FYI, following the LatAm business plan meeting Wednesday (November 18), Bob Berrellez and I were advised by F. Dunleavy and J. Guilfoyle that Mr. Geneen wished to chat with us about events in Chile and Latin America.

In response to his questions we expressed our views on the Chile situation, how it came to pass and what was happening—all of which you are familiar with. The conversation also swept broadly over other Latin nations, such as Argentina and Brazil.

Before it ended Mr. Geneen also raised some questions about State and Ambassador Korry. We expressed our opinions on both, including our belief that State more than any other government agency is responsible for the sad turn of events in the Latin area in general and Chile in particular. We mentioned that much of the blame in the latter must fall on Charles Meyer and his chief deputy, John Crimmons. He seemed unaware of Crimmons, but indicated we all might be better off without him. I mentioned that we had heard that Korry might be trolling for a position with ITT, since he is a dead duck at State, and after a discussion of him, he made it plain he wouldn't be interested in Korry.

Mr. Geneen also was very complimentary to Berrellez for his recent reporting on Chile. We mentioned that the news from Chile in the coming months likely would be rather grim, in spite of the wishful-thinking optimism prevalent in some circles. He cautioned us not to take personal or physical risks in obtaining our information but not to pull any punches in reporting, grim news notwithstanding.

Mr. Geneen also commented, saying we wouldn't believe it, that he had recently heard from Anaconda and they wanted to know what could be done to help salvage the situation in Chile. He noted it was a fine time for them to be waking up, considering his efforts to rouse them earlier.

Earlier, during the meeting, Mr. Geneen emphasized that contrary to rumors and speculation that ITT might be thinking of pulling back in Latin America because of recent political events in the area, we are to push ahead and look for new opportunities. He agreed with N. Theofel's comments that things have been equally as bad if not worse in Latin America in the last four decades and over-all we are in good shape. Mr. Geneen was especially complimentary to Theofel at the meeting.

cc: E. R. Wallace, K. Perkins

Exhibit 34

CHILE AD HOC COMMITTEE MEMBERS

Mr. Kimball C. Firestone
Firestone Tire and Rubber
  Company
1001 Connecticut Avenue, N. W.
Washington, D. C.
ME8-0300

Mr. Francis D. Flanagan
W. R. Grace and Company
1511 K Street, N. W.
Washington, D. C.
NA8-6424

Mr. William C. Foster
Ralston Purina Company
1730 Rhode Island Avenue, N. W.
Washington, D. C.
223-5303

Mr. Jack Gilbert
Charles Pfizer and Company
1700 Pennsylvania Avenue, N. W.
Washington, D. C. 20006
659-3515

Mr. Robert L. James
Bank of America
730—15th Street, N. W.
Washington, D. C.
NA8-8181

Mr. C. T. Mark
Dow Chemical Company
408 Executive Building
Washington, D. C.
296-1915

Mr. Ralph Mecham
The Anaconda Company
1511 K Street, N. W.
Washington, D. C.
393-5867

Mr. Lyle Mercer
Kennecott Copper Corporation
1775 K Street, N. W.
Washington, D. C. 20036
293-7090

Mr. Jack D. Neal
ITT Corporation
1707 L Street, N. W.
Washington, D. C. 20036
296-6000

Mr. William R. Merriam
ITT Corporation
1707 L Street, N. W.
Washington, D. C. 20036
296-6000

Mr. Bill Wickert
Bethlehem Steel Corporation
1000—16th Street, N. W.
Washington, D. C. 20036
393-4720

Exhibit 35

TO: Hendrix
FROM: Berrellez
DATE: March 24, 1971

cc: Gerrity, Wallace, Perkins, Guilfoyle, Dunleavy, Stimson, Goldman, Dunnett

URGENT
PRIVATE AND CONFIDENTIAL

N.C.D. (NO COPIES DISTRIBUTED)

1. A strong hint that the Chilean government may offer to buy out Chiltelco on a Peru-ITT type formula in the first round of future negotiations has emerged from reliable information reaching us from the Public Service Commission (Servicios Electricos).

2. Based on this information, the belief now is that for future political and financial strategy considerations, the government will concede to ITT the full rate increase requested. Thus, when they do take over—as this is the ultimate plan—the rate increase onus will be on ITT, not on them.

3. The Public Service Commission has asked Chiltelco for figures for the preparation of what they call a "definitive report" on the company's real value to serve as a base for the purchase offer.

4. The requested Chiltelco information will be turned over to Interior Minister Jose Toha and the Public Service Commission Superintendent Jaime Schatz, by Friday, March 27. Toha and Schatz are on the commission named by President Allende to look into the rate matter.

5. The Public Service Commission has exhaustively documented itself on ITT's settlement with the Peru government which they regard as extraordinarily favorable to the national interest and ITT.

6. From all this, we gather that the government will come up with an offer to buy the company. The price offered will be based on the book value less the total remitted abroad for loan interest repayments and profits since 1931. This total, we understand, runs to more than eighty million dollars, which means their offer will be under 100 million, if that.

7. What remains obscure at this stage is just how the government will finance the purchase package. From A.I.D. we have learned their balance of payments position is currently sound, running over 600 million dollars. Smaller recent settlements with foreign companies have been made in dollars.

8. The prospects are that the government will grant the rate increase behind a news media barrage justifying it as a move forced upon the government to prevent Chiltelco's bankruptcy caused by ITT mismanagement which could lead to more unemployment. The emphasis will be on ITT rather than Chiltelco mismanagement.

9. At the same time, the government will announce it will nationalize Chiltelco as a measure in defense of the national interest. This would pacify the hotheads, those with short memories who have probably forgotten the copper mines lesson: the threat followed by quiet, prolonged negotiations.

10. The rate increase concession would not be a politically unpopular move because its effects would be felt largely by the upper middle and upper classes that can afford telephone service and where the bulk of government opposition is concentrated.

11. Just how the Peru formula would be applied remains vague. The government may decide there's an area of investment in which we would be interested, but there's nothing immediately visible. Could OSESAC be enlarged as a factory concept embracing other electronic products with a government-guaranteed annual sales volume? This is a possibility we considered.

12. All this leaves unanswered the question of the hotels. State-controlled news media pressures toward nationalization of the San Cristobal Sheraton have been increasing.

13. Equally strong attacks against Chiltelco's service also have been more frequent with the emphasis as the culprit on ITT rather than Chiltelco. A related recent development was this:

14. Replying to an official request from a Christian Democrat Senator (Fernando Sanhueza), Jaime Schatz sent in a formal (written) reply in which he said he had documentary evidence of company lapses in providing better service. Senator Sanhueza said he had made his official request to Schatz because of continuous complaints of poor service. He did not identify the complainants.

15. As published in the local news media on March 23, the report indicated Sanhueza's request for the Schatz report was made in January. There was no indication when Schatz replied—whether it was before or after the March 10 meeting of ITT executives with Allende.

16. In essence, Schatz reported that his investigation revealed "negligence in the direction of technical aspects. Incomplete training of personnel and failure to maintain an adequate maintenance program." Specific faults mentioned were inferior service during peak load period (11:30A-10:30P) when wrong and busy numbers proliferated. He also said Chiltelco had not invested in or replaced equipment required by Santiago's growth.

17. A political report will follow separately updating the situation.

Regards.

Berrellez

END OF MESSAGE

PERSONAL AND CONFIDENTIAL

Original to Mr Hendrix/YPN
Copies to Mr Gerrity/33rd. Fl.
           Mr Wallace
           Mr Perkins
           Mr Guilfoyle
           Mr Dunleavy
           Mr Stimson
           Mr Goldman
           Mr Dunnett
           Mr Bennett

Exhibit 36

THE ANACONDA COMPANY
1511 K Street, N.W., Washington, D.C. 20005

Director
Government Affairs

February 10, 1971

CONFIDENTIAL

Mr. C. Jay Parkinson
Chairman of the Board
The Anaconda Company
25 Broadway
New York, New York 10004

Dear Jay:

A month ago, I initiated a series of meetings with Washington Corporate Representatives, whose companies have major investments in Chile or other Latin American countries. I suggested to Bill Merriam of ITT that he take the lead, which he did. The plan is to keep the pressure on Kissinger and the White House and to get frequent speeches in the *Congressional Record,* calling attention to the seriousness of the problem in Chile and in Latin America generally.

As part of the plan, I visited with Arnold Nachmanoff, Henry Kissinger's principal aide for Latin American affairs, particularly Chile. This was followed Friday by a similar visit from Jack Neal of ITT. We gave him a list of questions and points to make. Nachmanoff confirms the Juan de Onis *New York Times* article of January 27th, and indicated that this strong U.S. position was communicated to the highest levels of the Chilean government. He was pleased with Senator Javits' talk on OPIC to the American Management Association, and felt that it was particularly appropriate for Javits to speak out, rather than the Executive Branch of the government. He shares the common concern that I have run into everywhere in the Administration—mainly that it is important to avoid open challenges to Allende which would have the effect, in the Administration's view, of strengthening him.

Basically, Nachmanoff describes the U.S. policy now as being quiet but strong, doing nothing to provoke Allende. If Allende should attack the United States, however, then our government would reply in kind.

Since the AID cut-off, Nachmanoff sees very few pressure points where we can gain leverage with Chile. He believes that foreign capital will avoid that country and that Allende will feel the pinch. He believes the best way to get at Chile is through her economy; however, the question was raised—what happens to the companies which are sacrificed while this lesson is being taught to Chile? He didn't have a good response.

The next question was why the Inter-American Development Bank made two multi-million dollar loans to Chilean universities in the last month? Again, it was the old rationalization—namely, we wish to avoid an open challenge, particularly when the projects were already in the pipeline.

The meetings of our group will continue along with our tactics unless you instruct me otherwise.

Sincerely yours,

L. Ralph Mecham
(original signed "Ralph")

LRM/dp

cc:

W. E. Quigley
John G. Hall
Guillermo Carey
W. M. Kirkpatrick
H. L. Edwards
Paul Bilgore
Julian Hayes

Exhibit 37

July 19, 1971

Mr. E. J. Gerrity

J. V. Horner

Situation in Chile

As we mentioned during your visit here last week, we already had started soft sell discussions on Chile with various media interested in Latin America. We are continuing those discussions and preparing to step up the program.

At lunch today, I talked with Carl Migdail, an old friend of ours who is an expert on Latin America for U.S. News & World Report. When I said we wanted to get together with him and Howard Handleman and other members of the staff to point up the problems ITT and other American companies face under the Government of Allende in Chile, specifically the accusations of mismanagement, poor service, etc., Migdail said to me this is precisely what U.S. News & World Report had in mind in its reference this week (July 26 issue) at the bottom of the roundup on "Business Around the World."

I am attaching a copy of that roundup. Specifically call your attention to the latter part of it in which U.S. News & World Report states "President Allende already has accused the U.S. companies of mismanagement, misuse of copper resources, and 'excessive profits.'"

Migdail, who will be eager to talk to us later, said he and his colleagues are well aware that the allegations now being directed at the copper companies will be directed later at Chiltelco. We will keep you advised of developments with Carl and others.

cc: W. R. Merriam
     J. D. Neal
     J. P. Ryan
     B. A. Goodrich
     B. Schmidt

Exhibit 38

J Ryan   PERSONAL   July 20, 1971

R V O'Brien

LATIN AMERICA—"PLANS"

I spoke with Bob Schmidt this morning regarding our Congressional plans relative to Chile. We will prepare draft letters to be sent by appropriate members to key administration personnel inquiring as to what is being done to halt the continuous expropriation in Latin America; why the Hickenlooper Amendment and other protective statutes are not being used, and as to what the U.S.'s Latin American policy is.

Members to be approached for assistance will include:

> Senator John McClellan
> Senator John Sparkman
> Rep Otto Passman
> Rep Thomas Ashley
> Rep Dante Fascell
> Rep Thomas Abernethy

All of the above either chair or serve on committees and subcommittees which are concerned with Latin American and American investment abroad.

cc: R L Schmidt
      B A Goodrich

PERSONAL AND CONFIDENTIAL

Exhibit 39

July 22, 1971

MEMORANDUM TO: Messrs. Mecham and Mercer

FROM: W. R. Merriam (original signed by William R. Merriam)

As you know, ITT doesn't sit still when its future is being jeopardized. All of us are surprised that Kennecott and Anaconda aren't raising more hell publically [sic] about the hosing they are about to get in Chile.

We have started an all-out educational campaign with the press to carry our points forward, and we are beginning to mount a letter-writing campaign from selected members of Congress to various members of the Administration to strengthen their backs on Latin American matters. I, of course, would ask you to hold all of these memos close to the chest, but I don't think that either of you can sit back and wait for something to drop in your lap.

Incidentally, our people in New York are trying to stir up your people in New York.

/vdf

Exhibit 40

July 26, 1971

Mr. W. E. Quigley
Vice Chairman of the Board
The Anaconda Company
25 Broadway
New York, New York 10004

Re: *Chilean situation*

Dear Bill:

For some time Bill Merriam, Vice President of ITT here in Washington, has needled me about our Chilean stance, or at least what he believes it to be. He thinks we are too placid and if we are going to get whipped we might just as well fight. I have told him that based on my personal experience and what I have read about Marxists' takeovers in other countries he is probably right. However, there are some differences in Chile and I am not sufficiently informed on the situation there to know if the general rule applies in Chile. He has finally placed some of his views in writing and I am enclosing a copy of his memorandum to me of July 23rd, together with other material that he sent.

You will note that Lyle Mercer of Kennecott indicates that his company is going to go all out on Chile, whatever that may mean. However, I will continue to take no action until I hear from you.

Sincerely,

L. Ralph Mecham

cc: C. J. Parkinson
    J. B. M. Place   ba: W. M. Kirkpatrick
                        J. L. Hayes

Exhibit 41

TRANSLATION OF SPANISH-LANGUAGE PART OF TELEX 1403/S M

August 20, 1971

The Telephone Company has broken its commitment to provide efficient service. The Ministry of the Interior issued the following statement:

The telephone company of Chile obtained and was given the telephone service concession under an agreement detailing the basic stipulation that it must give the people of the country "modern and efficient" service as stated in the respective contract. By virtue of said concession contract, approved by law in 1930, that company received exceedingly favorable economic conditions from the state, enabling it to obtain stable currency benefits and to have recourse to special benefits or exemptions. But all this was based on the understanding that the company had to comply with the obligation to provide the country with very efficient service. The government, since it assumed control, has been concerned how best to see to it that the telephone company fulfill its legal obligations. Thus at the beginning of the year, one of the fiscal delegates asked the executive board to have the responsible parties at the company explain the reasons for the poor attention given to subscribers and for the unacceptable procedures it employs against them and made it known for the record in formal protest that the subscribers and the public in general are receiving deplorable service.

END OF PART ONE OF TWO PARTS

PART TWO OF TWO PARTS

Immediately, the technical departments of the superintendent of electrical power, gas and telecommunication services submitted reports proving that the services of the telephone company do not meet the minimum requirements under the international technical standards that are the applicable criterion in this case. Moreover, it does not take much effort to demonstrate to the country, which is suffering the consequences of such bad service, that the company is not providing the efficient quality service that it had promised. What is manifest indeed is that the concessionaire has violated the most important obligation to which it agreed under the contract, and it should be noted, moreover, that the government is cognizant, as the result of a denunciatory report by one of the fiscal delegates, of gravely irregular acts on the part of the Chilean Telephone Company, that are tantamount to open violation of the contract by subterfuges tending to directly elude its obligations. Specifically, it concerns the fact that the Telephone Company of Chile has separated its former directories department, delivering over all functions hitherto performed by this department and in particular the contracting for ads in the telephone directories, to a fictitious corporation called "Guías Y Publicidad de Chile" organized and designated by a foreign subsidiary of its real master. With this action the Company is attempting to prevent the State of Chile which has authority under law to intervene in and supervise the Company's activities, from controlling operations and very substantial profits collected through the fictitious company. The government, conscious of its duty to ensure efficient service for the country, has for some time tried to reach an agreement with the company on the latter's acquisition. It has not been possible to achieve such an agreement.

Under these circumstances, the company has submitted a request to have the rates currently in effect raised 53.4% for every line of service it renders. By means of this exorbitant raise it claims, on the basis of calculations that the government rejects, to be able to achieve a net profit of 10% on its investments, although it has not completed the ones it says it did. The application was rejected by the fiscal delegates on the board and the company has insisted that it will go through all the proceedings to enable it to get this excessive rate hike.

The government will take all necessary measures to prevent a company that has violated its most basic commitments, that is responsible for irregularities that will be fully demonstrated at the appropriate time, and that provides a service that amounts to truly a national scandal, from making a mockery of the obligations it has contracted with the state and with all its citizens.

MINISTRY OF THE INTERIOR

SANTIAGO, AUGUST 19, 1971

UNQUOTE

Fernando Eguiguren is preparing a short reply which will be discussed with Ernesto Barros and Eulogio Perez Cotapos.

HOLMES

Original to   Mr Goldman
Copies to   Mr Guilfoyle
             Mr Stimson

Exhibit 42

EDITORIAL FROM *EL MERCURIO*, SEPTEMBER 24, 1971

Quote   SYSTEM CONFIDENTIAL

The government had two courses to take to nationalize the telephones. One was to send Congress a draft law allowing the executive to expropriate the private interests invested in that activity. The other was to adjust contractually the terms through which private investors would cede their property to the government.

Apparently the executive took the first course and the conversations with the representative of ITT did not lead to an agreement.

The government's alternative was evident. It should have sent Congress the respective draft in order to comply with the constitutional norms that guarantee in Chile the right of property.

Following the accustomed illegal procedure it again ignored Congress and, through administrative measures, went after the defacto seizure of the property of the Chile Telephone Company.

This is an act of force that adds another shadow to the political experiment initiated by President Allende under the reiterated promise to act within the constitutional norm existing when the current president was elected. The interest aroused by the Chilean case was due to the announcements that it signified a democratic way toward socialism. It isn't strange, therefore, that each expropriation carried out behind the back of Congress gives the so-called "Chilean Model" a similarity to the "International Model" put in practice so many times by the Communists throughout the world and thus weakening the support of democratic opinion toward the conduct of our government.

It will be absurd if at this moment we would deny the many public complaints against the telephone service in reality, there are few countries that don't have a congestion of telephone traffic and other inconveniences caused by the rapid growth of telephone service consumption and financial and technical problems created in satisfying them. Be it as it may, Chilean telephones have been insufficient and, despite the expansions of the last five years, many sectors of the territory have complained about the lack of service.

The formula chosen by the authorities is the nationalization of the company. This is equivalent to supposing that the insufficiences are due to the excessive profits that the foreign headquarters, the ITT, takes from its Chilean branch, which translates into the lack of investment and faults in the maintenance of equipment and installations.

Even accepting the objections with respect to the disinterest of the Chile Telephone Company and supposing, furthermore, that the remedy for all the public problems amid its increasing service requirements were state controlled, the path of expropriation without law continues to be worthy of reproach and highly prejudicial to the prestige and effectiveness of the Chilean judicial system.

If the government has good reasons for proceeding to nationalize, everything should have counselled that they be submitted to parliament, where surely they would have found a welcome just as the copper nationalization found obstacles. From that, the measure of administrative intervention results an unexplainable procedure, even from the political point of view, unless the real objective of the government is to forget what was discussed recently with the Democratic Christian Directorate and ignore the idea of framing within the law the abundant expropriatory procedures initiated outside the lawmaker. In this last eventuality the country should clearly know then that the democratic and legal "model" has failed and that the defacto courses are those that have priority in creating the areas of state control.

In any case, it is deplorable that a new expropriation is undertaken without law to seize a service whose improvement in the hands of the state no one could assure.

End Translations.

Unquote	Original to Mr. Gerrity
Regards	Copies to Mr. Geneen (3 copies)
Gerrity	Mr. Dunleavy
	Mr. Bennett
	Mr. Hamilton
(End page three of three pages)	Mr. Perkins
	Mr. Guilfoyle
	Mr. Stimson
SYSTEM CONFIDENTIAL	Mr. Goldman
	Mr. Bogie
	Mr. Connery
	Mr. Hendrix

Exhibit 43

INTERNATIONAL TELEPHONE AND TELEGRAPH CORPORATION
1707 L Street, N.W.
Washington, D.C. 20036

William R. Merriam
Vice President
Director, Washington Relations

October 1, 1971

The Honorable
Peter G. Peterson
Assistant to the President
for International Economic Affairs
Old Executive Office Building
Washington, D.C. 20500

Dear Pete:

When Mr. Geneen lunched with you a few weeks ago, he stated he feared ITT's seventy per cent owned Chilean Telephone Company (Chiltelco) would soon be expropriated. This has now happened! The take-over was on September 29, 1971.

As Mr. Geneen said, we anticipated this action and were attempting to delay or prevent it. However, during the past month, the Chilean government moved rapidly with its campaign of harassment which went far beyond our anticipation. The following demoralizing incidents leading to expropriation took place during September:

Bank Accounts Frozen

In early September, Allende froze Chiltelco's bank funds, thus depriving ITT of existing operating cash and blocking the daily flow of customer payments to our accounts at the banks.

Records Confiscated

A few days later, the Chilean Revenue Service entered Chiltelco's Santiago headquarters, confiscated records, and announced an immediate investigation of company accounts.

ITT Officials Jailed

Last Saturday, September 25, a sizeable group of special police surrounded the home of Senor Benjamin Holmes, the manager of Chiltelco. Aged 71, Mr. Holmes is a distinguished, highly respected and well-known native-born Chilean citizen. The police startled and arrested Holmes in his bedroom, then placed him in prison after a lengthy interrogation.

Senor Gonzalo Von Wersch, also a native-born Chilean who manages another of our companies—Guias y Publicidad—which publishes yellow page directories—also was arrested and jailed.

Dr. Fernando Eguiguren, our distinguished Chilean attorney, was taken into custody; as was Senor Leon Berstein, the manager of our telecommunication factory.

After considerable legal intervention, we were able to get three of the Chileans released on bail, but the government felt it must keep one of them under detention. Senor Von Wersch remains in jail.

The charge against the foregoing gentlemen is some trumped-up accusation termed "fraud against the government."

Management and Legal Counsel Compromised

The forementioned terror tactics against our company officials is a well-known Communist ploy but one not customarily experienced in Latin America. Chilean actions badly damaged our interest and our chances of restitution. Not only have ITT officials been intimidated and the safety of their families jeopardized, but also our top management team and legal counsel have been placed in an untenable position. In any future negotiations or dealings with the Marxist-extremist government, our Chilean officials naturally will be cautious, thus, their usefulness will be limited.

Security of American Citizens Jeopardized

After these Chilean events, and because of a recent action against our visiting U.S. officials in another Latin American country, ITT will be hesitant about sending into Chile any officials from its New York headquarters whether they be American citizens or other nationalities.

It is inconceivable that the lack of protection to U.S. private enterprise in foreign lands has reached the stage where not only its properties are confiscated without just compensation, but also foreign citizens working for American firms are unjustly intimidated and jailed as propaganda hostages by a supposedly friendly nation with which the United States has diplomatic relations.

When events degenerate to a level where U.S. corporations must hesitate before sending American officials into a supposedly friendly country for legitimate business reasons then the situation calls for corrective measures. We believe recent action in Chile demonstrates this low stage has been reached.

U.S. Aid Continues

While all of this action by the Marxist government against U.S. firms is taking place, money derived from the U.S. taxpayers is still flowing into Chile in the form of aid.

In a meeting with Assistant Secretary of State Charles A. Meyer and his staff only a few days ago—September 28—we were informed that up to $1 million (U.S. dollars) are going into Chile *each month* from funds in the "Aid pipeline!" We believe this U.S. taxpayer money to the Marxist government should be terminated.

Also, we were told that funds in several "Inter-American Development Bank pipelines," not previously utilized, have been reallocated into a so-called earthquake emergency fund and made available to Chile. Considering the heavy U.S. contribution to the IADB, and the lack of a real emergency, such action should not have been permitted and, if possible, should now be rescinded.

Action Suggested

Besides curtailing the above-mentioned sources of aid to Chile, we believe the U.S. government should take every action which will bring President Allende's regime to the realization that his Marxist methods are incompatible with international practices, and inform him that he is to be held responsible for action against U.S. private enterprise.

It is noted that Chile's annual exports to the U.S. are valued at $154 million (U.S. dollars). As many U.S. markets as possible should be closed to Chile. Likewise, any U.S. exports of special importance to Allende should be delayed or stopped.

The U.S. should consult with other governments which are being effected [*sic*] by Chile's Marxism. This would include countries to which Chile owes money. Allende's treasury reserve is depleting rapidly and he has already suggested a moratorium on servicing Chile's foreign debt.

There are numerous justifiable leverages which the U.S. government could use to counteract or retaliate in this instance. We believe these leverages should be utilized to the fullest.

Sincerely,

(original signed by W. R. Merriam)

APPENDIX C

U.S. FINANCIAL AID TO CHILE AND LATIN AMERICA

During the years 1961–68, a congressional report noted that U.S. official sources had channeled over $8 billion to Latin America. More than $1 billion of this total went to Chile in an effort to offset the country's rising Marxist tendencies. The State Department and AID stated in congressional hearings that "Chile is a country of major U.S. assistance emphasis because of its important political role in the Hemisphere." [1]

Assistance to Chile was in the form of direct aid, soft loans, military assistance, and earthquake and disaster relief, totaling approximately $1.5 billion between 1961 and 1971. [2] (This figure does not include private investment in Chile, or the country's exports to the United States, valued at about $154 million annually.) Figures for the period 1961–69 (later figures not given) are as follows, in millions of U.S. dollars:

1961	$ 132.8
1962	169.5
1963	83.7
1964	127.4
1965	130.9
1966	107.7
1967	284.6
1968	99.8
	$1,136.4

Figures for 1969 and 1970 were estimated to be over $100 million. [3] In addition, in 1971 the "Aid pipeline" was channeling up to $1 million per month into Chile, and the Inter-American Development Bank had made funds available to Chile from its earthquake emergency fund (Appendix B, Exhibit 43).

[1] *Congressional Record,* April 11, 1972. —
[2] *Ibid.*
[3] *Ibid.*

Coca-Cola and the Middle East Crisis

[It is] very disturbing indeed and very mischievous—when private groups or businesses or individuals take it on themselves, by act or omission, to alter or dictate or defeat official policies of the United States Government. This amateur policy making—or policy breaking—can be accomplished by almost any group or organization endowed with the conviction that it knows more about some aspect of foreign policy than anybody else and with the will to intimidate officials or other organizations that are not very hard to intimidate. It has been done by business interests seeking a competitive advantage, by organized labor, and by those sterling patriots whose self-designed task it is to keep the rest of us in line, loyal and true to the red, white, and blue . . .

—Senator J. William Fulbright

In late 1964 the management of the Coca-Cola Company was faced with a crucial policy decision concerning its overseas business—whether to grant a bottling franchise in Israel to its then distributor, the Tempo Bottling Company of Israel, thereby antagonizing its Arab customers who were, in effect, at war with Israel.[1]

[1] Irving Spiegal, "Coca-Cola Refuses Israelis a Franchise," *The New York Times,* April 8, 1966, p. 1.

In 1951, three years after the modern State of Israel was founded (May 14, 1948), the Arab nations set up an economic boycott against certain companies doing business with the Israelis.[2] In most instances the Arabs had not objected to ordinary trade with Israel but had enforced the ban when capital goods or military equipment was involved.[3]

Had Coca-Cola accepted Tempo's application for the bottling franchise, the Israeli company would have built its own bottling plant and purchased syrup but not the finished product from Coca-Cola.

In January 1965 the company decided that the potential demand for Coca-Cola in Israel did not justify a bottling plant at that time and therefore refused the franchise. Several important considerations were responsible for the company's decision.

The principal reason was profits: The potential Israeli market for Coke —some 2.5 million Israelis—was dwarfed by the 104.7 million Arab population in the Arab League countries.[4] The Arabs had been among Coke's heaviest consumers from the time the soft drink had been introduced in the Middle East during World War II. Even tiny Kuwait had a per capita consumption of 175 bottles a year—nearly double the average United States rate. The hot desert climate and the Arab taboo against alcoholic spirits combined to make Coke a widely consumed beverage in the Middle East.[5]

In contrast, early governments of Israel, to minimize their exchange problems, had yielded to local citrus fruit lobbyists and had abrogated Abraham Feinberg's contract to bottle Coke in 1949. Coca-Cola knew that American companies such as Zenith Radio Corporation and Ford Motor Company had been barred from doing business in Arab countries because they sold their products in Israel. Therefore, it seemed that Coca-Cola might be able to operate either in the Arab countries or in Israel, but not in both.[6] If business firms have an obligation to their customers as well as to their stockholders, then Coca-Cola certainly owed such an obligation to the Arabs who had long been devoted to its products.

Moreover, in view of the competitive conditions, the danger of losing the lucrative Arab market appeared very real. The Arab countries could shut down the twenty-nine franchised Coca-Cola bottling plants because they could easily substitute Pepsi-Cola for Coca-Cola. Psychologists have tested panels of regular cola drinkers and have concluded that people can-

[2] *MSU Business Topics,* Spring 1968, p. 74.

[3] "Business in Mideast Walks on Shifting Sands," *Business Week,* July 2, 1966, pp. 26, 28.

[4] Luman H. Long, ed., *The World Almanac and Book of Facts, 1967,* New York, Newspaper Enterprise Association, 1966, p. 630.

[5] "Bottled Up," *Newsweek,* April 18, 1966, p. 78. See also Thomas Buckley, "Coca-Cola Grants Israeli Franchise," *The New York Times,* April 16, 1966, p. 1.

[6] *Business Week,* July 2, 1966, pp. 26, 28.

not differentiate between colas by taste alone.[7] Pepsi competed with Coke
in the Arab market and would most probably capitalize on Coke's fall
from Arab-leader favor.

A second consideration in refusing the franchise to Tempo was the
company's dissatisfaction with its Israeli distributor. In 1963 Coke filed
suit in a Tel Aviv court against Tempo for infringing upon the Coca-Cola
trademark. Coca-Cola was also unhappy with Tempo because it bottled
other soft drinks. By custom, Coca-Cola franchises are granted in per-
petuity as long as the bottlers uphold rigid quantity standards specified by
the company. Although many Coca-Cola bottlers also manufacture and sell
other soft drinks, the company's tradition of granting franchises of indefinite duration made it necessary for them to choose only those companies
with whom they could get along.[8] Obviously, Tempo's past record did not
meet this criterion.

REPERCUSSIONS OF COCA-COLA'S REFUSAL TO GRANT
FRANCHISE TO TEMPO BOTTLING COMPANY OF ISRAEL

Tempo was not satisfied with Coca-Cola's contention of insufficient
market in Israel. They averred that Coca-Cola's management had set
arbitrary and unusually high quotas for Tempo, which were impossible to
meet. They charged that the main reason for the refusal of the franchise
was to support the Arab boycott and asked the Anti-Defamation League
of the B'nai B'rith to undertake an investigation.[9] If Coca-Cola was indeed
supporting the boycott, it would be violating United States government
foreign policy.[10]

In April 1966, after a fifteen-month investigation, the Anti-Defamation
League released a report stating that Israel was one of the few countries in
the free world without a Coca-Cola bottling plant. The reason for this, the
report alleged, was that the Coca-Cola Export Corporation was cooperating with the Arab League boycott. The report cited the three major pre-
requisites Coca-Cola had for granting a bottling plant franchise: a $1
million minimum investment, a "viable market," and "practically exclusive
manufacture of Coke." Tempo, which had $2.2 million in sales in 1965,
had supposedly met the first two requirements and had agreed to the
third.[11] The Anti-Defamation League stated that the Israeli market was

---

[7] James A. Myers and William H. Reynolds, *Consumer Behavior and Marketing
Management* (Boston: Houghton-Mifflin Company, 1967), Chap. 2.

[8] E. J. Kahn, Jr., "Profiles," *The New Yorker,* February 14, 1959, pp. 37–40ff.

[9] "Israel: Capping the Crisis," *Time,* April 22, 1966, p. 75.

[10] Spiegal, "Coca-Cola Refuses Israelis a Franchise," p. 1.

[11] *Newsweek,* April 18, 1966.

potentially more profitable than that of the Arab franchise. Therefore, "The deducible facts seem strongly to indicate that, while submitting to the Arab boycott, Coca-Cola has assiduously attempted to camouflage its submission as a pure nonpolitical, economic decision." [12]

The aftermath of the report was sheer confusion. James A. Farley (former United States postmaster general), chairman of the Coca-Cola Export Corporation, vigorously denied the charge of honoring "any boycott." He said that detailed surveys of economic and market conditions evidenced a low success potential in the Israeli market but indicated that "all decisions of this kind are constantly under assessment and reassessment." Farley also said that the Tempo Company "had been found guilty in a Tel Aviv court of infringing the Coca-Cola trademark and bottle design in the marketing of its own product, Tempo Cola." [13] Denying that the company had yielded to the threat of an Arab boycott, Robert L. Gunnels, Coca-Cola export vice-president, said that an Israeli bottling plant would not be "mutually profitable" to Tempo and Coca-Cola and added that a similar decision had been made regarding bottling franchises in Jordan and Syria.

Some of the information advanced by Coca-Cola was unknown to the Anti-Defamation League. Arnold Foster, who prepared the report, said that the league was unaware of Coca-Cola's granting Abraham Feinberg's earlier application for a franchise and also of Tempo's infringement on the Coke trademark. He said that these facts had not been mentioned when the league contacted Coca-Cola in regard to the franchise denial to Tempo. [14]

The managing director of Tempo, in turn, objected to Coca-Cola's statements, saying that Tempo had not been found guilty by the court as the case had been settled out of court and that the shape of the Tempo Cola bottle was not at issue. According to *The New York Times,* court records bore out the Tempo statement. [15]

Coca-Cola's basic position was that if it was to operate profitably at home and abroad it must cater to everybody. A year before the Anti-Defamation League report, Coca-Cola President J. Paul Austin had received a human relations award from the American Jewish Association. The company had a record of being a goodwill ambassador for the United States. In 1949, as a result of left-wing agitation, an anti-Coke bill had become law in France. This aroused anti-France feelings in the United States, leading to several proposals of boycotts of French products. How-

[12] Spiegal, "Coca-Cola Refuses Israelis a Franchise," p. 1.
[13] Buckley, "Coca-Cola Grants Israeli Franchise," p. 1.
[14] "Coca-Cola Unit Denies Charge It Is Supporting Arab Boycott of Israel," *The Wall Street Journal,* April 13, 1966, p. 11.
[15] Buckley, "Coca-Cola Grants Israeli Franchise," p. 1.

ever, the company refused to exploit the anti-France feelings; and James Farley succeeded, through persuasion and diplomatic negotiations, in getting France to repeal the law.[16] The company had also begun operations in Bulgaria in response to the United States government's policy of "building bridges to the East." [17]

Coca-Cola, of course, was aware that Congress had gone on record opposing foreign-initiated boycotts in the Williams-Javits law of 1965 [18] and pointed out that its decision was solely based on economic grounds and that it was not violating the statute or the intent of Congress.

The Anti-Defamation League had, since its founding, become a powerful force in the use of reason and moral suasion to eradicate prejudice against Jews. Despite Coca-Cola's arguments and the league's admission of ignorance of some of the facts, the company stood to lose the patronage of some 5.6 million Jewish people in America—since a rumor had spread that Coca-Cola was anti-Jewish. (It should be noted, however, that the 104.7 million Arab population at that time dwarfed the 13.3 million worldwide Jewish population; so, from the standpoint of income, the Arabs appeared to be more desirable friends than the Israelis.) [19]

Mount Sinai Hospital in New York stopped taking delivery of Coca-Cola for its cafeteria. A New York theater chain and Coney Island's Nathan's Famous Hot Dog Emporium threatened to follow suit, and the New York City Human Rights Commission called for an investigation of Coca-Cola. Within a week of the league's charges, and despite Coca-Cola's denial of them, the company again issued a bottling franchise for Israel to Abraham Feinberg, now a New York banker, president of the Israel Development Corporation, and a promoter of Bonds for Israel. The Anti-Defamation League said that Coca-Cola's decision "will show other American corporations the sham that the Arab boycott really is." [20]

Actually, Feinberg had contacted Coca-Cola about his "renewed interest" a week before the league's charges were made public. Feinberg commented that he would not have accepted any franchise "if I believed Coca-Cola bows to Arab boycott threats." [21]

Now it remained to be seen what the Arabs would do. Israeli officials predictably reported that the boycott's influence had declined in recent years, since the Arab governments had not invariably backed up their threats. The Israeli Consulate General stated there were more than two hundred American companies doing business with both Israel and the

[16] Kahn, Jr., "Profiles," pp. 37–40ff.
[17] "Thaw That Refreshes," *Time*, December 3, 1965, p. 98.
[18] Spiegal, "Coca-Cola Refuses Israelis a Franchise," p. 1.
[19] Long, *World Almanac*, pp. 332, 594–670.
[20] *Time*, April 22, 1966, p. 75.
[21] Buckley, "Coca-Cola Grants Israeli Franchise," p. 1.

Arab League nations. *Business Week* reported that although the rich nations—Saudi Arabia, Kuwait, Libya—were the strictest enforcers of the boycott, Egypt often "winks at boycotts" (Nasser was a heavy Coke drinker), and Tunisia, Algeria, and Morocco "ignore the boycott more than they observe it." [22] Despite these reassurances, however, the possibility of large sales losses was real.

The reprisals from the Arab countries were not long in coming. In July 1966 the Central Office for the Boycott of Israel of the Arab League asked the company about its plans for setting up bottling plants in Israel and warned Coca-Cola that it faced a ban on its product and that the bottling plants would be closed within three months if the Israeli plant was approved. In November the thirteen-country Arab League Boycott Conference met in Kuwait.[23] The Boycott Bureau told the conference it had received unsatisfactory replies from Coca-Cola.

The conference then passed a resolution to stop the production and sale of Coca-Cola within Arab League countries. Enforcement of the ban, however, was left to the discretion of the individual countries.[24] The Boycott Bureau established a nine-month time limit to allow Arab bottling plants to use up Coke concentrates in stock.

The company made some belated efforts to placate Arab opinion. One month before the Arab League meeting, the company ran an advertisement in a Cairo newspaper showing the important economic and social role played by Coca-Cola in the Arab countries. However, a month was apparently not enough time for the advertisement to have any effect. In December 1966 Baghdad Radio announced that Iraq had begun its ban on Coca-Cola. The company said that it had received no official notification from Iraq but that in the three months since the ban had been announced by the Arab League the boycott "has not manifested itself in production sales." [25]

In September 1967, nine months after Arab League representatives had met to approve the boycott, the Boycott Bureau announced that the ban was effective. Despite the ban and the Arabs' increased hatred of Israel after the six-day war, Coke was not deterred and a Coca-Cola bottling plant opened for business in Tel Aviv in February 1968.

[22] *Business Week,* July 2, 1966, pp. 22, 26.
[23] Composed of the United Arab Republic, Iraq, Jordan, Lebanon, Saudi Arabia, Syria, Morocco, Yemen, Algeria, Kuwait, Libya, Sudan, and Tunisia.
[24] Thomas F. Brady, "Arabs Vote to Bar Ford, Coca-Cola," *The New York Times,* November 21, 1966, p. 1. See also *Business Week,* November 26, 1966.
[25] "Iraq Plans to Boycott Three U.S. Companies," *The Wall Street Journal,* December 20, 1966, p. 11.

C.

INDIRECT/DIRECT USE OF THE PRESIDENT'S EXECUTIVE AUTHORITY

The Steel Price Controversy

Kennedy-Johnson and the
Discretionary Use of Presidential Power

Sometime ago I asked each American to consider what he would do for his country, and I asked steel companies. In the last twenty-four hours we had their answer.

My father always told me that all businessmen were sons of bitches, but I never believed it until now.

—President John F. Kennedy

The steel controversy was the result of a power struggle in which—either by accident or design—U.S. Steel openly challenged the office of the Presidency, and the President chose to meet that challenge with the full powers of the office of the Presidency—but . . . he paid a tremendous price for his "victory."

—Roy Hoopes
in *The Steel Crisis*

We have traveled quite some distance in the area of presidential "persuasion" and business "cooperation" since the classic confrontation between President Kennedy and Roger Blough of U.S. Steel. There have been "voluntary" restraints on foreign investments, which were not so voluntary to begin with, but eventually became compulsory restraints during President Johnson's term. In the Nixon administration various "game plans" and a series of "phases" of varying degrees of voluntariness emerged to direct the nation's economy. It is surprising to realize the extent to which businessmen have reconciled themselves to the inevitability of such persuasion. The dissent, if there is any, is so muted as to be ineffective.

Two basic questions raised by the steel price controversy still remain unanswered: How appropriate is the discretionary use of presidential power through the prestige of the office and what is the sociopolitical environment that makes it possible? What are its consequences on the economy and society? More recently, we have become aware of even more serious side effects that need careful study and analysis, among them those caused by the Watergate scandal and ITT's alleged use of political pressure and campaign contributions to gain a favorable settlement of its antitrust case and its interference in Chilean internal political affairs.

The primary focus of this study is the social and political environment in the United States as it affects vital industrial enterprises—the concepts of free market, competitive economy, and freedom of private enterprise notwithstanding—and the obligation of the government to protect the public interest as it sees it. What happens when the delicate balance between government and business spheres of activity is upset by changes in economic circumstances or by the outlook, beliefs, and actions of men who control these institutions? The ensuing struggle and the outcome are never confined to the immediate issues but have a lasting effect on all social institutions. The steel price controversy provides us with a classic example. Brewing since the Eisenhower days, it exploded with tremendous impact on the national horizon when, despite President Kennedy's urging, the U.S. Steel Corporation defied him and announced an across-the-board price increase on April 10, 1962. As one observer pointed out, the issues surrounding the price of steel were not of economics, but of power.[1] The complicated and controversial economics of steel pricing cannot be treated exhaustively here. Treatment of economic issues is limited to providing an understanding of some of the motivations of the parties involved in the controversy and the use or misuse of statistics to support various viewpoints.[2]

[1] Roy Hoopes, *The Steel Crisis* (New York: The John Day Company, Inc., 1963), p. 243.
[2] Some sources concerned with the economics of steel prices are Charles L. Schultze, "Study Paper No. 1, Recent Inflation in the United States," for the Joint Economic Committee's "Study of Employment, Growth, and Price Levels," United States Congress, September 1959; "Employment, Growth, and Price Levels: Report of the Joint Economic Committee," Congress of the United States, January 26, 1960; "Administered Prices: A Compendium on Public Policy," Subcommittee on Antitrust and Monopoly of the Committee on the Judiciary, U.S. Senate, 88th Cong., 1st sess., March 11, 1963; G. J. McManus, "Has Steel Turned Profit Corner?" *Iron Age*, November 7, 1968, pp. 57–58; Robert R. Miller, "Price Stability, Market

The steel industry has been involved for years in crises and confrontations with both its unions and the U.S. government. President Truman even "nationalized" it temporarily (but the Supreme Court ruled the action unconstitutional). Indirect attempts to keep down steel prices, called "jawboning," have been tried successively by Presidents Eisenhower, Kennedy, and Johnson. Nixon, although an active participant in Eisenhower's attempts to keep steel prices stable, opposed this policy in his election campaigns and by mid-1970 had refrained from interfering in price increases by steel and other industries in the face of unabating inflation, rising unemployment, and the nosediving stock market.

BACKGROUND: THE EISENHOWER LEGACY

In June 1959 the United Steelworkers Union called for a strike against the steel industry, and in the same month the Eisenhower administration, acting through Vice-President Richard M. Nixon and Secretary of Labor James P. Mitchell, began participating in the negotiations between industry and union. To both parties in the negotiations, who had been preparing for the talks for nine months, the government intervention came as a surprise. The government, calling for an agreement that would not necessitate a price increase in steel, said any wage increases should be justified on the basis of increased worker productivity alone. The contract not only did not prevent a price increase but the increase was rather long lasting. The contract, to extend until mid-1962, called for periodic wage increases—the final one being in October 1961.

By July 1961 both industry and union were planning ahead for the 1962 talks. According to *Business Week,* "the industry is uncomfortably aware that its every move will be under the close scrutiny of the Administration." In fact, these feelings began when John F. Kennedy was elected to the presidency, the previous November, for "both his position as a senator and his labor policies as a presidential candidate left no doubts about a quick end of any hands-off policy in disputes." The steel industry, always opposed to third-party intrusion in management-union relations, considered it potentially as dangerous to a continuing competitive free market society as compulsory arbitration. The steel industry became even more uneasy in July 1961 when Kennedy's advisory committee on labor-management relations began a study of "free and responsible collective bargaining and industrial peace." [3]

Control, and Imports in the Steel Industry," *Journal of Marketing,* April 1968, pp. 16–20; Gertrude Shirk, "The 5.94-Year Cycle in Steel Production," *Cycles,* May 1968, pp. 54–60; Richard S. Thorn, "The Trouble with Steel," *Challenge,* July–August 1967, pp. 8–13.

[3] "Steel Has Eye on Washington," *Business Week,* July 22, 1961, pp. 102–3.

STEEL PRICES AND THE LIBERAL DEMOCRATS

Inflation was a key concern of the 1961 Congress. The Democratic majority, determined to control it, was sure of sympathetic understanding in the New Frontier activism of the Kennedy administration. Therefore, when the steel industry publications speculated about a price increase of four to five dollars per ton to compensate for the union pay raise, there was a flurry of debate and activity in the Senate. The debate was significant because some saw it as an attempt by the liberal Democratic congressional majority to prevent a price hike by threatening the industry with government regulation.[4]

On August 22, 1961, Senator Frank E. Moss (D-Utah) contended that between 1947 and 1958, 40 percent of the rise in the wholesale price index stemmed from steel prices being pushed up faster and further than the average of all other commodity prices. He felt that steel's importance in the United States price structure could scarcely be overestimated as it was not only a truly basic commodity, upon which most of our industrial capability depended, but its price had an enormous psychological effect on the price-setting process in other industries and was traditionally a bellwether of the economy. Through pyramiding, a $6 per ton rise in the price of steel in 1958 raised the cost of a tractor using only half a ton of steel as much as $97!

Senator Albert Gore (D-Tenn.), by far the most vociferous Senate opponent of steel's pricing policies, charged that the steel industry administered prices—prices set without regard to economic laws of supply and demand. He cited a study by the Joint Economic Committee of the Congress [5] which "proved beyond reasonable doubt that administered prices played the key role in the inflation of recent years." According to Gore, the industry had "established something of a ritual when the time for administered price increase is upon them." Months before any increase, steel executives used their trade publications "as a medium of communications in their mock sparring" to see which company was to be the price leader and "how far it is safe to push up the price." All this was done, not by "collusive understanding," but almost by habit. "It almost reminds one of the mating season dances of the Gooney birds," said Gore.

Gore charged that there was a plan afoot for the steel companies, acting as always in concert, to raise the price of steel by an appreciable amount some time in the fall of 1961. He further contended that "market forces will not bring about, nor will they justify, this increase," since the industry

---

[4] For documentation of senators' statements, see the *Congressional Record* for the 87th Cong., 1st sess., 1961, August 22, pp. 16679–88, 16694–708, 16710–14; August 29, pp. 17324–25; September 7, pp. 18519–64.

[5] John F. Kennedy, while still a senator, was a member of this committee in 1959.

was earning a "good rate of return on low levels of production." The senator concluded that public welfare demands prevented a price rise and "the real question is how to prevent such a rise within the framework of our free enterprise system." This prevention would have to be the government's job and Gore indicated several ways it could act:

1. The president of the United States should use his great legal and moral powers in which he would be backed by the majority of the Congress. Should the steel industry show any recalcitrance, he should not hesitate to pursue many options open to him including "bringing to bear the vast weight of public opinion."
2. The Federal Trade Commission could move to police the steel industry according to the mandate laid down for it by Congress.
3. The Department of Justice, Antitrust Division, could investigate the steel industry in light of administered prices.

Gore made one of the more controversial statements of the debate when he said that large steel companies should possibly be divided into smaller units to restore true competition and free enterprise to the steel industry. And, if all else failed, steel prices could be brought under utility-type regulations. Few would favor this, but it might be necessary. The public and the government must not be victimized by either big business or big labor, or both.

Senators Gale W. McGee (D-Wyo.) and Paul H. Douglas (D-Ill.) also warned the steel industry against price increases, citing their adverse effect on the United States balance of payments, and suggested that higher revenues would accrue if prices were reduced instead of increased.

Senator Estes Kefauver (D-Tenn.), chairman of the Subcommittee on Antitrust and Monopoly which investigated the steel industry after the 1959 strike, also felt that the steel price rise was unjustified. He noted that between 1947 and 1959, according to the Bureau of Labor Statistics, average hourly earnings in the steel industry rose 113 percent while man-hour productivity increased only 43 percent. Thus the unit labor cost grew, but by only 70 percent, while steel prices jumped 109.7 percent.

Kefauver added that there was no basis for the industry's frequent claim that an increase in employment costs was accompanied by increases in nonemployment costs, since the industry had failed to show any such nonemployment cost increases. Moreover, the price of one steelmaking material, purchased scrap, had declined sharply since 1956. Kefauver noted that steel industry defenders often erroneously attributed uniform price increases in the industry to uniform increases in wage costs (all steel companies dealt with the same union):

. . . the fallacy in this argument is that while it may explain the uniformity of the increases, it does not explain the identity of price levels after the increases. Even if the wage increases were the same for each company, the costs bases to which they were applied were not, and are not, uniform.

Kefauver contended that a price hike in the face of unused capacity was "a violation of the consent order entered into in 1951 by the steel industry under Section 5 of the Federal Trade Commission Act," under which the industry was "ordered to cease and desist from entering into any 'planned common course of action, understanding or agreement' to adopt, establish, fix, or maintain prices." [6]

Kefauver began his argument by noting that when one steel company lowered its prices, competing companies also lowered theirs. However, illogically, the same rationale was used for price increases: prices were *raised,* to meet competition! Why, Kefauver asked, did firms with equal or greater efficiency invariably feel it necessary to go along with U.S. Steel's increases? And why, in view of the relationship between operating rate, as a percentage of capacity, and return on investment, did no major steel producer adopt a *smaller* price increase than the leader's?

By simply not participating in a general price advance, any major steel producer would in a very short time secure a sufficient volume of orders to significantly raise its operating rate and thus its profit rate. Yet in the recession year of 1958, when all of the leading firms were operating below 60 percent of capacity, none availed themselves of this opportunity.

A final economic point presented by Senators Albert Gore and Hubert H. Humphrey (D-Minn.) was the impact any steel price increase might have on the industry's talks with the United Steelworkers Union. They contended that "by refraining from raising prices of steel in October, the steel companies would improve their bargaining position when wage negotiations are again undertaken in 1962. . . . If steel prices rise in October it would be naive of the steel companies to believe that the advance in profit margins which results will last much longer than the end of the next series of labor-management negotiations in mid-1962."

[6] In 1948 the Federal Trade Commission issued a complaint against virtually all members of the steel industry, charging that there had been a conspiracy to fix prices in violation of Section 5 of the Federal Trade Commission Act. It was a major antitrust case. There were 1,237 exhibits and 5,458 pages of testimony. Finally, on June 15, 1951, the steel companies voluntarily entered into a consent decree which they themselves had proposed to the commission.

THE REPUBLICAN REPLY

The widespread and generally negative press reaction to the Democratic attack on the steel industry was variously used by the Republican senators to support their arguments. The press comments were divided into three main areas: The attack on the steel industry was also an attack on the free enterprise system, the attack was well planned, and the tactics used were those of intimidation and fear and were unworthy of the representatives of the people in a democratic society. The following comments were perhaps typical of those expressed by the news media in general.

A *New York Times* editorial attacked Gore's "threats" to break up the steel industry:

> The private enterprise system operates on the assumption that prices should be set in the marketplace, and reflect the force of competition among buyers and sellers. The Senate floor is not the marketplace. . . . Competition is probably a much more real force in the American economy than Senator Gore believes. . . .
>
> In the case of steel, for example, there is not only the elementary competition of different producers and sellers, but also the competition to steel from other metals and plastics, and the significant competition given domestic steel by imports of foreign steel.[7]

Senator Gore replied that steel price increases involved the public interest—they activated the price/wage spiral—and unless big industry and big labor used self-restraint, government would have to intervene to safeguard the public interest.[8]

The August 31 issue of *Iron Age,* a steel industry trade publication, said of the Democrats who led the attack on steel that the timing of "this well-planned attack" had a definite purpose. It added up like this:

> Congress will be adjourned soon for the fall recess; therefore, scare the steel companies out of increasing prices during the time Congress is unable to act.
>
> Although this type of moral suasion is not direct control, it can have the same effect. The importance of the group attack can not be over-emphasized. This group represents the Senate majority, the Administration, and the forces of trustbusting, small business, the

---

[7] "Price Fixing in Congress," *The New York Times,* August 24, 1961.

[8] "Gore Defends Steel Debate—Senator Opposes Price Increase as Spur to Inflation," Letters to the Editor section, *The New York Times,* August 27, 1961.

consumer, and labor. Like a single voice, they agreed the nation's steel companies could not justify price increases this fall.[9]

On September 7, 1961, the Republican minority in the Senate responded to the Democratic attacks on a possible steel price increase. Their rebuttal questioned the Democrats' use of intimidation tactics and the accuracy and appropriateness of their statistics and logic.

On the first point Senator Everett Dirksen (R-Ill.) said:

> This appears, so far as I know, to be the first attempt at psychological price control by using threats, and by using persuasion, as weapons and as appeals to a kind of fear instinct. . . . One has no business trying, through the powers of government and through threats, to tell the producers what the price shall be unless they have had an opportunity to present their case, because that is an ex parte action, if I have ever seen one.

Republican senators criticized the Democrats' economic reasoning. Senator Barry Goldwater gave the most complete and detailed answer to the attacks on the steel industry by counterattacking the Democrats' strategy, their analysis of inflation's causes, their contention that competition did not exist in the industry, their statistics, and their analysis of the balance-of-payments problem.

Strategy. Of the Democrats' strategy, Goldwater said that by attacking the industry before it had made any price increases the Democrats were "laying the groundwork for controls," and they should "explain why they have not [also] taken vigorous anti-inflation action on unnecessary government spending, or have not exerted equal pressure on current wage demands which, in the past, have proved to be the most contributory factor behind 'cost-push' inflation."

Causes of Inflation. Inflation, said Goldwater, must be attributed to three broad influences "far beyond the confines of a single company or industry" such as steel: government deficit spending; cost-push inflation; and "better business conditions," or "the reemployment of production resources which have been idle for the past year and a half."

When government blamed the wrong sources for inflation, it put the steel industry "in an economic-political dilemma." Economics prevented raising prices during bad market periods (although costs continued to

[9] R. W. Crosby, "Senators Launch Attack against 'Phantom' Steel Price Hikes," *Iron Age,* August 31, 1961, pp. 55–57.

rise), but in good periods the government tried to prevent a price-cost adjustment.

COMPETITION IN THE STEEL INDUSTRY

Goldwater contended that there *was* competition in the steel industry, that many large steel buyers frequently divided their orders, playing one steel company against another, and cited specific voluntary price cuts.

The Senators are really saying that free enterprise—the competitive marketplace—is not the proper place to set prices. They are also saying that American business is not public-interest minded, but is avaricious to the point where it must be broken into little pieces or completely regulated by a political body.

This, by any other name is socialism.

Statistics. Goldwater attacked the Democratic senators' use of statistics. The base years for their statistics, the senator said, were designed to favor their argument and were "nontypical."

As an example of what changing the base year would do for statistics, Senator Wallace F. Bennett (R-Utah) later noted that if 1940 were used as a base year, employment costs from 1940 to 1960 increased 322 percent and output per man-hour increased 40 percent. "This represents an inflationary gap of 282 percentage points. Prices were bound to increase under such pressures. And this they did, to the extent of 174 percent."

Iron Age criticized using 1947 as a base year as a "setup to prove one point alone—what the White House wanted to prove." During the Depression steel prices were "among the lowest in the century" due to a "bloodletting spate of price cutting" from 1932 to 1939. The industry was thus caught with its prices so low during the wartime price freeze that it "was in danger of financial chaos." The fast pace of wartime production resulted in an industry "hard up for money to expand its capacity, to repair its plants and equipment." [10] Steel began to raise its prices after the war, not to gouge the consumer but rather, in the words of *Business Week*, to "recover profitability and generate heavy retained earnings to help finance massive plant rehabilitation and expansion." Thus began a price spiral lasting until 1955. In 1958, however, U.S. Steel, feeling that it "might be pricing its product too high," refused to lead in any price increase after the labor settlement and "forced its competitors to take the

[10] Tom Campbell, "Steel Men Hot under the Collar at President's Price Attack," *Iron Age,* September 14, 1961, pp. 143–44.

initiative. . . . Thus began the price stability of the past 37 months." [11]
In addition, Goldwater said the Bureau of Labor Statistics' indexes were misleading as they were made up of one size and quality for each of the common forms of steel products and "tend to overstate the actual prices prevailing on the market." They did not reflect changes in freight absorption, in product quality, or in extras added by a steel company. In fact, if all factors were included, an excellent case could be made that steel prices had actually dropped in the face of rising costs.

Balance of Payments. Goldwater accused the Democratic senators of implying that the country's balance-of-payments problems were due solely to the excess of steel imports over exports when in fact the trend was paralleled by almost all of American industry. The American steel industry could not compete because employment costs had risen faster than the productivity level, but to compete and produce, industry needed the best of equipment, and that came only from private investment. Therefore, the profit incentive must be kept alive if the United States steel industry was to be competitive.

Finally Goldwater argued that "if the steel companies charged too much, they must have made too much money. Yet, every investment yardstick shows just the opposite." Securities and Exchange Commission figures demonstrated that steel was less profitable than many other industries, and in spite of all the power its antagonists ascribed to it, it had not been able to increase its profitability to the level of other industries.

> If it has that kind of power—and ended up with that kind of result—it is the most public spirited private enterprise in the history of this country. Certainly no amount of public control and regulation could do as well.

THE PRESIDENT ACTS

On September 6, 1961, the day before the Republican rebuttal in the Senate, President Kennedy sent telegrams to the chief executive officers of the twelve [12] largest steel companies, saying: "I am taking this means of

---

[11] "Steel Price Increase Hopes Are Dashed," *Business Week,* September 16, 1961, p. 25.
[12] Armco Steel Corporation, Bethlehem Steel Corporation, Colorado Fuel & Iron Corporation, Inland Steel Company, Jones & Laughlin Steel Corporation, Kaiser Steel Corporation, McLouth Steel Corporation, National Steel Corporation, Republic Steel Corporation, United States Steel Corporation, Wheeling Steel Corporation, and Youngstown Sheet & Tube Company.

communicating to you, and to the chief executive offices of 11 other steel companies, my concern for stability of steel prices. . . ."

Using 1947 as the base period he contended that between 1947 and 1958 steel prices rose by 120 percent—during the same period industrial prices as a whole rose by 39 percent, and employment costs in the steel industry rose by 85 percent—providing much of the inflationary impetus in the American economy and adversely affecting steel exports and United States balance of payments. He went on to say that although since 1958 the general price level and steel prices had stabilized, this was accomplished at the cost of persistent unemployment and underutilized productive capacity including that of the steel industry whose utilization rate during the preceding three years had averaged 65 percent. In consequence,

many persons have come to the conclusion that the United States can achieve price stability only by maintaining a substantial margin of unemployment and excess capacity and by accepting a slow rate of economic growth. This is a counsel of despair which we cannot accept.

For the last three years, we have not had to face the test of price behavior in a high-employment economy. This is the test which now lies ahead.

The amount of the increase in employment cost per man-hour [on October 1] will be difficult to measure in advance with precision. But it appears almost certain to be outweighed by the advance in productivity resulting from a combination of two factors—the steady long-term growth of output per man-hour, and the increasing rate of operations foreseen for the steel industry in the months ahead.

The Council of Economic Advisors has supplied me with estimates of steel industry profits after October 1, . . . and the steel industry, in short, can look forward to good profits without an increase in prices.

The owners of the iron and steel companies have fared well in recent years.

A steel price increase in the months ahead could shatter the price stability which the country has now enjoyed for some time. In a letter to me on the impact of steel prices on defense costs, Secretary of Defense McNamara states: "A steel price increase of the order of $4 to $5 a ton, once its effects fanned out through the economy, would probably raise the military procurement costs by $500 million per year or more. . . ."

In emphasizing the vital importance of steel prices to the strength of our economy, I do not wish to minimize the urgency of preventing inflationary movements in steel wages. I recognize, too, that the steel industry, by absorbing increases in employment costs since 1958, has demonstrated a will to halt the price-wage spiral in steel. If the industry were now to forego a price increase, it would enter collective bargaining negotiations next spring with a record of three and one-half years of price stability. The moral position of the steel industry next spring—and its claim to the support of public opinion—will be strengthened by the exercise of price restraint now.

I have written you at length because I believe that price stability in steel is essential if we are to maintain the economic vitality necessary to face confidently the trials and crises of our perilous world. Our economy has flourished in freedom; let us now demonstrate again that the responsible exercise of economic freedom serves the national welfare.

I am sure that the owners and managers of our nation's major steel companies share my conviction that the clear call of national interest must be heeded.

Sincerely,

John F. Kennedy

RESPONSE TO THE PRESIDENT'S LETTER

According to *Iron Age*,[13] Kennedy's letter stunned the industry. The steel executives thought that by refraining from a price rise for three years, despite employment cost boosts, they were already acting in the national interest and being competitive with foreign steel and domestic substitute materials.

Business Week said the response to the letter was "immediate anger and long-term alarm."[14] The steel industry scorned Kennedy's reasoning, resented his motivation, and the list of United States presidents it did not trust now read: Harry Truman, Dwight Eisenhower, John Kennedy. Compounding the resentment was the widespread belief that Kennedy would not act against any excessive wage demands by the United Steelworkers. Where only selective price boosts were the most any "realist" could have expected from the industry, now even that was extremely unlikely. Where would the industry with such a rapidly advancing technology get the $1 billion a year needed to replace obsolete plants and implement new efficiencies?

The recipients of the president's letter—who were generally critical of the steel industry's being singled out while other causes of inflation were ignored—were largely noncommittal in regard to steel prices. The most publicized reply came from Roger Blough, chairman of U.S. Steel:

I am certain, Mr. President, that your concern regarding inflation is shared by every thinking American who has experienced its serious

---

13 Campbell, "Steel Men Hot under the Collar," pp. 143–44.
14 *Business Week*, September 16, 1961, p. 25.

effects during the past 20 years. . . . First, let me assure you that if you seek the causes of inflation in the United States, present or future, you will not find them in the levels of steel prices or steel profits.

Blough then used 1940 as a base year and noted that although steel prices had risen 174 percent since that time, employment costs had risen 322 percent. Wage-earner costs had increased and "far exceeded any productivity gains that could be achieved," despite new investment. Blough continued:

So far as profits are concerned, your advisers have chosen to measure them in terms of the return on reported net worth; and again I am afraid that this does more to confuse than to clarify the issue in the light of the eroding effects of inflation on investments in steel-making facilities over the past 20 years. If we compare the 50-cent profit dollars of today to the 100-cent dollars that were invested in our business 20 years ago, the resulting profit ratio can hardly be said to have any validity. . . .

The most useful measurement of the profit trend in a single industry over an inflationary period, is, of course, profit as a percentage of sales. On this basis . . . profits in the steel industry have only once in the past 20 years equaled the 8% level at which they stood in 1940, and have averaged only 6½% in the past five years. . . . [Moreover] averages can be dangerously misleading. Some companies will earn more than the average, while some may be suffering losses which they cannot sustain indefinitely. So it was in 1960 that among the 30 largest steel companies the profit rate as a percentage of sales ranged from a plus 9.3% to a loss of 5.2%

Whatever figures your advisers may elect to use, however, the simple fact is that the profit left in any company, after it pays all costs, is all that there is out of which to make up for the serious inadequacy in depreciation to repay borrowings, to pay dividends and to provide for added equipment. If the profit is not good enough to do these things, they cannot and will not be done; and that would not be in the national interest.

So reviewing the whole picture, I cannot quite see how steel profits could be responsible for inflation—especially when their portion of the sales dollar over the last 20 years has never exceeded 8 cents and is lower than that today.

As for the admittedly hazardous task which your economic advisers have undertaken in forecasting steel industry profits at varying rates of operation . . . it might reasonably appear to some—as frankly, it does to me—that they seem to be assuming the role of informal price-setters for steel—psychological or otherwise. But if for steel, what then for automobiles, or rubber, or machinery or electric products, or food, or paper, or chemicals—or a thousand other products? Do we thus head into unworkable, stifling peacetime controls of prices? Do we do this when the causes of inflation—in a highly competitive economy with ample industrial capacity such as ours—are clearly associated with the fiscal, monetary, labor and other policies of Government?

Blough noted that steel prices were at a level "slightly lower" than two years previously and that competitive factors such as foreign steel and domestic substitute materials provided effective competition for steel. He argued that no company, industry, or for that matter, country could disregard the inexorable pressure of the market if it wanted to maintain its position in a competitive world. Furthermore, he contended that as far as inflation was concerned the price of steel was a symptom and not the major cause of the problem.

THE ADMINISTRATION AND THE STEEL TALKS [15]

That steel prices were not raised in October was attributed to economic forces and not to the president's letter. Kennedy's letter was not the final involvement of the government in the industry's affairs, however, for —although the United Steelworkers' contract was to expire on July 1, 1962—in November 1961 Labor Secretary Arthur Goldberg pointed out that the administration was willing to use its good offices to achieve an early settlement not only to prevent steel users from stockpiling but also to achieve a modest contract and thus prevent another wage-price spiral.

In January several union and industry officials met at the White House to discuss with the president the importance of an early settlement. Goldberg later contacted both union and industry and they began negotiating in early February—the first time since World War II that the two parties had met so early in the year. By discussing the new contract at this time, the union was setting aside its strongest weapon—the threat of a strike at the last minute if its demands were not met. The union also limited its demands to a seventeen-cents-per-hour job security package, forgoing a wage increase. The four industry representatives to the talks said that while the demands "cannot be considered moderate in any sense," they were more moderate than previously and were appropriate considering the problems the country faced.

[15] Documentation for this section appears in Hoopes, *The Steel Crisis,* especially pp. 45–52, which is a complete, almost moment-by-moment account of the administration's activities in regard to steel from Fall 1961 to Fall 1962. A shorter book of the same nature is Grant McConnell's *Steel and the Presidency, 1962* (New York: W. W. Norton & Company, Inc., 1963).

Apparently, after pressuring the industry, the administration was now pressuring the union (even on national television). Goldberg said that large-scale labor-management conflicts were intolerable because of the Soviet threat and the competition from the European Common Market. (George Meany, head of the AFL-CIO, was reported to have exploded with anger at Goldberg's statements and said that he was "infringing on the rights of a free people and a free society.")

During the talks, in an interview in *U.S. News and World Report,* Blough said that steel employment costs had risen 12 percent in three years:

> And you're asking me how long can that continue to increase and how long it can be borne without some kind of remedy. I would give you the answer that it's not reasonable to think of it as continuing. In other words, even now there should be a remedy. If any additional cost occurs, the necessity for the remedy becomes even greater.

Renewed negotiations fell flat on March 2, industry saying the benefit package cost was too high. Secretary Goldberg then talked to Roger Blough, who said that the union proposal was inflationary but agreed to resume talks if the union would lower its proposals. Upon Goldberg's intervention, David J. McDonald, president of the United Steelworkers Union, agreed to lower the demands.

Toward the end of March, agreement was reached for a contract which would add ten to eleven cents an hour in a job security package. The contract, signed on April 6, was to be effective at least until April 1963. President Kennedy said the settlement was "obviously noninflationary and should provide a solid base for continued price stability."

Even the business community praised the contract. Roy Hoopes said:

> Of course, the steel industry had given no commitment that it would hold the price line, but many people, including most businessmen, assumed that labor's restraint would be followed by no increase in the steel prices for at least six months to a year. Obviously the White House assumed this, and the settlement was considered not only a major victory for the Administration, but a long stride toward a historic transformation in labor-management relations.

THE SHATTERED MASTERPIECE [16]

With the strike threat averted most executives were optimistic about the near future. On April 9, 1962, *The Wall Street Journal* reported that most

---

[16] All statements in the ensuing discussion not otherwise specifically documented can be found in Hoopes, *The Steel Crisis* (page reference shown).

producers of steel doubted there would be a general rise in steel prices in 1962 (14). However, on Friday, April 6, U.S. Steel's operations policy committee—the company's top ten executives—unanimously decided to raise base steel prices about 3.5 percent. On the following Tuesday the Executive Committee of the Board of Directors approved the decision. The Public Relations Department prepared a press release announcing the "catch-up" price as "adjustment."

The reason given for the price increase was the profit squeeze facing the company. The company had spent $1.2 billion for modernization and replacement of plant and equipment since 1958 of which the two sources of money for this investment—depreciation and reinvested profit—contributed only two-thirds. The rest of the money had to be borrowed and "must be repaid out of profits that have not yet been earned and will not be earned for some years to come." The release concluded that the new resources that would be generated by the price increase would improve the company's products and would be "vital not alone to the company and its employees, but to our international balance of payments, the value of our dollar, and to the strength and security of the nation as well" (293).

When the board meeting broke up at 3:00 P.M., Roger Blough phoned for an appointment with Kennedy and after flying to Washington was admitted to see the president at 5:45 P.M. on his as yet unannounced business (220). With a minimum of amenities, Blough handed Kennedy the company press release which was at that moment being sent to newspapers in Pittsburgh and New York, explaining that it was a matter of courtesy to inform the president personally. Kennedy is reported to have said, "I think you have made a terrible mistake." Forthwith he summoned Labor Secretary Arthur Goldberg who raced to the White House and angrily lectured Blough on the effect of the company's decision on the administration's economic policy, in which U.S. Steel also had an important stake, and the effect of the decision on Goldberg's, indeed the whole administration's, credibility in its pleas to unions to restrain their wage demands.

Blough quietly defended U.S. Steel's price increase and left the president's office in less than an hour. Neither Goldberg nor the president asked him to rescind the increase.

As soon as Blough left, Kennedy was reported to have "exploded" with anger and called together high-level administration officials and the Council of Economic Advisers. During the meeting the president found that only a "gentlemen's agreement" and never a firm price commitment had been made during the negotiations. Indeed, a request for such a pledge might have violated antitrust laws. As the meeting progressed, the president called his brother, Attorney General Robert F. Kennedy, who later released the announcement that "because of past price behavior in the steel industry, the Department of Justice will take an immediate and close look at the current situation and any further developments." The president also called Senator Kefauver who agreed to issue a statement of "dismay" at U.S. Steel's action and to say that "I have ordered the staff of [my] subcommittee to begin an immediate inquiry into the matter" (22–26). Thus ended the opening moves of the war to hold steel prices. *The Wall Street Journal* said of the day's events, "Wage-price stability in steel was intended as the graven image of a total program of stability; the Kennedy sculptors unveiled it as a finished masterpiece—and then suddenly it was shattered" (53).

REACTION TO THE PRICE HIKE

At the very least, U.S. Steel's timing was extremely poor and clearly embarrassed the White House for, as expected, the United Steelworkers were later to say that they would have upped their demands if they had known prices would be raised. The business community was surprised at the move, since the early settlement meant that steel users had not stock-piled and that demand was expected to be low until fall. Even so, any price increases were expected to be selective—not across the board—and to occur *after* the union security package took effect on July 1.

The company's lack of understanding of the "gentlemen's agreement" angered administration officials because it had entered into labor-management negotiations to keep the price of steel down. The *St. Louis Post-Dispatch* was skeptical of U.S. Steel's motivations and said that "it looks very much as if the steel masters used the President and his Secretary of Labor, who happens to have been the steelworker's own agent in the 1960 settlement, for the purpose of beating down wage demands prior to a price decision they had in mind all along" (108).

The administration knew about Roger Blough's statement concerning the industry's poor profit situation but attributed it merely to the game of collective bargaining where each side attempts to justify its position. Regardless of Blough's actual reasons it appeared to the White House as either of two things: (1) a challenge to the administration on the broad issue of government intervention in labor-management disputes, or (2) a personal affront to Democratic President John F. Kennedy designed to demonstrate that American industry could be as tough as the much publicized toughness of the New Frontiersmen.

The president accepted the challenge. Rumors soon circulated in Washington that both the Justice Department and the FTC would be conducting antitrust investigations, that the Treasury Department would abandon plans to relax tax depreciation rules, and that the IRS was checking up on U.S. Steel's stock option plan.

In the Congress the Democrats attacked U.S. Steel's action and Speaker John McCormack called it "shocking, arrogant, irresponsible." Most Republicans were cautiously silent as the price hike had taken them by surprise. Senator Gore prepared legislation that would begin government regulation of the steel industry and would establish a cooling-off period before the new prices would be allowed to go into effect.

THE FIRST DAY OF BATTLE

On Wednesday morning, April 11, the president met with members of his administration at a regular pre-press-conference breakfast which was devoted entirely to what to do about steel. The decision was to concentrate on persuading a select group of the large steel companies to hold the price line. Industry sources friendly to the administration had told the White House that if companies producing 16 percent of the industry's output were to hold the line, they would soon capture 25 percent of the market. In a market as competitive as steel, this action would force the other companies to lower their prices. Everyone in the administration who knew anyone in the business world—especially in the steel industry—was urged to telephone him to explain the president's point of view. These calls were "an organized, strategic, integral part of the Administration's campaign." In none of the calls was there an attempt to coax or to threaten—the approach was to explain the government's position, nothing more. The callers discovered that important segments of the business community were far more opposed to the increase than they had been willing to admit publicly.

Inland Steel was deemed to be the key company in the dispute because of its close ties with the government through its board chairman, Joseph L. Block, and because it was probably the most profitable of the large steel companies. But Block was vacationing in Japan at the time.

The purpose of the calls was to get the industry to delay price increases long enough for the administration to launch a counterattack that would make other companies hesitate before raising their prices. The administration learned that if Inland or Armco Steel were to raise prices they would wait at least one or two days, but Bethlehem Steel did not wait. By noon Wednesday Bethlehem announced a raise of six dollars a ton, although less than a day before—at its annual meeting and before U.S. Steel raised its prices—its president had told reporters that Bethlehem would *not* increase prices.

According to *Business Week,* after Bethlehem's announcement, "it looked like a race against time for other producers to get themselves on record before Kennedy's press conference at 3:30 P.M. Most of them made it." [17] These were Republic, Wheeling, Youngstown, and Jones & Laughlin —half of the twelve largest companies had announced higher prices. The president felt that the steel company actions had blatantly and openly challenged the antitrust laws in the noon to 3:30 P.M. rush. Of the six large companies that had not yet raised prices, five had not reached a decision. The combined volume of these five was 14 percent of the market—close to the 16 percent the administration thought necessary to hold the price line.

That afternoon as Kennedy rode to the State Department where he usually held his weekly press conferences, he put the finishing touches on his statement.

Good afternoon, I have several announcements to make.

The simultaneous and identical actions of United States Steel and other leading steel corporations increasing steel prices by some six dollars a ton constitute a wholly unjustifiable and irresponsible defiance of the public interest.

In this serious hour in our nation's history when we are confronted with grave crises in Berlin and Southeast Asia, when we are devoting our energies to economic recovery and stability, when we are asking reservists to leave their homes and families . . . to risk their lives— and four were killed in the last two days in Vietnam—and asking union members to hold down their wage requests . . . the American people will find it hard, as I do, to accept a situation in which a tiny handful of steel executives whose pursuit of private power and profit exceeds their sense of public responsibility, can show such utter contempt for the interest of one hundred and eighty-five million Americans. . . .

In short, at a time when they could be exploring how more efficiency and better prices could be obtained, reducing prices in this industry in recognition of lower costs, their unusually good labor contract, their foreign competition and their increase in production and profits which are coming this year, a few gigantic corporations have decided to increase prices in ruthless disregard of their public responsibility.

Kennedy then praised the steelworkers' union for abiding by its responsibilities; announced that the FTC would conduct an "informal inquiry" into the possibility that its 1951 consent order with the steel industry had been violated; hinted that the Department of Defense might shift its contracts for steel to price-line holding companies; and mentioned that

[17] "The Storm over Steel," *Business Week,* April 14, 1962, pp. 31–33.

proposed tax benefits to the steel industry through liberalized depreciation schedules were being reviewed (77–86).

In response to the president's accusation that U.S. Steel had not acted in the public interest, Roger Blough declared: "I feel that a lack of proper cost-price relationship is one of the most damaging things to the public interest." Blough announced that he would be giving his own news conference the next afternoon, Thursday, April 12.

THE SECOND DAY, APRIL 12

The Justice Department, considering a possible antitrust suit against various members of the steel industry, was much interested in the reported Tuesday afternoon statement by Bethlehem's President Martin that his company would not raise prices. But when U.S. Steel raised its prices, Bethlehem was the first to follow suit. There were antitrust implications here—U.S. Steel, because of its immense size, might exercise undue influence over other steel producers—so at 6:00 P.M. Wednesday, Attorney General Kennedy ordered his department to proceed with all possible speed in gathering necessary information. Apparently the FBI overreacted to this order, and between 3:00 A.M. and 4:00 A.M. Thursday phoned several reporters who had been present at Martin's press conference and announced their intention to come calling immediately.

On Thursday morning, Kennedy asked every cabinet member to hold press conferences in the next few days to outline the effect the price increase would have on each department and on every citizen of the land. The Justice Department, instead of the FTC, was given the principal responsibility for investigating the steel industry. The investigation was to include possible price collusion and the extent to which U.S. Steel had monopoly powers dangerous to the national interest.

Also on Thursday two more steel companies, one in the top twelve, announced price increases. On Wall Street the stock market dropped to a new low for 1962, with steel leading the retreat. On Thursday morning Blough himself called Treasury Secretary Douglas Dillon for his assessment of the situation. At the same time FBI agents showed up at eight steel companies with subpoenas requesting information and a look at their files—all but two of these (Inland and Armco) had already raised their prices. Talk from the Pentagon was that exceptions to the Buy America Act might allow the Pentagon to increase its purchases of foreign steel. Secretary Luther H. Hodges gave a noon speech denouncing price fixing and other unethical business tactics (109–10).

THURSDAY AFTERNOON—BLOUGH'S PRESS CONFERENCE

On Thursday afternoon Blough held his news conference:

. . . We have no wish to add to acrimony or to misunderstanding. We do not question the sincerity of anyone who disagrees with the action we have taken. Neither do we believe that anyone can properly assume that we are less deeply concerned with the welfare, the strength, and the vitality of this nation than are those who have criticized our action. . . .

The President said, when questioned regarding any understanding not to increase prices, "We did not ask either side to give us any assurances, because there is a very proper limitation to the power of the Government in this free economy." Both aspects of this statement are quite right. . . . [118–20]

Our problem in this country is not the problem with respect to prices; our problem is with respect to costs. If you can take care of the costs in this country, you will have no problem taking care of the prices. The prices will take care of themselves. [133]

Blough also denied that U.S. Steel was in any way defying the president by its decision, which it had a right to make, and, on the White House role in labor negotiations said, "I have no criticism. I do believe that when the air clears a little bit, I think we will all realize that this type of, shall I say—assistance?—has some limitations."

Blough denied having an understanding with other companies about prices. That prices were raised in a Democratic administration but had been kept level during a Republican one was not significant: "You can readily see that I do not know anything about politics!" One reporter asked if the increase "coming as it did right on the heels of the labor pact—was timed to check expanded government influence in collective bargaining; in other words, that you acted politically as well as economically." Again Blough denied any political motivation. He did mention, though, that if other companies did not raise their prices, U.S. Steel would be obliged to reconsider. The administration interpreted this to mean that victory was possible and that U.S. Steel was seeking an escape route.

All in all, industry sources felt that Blough did not present the best possible case.

THE TURNING POINT

At seven o'clock Thursday evening Attorney General Kennedy announced that he had authorized the Grand Jury to investigate the steel price increases and to find out if U.S. Steel "so dominated the industry that it controls prices and should be broken up." At about the same time Walter Reuther, head of the United Auto Workers Union, proposed that a price board be created to hold hearings on important prices such as steel before they could be increased. Later in the evening Tyson (chairman of the Finance Committee of U.S. Steel's board of directors) and several other U.S. Steel executives met in New York. According to Hoopes, "If there was any single turning point in the steel crisis, it probably came at this meeting." Previously the executives had thought all the uproar political in nature and probably short-lived but were now "convinced that the Administration men meant business." The executives had noticed that Inland had not gone along with the increase, and if it did not soon, Bethlehem would rescind its price and others would naturally follow (145).

THE THIRD DAY

Early in the morning of Friday the thirteenth, Kennedy talked to Roger Blough who suggested that communications should be maintained. Seeing this as a hopeful sign, Kennedy then moved to restrain members of his administration and to preserve a mood of conciliation. Also on Friday morning, Inland's late-Thursday decision not to raise prices was made public. The statement by Joseph Block was that although "profits are not adequate, we do not feel that an advance in steel prices at this time would be in the national interest." Attention now turned to Armco Steel, which had led off the price increase in 1958 when U.S. Steel refused and had a reputation for unpredictability. The real maverick of the industry, Kaiser Steel, had also not yet raised its prices.

Meanwhile rumors circulated that Roger Blough would resign; Inland's stock prices rose; other steel stocks fell; Colorado Fuel and Iron intimated that any price increase would be selective; Youngstown and Reynolds Metals implied that they would wait and see before acting on price levels.

At 10:00 A.M. Defense Secretary Robert S. McNamara stated that "where possible, procurement of steel for defense production will be shifted to those companies which have not increased prices," but he put an end to speculation that the department might increase its purchases of foreign steel because of the resulting unemployment that it might cause in this country.

All during the battle between steel and the administration, public opinion was firmly behind the president as was shown by a number of newspaper polls and by telegrams received by the White House. According to Roy Hoopes, "the majority of the nation's most influential newspapers [were] critical of the steel companies' action, [and] the business community [was] only lukewarm in its support of the steel industry. . . ."

THE FINAL BATTLE

The direct result of Blough's telephone conversation with Kennedy on Friday morning was a meeting the same afternoon of Clifford and Goldberg, and Blough, Tyson, and Worthington (president of U.S. Steel). According to reports, Clifford (a Washington attorney who was friendly to the Kennedy administration) explained that many continuing investigations of steel would be very uncomfortable, especially since Kennedy would be in office for a number of years and doing business in Washington might be difficult. Clifford and Goldberg also explored ways U.S. Steel could roll back its prices and still save face. During the meeting the various members were kept informed of events as they occurred outside: one in particular came at 3:25 P.M. announcing that Bethlehem had rescinded its price increase in order to remain competitive. This was the final blow to the company, and before the meeting was over, Blough and his fellow executives told Clifford and Goldberg that they too would later be announcing a rollback (164).

Within a few hours, in the words of *Time* magazine, there was a "precipitous rush to surrender" as the other steel producers rolled back their prices. The reason given for the rollbacks was "to remain competitive" in spite of poor profit conditions.

GRANT AT APPOMATTOX

Naturally the administration's plans for further attacks on the steel industry and proposed legislation were canceled or filed away and, for once, the administration was not crowing about its victory. As *Business Week* aptly said, "The President went out of his way to assure there will be no public recriminations now that the mistake has been retracted. Like Grant at Appomattox, he is letting the vanquished forces keep their horses and sidearms."

The relationship between the White House and U.S. Steel returned to normal, and Roger Blough agreed to stay on the president's business advisory committee. On other fronts, although the Grand Jury probe would continue, it was obvious that the administration would not press too hard for any indictments. (However, a New York Grand Jury did indict U.S. Steel, Bethlehem, Erie Forge and Steel, and Midvale-Heppenstall on price-fixing charges from an investigation begun in March 1961.) The activities of the Justice Department and the FTC were effectively curtailed, and the House investigation of the steel industry was called off, but Kefauver's Senate subcommittee investigation did proceed as scheduled.

THE KENNEDY ANTIBUSINESS CRUSADE

Most of the steel companies held their annual meetings soon after the "price fiasco." All those that had originally raised prices and then backed down maintained that they were forced to do so because the competition did not follow. One element of agreement among all steel spokesmen was that the need for a price increase had not passed—even Joseph Block agreed on this point and said Inland had refused to raise its prices only as a concession to the national interest. One steel executive said, "No company or industry may now raise prices without harboring the fear, and justifiably so, that the Administration may decide to employ the crushing weapons so recently displayed." Despite the industry's unanimous cry for more profits, every company's profit picture for the first quarter of 1961 showed a substantial improvement over the recession-affected first quarter of 1961 (224–25).

Despite its campaign of conciliation, the administration persisted in its economic policies and announced that it might act to prevent a price hike in the aluminum industry. There then began to emerge a "growing hostility" by the business community toward Kennedy, and a stock market crash in the summer of 1962 was attributed by many businessmen to the "Kennedy crowd." According to Roy Hoopes, "By late June and early July, the 'hate Kennedy' mood in the business community had almost reached a state of hysteria" and even rated a cover story in *Newsweek*. Even the Kennedy jokes became bitter and personal.

The animosity collapsed, however, by mid-autumn, perhaps because the administration's attempts at dialogue eventually got through or because a number of business leaders (including Blough and Block) helped to restore the peace. During the summer the Congress passed an administration-backed investment tax credit law and the Treasury Department announced revised tax depreciation schedules.

KENNEDY'S LAST YEAR WITH STEEL

A year passed without steel's making any price increases, but in April 1963 Wheeling Steel Corporation, with less than 2 percent of the United States market, announced a selective price increase of $4.50–$10.00 per ton on six items. "It was as though an electric shock had hit the President and his aides. . . ."[18]

The president's formal reply to the hike was a surprise:

I realize that price and wage controls in this one industry, while all others are unrestrained, would be unfair and inconsistent with our free competitive market . . . and that selective price adjustments up or down—as prompted by changes in supply and demand as opposed to across-the-board increases—are not incompatible within a framework of general stability and steel-price stability and are characteristic of any healthy economy.

In a free society both management and labor are free to do voluntarily what we are unwilling to enforce by law—and I urge the steel industry and the steel union to avoid any action which would lead to a general across-the-board increase.[19]

Actually, throughout 1963 the government allowed increases on 75 percent of the industry's product mix—all without protest.[20]

LYNDON B. JOHNSON'S LESS-VISIBLE POWER

After President Johnson took office, government-industry crises took longer to reach the confrontation stage. During 1967 the administration did not really flex its muscles (saying it did not need to), but in 1968 it acted vigorously to roll back a price boost. The Johnson administration's actions were less visible than Kennedy's, but its victory was also less clearcut. The government criticized Bethlehem Steel's small ($5.00 a ton) increase in structural steel and piling prices on New Year's Day 1966. U.S. Steel, on the other hand, deliberated about a week before raising prices on the products $2.75 a ton and drew praise from Washington. Bethlehem thereupon trimmed back its announced increase. However, the industry's later increases in large volume steel and strip received "only a mild com-

---

[18] "Can Price Rise Help Steel?" *U.S. News and World Report,* April 22, 1963, pp. 35–37.

[19] *Ibid.,* p. 37.

[20] "Inflation Hassle," *The Wall Street Journal,* October 4, 1967, p. 16.

ment of displeasure," and the government "only privately urged stainless steel makers to eschew any price boosts" in the fall, although prices were raised anyway.[21]

The government said nothing publicly about price increases until late August 1967 when Republic Steel hiked its prices 1.8 percent on carbon and alloy steel bars and the administration finally began to move to head off another increase.[22]

1967: THE BIGGEST BINGE IN FOUR YEARS

In response to Republic's boost, Gardner Ackley, chairman of the Council of Economic Advisers, called on the rest of the industry not to follow suit, but U.S. Steel, Bethlehem, Armco, Inland, Jones & Laughlin, and Kaiser raised prices anyway.

Thirteen top industry executives met with Johnson and Ackley on September 13 (at a meeting scheduled before the price rise) and told of the need for increased prices. Ackley later said that discussion of specific price actions would be a violation of antitrust law, and Secretary of Commerce Alexander B. Trowbridge said that no pledge was requested or made.

The Wall Street Journal, analyzing the significance of steel's move, said that the steel industry had just treated itself to the biggest price-raising binge in four years and that the government had even encouraged steelmakers by allowing the previous increases:

> The increases so far this year covered 42% of the industry's volume. By contrast, once it became clear that the mills wouldn't back down on sheet and strip in August 1966, Johnson Cabinet members began to describe the increases as covering "only a small fraction" of industry sales and as being "within bounds." Yet those products account for almost 40% of the steel mills sales. . . . The Government may have encouraged more steel price increases but the decision to cover so many products was made by the mills themselves. Their enthusiasm is bound to broaden, at least to some extent, the inflationary movement in the economy.[23]

The *Journal* then went on to criticize the administration's fiscal attempts to control the inflation [tax surcharge and investment tax credit] as being too late or too little.

---

[21] *Ibid.*
[22] "What's News—Business and Finance," *The Wall Steet Journal,* September 1, 1967, p. 1.
[23] "Inflation Hassle," *The Wall Street Journal,* October 4, 1967, p. 16.

The *Journal's* predictions were right—a sizable increase in steel orders occurred late in the year. In the first week of December, U.S. Steel raised its base price for cold rolled sheet, the prime steel product by volume, five dollars at ton.

Ackley's response to U.S. Steel's move was to urge the other companies to "consider carefully" the "interests of the industry and the nation" before following suit.

THE PRESIDENT'S RESPONSE: VERBAL POWER

President Johnson's simple response to the increase was that "we have exercised such rights as we had" to keep prices on cold rolled sheet steel down, that Mr. Ackley had expressed the strongly felt views of the administration, and that wage and price controls might be required in the future to avoid inflationary increases.[24]

Clearly Johnson's style toward steel price hikes differed markedly from Kennedy's. A *Wall Street Journal* editorial complimented Ackley for not blaming inflation on steel and also for criticizing the auto union settlement. The editorial pointed out that the administration's pressure on the industry seemed to have been "largely verbal—so far, anyway," and noted the contrast with actions Kennedy took, saying, "At least this time they didn't try to hang Roger Blough from the nearest lamppost." [25]

WEDNESDAY, JULY 31, 1968:
TIME OF "DIRE CONSEQUENCES"

In May 1968, according to *The Wall Street Journal*, U.S. Steel began to cut prices in areas subject to foreign competition and attempted to keep these "reductions quiet, hoping to prevent them from leading to any general break in steel prices." Big Steel's actions broke with industry precedent which said that importers, backed up with lower labor costs, could easily win a price war, and indeed the price cut occurred as American industry was stocking up for a posible steel strike on August 1.

No strike occurred, however, and on July 30 labor won a rather hefty settlement—one union estimate was that it represented a 6.1 percent

---

[24] After the industry put through a $3-a-ton increase on hot and cold rolled sheet in August 1966—the previous rise on the product—auto prices rose by $5 to $100. *The Wall Street Journal,* December 4, 1967, p. 3.

[25] "The High Price of Inflating," *The Wall Street Journal,* December 12, 1967, p. 16.

increase in employment costs to the industry, the largest since the 7.5 percent increase in 1958.

Less than a day after eleven companies signed the contract several increased their prices, led by U.S. Steel which announced a limited hike on can-making steel. An hour later, Bethlehem brought on yet another crisis by raising its prices *across the board* by nearly 5 percent, citing the extra labor costs of the new contract. If the rest of the industry followed Bethlehem's general price increase, it would be the first since 1958.

Later that day (July 31, 1968) Armco Steel announced it too would soon make across-the-board increases, and Republic Steel announced a 4.5 percent increase on its principal mill products. Republic said its "substantial" labor cost increases and "other unreimbursed costs will be recovered only partially by the price increases announced."

Business Week said:

> All during the ballyhoo over passage of the tax increase, Administration officials felt they were making progress on selling the country on the dangers of inflation. Says one Administrator economist: "We were beginning to turn the corner, and were getting back to price stability." . . . And that explains the "jawboning" strategy emanating from Washington the past few days.[26]

At a hastily called press conference the president labeled Bethlehem's hike as "unreasonable" and said it "just shouldn't be permitted to stand." Johnson added that he was "very hopeful that other steel companies wouldn't join the parade" and he had singled out Bethlehem because its increases were "across the board," and he said that he was not opposed to "selective increases that individual companies have made gradually." He noted that if the industry did not follow Bethlehem's lead, "competitive factors would, as they have in the past, bring about a readjustment," but if followed "it will have dire consequences for our nation." Furthermore, Bethlehem did not need a price increase since it had increased its first half earnings by 41 percent over the previous year. According to *The Wall Street Journal,* when it announced its price increases, "Bethlehem also announced second quarter earnings of $49.7 million . . . up 47% from $33.8 million . . . a year before on a 29% sales rise to $869.5 million from $675.5 million." Also, "second quarter profit increases of other major steelmakers, buoyed by strike-hedge buying ranged from 36 percent to U.S. Steel's 79 percent." Though conceding the labor settlement terms were "high," Johnson felt that increased prices "far exceeded" these costs.

26 "Calling the Shots on Steel Prices," *Business Week,* August 10, 1968, pp. 26–30.

A government economist later explained the administration's position that although it was not justified, a 2 percent price increase would cover the industry's increased labor costs. The question was, the economist said, whether the steel *users* should be absorbing all of the cost increases or whether steel should absorb some of them—especially at a time when the United States was "trying to turn the corner" toward stable prices.

Bethlehem's Chairman Edmund F. Martin responded to the president saying, "our announcement this morning speaks for itself. In our opinion our price increase is absolutely necessary, and we don't intend to withdraw it." The general feeling was that if other producers were to follow Bethlehem's lead, the increases would stick—as they had before even in times of decreased demand.

THURSDAY: NO FBI AGENTS THIS TIME

On Thursday, August 1, the administration continued its quick response to the steel price increases: the chairman of the president's Council of Economic Advisers sent telegrams to twelve steel companies that had not raised their prices asking that they consult him before doing so, and the president wrote to both the Speaker of the House of Representatives and the Senate Majority Leader repeating his warning of the "dire" consequences that would result if Republic's and Bethlehem's increasse were followed by the rest of the industry. The president said, "The Congress, which has acted in the national interest to help stem inflation by passing the recent tax bill, should be informed of the inflationary threat that the actions of a few pose for us all." The letters, however, did not make any specific requests for congressional action.[27]

At this juncture the administration felt that U.S. Steel was the key factor in preventing across-the-board hikes from spreading throughout the industry, although later in the day both Inland and Pittsburgh announced general increases of nearly 5 percent, matching Bethlehem's move the day before. By evening the flurry of activity reached its peak, for "all within a matter of minutes" U.S. Steel again raised its prices, the government acted to buy steel only from firms not going along with the price hike, and the president called for a meeting with twenty congressional leaders. The U.S. Steel price boost, the second in two days, increased prices an average of more than 5 percent on items that, industry wide, accounted for 14 percent of all shipments. The company said that further increases on other products would be made soon.

---

[27] "Government, Steel Industry Escalate War over Prices; U.S. Steel Posts Second Rise, Says More Are Likely," *The Wall Street Journal,* August 2, 1968, p. 3.

Clark Clifford once again entered the battle of steel prices on the government's side—now as secretary of defense. Clifford ordered the military services to buy their steel only from those companies that had not increased their prices and said that in the future "there must be positive assurance that steel products are acquired only from those firms which offer the most advantageous terms." The orders were also to apply to defense contractors and subcontractors. (Department purchases of military goods using steel totaled approximately $600 million per year—about 3.7 percent of the nation's steel production.) In addition it was reported that the Transportation Department was considering similar action in regard to its steel purchases for highway construction.

Since industry requested and Congress considered import quotas, one high government official thought the price boosts were "incredible" and said, "It seems the American consumer is the one who needs protection" from the steel industry.

FRIDAY: THE MAVERICK MOVES

On Friday night, August 2, Kaiser Steel raised its prices on carbon-steel plates, structural shapes, and tin-mill products, saying it would make further increases on other products soon. According to *The Wall Street Journal:*

> Industry sources saw significance in Kaiser Steel's move, because they said, the company is particularly vulnerable to pressure from Washington [since its] defense-related production is estimated at 20 percent to 25 percent of its total volume. Moreover, they said, a price increase, if it holds, would clear the way for even further inroads by foreign steel into the West Coast market, in which Kaiser Steel is the major factor.[28]

OVER THE WEEKEND: "DOUBTFUL TACTICS"

Other companies raised their prices over the weekend and said the increase might mean employee layoffs because of declining demand. The president applied his order to buy steel "at the lowest possible price" to all government agencies. Their combined civilian requirements for steel totaled $700 million per year.

The Wall Street Journal said that the government's punishment of "those

[28] "More Steelmakers Boost Prices: Several Concerns Schedule Layoffs," August 5, 1968, p. 3.

nasty firms for spurring inflation" was "surely pretty stupid; if anyone deserves punishment for spurring inflation it's the government. . . . Washington, after all, is spending the taxpayer's money with considerable abandon. Last week's fanfare surely suggests that the only time the government shops carefully, looking for bargains and low prices, is when it wants to chastise someone for something or other." [29] A government official said that the government was considering increasing its purchases of foreign steel, although *The Wall Street Journal* said that using foreign steel was a "doubtful tactic" as "long standing requirements" prohibited purchasing foreign goods unless the price differential was "overwhelming."

Also over the weekend Senator Philip A. Hart, chairman of the Senate Antitrust Committee, wrote to the chairman of the FTC, Paul Dixon, asking for an investigation "in light of the [steel] industry's pricing practices."

MONDAY: SEEMING CONTRADICTIONS

On Monday morning the FTC commissioners decided to gather information on Senator Hart's request before going ahead with an investigation. Dixon said that any investigation would be concerned with whether or not the steel price boost was "cost justified" and that no investigation would be needed if a price rollback occurred and the commission action was taken solely at the request of Senator Hart.

Congressman Joe L. Evins, chairman of the House Small Business Committee, ordered a staff investigation preliminary to a "full inquiry" on steel price hikes and their effect on small businesses which would "square up to the dangers posed by the greedy actions of the steel industry."

Meanwhile the Department of Transportation, the General Services Administration, and HUD (Housing and Urban Development) took steps to insure that steel orders—direct and indirect through contractors—went to lower-priced steel. Secretary of Commerce C. R. Smith said that even existing contracts should be reviewed and amended wherever possible to obtain steel at the lowest possible price.

On Monday it was clear that the administration was still hoping to force a partial rollback through competitive pressures by keeping U.S. Steel and others who had announced selective increases from extending them across the board. Republic Steel promised not to increase prices on steel used to make items for the Vietnam War; Armco said its hike would not apply on two of the three items it sold to the department; Bethlehem said its

---

[29] "What's Going On Here?" *The Wall Street Journal,* editorial, August 5, 1968, p. 12.

increases did not include certain military items. However, Pittsburgh Steel stood firm on its hike, and Inland Steel said nothing—but its Defense Department shipments were less than 2 percent of its total sales.

Defense officials were "exultant" at the steel companies' promises, but the companies said that they had been planning to exempt defense items all along. Indeed these defense "rollbacks" were thought by some to be symbolic victories showing weakness in the industry's position, but they also raised the question: Why weren't government *civilian* steel prices also lowered?

Tuesday was uneventful in the battle of steel prices. As long as U.S. Steel held firm, the government could expect Bethlehem eventually to roll back its prices, for the Pentagon did 80 percent of its steel business with U.S. Steel, Bethlehem, Pittsburgh, and Republic.

WEDNESDAY: THE BOOST'S BROKEN BACK

On Wednesday, August 7, U.S. Steel raised some of its prices 2.5 percent on the average—not much above the 2 percent government guidepost —and thus "broke the back" of the Bethlehem-led 5 percent general increase. "Within minutes" Bethlehem and others (Inland, Armco, Youngstown Sheet and Tube, Pittsburgh, Jones & Laughlin) compared their prices to U.S. Steel's levels and rescinded increases on prices U.S. Steel "had omitted from its boosts." The actual increased prices would average 4 percent to 6 percent but would "cover only about 63 percent of the industry's products, and exclude such big volume items as tubular and wire products and galvanized sheet, which are minor items in U.S. Steel's product line. . . ." Some companies, on the other hand, also made price *increases* to bring their prices in line with U.S. Steel. U.S. Steel said that there would be other price adjustments from time to time over the following twelve months.

White House Press Secretary George Christian said the president welcomed the move by U.S. Steel, and Arthur M. Okun, chairman of the president's Council of Economic Advisers, found the developments "gratifying" and, "taking account of all recent developments in steel prices and costs, the nation has a right to expect renewed price stability in this basic product in the months ahead." The White House said that it expected no more U.S. Steel price hikes during the year and that price rises and productivity gains in the auto and appliance industries should temper temptations to raise these prices because of increased steel costs.[30]

[30] "U.S. Steel Increases Prices 2.5%, Spurs Partial Rollback," *The Wall Street Journal,* August 8, 1968, p. 3.

"NO ONE NOW WILL EVER KNOW"

A *Wall Street Journal* editorial said the administration's claim to victory in the war over steel prices was "strange" under the circumstances and expressed regret at its price-holding actions.

> In our supposedly free economy companies naturally try to set prices high enough to cover their costs and provide them with a reasonable profit. That, essentially, is what the steel companies did in the wake of the costly contract settlement with the United Steel-workers.
> [The Government's] extra-legal price control naturally distorts the workings of competition. With imports sizable and with steel users working off inventories built up in fear of a strike, it's more than possible that the original price increases would not have held for very long even if the Government had not said a word.
> Unfortunately, no one now will ever know.[31]

But the editor lamented too soon for reports in October were that "a price war has broken out in the domestic steel industry," as some high-volume products had their prices slashed as much as 20 percent. According to *The Wall Street Journal:*

> The price cutting has taken much of the significance from President Johnson's success two months ago. . . . But current selling prices, in many cases, are considerably below even the pre-August list prices.[32]

Also in October, according to *Business Week:*

> U.S. Steel initiated a 4% price increase on various types of steel pipe. Bethlehem refused to support all the boosts, holding firm on two categories. This forced Big Steel to retreat—but only partly. It deferred the effective date of the increases from November 1, 1968 to February 1, 1969.[33]

---

[31] "A Peculiar Price Victory," *The Wall Street Journal,* August 9, 1968, p. 6.
[32] "Makers Quietly Cutting Prices as Much as 20% in Bid to Unload Surplus," *The Wall Street Journal,* October 7, 1968, p. 1.
[33] "Steel Industry Hit by Major Price Cut," *Business Week,* November 4, 1968, p. 35.

One novel twist to the price war was that most mills were denying the price cuts, which went only to large-volume customers, while insisting that everyone else was cutting prices! In November the whole industry was jolted when Bethlehem "cut its price of hot rolled sheet—the industry's second largest tonnage product—by 22 percent. . . . Bethlehem stressed that it acted to meet domestic competition. Steel executives translate this into retaliation against covert price cutting by U.S. Steel." [34] The rest of the industry soon fell into line with Bethlehem's cuts. According to *Business Week,* "Steel executives couldn't recall a more drastic price cut since the rampant competition of the early 1930s, nor could they recall a more direct challenge to the industry's leader, U.S. Steel Corp." Indeed, said the magazine, the industry's "administered price structure may be disappearing. Competition from foreign steel as well as other materials such as concrete, aluminum, and plastic has put the industry in a different posture. No longer is the materials business a seller's market, and steel may finally be adjusting to this." [35] Indeed, "Price cutting has pushed the industry's traditionally stable pricing structure close to chaos." [36]

[34] *Ibid.*
[35] "Revolution in Steel Pricing?" *Business Week,* December 14, 1968.
[36] "Pittsburgh Expects to Be Happier," *Business Week,* December 14, 1968, p. 40.

D.

GOVERNMENT AND
BUSINESS AS PARTNERS

The Supersonic Transport (SST)

*A Case Study in Government-Industry Cooperation
and the Determination of National Priorities*

You're darn right. It's a patriotic program.

—William Magruder
Director of SST Development with the Nixon administration

The federal government is guaranteeing everything. . . . Would not a businessman fight for this kind of opportunity? . . . What would he have to lose? . . . And the taxpayer is the pigeon, the fall guy—as Texan Guinan or P. T. Barnum would put it, the sucker.

—Senator William Proxmire

On June 5, 1963, President John F. Kennedy announced to a startled world his decision to commit the United States and its government to develop and build a supersonic plane. This was clearly in response to the British-French joint effort in building a supersonic plane—the Concorde. The declaration was appropriately made in a speech on graduation day at the United States Air Force Academy in Colorado Springs, Colorado. Among other things, the president said:

As a testament to our strong faith in the future of airpower, and the manned airplane, I'm announcing today that the United States will commit itself to an important new program in civilian aviation. Civilian aviation, long both the beneficiary and the benefactor of military aviation, is of necessity equally dynamic.

Neither the economics nor the politics of international air competition permit us to stand still in this area. Today the challenging new frontier in commercial aviation and in military aviation is a frontier already crossed by the military—supersonic transport.

[After reviewing the recommendations of the leading members of this Administration] it is my judgment that this government should immediately commence a new program in partnership with private industry to develop at the earliest practical date the prototype of a commercially successful supersonic transport superior to that being built in any other country in the world. . . .

An open preliminary design competition will be initiated immediately among American airframe and powerplant manufacturers with a detailed phase to follow. *If these initial phases do not produce an aircraft capable of transporting people and goods safely, swiftly, and at prices the traveler can afford and the airlines find profitable, we shall not go further.* [Emphasis added]

. . . Spurred by competition from across the Atlantic and by the productivity of our own companies, the Federal Government must pledge funds to supplement the risk capital to be contributed by private companies. It must then rely heavily on the flexibility and ingenuity of private enterprise to make the detailed decisions and to introduce successfully this new jet age transport into world-wide service. . . . This commitment, I believe, is essential to a strong and forward-looking nation. . . .[1]

President Kennedy's statement came one day after Juan Trippe, president of Pan American World Airways, announced that the airline was taking options for six Anglo-French SST Concordes. Pan Am's action was clearly a competitive move and followed those of BOAC and Air France, both of which had earlier ordered eight Concordes each. Kennedy's decision to move on SST was not a spontaneous response to Pan Am's action but was the outcome of long deliberations and study of the social, economic, and political impact of SST on the United States position in aviation industry both at home and abroad.

The idea of a civilian SST has been around since the early fifties, but there were serious doubts about its economic and technical feasibility. In 1956 the National Advisory Committee for Aeronautics, which has since been transformed into the National Aeronautics and Space Administration

[1] *The New York Times,* June 6, 1963, p. 25.

(NASA), launched a research program to explore the possibility of developing an engine capable of flying airplanes at speeds of near Mach 3.[2] This was a prelude to the B-70 bomber program, the contract for which was awarded to North American Aviation Corporation in February 1958. Quite a bit of research work had already gone into the various aspects of the program, and the nation's aircraft industry hoped to rely heavily on the technology developed in the B-70 program for later exploitation in a civilian version of SST. However, by the end of 1959—and after spending more than $330 million—the B-70 program was on the verge of being scrapped, along with the hopes of aircraft manufacturers. In the interest of economy, the Eisenhower administration had decided to terminate the program when Dr. George Kistiakowsky, the president's scientific adviser, predicted that intercontinental ballistic missiles would make the development of manned bombers needless.

There were strong supporters of the SST program who advocated the development of the B-70 for both its military use and its benefits to the civilian SST program. These included Senator Lyndon B. Johnson, chairman of the Preparedness Investigating Subcommittee of the Senate's powerful Committee on Armed Services, Air Force Chief of Staff Thomas White, Senator A. S. (Mike) Monroney, and General Elmwood R. (Pete) Quesada, President Eisenhower's appointee to run the new Federal Aviation Administration (FAA).

During the summer of 1960, Quesada put together a high-level committee composed of the members of FAA, NASA, and the Department of Defense (DOD) to develop strategies for commencing the SST program. However, in October 1960, an FAA-sponsored SST feasibility study conducted by United Research of Cambridge, Massachusetts, predicted that United States plane makers would not enter into an SST race with Britain, France, and the Soviet Union without the intervention and support of the United States government. This prediction was based on the high development costs (estimated at over $1 billion), the high risk and uncertainty of the economic feasibility, and the prospect of getting government subsidies (which seemed highly probable because the government publicly advocated the program).[3]

As Quesada saw it, the United States could not afford to lose face or market dominance by letting the Russians or the Anglo-French win the SST race. In November 1960, shortly before his resignation due to change in the administration, Quesada recommended to President Eisenhower an initial FY-61 funding of $17.5 million. However, the Bureau of the Budget

[2] *National Aeronautics,* June 1966, p. 24.
[3] *United States Supersonic Transport Program Summary,* Federal Aviation Agency, Washington, D.C., July 1965, p. 1.

reduced this figure to $5 million. At the same time he awarded the first SST engine-design research contracts to General Electric and Pratt & Whitney.[4] President-elect Kennedy's appointee to succeed Quesada as the chief of FAA was Najeeb Halaby who recommended that Congress spend $12 million a year for SST studies. Despite President Kennedy's support, the Senate only narrowly defeated amendments to the administration's appropriation bills which would have eliminated the SST studies.

In March 1961 President Kennedy asked Halaby to develop a program of national priorities to give the nation the "safest, most efficient and most economical national aviation system attainable." [5]

The Halaby report, titled" Project Horizon," was submitted to President Kennedy on September 5, 1961. It painted a picture of a fast-growing and changing world in glorious terms and described the role of air travel in it. "Faster, bigger aircraft have shrunk the globe to the point where the capitals of the world are almost as accessible to an American as the county seat of a few decades ago. . . ." [6] Recommending government participation in the SST program, the report said: "Government funds should be utilized through the research, design, development, prototype and probably production stages. Every effort must be made to recoup the Government's financial investment through some type of royalty system to be paid by the operators." [7]

In November 1961 the Supersonic Transport Advisory Group (STAG) was created by Halaby to advise the SST steering group. STAG developed technical guidelines for the SST, visited various aircraft plants, advised members of Congress, and shortly before its dissolution recommended to the president that he publicly announce the development and production of commercial SST as a national policy objective.[8]

In 1962 President Kennedy established a cabinet-level committee headed by Vice-President Johnson to report on all aspects of the SST program. The committee included the heads of the Atomic Energy Commission (AEC), Bureau of the Budget (BOB), Civil Aeronautics Board (CAB), Council of Economic Advisors (CEA), FAA, Department of Labor (DOL), NASA, Office of Science and Technology, Department of State (DOS), and Treasury Department. The report of the committee strongly recommended a go-ahead on the SST program and formed the basis of Kennedy's June 5, 1963, announcement.

[4] *Ibid.*
[5] *Supplementary Report to the Supersonic Transport Steering Group,* FAA, May 14, 1963, p. 8.
[6] *Report of the Task Force on National Aviation Goals—Project Horizon,* FAA, September 1961.
[7] *Ibid.*
[8] *US/SST Program Summary,* FAA, July 1965, p. 4.

THE POTENTIAL THREAT OF BRITISH-FRENCH AND
RUSSIAN SSTs

Since the early fifties both British and French aircraft and engine manufacturers had been working separately on a commercial SST for the world markets, the British to develop a long-range and the French a medium- and short-range version. However, the tremendous financial costs and the fear of American and Russian domination brought the British and French governments together. On November 29, 1962, the two countries agreed to establish a consortium of British and French interests (Concorde) to develop an SST jointly. The Anglo-French SST, called the Concorde, was to have a top speed of Mach 2.2 (1450 mph), thus staying within the present state of the technology. The Concorde is heavily dependent on the financial subsidies provided by the French and British governments.

The goal of the program was to get the Concorde into airline service by 1971, thus giving it a three to four year time lead over the United States SST. Despite various doubts as to its economic feasibility, several airlines ordered Concordes. BOAC and Air France were first, with orders of eight each, and by 1967 orders for seventy-four Concordes worth $1 billion had been placed. The market projections were for two hundred to three hundred Concordes by 1980 with most of the sales coming in the early years.

The original plans called for a "dual purpose" SST with long- and short-range versions to meet the differing primary needs of BOAC and Air France respectively. The British share of the costs was estimated at £50 million. As can be expected with any technical project of the Concorde's size and complexity, the program ran into serious technical problems which resulted in increased costs and time delays. Furthermore, BOAC, fearing that the contemplated long-range version would not adequately meet its requirements, insisted on a still longer range for the aircraft, thus causing a major redesign effort and escalating the costs to £140 million for England alone.

The rising costs of the program, the unfavorable balance of payments, and other domestic problems caused England to review her commitment to the Concorde when the Labour Government came into power in the fall of 1964. Fearing a jettisoning of the program, BOAC reserved a position for six US/SSTs. Air France immediately followed suit. However, by January 1965, when the British Government discovered that the agreement with the French was irrevocable, estimates for the British share of the cost had gone to £165 million.[9] The cost estimates for the Concorde kept rising, and in November 1966 it was estimated that the program would cost $1.4 billion—up from the original estimate of $400 million—and that eventual costs might go as high as $2.4 billion! [10]

The first Concorde 001 (the French version) was test flown on March 2, 1969. Concorde 002 (the British version) was flown a few weeks later. Neither was flown at supersonic speeds, for the requisite more-powerful engines were not slated to be completed until late 1970 or early 1971. A model of the Russian SST TU-144 was first shown to the West at the Paris Air Show in 1955 and was test flown in Russia on December 31, 1968.[11] The Soviet plane was designed to operate at 1550 mph carrying more than 90 passengers (Concorde's estimates were 126 passengers for short-to-medium range and 112 for distances of four thousand miles). TU-144 was expected to cost about $20 million, or the same as Concorde. Most aviation officials in the West, however, believed that TU-144 would not offer much competition because in the past Soviet planes had proved uneconomical.[12]

PROGRESS OF THE US/SST—THE KENNEDY-JOHNSON ERA

On June 14, 1963, following his Air Force Academy announcement, President Kennedy sent a message to Congress in which he flatly stated that "in no event will the Government investment be permitted to exceed $750 million [and] the Government does not intend to pay any production, purchase or operating subsidies to manufacturers or airlines." [13] The development costs of the program were estimated as approximately $1 billion over the next six years, of which the manufacturers were expected to pay a portion of the government's development costs through royalties.[14]

The government proposed to pay 75 percent of the development costs with the manufacturers paying the balance. This three-to-one formula prevailed in the early phases of the design but was raised to nine to one when the manufacturers balked at paying 25 percent because of increasing technological difficulties and rising costs.

President Kennedy's request for a $60 million appropriation to fund the government's share of SST design ran into some sharp congressional criticism. One of the program's critics, Senator Fulbright, remarked:

[9] *Los Angeles Times,* January 20, 1965.
[10] "Race for a Superjet—Can U.S. Catch Up?" *U.S. News and World Report,* March 17, 1969, pp. 38–39.
[11] *Ibid.*
[12] *Ibid.*
[13] *Congressional Record,* July 9, 1963, pp. 12283–84.
[14] *Ibid.*

This Congress has been asked to demonstrate that a "democratic, free enterprise system" in the President's words, can compete with Britain and France. . . . I had always thought that the outstanding virtue of our free enterprise system was that it was free and that it rested on the enterprise of individuals. Thus, I fail to see how a Government subsidy of three-quarters of a billion dollars to the airplane builders is going to represent a triumphant vindication of free enterprise.[15]

On another front, Stanford Research Institute (SRI), in a study of the SST program conducted for the FAA, concluded that there was "no economic justification for an SST program." [16] Despite criticism, both in Congress and in some well-informed public quarters, the House voted $60 million for the program in the fiscal year 1964 as requested by the president.

In January 1964 three airframe and three engine companies submitted initial design proposals. The proposals were evaluated independently both by the government and by a panel of ten airlines. The government's evaluation found that none of the airframe designs met range-payload, economic requirements. In May the president directed the FAA to award contracts for further design to two airframe companies (Boeing and Lockheed) and two engine companies (General Electric and Pratt & Whitney, a division of United Aircraft), which ranked best in the evaluation. The president also asked the Department of Commerce to conduct economic studies and the National Academy of Sciences to continue its supervision of the sonic boom studies. The selected airframe designs: (1) Boeing proposed a swing-wing (which would fold back during supersonic flight) and would carry 150 passengers at Mach 2.7 for four thousand miles; and (2) Lockheed proposed a double delta wing design and would carry 218 passengers at Mach 3.0 for four thousand miles. In November the airframe and engine competitors submitted their revised designs. After more than six months of review by various technical committees and the President's Advisory Committee on Supersonic Transport (established in March 1964 under the chairmanship of Secretary of Defense Robert McNamara), President Johnson, in July 1965, announced an eighteen-month design program running to the end of 1966. He also requested that Congress appropriate $140 million for the program for the fiscal year 1966.

Criticism in Congress became more severe and the public arguments both for and against the program more vocal. President Johnson's request for $140 million to get the eighteen-month Phase II of the program

[15] *Congressional Record*, June 26, 1963, pp. 11706–7.
[16] *Final Report: An Economic Analysis of the Supersonic Transport*, SRI Project No. ISU-4266, p. 1.

finished in only eleven months raised eyebrows in Congress. Was this only a "speed-up," or was it an indirect way of committing the government to the program? To secure congressional approval, and also to put the program in more favorable hands, the administration did two things: Considerable pressure was brought to bear upon various senators and congressmen to vote for the appropriation, and the president nominated, and the Senate approved, General Seth J. McKee as FAA administrator to replace Najeeb Halaby who was retiring. To do this, the FAA act which specified that the FAA administrator must be a civilian had to be amended. This was done at a time when the FAA was already top-heavy with military personnel with ninety-four retired and active officers holding down key jobs.[17]

Between July and December 1966, the SST prototype designs of Boeing, Lockheed, General Electric, and Pratt & Whitney were submitted and evaluated. In October 1966 Congress appropriated another $140 million for the fiscal year 1967. On December 31, 1966, the FAA announced that Boeing and General Electric had been selected to construct the SST airframe and engine respectively. Thus, after a government commitment of $311 million and expenditure of $244 million, in addition to $70 million spent by the plane manufacturers, the program was finally on the go. In the process, it had been reviewed by three presidential committees, the National Academy of Sciences, seven congressional committees, and thirteen federal agencies and departments.[18] It had also been analyzed and pronounced ill-advised and uneconomical by SRI, the Rand Corporation, and a host of other profit and nonprofit consulting organizations.

Construction contracts were signed on May 1, 1967, at which time Congress was also requested to appropriate $198 million for the fiscal year 1968 to help finance the prototype construction phase of the program. It was, however, still not clear how the $4.5 billion program would eventually be paid for.

President Johnson and the other supporters of the program notwithstanding, the SST program kept encountering new technological problems.

In the fall of 1968, after a year and a half and millions of dollars had gone into the swing-wing design, Boeing announced that its design would have to be scrapped. The corporation said it had found that the swing-wing, and especially its pivots, had made their 2707 (FAA-Boeing contract-designated name for Boeing's SST) too fat by twenty-five tons. Thus, the design would have to be rejected in favor of a fixed-wing after all. Unfortunately, Boeing's design was now even less well along than Lockheed's had been a year and a half earlier, *before the contract had even been*

[17] *Los Angeles Times,* July 12, 1965.
[18] *Newsweek,* August 29, 1966, p. 48.

awarded! Had Lockheed's more realistic fixed-wing design been awarded the contract, it is safe to say that much time and money would have been saved. This, however, is only one of the unforeseen technical problems which constantly blocked progress on the SST and threatened it with ultimate failure. As early as 1965, some of the airline executives had expressed doubts on the desirability of depending on the construction of one prototype based essentially on a paper design. In a report, R. W. Rummel, TWA's vice-president for planning and research, had recommended the construction of two prototypes, one each based on Boeing's and Lockheed's SST designs. This approach, in his view, could save a minimum of $480 million in the long run.[19]

THE NIXON ERA

When Richard Nixon was elected president in November 1968, the future of the program once again became clouded as both friends and foes hoped for a fresher and, from their point of view, more favorable consideration from the new administration. The Nixon administration obliged both groups. Soon after his inauguration, President Nixon, on February 19, 1969, announced yet another ad hoc committee to review the Supersonic Transport Program and to "investigate the national interest questions associated with the pending SST decision." [20] The presidential guidance was that the "SST must be safe for the passenger, profitable for the manufacturers and airlines, and superior to any other aircraft." [21] The Ad Hoc Committee, chaired by Undersecretary of Transportation James M. Beggs, included high-ranking representatives from the Departments of Commerce, Defense, Justice, HEW, State, and Treasury, the Council of Economic Advisors (CEA), NASA, and Dr. Lee A. DuBridge, the National Science Advisor. The committee held hearings and heard expert testimony during February and March 1969. As it turned out, the report of the committee was highly critical of the SST program. Consequently, the Department of Transportation, which had consistently advocated continuance of the SST program, kept the report secret until October 31, 1969, when it was released at the request of Congressman Henry S. Reuss (D-Wis.).[22]

---

[19] L. Stewart Rolls, David G. Koenig, and Fred J. Drinkwater III, "Flight Investigation of the Aerodynamic Properties of an Ogee Wing," NASA Technical Note D-3071, December 1965, p. 1.

[20] *Congressional Record,* October 31, 1969, H10432.

[21] *Congressional Record,* November 17, 1969, H10950.

[22] "Reuss Bill Would Ban Commercial Supersonic Flights in U.S.," Press Release from the Office of Congressman Henry S. Reuss, November 11, 1969, p. 2.

REPORT OF THE AD HOC COMMITTEE

The committee created four panels to examine the impact of the SST program in four specific areas: balance of payments and international relations, economics, environmental and sociological impact, and technological fallout. A summary of their findings follows.[23]

Balance of Payments and International Relations

The SST's balance-of-payments effect (BOP) was analyzed in terms of its overall impact on the United States BOP. This included both import and export of aircraft (the Commerce Department wanted to consider only the aircraft account), and increase in international air travel and its distribution between United States and foreign carriers (the Treasury and State departments wanted to include all aspects of BOP). The panel observed that on aircraft sales alone the United States BOP was likely to improve by between $11 billion and $18 billion (depending on competition from a commercially viable Anglo-French Concorde) from introduction in 1978 through 1990. The committee then analyzed the effect of SST on air travel expenditure. The current United States deficit in this category was estimated at $1.6 billion and "even in the absence of any commercial supersonic aircraft, it is expected to increase in absolute amount . . . totalling around $70 billion for the period 1970 through 1990." After taking the impact of SST and even revising their estimates of deficit downward, the committee concluded that "an adverse impact of speed-induced supersonic travel on the U.S. travel account [was likely to be] considerably greater than the estimated beneficial impact of supersonic aircraft sales on the U.S. aircraft account."

In terms of foreign relations impact the committee observed that the United Kingdom and France would frown at hasty action on the SST as designed to scuttle the Concorde. Similarly, strict noise standards could bar the Concorde from major United States airports. The committee recommended that both the United Kingdom and France be kept advised of "U.S. noise developments to ensure their full understanding if not acceptance of the U.S. position on noise."

Economics

The Economic Subcommittee expressed deep concern on the grave uncertainty associated with all economic aspects of the program: develop-

[23] *Congressional Record,* October 31, 1969.

ment and production costs, financing costs, and employment potential. The subcommittee observed that "almost every economic aspect of the program reflects unverifiable matters of judgment with great variance in the opinion of experts. Probably the single most uncertain aspect of the whole program relates to the uncertainty as to whether an SST can be built in the given time that will meet the specifications of being efficient, safe, and economical." [24]

The subcommittee did not put much faith in the assurances given by the manufacturers, FAA, and other interested government agencies and private business interests in view of similar assurances given to earlier investigating committees and also past experience with plane developments. It noted that even where commercial plane development, such as the Boeing 707, was based on well-established technology of military planes, "production costs have often been more than three times what they were predicted to be." The SST represented a jump of unprecedented magnitude in new technology, and even if all technical problems were solved, there was little doubt that costs would escalate considerably.

Demand for the SST was another uncertain area. Assuming that consumers value their time at one and one-half times their hourly earnings, the FAA projected that 500 SSTs would be sold. However, the Institute of Defense Analysis (IDA) model for forecasting demand, which estimates that passengers value their time as equal to their hourly earnings, reduced sales estimates to 350.

Similarly, in a 1967 Columbia Ph.D. study, Ruben Granau "concluded on the basis of a very detailed statistical study of air travel time from New York City to other points that businessmen value their time in air travel at 0.4 times their average hourly family income and that pleasure travellers valued their time in aircraft travel at zero."

The FAA in its base case assumed that supersonic transport would have a 25 percent passenger fare premium over subsonic planes. The FAA estimated that 1978 SST fares would equal 1965 subsonic fares and that subsonic fares would decline 25 percent in real terms between 1965 and 1978, thus producing the rate differential. However, subsonic fares declined 18 percent between 1965 and 1968, so—if we accept the IDA and FAA estimates of 1.8 percent per year fare decline—the relative difference between supersonic and subsonic fares would increase to 36 percent, thus reducing SST sales estimates to 200.

These highly speculative estimates are based on an untenable assumption—that American SSTs and British-French Concordes will not compete in the same markets. However, Concorde will be introduced five years before SST and may secure a considerable foothold in the market, and

[24] *Ibid.*

SST, despite its lower operating costs, may not be able to lower fares and obtain a greater market share. The subcommittee noted that

international fares are set by unanimous agreement of IATA in which each airline has a vote. With many airlines having the Concorde and with two airlines being intimately connected with its production—BOAC and Air France—it seems unlikely that the SST will force supersonic fares below those that are economical for the Concorde and drive the Concorde out of the market—the FAA assumption. The Concorde will be sold for about half the price and will have the seating capacity of an SST. Thus, two Concordes can be secured for each SST giving airlines an additional flexibility in scheduling. If fares are kept high enough to protect the Concorde so that both types of supersonic planes operate in the same markets at the same price, then they may split the market which will reduce SST sales from 500 to 250.

In terms of rate of return on investment to the United States government, the subcommittee observed that

by the terms of the FAA-Boeing contract, Boeing establishes the price of the plane. Given the demand model specified, Boeing . . . could make more money at a price of $40 million than at a price of $37 million. In fact, Boeing could maximize its profits if it charged about $48 million. Such a price would reduce sales of planes to something under 350. This would in turn reduce government royalties to the point that the government barely got its money back.

The return on investment (ROI) for the airlines was based on a load factor of 58 percent which is unrealistically high when compared with the industry average of 52.6 percent in 1968 or 55 percent achieved during 1962–68.[25] Assuming the more realistic 55 percent load factor, it is estimated that airlines would earn a ROI of 25.2 percent before taxes. In view of the recent declines in ROI after taxes (8.9 percent in 1966, 7.7 percent in 1967, and an estimated 6 percent in 1968), it is likely that the airline industry may already be overcapitalized and therefore declining ratios would make the problem of financing the purchase of SSTs quite difficult.

The subcommittee also questioned FAA's estimates of additional direct and indirect employment of more than one hundred thousand workers. First, an unknown proportion of this number was to result from relative

[25] The load factor for domestic airlines in the U.S. was reduced to 50 percent in 1969. *The New York Times,* January 11, 1970, Sec. 12, p. 17.

declines in other parts of the aerospace industry. Second, this employment would be concentrated in highly skilled and semiskilled managerial and professional occupations which are in short supply and in periods of full employment may prove inflationary. "The net employment increase from SST would likely be negligible and . . . the project would have practically no employment benefits for the disadvantaged hard-core unemployed with low skill levels."

After considering all the evidence, the subcommittee recommended that

no funds for prototype construction be included in the 1970 budget. The funds still available under the old design contract, and possibly some additional funds for research, should be used to clarify the characteristics of the SST. . . . We would also suggest that any further research on this plane be done under the responsibility of an agency other than FAA. While we do not wish to suggest that the role of FAA in the development of the aircraft has been improper in any way, we are concerned about possible conflicts of interest in the future.

Environmental and Sociological Impact

The subcommittee considered four areas of environmental and sociological impact of SST to be its main concern. These were sonic boom, airport noise, hazards to passengers and crew, and effects of water vapor in the stratosphere. On all these counts it was concluded that major problems remained to be solved and "should be the subject of further intensive research before proceeding with prototype construction."

Technological Fallout

The subcommittee considering the effects of technological fallout from the SST program concluded as follows:

The SST program will advance many areas of technology and will result in technological fallout both to the aircraft industry in general and to other industrial and military applications. The magnitude of this effect is very difficult to assess, but it appears to be small. Nevertheless, there are a number of areas which can be identified as having a high probability of potential benefit, such as: flight control systems, structures, materials, aircraft engines, aerodynamics.

While technological fallout will inevitably result from a complex, high technology program such as the SST development, the value of this benefit appears to be limited. We believe technological fallout to be of relatively minor importance in this program and therefore should not be considered either wholly or in part as a basis for justifying the program. In the SST program, fallout or technological advances should be considered as a bonus or additional benefit from a program which must depend upon other reasons for its continuation.

Following the deliberations of the Ad Hoc Committee and its subcommittees, Chairman James Beggs prepared a draft report purportedly summarizing the views of the members of the committee. This draft report was later to be submitted to the secretary of transportation and President Nixon. The draft was highly biased in favor of the SST program; it completely ignored or sharply toned down the criticism leveled at the SST program by various panels and greatly exaggerated the positive findings. Understandably the reaction of the committee members was sharp and bitter. Here are some examples:

1. The draft report, transmitted with your memorandum of March 18, has just been received. In my opinion the summary does not convey the sense of the Environmental and Sociological Panel report, and does not adequately reflect the concerns of the members of this panel.

   On the contrary, the editorial comments, interpretations and implied conclusions in the draft summary tend to convey the impression that the panel considered the environmental factors to be of small moment. Quite to the contrary these must be recognized as being of significant concern and emphasized at every step leading to a final decision in this matter.
                                             CHARLES C. JOHNSON, JR.
                                             Assistant Surgeon
                                             General Administrator

2. I believe that your draft report attaches more significance to technology fallout from the program than does the actual report of that subcommittee.
                                             RUSSELL E. TRAIN
                                             Under Secretary of the
                                             Interior

3. My reaction to the draft report at this time is negative.

   First, it is my understanding that "The objective of the Committee is to assess the impact of the SST on the national interest." The draft report fails to make this assessment. It neither reflects a Committee consensus concerning the net effects of proceeding with the SST, nor does it provide a basis for such a conclusion for Committee consideration. Instead, it merely reviews and summarizes some of the material presented by the subcommittee.

Second, the draft report presents a possibly misleading summary of the subcommittee reports. These raised numerous problems which bring into serious question the wisdom of proceeding with the SST; these problems are understated in the draft report.

ARNOLD R. WEBER
Assistant Secretary
of Manpower

4. I have carefully reviewed the Draft Report of the SST Ad Hoc Review Committee and have found that it does not adequately reflect the views of the working panels and of the members of the Committee. It contains primarily the most favorable material, interspersed with editorial comments, and thus distorts the implications and tenor of the reports. Unfortunately, you have not given us time enough to rewrite this draft. The report as it stands cannot be accepted as an accurate representation of either our views or those of other members. . . .

If the committee is not to be allowed to make joint recommendations to Secretary Volpe, I want to make clear our views. While the risks both economically and technically are great, the potential benefits are uncertain. With budget needs so great, I cannot see how this program can be justified at the present time and would recommend that no new funds be devoted to the project for at least FY 1970. This would mean that about $70 million would be available after April 15 [1969] for research on noise suppression, environmental effects, and market studies.

HENDRIK S. HOUTHAKKER
Council of Economic
Advisors

5. There are no overriding foreign policy grounds either for pushing ahead with the SST project now, or for delaying it, or for dropping it altogether. One specific aspect of this position is our view that it would not be proper to base the decision to go ahead with the project on any generalized concept of enhancement of U.S. prestige, or the like.

U. ALEXIS JOHNSON
Under Secretary
for Political Affairs

AIRLINES' REPORT ON SST

The FAA also sought the views of nine major American airlines concerning the SST program. All these airlines were holding positions on the reservation list for the SSTs. While all of them were agreed that a prototype of SST should be built, they were at best less than enthusiastic about the current design, timing of delivery, and sharing of development. None indicated any increase in its reservation positions and most of them wanted the government to bear the major financial burden. Here are some examples of the early 1969 comments:

AIRLINE 1

The recent SST review along with an assessment of the environment in which we are currently operating has led us to take a different posture than has been the case to date. The factors influencing this change are:

First, the operating economics of the presently proposed SST indicate that a substantial fare premium undoubtedly will be required to match the economic performance of the present generation of subsonic jets.

Second, there appears to be serious doubt that the proposed SST can meet existing or proposed airport noise criteria.

Third, the SST undoubtedly will be limited to overwater operation because of the sonic boom problem.

Fourth, the final cost per airplane will undoubtedly fall in the $40–50 million area representing an enormous risk per single vehicle.

Fifth, important and costly improvements are immediately required to bring both our airways and airports up to a capacity compatible with the current and future traffic demand.

There are other factors which weigh against unqualified commitment to the SST development schedule, but the above are the most important ones in my view. In light of the somewhat negative aspects bearing upon the SST program as of now and our existing capital commitments, I would be unwilling to recommend to Board of Directors the venturing of any additional risk capital. . . .

If our government's assessment of this program indicates that the United States must retain its dominant position in the aircraft manufacturing industry for national reasons, then it is my opinion that the development cost risks must be assumed by the government. Finally, if our country must make a choice between appropriations for improvements of our airways-airport systems or furthering the development of the SST, then there is no question that airways-airports must be the choice.

In summation, the provision of completely adequate airways and airports in this country must take precedence over any other consideration if the vigor of our economy is to be maintained. If there are funds available after the above need is satisfied, then these funds should go toward the orderly development of an SST at whatever rate of progress is possible.

I hope that the above may be helpful to Secretary Volpe in arriving at a sound decision on the future of the program.

AIRLINE 2

It is obvious that there are still some serious problems in the areas of community noise and economics. It also appears certain that the operation of the SST will be restricted to subsonic speeds over inhabited areas because of sonic boom. This will limit utilization and place an arbitrary ceiling on the total market for supersonic aircraft, increasing the unit cost.

AIRLINE 3

The 5-abreast 234 passenger prototype airplane design currently proposed by Boeing and validated by the FAA is not an airplane that embraces sufficient weight or space payload to be economically viable at other than substantially increased fare levels over those which we know today. The unknown changes in our economy between now and the planned availability of a production SST in 1978 or 1979 make the economic factors in this regard even more difficult to assess.

AIRLINE 4

We continue to be concerned about many of the technical aspects of the program, including weight and balance, flutter and dynamics, engine inlet design, and airport and community noise. Experience has indicated that solutions to problems of this type invariably add complexity and weight to an aircraft. Since the design payload-range characteristics already appear marginal, we question whether an economically viable airplane can be produced until these solutions are accurately defined.

AIRLINE 5

Present indications are that the SST program will not produce a vehicle as economically viable for airline use as formerly was believed to be the case. Nevertheless, in view of the efforts of other nations in the SST field . . . we remain convinced that national interest considerations, relating to the balance of payments and the competitive position of our aeronautics manufacturing industry, would be served by development and production of U.S. SSTs at an early date.[26]

[26] *Congressional Record,* October 31, 1969, H10444–45.

The differences between Chairman Beggs's draft summary report and those of the individual members were so strong that a meeting of the full committee was called and, when reconciliation proved impossible, it was decided that the entire record of the proceedings should be sent to the president for his consideration.

Despite the highly critical and unfavorable findings of his own committee, on September 23, 1969, President Nixon announced that he would ask Congress for a $96 million appropriation for the fiscal year ending June 30, 1970, for the "start of construction of two prototype SST aircraft." [27] Mr. Nixon said the decision was "based on need to keep the U.S. as world leader in air transport and to shorten flying times" [28] between the United States and the rest of the world. "Transportation Secretary and other department officials said *the SST won't be permitted to fly over the U.S. mainland because of the sonic booms.*" [29] (Emphasis added.) There were also indications that the project would be removed from FAA jurisdiction and be placed directly under Secretary Volpe. The government, which had already spent $600 million, estimated that its cost burden for the development phase would be $1.29 billion out of a total estimate of $1.51 billion, the remainder to come from the manufacturers and the airlines. It might be noted here that in 1963 when the SST project was launched President Kennedy said: "In no event will the government investment be permitted to exceed $750 million." [30]

On November 13, 1969, the House Appropriations Committee approved the Nixon administration request for $96 million funding for the SST program in the fiscal year 1970. A motion by Congressman Yates (D-Ill.) to delete the SST appropriation from the Transport Department budget was defeated by twenty-six to thirteen votes.[31]

During the debate on the House floor it further appeared that the Department of Transportation (DOT) had tried to keep from Congress the highly unfavorable views of Lt. Gen. Elmwood L. Quesada, the former head of FAA (1958–61) and currently a director of American Airlines. Congressman Henry S. Reuss (D-Wis.) reported to the House that he had tried to obtain a copy of General Quesada's testimony from DOT before the SST Ad Hoc Review Committee in March 1969. According to Reuss, "DOT at first told me that no transcript of the General's testimony even existed, but finally, after repeated requests, they were able to produce one

[27] "SST Faces Hard Fight in Congress but Chances of Funding Seem Good," *The Wall Street Journal,* September 24, 1969, p. 3.

[28] *Ibid.*

[29] *Ibid.*

[30] *Congressional Record,* July 9, 1963, pp. 12283–84.

[31] "House Panel Approves $96 Million SST Sum for This Fiscal Year," *The Wall Street Journal,* November 14, 1969, p. 21.

copy. It had been found in a safe in the office of the Under Secretary of Transportation." [32]

In his testimony, General Quesada stated that the SST program as originally conceived was never intended to develop an entirely new technology but to adapt commercially the know-how that was being developed for the B-70 program. As it turned out, the B-70 program was later canceled, thus bringing about a significant change in the circumstances which must cause us to reevaluate the program priorities for the SST.

It was never anticipated that the Federal Government would be the major sponsor of a supersonic transport. It was anticipated that a major sponsor of the supersonic transport would be economic demand and when economically feasible a supersonic transport program would proceed, hopefully helped by the government.[33]

(We might recall here that Boeing 707 was more than two years behind British turboprop Electra in coming into the market. Electra was a combination prop-jet while Boeing was a pure jet. Despite its delay in entering the market, Boeing was successful in capturing the world markets for its plane because of a superior product and lower operating costs.)

In terms of world competition, Quesada stated that our competition with the Anglo-French Concorde or the Russian TU-144 must be on the basis of the product quality and economic feasibility alone. Finally, he urged a more judicious use of the country's scarce economic resources while continuing the SST program on a more orderly basis:

There are limited funds that this country or any other country has; and they seem to be more limited all the time. And I would urge those of you who are struggling with this problem to bear in mind, as I am sure you do, that there are many other sources of demand that are reasonable and justified and this can very well be pitted against them, hopefully not eliminated. It would be a great tragedy if this program were ever eliminated.[34]

Boeing's Representation to the Ad Hoc Committee

The Boeing Company also submitted its views [35] to the Ad Hoc Committee, supporting the continuation of the SST program, the government

[32] *Congressional Record,* November 17, 1969, H10947.
[33] *Ibid.,* H10948.
[34] *Ibid.,* H10948.
[35] *The SST Program and Related National Benefits* [*The Boeing Report*], Boeing Company, Seattle, Washington, February 12, 1969.

participation in it, and has since then continuously defended its position in the news media and before various public and private bodies. A summary of Boeing's position follows:

1. Traffic forecasts by various independent analysts indicate that revenue passenger miles in the free world will increase at least sixfold between 1968 and 1990, and $125 billion of new aircraft will be needed to carry this traffic.

2. Supersonic transports will constitute a significant part of this $125 billion market. A comprehensive analysis of operating costs, competing equipment, and appropriateness to various routes shows that even without flying over populated areas to avoid sonic boom effects, the SST market will total $25 billion by 1990.

3. SSTs will be built whether we like it or not. Because of our technical capacity, the United States is now in a position to obtain $20 billion of this $25 billion market through the sale of an estimated 500 SSTs, 270 of them to foreign airlines.

4. In terms of balance of payments, the SST program (aircraft account) would bring in an additional $11.9 billion between 1975 and 1990. Conversely, if a timely US/SST is not introduced, the negative effect on aircraft account in the balance of payments could reach $16 billion by 1990.

    To counteract the argument of balance-of-payments deficits in travel account, Boeing argued that "if so inclined, U.S. tourists will travel overseas in Concordes (or even TU-144s) to spend their money. Actually, the foreign tourist coming *to* the U.S. also spends money, and the number of foreign visitors coming to the U.S. has been increasing in recent years." [36]

5. On a direct business venture basis, the government will be paid royalties on the sale of production airplanes in an amount returning the original investment of ($1.2 billion) by approximately the three hundredth plane and producing in excess of investment by the five hundredth delivery. In addition, it will bring in an additional $5.4 billion to the federal government and $1.3 billion to various state and local governments through corporate and personal income taxes of program participants and secondary employment through the "multiplier" effect. [37]

6. The production phase will yield prospective employment of approximately five hundred thousand highly skilled, high-wage persons

---

[36] Communication to the author by the Boeing Company, November 12, 1969.

[37] *Development of a National Asset—The American SST,* Boeing Company, Seattle, Washington, October 1969, p. 9.

at peak production. It will also provide secondary employment of over one hundred thousand in trade and professions including substantial numbers in semiskilled and unskilled categories.

7. There are impressive technological effects of the program for the nation which alone could justify the development of the prototypes. The benefits will, furthermore, not be confined to the transport industry but will be spread in all phases of industry through the development of new materials, manufacturing techniques, and electronics equipment.

8. The program will relieve congestion both at the airports and in the air by providing speedier movement at higher altitudes not presently used and quicker turnaround.

The company argued against the need for additional expenditure for airport modifications because of SSTs by stating that the SST was designed for operations from existing international airports. No modifications to runways would be necessary. By the time it entered commercial service in 1978, airports and loading docks would have been developed to take care of the 747 and the other large capacity subsonic jets. The SST would use these same facilities.[38]

THE HOME STRETCH—DEFEAT OF THE SST PROGRAM

Since Congress appropriated $85 million for the SST for fiscal year 1970 (although the House Appropriations Committee initially approved a funding request for $96 million), there had been significant changes in the congressional attitude toward the SST.

In his budget request, President Nixon asked for $290 million for the SST for fiscal year 1971. The winds of change, however, were blowing strongly against the SST. Ecology had become a potent public issue and had considerably strengthened the hand of the SST's opponents in Congress. SST backers moved to eliminate one criticism constantly made by the opponents, namely, the dual role of the FAA. Consequently, the SST program was "transferred from the FAA to the office of the Secretary of Transportation. . . . This transfer will remove the direct responsibility for prototype development away from the administration which is directly responsible for the aircraft's certification, thus eliminating possible concern about FAA conflict of interest." [39]

President Nixon had personally backed the SST program strongly and

[38] Communication to the author by the Boeing Company, November 12, 1969.
[39] U.S., Congress, House, Committee on Appropriations, Department of Transportation and Related Agencies Appropriation Bill, 1971, p. 9.

had appointed William Magruder, a former test pilot for Lockheed, to head the program. At the same time, several opinion surveys showed that a majority of the public opposed the SST. It became an issue in the 1970 congressional campaigns, when many candidates pledged that if elected they would vote against the project.[40] Throughout 1970 Magruder campaigned for the project, visiting cities all over the country and implying the SST was so important to the nation's economy, future, and prestige abroad that it would be unpatriotic to vote against the project.

Despite the efforts of the pro-SST forces, the Senate, on December 1, 1970, voted 52 to 41 (the preceding year the opposition had numbered only twenty-two votes) to deny the administration's request for funding to continue development of two SST prototypes through June 30, 1971. This apparent about-face in the Senate (admittedly a pleasant surprise for anti-SST legislators) is not difficult to interpret; environmentalists had formed extremely strong lobbies against the SST.[41] On December 8, 1970, however, the House voted to appropriate the full amount. Because the Senate and the House were unable to agree on the SST funding, the bill had to go to the Joint Economic Committee. Of the seven senators on the committee, four were in favor of the SST and three opposed it. Senator Proxmire, the Senate leader of the opposition, reluctantly agreed to stop his filibuster—after the committee agreed to fund the project with $210 million—by extracting a commitment from the pro-SST forces that allowed for a vote solely on the SST in March in return for three months' additional funding for the SST during that time ($52.5 million). (Previously the filibuster had been holding up the entire Department of Transportation budget.)

But the fight for SST was far from over. Program director Magruder chided the aerospace industry and labor groups for not pushing hard for the program. Consequently, an industry-union group called the National Committee on an American SST launched a nationwide drive with a budget of $350,000. Its primary aim was to develop a grass-roots letter-writing move by citizens urging their congressmen to vote for the plane.[42]

The committee's industry cochairman was Donald J. Strait, a vice-president of Fairchild Hiller Corporation, which was a major Boeing subcontractor with $34.5 million in SST contracts. Floyd E. Smith, president of the AFL-CIO International Association of Machinists, was the committee's labor cochairman. Members of the group ranged from twenty-two big corporations, such as Boeing, other aerospace companies, and defense

[40] "Senate Votes to Cut Off Money for SST Project; Cancellation Clauses Will Soothe the Affected Firms," *The Wall Street Journal,* March 26, 1971, p. 3.

[41] *San Francisco Chronicle,* May 11, 1970, p. 41.

[42] "A New Drive for SST Support," *San Francisco Chronicle,* February 23, 1971, p. 10.

contractors, to thirty-one unions, including the Retail Clerks of America, which had little visible interest in the project. The major notable exception in the labor ranks was the United Auto Workers Union, which refused to go along.

The drive started with full-page ads in the three Washington, D.C., daily newspapers, primarily directed at Congress. These were followed by a massive advertising campaign in the nation's other newspapers (the ad appeared in *The New York Times* on March 8, 1971) and in labor publications.

All these efforts came to naught, however. The first blow came on March 18, 1971, when the House voted 215 to 204 to deny the SST further funding. The final death knell was sounded on March 25, 1971, when the Senate voted 51 to 46 against appropriating additional funds for the SST. After the Senate vote, Senator Henry Jackson (D-Wash.), a leader of the Senate's pro-SST forces, said, "The program is over— period. There's no legal authority to continue beyond March 30, midnight."

The program was supported by the airlines to the extent of $80.9 million. Of this amount, $22.4 million was on deposit for 122 SSTs.[43] Additionally, nine U.S. airlines and KLM Royal Dutch Airlines had put up $58.5 million in risk capital for SST development on a matching grant basis with the U.S. government.[44] The $22.4 million on deposit was refunded immediately. The remaining $58.5 million was returned in August 1971.[45]

EPILOGUE

Activities on many fronts have continued since the defeat of the U.S. SST effort by Congress. The desire of the Nixon administration to revive the SST program has continued unabated while the opposition, if not actually growing, is equally determined, with Senator Proxmire keeping a watchful eye to make sure that the administration does not hide money for the SST under some other program. A flurry of bills has been introduced in Congress to control aircraft engine noise. The Coalition Against the SST has opened a permanent office in Washington, and there are reports that thirty groups have formed an anti-SST lobby in Washington,

[43] "Hopes Fade for SST; Termination-Sparked Lay-Off Surge," *Aviation Week & Space Technology*, April 5, 1971, p. 30.
[44] "Chances Improve for SST Airline Refund," *Aviation Week & Space Technology*, July 19, 1971, p. 24.
[45] *The New York Times*, July 30, 1971, p. 6.

one of which is Friends of the Earth, a New York-based environmental group.[46] And, finally yielding to congressional and public pressure, the administration agreed to transfer the jurisdiction of aircraft noise standards from FAA to the newly created Environmental Protection Agency.[47]

Research on the various aspects of supersonic flight continues in the United States, however. The Department of Transportation has funded a $21 million Climatic Impact Assessment Program (CIAP) which began in May 1973. Under this program, Concorde will carry instruments to measure ozone density as part of the study. The National Academy of Sciences and the National Academy of Engineering will oversee the research analysis of the CIAP data. A series of monographs are to be completed and published by the summer of 1947.[48]

NASA and the U.S. Air Force are pooling their research and technology. NASA's Langley Research Center at Hampton, Virginia, is conducting an $11 million study on wing designs, fuselage shapes, air frame and engine metals, and a "variable cycle" engine related to supersonic transport. In April 1973, during appropriations hearings on NASA's $3 billion budget for fiscal year 1974, NASA's Administrator James C. Fletcher told the committee members that NASA was studying the economics, potential pollution of the stratosphere, and noise effects of supersonic transport. He said: "We are doing fundamental research into supersonics. We are not developing an SST. That is not our mission." Fletcher also said that supersonic transport is a "way of life." [49]

Meanwhile, the fortunes of the Anglo-French Concorde and the Russian TU–144 have not been booming. Due to constantly increasing costs, estimates of the Concorde sales price keep going up and now stand at $46.7 million (over $60 million with parts and ground equipment), up from $31.2 million in December 1971 and $45.0 million as late as December 1972.[50] This has coincided with one of the worst periods in the financial health of U.S. airlines, which reported heavy losses in 1971 and 1972, with Pan Am leading the list. The first blow came on January 31, 1973, when Pan Am, citing cost as the major factor, dropped its eight options for Concordes. This opened the floodgates and, in short order, other airlines followed by canceling their options on a total of twenty-five Concordes: TWA, American, and Eastern Airlines each canceled six, Continental and Japan each canceled three, Sabena canceled two, and El Al

[46] J. Samuel Butz, Jr., "The Inevitable SST," *World,* June 5, 1973, p. 34.
[47] *Aviation Week & Space Technology,* November 20, 1972, p. 63.
[48] "U.S. Study of SST Impact to be Aided by Concorde," *Aviation Week & Space Technology,* February 19, 1973, p. 15.
[49] Butz, "The Inevitable SST."
[50] "Concorde Price at $46.7 Million," *Aviation Week & Space Technology,* May 7, 1973, p. 34.

one.[51] As of July 1973 Concorde had firm orders for only nine airplanes (BOAC, five; and Air France, four), and options for another fourteen planes.

Regardless of the bleak sales future, the Concorde manufacturers are pushing ahead on their manufacturing plans and the flight-testing necessary for certification from various governments. Hoping to interest U.S. airlines, the Anglo-French combine announced, in May 1973, a redesigned body for the Concorde aimed at the low-fare, high-volume market. In June 1973 FAA announced that certification for the Concorde was about 85 percent complete and that it foresaw no problems in the plane's receiving U.S. certification.[52]

TU-144 is also making progress, with domestic commercial service scheduled in 1975. To date Aeroflot has ordered thirty planes, with eventual requirements estimated at between sixty and seventy-five.[53] Despite the crash of one TU-144 at the Paris Air Show on June 3, 1973, observers do not believe that the manufacturing or commercial operation plans will be delayed.[54]

It would be presumptuous to say that the opponents of the supersonic transport have succeeded in permanently blocking its development. Nor can it be said that all the opposition has been futile and purposeless. Perhaps the SST *is* the aircraft of the future. No one can say for sure. However, one thing is certain. The opposition has forced both industry and government to consider the environmental and socioeconomic aspects of introducing new technology into the lives of people after basing their decisions only on the narrow economic and technological considerations of the companies involved. If and when the SST comes, it is likely to be a better aircraft, and it will be introduced with the voluntary approval not only of its users but of the affected public.

---

[51] "Slowdown of Concorde Production Seen," *Aviation Week & Space Technology,* February 5, 1973, p. 30; "Three More Airlines Drop Concorde Options," *Aviation Week,* February 19, 1973, p. 19.

[52] "Concorde Certification About 85% Complete," *The Wall Street Journal,* June 18, 1973, p. 16.

[53] "Top Priority Speeds TU-144 Production," *Aviation Week & Space Technology,* June 25, 1973, p. 12.

[54] "TU-144 Crash and Concorde," *San Francisco Chronicle,* June 5, 1973, p. 5.

III
CORPORATE INTERESTS AND SOCIAL AND ECONOMIC NEEDS OF ETHNIC MINORITIES

A.

SOCIAL AND
ECONOMIC PRESSURES

Eastman Kodak Company (A), Rochester, New York

Conflict with a Minority Group—FIGHT

It is beneficial for businessmen to indulge in introspection and in the words of Robert Burns, "see ourselves as others see us." It seems ironically fitting that the line should be from Burns' poem "To a Louse," because that is precisely how some people do see businessmen . . .

—George R. Vila,
Chairman and President, Uniroyal Inc.

Eastman Kodak is the largest producer of photographic equipment and supplies in the world. In *Fortune's* list of five hundred corporations in 1972 Kodak ranks twenty-third, with yearly sales in excess of $3.47 billion. It has over 114,000 employees in all its plants and offices.

Kodak, headquartered in Rochester, New York, is that city's largest employer, its more than 44,000 employees being about 13 percent of the entire work force in the area. Kodak's influence on the Rochester com-

---

This case material has been adapted from S. Prakash Sethi, *Business Corporations and the Black Man* (Scranton, Pennsylvania: Chandler Publishing Company, 1970). Copyright © 1970 by Chandler Publishing Company. Used by permission.

279

munity is such that merchants schedule sales to coincide with Kodak bonus checks.[1]

In 1918 founder George Eastman started the Rochester Community Service (later the Community Chest).[2] He also founded the Eastman School of Music and made large grants to medicine and to the community theater.[3] The company enjoys a close relationship with Rochester University and other local organizations,[4] donates employee time to work in civic causes, and is considered both a good place to work and a good corporate citizen. "Evidence of the company's philanthropy is visible everywhere." In the decade of the sixties Kodak pumped nearly $22 million into the city's hospitals, schools, and Community Chest. The company sponsors a fellowship program for black teachers, and in 1964 alone it gave $1.5 million for aid to education.

Because it is nonunionized, Kodak is unusual. More than half the companies in Rochester (including General Motors, General Dynamics, and Xerox) are unionized. One Kodak executive says, ". . . the only explanation is that . . . the laws being what they are . . . people don't feel the need to be represented." The company says that "Kodak continually reviews its employment policies to assure that they do not present any barriers to the employment of anyone because of race, creed, color, sex, or age. Pre-employment testing is limited to a few jobs which require specific skills or aptitudes." [5]

The company has long had a skilled trades apprentice program which, according to one Kodak brochure, consists of up to four years of "combined classroom and on-the-job training leading to a skilled craftsman career as an electrician, instrument mechanic, machinist, pipe fitter, sheet metal worker, or tool or instrument maker. A high school diploma or equivalent and demonstrated mechanical ability are required." [6]

Kodak was one of the first one hundred companies to join President Kennedy's Committee of Equal Employment Opportunity "Plans for Progress Program," in June 1962.[7] Its brochure "How Kodak People Are Selected" says, "For any particular job, the person is chosen who appears best fitted to do that job. . . . Such things as race, creed, color or national origin neither help nor hinder in getting a job at Kodak."

[1] Jules Loh, Associated Press for Sunday A.M. papers, April 23, 1967.

[2] "There's a FIGHT in Kodak's Future," *Factory*, June 1967, p. 69.

[3] "Meeting of Minds," *Forbes*, October 1, 1965, pp. 37–38.

[4] *Ibid.;* also see *Yearbook of American Churches* (New York: National Council of Churches of Christ in the U.S.A., 1965).

[5] "Equal Employment Opportunity. Eastman Kodak Company's Positive Program" (Rochester, New York: Public Relations Department, Eastman Kodak Company, 1967).

[6] *Ibid.*

[7] *Ibid.*

Kodak has been making efforts to ensure that blacks are aware of opportunities at Kodak. In recruiting nonprofessionals, the company uses a number of community agencies, such as the Human Relations Commission, the New York State Employment Service, the Urban League, Rochester's five settlement houses, high school counselors (with emphasis on inner-city schools), and adult education program administrators. In 1966 Kodak, which contributes to the Negro College Fund, expanded the range of its recruitment of professionals to include thirteen predominantly black colleges. During that year the company was involved with career centers in a program to help place college-trained Negroes.

A former Eastman Kodak board chairman stated in a letter of April 25, 1966:

You will recognize that our efforts to provide equal employment opportunities are increasingly more positive and far-reaching than in past years. Previously our policy had been simply to try to employ the person best fitted to do the work available without regard for his or her background. We have moved actively beyond that position. We now seek to help the individual who lacks the necessary qualifications *to become qualified*. In other words, we are contributing to the training of the individual so that he or she can qualify for employment.

However, Kodak's sense of social responsibility, though contributing to the betterment of community life, resembles that of the benevolent Puritan father who, while making sure of his children's welfare, does not hesitate to discipline them should they fail to measure up to his standards and values. By keeping its employees happy with generous bonuses, good working conditions, and other benefits, the company has remained free of unions and has carefully guarded the established prerogatives of management.

The benevolent father image is very strong in Rochester and has been fostered so assiduously and for such a long time that to some extent both the community and the company have become its captives. As William C. Martin puts it: "It is inaccurate to think of Rochester as a company town but he who underestimates the devotion Rochesterians feel toward Eastman Kodak does so at his own peril. . . ." [8]

ROCHESTER

According to the 1970 United States census, Rochester is the forty-ninth largest city in the country. *The World Almanac* says that New York's third

[8] William C. Martin, "Shepherds vs. Flocks, Ministers vs. Negro Militancy," *Atlantic*, December 1967, pp. 53–59.

largest city is a "world leader in the manufacture of precision goods and a major eastern U.S. cultural center. Located on Lake Ontario, it leads the world in the manufacture of photographic film and cameras, optical goods, dental equipment, and thermometers." [9] Rochester's largest employers are Eastman Kodak (41,757), Xerox Corporation (13,000), and Bausch and Lomb (5,300).

In a public relations ad in *The New York Times* Rochester said of itself that it was "a community of [metropolitan area] more than 700,000 people with the highest percentage of skilled, technical and professional employees of any major U.S. metropolitan area: more engineers than any one of 23 states: the highest median family income of any city in the state, sixth highest in the nation . . . 67 percent of the residents owning their own houses. For the Negro, it would seem that things never looked better. Employment of whites in the county had increased by 11 percent since 1960 but employment of nonwhites had gone up 43 percent—more than four times the national average." [10] The city housed some of the most enlightened corporations in the nation, with enviable records in labor relations and social welfare policies.

Rochester, in 1966, was suffering from all the malaise of a city in the doldrums. The vigor of its industry, high income, and employment for the majority of its work force were matched by the recurrent and persistent problems of its poor, whose lives were not being improved by the city's antipoverty and civil rights programs. Significantly, public housing units numbered 450, with only 1,400 more in the planning stage. One school board member stated that school segregation was "more severe than ever." [11] A few organizations, such as the NAACP and the Urban League, spoke for the poor and underemployed, but according to a *New Republic* article "the other civil rights organizations don't amount to much. An NAACP rally last year [1966] drew eight people." [12]

Reporting for *The New York Times* on June 20, 1966, John Kifner quoted the Reverend Herbert D. White, a young clergyman who headed the Rochester Area Council of Churches Board of Urban Ministry, on the state of the city:

This is a city with five settlement houses, whose Community Chest Drive always goes over the top, and which prides itself on having every available service. And it's a city which has gone on line—

[9] *The World Almanac, 1970* (Cleveland, Ohio: Newspaper Enterprise Association, Inc., 1970).

[10] Barbara Carter, "The Fight against Kodak," *The Reporter,* January 21, 1967, pp. 28–31.

[11] *Ibid.*

[12] James Ridgeway, "Attack on Kodak," *New Republic,* January 21, 1967, pp. 11–13.

against a lot of opposition—to have an open enrollment plan in the school and a police review board. But one thing that is crucial here is the high degree of affluence in this community. If you are poor in this town, you really know you are poor.[13]

Affluence was everywhere—for the whites. For blacks it was a mirage, unreal, unattainable. In April 1965 there were no blacks on the city council, none on the board of education or the planning commission. In the fire department 2 of 604 were blacks and on the police force 25 of 515.[14]

BIRTH AND GROWTH OF FIGHT

Rochester's race riots (July 23–26, 1964) had made it evident that something must be done to avoid a recurrence. Most citizens of Rochester were embarrassed and shocked that this could happen in "their" city. They believed that Rochester had adequate welfare programs, far superior to those of most other cities. Most leaders were against any radically different or innovative measures, believing that the 1964 riots could not happen again.

The majority of the local clergy felt differently. They felt it necessary to inspire in the black a feeling that he had some control over his own destiny, and they believed that this could best be achieved through a viable local organization.

The Rochester Ministers' Conference (RMC), an association of black church leaders, sought assistance from Dr. Martin Luther King's Southern Christian Leadership Conference.

As the standard "King" approach did not spark much fervor among the black community, the SCL team suggested that Saul Alinsky might be able to help.

The RMC obtained help from the interdenominational Board for Urban Ministry, which was affiliated with the Rochester Area Council of Churches. The board believed that the crux of the black problems was the "lack of a potent organization to raise his hopes and needs." [15] They felt that Alinsky could channel black hatred toward whites into constructive action through an organization similar to those he had started in other cities. The Board for Urban Ministry, with help from the Council of Churches, raised $100,000 for a two-year contract ($90,000 for expenses

---

[13] John Kifner, "Negro Federation Points to Advances in Its First Year in Rochester," *The New York Times,* June 20, 1966, p. 26.

[14] James Ridgeway, "Saul Alinsky in Smugtown," *New Republic,* June 26, 1965, pp. 15–17.

[15] Loh, Associated Press.

and $10,000 for salaries). The necessary funds flowed in from local and national church bodies and from many white liberals.

Alinsky's fame was based on his Woodlawn Organization which began in the Chicago slums in 1960. Alinsky later expanded his activities to Detroit and Kansas City. Alinsky's *modus operandi* was to seek out "natural leaders" and aid them in forming a "people's organization" whose goal was "self-determination." Alinsky's methods might polarize a community, nevertheless they were defended as being the only hope for ethnic minority poor. Alinsky believed that "people do not get opportunity or freedom or equality or dignity as a gift. . . . They only get these things in the act of taking them through their own efforts. . . . The haves never do anything unless forced."

In April 1965 FIGHT (Freedom-Integration-God-Honor-Today) was formed, allying 134 black organizations. The press warned that Alinsky's methods would result in future riots. Alinsky made an analogy between Rochester and a Southern plantation in his reply.

On June 11, 1965, the first FIGHT convention was held. The 1,000 delegates adopted a constitution, set policy goals, and elected a minister, Franklin Delano Roosevelt Florence, as temporary chairman.

Shortly after Alinsky arrived, local businessmen raised $40,000 to open an office of the moderate Urban League. In the past, funds for such an office had been unavailable. The manager of the Community Chest, threatening to withhold previously committed funds from a settlement house that had tried to join FIGHT, stated: "Chest funds could not be used to support FIGHT . . . in fulfillment of promises made to contributors." Florence accused the Community Chest of discrimination.

The *New Republic* quoted Florence as saying: "The establishment feels it can plan for us and not with us. . . . The only thing the white paternalists want to know about Negroes is whether they will riot again this year. And that all depends," he added, "on how soon the whites learn black men are human beings. They are not their simple children." [16]

In the beginning, Florence's leadership and indeed FIGHT's very survival were in jeopardy. Opposition was not only from the "white establishment" but from the "black community" as well, largely from middle-class blacks who felt that FIGHT's leadership was too militant. During its first eighteen months, FIGHT concentrated on federal antipoverty programs and urban renewal. It succeeded in getting the city to increase the number of planned low-cost housing units and also gained control of the urban renewal Citizens Committee. FIGHT obtained a $65,746 federal antipoverty grant for an adult education program and three seats on Roches-

[16] Ridgeway, "Saul Alinsky in Smugtown."

ter's antipoverty board. FIGHT's picketing of landlords was successful in getting slum apartment buildings fixed up.

FIGHT organized a recruitment and training program with Xerox, starting with sixteen trainees and expanding to thirty the number of jobs for hard-core unemployed workers in 1967.

FIGHT claimed to represent three-quarters of Rochester's black community through its component Negro organizations—churches, settlement houses, and Black Panther clubs. Many disputed this claim. FIGHT accepted few whites, but a "Friends of FIGHT" was formed to give whites a chance to lend support. Before December 20, 1966, FIGHT's active membership was small, but it eventually increased to about three hundred. According to an Associated Press feature story, directors of a settlement house that belonged to FIGHT said that the organization represented less than one percent of the black community. Florence denied this but offered no hard membership statistics.

In its June 1966 convention, FIGHT resolved that "Eastman Kodak be singled out for special investigation this year." According to Alinsky, "Rochester . . is under the thumb of Eastman Kodak, which also controls the banks, local university, hospitals, etc. The effect of its rule is to shut Negroes away from the rest of the community."

THE CONFRONTATION

Florence's first meeting with Kodak Board Chairman Albert Chapman, President William Vaughn, and Executive Vice-President Louis Eilers, which took place on September 2, 1966, was deceptively harmonious. Florence talked about the problems of the ghetto blacks. He demanded that Kodak implement a new training program to recruit and train blacks who could not meet regular recruitment standards. Vaughn stated that Kodak had such a program and suggested that they talk further on the proposal.

In preparation for the second meeting on September 14, 1966, Alinsky put FIGHT's proposal in writing. At the meeting, Florence read from a written statement that was distributed to everyone present. He admitted that Kodak's special preemployment training programs were a start but that the number of persons had to be increased to between five hundred and six hundred over an eighteen-month period so that they could qualify for entry level positions across the board. Florence further stated that FIGHT, as the only true representative of the unemployed in the Rochester area, should be solely responsible for recruiting and counseling the trainees. Vaughn's reply, also in writing, neither accepted nor rejected

FIGHT's demands. Vaughn described the existing programs for the un-qualified and spoke of plans to expand them:

> The company hopes to benefit from suggestions which FIGHT may offer, as it has in the past been helped by the advice of a number of organizations on these matters. FIGHT and other interested organizations are invited to refer possible applicants for all these programs.

Vaughn noted that the FIGHT proposal and Kodak plans had much in common and that the company would be interested in meeting again to discuss ways in which "FIGHT might cooperate in the implementation of Kodak's plans."

Kodak seemed in no way to want to end the talks. It was obvious that Kodak had stiffened its resistance to the FIGHT proposal by repeatedly stating "its intention to retain control of all hiring. At the same time, it urged FIGHT to refer people to existing programs designed for the under-skilled." [17] FIGHT rejected Vaughn's proposal to work within the existing Kodak framework for assisting hard-core unemployed. Vaughn refused to bind the company to hiring a specific number of people, pointing out that "jobs aren't something you turn out on a machine." [18] Among the reasons given by Kodak for not accepting FIGHT's demands were:

1. Kodak could not enter an exclusive arrangement with any organization to recruit candidates for employment and still be fair to the more than sixty thousand people who apply each year.
2. Kodak could not agree to a program that would commit it to hire and train a specific and substantial number of people in a period that would extend so far into the future.[19]

Florence and Vaughn agreed to meet the following day, but further talk was doomed. The unreconcilable difference was whether FIGHT could *demand* anything by right and whether Kodak could concede FIGHT's demands without abrogating its own rights and obligations. At future meetings, Kodak's leading representative was a second-echelon executive, Kenneth Howard of the Industrial Relations Department.

At one of the meetings, while Howard was explaining Kodak's training program, Florence repeatedly interrupted, asking, "Are we talking about

[17] Martin, "Shepherds vs. Flocks, Ministers vs. Negro Militancy."
[18] "The Fight That Swirls around Eastman Kodak," *Business Week*, April 29, 1967, pp. 38–41.
[19] "And Kodak Will Ask, 'How High?'" *Fortune*, June 1, 1967, p. 78.

FIGHT's proposal?" [20] Howard unequivocally expressed Kodak's view that the subject was the ways in which FIGHT might cooperate in Kodak's expanded recruitment and training plans. Florence made it clear that he was "not interested in Kodak's plans." He insisted that the discussion be limited to the FIGHT proposal. Howard restated Vaughn's reasons; nothing was accomplished.

The fourth meeting was held September 19. Howard called upon Florence in FIGHT's headquarters. Florence declared that he would deal with no one lower in rank than President Vaughn. Howard then presented a letter from Vaughn to Florence restating Kodak's position and informing him that if FIGHT were willing to cooperate, further discussion could be held, otherwise Kodak would proceed without FIGHT.

Between September 22 and October 22 two letters were exchanged. In one letter Florence stated:

> Use of terms like "exclusively," "monopolistic," "arbitrary demands," etc., in reference to the FIGHT proposal does an injustice to the careful thought and consideration that has gone into our suggestions. We have not even had opportunity to discuss the details of our approach with Eastman Kodak.[21]

Vaughn replied that:

> Meanwhile, you and other members of FIGHT might be interested in knowing that while these discussions and subsequent correspondence have been going on the Kodak company has continued to employ a substantial number of people in this community, including many Negroes.[22]

Negotiations broke down completely.

On October 22 Kodak announced that it had made arrangements with the Board of Fundamental Education (BFE), a professional adult education concern, for help in expanding Kodak's training programs. One hundred people would be enrolled. FIGHT was enraged and declared the "deal" to be a fraud perpetrated on the poor. Florence then led a forty-five–man group to Kodak's office to seek "clarifications" of the program. On his arrival, he found that all the trainees had already been selected.[23] "It's a

---

[20] *Business Week,* April 29, 1967.
[21] Letter to William L. Vaughn, president of Eastman Kodak, from Minister Franklin D. R. Florence, president of FIGHT, October 7, 1966.
[22] Letter to Mr. Florence from William L. Vaughn, October 21, 1966.
[23] Carter, "The Fight against Kodak."

fraud—It's a trick," Florence immediately declared. And he went on the radio to say: "We can't understand, for our lives, how a company with their creative ability can . . . take pictures of the hidden side of the moon . . . but can't create Instamatic jobs." Saul Alinsky, who was with Florence on the program, said: "I can tell you this. Eastman Kodak has plenty to be concerned about, because this kind of an issue . . . if it ever develops . . . and it may well develop . . . will become a nationwide issue across the board to every Negro ghetto in America." [24]

FIGHT retaliated with an intensive campaign in the news media abusing Kodak and threatening dire consequences for the peace of the city and other ghettos all over America.[25] Alinsky bitterly accused Kodak of playing "an out-and-out public relations con game with FIGHT" and considered the hiring of BFE (rather than the acceptance of FIGHT's programs) a "backdoor deal." [26]

To the management of Kodak, it was inconceivable that their organization, with its enviable record of good corporate citizenship and assistance to minority groups, should be accused by a militant group backed by local churches and other community organizations of not helping the cause of the Negro. Kodak's incredulity was reinforced by growing evidence that the company was not holding its own in the contest. In the public forum, FIGHT repeatedly outmaneuvered and outclassed Kodak.

The human element played its role, too. Florence—described in an AP story [27] as stocky, bullnecked, with a dry voice and unpolished manners—used communications media with dramatic effect on every possible occasion. He held press conferences after every meeting with company officials, sometimes in the lobby of Kodak's headquarters building. Vaughn, on the other hand, a quiet and somewhat aloof man who found Florence's manner "intimidating—a lot of finger-pointing and all that," [28] maintained a cool, dignified posture. Some Kodak employees attempted to help break the impasse between Kodak and FIGHT. In early December, for example, John Mulder, a Kodak assistant vice-president, met for lunch with his friend the Reverend Marvin Chandler, a member of FIGHT, and considered ways in which discussions might be resumed. Mulder had been active in civil rights causes, and his wife was a member of the Friends of FIGHT.[29] He felt that men directly responsible for hiring and training might be the most appropriate company representatives in future discussions with FIGHT.[30] He submitted this idea to Vaughn, who agreed, and on December 16, 1966, he appointed Mulder to head a new Kodak team.

[24] *Ibid.*
[25] *Ibid.*
[26] *Rochester Times-Union*, October 24, 1966.
[27] Loh, Associated Press.
[28] *Business Week*, April 29, 1967.
[29] Loh, Associated Press.
[30] Ridgeway, "Attack on Kodak."

KODAK'S ABORTIVE AGREEMENT AND ITS REPERCUSSIONS

On December 19 and 20, Mulder and other Kodak representatives met secretly with FIGHT spokesmen. Mulder had expected to meet with Chandler to pursue further their earlier luncheon discussion. Instead, although Chandler was present, Florence took charge.

At 2:00 P.M., December 20, the two parties signed the following agreement:

> A special committee appointed by Eastman Kodak president, William Vaughn, has been meeting Monday and Tuesday with officers of the FIGHT organization.
>
> Kodak representatives stated that they have not employed traditional standards of hiring for the last two years. FIGHT hailed this as a step in the right direction as well as Kodak officers' statement that they will deal with the problem of hard-core unemployed.
>
> Job openings, specifications, and hourly rates were discussed and agreed upon by the joint group.
>
> January 15th was agreed upon as the date for a beginning of the referral of 600 employees, the bulk of which would be hard-core unemployed (unattached, uninvolved with traditional institutions).
>
> Under the agreement, the FIGHT organization and Kodak agreed to an objective of the recruitment and referral (to include screening and selection) of 600 unemployed people over a 24-month period, barring unforeseen economic changes affecting the Rochester community. FIGHT, at its own expense, would provide counseling for the employees selected by Kodak.
>
> Kodak agrees to the following: join with FIGHT in a firm agreement to

A. Continue semi-monthly meetings between Kodak and FIGHT to increase the effectiveness of the program.

B. Kodak will familiarize FIGHT counselors with the foremen and work skills required, and in turn FIGHT will familiarize Kodak foremen with the life and environment of poor people.

C. Kodak and FIGHT will share information on the referrals.

D. Kodak and FIGHT will issue a 60-day community progress report.

> JOHN MULDER
> Asst. Vice President,
> Eastman Kodak
> Asst. General Manager,
> Kodak Park Works
> FRANKLYN D. R. FLORENCE
> President of FIGHT

Florence was extremely pleased and repeatedly asked Mulder if he was authorized to sign for Kodak. Upon Mulder's confirmation, FIGHT made a radio announcement of the agreement.

The nature of the content and timing of the agreement were most unusual and were indicative of Kodak's inexperienced negotiating personnel and their general handling of the situation. As Barbara Carter pointed out:

It was a strange agreement at best. One of the six paragraphs mentioned the "referral of six hundred unemployed people," another the referral of "six hundred employees," a distinction of some importance. For a non-union company, the briefest paragraph was by far the oddest. It said simply, "Job openings, specifications, and hourly rates were discussed and agreed upon by the joint group." Moreover, semimonthly meetings on the program's "effectiveness" were also agreed on.

On December 21, 1966, Kodak's Executive Committee met and voted unanimously to repudiate the agreement. The following day the board of directors met and concurred with the Executive Committee's decision. In a statement issued by the company the Executive Committee stated that "for all its ambiguities [the December 20 document] violated antidiscrimination laws." [31] The committee stated that Mulder had not had the authority to bind the company. The company apologized profusely for the mix-up but flatly repudiated the whole arrangement.[32] There was no record of any written instructions from Vaughn to Mulder about the extent of the latter's authority in conducting the negotiations. Mulder, after the incident, did not talk to the press or anyone else and his side of the story remained a mystery.

William S. Vaughn, newly elected chairman of the board, said that Kodak had

two fundamental and critical objections to the FIGHT proposal: (1) We could not enter into an arrangement exclusively with any organization to recruit candidates for employment and still be fair to the more than 60,000 people who apply each year. . . . (2) We could not agree to a program which would commit Kodak to hire and train a specific and substantial number of people in a period which would extend so far into the future. Obviously, our employment needs depend on the kinds of jobs available at a particular time, and on the demand for our products.[33]

[31] Loh, Associated Press.
[32] "Fight at Kodak," *Newsweek*, May 8, 1967, pp. 81, 83.
[33] *Fortune*, June 1, 1967.

According to an Associated Press release describing the events directly following December 20, 1966, "another aspect of the agreement plainly horrified at least one high Kodak executive, who detected the faint odor of a 'labor contract.' " [34]

The community reaction ranged from incredulity to anger. The involvement of a large corporation and the controversial Alinsky resulted in national attention to what Kodak believed was a local issue.

Kodak took double-page advertisements in both morning and afternoon papers and said that it "sincerely regrets any misunderstanding." The ads repeated the company's earlier position that it could not have "an exclusive recruitment" with any group nor could it commit itself to any specific number of jobs "owing to the uncertainties of economic conditions." Furthermore, the ads gave the company's oft-stated position on social responsibility—Kodak was "deeply concerned to do all that we reasonably can to meet a pressing social need in this community, namely, to try and develop employment opportunities" and "many positive steps" had already been taken by the management.[35]

Although neither FIGHT nor Kodak made it public at this time, it seems that immediately following the repudiation of the agreement by Kodak, and after Kenneth Howard was back in control as Kodak's chief negotiator, FIGHT desperately tried to patch things up and salvage the agreement almost on *any terms acceptable to Kodak but was rebuffed by company officials.* Earl C. Gottschalk, Jr., writing in *The Wall Street Journal* on June 30, 1967, gave the following account of Kodak's attitude:

> On December 23, a delegation headed by Mr. Chandler met with the executive committee. According to Mr. Chandler's account of the meeting—which Kodak agrees is accurate—FIGHT asked Louis D. Eilers, president of Kodak to sign the agreement. He declined, saying the company simply could not give a second party any voice in determining its labor relations and employment practices. Then, says Mr. Chandler, "We asked them to put into the agreement anything they wanted to, or to change it in any way they desired. Again, Mr. Eilers said no."
>
> "At that point," says Mr. Chandler, "Mr. Florence even suggested that the entire document could be dispensed with if he and either Mr. Eilers or Mr. Vaughn could go on television and make a joint statement saying simply that FIGHT and Kodak would work together to get more jobs for ghetto Negroes. This idea met with no enthusiasm either." [36]

---

[34] Loh, Associated Press.

[35] "Sheen Appoints a Vicar for Poor," *The New York Times,* January 4, 1967, p. 4.

[36] Earl C. Gottschalk, Jr., "Kodak's Ordeal," *The Wall Street Journal,* June 30, 1967, pp. 1, 14.

The issue of whether Kodak should accept FIGHT demands merged, in some people's minds, with the personality of Ken Howard. Howard said that he didn't know how widespread this feeling was. "I am aware of some of it, but most of the people who are mad at me do not talk to me about it. It has been the same here since I got this assignment. People who do not agree with you do not talk with you about it because essentially you are following the management policy and position in this area."

It would be erroneous to assume that Howard had something to do with the repudiation or that he was a better negotiator than Mulder. It would be more accurate to say that Howard's views of the situation and what Kodak ought to do were more congruent with those of the top management than Mulder's. Howard may have been wrong for the situation but he was right for the management. Being a second-echelon official he was simply presenting the management's views as well as he could. The fact that he happened to agree with the position only made him more suitable for the job.

Kodak did not visualize the effect of its repudiation on the nation. For a company of its size and resources it is hard to see how it could have been so wide of the mark in taking the pulse of the social system. While the company was handling the problem as a local issue, the controversy received national attention largely because of the efforts of FIGHT and its supporters, the National Council of Churches, the Catholic Church, and the very fact that it involved a large United States corporation. To an outsider it seemed like a fight between David and Goliath. According to Edward L. Bernays, a well-known public relations counsel and author:

> [It] fell like a bombshell into the pro-civil rights milieu of contemporary America. A company dependent on good will went against all the current social mores and folkways. It was a colossal public relations blunder that will go down in history.[37]

Alinsky caustically suggested, "Maybe their executives ought to enroll in the Head Start Program and learn to read." He charged Kodak with "playing into the hands of those who say you can't trust the white man. I don't know how much [strife] Kodak will be responsible for this summer."

Both Kodak and FIGHT held news conferences in which angry words were exchanged. In his news conference on January 6, 1967, Kodak's new president, Dr. Louis D. Eilers, charged that FIGHT's "talk about employment" was "being used as a screen" for "making a power drive in this community."[38] As reported by *The New York Times,* Dr. Eilers stated that

---

[37] *Ibid.,* p. 14.

[38] John Kifner, "Critics Assailed by Head of Kodak: He Accuses Negro Group of Power Drive Upstate," *The New York Times,* January 7, 1967, p. 25.

"since the Alinsky forces were brought to Rochester, FIGHT has run a continuing war against numerous institutions that help build Rochester— the school system, the Community Chest, the city government, and even organizations especially set up to help solve minority group problems." Dr. Eilers's statement characterized FIGHT's demands as "arbitrary and unreasonable," and he asked if the group's "goal was really to get jobs for those who need them. . . . To the best of our knowledge, FIGHT has not sent anyone to us to apply for work." Concerning Mr. Mulder, Dr. Eilers said, "We all expressed the greatest of displeasure at the signing," but added that he "didn't envision any change in Mr. Mulder's job."

In a news conference held later in his storefront office, Minister Florence (he insisted on being addressed as "Minister," rather than "Reverend") said that Dr. Eilers's statement was that "of an hysterical and insecure man." He said that his group was trying to get Negroes into the "[melting] pot at Kodak." As to Eilers's statement that no one had applied for jobs through FIGHT, Florence flourished what he said were duplicates of the applications of forty-five people.

Eilers and Florence met twice, but on the third meeting Eilers was not present and Kodak's representatives were members of the Industrial Relations Department. Florence left in a huff saying, "We thought we were going to meet with Dr. Eilers, and they sent in a group of janitors." [39]

In January Saul Alinsky began a campaign to round up national support for FIGHT. On January 3 representatives of the National Council of Churches Commission on Religion and Race, the Board of National Missions of the United Presbyterian Church, and the Board for Homeland Ministries of the Church of Christ visited Rochester and expressed their support of FIGHT in the Kodak dispute.[40] On January 10 the Citizens Crusade Against Poverty, a private group working with funds of the United Auto Workers Union, convened a closed meeting where it was decided to support FIGHT. At the meeting were delegates from the National Association for the Advancement of Colored People, the National Council of Churches, the Protestant Episcopal Diocese of New York, and the United Presbyterian Church.[41]

Hoping to make peace, the Area Council of Churches took a full-page ad urging FIGHT to endorse Kodak's training programs and Kodak to endorse FIGHT's proposal. A few days later the president of the council, a Kodak employee, and two directors, one also a Kodak employee, resigned from the council in protest against the ad, which they felt favored FIGHT. FIGHT became more "hardnosed":

[39] "Kodak Job Plan Rejected," *The New York Times,* January 11, 1967, p. 19.
[40] *The New York Times,* January 4, 1967, p. 4.
[41] *The New York Times,* January 11, 1967, p. 19.

"We're not interested in white hope," Florence told a FIGHT meeting. "FIGHT asks Kodak where is the black hope for the under-privileged and unemployed in Rochester."

"Tell it, Brother," yelled the crowd. "Sock it to 'em."

"They talk about America being a melting pot," said Florence, "but the question right now is not whether black can melt, but whether they can even get into the pot. That's what FIGHT has been trying to do—get some of them into the pot at Kodak." [42]

As a result of its abrogation of the December 20 agreement, Kodak's corporate image was extremely tarnished. As a letter to the editor illus-trates: "It is inconceivable that a man of Mr. Mulder's position could so misunderstand what he was or was not authorized to do." [43] Despite Kodak's insistence that it had not intended Mulder to initiate a new policy, *Business Week* quoted Vaughn as saying that Chandler and Mulder's de-cision to resume talks between FIGHT and Kodak "gave us some hope that there was a new deal here." [44]

On January 19 television reporters followed Black Power leader Stokely Carmichael into town. That night the leader of the Student Nonviolent Coordinating Committee told a FIGHT rally (approximate attendance, two hundred) of plans for a national boycott of Eastman Kodak products, vowing to "bring them to their knees." [45] Carmichael said, "We have been looking for a fight against a big company, and you've got everything we want. . . . When we're through, Florence will say 'Jump,' and Kodak will ask 'How high?' " [46] Carmichael's national boycott turned out to be picket-ing in four cities and involved only several dozen citizens of Detroit, Chicago, San Francisco, and Atlanta.[47]

During the first week of February Kodak announced openings for 137 to 158 unskilled persons in training programs leading to regular jobs. Kodak requested referrals from eleven agencies including settlement houses, the State Employment Service, the Urban League, and FIGHT.[48]

Four days later, Florence brought 87 people to the Kodak employment office. Kodak interviewers were ready with application forms. Describing the meeting, a Kodak official said the FIGHT people engaged

[42] Ridgeway, "Attack on Kodak."
[43] Paul A. Mallon, "But and Rebut," Letters to the Editors of *America*, May 6, 1967, p. 37.
[44] *Business Week*, April 29, 1967.
[45] Loh, Associated Press.
[46] Carter, "The Fight against Kodak."
[47] *Ibid.*
[48] *Ibid.;* also see Loh, Associated Press.

in an hour long demonstration, constantly interrupting our attempt to describe these programs to the group, they demanded that we provide jobs on the spot for those present. Our industrial relations people offered to accept applications and interview that day any members of the group who were seeking employment. Several stepped forward to volunteer only to be warned by Minister Florence, President of FIGHT, that they should not accept the offer.

The Associated Press reported that "after an hour and a half in a closed conference room, Minister Florence said his group had been offered neither jobs nor interviews, and if Kodak claimed the opposite, which Kodak did, it was 'an out and out lie.' " (The Associated Press learned that a Kodak spokesman had in fact told Minister Florence that applicants must first be interviewed and offered the chance. Minister Florence had replied, "We didn't come here to talk about interviews, we came for work.")[49] Florence also said that agencies who cooperated with Kodak in referring people for jobs were joining in a "conspiracy" (FIGHT had such an arrangement with Xerox at the time)[50] and that Kodak's training programs were "a sham and a disgrace."[51] Referrals were made and the program moved along.

Kodak decided to break off the meetings. Florence warned Kodak that it might be to blame for a "long, hot summer" in 1967.

Eilers regarded such threats as irresponsible and stated:

To tell the truth, I don't know what they want. Certainly not jobs—they could have had those, and still can. Every one of the ten referring agencies in Rochester has placed people in jobs at Kodak and none has asked for an exclusive deal. This year we'll have about 300 more in our training program. It's too bad FIGHT doesn't want to participate.

"We don't want any of Kodak's paternalism," said Florence. "The training program we've proposed is something we can do ourselves. We know ourselves better than anybody from Kodak does, and better than any Black Man who goes home to the suburbs every night and pretends he's white. We have to help ourselves by ourselves. That's what self-determination is."[52]

[49] Loh, Associated Press.
[50] Carter, "The Fight against Kodak."
[51] "Equal Employment Opportunity. Eastman Kodak Company's Positive Program" (Rochester, N.Y.: Public Relations Department, Eastman Kodak Company, 1967).
[52] Loh, Associated Press.

The New York Times described FIGHT's next move:

In March, FIGHT bought ten shares of Kodak stock, at a cost of $1,442.65 to gain a voice at the stockholders' meeting. The organization sent out 700 letters to clergymen and civil rights groups urging them to contact fellow stockholders to protest the company's action at the annual meeting.[53]

In response to FIGHT's call, various church organizations announced that they would withhold from the management their proxies for more than 34,000 shares. In addition, twenty-one private investors accounting for 5,060 shares announced that they would withhold proxies from the management. John Kifner, writing in *The New York Times,* pointed out that "those proxy withholdings (about 40,000 shares in all) are largely symbolic since the company's latest annual report lists 80,772,718 shares of stock." [54]

A group of influential ministers developed a compromise program that they believed would bring an end to the Kodak-FIGHT controversy. Representatives from many local industries joined the ministers and agreed to hire and train fifteen hundred hard-core unemployed over an eighteen-month period. Kodak also agreed to join Rochester Jobs, Inc., as this program was known.

FIGHT complained that this was another example of the white establishment's doing something for the poor without giving them an adequate voice in the process but finally joined the program. Florence was elected a vice-president and named to key committees. Clearly, FIGHT had gained an impressive victory and was undeniably, if indirectly, responsible for a precedent-setting partnership between private industry and the poor. Though no hiring quotas were announced, Kodak's share was approximately six hundred. The poor—not six hundred, but fifteen hundred—had the promise of jobs; FIGHT had its victory; and Kodak was apparently doing all FIGHT had ever asked of it. Florence announced that the new program would not affect FIGHT's dispute with Kodak and that the protest at the stockholders' meeting at Flemington would occur as scheduled. *FIGHT wanted some kind of direct concession from Kodak.*[55]

As far as Florence was concerned the issue was no longer jobs but dignity. He maintained that Kodak had arrogantly broken a moral agree-

---

[53] John Kifner, "21 Churches Withhold Proxies to Fight Kodak Rights Policies," *The New York Times,* April 7, 1967.

[54] John Kifner, "21 Kodak Investors Withhold Proxies," *The New York Times,* April 17, 1967, p. 25.

[55] Martin, "Shepherds vs. Flocks, Ministers vs. Negro Militancy."

ment. He said that FIGHT was only trying to solve local problems in partnership with business, instead of by resorting to the federal government. He recalled that in a previous crisis situation, during World War II, industry had turned farmers into tradesmen overnight because the national good demanded it. A similar crisis situation, he said, exists today.[56]

On April 25 Kodak's annual stockholders' meeting was held in Flemington, New Jersey. Buses and carloads of white and black demonstrators from Rochester and other cities and from Cornell, Princeton, Yale, and Dartmouth arrived in Flemington during the morning, and were met by a force of state troopers, local police, and Kodak guards. There were no incidents.

Also in attendance were the ten FIGHT members who had each purchased one share of stock plus the stockholders who had withheld their proxies in support of FIGHT. William S. Vaughn, chairman of the board, opened the meeting at one o'clock.

Florence was on his feet immediately. "Point of order," Florence shouted. "I'll be heard as long as I'm on the floor." To cries of "Throw him out," Florence shouted, "We will give you until two o'clock to honor that agreement," and then walked out of the building. Outside, Florence told his followers, "This is war."

Precisely at 2:00 P.M. Florence returned to the meeting, crying "point of order" until he had Vaughn's attention.[57] Florence pointed a finger at the chairman and asked, "Are you going to recognize the December 20 agreement?" Vaughn's reply was firm: "No sir, no we are not." [58] With this Florence and some of his followers walked out. FIGHT's attempts to disrupt the meeting were not successful. The meeting was not halted nor was the management challenged.

Vaughn's defense of Kodak's record as well as its reasons for repudiation drew cheers from most stockholders present.[59] Nor did the withholding of proxies present any serious difficulties for management. Of Kodak's 80.8 million shares, 84 percent were voted for management. All Kodak officers were reelected. A month later the company took away from John Mulder his assistant vice-president title, although he retained his job as assistant general manager of Kodak's Park Plant.

Outside the meeting Florence's and Alinsky's statements received national coverage from television, radio, and the press. Kodak's corporate image suffered considerably.

Following the annual meeting Kodak tried to upgrade its public image

[56] Raymond A. Schroth, "Self-Doubt and Black Pride," *America,* April 1, 1967, p. 502.
[57] *Business Week,* April 29, 1967.
[58] "Fight at Kodak," *Newsweek,* May 8, 1967.
[59] *Ibid.*

by hiring Uptown Associates, a Manhattan-based black public relations and advertising concern specializing in "ethnic marketing." According to a story in *The New York Times:*

"A Kodak official in Rochester said the company contract with Uptown Associates was not related to its current conflict with FIGHT."

Reuben J. Patton, head of Uptown Associates said "the company did not seek me out" because of the FIGHT controversy. He stated that he had first offered his services to Kodak in June 1964 when they were turned down by the company advertising director who wrote to Patton saying:

As you know we are very much interested in the Negro market. . . . At the moment we do not require extra services. . . . and if the occasion arises where we feel you can be of additional service to us, please be assured that you will hear directly from us.

Florence said he was "glad to hear that Kodak can sign contracts with Negro firms specializing in face-saving. This is proof that Kodak was never in good faith with the poor, but only wanted to hire 'instamatic' Negroes." [60]

Kodak eventually realized the ineffectiveness of its public relations strategy and consequently tried to amend it by hiring outside agencies such as Carl Byoir and Associates for help in dealing with ethnic groups. Kodak also approached other professional experts in urban and ghetto problems to help it specifically in dealing with FIGHT. Consequently, in May 1967, Kodak invited Daniel P. Moynihan, former assistant secretary of labor and then the chairman of the President's Council on Urban Affairs, for consultation. Mr. Moynihan talked with both Kodak officials and FIGHT members to seek out ways of possible compromise. A week of secret meetings followed between the two parties, which resulted in an agreement.

On June 23 President Eilers sent a telegram to Minister Florence in which Kodak recognized

that FIGHT, as a broad-based community organization, speaks on behalf of the basic needs and aspirations of the Negro poor in the Rochester area . . . that both FIGHT and Kodak support RJI which promised to be an effective way of providing job opportunities for the hard-core unemployed . . . that FIGHT and Kodak establish a relationship under which Kodak would send employment interviewers into selected places in inner-city neighborhoods in cooperation

[60] John Kifner, "Negro Ad Agency Hired by Kodak," *The New York Times,* April 28, 1967, p. 46.

with FIGHT . . . that it may be helpful to the people referred by FIGHT and employed by Kodak to have special guidance and advice from your organization [and that there be a] continuing dialogue between FIGHT and Kodak [to] cover various areas bearing on the economic needs and aspirations of the Negro community.[61]

At FIGHT's third annual convention, held that same evening, Kodak's telegram was endorsed.

In the fall of 1967 talks were renewed on Kodak's promotion of inner-city small business. FIGHT suggested that Kodak build a plant in a ghetto area and allow FIGHT to operate it. Kodak refused to do this but suggested something in the scope of small business. FIGHT was interested, so Kodak prepared a forty-page booklet entitled "A Plan for Establishing Independently Owned and Operated Business in Inner-City Areas." [62] The plan stated that Kodak would take the initiative in organizing a Community Development Corporation (CDC) and would assist in its financing along with other organizations that would be encouraged to join it. The objective of the CDC would be to support small businesses, and the plan suggested three types: wood products, vacuum-formed plastic items, and equipment service. In addition, Kodak suggested forming a microfilming service, which the company considered particularly desirable since it was labor-intensive, equipment could be rented, and required training took only a few weeks. The jobs involved would not be menial. Kodak foresaw a good-sized market in microfilming government documents.

FIGHT showed interest in the microfilming service, was disappointed that under 150 jobs were involved, and suggested an operation that would employ 500 people. Kodak estimated that it would need between $2 million and $3 million in sales to employ 500 people and emphasized that it considered such an operation unrealistic as there was no possibility of finding such a large market.

On November 4 *The New York Times,* giving FIGHT as its source, stated that Kodak would build a finishing plant for photographic facilities, employing 100 to 150 people and that the factory would be "black-operated." A November 18 article quoted the new FIGHT president, DeLeon McEwen, as saying, "Kodak will join FIGHT in developing a microfilming factory that will hire and train 400 to 500 unskilled Negroes."

The two stories put Kodak in an awkward position: to continue talks with FIGHT would be by "deeds reinforcing their exaggerated claims"; to

[61] From copy of telegram dated June 23, 1967, sent by Dr. Louis K. Eilers, president of Eastman Kodak, to the Reverend Franklin D. R. Florence, president of FIGHT.

[62] "A Plan for Establishing Independently Owned and Operated Business in Inner-City Areas" (Rochester, N.Y.: Eastman Kodak Company, November 1967).

break off talks would contradict Kodak's desire to help FIGHT. Kodak asked FIGHT to announce the misunderstanding, but it refused—even after Kodak said it would not be able to continue talks if this were not done. FIGHT, in preserving this "barrier" to talks, kept the issue alive.

On December 5 Kodak announced the "details of a plan to combat poverty in Rochester." The plans called for starting small businesses in the city's predominantly black slums, with each business employing nine to fifteen workers. Although these businesses would be started with Kodak's help, they "would eventually be independently owned and operated by employees." [63]

On April 1, 1968, Kodak announced that its program to train jobless persons from Rochester's inner city would continue in 1968. Monroe V. Dill, Kodak director of industrial relations, said that the company expected to hire two hundred persons for the program during the coming year, the same number as the preceding year. He also said that since the inception of the on-the-job program in 1964, five hundred men and women, many lacking industrial skills or adequate education, had been trained in special classes. FIGHT's president, DeLeon McEwen, responding to Kodak's announcement, said that the results of the education program were "known only to Kodak" and "they have not been enlarged to the black hard-core unemployed." [64]

This program was not connected with Rochester Jobs, Inc. (RJI). Earlier, in January, Rochester Business Opportunity Corporation (RBOC) had been formed "to promote and encourage independent business in and for the inner-city." Kodak joined with sixty of the city's largest companies to provide collateral to guarantee bank loans to finance business among the inner-city residents. RBOC's twenty-eight–member board also included several blacks and a Puerto Rican.

On April 17 Kodak announced a gift of $150,000 to the Community Chest's Martin Luther King Memorial Fund. RBOC's largest venture has been a $600,000 joint venture by FIGHT, the U.S. Department of Labor, and Xerox to start a FIGHT-managed metal stamping and electrical transformer manufacturing factory expected to employ one hundred people.

---

[63] "Handicraft Plan Offered by Kodak," *The New York Times,* December 16, 1967, p. 37.

[64] "Kodak to Continue Training Program," *The New York Times,* April 2, 1968.

B.

DISCRIMINATION

Crown Zellerbach Corporation, San Francisco

Conflict with the Equal Employment Opportunity Clause of the Civil Rights Act, 1964

> I dreamed that I had died and gone to my reward,
> A job in heaven's textile plant on a golden boulevard,
> The mill was made of marble, the machines were made of gold,
> Nobody ever got tired, and nobody ever grew old.
>
> —Joe Glazer,
> "Song for the Workers"

INTRODUCTION

On January 30, 1968, the United States filed action against Crown Zellerbach Corporation (C-Z) and against both the International and Local 189 of the United Papermakers and Paperworkers, AFL-CIO, CLC. The suit alleged that the defendants had, both jointly and independently, engaged in employment practices that discriminated against Negroes at C-Z's Bogalusa, Louisiana, paper mill. This violated Title VII of the Civil Rights Act of 1964 and contractual obligations that C-Z had undertaken pursuant to Executive Order 11246 which ensures nondiscrimination in employment by government contractors.[1]

In the complaint, the United States asked the district court to enjoin the local and international unions from striking. The strike was threatened to prevent C-Z from effecting certain changes in its seniority system. C-Z had agreed with the Office of Federal Contract Compliance to implement these changes in partial fulfillment of its contractual obligations to afford black employees equal employment opportunities, as required of government contractors by Executive Order 11246. The complaint also sought an order requiring that C-Z and the unions implement a seniority and recall system which would eliminate the present effects of past discrimination.[2]

The suit against C-Z came at the end of a civil rights turmoil which had been shaking the small Louisiana town of Bogalusa since early in 1965. According to *Business Week,* "Probably no major corporation, not even U.S. Steel, with its Birmingham (Ala.) problems, has had civil rights issues more forcefully thrust into its executive offices." [3] The company had always had a very favorable civil rights reputation. Former Secretary of Labor James Mitchell, when a C-Z vice-president, had even helped to organize San Francisco's Human Relations Commission.[4] Nondiscrimination had always been the traditional policy of the company. The company, therefore, was very proud of its record.

HISTORY

Bogalusa, a town in eastern Louisiana, was founded by the Great Southern Lumber Company in 1906 and grew up around one of the largest lumber mills in the world. It originated as a company town—the company owned the houses and operated the general store, the hospital, and the utility system. In time, the lumber operation shifted to pulp and paper. The lumber mill itself closed in 1938, and the properties of Great Southern were taken over by Gaylord Container Corporation of St. Louis. C-Z became a corporate resident of Bogalusa in late 1955 when it merged with Gaylord. As a result of this merger, Gaylord's large pulp and paper mill in Bogalusa and some half million acres of pine timberlands became part of the C-Z organization.[5]

[1] Brief for the United States on appeal from the United States District Court for the Eastern District of Louisiana in the case *United States* v. *Local 189,* United Papermakers and Paperworkers, AFL-CIO, CLC; and Crown Zellerbach Corporation; No. 25956, p. 13.

[2] *Ibid.,* p. 14.

[3] "Caught in the Civil Rights Crossfire," *Business Week,* August 7, 1965, p. 102.

[4] *Ibid.*

[5] "Equal Employment Opportunity in Bogalusa, Louisiana," statement delivered by Reed E. Hunt, chairman of the board of Crown Zellerbach Corp., April 22, 1965.

The mill and its three converting plants sit literally in the middle of Bogalusa. Partly because of the summer heat and humidity, but also because of the mill, stepping into Bogalusa has been described as stepping into "a hot, musty cellar, where old paper, boxes and charred lumber have steeped in stagnant pools for months and years." [6] As the largest employer and industry in this community of 23,000, employing 2,900 people (including 390 blacks out of a 30 to 40 percent black population), Crown Zellerbach has been prominently identified with Bogalusa.[7]

"The racial bias was very typical of a small southern city—separate schools for the 9,000 Negroes and 14,000 whites; Negroes in the balconies of the two movie houses; separate cemeteries; separate hospitals; white restaurants off limits to Negroes; limited job opportunities to the colored." [8] In other words, "the air in Bogalusa is almost the only thing in Bogalusa that's spread around without regard to race, creed or color." [9] Violence was part of this town long before the civil rights struggle erupted. Yet, that streak of violence and meanness could also be interpreted as a streak of stubbornness. Once sides were chosen, the game was played for keeps.[10]

RACIAL BIAS IN THE PLANT—JOB ASSIGNMENT AND PROMOTION

The racial segregation practiced in the town was also practiced at the C-Z plant—separate jobs for blacks and whites, separate unions, separate facilities. Each job was absolutely restricted to either white or black employees. All jobs in several departments in the plant were restricted to white employees only. In other departments, some jobs were restricted to white employees and others to blacks. With a single exception, all the white jobs in the mixed racial departments were more highly paid and involved greater responsibility than the best job allotted to blacks.[11]

The permanent jobs in the Bogalusa mill were organized into groups known as progression lines, with the lowest paying jobs at the bottom and the highest at the top (the usual method of mill organization practiced by the paper mill industry in the United States). Generally, an employee entered a progression line at the lowest job and was promoted to the next higher job in the line. When a vacancy occurred in a line job, the incumbents immediately below competed for it. According to job seniority, the

---

[6] Jude Wanniski, "The Smoke Hangs Heavy over Bogalusa," *National Observer,* July 1965.

[7] Hunt, "Equal Employment Opportunity in Bogalusa, Louisiana."

[8] Wanniski, "The Smoke Hangs Heavy over Bogalusa."

[9] *Ibid.*

[10] *Ibid.*

[11] Brief for Local 189a, United Papermarkers and Paperworkers, AFL-CIO, CLC; *U.S.* v. *Local 189,* No. 25956, p. 2.

contestant who held the lower job for the longest time usually obtained the promotion. Demotions were also based on job seniority. If demotions resulted in the demotion of an employee out of the line of progression, he had the first right to return to the progression line when a vacancy occurred. The right to return was called the "recall right." [12]

In addition to the progression lines there was a labor pool, known as the extra board of permanent employees, who were available to fill temporary vacancies in the permanent jobs. A new employee was usually assigned to the extra board until a vacancy occurred in the existing jobs of the progression line, at which time the members of the extra board and employees in other progression lines would bid for the permanent assignment. The position was awarded to the qualified employee with *the greatest seniority* in the mill. Any individual previously demoted out of that particular progression line had the recall right over any other employee.[13]

The job seniority system at Bogalusa had long been in effect in paper mills throughout the country. The system, according to C-Z, particularly reflected the needs of the paper industry by ensuring the greatest amount of on-the-job training for employees before they were promoted to higher positions. Extensive training was particularly important in the paper industry where mistakes in the operation of expensive machinery could cause tremendous financial losses. In addition to the economic considerations, there were safety factors which dictated the necessity of a seniority system that maximized on-the-job training.[14]

Due to the segregation practice at the mill before the merger, there were two unions—one for whites and the other for blacks, Locals 189 and 189a respectively, with separate extra boards and separate progression lines. A new white employee, under the jurisdiction of Local 189, would be assigned to the white extra board from which he could then reach the white progression line. A black employee would fall under the jurisdiction of Local 189a which could assign him only to the black extra board from which in turn only the black progression lines could be reached. Thus, a black person could never reach a white position, regardless of how long he had worked in the plant.[15] The company had not faced such a civil rights problem before as it was relatively new to the south.

TROUBLE AT THE PLANT

The first problem C-Z encountered at the mill was not racial but a conflict with the union. When C-Z took over, the mill studies undertaken

[12] Brief for Crown Zellerbach Corporation, *United States* v. *Local 189*, No. 25956, pp. 3–4.
[13] *Ibid.*, p. 4.
[14] *Ibid.*, p. 4.
[15] *Ibid.*, p. 5.

showed that to make the mill fully competitive in the industry, it had to be extensively modernized. It was also clear that the mill was greatly over-staffed and that the work force would have to be reduced. According to the former owner of the Bogalusa radio station:

The paperworkers had little knowledge of a real, working day. At one time or another, practically all of the men had established the habit of punching the time clock in the morning, then, either going back out and going fishing or finding a place in the building to go to sleep, and then punching out at night. This had been going on for years. C-Z, therefore, not only had to modernize the mill, but the workers as well.[16]

Although the company made every effort to explain the competitive situation to the union, tensions developed when the company started its $45 million modernization program and discharged employees because of increased plant efficiency. In August 1961 the union struck the mill. It was a costly strike to the company, the employees, and the community because it lasted for seven months.

Once the strike was settled, the company moved toward a solution of the segregation problem at the plant. Not only was discrimination against company policy but, as contract supplier to the federal government, Crown Zellerbach was subject to Executive Order 11246. The order at that time required not overnight compliance but progress toward a solution. Coming off the long labor dispute, the company moved slowly to introduce to the unions the first measure to alter the accepted pattern of race relations in the community, as the matter had always been part of a union contract.[17]

On May 17, 1964, the two extra boards were merged and, under the terms of that merger, any black employee then on the extra board or any newly hired black employee was eligible to move into any progression line in the mill, including those formerly restricted to white employees.[18] Also following the strike, Bogalusa had in consecutive years its first flood, first drought, and first freeze. In May 1964, with the conflict solved at the plant, the community began to relax because it appeared that Bogalusa had finally weathered the last of its pains.[19] In fact, this summer was only the quiet before the storm, during which the city through nationwide publicity became notorious as the Ku Klux Klan center of America, and Crown

[16] "A Broadcaster's Nightmare," speech by Ralph Blumberg at the Deadline Club, Sigma Delta Chi Professional Chapter, New York, January 28, 1966, reproduced in *Quill,* April 1966, pp. 12–16.
[17] Hunt, "Equal Employment Opportunity in Bogalusa, Louisiana."
[18] Brief for Crown Zellerbach Corporation, p. 5.
[19] Blumberg, "A Broadcaster's Nightmare," p. 12.

Zellerbach Corporation, identified with Bogalusa, became embroiled in the civil rights struggle.

THE EXPLOSION

The civil rights movement had gathered steam in Bogalusa. To avoid trouble, the city had kept its lines of communication open to both black and Klan leaders. As the makeshift biracial committee was making no apparent progress, the blacks began to get restless and started to plead with Washington to send CORE or the NAACP into Bogalusa.[20]

The first sign of trouble was the show of strength exhibited by the Klan. As described by Ralph Blumberg, former owner of the Bogalusa radio station:

> On May 30th, 1964, the Ku Klux Klan held a huge open meeting within the city limits of Bogalusa which actually is against the law in Louisiana. They were in full regalia . . . the multi-colored hoods and white sheets, 20-foot flaming crosses, guards on horseback armed with shotguns, and about 3,000 Klansmen. The traffic that night was so heavy that the city police were out there directing traffic. Everyone in Bogalusa and the surrounding area had come to get a look at the Ku Klux Klan in action and they weren't disappointed. . . . it was quite a show. This was the Klan's way of displaying a real show of strength.[21]

The evening was not publicized by the national media and thus received only local coverage. To avoid the racial pitfalls that had torn other communities apart, six leading citizens of Bogalusa—three clergymen, the leading attorney, the editor of the newspaper, and Ralph Blumberg—invited Brooks Hays to Bogalusa to speak to the business and professional community. Mr. Hays, a former congressman and prominent Baptist layman, had seen many racial problems firsthand in the South. As he was now working for the federal government and was thus required to speak to integrated audiences, the group decided to invite eight black leaders. The mayor and the city officials refused to be associated with the plan.[22]

The Klan received knowledge of the planned meeting—the city attorney was a Klansman—and opposed the meeting, labeling Hays a communist. Through pamphlets and direct threats, the six members of the group and

[20] *Ibid.,* p. 12.
[21] *Ibid.*
[22] *Ibid.,* p. 13.

owners of facilities suitable for such a meeting were pressured to call off the meeeting. Leaflets such as the following were being distributed:

The Ku Klux Klan is strongly organized in Bogalusa and . . . being a secret organization, we have Klan members in every conceivable business in this area. We will know the names of all who are invited to the Brooks Hays meeting and we will know who did and did not attend this meeting. Accordingly, we take this means to urge all of you to refrain from attending this meeting. Those who do attend this meeting will be tagged as integrationists and will be dealt with accordingly by the Knights of the Ku Klux Klan.[23]

The Klan in this community was able to exert so much pressure and to intimidate so many people that the meeting had to be canceled. Blumberg's station broadcast an editorial critical not of the Klan or its goals but of its methods. An organized campaign of terror followed, which included threats to Blumberg's life and family. Patrol cars watched his house every night. The Klan was so effective in intimidating other businessmen in the community that all but one boycotted his station. His automobile's windows were smashed and seven bullets were fired into his radio equipment. The transmitter door was sprayed with shotgun blasts. Although he received outside contributions, he was finally forced to sell his station. The three ministers who were part of the group had already left Bogalusa. Blumberg said that the only reason he survived was because of the FBI.[24] He was later an important witness against the Klan in the 1966 hearings of the House Committee on Un-American Activities and his story received nationwide publicity.[25]

The cancellation of Hays's speech brought national publicity. The *Nation,* a liberal magazine, "exposed" Bogalusa as "Klantown" U.S.A., pinpointing it as the heart of the KKK. According to Mr. Cutrer, then mayor of Bogalusa, it was the *Nation* article that had started all the trouble.[26] The speech had been planned for January 7, 1966. In late January the local black group, the Bogalusa Civic and Voters League (advised by outside members of the Congress of Racial Equality), carried out a test of public accommodations. Although, due to the careful planning of Mayor Cutrer, the test was carried out peacefully, ten days later two CORE workers stated that they had been attacked by a mob of white men. The attack received nationwide newspaper coverage and CORE officially

---

[23] *Ibid.*
[24] *Ibid.,* p. 14.
[25] "Klan Said to Retain Its Control of Bogalusa Despite Court Order," *The New York Times,* January 6, 1966, p. 13.
[26] Wanniski, "The Smoke Hangs Heavy over Bogalusa."

entered the struggle.[27] In April A. Z. Young, for fifteen years a forklift operator at the box plant of the paper mill, a former president of the black union, Local 624 of the International Brotherhood of Pulp, Sulphide and Paper Mill Workers (IBPS), and considered a militant by many people, took over as president of the Voters League.[28]

The race problems that had smoldered below the surface in Bogalusa now burst into the open. Since the first incident that brought national coverage, a week seldom went by that Bogalusa did not make headlines. Marchers participating in civil rights demonstrations were openly attacked and severely injured while the police watched.[29] The first two black deputies ever hired in the area were ambushed by night riders while on patrol; one was killed and the other critically injured.[30] A white man bent on further assault attempted to force his way into a car that was carrying an injured demonstrator and was shot by a black man. The Bogalusa park had to be closed when attempts to integrate it resulted in violence.[31]

The moderate elements and local businessmen were conspicuous by either their silence or lack of enthusiasm in helping to solve the city's racial problems and to cool the tensions between the black and white communities. Mayor Cutrer, who had claimed that a sizable number of Bogalusa's citizens were indeed moderate, nevertheless conceded privately that he was dismayed that so few ever came out to support his moderate position. Early in June 1965, a group of moderates tried to gather signatures for a statement affirming the city's belief in law and order. The project had to be abandoned for want of enough endorsers.[32] However, some eight months later, on February 24, 1966, a full-page ad appeared in the local newspaper. The ad, sponsored by 225 business firms, strongly advocated the cause of racial cooperation.

The city's moderate white businessmen had been keeping silent for fear of revenge from the Ku Klux Klan. Similarly, the black moderates failed to counsel patience for fear of being labeled "Uncle Toms," while "teachers, lawyers, physicians, and other professional people have largely kept silent because they say they would prefer not to get involved." [33] On the other hand, Saxon Farmer, a Bogalusa distributor for a major oil company and a

---

[27] *Business Week,* August 7, 1965, p. 102.

[28] Wanniski, "The Smoke Hangs Heavy over Bogalusa."

[29] "U.S. Sues to Halt Bogalusa Strife," *The New York Times,* July 20, 1965, p. 16.

[30] "Moderates Fail to Aid Bogalusa," *The New York Times,* July 11, 1965, p. 1. After a lapse of over eight months, the city hired another black policeman, and the two black deputies began patrolling their area on April 1, 1966. "Negroes Put Back on Duty at Bogalusa," *Baton Rouge Morning Advocate,* April 2, 1966.

[31] "Bogalusa Mayor Very Troubled," *The New York Times,* May 24, 1965, p. 1.

[32] *The New York Times,* July 11, 1965, p. 1.

[33] Allan Katz, "Race Ordeal Teaches City Vital Lesson," *New Orleans States-Item,* August 11, 1965.

known KKK leader, said that a majority of the city's businessmen believed "whites should resort to violence if necessary to prevent desegregation." [34] What about the executives in the large plants owned by big United States corporations? According to an article by Allan Katz, a staff writer for the *New Orleans States-Item,* "A number of executives of a large plant in the area have said they have not become involved because the company does not encourage it, and besides they are transients who may be transferred at any time." [35]

As the Crown Zellerbach Corporation was prominently identified with Bogalusa, its name was constantly in the news. The Bogalusa Civic and Voters League and CORE representatives picketed the plant. They charged C-Z with discriminatory practices and specifically demanded that more black women be hired. Many black women worked as maids for three dollars a day for white women who were working in the plant for fifteen dollars a day. Because of the modernization process in the plant, women had been and were still being laid off. As per union contract and general custom in industry, the people laid off had first recall to any new opening.

Although C-Z was seldom attacked editorially, its identification with Bogalusa, the picketing outside the plant reported in the newspapers and shown on television, and the attacks on the company by representatives of civil rights groups created a mental association of C-Z with the acts of the KKK and other racist extremists.

COMMUNITY PRESSURES AT CROWN ZELLERBACH'S HOME OFFICE IN SAN FRANCISCO

The unfavorable publicity associated with the events in Bogalusa, as reported in both national and local media, brought pressure on C-Z's San Francisco headquarters. A committee of fifty-three San Francisco civil rights and religious leaders publicly urged C-Z to use its economic strength to bring racial harmony to troubled Bogalusa. However, in a stroke of reverse segregation, it was demanded that C-Z release all employees who were members of the KKK or had participated in antiracial activities such as cross burnings or beatings. The demand was made through a press conference held by the group. W. T. Ussery, a San Francisco vice-president of CORE, had earlier sent a telegram asking C-Z officials to contact President Johnson, Attorney General Katzenbach, and other state and Bogalusa officials to press for the rights and safety of Bogalusa citizens and to appeal publicly for the end of "mob rule and control" by the Klan. It also asked

[34] Jack Nelson, "Some Bogalusa Whites Said to Favor Violence," *Los Angeles Times,* July 13, 1965.
[35] Katz, "Race Ordeal Teaches City Vital Lesson."

for an immediate meeting with CORE officials to discuss the exact action undertaken by C-Z to ease and correct the situation.[36]

When the company did not respond to the appeals, pressure was increased by picketing C-Z's head office and by news releases from the committee, now headed by Mr. Ussery. Other civil rights groups joined in the activities. In June 1965 the Midpeninsula Catholic Interracial Council demanded that Reed E. Hunt, chairman of the board of Crown Zellerbach, be removed from the University of San Francisco Board of Regents.[37] The events received wide coverage in the Bay Area. The message in all the interviews with civil rights leaders, as reported by television, radio, and the newspapers, was always the same: Crown Zellerbach should use its economic strength in Bogalusa by taking a firm stand on civil rights and thus help to resolve many of the problems.

Besides protests, the civil rights groups also attempted to use economic boycott to pressure the company into taking a tougher stand in Bogalusa. Leaders asked Philco's Western Development Laboratories in Palo Alto to cease purchasing paper products from C-Z.[38] The NAACP, at their convention in Denver, adopted a resolution urging its members to boycott all Crown Zellerbach Corporation products because of discrimination at the company's plant at Bogalusa.[39]

CROWN ZELLERBACH'S RESPONSE

When the racial strife erupted in Bogalusa, the company was caught in a situation unfamiliar to its executives. There was no precedent that could be used as an example for action. The company to some extent had to improvise.[40]

R. R. Ferguson, a Canadian with a background in production who was sent to the mill in 1964 as resident manager, believed that the company did not have the right to run the town or the right to tell the people what their community and social policies should be and how they should conduct themselves. He believed that the company should comply with civil rights legislation but that management should take part in community affairs as individuals.[41] Since the start of the strife in January 1965, he had spent half his time on civil rights problems inside and outside the mill.[42]

---

[36] *Business Week*, August 7, 1965, p. 102.
[37] "Ouster of USF Regent," *Palo Alto Times*, June 22, 1965.
[38] *Ibid.*
[39] "NAACP Urges Zellerbach Corporation Boycott," *San Francisco Chronicle*, July 4, 1965, p. 1A.
[40] *Business Week*, August 7, 1965, p. 102.
[41] *Ibid.*
[42] *Ibid.*

Much of his activity consisted of meeting with all kinds of groups, with these meetings usually being open. He explained his policy to the white union group as follows:

We offer jobs in the mill on a nondiscriminatory basis. This is a national policy. This is a company policy. It is fair policy. . . . There are those who want us to tell you what to do . . . to dictate a program of social reform here, to lay down the law at Bogalusa. . . . We will not do this.[43]

Ferguson felt that such appearances were effective because C-Z was the largest employer and C-Z's explanation of the requirements of the law would have an effect.[44]

Ferguson also helped to organize a broadly based Community Affairs Committee, which eventually included six C-Z officials, to advise the mayor and city council. It was difficult to form the group in Bogalusa because few wanted to become publicly involved. The committee succeeded in getting the other members and the mayor, Cutrer, a white moderate, to accept a few proposals. It also attempted to persuade restaurants to serve blacks but failed to obtain unanimity.[45]

At the same time, a process was underway to integrate the facilities at the plant, such as locker rooms, rest rooms, pay lines, and so forth, to meet the civil rights deadline of July 2, 1965, set by the federal government under the Civil Rights Act of 1964.[46] The old traditions of segregation were hard to change. When the company ordered a concessionaire operating on the plant's property to integrate, whites stopped eating there, and within a few days the operator went out of business.[47]

At the company's national headquarters in San Francisco, management had to decide how to balance Ferguson's position at the plant against the posture of Crown Zellerbach as an internationally known company. At times the possibility of taking strong action to protect the good civil rights reputation of the company was considered. One of the possibilities discussed was "to send a task force to Bogalusa and take a firm pro-civil rights stand with the local people." The company decided, however, that it had to back its manager "wholeheartedly," and he, in turn, was strongly supporting Mayor Cutrer, whose moderate stand drew fire from both sides. The decision meant that the company would not use its economic weight to force desirable social objectives. According to Hunt, "the surest way to

[43] *Ibid.*
[44] *Ibid.*
[45] *Ibid.*
[46] Hunt, "Equal Employment Opportunity in Bogalusa, Louisiana."
[47] *Business Week,* August 7, 1965, p. 102.

get into trouble in a community is to set yourself up as a political leader.
. . . This office is not going to dictate to a community 2,000 miles away." [48]

Because of this policy of noninterference by the home office in local community affairs and the "peremptory tone" of the wire sent by Mr. Ussery, C-Z's management in San Francisco had decided to ignore it, along with other messages and phone calls sent from CORE. When the company received a letter from the Committee for Concern for Bogalusa (the San Francisco civil rights group), of which Mr. Ussery was now chairman, Crown Zellerbach president Peter T. Sinclair wrote to Ussery stating the company's support of the civil rights act and pointing out that C-Z officials in Bogalusa had signed a statement the previous day calling for "restraint" and expressing support for the mayor.

Sinclair's letter drew more demands for meetings and discussions on points outlined by CORE and the committee. The company continued to refuse to meet with the San Francisco groups, which they held to be acting in bad faith, having used the meeting with C-Z only as a tool to strengthen the hands of the Bogalusa blacks in dealing with the mayor. [49]

To answer attacks on the company made by the civil rights groups, Hunt appeared on a news program and stated company policy regarding Bogalusa:

> The committee wants us to dictate a program of social reform. We do not think that this is the proper function of a private corporation and we do not propose to dictate to any community, San Francisco or Bogalusa. . . . So far as civil rights issues are concerned, we feel that a private company should deal with them in ways which are appropriate to its role as a private employer in the community. [50]

The declaration of company policy received wide coverage. To clear the situation further, a statement delivered at the company's Annual Share Owner's Meeting in San Francisco, April 22, 1965, was mailed to company stockholders. In the statement, the company's basic position was again outlined as well as the company's emphasis on equal employment opportunity, with the following addition:

> But we recognize that we have wider responsibilities and obligations in Bogalusa. These take the form of support for community institutions, support of law and order, living up to the requirements of good corporate citizenship. We are members of the Community

[48] *Ibid.*
[49] *Ibid.*
[50] "Company's 'Hands Off' Policy in Racial Strife," *San Francisco Examiner,* March 6, 1965, p. 8.

Affairs Committee. We have expressed our point of view. We will continue to voice our opinions within this democratic forum. We listen to the opinions of others and we hope we will be listened to. The company will do its part. We will cooperate to the utmost, in ways which are appropriate to a private corporation. We have every confidence in the integrity of the people of Bogalusa and that, given the facts, they will so conduct themselves as to reflect credit on the community.[51]

Crown Zellerbach also rejected the request that the company fire Klan members or those participating in violent acts against blacks. Ferguson, the plant manager, had rejected such steps, stating: "An employee's private life is his own. . . . If he comes into conflict with civil authorities, they take over." Hunt, as the chairman of the board, agreed with Ferguson and pointed out that the president and the vice-president of the Bogalusa Civic and Voters League, A. Z. Young and R. Hicks, had continued to work at the plant.[52] The company had also stated that "discharging an employee for membership in outside organizations, especially employees covered by labor contracts, is another question. Dismissal of the employee under such circumstances has been construed as unfair and discriminatory." [53]

The company's response was not satisfactory to the civil rights groups, which increased their pressure through the sit-ins and threatened boycotts. The demonstrations and civil rights activities in front of the C-Z headquarters received wide newspaper coverage in the Bay Area while the violence of the civil rights struggle in the South was being broadcast via national media. On July 6, 1965, C-Z agreed to meet in Bogalusa with the Civic and Voters League of Bogalusa to discuss company policy.[54] With the agreement to meet with the Bogalusa civil rights groups, tension in San Francisco subsided.

The meeting took place on July 15. Before the meeting, the two major international unions representing the production employees in the Bogalusa plant issued public statements calling attention to "their exclusive rights to bargain with the company under the provisions of the National Labor Relations Act." They further emphasized the responsibilities and obligations of organized labor under Title VII of the Civil Rights Act, which applied equally to employers and unions.[55] In a joint statement

[51] Hunt, "Equal Employment Opportunity in Bogalusa, Louisiana."
[52] *Business Week,* August 7, 1965, p. 102.
[53] "Coast Unit Fights Louisiana Racism," *The New York Times,* March 6, 1965, p. 9.
[54] "C-Z Will Meet with Rights Unit," *San Francisco Examiner,* July 18, 1965, p. 4.
[55] Reed E. Hunt, "Crown Zellerbach, Bogalusa and Civil Rights," sequel to the statement of April 22, 1965 (annual shareowners' meeting).

released after the meeting, both sides expressed the feeling that the discussion had been a "useful exchange of views." [56]

On July 30, 1965, the company released another statement which was a sequel to the one of April 22, 1965. The company again stressed adherence to the civil rights legislation and pointed out that because of the integration of the extra board both blacks and whites had worked on temporary assignment in every progression line in the mill. The pamphlet also pointed out that:

> Equal opportunity as it applies to new hires can be an empty phrase if jobs themselves are not available. . . . During the past years only white women have been hired for hourly production jobs in the bag and box plants. The continuing reduction in the work force has decreased the number of women employed in these operations. Women production employees who were laid off have the contractual right to be recalled to work before any additional new workers can be hired.
>
> We can conclude, therefore, that the principle of equal employment opportunity alone will not be sufficient to solve the long-range employment situation in Bogalusa. In the absence of new industry the community faces the prospect of a declining rate of employment.[57]

To show the company's good faith in its intent to deal with segregation at the plant, two clerical openings had been filled by black women.[58]

While the company was struggling at its headquarters with the racial problem, the intensity of the strife in Bogalusa was increasing. CORE, at its twenty-first annual convention, voted to make a major assault against segregation in Bogalusa. The delegates unanimously passed a resolution urging its members "to go to Bogalusa and stay as long as necessary." The resolution also authorized "full legal assistance" for civil rights workers in Bogalusa. The chief aim of the demonstrations was to end police brutality, obtain jobs for blacks in Bogalusa stores, and win broader employment opportunities for women.[59] A further complaint was that although the new nondiscriminatory policies dealt fairly with new employees, they did nothing for older black employees who were held back by the company's former policies.[60]

The civil rights organizations were not the only ones preparing for new

---

[56] *Ibid.*

[57] *Ibid.*

[58] *Ibid.*

[59] "CORE Will Seek Jobs in Bogalusa," *The New York Times,* July 4, 1965, Sec. 7, p. 4.

[60] "Negroes Resume Bogalusa Drive," *The New York Times,* July 8, 1965, p. 19.

pressures. Representatives of the National States Rights party, a front of the KKK, held rallies at the edge of town. The meetings attracted crowds up to two thousand out of the town population of twenty-three thousand, of which 30 to 40 percent were black. One representative made the following statement to the crowd:

> The nigger is not a human being. He is somewhere between the white man and the ape. We don't believe in tolerance. We don't believe in getting along with our enemy. Every time a nigger gets a job, that's one more job that you can't have.[61]

The ensuing marches, demonstrations, and counterdemonstrations grew in violence and intensity. On July 10 Federal Court Judge Herbert W. Christenberry enjoined the Bogalusa police from using violence or threats of violence to prevent blacks from exercising their civil rights. He further ordered the police "to protect Negroes and other civil rights advocates from harassment by white townspeople."[62] Fuming about the federal court injunction, one officer of the Bogalusa police department tore up one of the law-and-order stickers, stamped on it, and declared: "A nigger is a nigger and that's what he's gonna be till I die."[63]

By mid-July the violence had increased to such an extent that both the city council and the civil rights leaders in Bogalusa appealed directly to President Johnson for assistance. Although the president declared that the Bogalusa problem was a local community matter, he sent the chief of the civil rights division of the U.S. Justice Department, John Doar, to represent the federal government in working out a solution.[64]

John Doar arrived in Bogalusa on July 15 at the height of the struggle. The civil rights advocates had just rejected a proposed thirty-day cooling-off period, explaining on the Huntley-Brinkley NBC network news:

> Let them quit shooting and killing and knocking and beating and refusing us for thirty days. Let them cool off for thirty days. If they want to bring peace to town, tell them to open the parks for thirty days, feed us for thirty days, integrate the schools for thirty days. Let them do something for a change. The black man in America has been giving and giving and giving for five hundred years. And, baby, we've given all we've got. There ain't no more left.[65]

[61] *The New York Times,* July 11, 1965, p. 1.

[62] "U.S. Court Enjoins Bogalusa Police," *The New York Times,* July 11, 1965, p. 1.

[63] Nelson, "Some Bogalusa Whites Said to Favor Violence," p. 5.

[64] Hunt, "Crown Zellerbach, Bogalusa and Civil Rights."

[65] "Federal Government Intervenes," Huntley-Brinkley Report, NBC, July 15, 1965, Radio TV Reports, Inc.

The confrontation of the two opposing forces was again receiving national coverage—television, newspapers, and radio. The White House also named Lee White, a presidential counsel, to serve as special adviser to Mr. Johnson on developments in Bogalusa.[66]

On July 19 the attorney general initiated in the Federal District Court in New Orleans a program of broad legal action against three local law enforcement officials, the Original Knights of the Ku Klux Klan, and thirty-five white extremists to halt the racial violence. The three law enforcement officers were the Public Safety Commissioner, Police Chief Claxton Knight of Bogalusa, and a deputy sheriff of the county.[67] The two Bogalusa officials were later found to be in criminal contempt of court for not obeying the injunction of July 10 ordering them to protect civil rights demonstrators. The action against the Klan and the other group was to restrain them from threatening or assaulting civil rights workers or intimidating public officials and businessmen.[68]

Following the injunctions against the Klan and other white extremists and the contempt trial of the city officials and other law enforcement officers, the intensity of the struggle decreased. Marches for integration of schools, boycotts, and picketing of Bogalusa businesses—including Crown Zellerbach—to obtain more jobs continued. By the fall of 1965 the civil rights groups had made some progress in such areas as housing, street lighting, and integration of restaurants and other facilities, but they had failed to make serious headway in the area of employment.[69]

Bogalusa, as part of the civil rights struggle, continued to get attention from the national media. Drew Pearson, on his program from Newark, New Jersey, which was carried over a number of stations, commented:

> After all the civil rights demonstrations in Bogalusa lasting all summer, here is the net result. Two Negroes have been hired on the police force, seven children are in the schools, and one extra woman is working at the Crown Zellerbach Paper Company. Crown Zellerbach could have improved the situation, but it didn't.[70]

Walter Cronkite on CBS Evening News also discussed Bogalusa; correspondent Bert Quint reported:

[66] "Bogalusa Plans Parley on Crisis," *The New York Times,* July 10, 1965, p. 9.
[67] "U.S. Sues to Halt Bogalusa Strife," *The New York Times,* July 20, 1965, p. 1.
[68] "Two Bogalusa Aids Held in Contempt," *The New York Times,* July 30, 1965, p. 1.
[69] "Mix Strife Leaves Scars on City," *New Orleans States-Item,* August 9, 1965, p. 1.
[70] "Drew Pearson," WVNJ and other stations; September 12, 1965, Radio TV Reports, Inc.

They are picketing in Bogalusa, picketing for what civil rights leaders here say is the best Christmas gift of them all, a decent job that anyone, black man or white, can be proud of.

They have been boycotting the downtown stores for months without notable progress in their drive to get them to hire Negro clerks.[71]

In the latter part of 1965 an agreement was reached at the plant which provided an additional method by which black employees could obtain entry jobs in white lines of progression. Under the agreement, employees in black lines could compete on the basis of mill seniority for white entry jobs without first returning to the extra board and sacrificing accrued seniority against reductions in the work force. However, regardless of the length of time the successful black bidder had spent in a black job or in the plant (according to the job seniority system in force), when transferring into the white line, he was no better off for purposes of future promotions or demotions in that line than the newest white employee in the line. Although the agreement provided a new opportunity for the black employees, in practice the potential transfer was associated with considerable risk.[72]

CROWN ZELLERBACH AND U.S. GOVERNMENT AGENCIES

In late 1965 a newly organized federal agency, the Equal Employment Opportunity Commission (EEOC), created under Title VII of the Civil Rights Act, entered the civil rights struggle. The agency charged that the system of promotion and demotion was still discriminatory.[73] On December 18, 1965, the company and the unions agreed on a new proposal which was enacted on January 16, 1966, and provided for the merger of some of the white progression lines with functionally related black progression lines. In theory, the merger was to provide access by promotion to higher-paying white jobs that bore a functional relationship to lower-paying black jobs. Once the merger was effected, the job seniority system would continue to operate.[74]

The union's resistance to change was seen by many as a principal barrier to harmony in Bogalusa. On C-Z's initiative, the unions met in New

[71] "Walter Cronkite, CBS Evening News," December 7, 1965, Radio TV Reports, Inc.

[72] Brief for the U.S., p. 9.

[73] "F.D.R. Jr., Blasts Race Question in Promotion," *New Orleans States-Item,* December 18, 1965, p. 1.

[74] Brief for the U.S., p. 10.

Orleans with the EEOC and the above agreement was reached. Franklin D. Roosevelt, Jr., son of the late president and chairman of the commission, came himself to work toward an agreement. The unions' agreement came despite the presence of Ku Klux Klansmen on the executive board of the plant's main local.[75] Given the obstacles, the agreement was hailed as a major step forward and a breakthrough in Deep South racial employment patterns, and Roosevelt congratulated Crown Zellerbach and the union leadership for making a major contribution to the welfare of the country.[76]

Although the agreement worked out under the auspices of the EEOC was hailed as a major breakthrough, the black workers at the plant rejected the new plan of dovetailing the progression lines by a vote of 162–0, declaring that the company had merged only two of the eleven lines of job progression.[77] Furthermore, the order in which jobs were placed in the merged progression lines was based on rates. This resulted in all but two of the newly merged lines having the highest-paying black jobs placed below the lowest-paying, entry-level white jobs. The lowest-paid, most junior position held by a white employee was placed for the purpose of promotion and demotion above the highest-paid, most senior position held by a black employee.[78]

Access to the newly opened white lines of progression was further inhibited by the contract recall right. Because of the reduction in force, many white employees who had formerly worked for some time in the white progression lines had been demoted but continued to hold recall rights to those jobs that were formerly entry jobs to the white progression lines. The presence of these recall rights meant that a vacancy in a former white entry job that now fell in the *middle* of the merged line would not be filled by the most senior black employee in the job below the vacant job as long as there was a white employee with a recall right to that job. The white employee could exercise that recall right regardless of whether the black employee had more mill seniority. Despite the structural changes in the lines of progression, the incumbent black employee therefore had little chance to compete for the better-paying and more desirable white positions.[79]

The local black civil rights organizations continued to demonstrate in Bogalusa for their goals, which included more employment at the C-Z mill, and CORE and other groups continued to support the local efforts to focus attention on the civil rights movement. Although the civil rights

[75] "EEOC Considers Bogalusa Efforts as Step Forward," *Morning Advocate,* Baton Rouge, January 29, 1966, p. 2A.

[76] "Hiring Violation Is Charged at Bogalusa Mills," *Washington Post,* January 29, 1966, p. 2.

[77] *Ibid.*

[78] Brief for the U.S., p. 10.

[79] *Ibid.,* pp. 10–11.

marches continued and the Klan continued to hold its meetings and marches, the frequency of confrontations and the intensity of the struggle had somewhat diminished, partially because of the protection afforded civil rights personnel and black marchers by the local and state police. The marches, did, however, continue to focus public attention on Bogalusa, Crown Zellerbach, and the civil rights struggle.

CROWN ZELLERBACH AND THE OFCC

The Office of Federal Contract Compliance (OFCC), placed under the secretary of labor by Executive Order 11246, was responsible for achieving nondiscrimination in employment by government contractors. On February 8, 1967, the director of the OFCC wrote to C-Z alleging, among other things, that C-Z was "operating racially segregated but functionally related progression lines" and "permitting discriminatory use of recall and seniority rights," [80] although C-Z had implemented all requirements and suggestions made by the EEOC. The OFCC demanded that C-Z implement a newly conceived and hitherto untried combination seniority system under which promotions within the lines of progression would be based on a combination of an employee's job and plant seniority.[81] The OFCC threatened to terminate C-Z's contract with the government and debar the company from further contracts.[82]

Meetings were held regarding the seniority procedure during March 1967, which representatives of other government departments attended, including the Justice Department and EEOC. Although the subject discussed was part of the collective bargaining agreement between C-Z and the unions and was usually recognized by the courts to be a matter commonly restricted to collective bargaining, the unions were not allowed to participate because the OFCC "did not recognize the right of the union to participate." [83] However, at the insistence of the company, which brought eleven local union leaders—black and white—to Washington, D.C., at its own expense, the union representatives were allowed to sit in, but not participate in, one of the meetings. On March 19, 1967, C-Z agreed to "bargain in good faith with the unions to secure their acceptance of the OFCC mill-plus-job seniority proposal." The unions were not permitted to be a party to the agreement under the OFCC's rule.[84]

During March 1967 C-Z made an alternative proposal under which

[80] Brief on Behalf of Local 189, United Papermakers and Paperworkers, *AFL-CIO, CLC; and its International* v. *U.S.;* No. 25956, p. 7.
[81] Brief on Behalf of Crown Zellerbach, p. 7.
[82] *Ibid.*
[83] Brief on Behalf of Local 189, p. 8.
[84] *Ibid.*, p. 8.

blacks would be given seniority credit dating back to July 2, 1965, the effective date of the Civil Rights Act. Under the proposal, according to a six-year projection, 235 advances in the line would be made by black employees against 204 advances under strict seniority as against 278 advances under the new and untried combination system devised by OFCC. The OFCC rejected the C-Z proposal.[85]

When no progress had been made on the negotiation during April, after C-Z and the OFCC had signed the agreement on March 19, 1967, "The OFCC by letter alleged that Crown was in violation of the March 19 agreement and a memorandum was circulated to the heads of all government agencies, directing their contracting officers to consult with OFCC before awarding any government contract to Crown." [86] This memo was withdrawn the following month.

On June 16, 1967, a new contract was signed, again without union participation, between C-Z and the OFCC.[87]

The system proposed by the OFCC constituted a radical departure from the system of progression prevailing in the industry throughout the United States and Canada. According to C-Z:

> The mill-plus-job seniority proposal was developed by the OFCC staff without the benefit of sufficient information as to how it would operate at the Bogalusa mill and without consultation with experts in industrial relations. Under the OFCC formulation, the system would not only govern the promotion of Negro employees who had suffered discrimination, but it would also operate in progression lines in which there were no Negro employees thereby governing the promotion of white employees who were competing only against other white employees.[88]

Concurrent with the OFCC–C-Z negotiations, black employees of the Bogalusa plant were filing suit in the federal district court, charging Crown Zellerbach Corporation with racial discrimination in employment practices. At the same time marches in the Bogalusa area again drew the attention of the national media.[89]

C-Z intended to put the OFCC proposal of the combination seniority into the negotiations for a new union contract (the current contract was to expire August 1, 1967). About July 1, 1967, C-Z and the union began

---

85 *Ibid.,* p. 9.
86 Brief on Behalf of Local 189, p. 9.
87 *Ibid.,* p. 10.
88 Brief on Behalf of Crown Zellerbach, p. 6.
89 "Suit Charges Bias in Bogalusa Mills," *The New York Times,* July 30, 1967, p. 45.

bargaining for a replacement collective agreement. As expected, part of C-Z's proposal to the union, in accordance with its agreement with the OFCC, was the combination seniority system for promotion and demotion in the plant. Despite intensive bargaining extending into the latter part of August, C-Z was unable to secure union acceptance on the changes in the seniority system, although the parties had agreed upon some 150 items, including many of those contained in the agreement between C-Z and OFCC. Thereafter, the membership of Local 189 voted 777–14 to strike and Local 189a voted 82–51 to strike. On September 7, 1967, the unions notified C-Z that the strike would begin on September 19.[90]

On September 9, 1967, seven sticks of dynamite taped together in what appeared to be a homemade bomb, hidden in a brown paper bag, were discovered in a locker room of the mill. The fuse had been lit but had gone out. Although the plant had generally been integrated, the locker and the shower room had continued to be segregated. The rooms had been de-segregated in April upon OFCC demand, but white employees had turned in their keys, thus creating a black washroom. White employees no longer showered at the plant. The FBI was called in to investigate.[91]

The strike was avoided when the two parties with the aid of a repre-sentative of the Federal Mediation and Conciliation Service reached an agreement on a new contract September 18. The new contract, however, did not include an agreement by the union to accept the combination seniority system proposed by the OFCC. Instead, C-Z and the union agreed to leave the issue open to further collective bargaining. Because of the mill's economic importance in the community—and having experi-enced a long strike in the early sixties—the agreement was received with much relief in Bogalusa.[92] The members of Local 189a, the black union, abstained from voting on the acceptance of the contract proposal until the seniority provisions were negotiated.[93]

Negotiations on the combination seniority issue resumed in early No-vember with the parties reaching an alternative proposal suggested by the union. As before, the OFCC found the new proposal unacceptable. "De-spite Crown's persistent effort to secure union acceptance of the mill-plus-job seniority proposal," [94] the OFCC still threatened to debar C-Z from government contracts if the company was unable to secure an agree-ment from the unions by December 9, 1967. C-Z was thus caught between a union-threatened strike and an OFCC debarment.[95] The uppermost con-

---

90 *Ibid.,* p. 11.
91 "Dynamite Is Discovered in Bogalusa Mill," *Sunday Advocate,* Baton Rouge, September 10, 1967.
92 Brief on Behalf of Crown Zellerbach, p. 6.
93 "C-Z, Union to Sign Pact," *Bogalusa Daily News,* September 17, 1967.
94 Brief on Behalf of Crown Zellerbach, p. 8.
95 *Ibid.*

cern in the minds of the C-Z officials at that time was the possibility of another "prior consultation" memo such as the one the OFCC had issued in May, which the company felt was an attempt to deprive it of government business without due process.

To extricate itself, C-Z and the union filed actions in the United States District Court for the District of Columbia against the secretary of labor, W. Willard Wirtz, and Edward C. Sylvester of the OFCC. The court issued a temporary restraining order on December 12, 1967, and a preliminary injunction on January 2, 1968, restraining the defendants from imposing sanctions on C-Z without first granting it a hearing.[96]

On January 3, 1968, C-Z entered into an agreement with OFCC by which it committed itself to install unilaterally the mill-plus-job seniority system. (C-Z reserved the right to contest the legality of the OFCC's action.) Under the provisions of the new labor contract, C-Z notified the unions on January 16, 1968, that it would institute the system requested by the OFCC on February 1, 1968. The unions in turn voted to strike on that same date to prevent the institution of the new system and thus prevent any change of the "job seniority system" in force prior to the OFCC action.[97]

On January 30, 1968, the United States filed action against Crown Zellerbach Corporation and Local 189, alleging that "the defendants had both jointly and independently engaged in employment practices which discriminated against Negroes on account of their race at the paper mill in Bogalusa." The complaint also asked the court to "enjoin the Local and International unions from engaging in a threatened strike in order to prevent the implementation by Crown of certain changes in the seniority system." An order restraining a strike was issued on January 31, 1968, and the mill job seniority system was placed into effect on February 1, 1968.[98]

ARGUMENTS IN COURT

During the hearings starting on March 20, 1968, the following issues were to be decided:

1. Whether, under the facts and circumstances of this case, the job security system which was in effect at the Bogalusa paper mill prior to February 1, 1968 was unlawful.
2. If the answer to the above question is in the affirmative, what is

---

96 *Ibid.*
97 *Ibid.*
98 *Ibid.,* p. 9.

the necessary or appropriate standard or guideline for identifying the seniority of employees for purposes of promotion and demotion? [99]

THE GOVERNMENT'S ARGUMENT

As expected, the government argued that the seniority system then in effect was discriminatory, but instead of requesting the implementation of the job-plus-mill seniority system, the government demanded that promotions and demotions should be made strictly on the basis of yet another new and untried seniority system—mill seniority. During the six weeks after February 1, the job-plus-mill seniority system had proved itself useless, "causing whites to jump whites and Negroes to jump Negroes without significant advancement of Negroes to higher paying jobs." [100] Therefore the Justice Department, through its representative, demanded mill seniority (that is, length of in-plant service) as a criterion for promotion and demotion. To prove the job seniority in force at the plant unlawful, it argued as follows:

Because, in the past, Negro employees were assigned to the lower-paying, less desirable jobs and white employees were assigned to higher-paying, more desirable jobs, a system of "job seniority" deprives Negro employees of the opportunity to compete with their white contemporaries for the higher-paying, more desirable, previously white jobs; for the white employee receives credit for the period of time he served in the white lines of progression and white jobs, at a time when Negro employees were denied access to these jobs. Indeed, as we have shown more fully in the Statement above, the result of the merger of the lines of progression in January, 1966, was to make virtually all the Negro employees in the plant, including those with 20 or 30 years of service, junior for the purposes of promotion, transfer and demotion, to the most junior white employees. The main issue for decision here is whether such a seniority system which, although racially neutral on its face, perpetuates the results in present and future discrimination, is lawful under the equal opportunity requirements of Title VII of the Civil Rights Act of 1964 and the contractual obligations imposed by and pursuant to Executive Order 11246.
. . . The fundamental proposition underlying . . . the government's position in this and similar cases is that Title VII of the Civil Rights Act and Executive Order 11246 cast upon those subject to

[99] Brief on Behalf of U.S., p. 15.
[100] Brief on Behalf of Local 189, p. 12.

their provisions not merely the duty to follow racially neutral employment policies in the future, but also an obligation to correct and revise any practices which would perpetuate into the period of time subsequent to their effective dates the racially discriminatory policy pursued prior thereto. In our view, the discrimination prohibited includes not merely conduct which directly or expressly distinguishes among employees on the basis of race, but also practices which appear to be even-handed on their face, but which in actual effect, perpetuate past racially discriminatory practices . . .

. . . While past discriminatory conduct is not *eo ipso* a violation, its deliberate absorption as an integral part of a policy implemented or continued after the effective date of the Act warrants judicial relief. . . .[101]

In conclusion, the government's argument can be stated briefly in one sentence:

The "Job Seniority" system in effect at the Defendant Crown Zellerbach's Bogalusa paper mill prior to February 1, 1968, was unlawful because it perpetuated the effects of prior racially discriminatory practices and resulted in present and future discrimination.[102]

As can be seen, the government in its argument does not deal with the advantages of the present job seniority system or with the potential dangers of changing an industry-wide system but only with discriminatory policies and discriminatory effects of the current system.

CROWN ZELLERBACH'S ARGUMENT

Crown Zellerbach's argument can be divided into three parts:

1. Because while the action was pending the government demanded mill seniority rather than the mill-plus-job seniority system which had been agreed upon by C-Z and OFCC, it had repudiated the contract with C-Z. The court therefore should return the parties to the time when the job seniority system was in effect prior to the filing of the complaint by OFCC.[103]

---

[101] Brief on Behalf of U.S., pp. 17–19, 21.
[102] *Ibid.,* p. 17.
[103] Brief on Behalf of Crown Zellerbach, p. 19.

2. The government case has never implied "that the job seniority system in effect . . . prior to February 1, 1968 was adopted for discriminatory practices." [104]

   The system was adopted at a time when the progression lines were either under the exclusive jurisdiction of Local 189 or Local 189a. As there was at that time no competition between white and black employees within the progression lines, "it is obvious that the job seniority system was adopted for legitimate business purposes rather than for racial consideration." [105] The job seniority system was therefore not illegal at that time, and therefore the continuation of the system cannot be illegal.

3. The job seniority system was not chosen at random or for any reason but valid business purposes. Dr. Northrup, an expert witness called by C-Z, "testified that the job seniority system was the seniority system generally found throughout the country in the paper industry." [106] He further testified that the job seniority system "maximizes the training of employees given in one job before promotion to a higher job, and in most instances maximizes the training of employees in the higher jobs to which they will be promoted." [107] He continued by stating that "there are particular characteristics of the paper mill which make this [job] seniority system most appropriate in the paper industry: a paper mill contains very expensive and highly sophisticated machinery which when operated improperly can cause tremendous financial losses." [108] The testimony of Dr. Northrup was not contradicted at the trial.[109]

LOCAL 189'S ARGUMENT

The union of white employees, Local 189, argued somewhat the same as C-Z had previously, stressing the importance of retaining the job seniority system:

1. It pointed out that the job security system was not inherently discriminatory and its use was not to continue discrimination but to continue accepted labor practices.

---

104 *Ibid.*, p. 23.
105 *Ibid.*
106 *Ibid.*, p. 21.
107 *Ibid.*
108 *Ibid.*, p. 22.
109 *Ibid.*

2. To change the seniority system to grant preferential employment rights to Negroes would be to contravene the intent of Congress by applying the statute retroactively.[110]

3. The job seniority system was developed in part on considerations of safety, as testified by Mr. Vrataric, an expert witness called by the defendant union.[111]

The union's argument was best reflected in the emotional appeal made, part of which was as follows:

In its zeal to eliminate one type of injustice Congress clearly did not intend to establish a right of racial preference or to create another and all-pervasive injustice for other employees. . . .

Selective compassion for one group at the expense of another group by inept and amateur tinkering with a seniority system concededly not inherently discriminatory and standard in the paper industry, not only fails in this instance to guarantee the legitimate aspirations of the Negro employees; it also tends to reduce wholesome efficiency of plant operations and to alienate further other employees whose reasonable expectations of job progression are destroyed.

Through the collective bargaining efforts of this Union the lowest rate of pay at Bogalusa for a newly hired unskilled common laborer is now $2.69 an hour, substantially higher than the average rates of pay in most other industries in the South.

Governmental imposition of a seniority system which ignores the factors of efficiency, safety and the reasonable expectations of other employees in order to give preferential treatment to Negroes will in the long run only exaggerate the feeling of frustration and inadequacy which a culturally disadvantaged group may experience as its members struggle to qualify for jobs for which their previous job training and literacy have not qualified them. It is of dubious value to colored and white men alike in the Bogalusa area if misguided manipulations of the seniority system ultimately force the employer into a personnel policy which excludes all but the better educated from opportunities for employment. . . .

. . . Equal employment opportunity has existed at Bogalusa since May of 1964; equal employment in any society cannot be mandated for any one group at the expense of another and Congress did not so intend.[112]

---

[110] Brief on Behalf of Local 189, p. 22.
[111] Brief on Behalf of Crown Zellerbach, p. 21.
[112] Brief on Behalf of Local 189, pp. 35–37.

LOCAL 189A'S ARGUMENT

As the hearing affected the members of the union of black employees, and as cases against C-Z and Local 189 on charges of discrimination were pending, the judge also decided to hear the arguments from the representatives of Local 189a. Their arguments were similar to those of the Justice Department with special emphasis on the following three points:

1. They conceded that Congress did not require reverse discrimination for wrongs committed prior to the act. But in their opinion, neither did Congress intend "to freeze an entire generation of Negro employees into discriminatory patterns that existed before the act." [113] The continuation of the present job seniority system, in their opinion, would result in such a freezing through no fault of their own, but because of their color.

2. They further conceded "that if job seniority was necessary to the proper operation of the plant, Title VII would provide no obstacle to its continued use, regardless of the effect on Negro employees." [114] If the role of the job seniority system was to ensure that the senior man was sufficiently prepared for the promotion, then the seniority system could be replaced by a requirement that "a man must spend a given amount of time in a job before he is eligible to compete for promotion." [115] The length of time would be determined by the difficulty of learning each job. Given the implementation of such a "residence requirement" the job seniority would no longer be required for the efficient running of the plant and the mill seniority system could be introduced.

3. Irrespective of what system was used for promotion "the collective bargaining agreement between the parties reserves to C-Z the paramount right to deny a promotion to any employee, if he is not 'equally capable and efficient' as any other employee eligible for promotion, regardless of his seniority." [116] The company was, therefore, never obligated to advance any employee until it was convinced that the employee was qualified for the promotion and thus would not endanger the efficiency of the plant operation or the safety of fellow employees.

[113] Brief for Local 189a, United Papermakers and Paperworkers, *AFL-CIO, CLC; David Johnson, Sr., and Anthony Hill; 189a* v. *189 and C-Z*, p. 24.
[114] *Ibid.*, p. 29.
[115] *Ibid.*, p. 30.
[116] *Ibid.*, p. 32.

CONCLUSION

To summarize the arguments:

The thrust of the government's argument was the acceptance of a seniority system to provide the greatest chance of advancement of black employees to better and high-paying jobs, regardless of the desires of the parties to the collective bargaining agreement. The mill seniority system provided the desired results.[117]

Local 189 and Crown Zellerbach argued that the mill seniority system or the mill-plus-job seniority system decreased the efficiency of the plant and the safety of the employees, upset existing plant relations and employee expectations, and only incidentally accelerated black promotion. The job seniority system, on the other hand, fit the needs of the industry.[118]

Local 189a argued that job seniority was not required for the efficient running of the plant or for the safety of the employees because the promotion of capable employees was ensured by other means. The use of the mill seniority system, however, would eliminate present and future discrimination by providing each employee, regardless of race or color, the same chance of promotion.

On March 26, 1968, the court ruled that "in view of the racially motivated practices of denying to Negroes access to better-paying jobs in which Crown had engaged with the cooperation of Local 189, the job seniority system in effect prior to February 1, 1968, was unlawful. The court ordered defendants to replace that system with one which incorporated mill seniority as the sole determinant of promotion eligibility for qualified Negro employees who had previously been discriminatorily assigned." [119]

The court had determined that "only Negro employees hired prior to January 16, 1966, had been discriminated against." [120] Accordingly, mill seniority would only apply in situations "wherein this class of Negro employees were in competition in regard to training, promotion and demotions." [121]

Crown Zellerbach and Local 189 appealed the decision. The Fifth Circuit Court of the United States Court of Appeals rendered its opinion on July 28, 1969. The court stated that the major issue in the case was "how to reconcile equal employment opportunity *today* with seniority expectations based on *yesterday's* built-in racial discrimination." The court affirmed the decision of the district court, holding that C-Z's job seniority system in

[117] Brief on Behalf of Local 189, p. 13.
[118] *Ibid.*, p. 19.
[119] Brief on Behalf of U.S., p. 16.
[120] *Ibid.*, p. 27.
[121] *Ibid.*, p. 27.

effect at its Bogalusa paper mill prior to February 1, 1968, was unlawful and stated that the act required that "Negro seniority be equated with white seniority." [122]

[122] Opinion of the U.S. Court of Appeals for the Fifth Circuit in the case of Local 189 United Papermakers and Paperworkers AFL-CIO; United Papermakers and Paperworkers, AFL-CIO, CLC; and *Crown Zellerbach Corporation* v. *U.S.*, "Appeal from the United States District Court for Eastern District of Louisiana," July 28, 1969, pp. 2–3.

IV

CORPORATIONS, THEIR DEPENDENCIES, AND OTHER SOCIAL INSTITUTIONS

A.

CORPORATIONS AND
THE STOCKHOLDERS

Securities and Exchange Commission
versus Texas Gulf Sulphur Company

Use of Material Information by Corporate Executives
and Other "Insiders" in the Sale and Purchase of
Company Stock for Personal Gain

When the history books are written, the Texas Gulf case may turn out to be a landmark in the evolution of capitalism from the original "public-be-damned" to capitalism as a public trust.

—Business Week

This is not regulation—it is bureaucracy run wild. . . . At each fresh aggrandizement of the agency's power, each assault on personal freedom, brokers and businessmen have beat a retreat under the ignoble standard, "we can live with it." Gentlemen, can you live with the police state?

—Barron's

At 10:00 A.M. on April 16, 1964, Texas Gulf Sulphur Company (TGS) issued a press release announcing a major strike of zinc, copper, and silver on its properties in the Timmins area of Ontario, Canada. The news culminated in the confirmation of a long circulating, but recently intensified, rumor of the presence and discovery of sizable ore deposits by TGS on the Timmins property. The press release stated, in part:

Texas Gulf Sulphur Company has made a major strike of zinc, copper and silver in the Timmins area of Ontario, Canada. . . .

Seven drill holes are now essentially complete and indicate an ore body of at least 800 feet in length, 300 feet in width and having a vertical depth of more than 800 feet. . . .

This is a major discovery. The preliminary data indicate a reserve of more than 25 million tons of ore. The only hole assayed so far represents over 600 feet of ore, indicating a true ore thickness of nearly 400 feet. . . .

Visual examination of cores from the other holes indicates comparable grade and continuity of ore. . . .

The ore body is shallow, having only some 20 feet of overburden. This means that it can easily be mined initially by the open pit method.[1]

The events that led to the press release started in 1957. At the time of the press release none of the participants knew that these events were but the beginning of a long, arduous travail, which would expand the fiduciary responsibilities of the corporate management and those who might have access to inside information in exploiting that information for their personal gain.

BACKGROUND

TGS, which was incorporated in 1909, is the world's major supplier of sulphur. However, in 1963 the company's annual earnings ($9 million) showed a dramatic decline from 1955 ($32 million).[2] TGS attributed this decline in earnings (as well as sales of $93 million in 1955 against $62 million in 1963) to an oversupply of sulphur on the world markets, with the resulting implications of declining prices ($28 per ton in 1956 against $20 per ton in 1963). However, in late 1963 the price decline was reversed, so that by April 1, 1964, TGS announced an increase of $2 per ton. This announcement followed the disclosure on February 8, 1964, of the company's increased production plans. One of the consequences of this general decline in profitability was TGS's entry into a diversification program in phosphate, potash, trona, oil, and gas (phosphates, potash, and nitrogen are the main components of fertilizer).

---

[1] "Major Ore Lode Hit by TGS in Canada," *The Wall Street Journal,* April 17, 1964, p. 2.

[2] Earnings per share 1960—$1.27, 1961—$1.26, 1962—$1.21, 1963—$0.93, 1964—$1.15. The large decline in 1963 was due to extraordinary loss of one of TGS's seagoing tankers.

As part of its worldwide exploration for increased supply, TGS initiated in 1957 a search for sulphides [3] on the Canadian Shield, the vast, flat, and mostly barren area of eastern Canada, which is composed of Precambrian (very complex and distorted) rock formations. After the initial surveys, an aerial geophysical survey was begun in March 1959. This survey, conducted by an exploration group consisting of Richard D. Mollison, Walter Holyk, Richard H. Clayton, and Kenneth H. Darke (see cast of characters), detected several thousand anomalies (unusual variations in the conductivity of the rock). These were reduced to several hundred that merited further study. One of these anomalies was located in Kidd Township, near Timmins, Ontario (hereafter referred to as Kidd 55).

Cast of Characters (1,269)

Name	Position
Claude O. Stephens	President and director
Charles F. Fogarty	Executive vice-president [a] and director
Thomas S. Lamont	Director
Francis G. Coates	Director
Harold B. Kline	Vice president and general counsel [b]
Richard D. Mollison	Vice-president
David M. Crawford	Secretary [c]
Richard H. Clayton	Engineer
Walter Holyk	Chief geologist
Kenneth H. Darke	Geologist
Earl L. Huntington	Attorney
John A. Murray	Office manager

[a] Prior to February 20, 1964, was senior vice-president.
[b] Prior to January 31, 1964, was vice-president—administration, and secretary.
[c] Employed by TGS in January 1964 and became secretary on February 20, 1964.

Kidd 55 Segment

As a result of the aerial survey of the Kidd 55 segment, TGS acquired an option to buy for five hundred dollars the northeastern quarter section of 160 acres on June 6, 1963. Clayton, in conducting a ground survey on October 29 and 30, 1963, confirmed the indicated presence of conductive subsoil material. After consultation with Holyk and Darke, a drill site,

---

[3] Certain minerals combine with sulphur, some of which, such as copper sulphide and zinc sulphide, may be mined commercially if found in quantity. Sulphides conduct electricity better than most other rock types and thus can be detected by aerial survey if in sufficient quantity and not buried too deeply.

K-55-1, was chosen, and drilling operations began November 8, 1963.[4] Darke telephoned Holyk on November 11 at his home in Stamford, Connecticut, to report findings of a strong initial evidence of mineralization in the core sample. Holyk left for Timmins the same day. Prior to his departure he called Mollison, who passed on the findings to Charles F. Fogarty, the company's executive vice-president. Fogarty in turn called Claude O. Stephens, the company's president. The drilling was terminated the following day after work had been done on a core section 655 feet in length. In a visual mineralization estimate, Holyk predicted an average copper content of 1.15 percent and a zinc content of 8.64 percent over a length of 599 feet. On November 13 Mollison and Fogarty flew into Timmins for consultation with the exploration group. The following morning they returned to New York with Holyk. For confirmation a split core sample was flown by TGS to the Union Assay House in Salt Lake City for a detailed chemical analysis. The results of this analysis later indicated (mid-December) a copper content of 1.18 percent, a zinc content of 8.26 percent, and a silver content of 3.94 ounces per ton over a length of 602 feet (1,271).

Secrecy of Drilling Operations

The company instituted standard exploratory security measures to insure that its findings remained secret. The drilling crew was told to keep the results and the site confidential. Drilling on the K-551 anomaly was terminated, and the drilling rig was moved to a new drill site, K-55-2, located off the anomaly (Figure 1). Drilling was begun on November 20 and was completed ten days later. The rig was then moved out, leaving behind an obvious drill site, but a barren core. Small saplings were planted in the core area of K-55-1 to conceal its location. A convenient snowfall completed the concealment of drilling activities. During this time and in subsequent months strong rumors of a major nickel find by TGS began to circulate.

Land Acquisition

Based on Holyk's estimates, and without the confirming analysis of the official assay, TGS decided to acquire the three remaining quarter sections of K-55. Under the direction of Darke, TGS began to stake claims in the area surrounding the Kidd site. This work was completed on March 27,

---

[4] *Securities and Exchange Commission* v. *Texas Gulf Sulphur Company*, S.D.N.Y. 258 F. Supp. 262 (1966), 288. All subsequent references in the text to this citation will be shown as (1. page number).

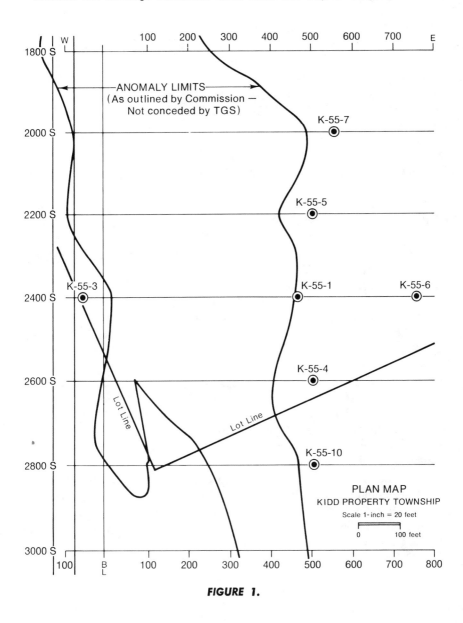

FIGURE 1.

1964. Three days later a TGS legal team, including Harold B. Kline, vice-president, consummated the purchase of the remaining Kidd-55 sections.[5] The company purchased one section outright for $7,500 and obtained

[5] Morton Shulman, *The Billion Dollar Windfall* (New York: William Morrow & Co., Inc., 1970), p. 107.

options on the two remaining quarter sections for $7,000 based on a purchase price of $45,000 (1,271). Because of TGS's drilling activity, the growing rumors, and the claim-staking activity, there was increased trading in mining claims and stocks on the Toronto Stock Exchange. Many of the claims in the area surrounding Timmins and the Kidd site had been reviewed by TGS's exploration team and deemed worthless. These in turn had been bought up by a Timmins partnership, including Darke, which began to sell them off. Worthless or not, a "traditional" Canadian mining frenzy was on.

After obtaining the rights to the full Kidd Township section, drilling was resumed on March 31, 1964, at the K-55-3 drill site. That same day in New York, TGS announced a $2-per-ton increase in the price of sulphur. The drilling operation was completed on the evening of April 7 at a length of 876 feet. The visual estimates showed an average copper content of 1.12 percent and a zinc content of 7.93 percent over 641 feet. Throughout the drilling operation, Mollison and Holyk gave daily progress reports to Stephens and Fogarty in New York.

TGS brought in additional rigs so that test drilling could proceed at a faster pace. Drilling at the K-55-4 site was begun on April 7. Two days later the operation was completed over a length of 420 feet. The visual estimates showed a copper content of 1.14 percent and a zinc content of 8.24 percent over 366 feet. Additional drilling, to a length of 579 feet, did not show any additional mineralization (1,272). Combined with the results of K-55-1 and K-55-3, the evidence to date showed the existence of substantial mineralization on the eastern edge of the K-55 anomaly, which was the first time TGS had a firm indication, if not solid geophysical proof, that the discovery was minable (i.e., was three dimensional in sufficient size). (See Figure 1.)

Drill site K-55-6 was begun on April 8, and by April 10 it was evident that substantial copper mineralization existed over the last 127 feet of the total 569-foot length. No visual estimates were made, as none of the geologists were on the site. Drill site K-55-5 was begun on April 10, and by that evening evidence of strong mineralization was apparent over the last 42 feet of the 97-foot core length (1,272).

Rumors and Reality

On April 9, 1964, several Toronto newspapers reported that TGS had discovered what was termed "one of the largest copper deposits in North America, [and] a major copper strike" (1,293). Similar stories circulated in the *Northern Miner* and the *Toronto Star* which stated that "the Moccasin telegraph has Texas Gulf's activity centered in Kidd township. . . . Timmins was . . . bug-eyed with excitement." [6] Alerted to the Toronto news stories, Stephens telephoned Thomas S. Lamont, a company director, on the tenth for advice on handling the Canadian rumors. Lamont recommended that TGS take no action as long as the rumors remained solely in Canada or at least until TGS had enough information about the implications of the drilling results to issue an appropriate statement to the press. However, he said, should the rumors reach New York, a press release would be necessary.

The following day, April 11, Stephens read the articles that appeared in *The New York Times* and the *New York Herald Tribune*. The *Herald Tribune* stated in part that the K-55 discovery was "the biggest ore strike since gold was discovered more than 60 years ago in Canada. . . . A bed of copper sulphide 600 feet wide with a possible over-all copper return of 2.87% through most of its width" (1,293). The article also stated that TGS had four drilling rigs in operation on the K-55 site and that the cores' richness was such that they had to be flown out of Canada for assay.

Immediately after reading the articles in the New York papers, Stephens phoned Fogarty at his home in Rye, New York, and asked Fogarty to read the articles and call him back. Later Fogarty called Stephens at his home in Greenwich, Connecticut, and told him that he was "quite upset . . . because certainly they [the articles] were full of exaggerations and what I considered to be erroneous statements" (1,294). Stephens indicated that TGS should issue, as soon as possible, a press release to clarify the situation and to dispel the rumors. Fogarty then contacted Carroll of TGS's public relations firm, Doremus and Company, and Carroll agreed that a press release was necessary.

That evening Fogarty went to Greenwich to discuss the situation at the drill site with Mollison, who had flown in from Timmins to spend the weekend at home. Mollison advised that, based on the information he had up to the time he left Timmins on the morning of April 10, it was too early to determine what type of discovery TGS had made. He said that "it was impossible at that time . . . to understand the structure [of the discovery or] . . . to make projections from one hole to another" (1,294).

Fogarty returned to New York City, and with the help of Carroll and David M. Crawford, the company's secretary, drafted a statement for release to the press on April 12. The draft was given to Earl L. Huntington, the company's attorney, to verify the legalities of the press release.

April 12 Press Release

On the morning of April 12, Fogarty called Mollison at his home and told him to return as soon as possible to Timmins, along with Holyk (who

---

[6] John Brooks, "Annals of Finance: A Reasonable Amount of Time," *New Yorker*, November 9, 1968, p. 171.

had also returned to New York for the weekend), to "move things along" (1,294). Fogarty then called Stephens and read the statement to be released at three o'clock that afternoon for publication Monday morning:

During the past few days, the exploration activities of Texas Gulf Sulphur in the area of Timmins, Ontario, have been widely reported in the press, coupled with rumors of a substantial copper discovery there. These reports exaggerate the scale of operations, and mention plans and statistics of size and grade of ore that are without factual basis and have evidently originated by speculation of people not connected with TGS.

The facts are as follows. TGS has been exploring in the Timmins area for six years as part of its overall search in Canada and elsewhere for various minerals—lead, copper, zinc, etc. During the course of this work, in Timmins as well as in Eastern Canada, TGS has conducted exploration entirely on its own, without the participation by others. Numerous prospects have been investigated by geophysical means and a large number of selected ones have been core-drilled. These cores are sent to the United States for assay and detailed examination as a matter of routine and on advice of expert Canadian legal counsel. No inferences as to grade can be drawn from this procedure.

Most of the areas drilled in Eastern Canada have revealed either barren pyrite or graphite without value; a few have resulted in discoveries of small or marginal sulphide ore bodies.

Recent drilling on one property near Timmins has led to preliminary indications that more drilling would be required for proper evaluation of this prospect. The drilling done to date has not been conclusive, but the statements made by many outside quarters are unreliable and include information and figures that are not available to TGS.

The work done to date has not been sufficient to reach definite conclusions and any statement as to size and grade of ore would be premature and possibly misleading. When we have progressed to the point where reasonable and logical conclusions can be made, TGS will issue a definite statement to its stockholders and to the public in order to clarify the Timmins project.[7]

K-55 Revisited

When Mollison left Timmins for New York on the morning of April 10, he had the up-to-date results of the drilling operations. However, drill-

[7] "TGS Calls Talk 'Premature' on Canada Copper Lode," *The Wall Street Journal,* April 13, 1964, p. 12.

ing did not stop while he and Holyk were absent. Rather, operations had intensified.

At site K-55-5 drilling resumed on the evening of April 10 and was completed on April 13. The core sample indicated mineralization to the 580-foot level, and the visual estimates over a 525-foot section indicated an average copper content of 0.82 percent and a zinc content of 4.2 percent. At site K-55-6 drilling also resumed on April 10 and was completed at 7:00 A.M. on April 13. The visual estimates showed mineralization over 504 feet of the 946-foot core, with a copper content of 1.72 percent and a zinc content of 6.60 percent (1,272).

On April 11 drilling on K-55-8 was begun. This particular site differed from the others in that it was a mill test hole.[8] The bore was completed on April 13. No visual estimates or other geological evidence was available or reported prior to April 16 because a mill test requires more detailed analysis (1,273).

A new site, K-55-7, was begun on April 12 and by the following day had encountered mineralization of 50 feet over its 137-foot length. By April 15 the core had been drilled to 707 feet, but with only an additional 26 feet of mineralization between the 425- to 451-foot level. The last site drilled by the exploration group, K-55-10, was begun on April 14. By 7:00 P.M. the following day, substantial mineralization was evident over the last 231 feet of the 249 feet of drilling (1,273).

The Northern Miner

Because of the rumors sweeping Canada in early April, the *Northern Miner,* a weekly mining trade journal published in Toronto, asked TGS for an inspection tour of the Kidd site and interviews with the exploration team so that it could gather information for an article that might clarify the rumors. The circulation of the journal in the United States was very small (7,400 subscribers, of whom 1,412 were in New York, plus a small newsstand circulation) (1,285). TGS agreed and made arrangements to have one of the paper's reporters, Graham Ackerley, visit the site on April 12. However, because of the printing of the articles in the Toronto press, Stephens and Fogarty on April 11 asked that Ackerley's visit be postponed to April 13 so that it would not coincide with the April 12 press release.

Ackerley visited the Kidd site and inspected the drilling records to date and the core samples, and he interviewed Mollison and Holyk (both of whom had returned to Timmins from New York), and Darke. While at

---

[8] A mill test hole differs from the others in that the diameter is twice the normal drill core size (2¼″ vs. 1⅛″). It is used to determine the amenability of the mineral material to routine mill processing.

the site Ackerley wrote the draft of his article, which he submitted to Mollison for clearance. Both Mollison and Holyk read the proposed article and decided that "some conclusions were too optimistic . . ." (1,285). However, they did not require any major revisions of the draft. The article stated, in part, *"The Northern Miner* can say that a major zinc-copper-silver mine is definitely in the making, one that has all the earmarks of shaping into a substantial open pit operation . . . something in excess of 10 million tons of ore is indicated." [9]

Mollison returned the draft to Ackerley on the evening of April 15 with his clearance for publication. The article was published in the paper's April 16 morning edition. The paper hit the streets in Toronto between 7:00 A.M. and 8:00 A.M. Reports of the article were telephoned and telexed to New York City from Toronto prior to the opening of the New York Stock Exchange (10:00 A.M.) on April 16, 1964 (1,285). By 9:15 A.M. the TGS discovery was the talk of the financial community in New York.[10]

Ontario Minister of Mines

During the period between the two press releases, the Canadian Institute of Mining and Metallurgy held its annual convention in Montreal (April 13–15). The main subject of conversation throughout the meeting was the rumors of the TGS discovery which were sweeping the Canadian mining and business communities. One of the participants of the convention was Ontario Minister of Mines George Wardrope.

First contacted by Holyk in Montreal, Wardrope arranged a meeting for Tuesday, April 14. Mollison and Holyk arrived for the meeting to find themselves celebrities, with a press conference waiting. Since they had no authorization to make a public statement, they went back to their hotel. It was then agreed that they would fly the minister and his deputy to Toronto the following day (9:30 A.M.). During the flight Wardrope was informed of the current developments at the Kidd drilling site. He was enthusiastic over the scope of the discovery and expressed a desire to make a public statement concerning the exploration operation, and both Mollison and Holyk agreed that such a statement was desirable.

With the assistance of Mollison, Wardrope drafted a statement which concluded: "The information in hand . . . gives the company confidence to allow me [the minister] to announce that Texas Gulf Sulphur has a minable body of zinc, copper, and silver ore of substantial dimensions that

---

[9] "TGS Comes Up with Major Find Carrying Important Copper, Zinc, Silver Values," *Northern Miner,* April 16, 1964, p. 1.
[10] Brooks, "Annals of Finance," p. 174.

will be developed and brought to production as rapidly as possible" (1.285–86).

It was decided that the minister would issue the statement in Toronto on radio and television at 11:00 P.M. (April 15). Mollison phoned Stephens and Fogarty in New York about the timing of the statement's release. Mollison and Holyk went on to Timmins, took a quick look around (by this time Timmins was a boomtown), conferred with John A. Murray, the company's office manager, and then returned to New York, arriving late that evening. For some undisclosed reason, the minister's statement was not made that evening but, instead, the following morning (April 16) at 9:40 at the Ontario Parliament in Toronto.

April 16 Press Release

At 9:00 A.M. on April 16, the TGS board of directors held its regularly scheduled monthly meeting at its offices in the Pan American building. Copies of the press release were distributed and read to the members of the board (all fifteen of whom were present). For most of them this was the first confirmation of the rumors that had appeared in the Canadian and the New York press. Stephens also told the board that the Ontario minister had made a statement the previous evening (this had not been confirmed by TGS). They were then briefed by Holyk and Mollison on the Kidd operations. After a short meeting Stephens called the reporters into the boardroom at 10:00 A.M. and then read the press release (see pages 333–334 of this book).

The reporters rushed from the room to call in the story to their respective services. The first summary of the release was carried over the internal wires of the brokerage house Merrill Lynch, Pierce, Fenner and Smith at 10:29 A.M. The Dow-Jones broad tape carried parts of the release between 10:45 A.M. and 11.02 A.M. (1,289).

Purchase of Stocks Options and Calls

In March 1961 TGS instituted the Restricted Stock Option Incentive Plan, which was for management personnel making an annual salary of over $24,000. On February 20, 1964, the board of directors voted to grant stock options to twenty-six members of TGS. This was done on the recommendation of a committee composed of J. H. Hill, chairman of the board of Air Reduction and other companies, and Francis G. Coates—the third member, L. M. Cassidy, was not present. Twenty-one of the options were granted to personnel making more than $24,000 (which included Stephens, Fogarty, Kline, and Mollison). The other five options were granted to personnel making between $15,000 and $21,000 (which included Holyk). The plan stated that the options would be granted at a minimum of 95 percent of the fair market price of the shares on the day of their approval. The options were to be based on the average of the high and the low quote for TGS stock on February 20, 1964—$23.81 per share (1,290–91).

In making the stock options, neither the committee nor the board of directors asked, or were they told, if any of the prospective recipients had any special knowledge that might affect the market performance of TGS shares. However, each of the named recipients was aware of the developments to that point at the Kidd site.

Individual Actions of the Principal Characters

1. *Thomas S. Lamont.*   Lamont, who in addition to being a director of TGS was also a director of the Morgan Guaranty Trust Company and was on its executive committee and its trust and investment committee, first heard of the Kidd operations on April 10 when Stephens called to ask him for advice on handling the Canadian rumors. Lamont recommended that nothing be done at that stage. On April 11 he read the *Herald Tribune* article; and on April 12, the TGS press release. On April 13 and 14 Lamont talked with Executive Vice-President Hinton of Morgan Guaranty about the articles in the press and TGS's public statement that Lamont knew "nothing more than what was in the papers." On April 15 Stephens phoned Lamont and informed him of the press release to be issued the following day. At the meeting of the board of directors, Lamont read the full text of the release. At 10:40 A.M. he called Hinton at Morgan Guaranty and advised him of impending good news on the "tape." Hinton immediately called the bank's trading department and was told that the market for TGS was active and up three points. He then placed orders for twelve thousand shares for various bank customers. At approximately 12:30 P.M. Lamont placed a buy order for three thousand shares for himself and his family.

2. *Francis G. Coates.*   Coates, who was in Houston, Texas, telephoned Stephens in New York after reading the April 11 article in the *Herald Tribune*. He was informed of the TGS position with regard to the rumors and of the press release scheduled for the following day.

On April 13 Coates called Stephens again in New York and asked if it was necessary to return for the directors' meeting. He was told that he should be present, but he was not told why. On April 15 Coates flew to New York and saw a draft of the April 16 press release. He attended the directors' meeting on the sixteenth. At 10:20 A.M. he left the room and called his son-in-law, H. Fred Haemisegger, a stockbroker in Houston, and after informing him of the TGS discovery, placed an order for two thousand shares for the accounts of four family trusts of which he was a trustee. Haemisegger told four of his customers of the TGS announcement, and they bought fifteen hundred shares of TGS.

3. *David M. Crawford.* Crawford read the April 11 article in the *Herald Tribune* on the way to Houston to prepare for the annual stockholders' meeting scheduled for April 23. He returned to New York either late on April 14 or early on April 15. Along with Fogarty and Orlando of Doremus and Company—TGS's public relations firm—he helped to draft the press release on the afternoon of April 15. This was the first time that he was made aware of the developments at the Kidd site.

Crawford spent that night in New York. At midnight he telephoned his broker in Chicago and ordered three hundred shares for himself and his wife to be bought at the opening of the exchange. In the morning, at 8:30, he called Chicago again and increased his order to six hundred shares.

4. *Richard H. Clayton.* In Timmins on April 12 and 13, Clayton returned to New York on April 14. He spent April 15 in TGS's offices. That day he called his broker in Toronto and ordered two hundred shares.

Reaction to the Press Release of April 16

The public reaction to the confirmation of the rumors about the Kidd discovery caused the price of TGS shares on the New York Stock Exchange to soar "$7 to close at $36.375 a share. It was the most active Big Board Stock, with 444,200 shares traded." [11] The news created active trading in mining shares throughout the next week, on both the American and the Canadian exchange.

Public reaction to the April 12 announcement and the company's negation of the "premature and possibly misleading" [12] rumors came under public criticism. Fogarty stated in an interview that "it wasn't until the middle of last week that the company knew it made the mineral discovery in Timmons." He also stated that TGS only made its announcement after a fourth drilling rig that went into operation the preceding week had gathered information at a very rapid pace. "By Wednesday," he said, when seven drill holes were nearly completed, "we felt we had enough informa-

[11] *The Wall Street Journal,* April 17, 1964, p. 2.
[12] *The Wall Street Journal,* April 13, 1964, p. 12.

tion to hang our hat on." Fogarty further elaborated that the April 12 press release was issued because so much misinformation was coming out about the company that it was "in the best interest of the public and the company to clarify the situation." [13]

TABLE 1

Market Activity of Texas Gulf Sulphur Common Stock on the New York Stock Exchange in April 1964

Date	Sales in 100s	Open	High	Low	Close	Net Change
4/9	798	29¾	30⅛	28⅝	29	− ⅝
4/10	921	29⅜	30⅛	29⅛	30⅛	+1⅛
4/13	1,265	32	32	30⅛	30⅞	+ ¾
4/14	769	30⅞	30⅞	29⅜	30¼	− ⅝
4/15	438	30⅛	30¼	28⅞	29⅜	− ⅞
4/16	4,442	30⅛	37	30⅛	36⅜	+7
4/17	4,992	39¾	42	38¾	40¼	+3⅞
4/20	3,785	42	44	41½	42¼	+2
4/21	2,201	41	41¼	39⅛	40⅛	−2⅛
4/22	3,265	40½	47	40½	45½	+5⅜
4/23	5,696	47¾	48¼	42⅛	42⅝	−2⅞
4/24	2,438	44	44¾	42¾	44¼	+1⅝
4/27	2,336	44⅛	47½	44⅝	47	+2¾
4/28	4,712	47¾	52⅜	47¾	52⅜	+5⅜
4/29	9,067	54½	59	53½	56¾	+4⅜

On Monday, April 20, the NYSE announced that it "was barring stop orders in Texas Gulf Sulphur . . . effective at today's market opening [Tuesday, April 21]." [14] The same day TGS announced an increase of 19 percent, to $2,764,000, of its first-quarter earnings, or twenty-eight cents a share (from $2,320,000, or twenty-three cents a share, during the first quarter of 1963). Sales climbed to $15,237,000 for the quarter, from $14,723,000. It stated that the improved earnings "resulted mainly from economies in the delivery of sulphur and in the operation of the Texas

[13] "Texas Gulf Sulphur Ore Discovery Still Has Mine Stocks, Claims Flying," *The Wall Street Journal*, April 20, 1964, p. 32.

[14] A *stop order* is an order an investor places with his broker to buy a specified number of shares of a stock if the price of the stock rises above a specified level or to sell if it falls below a specified level. When the stop price is reached, a stop order becomes a market order, or an order for the broker to get the best possible price. Stop orders tend to increase the price fluctuations of a volatile stock.

Gulf facilities and in some price improvement abroad." [15] Fogarty also said that TGS expected a continued favorable trend.

Two days later, Fogarty announced that "Texas Gulf Sulphur Company's mineral discovery in Canada won't benefit the company's earnings this year [1964]," adding that any increased earnings would "probaby start in 1965." [16]

At the annual stockholders' meeting in Houston, Stephens announced that it would be another six months before the company's copper, zinc, and silver discovery in Canada could be fully evaluated. He also indicated that the initial announcement of the discovery's size on April 16 was a conservative one.

Public Disclosure of Stock Purchases by Insiders

Approximately one month after the public announcement of the TGS discovery, news began to surface that executives of TGS had purchased shares in the company on the open market on or about the date of the announcement. On May 14, 1964, an article in *The Wall Street Journal,* quoting NYSE sources, reported that two officers and a director of TGS had purchased a total of 3,730 shares of TGS common in April 1964. The officers named were Crawford (530 shares) and Lamont (3,200 shares). [17]

Lamont informed the *Journal* that his purchase on April 16 had been made "in the afternoon long after the public announcement" and that "for obvious reasons I wouldn't dream of buying stock before the news got out." The same article stated that Fogarty had purchased four hundred shares on April 1 and another four hundred on April 6. He later purchased an additional one hundred shares on April 21 and another one hundred on April 22. When reached for comment, Fogarty stated that his purchases at the beginning of April had been made "after public announcements of other Texas Gulf Sulphur activities that have been overlooked amid the recent attention focused on the ore discovery." This reference was to TGS announcements at the beginning of April that the company was undertaking a major potash development in Utah, that a $2-per-ton price increase for sulphur was being introduced, and that a $45 million phosphate development was being initiated in North Carolina. He further stated that

---

15 "Texas Gulf Sulphur and Curtis Stock Prices Climb Again in Wake of Ore Find in Canada," *The Wall Street Journal,* April 21, 1964, p. 6.

16 "Texas Gulf Believes Find Won't Lift Net Until '65," *The Wall Street Journal,* April 23, 1964, p. 32.

17 "Texas Gulf Sulphur Co. Stock Bought in April by Two Officers, Directors," *The Wall Street Journal,* May 14, 1964, p. 15.

"his purchases were made in the belief that these activities would benefit future earnings and were made only after the activities had been announced." [18]

The next day, May 15, it was further revealed that another TGS employee had disclosed purchases of TGS stock on or about the date of the discovery's public announcement. The NYSE reported that Francis G. Coates, of Baker, Botts, Shepherd, and Coates, a Houston law firm representing TGS, and a TGS director, had purchased two thousand shares of TGS common on April 16. The NYSE further stated that the purchases were executed after the public announcement.[19]

On June 18, 1964, TGS announced its plans for developing the Kidd site and stated that the ore body appeared to be twice the size of the original estimate. The announcement set off such a flurry of trading on the NYSE that activity had to be halted briefly.

SECURITIES AND EXCHANGE COMMISSION SUIT

On April 19, 1965, the SEC filed a thirty-four-page civil suit against TGS and thirteen "insiders" (see cast of characters) in the United States Court for the Southern District of New York.[20] The complaint alleged that twelve of the defendants used inside information about the discovery on the Kidd site to make illegal gains in market activity in TGS common stock before word of the find was made public. The other defendant, Thomas S. Lamont, was accused of giving the Morgan Guaranty Trust Company advance knowledge of the ore discovery on April 16. The complaint covered the period between November 12, 1963, when drilling first indicated an ore find, and April 16, 1964, when the find was made public.[21]

The defendants were alleged to have made outright purchases of 9,100 TGS shares and to have bought call options on an additional 5,200 shares. They were also alleged to have received stock options on 31,200 shares. Additionally, the complaint charged that TGS personnel tipped off other individuals who bought 14,700 shares outright and calls on another 14,100 shares.[22] Furthermore, the suit was supposed to alert investors who had

---

[18] *Ibid.*

[19] "Another Texas Gulf Sulphur Aide Bought Stock April 16," *The Wall Street Journal,* May 15, 1964, p. 4.

[20] The case was heard only against twelve defendants. One defendant, Thomas P. O'Neill, an accountant with TGS, was served with a summons but failed to appear. His case was separated from the rest of the defendants.

[21] "Texas Gulf Sulphur Officers Accused by SEC of Profiting by Inside Data," *The Wall Street Journal,* April 20, 1965, p. 3.

[22] "Texas Gulf Suit Opens New Door for SEC," *Business Week,* April 24, 1965, pp. 24–25.

sold TGS stocks to insiders that they had the right to sue the TGS insiders for their losses.[23]

Offer to Return Profit to the Company

During the last week of April 1965, TGS again held its annual stockholders' meeting in Houston. Frequently interrupted by applause, TGS President Stephens addressed the meeting and said that the company was satisfied that no element of bad faith or overreaching was involved in any purchases by officers or directors. However, he recognized that others, influenced by hindsight and the magnitude of the Timmins discovery, might be concerned. Stephens also revealed that officials of the company had offered to return to the company any profits made on stock purchases since the ore discovery on the Kidd site, but that these offers had been summarily rejected by the SEC. In a press interview, Fogarty suggested that this refusal was part of an attempt "to strengthen their [the SEC's] policing powers. They are interested in getting broad legislation to prevent anyone in a company from buying that company's stock." A spokesman for the SEC promptly denied the charge, stating that "present legislation completely covers this kind of situation." [24]

Stockholder Suits

With the filing of the SEC suit in the New York federal court, the doors were opened for private civil suits instituted by former stockholders. By the middle of June 1965, at least fifteen major damage suits naming TGS and various company officials had been filed: twelve in the U.S. District Court in New York (in addition to the SEC complaint), one in the U.S. District Court in Chicago, one in the New York State Court, and one in New York Supreme Court. The total damages demanded in the various actions ran into the millions. The suit in Chicago, on behalf of fifty stockholders, asked punitive damages of $1.5 million. Another in the New York Supreme Court, on behalf of thirty-five former stockholders, sought punitive damages of $2.52 million and actual damages of $200 thousand.[25]

Summary of SEC Complaint

The SEC complaint charged each of the defendants with violations of Section 10b of the Securities and Exchange Commission Act of 1934 (15

[23] "Offer Declined," *Forbes,* May 1, 1965, p. 16.
[24] "Texas Gulf Says SEC Rejected Profit Turnback," *The Wall Street Journal,* April 23, 1965, p. 3.
[25] "Stock Suits Pile Up," *Chemical Week,* June 12, 1965, p. 38.

U.S.C. § 78j(b)) and Rule 10b-5 promulgated thereunder by the commission. Section 10 of the act reads, in pertinent parts, as follows:

It shall be unlawful for any person, directly or indirectly, by the use of any means or instrumentality of interstate commerce or of the mails or of any facility of any national securities exchange . . .

(b) To use or employ, in connection with the purchase or sale of any security registered on a national securities exchange or any security not so registered, any manipulative or deceptive device or contrivance in contravention of such rules and regulations as the Commission may prescribe as necessary or appropriate in the public interest or for the protection of investors.

Rule 10b (17 C.F.R. 240) provides that

it shall be unlawful for any person, directly or indirectly, by use of any means or instrumentality of interstate commerce, or of the mails, or any facility of any national securities exchange,

(1) to employ any device, scheme or artifice to defraud,
(2) to make any untrue statement of a material fact or to omit to state a material fact necessary in order to make the statements made, in the light of the circumstances under which thus were made, not misleading, or
(3) to engage in any act, practice, or course of business which operates or would operate as a fraud or deceit upon any person, in connection with the purchase or sale of any security.

The commission specifically charged that:

1. TGS violated Section 10b and Rule 10b-5 by issuing a false press release on April 12, 1964, concerning its exploratory activities on the Kidd 55 segment near Timmins, Ontario, between November 12, 1963, and April 16, 1964.
2. Each defendant was charged with similar violations, for purchasing stocks or calls on TGS stock or recommending such purchases to others between November 12, 1963, and April 16, 1964, on the grounds that defendants used to their own advantage *material information,* which they possessed, as to TGS's exploratory activities, which material information *had not been disclosed to or absorbed by the stockholders or the public.*
3. Five of the defendants were further charged with similar violations

for accepting stock options granted by TGS on February 20, 1964, on the grounds that they used *material information* in their possession to their own advantage by failing to disclose it to the directors' committee that granted the stock options.

In seeking remedy against these violations, the SEC sought to have the court decree:

1. Cancellation of stock purchases made by the thirteen defendants
2. Cancellation of the stock options
3. An injunction against further insider transactions based on inside information
4. An injunction against issuing misleading press releases
5. Additional relief not yet specified

The central precedent for SEC's suit of the alleged violation of Rule 10b-5 was the 1961 *Cady, Roberts* case, in which a representative of that brokerage house, who was also a director of Curtis-Wright Publishing Company, told an associate, thirty minutes before public release of the information, that Curtis-Wright was reducing its dividend rate. The associate used this information to make a financial gain. The decision, written by the then SEC Chairman William L. Cary, found this to be a violation of Rule 10b-5, stating that insiders must disclose material facts known to them by virtue of their positions but not known to persons with whom they deal and that, if known, would affect their investment judgment. Failure to make disclosure in these circumstances constitutes a violation of the antifraud provisions.[26]

The SEC provided evidence to show that all the individual defendants purchased shares of TGS or calls on TGS stock between November 12, 1963, and April 16, 1964. Evidence also showed that certain persons, called "tippees" by the SEC counsel at the trial, purchased shares of TGS or calls on TGS stock on the basis of advice received directly or indirectly from defendants Darke, Coates, and Lamont (see Tables 2 and 3).

The SEC suit charged that the defendants had failed to disclose "material facts" in the sale or purchase of TGS securities and asked the defendants to reimburse for their losses those individuals who sold TGS stock based upon the "false and misleading" April 12, 1964, press release concerning the Kidd discovery. The SEC contended that the defendants had engaged in a "course of business" that operated "as a fraud or deceit" on the stockholders. The suit would require the defendants to either sell

[26] *SEC* v. *Cady, Roberts & Co.* (S.D.N.Y. 1962).

TABLE 2

Number of Shares and/or Calls Purchased by Defendants and Their "Tippees"

Purchase Date	Purchaser	Shares Number	Shares Price	Calls Number	Calls Price
HOLE K-55-1 COMPLETED NOVEMBER 12, 1963					
1963					
Nov. 12	Fogarty	300	17¾–18		
15	Clayton	200	17¾		
15	Fogarty	700	17⅝–17⅞		
15	Mollison	100	17⅞		
19	Fogarty	500	18⅛		
26	Fogarty	200	17¾		
29	Holyk (Mrs.)	50	18		
CHEMICAL ASSAYS OF DRILL CORE OF K-55-1 RECEIVED DECEMBER 9–13, 1963					
Dec. 10	Holyk (Mrs.)	100	20⅜		
12	Holyk (or wife)			200	21
13	Mollison	100	21⅛		
30	Caskey *			300	22¼
30	Fogarty	200	22		
31	Fogarty	100	23¼		
1964					
Jan. 6	Holyk (or wife)			100	23⅝
8	Murray			400	23¼
16	Westreich *	2,000	21¼–21¾		
24	Holyk (or wife)			200	22¼–22⅜
Feb. 10	Fogarty	300	22⅛–22¼		
17	Atkinson *	50	23¼	200	23⅛
17	Westreich *	50	23¼	1,000	23¼–23⅝
20	Darke	300	24⅛		
24	Clayton	400	23⅞		
24	Holyk (or wife)			200	24⅛
24	Miller *			200	23¾
25	Miller *			300	22⅜–23½
26	Huntington	50	23¼		
27	Darke (Moran as nominee)			1,000	22⅝–22¾
Mar. 2	Holyk (Mrs.)	200	22⅜		
3	Clayton	100	22¼		
3	E. W. Darke *			500	22½–22⅝
16				100	22⅜
16	Holyk (or wife)			300	23¼
17	Holyk (Mrs.)	100	23⅞		
17	E. W. Darke *			200	23⅜
23	Darke			1,000	23¾
26	Clayton	200	25		

TABLE 2—Continued

Purchase Date	Purchaser	Shares		Calls	
		Number	Price	Number	Price

LAND ACQUISITION COMPLETED MARCH 27, 1964

Purchase Date	Purchaser	Number	Price	Number	Price
Mar. 30	Atkinson *				
30	Caskey *	100	25⅞	400	25¾–25⅞
30	Darke			1,000	25¾–25⅞
30	E. W. Darke *			1,000	25½
30	Holyk (Mrs.)	100	25⅞	200	25½
30–31	Klotz *				
30	Miller *			2,000	25½–26⅛
30	Westreich *	500	25¾	500	25½–25⅞

CORE DRILLING OF KIDD 55 SEGMENT RESUMED MARCH 31, 1964

Purchase Date	Purchaser	Number	Price	Number	Price
Apr. 1	Clayton	60	26½		
1	Fogarty	400	26½		
2	Clayton	100	26⅞		
6	Fogarty	400	28⅛–28⅞		
8	Mollison (Mrs.)	100	28⅛		

421 FEET KIDD-55-4 COMPLETED APRIL 9, 1964, 7 P.M.
TGS PRESS RELEASE ISSUED APRIL 12, 1964

Purchase Date	Purchaser	Number	Price	Number	Price
Apr. 15	Clayton	200	29⅜		
16	Crawford (and wife)	600	30⅛–30¼		

TGS PRESS RELEASE AND PRESS CONFERENCE APRIL 16, 1964, 10 A.M.

Purchase Date	Purchaser	Number	Price	Number	Price
Apr. 16	Coates (for family trusts)	2,000	31–31⅝		
16	Haemisegger **	300	32½		
16	Robert L. Armstrong **	200	32¼–34½		
16	Charles Callery **	300	32½		
16	James A. Baker III **	200	32⅝		
16	Malcolm G. Baker, Jr.**	500	34½–35		
16	Morgan Guaranty Trust Co.***	10,000	32⅝–34		
16	Lamont and family ****	3,000	34½		

Source: 258 F. Supp. 262 (1966), 273–75.

* Darke visited Mrs. Caskey and her daughter Miss Atkinson in Washington between Dec. 25 and Dec. 30, 1963, and recommended TGS. They in turn recommended TGS directly or indirectly to others marked with *, with the exception of E. W. Darke, K. H. Darke's brother, who purchased calls on K. H. Darke's recommendation.

** Purchased by Haemisegger, Coates's son-in-law, for himself and customers (**) following telephone call from Coates before 10:20 A.M.

*** Purchased for its customers' accounts following call from Lamont to Hinton at about 10:40 A.M.

**** Purchased through Morgan Guaranty Trust Co. after 12:33 P.M.

TABLE 3

Estimated Profits of Defendants and Their "Tippees" on the Purchase of Shares
and/or Calls of Texas Gulf Sulphur Stock from November 12, 1963,
To Close of Business April 16, 1964

Defendants (and associates)	Estimated Dollar Profits			
	From 11/12/63 to 7:00 P.M., 4/9/64	From 7:00 P.M., 4/9/64 to 10:00 A.M., 4/16/64	From 10:00 A.M., 4/16/64 to close of business, 4/16/64	Total
Charles F. Fogarty	39,384			39,384
Thomas S. Lamont			41,150	41,150
Francis G. Coates			15,086	15,086
Richard D. Mollison	4,200			4,200
David M. Crawford		3,712		3,712
Richard H. Clayton	13,953	1,400		15,353
Walter Holyk	21,154			21,154
Kenneth H. Darke	127,205			127,205
Earl L. Huntington	2,562			2,562
John A. Murray	4,086			4,086
Total	212,544	5,112	56,236	273,892

back stock at the original prices or make up the difference in cash for those who sold their holdings in TGS based on the April 12 statement. It was this aspect of the suit that generated the most interest in the financial and legal community because, for the first time, the SEC was levying damages against "insiders." The suit also tended to break new ground in four major aspects, namely: (1) What is material information? (2) What is false and misleading information? (3) Who are the insiders? (4) What is a reasonable time that must elapse before a piece of information can be said to have become public knowledge?

In its briefs and at the trial, the commission made no distinction among the three sections of Rule 10b-5 as to violations, relying on precedents which noted that as long as a violation of the rule was alleged, it was immaterial which section of the rule was invoked (1,276).

Summary of Defendants' Response

By the middle of July, TGS filed an answer to the SEC complaint, denying that the purchases made by the defendants were made "with knowledge and information or material facts that were not disclosed to sellers of stock . . . or that the company issued a misleading press release concerning the extent of the copper and zinc minerals strike at Timmins, Ontario." TGS further spelled out the history of the Kidd site, specifically stating that K-55-1 "could not indicate that there was a mineable body of ore, much less that there was a major sulphide deposit . . . in that the core sample . . . didn't show whether mineralization occurred in thin, intermediate, or wide zones, or discontinuous zones." The company also stated that the unsubstantiated "rumors compelled TGS to make an immediate public statement [April 12] . . . indicating that it was not the source of these rumors." [27]

In addition to the company's answer to the SEC complaint, each defendant filed a separate answer. The defendants further asserted that:

1. The commission must first "establish the elements of common law fraud—misrepresentation or nondisclosure, materiality, scienter, intent to deceive, reliance, and causation citing decisions in private actions brought under Section 10(b) requiring proof of one or more of these traditional elements as a condition precedent to relief" (1,277).

2. The commission cannot broaden the definition of "insiders" or the limits of their liabilities to the sanctions beyond what Section 16 of the Act (15 U.S.C. 78p) specifies relating to directors, officers, and principal stockholders (1,278).

3. The facts do not prove the commission's allegations.

SUMMARY OF THE LOWER COURT'S DECISION

District Court Judge Dudley B. Bonsal rendered the lower court's decision on August 19, 1966. For easier understanding, the decision is divided into two parts—questions of law and questions of the facts in the case.

Questions of Law

The court held that in a regulatory or enforcement proceeding, the commission was not required to prove common law elements. "It is only necessary to prove one of the prohibited actions such as the material statement of fact or the omission to state a material fact" (1,277). Furthermore, the court cited the following Supreme Court decision:

It would defeat the manifest purpose of the Investment Advisers Act of 1940 for us to hold, therefore, that Congress, in empowering

[27] "TGS Fights Back," *Chemical Week,* July 17, 1965, p. 28.

the courts to enjoin any practice which operates "as a fraud or deceit," intended to require proof of intent to injure and actual injury to clients (375 U.S., at 192, 84 S. Ct., at 283). . . .

Congress intended the Investment Advisers Act of 1940 to be *construed like other securities legislation* "enacted for the purpose of avoiding frauds," not technically and restrictively, but flexibly to effectuate its remedial purposes (375 U.S., at 195, 84 S. Ct., at 284). [1,277]

The court also rejected the defendants' arguments regarding the definition of insiders and the limits of their liability under Section 16 of the act, citing various legal precedents that the scope of Secton 16 was narrower and was intended only as a "crude rule of thumb" to make unprofitable all short-swing speculation by a *specifically defined group of insiders* (1,278). Section 10b, on the other hand, applied to "any person" claiming to have been defrauded and was *not* limited to the purchase or sale of a listed security as in Section 16. Therefore, Section 16 imposed no limitations on the enforcement of Section 10b.

To establish violations of Section 10b and Rule 10b-5(3), the commission had to prove that the defendants engaged in a course of business that operated as fraud or deceit in connection with the purchase or sale of any security. The court then turned its attention to the question of whether insider purchases based on material undisclosed information did indeed constitute such violations. If such a contention were granted, then it must be decided as to who the insiders were, whether the act and the rule were limited to "face-to-face" transactions, and what constituted material information (1,278).

After citing various legal precedents and earlier court decisions, the court concluded:

1. The failure of the director and general manager of a corporation to disclose special facts in purchasing its securities operated as a fraud on the seller. The U.S. Supreme Court had stated in a decision:

> If it were conceded, for the purpose of the argument, that the ordinary relations between director and shareholders in a business corporation are not of such a fiduciary nature as to make it the duty of a director to disclose to a shareholder the general knowledge which he may possess regarding the value of the shares of the company before he purchases any from a shareholder, yet there are cases where, by reason of the special facts, such duty exists (213 U.S., at 431, 29 S. Ct., at 525). [1,278]

The court applied this "special facts" doctrine to Section 10b and Rule 10b-5 and declared that trading by an insider on the basis of undisclosed information was indeed a violation of the act and the rule.

2. *Insiders* might include employees of a company as well as directors, officers, and major stockholders who were in possession of material undisclosed information obtained in the course of their employment or engagement with the company.

3. As far as the court was concerned, *material information* was any "important development which might affect security values or influence investment decisions [of] reasonable and objective" investors.

4. The obligation to *disclose* material information rested on two grounds:

   (a) there must exist some basis for access to information intended for corporate purposes only and not for the personal gain of anyone; and

   (b) there must be some "inherent unfairness" involved where one party take advantages of such information, knowing that it is not available to those with whom he is dealing.

5. An insider's *liability* for failure to disclose material information that he used to his advantage in the purchase of securities extended to purchases made on national securities exchanges, as well as to face-to-face transactions.

6. *Fraud* might be accomplished by false statements, by failure to correct a misleading impression left by statements already made, or, as in the present case, by not stating anything at all when there was a duty to come forward and speak.

7. The court also rejected the defendants' argument that it would be impossible for an insider trading on a national exchange to locate the buyers or sellers to disclose material information to them. The court maintained that there were other ways to disclose significant corporate developments. For example, the New York Stock Exchange stated in its *Company Manual* that important developments that might affect security values or influence investments should be promptly disclosed. However, where material information was available to the employees of the corporation that was only for corporate use and could not be disclosed, even to stockholders, then the employee must avoid using it to his own advantage. However, to establish a violation of Section 10 and Rule 10b-5, the undisclosed information must be material. Nothing in the act would prevent

insiders from buying their company's stock or benefiting from the company's incentive stock option plan:

> On the contrary, it is important under our free enterprise system that insiders, including directors, officers, and employees, be encouraged to own securities in their company. The incentive that comes with stock ownership benefits both the company and its stockholders.
>
> Moreover, it is obvious that any director, officer, or employee will know more about his company or have more specialized knowledge as to at least some phase of its business than an outside stockholder can have or expect to have. Often this specialized knowledge may whet the speculative interest of the insider, particularly if he believes in the future of his company, and may lead him to purchase stock. Purchases under such circumstances are not encompassed by Section 10(b) and Rule 10b-5. [1,280]

Nevertheless, the court maintained that where an insider came into possession of material information that he used to his own advantage by purchasing stock of his company prior to public disclosure, he was indeed violating Section 10b and Rule 10b-5.

Information is not material merely because it would be of interest to the speculator on Bay Street or Wall Street. Material information has been defined as information which in reasonable and objective contemplation might affect the value of the corporation's stock or securities. . . .

Material information need not be limited to information which is translatable into earnings, as suggested by defendants. But the test of materiality must necessarily be a conservative one, particularly since many actions under Section 10(b) are brought on the basis of hindsight. As stated by a former member of the staff of the Commission:

> It is appropriate that management's duty of disclosure under rule 10b-5 be limited to those situations which are essentially extraordinary in nature and which are reasonably certain to have a substantial effect on the market price of the security if disclosed. A more rigorous standard would impose an unreasonable burden on management in its securities trading. [1,280]

The court therefore decided that all the defendants were indeed subject to the jurisdictional requirements of Section 10b and Rule 106-5.

Questions as to Facts

The court then turned its attention to the issue of whether any of the defendants, in purchasing TGS stock or calls, were using, to their own advantage, material information as to the drilling on the Kidd-55 segment not disclosed to the public. To analyze this issue, the court divided the total time period into the following three segments:

1. From November 12, 1963, to 7:00 P.M., April 9, 1964
2. From 7:00 P. M., April 9, 1964, to 10:00 A.M., April 16, 1964
3. From 10:00 A.M., April 16, 1964, to the close of business on that day

November 12, 1963, to 7:00 P.M., April 9, 1964. Regarding the materiality of information on Kidd-55-1, there was no doubt that the drill core was unusually good. However, all the experts agreed that one drill core does not establish an ore body, much less a mine. The SEC contended that the results of K-55-1 were material because of the significance certain defendants attached to those results. Between the completion of K-55-1 on November 12, 1963, and the completion of K-55-3 on April 7, 1964, defendants Fogarty, Mollison, Holyk, Clayton, and Darke spent more than $100,000 in purchasing stocks and calls on the stock of TGS. However, the court maintained that those purchases were made on the basis of educated guesses, which were not proscribed under Section 10 or Rule 10b-5.

As to K-55-3, the court stated that K-55-1 had not gone down dip, and indicated a vertical plane on Section 2400 S containing mineralization. However, there was an indication that the mineralization extended beyond the plane. The results of K-55-3 added to the information previously known but did not constitute material information.

The court concluded that there was strong evidence that TGS had a commercially minable area, since the drilling of K-55-4 to 7:00 P.M. on April 9, 1964, had indicated that the mineralization encountered on the vertical plane between K-55-1 and K-55-3 extended southward 200 feet (Figure 2). But the court felt that the total drilling results up to 7:00 P.M. on April 9, 1964, did not provide material information that, if disclosed, would have had a substantial impact on the market price of the company's stock.

Accordingly, the purchases made by certain defendants prior to 7:00 P.M. on April 9, 1964, were not based on material information. The fact that subsequent drilling established a major ore body was immaterial (1,285).

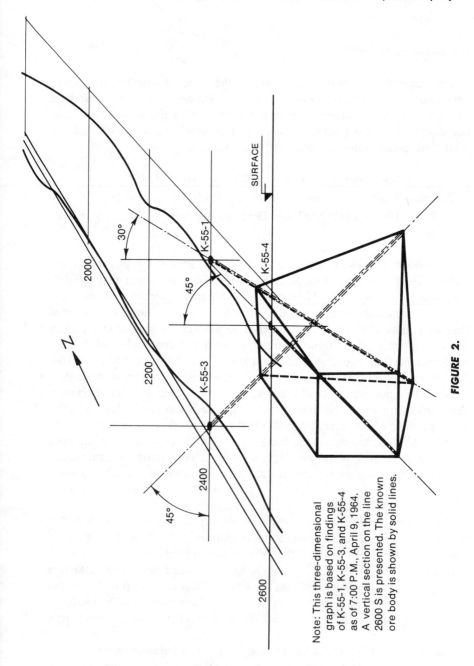

Note: This three-dimensional graph is based on findings of K-55-1, K-55-3, and K-55-4 as of 7:00 P.M., April 9, 1964. A vertical section on the line 2600 S is presented. The known ore body is shown by solid lines.

FIGURE 2.

7:00 P.M., April 9, 1964, to 10:00 A.M., April 16, 1964. This period starts with the completion of K-55-4 and the firm establishment of the availability of commercially exploitable ore. The SEC's experts contended that K-55-4 established the third dimension to the mineralization zone. Therefore, on the basis of work done up to 7:00 P.M., April 9, 1964, TGS should have realized a mine, and, furthermore, TGS could have calculated the ore reserves up to 7.7 million tons with a gross assay value of $204.2 million.

The court rejected the defendants' argument that if the information were indeed true, it had already become public knowledge through the story in the *Northern Miner*, the rumors in Canada, and the pending announcement by the Canadian minister of mines. The court maintained that if TGS officials did believe that the news had already become public, there was "little purpose in making the arrangements for a press conference and issuing a detailed announcement on April 16" (1.286).

Therefore, the court held that information on the Kidd property during this period was *material undisclosed information,* and hence its use by any of the defendants for their personal gain would constitute a violation of Section 10b and Rule 10b-5.

10:00 A.M., April 16, 1964, to Close of Business on That Day. The court held that any material information became public knowledge *as soon as* the announcement had been made: "It is the making of the announcement that controls" (1.288). The court rejected the SEC's contention that although the information was announced it was not absorbed by the public for some time. First, if the commission's argument were to be accepted, its application should be extended beyond corporate insiders to those people who might be in a position to take unfair advantage of the stockholders —for example, brokers, press reporters, or telephone operators who received the news in the course of their work before the general public did. Second, if the courts were to decide what was a reasonable elapsed time after the fact, to take into consideration specific circumstances in individual cases, it would lead to uncertainty because no insider would know if he had waited long enough after an announcement had been made.

Therefore, the court held, purchases of TGS stock by any of the defendants after the press announcement had been made did not constitute a violation of Section 10b or Rule 10b-5.

The Issue of Stock Options

Five of the defendants—Stephens, Fogarty, Kline, Mollison, and Holyk —were charged with violation of Section 10b and Rule 10b-5 by accepting stock options voted to them on February 20, 1964, by the directors' committee. The SEC contended that these defendants violated the section and the rule because they had knowledge of K-55-1 and its results, which they failed to disclose to the committee or to the board of directors prior to accepting the options.

The court agreed that the committee necessarily relied on information furnished it by the higher echelon of TGS's management (which would include defendants Stephens and Fogarty, but not Kline, Mollison, or Holyk). The court agreed that Mollison and Holyk knew the results of K-55-1 and reported these results to their superior, defendant Fogarty. Kline, Mollison, and Holyk had no duty to inform the committee of information already known to their superiors, since they could assume that such information would be reported to the committee by the management. However, defendants Stephens and Fogarty *were* management and, therefore, were under an obligation to inform the committee of material information affecting the issuance of the stock options.

Notwithstanding, the court held that since this information was not material, the defendants did not violate Section 10b and Rule 10b-5 in accepting the stock options.

The Press Release of April 12

The SEC charged that the press release was materially misleading in characterizing the Kidd discovery as a prospect and in saying that any statement as to size and grade of ore would be premature and, therefore, in violation of the section and the rule. TGS denied this charge, further contending that no violation had occurred, since the press release had not been issued "in connection with the purchase or sale of any security" (1,293).

In reviewing the circumstances surrounding the press release, the court noted that the purpose of the April 12 press release was an attempt by TGS to meet the rumors that were circulating with respect to the Kidd 55 segment. There was no evidence that TGS derived any direct benefit from the issuance of the press release or that any of the defendants who participated in its preparation used it to their personal advantage. Moreover, defendants Fogarty and Mollison were under so much pressure prior to the press release, due to the rumors, that no matter how much or how little they said, they were likely to be criticized after the fact, and this, indeed, is what happened.

Consequently, the court held that in the absence of any evidence that the April 12 press release was deliberately deceptive or misleading or was intended to affect the market price of TGS stock to the advantage of TGS or its insiders, the issuance of the press release by TGS did not violate Section 10b or Rule 10b-5.

Conclusion

The court dismissed the SEC complaint against defendants Texas Gulf Sulphur Company, Charles F. Fogarty, Richard D. Mollison, Walter Holyk, Kenneth H. Darke, Thomas S. Lamont, Francis G. Coates, Claude O. Stephens, John A. Murray, Earl L. Huntington, and Harold B. Kline. Defendants Richard H. Clayton and David M. Crawford were found to have violated Section 10b and Rule 10b-5 by purchasing TGS stock or calls during the period between 7:00 P.M., April 9, 1964, and 10:00 A.M., April 16, 1964.

NOBODY IS HAPPY WITH THE DECISION—
EVERYBODY APPEALS

The SEC immediately began to plan its appeal to the U.S. Court of Appeals, Second District (New York). Although disappointed with the findings of the district court, the SEC actually had many of the basic principles of its case accepted in Judge Bonsal's decision. For the first time, explicit rules were established for management decision making concerning the public release of major corporate developments and the operation of corporate stock-option and investment programs.

The SEC filed its briefs in the court of appeals during the first week of December 1966. The first brief was against TGS and the ten exonerated individual defendants. The second was in response to the appeals of Clayton and Crawford. The appeals were argued before a panel of three circuit court judges, Waterman, Moore, and Mays, on March 20, 1967. It was then ordered that the case be submitted to the court in banc (all other judges of the appeals court review the evidence and arguments and then submit individual opinions).

The Appeals Court Decision

On August 13, 1968, the appeals court handed down its decision.[28] By a seven-to-two majority, the court affirmed the decision of the lower

[28] *Securities and Exchange Commission* v. *Texas Gulf Sulphur Co.; Securities and Exchange Commission* v. *Crawford and Clayton.* United States Court of Appeals, Second Circuit, No. 30882, August 13, 1968. Appeal from the United States District Court, Southern District of New York (Federal Securities Law Reports) No. 214-15, 8-16-68. Unless otherwise specified, all references to this citation in the text will be shown as (2. page number).

court in the cases of Clayton and Crawford. The court also affirmed the dismissal of charges against Murray. However, in the remaining cases, the court reversed the decision of the lower court and found TGS and the remaining eight defendants (Lamont having recently died) in violation of Rule 10b. All the defendants, with the exception of Murray, were remanded to the district court for determination of appropriate penalties.

In arriving at its decision, the appeals court considered the following questions:

1. Whether or not the drilling results prior to 7:00 P.M., April 9, 1964, were "material." Note that Judge Bonsal had decided that the drilling results during the remaining two periods—that is, 7:00 P.M., April 9, 1964, to 10:00 A.M., April 16, 1964; and 10:00 A.M., April 16, 1964, to the close of business that day—were material information. The appeals court concurred with the lower court's findings on this issue.

2. Whether the issuance of the press release of April 12 was lawful (as decided by the lower court) because it was not issued for the purpose of benefiting the corporation; there was no evidence that any insider used the release to his personal advantage, and it was not misleading or deceptive on the basis of the facts then known.

3. Whether or not information *becomes* public knowledge *immediately* on announcement to the press.

The court analyzed the activities of the defendants and the movements in TGS stock prices during the period under question. Between November 12, 1963, when K-55-1 was completed, and March 31, 1964, some of the defendants and their "tippees" (Table 2) increased their stock holdings from 1,135 to 8,135 shares and from 0 to 11,300 calls. The price of the stock rose from 17⅜ on November 8, 1963, to 20⅞ on December 13, to 24⅛ on February 21, 1964, to 26 on March 31, and to 30⅛ on April 10. On April 13, the day on which the April 12 release was disseminated, TGS opened at 30⅛, rose immediately to a high of 32, and gradually tapered off to close at 30⅞. It closed at 30¼ the next day, and at 29⅜ on April 15. On April 16, the day of the official announcement of the Timmins discovery, the price climbed to a high of 37 and closed at 36⅜. By May 15, TGS stock was selling at 58¼ (2,99177).

The court noted that the drilling results of K-55-1 (the first hole) were "so remarkable that neither Clayton, an experienced geophysicist, nor four other TGS expert witnesses, had ever seen or heard of a comparable initial exploratory drill hole in a base metal deposit." As a result, the trial court concluded, "There is no doubt that the drill core of K-55-1 was unusually good and that it excited the interest and speculation of those who knew about it." Based on the evidence presented, the trial court had also concluded "that the vertical plane created by the intersection of K-55-1 and K-55-3, which measured at least 350 feet wide by 500 feet deep, extended southward 200 feet to its intersection with K-55-4, and that there was real evidence that a body of commercially mineable ore might exist" (2,99174). (See Figure 2.)

The appeals court contended that, under the rule, the term *insider* applied not only to the officers, directors, and employees of the company but also to others who might possess inside material information and who might not be strictly termed *insiders* within the meaning of Section 10b of the SEC act. Thus, anyone so termed possessing material information must either disclose it to the public or refrain from using it to his own advantage.

So, it is here no justification for insider activity that disclosure was forbidden by the legitimate corporate objective of acquiring options to purchase the land surrounding the exploration site; if the information was, as the SEC contends, material, its possessors should have kept out of the market until disclosure was accomplished. [2,97178]

The appeals court agreed with the lower court that the insiders' regulatory obligation to disclose material information was that it must be enjoyed equally, so that outsiders might draw their own conclusions based on knowledge equal to that of the insiders. However, the appeals court disagreed with the lower court that "the test of materiality must be a conservative one" (1,280) but stated:

The basic test of materiality . . . is whether a *reasonable* man would attach importance . . . in determining his choice of action in the transaction in question. This, of course, encompasses any fact . . . which in reasonable and objective contemplation *might* affect the value of the corporation's stock or securities. . . . Such a fact is a material fact and must be effectively disclosed to the investing public prior to the commencement of insider trading in the corporation's securities. The speculators and chartists of Wall and Bay Streets are also "reasonable" investors entitled to the same legal protection afforded conservative traders. [2,99178]

Notwithstanding, the trial court's conclusions that the results of the first drill core, K-55-1, were "too remote" to have had any material impact on the market, knowledge of the possibility of the existence of a mine was surely more than marginal, as indicated by the remarkably rich drill core located rather close to the surface (suggesting minability by the less expensive open-pit method) within the confines of a large anomaly (suggesting an extensive region of mineralization). This might well have affected the price of TGS stock and would certainly have been an important fact to a reasonable, if speculative, investor in deciding whether he should buy, sell, or hold.

The appeals court stated that its disagreement with the district judge was not as to his findings of basic fact, but as to the application of a "clearly erroneous" rule to test the materiality of information.

A major consideration in determining whether the K-55-1 discovery was a material fact is the importance attached to the drilling results by those who knew about it. Stock purchases and purchases of short-term calls—in some instances by individuals who had never before purchased calls or even TGS stock—virtually compels the inference that the insiders were influenced by the drilling results. This insider trading activity, which surely constitutes highly pertinent evidence and the only truly objective evidence of the materiality of the K-55-1 discovery, should not have been disregarded by the lower court, in favor of the testimony of the defendants' expert witnesses, all of whom "agreed that one drill core does not establish an ore body, much less a mine" (1,282–83).

Therefore, the appeals court held that all transactions in TGS stock or calls by individuals with knowledge of the drilling results of K-55-1 were made in violation of Rule 10b-5. It further stated:

> Our decision to expand the limited protection afforded outside investors by the trial court's narrow definition of materiality is not at all shaken by fears that the elimination of insider trading benefits will deplete the ranks of capable corporate managers by taking away an incentive to accept such employment. [2,97180]

When May an Insider Act?

The appeals court contended that the effective protection of the public from insider exploitation of advance notice of material information required that the time that an insider placed an order, rather than the time of its ultimate execution, be determinative for Rule 10b-5 purposes. Otherwise, insiders would be able to "beat the news." Before insiders may act upon material information, such information must have been effectively disclosed in a manner sufficient to insure its availability to the investing public. Particularly here, where a formal announcement to the entire financial news media had been promised in a prior official release known to the media, all insider activity must await dissemination of the promised official announcement.

In the *Cady, Roberts* case, SEC set the standard by instructing insiders to "keep out of the market until the . . . public release of the information . . . is carried out instead of hastening to execute transactions in advance of, and in frustration of, the objectives of the release." The reading of a news release to the press was merely the first step in the process of dissemination required for compliance with the regulatory objective of providing all investors with an equal opportunity to make informed investment judgments. Assuming that the contents of the official release could instantaneously be acted upon, at the minimum the insiders should wait until the news could reasonably be expected to appear over the medium of widest circulation, the Dow-Jones broad tape, before entering the market to purchase shares in their company (2,97181–82).

The appeals court also rejected the arguments of "good faith" on the part of the defendants when they stated that their purchases before the April 16, 1964, news release were justified because they "honestly believed that the news of the strike had become public at the time they placed their orders" (2,991 82). Moreover, a review of other sections of the act, from which Rule 10b-5 seemed to have been drawn, suggested that the implementation of a standard of conduct that encompassed negligence as well as active fraud comported with the administrative and the legislative purposes underlying the rule. "This requirement, whether it be termed lack of diligence, constructive fraud, or unreasonable or negligent conduct, remains implicit in this standard, a standard that promotes the deference objective of the Rule" (2,897183). The court also held that "in an enforcement proceeding for equitable or prophylactic relief, the common law standard of deceptive conduct has been modified in the interests of broader protection for the investing public so that negligent insider conduct has become unlawful."

Insiders' Acceptance of Stock Options

The apeals court concluded that contrary to the lower court's findings, Kline (in addition to Stephens and Fogarty, directors of the corporation) also had a duty to disclose to the directors' committee his knowledge of the Kidd discovery before accepting stock options. Kline, a vice-president who had become the general counsel of TGS in January 1964, had been secretary of the corporation since January 1961. As such, he was a member of top management and was under an obligation, before accepting his option, to disclose any material information he may have possessed. Therefore, he was also in violation of Section 10b and Rule 10b-5.

TGS and the April 12, 1964 Press Release

TGS defended its actions by asserting that (1) the issuance of release produced no unusual market action; (2) no proof was offered by the SEC that the purpose of the press release was to affect the market price of the TGS stock for the benefit of TGS or its insiders; and (3) the issuance of the press release did not constitute a violation of Section 10b or Rule 10b-5, since it was not issued "in connection with the purchase or sale of any security" (2,97185).

The appeals court first took issue with the defendants' interpretation of the "in connection with" of the act. According to the court, a review of the congressional intent in passing the Securities and Exchange Act of 1934 would indicate that the dominant purposes underlying the act were to promote free and open public securities markets and to protect the investing public from suffering inequities in trading that follow from trading stimulated by the publication of false or misleading corporate information releases. The relevant congressional committee report on the bill stated:

> The idea of a free and open public market is built upon the theory that competing judgments of buyers and sellers as to the fair price of a security brings about a situation where the market price reflects as nearly as possible a just price. Just as artificial manipulation tends to upset the true function of an open market, so the hiding and secreting of important information obstructs the operation of the markets as indices of real value. *There cannot be honest markets without honest publicity . . .*

> Delayed, inaccurate, and misleading reports are the tools of the unconscionable market operator and the recreant corporate official who speculate on inside information. [2,97186]

Indeed, from its very inception, 10b was always acknowledged as a catchall and not to be narrowly construed. Congress intended to protect the investing public, in connection with its purchases or sales on exchanges, from being deceived by misleading statements of corporations, irrespective of whether the insiders trade in the securities of a corporation and irrespective of whether the corporation or its management has an ulterior purpose or purposes in making an official public release.

Accordingly, the court held that Rule 10b-5 is violated whenever assertions are made, as here, in a manner reasonably calculated to influence the investing public, that is, by means of the financial media. However, if corporate management "demonstrates that it was diligent that the information it published was the whole truth" and that such information "was disseminated in good faith, Rule 10b-5 would not have been violated" (2,97188).

As to the specific action of TGS in issuing the April 12 statement, the court held that TGS either should have made the statement on the basis of the facts known to it or should have delayed the presentation a bit until an accurate report of a rapidly changing situation was possible. According to the court, the choice of an ambiguous general statement rather than a summary of the specific facts could not reasonably be justified by any claimed urgency. The avoidance of liability for misrepresentation in the event that the Timmins project failed, a highly unlikely event as of April 12 or 13, did not prevent the accurate and truthful divulgence of detailed results that need not have been accompanied by definite assertions of success.

Thus, the court concluded that the release was issued in a manner reasonably calculated to affect the market price of TGS stock and to influence the investing public, and it remanded to the district court to decide whether the release was misleading to the reasonable investor, and if so, whether the court in its discretion should issue the injunction sought by the SEC (2,97190).

REACTION TO THE DECISION OF THE APPEALS COURT

The reaction to the decision and its implied expansion of the interpretation of Rule 10b was remarkable in its sedateness. Texas Gulf shares on the NYSE showed almost no effect from the decision. A Dow-Jones midweek financial news summary found relatively little concern among corporate executives questioned. Typical of the comments were the following: "This decision will do no more to us than to confirm our previous policy of care and scrupulousness in the dissemination of information. . . ." "We don't live on tips." "I don't think it's really going to hurt us in our work." However, the official reaction of the influential financial weekly, *Barron's,* was immediate and vociferous. In an article published on August 19, it found Wall Street's lack of concern disquieting. "Like other disaster victims, neither business nor financial circles seem to realize what has hit them." Predicting a stopping of the flow of corporate information to the public, the article stated that "in the end, as the flow of information, 'inside' and out, inevitably slows down, the chief victims will be the investors whom SEC is sworn to protect." It then took the court to task:

Only by riding roughshod over legislative history, legal precedent, simple logic and common sense could the court majority have reached its conclusions. . . . Nonetheless, if this shoddy decision stands, the consequences to the defendants, the financial community and the business world are frightening to contemplate. . . . The restraint constitutes not "double" jeopardy but "perpetual" jeopardy. What about a businessman's civil rights? . . . This is not regulation—it is bureaucracy run wild.[29]

Forbes, another weekly business periodical, saw the TGS court decision in an entirley different light:

The Texas Gulf ruling is not isloated: It is part of a growing trend on the part of the courts and of the laws to be increasingly strict and precise as to the nature of the relationship between a corporate management and its scattered and relatively powerless public stockholders. The issues raised in the Texas Gulf case go far beyond that company.[30]

Although stating that "the limits of the law have yet to be reached," *Forbes* concluded by finding that "it adds up to one more illustration of how capitalism is capable of becoming more democratic—and hence more durable." [31]

But the financial community was not so sure, especially the financial analysts. Corporate silence in divulging pertinent information was becoming deafening. However, early in October, the general counsel for the SEC, Philip A. Loomis, addressed a meeting of analysts directly on this point. He noted that much of the silence was due to nervousness among corporate lawyers and public relations men who overreacted to the TGS decision. He stated that companies should be willing to make information more available if just to avoid such actions and that the emphasis of the analyst's job should be on interpretation of the facts and not hot tips.[32]

On October 30, 1968, TGS filed a motion in the U.S. District Court, in connection with a stockholders suit, that its constitutional right of free speech was being abridged by the appeals court decision. This motion was seen as the foundation work for an appeal to the U.S. Supreme Court.[33]

Legal "Remedies" for the Defendants

Beginning in October 1969 and lasting through part of February 1970, Judge Bonsal of the U.S. District Court imposed "remedies" upon the

[29] "Perpetual Jeopardy," *Barron's,* August 19, 1968, p. 1.
[30] "The Law: Trouble for the Top," *Forbes,* September 1, 1968, p. 23.
[31] *Ibid.*
[32] "SEC Blows Away the Fog," *Business Week,* October 12, 1968, p. 111.
[33] "Abreast of the Market," *The Wall Street Journal,* October 29, 1968.

defendants, as outlined by the appeals court, finding the April 12, 1964, press release misleading to reasonable investors using due care and ruling that the framers did not exercise due diligence in its issuance. The judge denied the SEC's request that TGS, as a corporation, be enjoined from issuing or otherwise disseminating false, misleading, or inadequate information in that "no proper showing of any reasonable likelihood of future violations was evident." Judge Bonsal refused to issue injunctions against future illegal trading against Darke, Holyk, Huntington, Fogarty, and Mollison. However, the judge did enjoin Clayton and Crawford from future illegal trading "because they purchased during a period of nondisclosure, knowing beyond doubt that Texas Gulf had made a very important mineral discovery." [34]

The remaining defendant, Coates, had reached a court settlement in October, which became the guideline for the remedies imposed by Judge Bonsal. Coates paid $26,250 into a 6 percent escrow fund, $9,675 of which was the profit gained by his tippees. The formulation of the settlement was based on the difference between the purchase price of the stock and its price on April 17, 1964, plus bank rate interest.

In February the other defendants were ordered to make the following payments into the escrow fund (to be used for settlements in other suits against TGS): Darke—$41,794, plus $48,404 for the profits of his tippees; Holyk—$35,663; Huntington—$2,300; and Clayton—$20,010. Crawford had already surrendered to the company, at his cost, the stock he purchased, making any other penalty unnecessary. [35] Fogarty and Mollison surrendered to TGS, at their cost, the shares that they purchased.

At the time of the settlement of the SEC charges (and TGS was planning to appeal the decision), there were more than sixty stockholder suits pending. In the second week of February 1970, TGS filed an appeal to a Utah civil decision in which TGS was found guilty of issuing a misleading press release and ordered to pay $22,000 in damages to former shareholders. [36]

During early June 1971, the U.S. Court of Appeals for the Second Circuit upheld, under a TGS appeal, Judge Bonsal's penalties for all the defendants with the exception of Kline. The court stated that the district court had erred in ordering Kline's option canceled without giving him a chance to be heard on the matter. [37]

Eight years to the day after TGS's initial press release, Judge Bonsal upheld a proposed settlement of stockholder claims against TGS in the

[34] "Texas Gulf Ruled to Lack Diligence in Minerals Case," *The Wall Street Journal*, February 9, 1970, p. 26.

[35] *Ibid.*

[36] "Texas Gulf Tangle Unwinds—A Little," *Business Week*, February 14, 1970, p. 29.

[37] "Findings Upheld on Texas Gulf," *The New York Times*, June 19, 1971, p. 33.

New York District Court as being "fair, reasonable and adequate." Under the terms, TGS agreed to pay $2.7 million to former stockholders who sold their stock on the basis of the April 12, 1964, press release. The judge concluded the case by stating that "the settlement is in the best interests of all parties." [38]

[38] "TGS Terms of Settlement Called Fair by Court," *The Wall Street Journal,* April 12, 1972, p. 16.

B.

CORPORATIONS AND THE INDIVIDUAL

General Motors' Nadir, Ralph Nader

*Corporate Economic Interests
and Encroachment on an Individual's Privacy*

When a trout rising to a fly gets hooked on a line and finds himself unable to swim freely, he begins with a fight which results in struggles and splashes and sometimes an escape. Often, of course, the situation is too tough for him.

In the same way the human being struggles with his environment and the hooks that catch him. Sometimes he masters his difficulties, sometimes they are too much for him. His struggles are all that the world sees and it naturally misunderstands them. It is hard for a free fish to understand what is happening to a hooked one.

—Karl A. Menninger

A *New Republic* news story [1] about Ralph Nader confirmed rumors and summarized three months of 1966 news accounts about an investigation into the affairs of the well-known auto critic. The article implied that some unnamed source in the automobile industry was behind the investigation. The allegations are abridged here.

According to Nader, on January 10, 1966, it was in the Kirkwood Hotel in Des Moines, Iowa, where he was testifying at the state attorney general's

---

[1] James Ridgeway, "The Dick," *New Republic*, March 12, 1966, pp. 11–13.

inquiry into traffic safety, that he first thought someone was following him. Later that month he began receiving annoying and unidentified calls on his unlisted telephone.

Senator Abraham Ribicoff's auto safety subcommittee invited Ralph Nader to testify on February 10, 1966. On the evening before the hearing, harassing calls came with increasing frequency until 4:00 A.M.[2]

The subcommittee invited Ralph Nader to testify because he was campaigning to have automobile manufacturers remove design defects from their cars and to make them safer. On November 30, 1965, Nader's book, *Unsafe at Any Speed,* was published. It was "a meticulously documented (and as it turned out, best-selling) report on safety defects in Detroit's cars, primarily some of General Motors' early Corvairs." [3] The book criticized the industry's "over-emphasis of style, disregard for the safety of the driver and passengers, and engineering stagnation." *Unsafe at Any Speed* "received widespread and largely favorable reviews" and strengthened considerably the argument of auto-safety activists both on and off Capitol Hill.[4]

Nader made a great impression on the members of the subcommittee, and according to one staff member, "he [Nader] was a Congressional staffer's dream. . . . Nader wasn't selling anything . . . [and] he had the data—the names and phone numbers to substantiate everything." [5]

A series of events lent weight to Nader's conviction that he was being investigated. His landlady was asked about his promptness in paying bills. An attractive girl invited him to her apartment to discuss "foreign affairs with a few of her friends." Two men followed him from an airport. His old law school friend, Frederick Condon, was asked questions by an investigator supposedly representing a client who was thinking of hiring Nader.

---

[2] According to *The New York Times,* "the callers were never obscene or abusive, he said.

" 'Mr. Nader?' a voice would inquire.

" 'Yes.'

"Then suddenly, as if to a child:

" 'Cut it out now! Cut it out! You're going to cut me off I tell you! Cut it out!' "

Nader said that the phone calls caused him to oversleep and hence he was late in giving his testimony to the subcommittee.

Walter Rugaber, "Critic of Auto Industry's Safety Standards Says He Was Trailed and Harassed; Charges Called Absurd," *The New York Times,* March 6, 1966, p. 94.

According to Ridgeway, "The Dick," ". . . on the evening of February 9, when he was trying to put the finishing touches on a prepared statement, Nader got half-a-dozen phone calls. A voice would say, 'Mr. Nader, this is Pan American,' and then hang up. Or, 'Mr. Nader, please pick up the parcel at Railway Express.' And finally, 'Why don't you go back to Connecticut, buddy-boy.' "

[3] "Meet Ralph Nader, Everyman's Lobbyist and His Consumer Crusader," *Newsweek,* January 22, 1968, pp. 65–73.

[4] Elizabeth Brenner Drew, "The Politics of Auto Safety," *Atlantic,* October 1966, p. 95.

[5] *Newsweek,* January 22, 1968, p. 65.

Other friends and associates were asked all kinds of questions by investigators from different agencies, *including whether or not he led a normal sex life, possible anti-Semitism, and political affiliations.*[6] A blonde in a supermarket asked him to help her move some furniture (and asked no one else when he refused). By this time Nader thought that girls were being used to try to lure him into a compromising situation and that someone, most likely connected with the auto manufacturers, was attempting to dig up some sordid past episode to discredit him as a congressional witness.[7]

Employees of the *New Republic,* for which Nader had written articles, contacted Allied Investigating Service, which supposedly had questioned Nader's stockbroker. After much prodding, they denied investigating Nader. Management Consultants in Boston, which sent a representative to see Thomas F. Lambert, Jr., editor in chief of American Trial Lawyers Association (ATLA) publications, declined to discuss the matter. Vincent Gillen of Vincent Gillen Associates, however, admitted investigating Nader but would not name his client.[8]

The New York Times on March 6 stated that unnamed sources in the auto industry said the investigation was "too clumsy" to have been initiated by an automobile manufacturer and was probably done by other Nader targets in the "traffic safety establishment"—the National Safety Council or the American Association of Motor Vehicle Administrators. One informant added, "think of what a blunder it would be if a company was caught at it," and another said that if the manufacturers were doing it, Nader would not even be aware that he was being investigated. The major auto companies had special investigation bureaus for "high level security work" and preemployment investigations.[9]

On March 8 Senators Gaylord Nelson (D-Wis.) and Abraham Ribicoff (D-Conn.) asked the Justice Department to look into Nader's being "investigated by private detectives" and the late telephone calls since his appearance before a Senate hearing. Nader was scheduled to appear before the subcommittee again and Nelson said that "the clear implication of

[6] Ridgeway, "The Dick."

[7] *Ibid.,* also see "The Nader Caper," *Newsweek,* March 21, 1966, p. 83.

[8] According to Ridgeway, "The Dick," Gillen said:
"I am a private investigator. We have hundreds of clients; we write thousands of reports, primarily on employment matters. I was asked by a client to make an investigation of Ralph Nader. I understand that he is an intelligent, articulate fellow. And my client told me he was considering him for an important job, to do research on something, I don't know what."

[9] "Investigation Asked," *The New York Times,* March 9, 1966, p. 38; "Ribicoff Summons GM on Its Inquiry of Critic," *The New York Times,* March 11, 1966, p. 18; "Critic of Auto Industry's Safety Standards Says He Was Tailed and Harassed; Charges Called Absurd," *The New York Times,* March 6, 1966, p. 94.

everything reported so far is that the automobile industry has hired at least three different firms of private detectives to shadow and investigate . . . a witness before a Congressional committee." [10]

Nelson added that both the auto makers and Congress should welcome an investigation to "clear the air." Ribicoff stated that the incidents were "an apparent attempt to harass and intimidate a subcommittee witness," for which federal laws provide penalties of up to five years in jail and a $5,000 fine. The senator added, "no citizen of this country should be forced to endure the kind of clumsy harassment to which Mr. Nader has apparently been subjected since the publication of his book. Anonymous phone calls in the night have no place in a free society." [11]

On March 9 the vice-president and director of the Ford Motor Company, John S. Bagas, sent a telegram to Senator Ribicoff saying that the "Ford Motor Company has not been nor is it now directly or indirectly involved in any alleged investigation or harassment of Mr. Nader, nor has it any knowledge of or connection with the alleged incidents concerning him." [12] After the Ford statement was issued, newspaper reporters received denials from Chrysler and American Motors. General Motors would not comment. Put on the spot, GM spokesmen "shortly before 11 P.M. [and] after the first editions of most morning newspapers had been printed . . . delivered a statement to newspaper offices." The statement admitted that the company had directed the investigation.[13] Indications were that GM's president, James Roche, had not learned of GM's true involvement until late in the afternoon and had personally ordered that an admission be made:

> Following the publication of Mr. Ralph Nader's criticisms of the Corvair in writings and public appearances in support of his book . . . the office of its general counsel initiated a routine investigation through a reputable law firm to determine whether Ralph Nader was acting on behalf of litigants or their attorneys in Corvair design cases pending against General Motors. The investigation was prompted by Mr. Nader's extreme criticisms of the Corvair. . . . Mr. Nader's statements coincided with similar publicity by some attorneys handling such litigation. . . .
>
> The investigation was limited only to Mr. Nader's qualifications, background, expertise and association with such attorneys. It did not include any of the alleged harassment or intimidation recently reported in the press. If Mr. Nader had been subjected to any of the incidents and harassment mentioned by him in newspaper stories,

---

[10] "Investigation Asked," *The New York Times,* March 9, 1966, p. 38.

[11] *Ibid.*

[12] "GM Admits Investigating Auto Critic," *Washington Post,* March 10, 1966, p. A7.

[13] *The New York Times,* March 11, 1966, p. 18.

such incidents were in no way associated with General Motors' legitimate investigation of his interest in pending litigation.

At General Motors' invitation, Mr. Nader spent a day at the GM Technical Center . . . early in January visiting with General Motors executives and engineers. . . .

Mr. Nader expresed appreciation for the courtesy in providing him with detailed information, but he nevertheless continued the same line of attack on the design of the Corvair. . . . This behavior lends support to General Motors' belief that there is a connection between Mr. Nader and Plaintiff's counsel in pending Corvair design litigation.[14]

Senator Nelson, "shocked" by the GM announcement, said that the investigation was "a pretty scandalous business"[15] and that he thought the auto safety subcommittee should determine if GM's law firm was in contempt of Congress. Senator Ribicoff said he would invite Roche, Nader, and the private detectives to testify before his auto safety subcommittee on March 22:

I have not discussed this matter with any of the parties concerned, but I suggest that they come before the committee to discuss the entire matter.

The safety of the American driving public is the basic issue before the committee. To this must now be added the additional issue of a witness's right to testify before a committee of the United States Congress without fear of character assassination or intimidation.[19]

Nader told *The New York Times* that he had not represented clients involved in Corvair litigations. A number of lawyers had asked him for Corvair information, but he had never been paid for it and had left his law practice "to pursue the cause of safer designed automobiles for the motoring public." Therefore, he asked GM to admit that it could not have evidence linking him with the Corvair lawyers.[17] GM implied in a *New York Times* story[18] that it could prove the case against Nader and that the proof would be presented before the Ribicoff committee.

[14] U.S., Congress, Senate, "Federal Role in Traffic Safety," *Hearings before the Subcommittee on Executive Reorganization of the Committee on Government Operations,* 89th Cong., 2nd sess., March 22, 1966, p. 1389.

As extensive use is made of the Senate Hearings, citations from this source will henceforth appear in the text set off by parentheses or brackets enclosing page references.

[15] *The New York Times,* March 11, 1966, p. 18.

[16] *Ibid.*

[17] "GM Acknowledges Investigating Critic," *The New York Times,* March 10, 1966 p. 1.

[18] *The New York Times,* March 11, 1966, p. 18.

THE HEARING

On March 22 Senator Ribicoff's subcommittee conducted hearings into the investigation of Nader and, in spite of the confidence GM had displayed in its March 8 statement, the only case it proved was Nader's. According to *Newsweek:*

The scene had all the fascination of a public whipping, and the huge old Caucus Room of the Senate Office Building was appropriately jammed with reporters, cameramen, television crews and Washington citizens. In the seats of power, ranged against a white marble wall, were a tribunal of Sen. Abraham Ribicoff's traffic-safety subcommittee. At the witness table was the president of the world's largest manufacturing company.[19]

The hearing had political overtones: It was good publicity for Democrat Ribicoff and only one of three Republicans on the subcommittee even showed up briefly. One subcommittee member, Robert F. Kennedy, recognized an old friend, Theodore C. Sorensen, who appeared but said little as Roche's legal counsel.[20]

Ribicoff sternly opened the meeting:

There is no law which bars a corporation from hiring detectives to investigate a private citizen, however distasteful the idea may seem to some of us. There is a law, however, which makes it a crime to harass or intimidate a witness before a congressional committee.

. . . [the] right to testify freely without fear of intimidation is one of the cornerstones of a free and democratic society. Any attempt to jeopardize this right is a serious matter.

I have called this special meeting today to look into the circumstances surrounding what appeared to be an attempt by General Motors Corp. to discredit Mr. Ralph Nader, a recent witness before the subcommittee. . . . [GM] has admitted responsibility for undertaking a determined and exhaustive investigation of a private citizen who has criticized the auto industry verbally and in print. [1380]

[19] "Private Eyes and Public Hearings," *Newsweek*, April 4, 1966, pp. 77–78.

[20] *Ibid.* Sorensen had been White House counsel under John F. Kennedy, and Sorensen's law firm was aiding GM's defense in the Corvair design suits. "Sorensen Expected at Nader Quiz Today," *Washington Post*, March 22, 1966, p. A2.

GM'S POSITION

Mr. Roche testified as follows:

Let me make it clear at the outset that I deplore the kind of harassment to which Mr. Nader has apparently been subjected. I am just as shocked and outraged by some of the incidents which Mr. Nader has reported as the members of this subcommittee.

As President of General Motors, I hold myself fully responsible for any action authorized or initiated by any officer of the Corporation which may have had any bearing on the incidents related to our investigation of Mr. Nader. I did not know of the investigation when it was initiated and I did not approve it.

While there can be no disagreement over General Motors' legal right to ascertain necessary facts preparatory to litigation . . . , I am not here to excuse, condone or justify in any way our investigating Mr. Nader. To the extent that General Motors bears responsibility, I want to apologize here and now to the members of this subcommittee and Mr. Nader. I sincerely hope that these apologies will be accepted. Certainly I bear Mr. Nader no ill-will.

To the best of my knowledge . . . the investigation initiated by General Motors, contrary to some speculation, did *not* employ girls as sex lures, did *not* employ detectives using false names, did *not* employ Allied Investigation, Inc., did *not* use recording devices during interviews, did *not* follow Mr. Nader in Iowa and Pennsylvania, did *not* have him under surveillance during the day he testified before this subcommittee, did *not* follow him in any private place, and did *not* constantly ring his private telephone number late at night with false statements or anonymous warnings. [1381]

Mr. Roche said that the investigation was initiated before Nader became a congressional witness and that it was wholly unrelated to the proceedings of the subcommittee and Mr. Nader's connections with them (1382).

He went on to say that no "derogatory information of any kind along any of these lines turned up in this investigation" (1383).

Roche also reiterated the company's right to investigate certain facts in relation to its defense of the one hundred Corvair design suits:

First, to ascertain whether any actions for libel . . . should be instituted against members of the bar (including Mr. Nader) who publicly discussed pending or anticipated litigation; *second,* to ascertain whether any witness, or author of any book or article which might be offered as evidence in any court (including Mr. Nader) was entitled to the legal definition of "expert"; and *third,* to ascertain whether [these individuals] . . . show bias, lack of reliability or credibility, [or] . . . if . . . they had a self interest in the litigation or had been attempting deliberately to influence public opinion. [1384]

Roche said the company had the legal right and duty, in protecting its stockholders' interests, to make an investigation within the framework of these three points.

GM's president added that investigation into an individual's personal life, a very "uncommon occurrence" at GM, was usually for preemployment or possible embezzlement. It would be initiated by the general counsel, usually "in consultation with other executives familiar with the particular problem involved. But, if it were a serious enough matter, then it would be called to the attention of the other officials in the corporation, or perhaps some of our top committees" (1385–86).

Several members of GM's legal staff testified before the committee to explain in greater detail the necessity GM felt to investigate Nader.

INVESTIGATION STORY: GM'S VERSION

General Motors introduced its rear-engine compact car, the Corvair, in the fall of 1959, and by November 1965 the company had been plagued with over one hundred suits alleging injuries arising from Corvair failures due to basic design defects. Although GM had won two Corvair design suits, it settled another out of court (without admitting legal liability) because the jury's emotions had been aroused by gruesome photographs of the plaintiff's injury (1509–10).[21] This settlement further aggravated the situation as it was heralded in various news media "as a victory for the plaintiffs" (1408). It was followed by a flood of letters from Corvair owners and GM stockholders. Thus the company became apprehensive that "false" publicity might adversely influence future cases.

By 1962 various attorneys and law firms (many of whom were handling Corvair cases) began exchanging information, and by 1965 they were speaking publicly about Corvair's design defects. In June and July 1965 Thomas F. Lambert, Jr., of ATLA suggested to those seeking more in-

---

[21] Ralph Nader's version of the reason GM settled is somewhat different from the company's version. GM discontinued the manufacture of the Corvair in May 1969. "The Last of the Troubled Corvairs," *San Francisco Chronicle*, May 13, 1969, p. 10.

formation about Corvair design that they contact a then unknown Ralph Nader:

We also suggest that you write to Ralph Nader, . . . Winsted, Connecticut. Ralph is a lawyer who has developed expertise in the area of automobile manufacturer's liability. Ralph has a substantial amount of information on the Corvair. [1416]

According to Aloysius Power, GM's general counsel, the company wondered,

Who was this "lawyer" with whom the ATLA editor was on a first-name basis? At that time, Mr. Nader was not listed as counsel in any pending Corvair case. Where did he obtain such a "substantial amount of information on the Corvair," and how had he "developed expertise"?

Was he an engineer, a paid consultant to the ATLA Corvair counsel? Or was he preparing to file another one of these cases?

Practically all of the material he was using in his writings to attack the Corvair appeared to come from material collected or obtained by plaintiff's counsel in pending Corvair litigation. [1420–40]

In addition, Nader wrote an article for the January 1965 ATLA magazine, *Trial,* outlining often overlooked sources of evidence of unsafe automobile design, and in October 1965 advance reviews and excerpts from the book began appearing in national magazines.

According to Power, pretrial investigation was crucial if they were to fight these pending cases effectively (1420–38).[22] The company must know how valid was Nader's claim to be an "expert," since expert testimony was vital in such cases. Second, had Nader violated Canon 20 of the Canons of Professional Ethics of the American Bar Association, which "condemns public discussion or statement by a lawyer concerning pending or anticipated litigation"? (1404). Therefore, Power felt that an investigation of Nader was a "prudent and appropriate measure" to take. "In the light of the situation existing at that time, I could not have arrived at any other decision consistent with my responsibilities as the general counsel of General Motors" (1403).

On November 18, 1965, GM's legal department asked its product liability insurer, the Royal-Globe Insurance Company, if it had ever employed any private investigators in Connecticut who might have looked into

---

[22] At the time of the hearings, GM had not lost any Corvair design suits.

Nader's qualifications. They had not, and a Hartford, Connecticut, investigator, Mr. O'Neill, was commissioned by Globe to "obtain whatever information he could with respect to his [Nader's] qualifications and whether or not he was a trial lawyer in Winsted, Conn." The report stated that Nader had only briefly practiced law in Hartford, that his family lived in nearby Winsted, and that he might be in Washington, D.C., although no legal directory listed him there. No information as to his technical competence was uncovered (1439).

On December 22, 1965, Miss Eileen Murphy, who was working in GM's law library and who had earlier worked in Washington, phoned Richard Danner of Alvord and Alvord, a Washington law firm, to ask if he could recommend a good investigating agency for some "background information" on Nader. Danner in turn called Vincent Gillen in New York, president of Vincent Gillen Associates, Inc., to ask if he could handle an investigation covering several Eastern states. On January 11, 1966, Miss Murphy came to Washington and gave Danner what little information GM had obtained on Nader, reiterating GM's suspicions but adding that no compelling proof had been found (1515–16, 1524). According to Power, Miss Murphy said the investigation should cover:

> Where does Mr. Nader live and where does he practice law if he is practicing? Had he been employed by the Federal Government? What other employment? Where is the source of his income? What were the details of his background that might affect his writings? Especially does he have any engineering background . . .
>
> What would account for the absence of objectivity unusual in a lawyer writing about the Corvair? Does he have any connection at all with ATLA or ATLA attorneys? Are there any indications that he might be working as a consultant to lawyers handling Corvair cases against General Motors? [1440–1516]

According to Danner, however, Miss Murphy also requested "a complete background investigation of Mr. Nader's activities." The instructions given were described by those agents actually investigating Nader: ". . . Our job is to check his life, and current activities to determine 'what makes him tick,' such as his real interest in safety, his supporters, if any, his politics, his marital status, his friends, his women, boys, etc., drinking, dope, jobs— in fact, all facets of his life" (1506).

Danner testified at Ribicoff's subcommittee hearing that he then told Miss Murphy that the investigating agency would have to use a suitable pretext as Nader would most likely learn of the investigation through the people being questioned. Danner also said that "all instructions to the investigative agency were to be handled by me, and all reports submitted by the agency were to be sent to me for transmittal to General Motors" (1440–42, 1516, 1524).

Gillen flew to Washington on January 13, 1966, to get his assignment from Danner. In his testimony before the subcommittee, Gillen said that it was the first time that he had heard of Nader. Gillen told Danner that if he were to ask questions about Nader's connection with Corvair cases, his expertise in safety, and his associates in the legal profession:

> . . . the implication would be immediate, the onus would immediately be on General Motors if Nader heard of this, and I tried to dissuade them or told them "Are you prepared for what may happen, because you cannot investigate someone without their hearing about it talking to their friends." I told them right from the beginning.
>
> Danner said, "Don't worry about it." So I did it as gently and discreetly and fairly to Nader as could possibly be done. [1549]

Since it was necessary to conceal the nature of the investigation and the identity of the client, it was agreed that all information would be collected under the pretext of preemployment type of inquiry instigated by a company of a prospective employee.

In defending his belief that a preemployment pretext was the best strategy to use to get the desired information, Gillen told the subcommittee:

> As you gentlemen are aware, whenever any investigation is made, people interviewed invariably jump to the conclusion that something is wrong with the person being investigated, especially if no reason for the inquiry is given. On the other hand, if people are told the person is being investigated for a position, no stigma is attached to the inquiry. We do it everyday. [1525]

Danner told the senators that Gillen and he had agreed that Nader was not to be placed under surveillance unless absolutely necessary (1517).

On January 17 Senator Ribicoff officially announced that Nader would be a witness at one of the subcommittee hearings on February 10.

On January 20 Gillen requested his Washington associate, D. David Shatraw, president of Arundel Investigative Agency of Severinia Park, Maryland, to investigate Nader, warning him "not to arouse the ire of Nader . . . it is important that interviews be handled with great discretion and under a suitable pretext" (1525).

From January 25 to January 27, Gillen's men conducted their investigation in the Winsted-Hartford, Connecticut, area. Gillen later said that all his men used their own names and identified Gillen as their employer (they didn't know who the real client was). No one in Connecticut could say where Nader was "except possibly in Washington." Little was discovered as to his sources of income or activities, so it was decided on January 26 that surveillance would be necessary. Shatraw began his end of the investigation on February 3, which according to Gillen showed that Nader's assertions to the press that he was harassed in January, if true, were not the result of Gillen's or Shatraw's work. One of Shatraw's men called an address that Nader had put on some legal papers many months before to "ascertain if anything was known of Mr. Nader. To his surprise, the landlady said he was rooming there but was not in" (1525–26).

On Friday, February 4, two Arundel Investigative Agency men began a surveillance on Nader, which because of the agency's heavy workload was ended the following morning. On Sunday, at 4:00 P.M., Gillen had two of his own men resume the surveillance and investigation in Washington. Gillen said that "all other surveillance and investigation in Washington thereafter was conducted by our own employees. We conducted no surveillance outside Washington" (1527).

On February 9 Danner suggested substituting "spot checks" for the unproductive and expensive surveillance. He thought a good time to pick up Nader would be directly after he testified on February 10. The "tailing" didn't begin until the eleventh at 11:00 A.M. when one of Gillen's men followed Nader into the new Senate office building but left when challenged by the guards. This ended the surveillance, but one man continued openly to interview Washingtonians about Nader. Newspapers reported the episode in the building on the thirteenth, saying that Gillen's men "clumsily" mistook a newspaper reporter for Nader (which Gillen denied). On the fourteenth, GM's Power, ex post facto, ordered the surveillance stopped (1543–44).

Gillen's man left Washington on February 18. Thus, Gillen said, the alleged incidents of women approaching Nader on Sunday, February 20, and Wednesday, February 23, were unrelated to his investigation. "Neither I, nor any of my former FBI colleagues, used any women during this investigation. I had no one, male or female, working on this case those days in Washington" (1528).

On February 28 Power instructed Danner to cease the entire investigation.

According to the testimony given at the hearings, Nader was investigated by various agencies for five or six days in mid-November 1965, and between January 25 and February 28, 1966. People from all walks of life who were even remotely connected with Nader were questioned. Frederick

Condon and Thomas F. Lambert, Jr., wrote letters to the subcommittee and gave details of their interviews.

Condon, who had gone to law school with Nader, was at that time assistant counsel for the United Life and Accident Insurance Company of Concord, New Hampshire. Nader had dedicated his book, *Unsafe at Any Speed,* to Condon. According to Condon, Gillen came up to talk to him under the pretext of preemployment inquiries concerning Nader. However, the nature of his questioning made Condon suspect that Gillen was investigating Nader on behalf of some automobile company. Gillen asked questions slanted toward finding out if Nader was a homosexual. Gillen also inquired if Nader was anti-Semitic because of his "Syrian" ancestry (Nader is of Lebanese descent) or had participated in or belonged to any left-wing organization. Condon thought that Gillen had a tape recorder in his attaché case as he was hardly taking any notes. Gillen, in his testimony, however, denied having any tape recorder with him and also gave a different version of his questioning of Condon. Gillen said that the sole purpose of his interview with Condon was to find out if Nader had ever had a driver's license, as official Connecticut records contained conflicting information and no one had ever seen him driving a car (1521–47).

Thomas F. Lambert, Jr., of ATLA publications wrote to Senator Ribicoff and described his interview with Mr. Dwyer of "Management Consultants." Gillen said that he had sent Dwyer on the interview. In response to Dwyer's questions, Lambert told him that it was

> our belief that Nader had done the best writing on unsafe design of automobiles of which we were aware . . . I [Lambert] suggested that Nader may have acted as a consultant to three very able and experienced trial lawyers who had handled or are currently handling Corvair cases. I suggested that he might be able to verify Nader's actual experience in such consulting work by directly contacting these three lawyers (David Harney, Los Angeles; Barney Masterson, Clearwater, Fla.; and Louis B. Davidson, Chicago). [7551–52]

Almost everyone denied using girls at any point or intending intimidation or harassment of any Senate subcommittee witness. Danner was unaware that Nader was to testify, and Gillen stated that the investigation would never have been initiated had he known that Nader was to testify. Furthermore, only two phone calls were supposedly made to Nader, neither during early morning hours. Gillen's reports were forwarded to Detroit by Danner, the final report being sent on March 14. Gillen was the only one in his organization who knew the real client's identity. Hence, he did not edit much irrelevant material from the investigators' reports. "To do so would have indicated the real client to my own staff. I even left in some rather harsh statements about General Motors and some of its officials" (1532). Miss Murphy at GM received the reports. The company was billed $6,700 for the investigation (1539).

GILLEN'S PRETEXT: WAS IT ETHICAL?

Much of the subcommittee's attention was concerned with the questions asked Nader's friends and associates. Since a preemployment pretext was used, the investigators asked about things GM was supposedly not interested in. Gillen stoutly defended his investigative technique and denied any unethical practice or moral wrongdoing. Gillen said the motto of his company was "There is no substitute for quality and integrity. I stand on the quality of our reports. I submit my integrity to the scrutiny of all" (1532). According to Danner, who hired Gillen, it was GM's idea that the investigation go into the "detail and background" of Nader's life, including anti-Semitism and marital status and the kind of girl friends he had. Danner said it couldn't have been his idea: He had never heard of Nader before Miss Murphy called him (1520–21).

Senator Robert F. Kennedy, a member of the subcommittee, questioned Gillen persistently on the use of the preemployment pretext, false names, and personal questions when Nader wasn't really being considered for a job. He was further concerned about harassing Nader. Gillen's position was that the objectives might differ but investigative methods for either objective were identical and did not constitute harassment. After all, Gillen said, pretexts "are used all the time. I know the government uses pretexts in connection with applicant investigations" (1519–20).

Gillen maintained that others were also investigating Nader a month before the subcommittee met. He suggested that the subcommittee find out who did vex Nader with phone calls, use girls as sex lures, and follow him in Iowa and Philadelphia. These were the real harassing agents (1550–51).[23]

Furthermore, our investigation uncovered absolutely no indication of any abnormality on the part of Ralph Nader. On the contrary, he obviously is an intelligent, personable young man.

The same thing applied to the questions regarding anti-Semitism. Virtually everyone we talked with in Winsted cautioned us not to attribute to Ralph the attitude and obvious feelings of some members of his family. In fairness to Ralph, we had to ask that question of all those with whom he associated during his adult life. I am happy

[23] *The New York Times*, March 6, 1966, p. 94.

to state that none of the people we interviewed believes Ralph Nader is anti-Semitic. [1532]

The possibility of anti-Semitism was not the only thing Gillen felt it necessary to pursue "in fairness to Ralph." Nader's high school principal showed Gillen's men a yearbook which said, "Ralph Nader—woman hater." He said:

Now some people get the wrong impression about Ralph and this stuff. Do not pay any attention to it.
According to Gillen, "There is where it first raised its head and we had to pursue it in fairness to Ralph." [1549]
"What the hell's this 'fairness to Ralph'?" Kennedy barked. "You have to keep running around the country proving he's not anti-Semitic or not queer? Ralph's doing all right." [24]

Nader was not the only one to fall under the vast network of Gillen's operatives. Even Senator Ribicoff himself was checked to verify that he had never met Nader before he testified.[25]

GENERAL MOTORS' MARCH 9 PRESS RELEASE: WAS IT DELIBERATELY MISLEADING?

Another issue raised by the subcommittee hearing was the statement released by General Motors on March 9, in which the company admitted its responsibility for the investigation but said that it was limited to Mr. Nader's qualifications, background, expertise in car safety, and possible association with those handling Corvair cases against GM. Senator Kennedy, however, maintained that GM denied things that they were indeed responsible for and the statement "misled and in fact, was really, I might say, false" (1398).

GM's President Roche, in New York on March 6, saw *The New York Times* article describing Gillen's admission of the investigation. At the time, Roche was unaware of GM's instigation. On March 8, when Roche called his legal department in Detroit asking them to deny any GM involvement, he was told that GM was indeed responsible. He flew back to Detroit and with his legal staff worked on various drafts of the press release from 2:30 P.M. until 8:30 P.M. The mechanics of preparing it were

[24] *Newsweek*, April 4, 1966, pp. 77–78.
[25] *Ibid.*

such that it missed most morning papers' 10:00 P.M. deadline (1402). While the release was being prepared, Roche's legal staff informed him that GM had hired Gillen, but he was not told of the preemployment pretext (1393). In fact, Roche saw none of Gillen's reports before he signed the statement, and he relied entirely on the assistant general counsel, Mr. Bridenstine (1402). Bridenstine assured Roche that the investigation was "made solely for the purpose of determining Mr. Nader's connection tion . . ." (1397).

GM's general counsel, Aloysius F. Power, who had originated the investigation, was out of town when the statement was prepared, and the press release was read to him over the phone. He did not object to any inaccuracies even though he "was aware of the reports and the investigation . . ." (1379).

Roche admitted that the statement might be somewhat misleading and that he had learned a great deal about the investigation of Nader since the March 8 statement:

> But I thought our first responsibility was to put out a statement that admitted our responsibility for conducting an investigation. . . .
> As I indicated earlier, were I writing this statement, this press release, today, I think it would be in different language. [1392]

Roche added, however, that there was no intent to mislead. Roche acknowledged that certain people on the GM legal staff were receiving reports and knew the full extent of the investigation. Senator Kennedy thought it was "terriby serious, almost equally unfortunate, if not more unfortunate, that General Motors permitted this statement to go out on March 9 which so misled the general public and misled members of Congress and the press of the United States . . ." (1399–1400).

Kennedy, however, was far from satisfied with this explanation. In speaking to Roche, he commented:

> What I don't understand is why people in your office would permit the release of a false statement. I mean, when you call in someone and say, we want to put the facts out, we want to be candid and honest with the general public. Because, nobody has a greater responsibility than General Motors. They are the leading corporation in the United States, they stand for something not only in this country but all over the world.
> Mr. Roche: This is certainly not like General Motors, Senator Kennedy, and I understand what you mean. This is a new and strange experience for most of our people with whom I am associated. And we do not like this kind of approach to a problem of this kind. [1399]

Power also testified before the subcommittee, joined in Roche's apology, and said he thought the surveillance was ordered because the investigators thought it appropriate. According to Power, he had not read all available reports relayed by Mr. Danner, but he thought they contained nothing detrimental to Nader's character. However, they did "indicate that Mr. Nader had no educational background or work experience in the field of motor vehicle engineering or technical research, that he did not appear to have the background to qualify as an expert witness in Corvair design cases and that he was reported to have very little trial experience as an attorney" (1442).

The last report was sent to GM on March 14. According to Power, GM was wrong in having Nader followed, but he felt that the investigation was still "limited" and that the press release was not misleading. Power admitted that Nader's character was not helped by the intimate questions asked but thought that the seriousness of the charges against GM by Nader's book and articles should be kept in mind.

Only after extensive questioning by Senator Kennedy did Power say that maybe GM should have added after "initiate a routine investigation" the words "which developed into an intensive investigation" (1453).

Kennedy also relentlessly pursued the same line of questioning with Assistant Counsel Louis H. Bridenstine, who helped draft the March 9 statement. Bridenstine based that statement on "the people in the office who were working on the Corvair, and who knew about the investigation . . ." (1454).

The purpose of the statement was to admit GM's initiating an investigation but to disclaim instances reported by the press for which Bridenstine knew GM was *not* responsible (1457–60). Bridenstine, who struck Kennedy as being evasive, said that the investigation was intended to be routine.[26] However, Senator Kennedy said:

> But that is not what you said [in the press release]. You didn't say the investigation was "intended." You state categorically that it was limited. . . . And, certainly anybody reading that statement would arrive at the conclusion that it was in fact limited and didn't go into all these other matters that had been reported in the press. Wouldn't you agree that it was misleading?
>
> Mr. Bridenstine: It certainly can be construed as that, sir, and if it will help us any, I will agree that it was misleading, but I will say it wasn't intended as such. [1460]

Bridenstine knew that Nader had been followed, admitted that he should have known more about the investigations, but said that he did not have time to read the reports carefully.

[26] *Newsweek,* April 4, 1966, pp. 77–78.

Thus, the staff members at GM who initiated the investigation and who were responsible for it were not aware of its extent. The first report Gillen sent to GM via Danner stating that surveillance had taken place was on March 3. Power had heard about it on February 14, some eight days after it started, and ordered it stopped, but by then it was too late. But the very first report sent to GM, received midway during the surveillance, mentioned the possibility of surveillance as per Gillen and Danner's discussion, yet GM took no immediate action (1446, 1449, 1463).

Senator Ribicoff was curious why GM couldn't hire its own investigative agency directly. Danner, who had never handled investigative work before (1518), was an intermediary in the truest sense—Gillen never spoke to anyone at GM, and Danner spoke only to Miss Murphy at GM. Gillen's reports were certainly detailed, but no one high in GM's legal hierarchy read them carefully. The multiplicity of links between Gillen and Roche certainly made for a large gap of ignorance (1521).

THE ISSUE OF AN INDIVIDUAL'S PRIVACY VS. CORPORATE POWER: NADER'S POSITION

The price paid for an environment that required an act of courage for a statement of truth has been needless death, needless injury and inestimable sorrow.

How much has this Nation lost because there are men walking around today with invisible chains?

The trademark of modern society may be the organization, but its inspiring and elevating contributions still flow from individual initiatives. Unless multiple sources of initiative and expression are kept open and asserted, the creative and humanizing infusions of a peoples' energies will atrophy.

Yet in a confrontation between an individual and a corporate organization, between myself and General Motors, if you will, the systematic immunities accrue to the corporation which has outstripped the law that created it. This problem of legal control over corporate action is one of increasing interest to a number of legal and economic scholars. I am responsible for my actions, but who is responsible for those of General Motors? An individual's capital is basically his integrity. He can lose only once. A corporation can lose many times, and not be affected. This unequal contest between the individual and any complex organization, whether it is a corporation, a union, government, or other group, is something which bears the closest scrutiny in order to try to protect the individual from such invasions.

The requirement of a just social order is that responsibility shall lie where the power of decision rests. But the law has never caught up with the development of the large corporate unit. Deliberate acts emanate from the sprawling and indeterminable shelter of the corporate organization. Too often the responsibility for an act is not imputable to those whose decision enable it to be set in motion. The president of General Motors can say he did not know of the specific decision to launch such an investigation. But is he not responsible in some way for the general corporate policy which permits such investigations to be launched by lower-level management without proper guidelines? The office of the general counsel can put forth a document outlining the limits of a "routine" investigation merely to protect the interest of the company's shareholders. A second shield in front of the corporate shield comes in the form of a law firm commissioned in the nonlegal task of hiring a private detective agency. In this case, apparently, GM did not wish to hire agents directly. The enthusiasms of their detectives, the law firm would have us believe, were unauthorized frolics and detours. Besides, the law firm could assume responsibility in the last analysis since there was little burden to such an assumption. Aside from the Federal statute under which this subcommittee is proceeding in this matter, there are few sanctions to protect the principle of privacy in American society against such new challenges largely unforeseen by the Founding Fathers. [1466–67]

Nader said the investigation was indeed a harassment, to his family and to himself, for it sought "to obtain lurid details and grist for invidious use," [27] and

it certainly took up a lot of my time and concern, and particularly concern over where was it going to end. One can possibly take harassing phone calls. One can take surveillance. But what is quite intolerable is the probings and what possibly might be done with these probings. One never has a chance to confront the adversary in a sense. It is faceless, it is insidious, and individuals, not only myself, can be destroyed in this manner, quite apart from discomfort. And so I was quite fearful of what was going to be the end of this. How was this information going to be used, and whether there was going to be even more overt foul play, perhaps of a physical nature.

I am not particularly sensitive to criticism at all. In fact, I probably have an armor like a turtle when it comes to that. I like to give and take. As an attorney, one is used to it. I don't intimidate easily, but I must confess that one begins to have second thoughts of the penalties and the pain which must be incurred in working in this area.

I think the thing that has persuaded me to continue in this area is

[27] "GM Apologizes for Harassment of Critic," *The New York Times*, March 23, 1966, p. 1.

that I cannot accept a climate in this country where one has to have an ascetic existence and steely determination in order to speak truthfully, candidly, and critically of American industry, and the auto industry. I think if it takes that much stamina, something is wrong with the enabling climate for expression in our country. I don't think it is generally wrong, but I think that we need to look into these areas and see how we can continually improve this climate. And it goes way beyond ideological considerations. This is not an ideological problem. This is a problem of individuals confronting complex organizations, whether they are complex organizations in the United States—corporations, labor unions or what not—or whether they are complex organizations in other countries of the world. [1512]

The complex organization need not have the upper hand against the individual, Nader said. Improvement of public education in this regard can become "a built-in check" against invasion of privacy. According to Nader, protection of privacy involves social sanctions as well as legal penalties so that

when somebody comes in and probes, and just flashes a badge without even showing it, people don't surrender and say, "I'll tell you everything." They will say, "Who are you? Who do you represent? Who is your client? Why are you asking these questions? What is your name? What is your detective serial number?" I am amazed how many people in this country are in a sense subtly restrained from that, as if they had better talk. [1513]

Glancing at the thick sheaf of detective reports, Ribicoff told Nader, "You and your family can be proud. They have put you through the mill and they haven't found a damn thing wrong with you" (1513).

Nader stated that he did not represent clients involved in Corvair design suits or work for their attorneys. Nader in fact had said this to GM executives when he visited the Technical Center in January; apparently, involvement would have prohibited his seeing certain Corvair technical exhibits at the center. According to Nader, Bridenstine had indicated that he believed what Nader said. That GM's actions proved they did not take him at his word only demonstrated to Nader that

General Motors' executives continue to be blinded by their own corporate mirror-image that it's "the buck" that moves the man. They simply cannot understand that the prevention of cruelty to humans can be a sufficient motivation for one endeavoring to obtain the manufacture of safer cars. [1469]

Nader added that contrary to Roche's earlier statement, he was "singularly unimpressed" at GM's presentation, which included an "outrageously erroneous assertion" and "evasive responses" (1469).

As for the similarity of his writings and plaintiffs' language in design cases, Nader said these resulted from "a common design defect" in the cars. Indeed, some of Nader's material came directly from GM's patents and trade journals! (1507).

THE CASE IN RETROSPECT

Despite Nader's tormenting by the investigation and hearings, Ribicoff said he could not help "but feel that what this hearing has achieved will have a salutary effect on business ethics and also the protection of the individual" (1513). Kennedy felt that Roche had raised his stature by appearing (1564). Perhaps the most important results of the hearings were the auto safety laws. Kennedy said that were it not for Nader and Ribicoff, Congress would not even have considered an auto safety law (1515).

According to the *Atlantic,* the March 22 hearings

did as much as anything to bring on federal safety standards. One Senator said, "Everybody was so outraged that a great corporation was out to clobber a guy because he wrote critically of them. At that point everybody said what the hell with them." Another Capitol Hill man said, "When they started looking in Ralph's bedroom, we all figured they must really be nervous. We began to believe that Nader must be right." [28]

As for Nader, the hearings made him frontpage material, the underdog miraculously defeating the giant automotive industry. According to *Newsweek,* "After his confrontation with GM, Nader's public image was more like that of a knight in shining armor." One auto man grumbled, "If GM hadn't beatified him, where would he be today?" [29]

Although the Justice Department decided that "criminal prosecution is not warranted in this matter" (1591), in November 1966 Nader filed a $26 million invasion of privacy suit in the Manhattan State Supreme Court of New York. He named General Motors, Vincent Gillen, Vincent Gillen Associates, Inc., and Fidelifacts, Inc. (a nationwide investigative firm for which Gillen holds the New York franchise).[30]

[28] Drew, "The Politics of Auto Safety," p. 99.
[29] *Newsweek,* January 22, 1968, pp. 65–66.
[30] "Nader Sues GM for $26 Million," *The New York Times,* November 17, 1966, p. 35; and "Ralph Nader Sues GM over the Investigation Made of Him," *The Wall Street Journal,* November 17, 1966, p. 5.

The papers filed in the suit said that General Motors "decided to conduct a campaign of intimidation, smearing and otherwise severely injuring [Nader]," [31] and subjected him to "harassment and intimidation [and] intruded into and invaded his seclusion, solitude and private affairs." The papers added that he had been "accosted by girls for purposes of entrapment and extortion" and that he had received phone calls "of a threatening, obnoxious and harassing nature." Furthermore, the defendants used "wiretapping, electronic or mechanical equipment . . . [for] eavesdropping" and interviewed his friends under false pretenses, casting aspersions on his "political, social, economic, racial and religious views, tendencies and possible prejudices" by questioning his integrity, "his sexual proclivities and inclinations; and his personal habits, such as the use of intoxicants, narcotics and the like." [32]

GM responded that it had no legal liability to Nader and that the courts would "vindicate" its position.[33] Gillen denied being concerned, saying the suit was "a lot of nonsense." He added that Fidelifacts, staffed by twenty-six former FBI agents in nationwide offices, "specialized solely in pre-employment investigations and had nothing to do with the case." [34] Nader said the suit was brought to "remedy a wrong inflicted upon one individual and the public interest, in the freedom to speak out against consumer hazards." Accordingly, any court awards would be used for the cause of auto safety.[35]

Meanwhile, as a result of a statement Gillen made to a Detroit newspaper, and unknown to GM, Nader brought a separate defamation of character suit against Gillen.[36] On the basis of Gillen's testimony in the suit's depositions, Nader's attorneys found information to make up "a list of more than 300 controversial statements about the facts in the larger suit against General Motors, and demanded that both Gillen and GM either confirm them or deny them." Within four of the twenty-nine days allowed to do so, Gillen responded. His response again made the Nader case front-page news and prompted Senator Ribicoff to ask the Justice Department to reinvestigate the possibility that perjury had been committed during his subcommittee hearings.[37]

[31] *The Wall Street Journal*, November 17, 1966, p. 5.
[32] *The New York Times*, November 17, 1966, p. 35.
[33] *Ibid.*
[34] *Ibid.*
[35] *Ibid.*
[36] "GM Aide Is Said to Assist Nader," *The New York Times*, February 7, 1967, p. 29; "Nader Again," *Newsweek*, February 20, 1967, p. 86; and Sidney Zion, "Ribicoff Seeking New GM Inquiry," *The New York Times*, February 6, 1967, p. 1.
[37] Zion, "Ribicoff Seeking New GM Inquiry"; and *Newsweek*, February 20, 1967, p. 86.

GILLEN'S ALLEGATIONS

Gillen swore in the court papers that "General Motors caused the original version of the first page" of one of Gillen's reports to GM to be withheld from Ribicoff's subcommittee and substituted an altered version. The original version showed that the true purpose of the investigation was to "discredit" Nader and to "shut him up." Gillen cooperated with GM in changing the document as it "did not coincide" with GM's "announced purpose" for the investigation. Gillen added that he did not look into Nader's connection with Corvair suits but delved "deeply into [his] past and present life . . . covering all facets thereof, including his movements." The original version of the first page of his report on Nader was destroyed on Danner's request, and the new version stated that the primary objective of the investigation was to fill in missing details on Nader "with emphasis on anything showing prejudice against automobiles or their manufacturers, or any subsidy involved in his writings." Both the investigation and the preemployment pretext "had been approved by General Motors' legal department." [38]

Furthermore, Gillen said he secretly taped his first meeting with Danner (another former FBI agent) on January 13, 1966, when Danner gave Gillen his instructions. Danner allegedly told Gillen:

They want to get something somewhere on this guy to get him out of their hair and to shut him up.

He's Syrian, or something, and maybe you will find an anti-Semitic angle . . . that will be interesting to Ribicoff.

There's something somewhere; find it so they can shut him up. His stuff is pretty damaging to the auto industry.

Gillen said that he had told GM, before the March 22 hearing, that he had recorded the discussion, but the company made no request for a transcript. [39]

[38] "Ribicoff Wants Study of Possible Perjury in GM-Nader Hearings," *The Wall Street Journal*, February 6, 1967, p. 4; and "Detective in Nader Case Says GM Altered Papers," *The New York Times*, February 5, 1967, p. 1.

[39] *The New York Times*, February 5, 1967, p. 1. Perhaps GM did not request a transcript of the meeting between Danner and Gillen because Danner may have recorded it himself. In any case, Gillen's admission certainly is an indication of his tendency to use recording devices in his investigations. It was said during Ribicoff's hearing that such devices were not used in the investigation. See pp. 378 and 385 of this book.

Sometime after this interview, a letter written on blank stationery, signed "Eileen," complained about the investigation's progress and requested specific kinds of information—Nader's savings accounts, stocks, accidents, and driver's license.[40] According to the *New Republic*, "Eileen" was Miss Eileen Murphy, of GM's legal department, and the letter was the seven-page investigation "guide" Gillen referred to in his court statement.[41] The "guide" made no mention of Corvair litigation but suggested possible anti-Semitism, dope, and asked, "Dose he drink?" [42] According to the *New Republic,* the letter was dated February 1966, addressed to Danner, and read in part:

> Dear Dick,
>   . . . everyone is going overboard to impress us with what a great, charming, intellectual this human being is—Eagle Scout type. There are too many variances for this to be accurate. . . . What is his Army record? What did he do for six months in the Army? . . . He mentions an accident which happened a decade ago. *He saw* a child decapitated. See if this gem can be uncovered as to where, when or how he was involved. . . . Well, friend, have fun. . . .[43]

Gillen's court statement said that when he visited Detroit, shortly before the hearing, the company took the letter from him so that a copy would not fall into Ribicoff's hands.[44]

Gillen felt that one of the reasons for injecting anti-Semitism into the investigation "was to attempt to discredit Ralph Nader in the eyes of Senator Abraham Ribicoff, who is Jewish." He said that some members of GM's legal department thought Ribicoff and Nader had "some fairly close relationships" and they found it difficult to believe Ribicoff's statement that he saw Nader for the first time on February 10, 1966. Thus, Gillen was told to investigate the senator's "credibility." In fact, when Gillen visited Detroit before the hearings, a GM lawyer "attempted to convince" him that he should deny any charges of investigating Ribicoff. Indeed, the night before the hearings, GM's Power, in getting Gillen to cooperate with GM, allegedly said, "I threatened to resign, but they're afraid to let me resign. If I can take this, you can take it too." [45] Power would not com-

[40] *Ibid.*
[41] James Ridgeway and David Sanford, "The Nader Affair," *New Republic,* February 18, 1967, p. 16; and *The New York Times,* February 5, 1967, p. 1.
[42] Ridgeway and Sanford, "The Nader Affair," p. 18; and *The New York Times,* February 5, 1967, p. 1.
[43] Ridgeway and Sanford, "The Nader Affair," p. 18.
[44] *Ibid.;* and *The New York Times,* February 5, 1967, p. 1.
[45] "Nader Again," *Newsweek,* February 20, 1967, p. 86.

ment on Gillen's statements, saying, "It's unethical to discuss a case when it's at trial," referring questions to counsel representing GM in the suit.[46]

In the court statements, Gillen said that he had been conducting investigations for GM since 1959, including an investigation on entertainer Danny Kaye "to ascertain whether his morals, character and political beliefs were suitable for identification with General Motors." Kaye, like Nader after him, received a good report. Gillen also helped with a two-year surveillance on a woman who said that she had had an affair with an officer of GM.[47] Also on Gillen's list were United Auto Workers officials and a civil rights worker "in whom General Motors was interested." In addition, Gillen looked into a Harlem antipoverty group which had charged GM with discrimination against Negroes in the company's hiring policies.[48]

GM'S RESPONSE

The questions Nader's attorneys asked Gillen to answer were in the form of a "request for admission," which requires the other party to admit or deny certain statements under oath.[49] The same request was submitted to GM on January 25. Gillen signed the request within four of the twenty-nine days allowed for him to do so. Surprised at his speed in answering, GM asserted that he was in collusion with Nader against GM in the suit. Gillen filed the papers on a Friday and the next Monday, February 6, GM submitted court papers saying of Gillen's statements that "the most casual examination . . . makes it obvious that Gillen is cooperating." [50] The company then moved to strike the requirement for the "request to admit" citing it as improper, in violation of GM's rights, and not in line with established legal practice.[51] One week later, GM submitted court papers requesting that all suits involving Nader be merged, again charging Gillen-Nader cooperation. The company's stand was that the Detroit suit represented a vehicle for obtaining information against GM. Of Gillen's motive for collusion, the company's attorneys said that GM had advised Gillen the previous November that it could not commit itself to pay for his defense in the suit or to bear any of his losses. GM said, "That marked the end of any

[46] *The New York Times,* February 5, 1967, p. 1.
[47] *Ibid.*
[48] *Ibid.;* and Ridgeway and Sanford, "The Nader Affair," p. 18.
[49] *The New York Times,* February 5, 1967, p. 1.
[50] *The New York Times,* February 7, 1967, p. 29; and "GM Says Detective It Hired in Nader Case Now Helps Auto-Critic in Suit against Firm," *The Wall Street Journal,* February 7, 1967, p. 7.
[51] *The Wall Street Journal,* February 6, 1967, p. 4; and *Newsweek,* February 20, 1967, p. 86; and *The New York Times,* February 5, 1967, p. 1.

genuine effort on Gillen's part to defend himself . . . [beginning] fullest cooperation [with Nader]." [52]

Gillen labeled GM's claims of cooperation as "ridiculous." [53] He said he had counterclaimed against Nader in the Detroit suit for $2 million and had counterclaimed against both GM and Nader in the New York suit— for $21 million each. Gillen asked, "Is that what they call cooperation? I'm suing Nader for $2 million in one suit and $21 million in the other." He said of the court papers filed recently that "I was simply telling the truth." [54]

Nader's attorney said of GM's charges, "If they're implying collusion or a deal of any kind, we flatly deny it. If General Motors wants to send a 'request to admit' on that, Nader will deny it under oath." [55]

MANEUVERINGS

A long series of pretrial maneuverings followed the company's February 1967 court motions, which were not concluded until July 1968. By this time, the court had rejected GM's claims of collusion between Nader and Gillen and had refused to throw out Gillen's allegations.[56] It was expected that the company would appeal these *pretrial* decisions to the U.S. Supreme Court.[57]

EPILOGUE

On August 13, 1970, General Motors and Ralph Nader announced an out-of-court settlement of $425,000 for Nader's $26 million invasion-of-privacy suit against GM. In announcing the settlement, Nader's spokesman said that the proceeds of the settlement, after deducting legal fees and expenses, will be used to establish a "continuous legal monitoring of General Motor's activities in the safety, pollution, and consumer relations area." [58]

[52] "GM Would Merge Nader-Gillen Suits," *The New York Times,* March 14, 1967, p. 35.

[53] *The Wall Street Journal,* February 7, 1967, p. 7.

[54] *The New York Times,* February 7, 1967, p. 29.

[55] *Ibid.*

[56] "Collusion Rejected in Two Nader Suits," *The New York Times,* July 6, 1967, p. 22; and "GM Is Rebuffed in Suit by Nader," *The New York Times,* July 6, 1968, p. 42.

[57] *Ibid.;* and "The Critic," *San Francisco Sunday Examiner and Chronicle,* February 23, 1969, p. A9.

[58] *The Wall Street Journal,* August 14, 1970, p. 4.

Bethlehem Steel Company and the Woodroofe Incident

To What Extent Can a Corporation Control an Employee's Social and Political Activities?

> The fundamental tendency of the bureaucratic mind is to turn all problems of politics into problems of administration.
>
> —Karl Mannheim

On March 16, 1964, the Bethlehem Steel Company fired Philip B. Woodroofe, supervisor of municipal services at the Bethlehem, Pennsylvania, home office. The charge was that Woodroofe and his wife refused to comply with a company demand to resign from the Community Civic League, an organization to improve interracial relations. Woodroofe was a founder of the organization.

When pressed for an explanation, the company simply stated that Woodroofe had resigned and that it was not company policy to make statements on an individual employee's resignation. Woodroofe himself denied having resigned:

> I have never submitted my resignation, nor have I been asked to

399

submit one. . . . I was told I was through. . . . I was told I couldn't act as a private citizen, nor could my wife.[1]

This incident, which for a short time received national attention, brought into sharp focus the contradictions between a company's public posture and its private philosophy; the vulnerability of professional junior and middle-level managers—unprotected by unions or internal company due process against the arbitrary exercise of power by large corporations; and, still more important, the infringement of an individual's rights by the extension of the corporation's control over his actions in areas not directly connected with corporate activities.

THE COMPANY

Bethlehem Steel, the second largest steel company in the United States, dominates the economic and social life of the Lehigh Valley and the city of Bethlehem, Pennsylvania. It furnishes nearly 50 percent of the entire payroll of the town. Of Bethlehem's population of 77,000, about 1,000 are blacks, and a very small number are Puerto Ricans. (In the Lehigh Valley as a whole, with a population of 250,000, about 2,500 are blacks.) Schools have not been segregated, and there have been no civil rights demonstrations. There has been a problem of inadequate housing for the poor and a high rate of Negro school dropouts.[2]

Over the years [Bethlehem Steel] has demonstrated its consciousness of the civic well-being of its home office city in many ways. It has invested heavily, without any prodding, in air pollution controls, in neutralizing the manufacturing effluents which it dumps into the Lehigh River, and in expending heavy sums to beautify the city by buying up eyesores and staving off blight along approaches or property not used for steel manufacturing. Besides, it has increasingly encouraged its people to participate in a wide range of civic activity, even to the point of giving one of its junior executives a leave of absence to run for Congress last year.[3]

---

[1] Joseph A. Loftus, "Bethlehem Puzzled by Dismissal of Steel Aide over Racial Stand," *The New York Times,* March 22, 1964, p. 10.

[2] *Ibid.*

[3] "The Woodroofe Incident," *Bethlehem Globe-Times,* March 20, 1964, p. 6.

In its management policies, however, the company has long been regarded as one of the "most withdrawn and individualistic companies in a conservative industry." [4]

Bethlehem Steel is run by a board of directors made up entirely of company officers, without a single outsider. Situated far from the big steel centers, the "inbred and stratified social life" of the company executives centers on the Saucon Valley Country Club. To an outsider, the company "offers a cautious austere facade." [5]

Bethlehem is noted for being stingy with titles but generous with salaries. With $2.1 billion in sales, it has only 10 vice presidents. United States Steel, with $3.6 billion in sales, has 77.

The lowest-paid Bethlehem vice presidents received $113,866 last year, and the highest paid, John E. Jacobs, vice president for steel operations, drew $218,358. Mr. Cort, who was president and a director for five months, received $79,167 for the period, or payment at an annual rate of $145,000.

Mr. Martin, in his capacities as president and vice chairman, drew $251,726, and Mr. Homer, as chairman, received $301,860.[6]

The style of management has been strictly individual and authority has clearly been centralized at the top. In its fifty-nine-year history the company has had only three chief executives. The first died in office at the age of seventy-seven. The other two retired after serving for eighteen and for seven years at the ages of eighty-one and sixty-eight, respectively. The fourth chief executive officer, Edmund F. Martin, took over on March 17, 1964, at the age of sixty-one, moving up from his former position as the vice-chairman.

Arthur Homer, the retiring chairman, has been regarded as one of the most commanding figures in the steel industry:

He is a tall, lean simply-spoken man, whose demeanor has been described as that of an affable New England preacher. He enjoys a pipe and occasionally indulges in a little wit or whimsy. . . .

At his quarterly press conferences in New York he stood at the door to the 15th floor conference room greeting reporters as they

---

[4] John M. Lee, "1964: Year of Change for Bethlehem Steel," *The New York Times,* April 12, 1964, Sec. 3, pp. 1, 5.

[5] *Ibid.*

[6] *Ibid.*

entered. He then took a seat alone on one side of a 30-foot table and fielded questions from the newsmen arrayed opposite him.

Behind Mr. Homer, against the wall, sit all the directors. Only occasionally did Mr. Homer ask any of them to comment. During the conference, the directors' expressions seldom changed except to laugh at a Homer quip. There was no question of who spoke for Bethlehem.[7]

PHILIP B. WOODROOFE

Woodroofe, forty-five at the time of the incident, is the son of an Episcopal minister. He interrupted his studies at Lehigh University to enter the United States Air Force shortly after Pearl Harbor. He served in World War II and in the Korean conflict as a B-29 pilot and instructor. He left the service as a lieutenant colonel in the Air Force Reserve.[8]

In 1957, when he was director of residence halls at Lehigh University, he was hired to be Bethlehem's supervisor of municipal services. His duties at the company called for, among other things, cooperation in city planning.[9]

COMMUNITY CIVIC LEAGUE

In May 1963 the Right Reverend Arthur Lichtenberger, presiding bishop of the Protestant Episcopal Church in the United States, appealed to his church members to take positive action and assume responsibility in solving this country's racial problems. Woodroofe, an Episcopalian, took this appeal seriously and initiated informal meetings between local white and black leaders to develop the framework for an organization that could provide a forum where community problems could be brought into the open and discussed, thus avoiding the possibility of violent confrontation between various groups. Woodroofe took a leading role in mobilizing community support. As a result, the Community Civic League was formally organized on March 15, 1964, at the local YWCA. Participating were more than two hundred local citizens, including Bethlehem's mayor, H. Gordon Payrow, and a number of clergymen.

---

[7] *Ibid.*

[8] "Steel Company Ousts Municipal Aide," *Bethlehem Globe-Times,* March 17, 1964, p. 7.

[9] Loftus, "Bethlehem Puzzled by Dismissal of Steel Aide."

WOODROOFE'S TROUBLES WITH THE COMPANY

Two days before the organizational meeting of the league, Woodroofe was informed that his superiors were displeased with his involvement in league activities. According to a story in *The New York Times:*

On Friday, March 13, F. C. Rabold, manager of general services for Bethlehem Steel, said it had come to his attention through his superiors that Mr. Woodroofe was involved in the league. The instructions to Mr. Rabold were to "get me out" of the league, Mr. Woodroofe said.

One of Mr. Rabold's superiors is Russell K. Branscom, vice president for industrial and public reations. Nebraska-born, Mr. Branscom was graduated from the University of Alabama with the interfraternity award for outstanding service to the university. That was in 1935. He has been in Bethlehem since then.

Mr. Woodroofe was given until Sunday noon to make his decision. He talked with Mr. Rabold Saturday and was cautioned about the consequences of a wrong decision.

"Helen and I talked about exchanging places," she to go on the board of the league and he to be a rank-and-file member. "The company told me that wouldn't do," he said.

Mr. Woodroofe won an extension of the deadline until 4 P.M. Sunday so that he could talk to his friend, Bishop Frederick Warneke. The Bishop was away and Mr. Woodroofe gave his answer without that counsel. The answer was:

"Neither I nor Helen will disassociate ourselves from the Community League. What we started here is good. We must continue it."

Mr. Woodroofe said his superior's reply was: "I think you've made a mistake."

The company's view that the league would worsen rather than help the situation was conveyed to Mr. Woodroofe.

When Mr. Woodroofe reported for work Monday morning, Mr. Rabold told him, "I'm surprised that you are here."

"Do you mean to say really I'm through?" Mr. Woodroofe asked.

"Yes, you're through," was the reply.

"So I went to the board and punched my time card," Mr. Woodroofe said. He was through at 10:15 and left without cleaning out his desk.[10]

[10] *Ibid.,* p. **10.**

The town was shocked and dismayed. The story made the national newspapers. The local papers during the next few days were full of angry letters from readers and editorials condemning Bethlehem Steel's action. Not a single word could be found in either the local or the national news media justifying or supporting the company's action.[11]

THE COMPANY'S POSTURE IN THE AFTERMATH

Bethlehem's press statement that Woodroofe had resigned was clearly unsatisfactory to the community. It refused to accept the company's statement in view of Woodroofe's charge that he was indeed fired. Consequently, in response to local inquiries, the company issued two statements denying that it was against employee participation in community affairs and insisting that Woodroofe's dismissal was based on a clear case of conflict of interest.

The first statement was issued on March 24, 1964:

[As far back as] in 1955, for example, our Chairman and Chief Executive Officer, Arthur B. Homer, addressing the Bethlehem Chamber of Commerce, emphasized that "our employees are encouraged to participate as fully as they can in the life of the community, as citizens, irrespective of their status with the company."

This continuing policy was re-emphasized in a speech on March 16, 1960, by James V. Robertson, Manager of Community Relations, who said:

". . . Part of that job is encouraging employees—and I quote Mr. Homer on this—'to participate as fully as they can in the life of the community, irrespective of their status with the company.' "

Also, in 1961, in management conferences held in all the steel plants, employees were again encouraged to participate as fully as they cared to in the life of the community, as citizens, irrespective of whether or not the company provides financial support for a particular organization's activities. That policy has continued without change to the present time.[12]

A company spokesman also said that "the company would be glad, if invited, to designate an official representative to participate in the activities of the committee." [13]

[11] See *Bethlehem Globe-Times*, March 18, 20, 23–25, 27, 30, April 10, 1964; and *Allentown Morning Call*, March 27, 1964.

[12] "Company Says No Bar on Civic Activity," *Bethlehem Globe-Times*, March 25, 1964.

[13] "Steel Company Invites Bid to Interracial League," *Bethlehem Globe-Times*, March 24, 1964, p. 12.

The second statement, issued on March 25, 1964, dealt specifically with Woodroofe's dismissal:

> As supervisor of municipal services of this company, Mr. Woodroofe participated as the official representative of the company in certain municipal activities. When he became identified with the Community Civic League, it was the company's belief that his position on matters coming before that organization would be viewed as an expression of the official position of the company. This type of activity did not represent an area related to his responsibilities with the company and the company believed it inescapable that misunderstandings would result.
>
> Therefore, although the company does encourage employees to participate in affairs of their local communities, the circumstances in this case were such—and Mr. Woodroofe was so advised—that there was a clear conflict between his official representation of the company in certain community activities and his participation in the League. Mr. Woodroofe chose to resign from the company.[14]

In a later announcement, the company stated that Woodroofe was offered two other jobs with the company prior to his dismissal but that he refused to accept either of them.[15]

When asked to comment, Mr. Woodroofe said that he found it difficult to accept the company's statement at face value since it demanded that his wife also resign from the Community Civic League.[16] Mrs. Woodroofe added, "And I am on the Red Cross Board. I don't speak for the company there." [17]

COMMUNITY CIVIC LEAGUE'S RESPONSE

A league spokesman considered it an encouraging sign when Bethlehem Steel indicated interest in participating in the league's affairs. The Reverend R. Wakefield Roberts, the pastor of Saint John Zion Methodist Church and a member of the league's board of directors, said that he was positive that the league would extend an invitation to the company to join. He also stated that the board would adopt an official position on the Woodroofe incident.[18]

---

[14] "Steel Blames 'Conflict' in Woodroofe Case," *Bethlehem Globe-Times,* March 26, 1964.

[15] "Woodroofe Vetoed Two Other Jobs," *Bethlehem Globe-Times,* April 15, 1964, p. 1.

[16] *Bethlehem Globe-Times,* March 26, 1964.

[17] Loftus, "Bethlehem Puzzled by Dismissal of Steel Aide."

[18] "Steel Co. Bid to Interracial League," *Bethlehem Globe-Times,* p. 12.

The meeting took place on the evening of March 24, 1964. At the meeting the board turned down the company's bid to send an official representative to participate in the league's activities. In declining the company's request the board cited a provision of its constitution which limited the membership in the league to persons who were "willing to work as individuals towards improving conditions of minority groups in Bethlehem, rather than as representatives of any church, industry, business or profession." [19]

The board also unanimously decided not to take any official position on the Woodroofe incident. This was done at the suggestion of Woodroofe who requested that the board make no statement "public or private" as this "would not serve the league's purpose." [20]

On June 30, 1964, Philip Woodroofe resigned from the board of directors of the league as he planned to move to New York where he had reportedly accepted a real estate job. However, he retained his membership in the league. [21]

[19] "Civic League Fails to Offer Steel Bid," *Bethlehem Globe-Times,* March 25, 1969.

[20] *Ibid.*

[21] "Woodroofe Resigns Seat on Civic League Board," *Allentown Morning Call,* July 1, 1964.

Motorola v. Fairchild Camera

The Case of C. Lester Hogan et al.

All that clearly appears is that he undertook to use in his new employment the knowledge he had acquired in the old. This, if it involves no breach of confidence, is not unlawful; for equity has no power to compel a man who changes employers to wipe clean the slate of his memory.

—Justice Francis M. Scott
in *Peerless Pattern Co.* v. *Pictorial Review Co.*
(147 App. Div. 715, 132, N.Y.S. 37)

On August 8, 1968, C. Lester Hogan resigned from Motorola, Incorporated, to join Fairchild Camera and Instrument Corporation. At the time of his resignation, Hogan was a director and executive vice-president of Motorola and general manager of the Semiconductor Products Division. His new position was as a director and president of Fairchild. Soon after Hogan resigned, seven other top men in Motorola's semiconductor division joined him at Fairchild,[1] and by the end of September, another fifteen executives left Motorola.[2]

[1] *Motorola, Inc.* v. *Fairchild Camera and Instrument Corporation, et al.,* Civil Complaint No. 6808, U.S. District Court, Arizona, August 27, 1968, as amended by the Court Order of September 18, 1968, pp. 6–20.

[2] "The Fight That Fairchild Won," *Business Week,* October 5, 1968, p. 113.

On August 27, 1968, Motorola filed a civil suit in the Federal Court in Arizona charging Fairchild and seven other defendants with antitrust violations, unfair competition, interference with advantageous personnel relations, and unjust enrichment. Motorola sought relief in terms of compensatory and exemplary damages and also asked that Hogan and the other defendants hold in "constructive trust" (read, returnable to Motorola) all profits they derived from Fairchild. Named as codefendants were the wives of Hogan and of the seven other defendants for the reason that the financial benefits allegedly gained by the defendants "are or may constitute community property for which said defendants must account to plaintiff and as to which a constructive trust is prayed to enforce the rights of plaintiff therein." [3]

THE DEFENDANTS

1. Fairchild Camera and Instrument Corporation
2. C. Lester Hogan and Audrey Hogan
3. Leo E. Dwork and Bea Dwork
4. Eugene A. Blanchette and Valerie Blanchette
5. George M. Scalise and Dorothea Scalise
6. Andrew A. Procassini and Jean Procassini
7. William L. Lehner and Ella Lehner
8. Thomas D. Hinkelman and Winnie Hinkelman
9. Wilfred J. Corrigan and Sigrun Corrigan

MOTOROLA'S SPECIFIC CHARGES: AGAINST FAIRCHILD

1. Fairchild knew, or reasonably should have known, that Hogan and the seven other defendants were key members of the top management team of Motorola's Semiconductor Division; had harmonious relations with Motorola's management; and had each executed stock-option contracts with Motorola which stipulated remaining in Motorola's employ for one year (24). Its solicitation and employment of Motorola's key management employees in the Semiconductor Division would tend to restrain and lessen competition in the semiconductor industry, inasmuch as the wrongful wholesale defection of part of the latter's top management team to a competitor might well seriously weaken and render less effective

---

[3] Extensive use is made of Motorola's Civil Complaint No. 6808. Citations from this source henceforth appear in the text set off by parentheses or brackets enclosing page references.

Motorola's competitive position. This restraint of and injury to competition between Motorola and Fairchild violates the laws of the United States. "The products of both Motorola and Fairchild are sold and move in and are a part of the interstate and foreign commerce of the United States" (25,31).

2. Despite this knowledge, Fairchild enticed these defendants into breaking their employment relationships with and fiduciary duties owed to Motorola (26).

3. As part of this wrongful scheme, Fairchild expected that Hogan would directly and indirectly solicit the key employees—that is, the remaining named defendants, and others—to break their employment obligations with Motorola by leaving Motorola in a body and without notice and becoming employees of Fairchild. Furthermore, as part of this scheme, Fairchild authorized Hogan to induce Motorola employees to join Fairchild and for this purpose gave him written forms of stock options (26,30).

MOTOROLA'S SPECIFIC CHARGES: AGAINST HOGAN

In the middle of July 1968, after Fairchild approached him for the first time, Hogan assured Motorola that he was not interested in changing employers and that he intended to honor his commitment to Motorola. This was a misrepresentation, however, according to Motorola, as Hogan suddenly advised Motorola on August 7, 1968, that he was resigning and submitted his written resignation the next day, to be effective immediately. Without his employer's knowledge, Hogan had negotiated with one of Motorola's largest competitors in the semiconductor industry with intention to defect and to "take his 'team' of top management people in the Semiconductor Division with him." To accomplish this, Hogan met with his codefendants individually and in groups on various occasions between early July and August 7, 1968, in Maricopa County, Arizona (28–29).

MOTOROLA'S SPECIFIC CHARGES: AGAINST HOGAN AND HIS CODEFENDANTS FROM THE SEMICONDUCTOR DIVISION

1. Motorola charged that Hogan, Dwork, Corrigan, Blanchette, Hinkelman, Procassini, Scalise, and Lehner knew, or should reasonably have known, that the lavish salary increases and other financial benefits offered by Fairchild were

for the purpose of obtaining for Fairchild access to the trade secrets and "know how" of Motorola known to said employees by reason of their employment by Motorola for use by Fairchild. Each of said employees knew or should have realized that their knowledge and familiarity with said trade secrets and know how was so intertwined with their personal engineering and other skills that use by and disclosure of Motorola's trade secrets to Fairchild would be inevitable and unavoidable if said employees undertook to discharge and carry out duties for Fairchild which were similar to their duties while employed by Motorola. [30]

2. These defendants were part of the top management team of Motorola's Semiconductor Division. As such, they were privy to trade secrets,[4] information concerning Motorola's research, new product development, current products, pricing, and other policies in the highly competitive marketing of semiconductor products, both in the United States and abroad. They also had access to the confidential information supplied to the company by Motorola's customers for product research and development. These defendants had been informed and were aware that such information or know-how was confidential and was the sole and exclusive property of Motorola, could be used solely for the benefit of and in the cause of business for Motorola, and was to be kept confidential for period of two years after any termination of employment with Motorola (3).

3. Each of the individual male defendants had executed an agreement with Motorola with respect to inventions and other proprietary information, and these agreements were in force at the time of their unilateral resignations (3–4).

4. In March 1968 each male defendant was granted substantial salary increases and additional valuable stock options, in consideration of which

---

[4] The definition of *trade secret* as used by Motorola in its complaint (p. 9) and accepted by Fairchild and the other defendants in their answer to Motorola's complaint is as follows:

A trade secret may consist of any formula, pattern, device or compilation of information which is used in one's business, and which gives him an opportunity to obtain an advantage over competitors who do not know or use it. It may be a formula for a chemical compound, a process of manufacturing, treating or preserving materials, a pattern for a machine or other device, or a list of customers. A trade secret is a process or device for continuous use in the operation of the business. Generally it relates to the production of goods, as, for example, a machine or formula for the production of an article. It may, however, relate to the sale of goods or to other operations in the business, such as a code for determining discounts, rebates or other concessions in a price list or catalogue, or a list of specialized customers, or a method of bookkeeping or other office management.

It may be a device which is patentable but it need not be. It may be a device or process which is clearly anticipated in the prior art or one which is merely a mechanical improvement. It must at least be novel to the person receiving the disclosure.

he agreed, in writing, to remain in Motorola's employ for a period of one year from that date (20).

5. The defendants knew that their resignations without notice would constitute a wrongful breach of their employment obligation with Motorola (31).

6. They also knew that Fairchild would obtain, by its wrongful conduct, a top-management team of great value to Fairchild and the loss of such a team could be seriously damaging to Motorola as a competitor of Fairchild (31).

7. These defendants, between August 9 and August 14, 1968, wrongfully left Motorola to accept jobs with Fairchild. Furthermore, *these defendants' new jobs with Fairchild covered the same areas of responsibility as those of their previous jobs with Motorola* (31).

8. Motorola also charged that, since

It is impossible to separate out and segregate the amount of said inducements which might be considered as legitimate, if said defendants had not been under an employment obligation to Motorola, and hence the entire gain is infected with the evil purpose which actuated the offers by Fairchild.

Each therefore holds these gains as property secured by wrongful acts damaging to Motorola, as constructive trustee for Motorola. [Emphasis added] [31]

NATURE OF RELIEF SOUGHT BY MOTOROLA

Motorola asked the court that:

1. Fairchild, Hogan, and the other male defendants be enjoined from employing or agreeing to employ any present employee of Motorola and from soliciting, urging, or permitting the male codefendants to disclose or utilize any trade secret or information of Motorola and its customers in discharge of their duties as employees of Fairchild (36–37).

2. Hogan and other male defendants be enjoined from disclosing or utilizing, for the benefit of Fairchild, any trade secrets or confidential information of its customers gained while employed by Motorola (37).

3. All male defendants and their wives be enjoined from selling, encumbering, or otherwise lessening the monetary value of each of said defendants' financial gains and rewards realized by accepting

employment from Fairchild. That these defendants are to hold all "illicit gains made by them from Fairchild" as the price for breaching their agreements with Motorola as a "constructive trustee for Motorola and requiring that the same be paid over to Motorola" (38).

4. Motorola be awarded judgment "against *Fairchild and Hogan* for such damages compensatory and exemplary as the court may determine as appropriate to make Motorola whole and to deter other corporations and directors and officers thereof . . ." (emphasis supplied) (38).

SUBSTANTIATION OF CHARGES BY MOTOROLA

To substantiate its charges against Fairchild and other defendants, Motorola made the following points:

1. Both Motorola and Fairchild are manufacturers and sellers of semiconductor products and other devices and instruments that use these products. Motorola and Fairchild compete with each other in interstate and foreign commerce for the distribution and sale of these products.

2. Motorola is a pioneer in electronics industry, including the semiconductor field, and is recognized as such nationally and internationally.

3. Motorola has expended large sums of money on research and development in electronics, including the semiconductor field, and has maintained a large staff of scientists, engineers, and technicians. As a result of these activities, the company has developed certain novel products and processes which are trade secrets and are maintained as proprietary information in the operation of the Semiconductor Division.

4. All male defendants had been part of Motorola's Semiconductor Division. Within that division their duties and responsibilities were such that they had access to, and were familiar with, these trade secrets (6–20).

The brief job descriptions of these defendants, at the time of their resignations, will clarify this point:

C. Lester Hogan. As director and executive vice-president of Motorola, Inc., he was privy to, and had knowledge of, Motorola's corporate trade secrets. As general manager of the Semiconductor Division, he was familiar with all its trade secrets and knew of its product mix, marketing policies, and long-range plans for product development and marketing.

Leo E. Dwork. Vice-president of Motorola, Inc., and director of Products and Operations Group within the Semiconductor Division. Prior to an organizational change four months before the resignations in April 1968, Dwork reported directly to Hogan. Dwork was manager and director of discrete semiconductors, with some minor exceptions, and had supervisory and management direction and control of all research and development and manufacturing of these products. He was responsible for the activities of the Applied Sciences Group which performed basic research for both discrete semiconductor products and integrated circuit products; for overall management of quality control; for the important Materials Department which supplied materials for product manufacture throughout the entire division. Dwork was chairman of the division's Patent Committee and as such reviewed and had access to all new invention and patent disclosures emanating from all division departments; received confidential information on the various aspects of Motorola's basic research, product development and manufacturing, and marketing. Further, defendants Lehner and Procassini reported directly to Dwork.

Wilfred J. Corrigan. As director of Products Groups, he was in direct charge of product development and manufacturing operations pertaining to the majority of discrete semiconductors and related products and applications, which product area provides a large dollar volume of sales to Motorola at the present time.

Eugene A. Blanchette. As director of Integrated Circuits Operation, he was in direct charge of product development and manufacturing operations pertaining to integrated circuits and related products and applications. Blanchette had full knowledge of all of Motorola's integrated circuitry manufacturing equipment processes and technology much of which, including trade secrets, marketing and customer information, was confidential.

William L. Lehner. As manager of Equipment and Plant Operations, he had overall responsibility for designing, engineering, building, maintaining, and calibrating all special manufacturing and testing equipment used by Motorola in its Semiconductor Division.

Andrew A. Procassini. As director of Reliability and Quality Control, Procassini had frequent occasion to confer personally with Dwork, Corrigan, Lehner, and Blanchette with respect to quality control aspects of the entire Semiconductor Division. He was also responsible for translating customers' specifications (generally considered as confidential) to Motorola's format of specifications. Procassini had intimate knowledge of customers' special reliability requirements, which were also highly confidential.

George M. Scalise. As general manager of Semiconductor Division, European Operations, he had knowledge pertaining to all of the manufacturing and marketing operations, including, importantly, knowledge concerning the products that are or can be sold in the greatest volume and profitability in the European market. Additionally, Scalise had participated in the long-range planning of both manufacturing facilities and marketing in the European area.

Thomas D. Hinkelman. As director of Planning and Production Control, he was responsible for preparing long-range plans and recommendations with respect to capital expenditure requirements of the Semiconductor Division projected over a five-year period. He also participated in new-product planning for the European market and was responsible for processing all requests from all departments within the division for capital expenditures on a day-to-day basis. Hinkelman was also responsible for inventory control and warehousing operations in the domestic Semiconductor Division. In this capacity he had detailed knowledge of the volume of product types that Motorola manufactures.

EVENTS LEADING TO THE RESIGNATIONS
FROM MOTOROLA

Motorola maintained that relationships between the company and its top-management personnel were harmonious and that the latter worked together smoothly as a team. Moreover, the company contended that, as late as March 1968, each male defendant was granted a substantial salary increase, stock options, participation in Motorola's profit-sharing plan, and a host of other benefits which the company considered "as fair and reasonable compensation for their services to the company, and as a proper and fair inducement for said defendants to perform their corporate functions competently and loyally and as fiduciaries to their employer Motorola" (20). In return for these benefits, each defendant agreed in writing to remain with Motorola for at least one year from the date of the agreement. Thus Motorola implied that it clearly was the injured party and an innocent victim of the unfettered greed of the male defendants and of the ruthless and unprincipled temptations offered by Fairchild to entice these employees of a competitor to break their agreements with their employer in a manner that was tantamount to personnel raiding.

However, it appears from other accounts that things may not have been that smooth at Motorola, and although Fairchild did indeed make a very tempting offer to Hogan, it is not at all clear that he or the other male defendants would have stayed with Motorola for long even if Fairchild's offer had not been forthcoming.

Hogan joined Motorola's Semiconductor Division in 1958 when it was beset with start-up problems and had annual sales of less than $5 million. Prior to joining Motorola, Hogan had taught physics, had a fine technical background, and understood the making of semiconductors. He was able to build a superb organization at Motorola by attracting good men and keeping them together. Although he had no previous business experience, he lost no time in acquiring this knowledge under the guidance of vice-chairman Daniel E. Noble (who had hired him) and other Motorola people. Under Hogan's leadership, the Semiconductor Division took off and, in 1967, the division's sales amounted to $230 million, with profits of $30 million. In 1968 the company for the first time passed Texas Instruments (the perennial leader in the semiconductor industry) to become the biggest producer in the United States.[5]

Despite the tremendous success achieved under his guidance, Hogan became disenchanted with his job. He felt that Motorola's top management had not recognized his and the division's outstanding performance: He claimed that he had received only one voluntary raise during his ten years with the company. He also felt demeaned because he had to report to three other executives—Chairman Galvin, Vice-Chairman Noble, and President Elmer H. Wavering. The first confrontation between Hogan and the company came about in January 1968. At that time, Hogan was offered the presidency of General Instrument Corporation, a manufacturer of semiconductors and electronics with headquarters in New York. Although he turned down the offer, he used it as a lever to force Motorola's management to offer him and his staff greater salaries and benefits.[6] It might be noted that these were the increases granted the staff in March of that year which Motorola cited in its suit as an example of its generosity.

In the case of Hogan:

Motorola offered Hogan an increase in salary from $80,000 per year to $90,000 per year, which increase was effective with his January 16, 1968 check, and also agreed to give him a stock option for

---

[5] *Business Week,* October 5, 1968, p. 107.
[6] *Ibid.,* p. 112.

10,000 shares of Motorola stock which amount was substantially above the stock option policy of Motorola. (Subsequently, by mutual agreement, to avoid emphasizing the fact that Hogan received the very large stock option as compared with other officer employees, the option was reduced to 9,000 shares.) [In return Motorola received] Hogan's assurance and promise that he would remain in the employ of Motorola for at least a year and that he would not either entertain or accept any offers from other companies during such period. [23]

The incident, however, left the relationship between Hogan and Motorola's Chairman Galvin somewhat less than friendly. Furthermore, "Hogan, who until then had netted only $239,000 from previous stock options, made a discouraging discovery: The new stock options were useless because he lacked the money to exercise them, and he could not afford the interest on a loan to do so." [7]

While these events were taking place at Motorola, Fairchild—once the darling of the semiconductor and electronics industry—was experiencing difficulties due to a diversification program that had not been successful. In 1967 its chairman had resigned, sales had fallen 10 percent from the previous year's, and the company incurred a loss of $7 million. During the first half of 1968, Sherman M. Fairchild, the largest stockholder of Fairchild Camera, took over the chairmanship of the company as an interim measure. The active management was given to a four-man committee. However, the committee system failed and conditions deteriorated further. To keep the situation from worsening, Sherman Fairchild and his advisers started looking for a new president. Feeling that they needed a man experienced in the semiconductor industry, they offered the job to the president of a small company in this field. To make the job more attractive, Fairchild considered spinning off the semiconductor division into a separate company. When this man declined the offer, Hogan became the next choice. On June 25, 1968, Robert N. Noyce, group vice-president in charge of the semiconductor and instrumentation divisions at Fairchild, called Hogan and made an appointment for Walter Burke, a board member and personal financial adviser to Sherman Fairchild, to meet Hogan in Phoenix. According to a story in *Business Week:*

Hogan jumped to the conclusion that Burke wanted to talk about a Motorola license for planar technology and readily agreed to the visit. Motorola is the only major semiconductor maker that has not licensed this important Fairchild process, and Hogan feared that Fairchild would sue for patent infringement. . . . [Instead] Burke offered

<hr>

[7] *Ibid.,* p. 113.

Hogan a job—though it was somewhat vague in detail. Hogan, though receptive, turned it down.[8]

In the meantime, Noyce, who wanted to quit Fairchild Camera and start his own semiconductor company but had agreed to stay—at Sherman Fairchild's urging—until a new executive was found, decided that he could wait no longer. His lawyers had warned him of a possible conflict of interest if he continued to work with Fairchild while planning to start his own company. Consequently, on June 28, 1968, Noyce resigned formally, thus forcing Sherman Fairchild to act immediately. According to *Business Week:*

> A week later, Sherman Fairchild himself visited Hogan at his home in Phoenix and offered him a job—this time as president of Fairchild Camera. Hogan said he was dedicated to his career at Motorola and added that stock options were pie in the sky if one didn't have the money for them. His decision was left in abeyance.
> A few days later, when Hogan called to decline the job, Sherman Fairchild unfolded a new offer, complete with a personal loan to pay for the stock options. . . .

Meanwhile, Noyce paid a visit to Hogan and frankly spelled out the strengths and weaknesses of Fairchild Camera for his benefit.[9]

The offer, as disclosed to Motorola by Hogan, contained substantially the following terms:

1. Hogan would become director and president of Fairchild and his annual salary would be increased from the $90,000 paid him by Motorola to $120,000.
2. Upon becoming an employee of Fairchild, Hogan would be put in a position to reap an immediate financial gain of $250,000 either by a cash payment or immediately realizable stock options.
3. Hogan would receive a stock option on 90,000 shares of Fairchild at approximately $60 per share, and Sherman Fairchild would loan Hogan $5,400,000 for up to ten years, without interest, to enable Hogan to exercise this option. If the stock value slipped below the option price, Hogan was to have the right to repay the loan by surrendering the stock at the option price. (A 6 percent

[8] *Ibid.,* **p.** 112.
[9] *Ibid.*

loan for the same sum and duration would be worth $324,000 per year or $3,240,000 at the end of ten years.)

4. Fairchild would move the main office headquarters from Syosset, New York, to Mountain View, California, so that Hogan could live near San Francisco according to his preference.

5. Hogan would have the right to select the Board of Directors of Fairchild with the promised assistance and cooperation of one or more of Fairchild's major stockholders. [27–28]

Hogan was persuaded to accept the job because of the challenge of being the number one man and because, for once, he could be financially independent. He accepted the offer on August 3, 1968.

According to *Business Week:*

> On Aug. 7, Hogan turned in his resignation to Noble, the Motorola executive who had hired him in 1958. Noble was hurt because he had not known that Hogan had reopened negotiations with Fairchild after having once turned the company down. He urged Hogan to reconsider and to talk to Galvin.
>
> The next day in Chicago, an annoyed Galvin feared another ploy to raise salaries. He started the conversation by discounting Hogan's contribution to Motorola's success. Annoyed, Hogan spelled out Fairchild's deal and compared it to what he felt was Motorola's parsimony. The meeting grew more acrimonious. It finally ended with Galvin accepting Hogan's resignation and telling him not to return to the plant, not even to pick up his own checkbook, which Hogan had left in his desk.[10]

DEFENDANTS' REPLY TO MOTOROLA'S CHARGES

Fairchild and Hogan denied that there was "any wrongful raid upon plaintiff's employees." [11] Hogan maintained that, contrary to Motorola's allegations, his staff had visited him at his home, requesting him to take them with him to Fairchild. This, according to Hogan, took place over the weekend *following* Motorola's announcement of Hogan's resignation. The desire to leave Motorola was so great and so widespread that Hogan turned down seven or eight men for each one he accepted.[12]

---

[10] *Ibid.,* p. 113.
[11] "Complaint and Answers," *Motorola, Inc.* v. *Fairchild Camera and Instrument Corp., et al.,* Civil Action No. 6808, U.S. District Court, Arizona, p. 11.
[12] *Business Week,* October 5, 1968, p. 113.

Moreover, Fairchild contended that Motorola

> does not come into court with clean hands in that it has solicited and induced highly skilled and knowledgeable employees of its competitors, including Fairchild, to terminate their employment and work for plaintiff and has then obtained and used the trade secrets and confidential business information of said competitors; accordingly, the plaintiff is not entitled to equitable relief herein and may not maintain this action.[13]

According to *Business Week,* personnel raiding is common practice in the semiconductor industry. When Motorola was struggling to develop its semiconductor division, it hired eighteen engineers from General Electric, and every other company in the industry has done much the same thing.[14]

Hogan and the other male defendants denied any wrongdoing in resigning from Motorola. Although they were granted certain stock options in March 1968, not exercisable for one year from that date, they were compelled to execute an agreement in connection with accepting such stock options. The defendants alleged that such instruments, which compelled an employee to remain in the

> employ of Motorola for a stated period of time, are null and void and have no effect by reason of lack of valuable consideration for such promise, failure of consideration and lack of mutuality of obligation and remedy.[15]

Under this agreement Motorola was not obliged to employ the individual defendants for any definite period.

Fairchild, Hogan, and the other male defendants contended that Motorola presented no evidence to prove that any trade secrets had or would be violated by the defendants and that any of their actions were or would violate antitrust laws as being in restraint of competition or unfair trade practices.

The defendants contended that Motorola was not the real party allegedly injured because part of the trade secrets referred to were those of Motorola's customers, who had not joined Motorola in this complaint. Therefore, the plaintiff had, in any event, failed to comply with Rule 19(c) of the Federal Rules of Civil Procedure.[16]

[13] "Complaint and Answers," *Motorola v. Fairchild,* p. 52.
[14] *Business Week,* October 5, 1968, p. 106.
[15] "Complaint and Answers," *Motorola v. Fairchild,* p. 31.
[16] *Ibid.,* p. 53.

MAJOR DEFENSE

In addition to denying Motorola's charges, Fairchild and the other defendants rested their defense by attacking the basic premise of Motorola's contention that an employee can be forced to work for a given company, or not at all.[17] According to the defendants:

> If, as seems to be the position of plaintiff, a highly skilled and knowledgeable employee of plaintiff may not be employed by or work for a competitor but must remain an employee of plaintiff or not work at all, then in effect said employee would be placed in involuntary servitude in violation of public policy and in violation of Section 1, Amendment XIII of the Constitution of the United States; accordingly, plaintiff is not entitled to equitable relief herein and may not maintain this action.[18]

TRIAL AND JUDGMENT

Motorola revised its original complaint of 1968 and filed an amended complaint on May 29, 1969. The case came up for trial before Judge William Copple of the U.S. District Court of Arizona on May 30, 1971. The court's decision was rendered on March 13, 1973.[19]

The court ruled that the "plaintiff has failed to establish by any credible evidence that plaintiff suffered any damages proximately caused by the events of August 1968." The court also:

1. Dismissed Motorola's complaint and action for lack of proof of liability "with prejudice" [20] as to all defendants and granted defendants' claim to recover their taxable costs
2. Observed that, from the testimony, it appeared that Motorola's "primary reason for filing this action was to inhibit the freedom of

---

[17] It might be noted that such a practice, with few exceptions, is legal and prevalent in the sports profession, which is exempt from U.S. antitrust laws.

[18] "Complaint and Answers," *Motorola* v. *Fairchild,* p. 52.

[19] *Motorola* v. *Fairchild,* Civil Complaint No. 6808, U.S. District Court, Arizona, March 13, 1973.

[20] A dismissal "with prejudice" terminates the litigation in the trial court in favor of the defendants. This means that a new lawsuit may not be brought on the same "cause of action" (controversy) between the two parties. However, an appeal of the judgment can still be made on error of law.

other employees who might be desirous of leaving Motorola to take employment with a competitor"

Never before or since this action has Motorola sued other executives who also resigned during their one-year option period for either breach of contract or a "trade-secrets" injunction.

Motorola is appealing the decision to a higher court.

The following is a brief summary of the court's findings as to the law and the facts in the case:

The plaintiffs sought relief for unfair competition; interference with advantageous personnel relationships; antitrust violations; unjust enrichment; constructive trust upon benefits wrongfully obtained; damages—punitive and compensatory; and breach of fiduciary duty by officer and director.

The evidence showed that Robert Galvin, the major stockholder of Motorola and its chief executive officer, ran the company with a strong hand and had centralized management where "not even a division manager can implement any decision or plan with which Galvin disagrees."

Motorola Semiconductor Division was characterized by the evidence as a low-cost, mass producer rather than as an innovator. Fairchild Camera, on the other hand, was known more for research and development and less as a low-cost producer.

The industry is led by bright, relatively young, and highly ambitious scientists and is characterized by a high mobility of top-flight executives.

During his employment with Motorola, and especially during the period of his negotiations with Motorola and Fairchild, Galvin never advised Hogan that "he had an employment contract with Motorola and, in fact, told him that he was, of course, free to resign." And Hogan had correctly so informed the Fairchild negotiators when they specifically asked for this information. Consequently, "there was no evidence of any 'conspiracy' by defendants. . . ."

The court's interpretation of the law was that the mere fact of a stock-option agreement for one year between Hogan and other defendants and Motorola was not to be construed "as a binding contract of employment [and] because the employee-defendants were free to leave Motorola, Fairchild was free to employ them. *A competitor is privileged to hire away an employee whose employment is terminable at will*" (emphasis added).

Furthermore, no contract existed between plaintiff and its former employee-defendants restricting or limiting their employment in the same industry following termination.

The evidence also showed that Motorola was being run efficiently and profitably by the successors of the employee-defendants, and there was "no evidence of malice or bad faith showing intent to leave Motorola in a position where it could not function because key employees had left."

The court could also "find no facts which would support a claim under the antitrust laws on any theory, nor which would support a claim for unfair competition."

Claims Relative to Trade Secrets. At the time of their resignations, each Motorola employee-defendant had, in effect, an agreement with plaintiff regarding nondisclosure of trade secrets to unauthorized parties.

Motorola did not claim that any employee-defendant took with him any blueprints, invoices, customer lists, price lists, or written or printed data of any kind belonging to plaintiff.

Defendants contended that all of plaintiff's claimed trade secrets at issue in the trial were either fully disclosed by patents, domestic or foreign, issued prior to August 1968 or were generally known in the trade and were not secrets in fact.

The evidence showed that Fairchild, like most other companies in the electronics industry, purchased and studied all domestic and foreign patents as well as relevant trade literature and competitors' sales, promotional literature, and products.

The court stated the general guiding principles as to the law of trade secrets through a quotation from Judge Yankwich's decision in *Sarkes Tarzian, Inc.* v. *Audio Devices, Inc.,* supra, at 265:

Trade practices, to come within the obligation of secrecy, must be secret. While they need not amount to invention, in the patent law sense, they must, at least, amount to discovery. It follows that matters which are generally known in the trade or *readily discernible* by those in the trade cannot be made secret by being so labelled in an agreement.

Criteria to consider in determining whether given information is a trade secret are the following:

(1) the extent to which the information is known outside [the] business; (2) the extent to which it is known by employees and others involved in [the] business; (3) the extent of measures taken by [the employer] to guard the secrecy of the information; (4) the value of the information to [the employer] and to his competitors; (5) the amount of effort or money expended by [the employer] in developing the information; (6) the ease or difficulty with which the information could be properly acquired or duplicated by others. [*Restatement of Torts*

¶ 757, Comment *b*, at 6 (1939); *Accord Metal Lubricants v. Engineered Lubricants,* 411 F.2d 426 (8th Cir. 1969)]

Motorola had 140 different alleged trade secret items in litigation. It dropped 134 of these voluntarily before the case came to trial. Subsequently, it added four more items, making a total of ten alleged secrets in litigation.

The evidence and trial testimony showed that plaintiffs made no real effort, prior to trial, to keep the trade secrets secret. They were "either revealed in the marketed product; fully disclosed by issued patents; generally known to those skilled in the industry or trade; or consisted of information easily acquired by persons in the industry from patents, literature, or known processes freely available. . . . ." The court also held that trade secret claims must fail because plaintiffs "did not even know what it was intending to claim."

Although the Motorola employee-defendants had executed a nondisclosure agreement, they were not advised upon execution, *as is the general practice in similar companies in the same industry,* or during the term of their employment, either generally or specifically, what plaintiff considered "proprietary," or "covered by the restrictive nondisclosure agreement." Therefore, such a nondisclosure agreement was unenforceable as applied to these alleged claims for trade secrets. The court further stated that the law does not allow the protection of trade secrets to be used as "a sword . . . by the employers to retain employees by the threat of rendering them substantially unemployable in the field of their experience should they desire to resign. This shield is not a substitute for an agreement by the employee not to compete with his employer after the termination of employment" (*E. W. Bliss Co.* v. *Struthers-Dunn, Inc.,* supra, at 1112–1113).

C.

CORPORATIONS AND
THE NEWS MEDIA

A.B.C. + I.T.T. $\stackrel{?}{=}$ Free Press [1]

News is nothing more than any other thirty minutes of TV programming, and when it starts getting bad ratings it's going to go off the air.

—Anonymous Observation

Journalists were never intended to be the cheerleaders of a society, conductors of applause, the sycophants. Tragically, that is their assigned role in authoritarian societies, but not here—not yet.

—Chet Huntley

INTRODUCTION AND BACKGROUND

What exactly is the public interest in the news media? This question is open to many interpretations, but the news media themselves use the criterion that news be covered "fairly," with no one business, government,

[1] Title adapted from Eileen Shanahan, "Comment: Merger Issue. A.B.C. + I.T.T. = ?" *The New York Times,* July 30, 1967, Sec. 4, p. 5.

or interest group controlling media coverage.[2] Competition among enterprises engaged in the communications business insures the use of technological improvements and up-to-date services and helps to minimize the influence of any one group. Likewise, the public interest is served by corporations with sufficient financial resources to assume risks in introducing new processes and techniques and in expanding into pioneer communications fields.

The following case concerns the thwarted merger between two communications companies, ABC and ITT. In the events surrounding the proposed merger the issues involved in defining the public interest in news broadcasting were thoroughly scrutinized, with implications not only for the immediate question of the conformity of the merger to government regulations but also for the long-term issues of control, autonomy, and quality performance of broadcasting enterprises.

BACKGROUND OF ABC AND ITT

International Telephone and Telegraph (ITT) is one of the largest conglomerate corporations in the world. Since its formation about fifty years ago, it has primarily operated as a holding company for foreign telephone equipment and operating companies.[3] At the time of the proposed merger, ITT had interests in at least sixty-six countries and was engaged in domestic and foreign manufacturing, the operation of telecommunications utilities, and financial and other service activities. A leading international record carrier, ITT also claimed to be the world's largest manufacturer of telecommunications equipment.[4] Of its domestic manufacturing activities, about 40 percent was done under government contract related to space programs and defense. Sixty percent of its net income came from abroad and, according to the company, it had "extensive investment and responsibility in the economies and societies of the countries in which it operates."[5]

2 S. Prakash Sethi, *Business Corporations and the Black Man* (San Francisco: Chandler Publishing Co., 1970), Chap. 6.

3 "Dissenting Opinion of Commissioner Nicholas Johnson," Part IV of *ABC-ITT Merger Proceedings,* Federal Communications Commission, Washington, D.C., rev., December 21, 1966, p. 15.

4 *Ibid.,* "Dissenting Statement of Commissioner Robert T. Bartley," *ABC-ITT Merger Proceedings,* Part II, pp. 2–3.

5 *Ibid.,* Part IV, pp. 8, 11, 21. For example, directors of foreign ITT subsidiaries include three legislators, a former premier, and foreign ministry employees. Eventually seven of fifteen board members of the Chilean subsidiary will be government appointed [pp. 19–20].

The Indian government owns 75 percent of one ITT company, and the company cannot sell any of the stock to an Indian or to a citizen of a country not approved by the Indian government.

In 1959 ITT hired Harold Geneen as president. To balance the corporation's domestic and international operations, Geneen activated a vigorous policy of growth, primarily through the acquisition of domestic industries, including Alexander Hamilton Life Insurance, American Universal Life Insurance, Avis Rent-A-Car, and Aetna Finance Company. The goal of doubling sales and earnings in the first five-year period was achieved, and ITT's acquisitions have continued unabated. Much of the success of ITT's growth policy has been attributed to Geneen and the taut system of control that he exerted over ITT's previously autonomous operating managers.

The American Broadcasting Companies, Inc., is a child of the government's concern for the maintenance of freedom of the press. In response to the Federal Communications Commission's (FCC) chain broadcasting rules of 1941, the Blue Network Company, one of two networks owned by the Radio Corporation of America (RCA), was offered for sale and was purchased by Edward J. Noble, who created the "American Broadcasting Company." ABC has since substantially increased its operations and by 1966 owned 399 theaters in thirty-four states, five television stations (most ABC affiliates are independently owned as per government regulation), and six AM and FM stations in the top ten broadcasting markets. ABC was capable of reaching 93 percent of 50 million American homes with television sets and 97 percent of those with radios.

In addition, ABC subsidiaries produced records on six different labels, published three farm newspapers, and distributed filmed television programs to stations, networks, and advertisers. ABC was active in foreign markets through a wholly owned subsidiary which acted as program purchasing and sales representative for foreign stations in twenty-five nations.[6]

HISTORY OF THE MERGER

On December 3, 1965, ITT publicly announced that the two companies had met several times and agreed that ABC would be merged into ITT as a wholly owned subsidiary with control passing from ABC stockholders to a new group composed of both ABC and ITT stockholders.[7]

The two companies entered into the agreement on February 14, 1966, and on March 31, 1966, ABC filed the necessary applications with the FCC for its approval of transfers of licenses for ABC broadcasting stations to the new ITT subsidiary corporation. Proxy statements describing the details of the merger were sent to the shareholders of both companies who voted overwhelmingly to approve the merger.

In July 1966 the FCC requested information from the presidents of

[6] *Ibid.*, Part II, Attachment A; Part IV, pp. 12–15.
[7] *Ibid.*, Part IV, p. 85.

ABC and ITT regarding the proposed future operations of the new broadcasting company. Replies were soon received by the commission, which then accepted the bulk of the data as authentic and accurate statements of fact. The FCC then ordered that a hearing before the full seven-member commission be held on September 19, 1966; any party interested in the case could appear and be heard at that time.

As in all merger cases, the FCC considered the possibility of potential antitrust effects, and in keeping with policy, maintained a continuing liaison with the Antitrust Division of the Department of Justice with regard to the case. The division itself had been independently collecting data on the case since the two companies' first announcement but continually put off the commission when it requested Justice's views. Thus the department made no statement regarding the matter prior to the FCC's hearing on September 19, 1966, did not appear at the hearing, and commented only that it had the matter under study.[8]

It was not until November 3, after the commission had notified Antitrust Division Chief Donald Turner that an FCC decision was imminent, that Turner replied that there was a "sufficient possibility of significant anticompetitive effects"[9] which could result from the merger. He suggested that the commission hold off its decision until the department had arrived "at a final decision on the anticompetitive aspects of the merger."[10] The commission then asked the division to make a more definite statement and notified it that it was preparing to issue its decision on December 21, 1966. The commission noted, however, that whereas a Justice Department report would be significant, it would not be binding.[11]

Finally, on December 20, 1966, Turner submitted to the commission the Antitrust Division's decision that the department did not have the grounds to seek to block the merger in court, but it saw a number of possible anticompetitive consequences in the proposed merger that the FCC should explore.

The commission, having been prepared for weeks to act on the proposed merger, approved it the next day, noting that the questions Justice raised had already been carefully considered. The commission also criticized the

---

[8] *Ibid.*, "Memorandum Opinion and Order," Part I, pp. 1, 2, 5.

[9] *Ibid.*, Part IV, p. 80.

[10] *Order on Petition for Reconsideration,* Federal Communications Commission, February 1, 1967, Part I, p. 2.

[11] *ABC-ITT Merger Proceedings,* Part I, pp. 1, 5; Part IV, pp. 80–84.

This was the first time that the Justice Department had sought to intervene in a case involving FCC's handling of broadcast properties. Traditionally, the courts had recognized that in the regulation of broadcast media considerations other than competition should also prevail in the general public interest. For example, in the case of *FCC v. RCA Communications, Inc.,* the court agreed with FCC that "encouragement of competition as such has not been considered the single or controlling reliance for safeguarding the public interest." 346 US 86 (1953).

Justice Department for waiting as long as it had before expressing its views. The commission's vote was four to three, with Commissioners Bartley, Cox, and Johnson dissenting.

Promptly following the commissioner's decision, the Justice Department, in a Petition for Reconsideration, asked the FCC to review its decision and to hold a full and evidentiary hearing (which had not been done earlier) and to permit the Antitrust Division to participate as a party.[12] The department hinted that if the FCC did not reopen the case, it might bring suit under Section 7 of the Clayton Act to nullify the merger on anticompetitive grounds.[13]

On February 1, 1967, the FCC ordered ABC and ITT to delay the merger until a reconsideration hearing had been conducted.[14] The companies called the department's intervention an "unprecedented attack" on the commission's competence and urged the FCC to reject the department's allegations.[15] The FCC said that the delaying action was taken because of the unique status of the Justice Department and the particular nature of the case but pointed out that this procedure set no precedent whatsoever. The commission further indicated that Justice would have to supply it with documentary evidence to support its charges.[16]

The commission held a thirteen-day hearing during April 1967, in which the Justice Department was a party. The commission again approved the merger on June 22 and the vote was again four to three with the same dissenters.[17]

Subsequent to this second approval, the Justice Department appealed the case to the United States Court of Appeals in Washington, and the unlikely happened: The U.S. (Justice), as it were, was opposing the U.S. (FCC) in a court case.[18] Prior to a court decision, however, ITT withdrew from the ABC merger agreement on New Year's Day, 1968.[19] The merger agreement had given either party the right to cancel after New Year's Eve. ITT exercised this option because it felt that terminating the merger would best serve the interest of its stockholders as the stock price of ABC had tremendously risen during the long delays plaguing the

[12] *Order on Petition for Reconsideration,* February 1, 1967, p. 4.
[13] *ABC-ITT Merger Proceedings,* Part I.
[14] "Dissenting Opinion of Commissioners Robert T. Bartley, Kenneth A. Cox, and Nicholas Johnson," *The ABC-ITT Merger Case Reconsideration,* Federal Communications Commission, June 22, 1967, p. 135.
[15] Eileen Shanahan, "Merger Defended by ITT and ABC," *The New York Times,* February 24, 1967, p. 1.
[16] *Order on Petition for Reconsideration,* February 1, 1967, pp. 3–4.
[17] *The ABC-ITT Merger Case Reconsideration,* June 22, 1967, Sec. 2, pp. 137–38.
[18] "ITT-ABC Merger Is Held Up by Federal Court," *The New York Times,* July 22, 1967, p. 53.
[19] Jack Gould, "ITT Calls Off ABC Merger Bid," *The New York Times,* January 2, 1968, p. 1.

merger. The potential cost to ITT of the merger had risen from $380 million to $660 million.[20]

SOME KEY ISSUES

It would be impossible to present all the issues involved in the proposed merger, but some of the most important are discussed below.

During the first hearing, the majority of the commission was of the opinion that since ITT and ABC were not competitors in any market, the merger would not increase the concentration of control in the broadcasting industry, hence it would not have anticompetitive effects. Indeed the merger would benefit the public interest for three reasons. First, the increased financial resources available to ABC through ITT would result in better programming. ABC's financial need was great. Although NBC and CBS had been very profitable operations, ABC had been in the red for the past four years. Second, ABC stated that more cash would better its competitive position with respect to the other networks, and ITT promised to help in this area. Third, ITT had decided to attempt to make technological advances in UHF broadcasting, an area that would help the network to become more competitive with CBS and NBC.

Some observers felt that one reason for ABC's enthusiasm for the merger was the fear that a prominent industrialist, Norton Simon, was attempting to take control of the company. Simon had begun buying ABC stock in March 1964, and by July 1964 he was the largest single stockholder with 9 percent of the company's outstanding stock. It was rumored that he wanted a seat on the network's board of directors. Speculation abounded that ABC wanted to merge (which would dilute Simon's ownership percentage) to prevent his control of the company.[21]

Both the Justice Department and the dissenting commissioners raised another issue. The original hearing had consisted of only two days of oral hearings before the commission *en banc,* and not before an examiner who customarily heard the arguments. The FCC felt this to be a more direct and public way to study the issues. However, the antagonists said that the commission had "failed to conduct the type of full hearing required by the Federal Communications Act of 1934"[22] and had not given sufficient

---

20 "A Broken Engagement for ITT and ABC," *Business Week,* January 6, 1968, p. 24.

21 *ABC-ITT Merger Proceedings,* Part I, pp. 8–13; Part IV, pp. 15–17.

22 *Ibid.,* Part I, p. 4. According to dissenting Commissioner Johnson, the commission was not originally planning to hold hearings at all as the outcome had "been a foregone conclusion." Only Commissioner Bartley's insistent request for "a full evidentiary hearing" led to the compromise "oral hearing" (Part IV, p. 2).

warning for those opposed to the merger to prepare their arguments. Indeed, no opposing arguments were made.[23]

The antagonists felt that the merger would eliminate ITT as a potential independent entrant into broadcasting. They said that ITT was one of the relatively few firms with the resources, technical capability, interest, and incentive likely to make a significant contribution to diversification in broadcasting and to activities directly competitive with broadcasting. The merger would reduce the likelihood of such occurring. It was said that ITT had been considering entering the broadcasting industry prior to the merger agreement. Without the merger, the argument ran, ITT would have entered TV broadcasting on a significant scale.[24]

The same argument was said to apply to ITT's CATV and Pay-TV efforts. If the merger were approved, ITT would probably drop its efforts in this area as CATV would conflict with ABC's broadcasting aspirations.[25] That is, the company would have an interest in the *status quo* technology and would be less interested in research and development aimed at promoting Pay-TV and CATV. Merger opponents rejected this on the grounds of ABC's financial needs. They said that open-market financing was available and that despite ABC's rapid approach to the debt limit, the limit could probably be extended. Furthermore, ABC's deficient performance was not due to insufficient funds but to operational difficulties.[26] Finally, the opposition accused ABC and ITT officials of making misleading and erroneous statements and of lacking general candor while testifying.[27]

The commission majority replied that ITT's decision to merge with ABC came *after* its decision not to enter the broadcasting industry and *after* it had begun moving out of CATV. In addition, the majority held that there were "hundreds" of other companies capable of doing valuable research and development in broadcasting technology and that the merger would induce ITT to do research that might benefit ABC.[28]

The three commissioners who wrote the minority opinion disputed ITT's statement that it had decided not to enter the broadcasting industry,

[23] Department of Justice, *Proposed Conclusions and Brief*, May 29, 1967, p. 82. See also *ABC-ITT Merger Proceedings*, Part IV, Sec. 2, pp. 68–70.

[24] Department of Justice, *Proposed Conclusions and Brief*, May 29, 1967, p. 87. See also *ABC-ITT Merger Case Reconsideration*, June 22, 1967, pp. 43–47.

[25] CATV, or Cable TV, transmits programs by telephone wires rather than by air and usually increases the number of stations available to a particular area. James Ridgeway, "The Voice of ITT," *New Republic*, July 8, 1967, pp. 17–19.

[26] *The ABC-ITT Merger Case Reconsideration*, June 22, 1967, Sec. 2. See also Department of Justice, *Proposed Conclusions and Brief*, April 29, 1967.

[27] *The ABC-ITT Merger Case Reconsideration*, Sec. 2.

[28] "Opinion and Order on Petition for Reconsideration," *The ABC-ITT Merger Case Reconsideration*, Federal Communications Commission, Washington, D.C., June 22, 1967, Sec. 1, pp. 14, 38.

citing an offer the company had made to an independent television station. Also, if the merger were allowed, ITT would pursue research in general broadcasting which could help ABC, but it probably would not do research on Pay-TV and CATV, media competitive with ABC's general broadcasting. On the other hand, if the merger were prohibited, ITT would be one of the most likely contributors to Pay-TV and CATV technology.[29] Also, ABC should not look to ITT for help with its cash flow problem as ITT documents had projected a net cash flow *from* ABC to the parent company.[30]

THE ABC-ITT MERGER AND THE INDEPENDENCE
OF THE NEWS MEDIA

The primary issue of this case, and indeed one of the primary issues of the merger agreement, was the degree of autonomy that ABC would maintain as a wholly owned subsidiary of ITT. ABC President Goldenson, in an interdepartmental letter sent before the agreement, stated:

> While I cannot at this time discuss the details of these continuing negotiations, I thought you would like personally to know that a prerequisite of any proposed merger, as far as I am concerned, will be the continued autonomous management and operation of American Broadcasting Companies, Inc., and its divisions and subsidiaries.[31]

ABC later won assurances from ITT that it would remain autonomous under its present management and Goldenson's leadership. Doubts were expressed, however, that ITT President Geneen would stand idly by as a titular head of "that third network" after a record of wanting the top position in everything he did.[32] Shortly after the agreement was made, Wall Street observers anticipated "that the strong personalities of Mr. Geneen and Mr. Goldenson will clash and that the ITT image will intrude heavily into ABC, particularly in programming." [33]

In any case, the merger agreement provided that ABC would retain its own independent board of directors and management, with some cross representation on the two boards, for at least three years. During those

[29] *The ABC-ITT Merger Case Reconsideration,* June 22, 1967, Sec. 2, pp. 13–14, 43–45.
[30] *ABC-ITT Merger Proceedings,* Part IV, p. 10.
[31] Gene Smith, "Defies Merger Proposal," *The New York Times,* December 3, 1965, p. 55.
[32] Gene Smith, "New Role Looms for IT&T Chief," *The New York Times,* December 3, 1965, Sec. 3, p. 1.
[33] Gene Smith, "Personality: The Empire Builder at I.T.T.," *The New York Times,* December 20, 1966, Sec. 3, p. 3.

three years, however, matters of major ABC importance were to be submitted to the ITT board before becoming effective.[34]

THE FCC MAJORITY OPINION

The majoirty opinion in the FCC's first ruling of December 1966 pointed out that the key issue of the proposed merger was whether the extensive business interests of ITT might influence ABC's broadcasting activities, and particularly whether there would be any commercial influence on the journalistic function—the reporting of news and news commentary—or on the selection, scheduling, or treatment of public affairs programming. The majority recognized the large stake our society has in preserving the freedom of broadcast stations and networks from the intrusion of extraneous private economic interests upon programming decisions. Thorough, fearless, and unbiased collection, dissemination, and analysis of news is, they said, crucial to a free society. There is widespread and growing reliance by the public upon broadcast sources of news and news commentary and upon public affairs programming and other kinds of informative programming. They were, therefore, attentive to the positive assurances that both ABC and ITT gave the FCC and the public on this score.

The majority opinion affirmed that the commission's own criteria for freedom of the press would not be violated by the merger because of ABC and ITT's repeated assurances that ABC would operate as a substantially autonomous subsidiary and that ABC's operations as a broadcasting licensee would not be affected by the commercial, communications, or other similar interests of ITT. Both ITT and ABC officials were examined at length on this matter, and the assurances and representations set forth were considered sufficient guarantee that the autonomy of ABC's news department was not in jeopardy.[35]

As to the hazard of alien influence on the broadcasting operations of an American subsidiary of ITT, the majority opinion stated:

> We know from our experience in the regulation of communications that many of our large broadcasting licenses and the two other television networks also have substantial foreign interests, including subsidiary corporations in many countries. We have seen no evidence at any time that any of these foreign interests have influenced any of the programming presented in this country. There is no reason to assume or suspect that any such influence will occur in the case of ITT.

[34] "Dissenting Statement of Commissioner Robert T. Bartley," Part II, *ABC-ITT Merger Proceedings*, FCC, December 21, 1966, p. 8.
[35] *Ibid.*, Part I, p. 10.

Nothing of which we are aware in the history of ITT's operations abroad or in the United States suggests that it has ever been or would in the future be neglectful of its loyalties or responsibilities as an American company, or that aliens associated in the ownership and management of overseas ITT companies would by some sinister and unexplained means exert influence upon the interests of the United States broadcast public.[36]

THE DISSENTERS

The key difference between the majority and minority opinions was in regard to the *possibility* of dangers resulting from the merger as opposed to the *probability* of such. The minority was concerned with the *"potential* conflict of interest between the business interests which comprise ITT and ABC's broadcasting responsibility to the public, especially in news and public affairs," while the majority was concerned with the *likelihood* of such. This is why dissenting Commissioner Johnson felt that it was ITT and ABC's burden to show that the merger was in the public interest, and not as the majority felt, that any merger is in the public interest unless proof to the contrary is brought forth.

Johnson said:

ITT as owner of ABC constantly will be faced with the conflict between its profit maximizing goals—indeed obligations to shareholders—which characterize all business corporations, and the duty to serve the public with free and unprejudiced news and public affairs programming. The issue is both whether anything damaging to ITT's interest is *ever* broadcast, as well as *how* it is presented.

The number of such potential conflicts is "endless." How, for example, was ABC to report foreign affairs when 60 percent of ITT's earnings was from foreign subsidiaries and investments? More specifically, how should ABC report on the possible nationalization of ITT property in foreign countries? (It had occurred in eight countries.) In the past, ITT had encouraged such laws as the Hickenlooper amendment calling for reduction of United States aid in countries not paying for nationalized property. How should ABC News view such laws in the future? How should the network report widespread dissent movements in Brazil if the government outlawed reports favorable to the dissenters? "Would anyone in ABC News be in-

[36] *The ABC-ITT Merger Case Reconsideration,* June 22, 1967, Sec. 1, pp. 16–17.

clined or feel free to propose the show in the first place?" said Johnson. "Would they be able to withstand suggestions from within or without ITT that ABC news' resources might better be used on other assignments?" How should ABC report government defense and space policy when space-related contracts accounted for 40 percent of ITT's domestic income? Or, how should the network view truth-in-lending legislation while parent ITT operated several finance companies?

The mere promise of ITT officials that they would not interfere with ABC news and public affairs programming was not sufficient, Commissioners Johnson and Bartley asserted. Both Goldenson and Geneen might be out of a job tomorrow, but the corporation would continue. "These assurances are given by men—and we are turning these broadcast properties over to corporations," which would continue to influence the public after present officials were gone.

Even assurances by present management would not guarantee the independence of ABC during their periods in office:

> Subtle pressures on ABC officials to serve ITT interests cannot be eliminated by the most scrupulous adherence to formal independence for ABC and its editorial staff. ABC personnel will, on their own initiative, consider ITT's interests in making programming decisions. Institutional loyalties develop. These are often reinforced by the acquisition of stock in the employing company—now ITT stock, not ABC. And most important, it will be impossible to erase from the minds of those who make the broadcasting decisions at ABC that their jobs and advancement are dependent on ITT.[37]

With awareness of ITT's foreign interests, even the most conscientious news official would be less objective than he would be if ABC remained unaffiliated, and he would not forget that his future in the company could be affected by his handling of ITT-sensitive issues. Thus, the threat was less that items would be filmed, killed, or slanted, as that ideas or new coverage would never even be proposed. It was also possible that materials would be considered that were in essence simply public relations pieces for ITT or its interests. These were real threats, but the more probable abuse was that newsmen might overcompensate by stressing or suppressing developments embarrassing to ITT. Whichever way the programming leaned, the public would suspect that ITT interests governed ultimate selections. "The risks which this suggests are of a kind that should be taken

---

[37] All these quotations will be found in *ABC-ITT Merger Proceedings,* Part IV, pp. 6, 18, 20–29. See also Part II, p. 4.

only with the greatest caution and only with a showing of extraordinarily compelling countervailing benefits." [38]

Johnson added that ITT was like most companies that spend "vast sums to influence its image and its economic relations—through advertising, public relations, and Washington representation."

Are we to accept, on the parties' own self-serving assurances, that although ITT may continue to exert pressure as an advertiser on the programming of CBS and NBC, it will exert none as an owner on the programming of ABC?

I am afraid I must concede that the assurances we have been provided—that ITT will be totally oblivious to the image created for it by its own mass media subsidiary, ABC—simply strain my credibility beyond the breaking point.

It seems elementary to me that the only real way to find adequate safeguards for the public's interest in programming integrity is to give attention to the structure of the industry, not to assurances, albeit sincere, of interested parties who may be gone tomorrow.

[Thus] the best we can do is to try to provide as much insulation as possible for the industry's programming from extraneous economic considerations. The worst we can do is to encourage mergers like this, which expose businessmen to the daily temptation to subvert the high purpose and indispensable role of the broadcast media in a free society.[39]

Bartley, who agreed with Johnson that industry *structure* was paramount, in his dissent referred to other cases in which nonbroadcast corporate interests have intruded into broadcast operations. For example, RCA-NBC exerted pressure on Westinghouse to "swap stations in Cleveland and Philadelphia so RCA could have an outlet in Philadelphia where its laboratories were located." [40] Bartley concluded that "as bankers think like bankers, I believe we can expect that corporate conglomerates will think like corporate conglomerates rather than like objective professional broadcasters."

The majority did not feel structure to be that critical, as it did not

treat the matter as closed. It demands "eternal vigilance" by all broadcast licensees and will receive our continuing scrutiny for

[38] "Dissenting Opinion of Commissioners Robert T. Bartley, Kenneth A. Cox, and Nicholas Johnson," *The ABC-ITT Merger Case Reconsideration,* Federal Communications Commission, Washington, D.C., June 22, 1967, p. 85.

[39] *ABC-ITT Merger Proceedings,* Part IV, pp. 28, 30.

[40] *Business Week,* January 6, 1968, p. 14.

indication that our reliance upon the assurances and safeguards set out on this record was not warranted.[41]

To the majority's promised scrutiny, Bartley retorted:

> What tools do they have to make the vigilance meaningful? . . . Such policing would be a near impossibility. When such eternal vigilance demands our continuing scrutiny of the particular situation, I believe the better course is to protect the public interest by not allowing it in the first place.

The majority pointed out, however, that since the beginning of broadcast licensing, the commission had licensed enterprises involved in a vast number of activities. Proposals excluding particular business interests (such as those in foreign countries) could not now be adopted unless they were applied to other cases, which would require the FCC to restructure the broadcasting industry, in turn requiring the FCC to refuse to renew licenses held by other networks and by numerous large conglomerate corporations. The majority said that such actions would not be in the public interest. But Bartley was suggesting this restructuring of the industry when he said, "This merger presents the Commission with the very basic and fundamental question of whether licenses should be granted to corporations involved in business other than broadcasting."

ITT PRESSURE ON NEWS MEDIA

In April 1967 the FCC held hearings on the Justice Department's request for a reconsideration of the merger. During these hearings, ABC President Goldenson testified that the president of ABC-News would still have unquestioned authority over news programming and his decisions "wouldn't have to be cleared with anybody." [42] ITT President and Chairman Geneen testified before the commission that his company had "absolutely no intention of interfering in any way with the content of news programs" on ABC. The "composition and status" of ABC's board of directors would be unique among ITT subsidiaries, and present "operating personnel and general policies" would be continued. Geneen said, "We

---

[41] All the quotations will be found in the following sequence in *ABC-ITT Merger Proceedings:* Part II, p. 4; Part I, p. 10; Part II, p. 13; Part I, p. 18; Part II, p. 14.

[42] Fred L. Zimmerman, "Managing the News?" *The Wall Street Journal,* April 17, 1967, p. 18.

have considerable confidence in ABC's management or we wouldn't have entered into the merger."

This confidence in ABC's management, it turned out, was not unconditional. Geneen's original position was that, as a member of ABC's new board and executive committee, he would refrain from voting on matters likely to involve conflict of interest. However, *The Wall Street Journal* reported that Geneen, under pressure by an FCC attorney, admitted "it would be his duty to vote on all matters before ABC's board or executive committee." ITT would have the final say in the network's programming and selection of ABC directors. Geneen also said other "matters of major importance" would need his company's approval.[43]

Only a few days after Geneen testified that his company would not unduly influence ABC's news programming, an article in *The Wall Street Journal* quoted three reporters who said ITT officials had requested them to alter news stories in various ways. The article gained wide publicity for the issue of freedom of the press in the proposed merger.

THE JOURNAL ARTICLE

The Wall Street Journal article of April 17 quoted one reporter as saying, "It's incredible that guys like this want the right to run ABC's news operation." This criticism was in response to an ITT representative's complaint to the reporter's editor about his articles.[44]

A public relations official of ITT said, "We've been dissatisfied with some of the coverage. . . . Some of it has been incomplete and unfair." Indeed, by late February various company officials had complained about the coverage of *The New York Times,* the Associated Press, United Press International, *The Wall Street Journal,* and the *Washington Post.* According to *The Wall Street Journal:*

> The complaints were made through calls and letters to reporters and editors, and at meetings, with editors here [Washington, D.C.] and in New York. Occasionally factual inaccuracies were alleged, but more often the complaints were that reporters weren't writing balanced accounts or were obtaining information from unreliable sources.

Eileen Shanahan, who had been covering the proposed ITT-ABC merger for *The New York Times,* said that in January two ITT officials came to

---

[43] "ITT Says Its Control of ABC Won't Alter Network's News Policy," *The Wall Street Journal,* April 17, 1967, p. 3.
[44] Zimmerman, "Managing the News?" p. 18.

see her to complain about an article and to suggest "in imperious tones" that *The New York Times* carry the full text of a long FCC order issued that day. Later on, a third ITT representative telephoned her, criticizing an article and saying that the subject matter "wasn't worth a story." Miss Shanahan said, "He questioned my integrity and that of the *Times.*" The official in question, in denying Miss Shanahan's allegations, said he only "objected to one or two sentences."

Morton Mintz of the *Washington Post* found ITT's Public Relations Department's actions "rather unusual" when they first called him in November 1966 to suggest that he cover a certain congressman's speech which was expected to be favorable to the merger. Mintz replied that he was busy and did not intend to cover the speech. At that point the ITT representative asked to speak to the editor and executive vice-president of the *Post* who, however, never mentioned this to Mintz.

A UPI reporter said he was subject to "an obvious economic threat" from ABC, a big customer of the press service's radio and television news reports, after various stories he wrote concerning the merger appeared. Jed Stout, another reporter from UPI, said that John Horner, Washington, D.C., director of news media relations for ITT, telephoned him and cited a *Wall Street Journal* article dated February 6, which stated that the Justice Department would bring ITT to court if the FCC did not rule against the proposed merger. Stout said, "As I interpreted it he was asking me to write a story 'knocking down' the Journal piece. I declined to do so." [45]

The night that the FCC announced another delay of the ITT-ABC merger to hold further hearings regarding the Justice Department's evidence, a Washington-based AP reporter, Stephen M. Aug, was dictating the story over the phone. As he was in the middle of his sixth paragraph he was told that ABC had seen the story over the AP wires and had called from New York requesting he change his first paragraph.[46] Network officials wanted the paragraph changed from the FCC "ordered" a delay in the merger to the FCC "suggested" a delay. Aug refused to change the wording.[47]

REACTION TO THE WALL STREET JOURNAL ARTICLE

Two days later, on April 19, the Justice Department requested the FCC to subpoena three of the reporters quoted in the article, Messrs. Aug and

[45] *Ibid.;* see also "ITT Inquiry Calls Three Reporters," *The New York Times,* April 20, 1967, p. 28.

[46] Zimmerman, "Managing the News?" p. 18; see also Fred P. Graham, "3 Reporters Allege Pressures by ITT about Their News Coverage of Its Merger Plan with ABC," *The New York Times,* April 21, 1967, p. 45.

[47] Graham, "3 Reporters Allege Pressures by ITT."

Stout, and Miss Shanahan, to "explore matters raised by a *Wall Street Journal* article Monday, reporting on efforts to affect press coverage of these proceedings and the independent news judgment" of these reporters and their organizations.[48] According to the department such "alleged pressure" might be improper [49] and might be related to the company's promise not to interfere with ABC news coverage.[50] The FCC chief examiner complied with the department's wishes.[51] Also, an FCC Broadcast Bureau attorney said the bureau intended to call on John Horner, the ITT official mentioned in the article, to testify before the commission concerning his reported activities.[52]

The reporters were reluctant to give information to other reporters until after their testimony. Miss Shanahan did say, however, that the *Journal* article was "correct, as far as it went—there was more."

Horner issued a statement saying:

> . . . we have made no effort to manage the news. We at ITT believe wholeheartedly in the right of free speech and we have the greatest respect for members of the press and other news media. Historically, the company has been able to communicate its views to the press without any difficulty.
>
> As a publicly held company, we regard it as our duty to supply the fullest information possible on news stories and when occasional errors occur, to assist correspondents in correcting the record. In so doing over many years, we have enjoyed excellent cooperation from the media.

The day the subpoenas were issued, James Hagerty, an ABC vice-president who had been President Eisenhower's press secretary, said it would be "impossible" for ITT to influence ABC news coverage—and "if it did I would resign." [53]

THE REPORTERS TESTIFY

The three reporters testified at hearings held on April 20. Stout of UPI added greater detail to the allegations made in *The Wall Street Journal*

[48] "Reporters Are Subpoenaed for Hearing on ABC-ITT," *The Wall Street Journal,* April 20, 1967.
[49] *The New York Times,* April 20, 1967, p. 28.
[50] Graham, "3 Reporters Allege Pressures by ITT," p. 45.
[51] *The New York Times,* April 20, 1967, p. 28.
[52] *The Wall Street Journal,* April 20, 1967.
[53] *The New York Times,* April 20, 1967, p. 28.

article of April 17.[54] He said Horner had talked to him in February about the *Journal* article of February 6 and had asked him about the *Journal's* sources of the rumor that the Justice Department would probably challenge the merger in court if the FCC approved it. The article was not free to name the officials who had given the information. Stout, who regularly covered the Justice Department, said at the hearings that Horner "asked me to make inquiries in the Department of Justice as to whether or not this decision [to go to court] had [actually] been made." Stout refused Horner [55] and told the FCC he had never before received such a request.[56]

ITT had already complained to *The Wall Street Journal* about the February 6 article. The *Journal* said of the complaint that

> Mr. Horner said then that it was a "speculative story" and that it didn't seem right for the Journal to print "speculative" stories.
> He said the Journal shouldn't write stories having an adverse effect on the stock market. He noted that ABC stock had dropped $4.50 a share the day after the article was printed. The same day, however, ITT common stock rose $1.625 a share.
> ITT succeeded in getting the Justice Department to send the company a telegram stating that a decision hadn't been made on whether to take the case to court. ITT itself promptly issued the telegram to the press. But a Justice Department official told the Journal privately that the telegram to ITT shouldn't be construed as a denial of the Journal's report.

Stout said that Horner telephoned him again concerning the *Journal* article, calling its author a "hipshooter" and saying "there had been a great deal of inaccurate reporting on the merger." Also, Stout's own reporting came under fire. On February 3, two of his superiors discussed his "choice of words" in a story concerning the merger proposal. They explained to him that "there have been complaints received from officials of ABC about the accuracy of the story." The reporter's superiors told him the phrase in question was not accurate.[57]

Miss Shanahan testified that ITT representatives had contacted her five or six times. During one brief encounter, an official, whose identity the reporter did not remember, talked to her of a recent development in the merger case favorable to ITT saying, "I expect to see that in the paper, high up in your story." [58]

[54] Graham, "3 Reporters Allege Pressures by ITT," p. 45.
[55] "Reporters Tell FCC That ITT, ABC Tried to Influence Press Coverage of Merger," *The Wall Street Journal*, April 21, 1967, p. 10.
[56] Graham, "3 Reporters Allege Pressures by ITT," p. 45.
[57] *The Wall Street Journal*, April 21, 1967, p. 10.
[58] *The ABC-ITT Merger Case Reconsideration*, June 22, 1967, Sec. 2, p. 29.

On February 1, at about 8 P.M., Edward Gerrity, senior ITT vice-president for public relations, and another ITT official delivered a company statement to Miss Shanahan's office.[59] According to the reporter, Gerrity indirectly requested to see the story Shanahan was then writing, which she thought he should have known was "an improper thing to ask a reporter." He asked if her paper was going to run the text of a recent FCC statement criticizing the Justice Department for being late with its evidence in the case. Shanahan thought that document insufficiently important, but Gerrity asked in an "accusatory and certainly nasty" tone, "you mean you did not even recommend the use of text?" Shanahan said, "He badgered me again to play up favorable developments in the case." Gerrity also inquired if she had been following the stock market prices of ITT and ABC. Shanahan told him she had not [60] and later told the commission that "he asked if I didn't feel I had a responsibility to shareholders who might lose money from what I wrote. . . . I told him no.[61] . . . My responsibility was to find out the truth and print it." [62]

Gerrity then asked if she was aware "that Commissioner Nicholas Johnson was working with some people in Congress on legislation that would forbid any newspaper from owning any broadcast property." [63] (*The New York Times* owns an AM-FM radio station in New York.) When she told him she was unaware of such a bill he replied, "I think this is some information you should pass on to your publisher before you write any more about Commissioner Johnson's opinions." [64]

During the hearings the *Times* reporter identified one of the congressmen alleged to be working with Johnson as Senator Gaylord Nelson of Wisconsin.[65] In response to this testimony the FCC later issued a statement saying:

> Commissioner Johnson will have no statement to make on this charge, at this time, while the merger case is under consideration by the Commission. Neither Mr. Johnson nor any other official Commission spokesman has ever talked with any person at any time about legislation prohibiting newspaper ownership and no change in that policy is now under consideration.[66]

[59] *Ibid.;* see also *The Wall Street Journal,* April 21, 1967, p. 10.
[60] *The ABC-ITT Merger Case Reconsideration,* pp. 29–30. See also Graham, "3 Reporters Allege Pressures by ITT," p. 45.
[61] *The Wall Street Journal,* April 21, 1967, p. 10.
[62] *The ABC-ITT Merger Case Reconsideration,* June 22, 1967, Sec. 2, p. 30.
[63] *Ibid.*
[64] *The Wall Street Journal,* April 21, 1967, p. 10.
[65] *The ABC-ITT Merger Case Reconsideration,* June 22, 1967, Sec. 2.
[66] *The Wall Street Journal,* April 21, 1967, p. 10.

Johnson later personally denied "collaboration" with Nelson, and Nelson denied ever having met Johnson.[67] According to the July 8, 1967, issue of the *New Republic, Variety* discovered that ITT public relations officials had given the same story about Senator Nelson to reporters for the *Milwaukee Journal* which owns a radio and TV station. The newspaper, however, discovered that the ITT information was incorrect.[68]

According to the reporter's testimony, later in February the Justice Department filed its report with the FCC and Miss Shanahan wrote an article on the department's evidence.[69] John Horner then told her that her coverage of the merger "has been unfair right from the beginning." [70] According to Horner the most objectionable part of her recent story was her statement that the department would take the merger to the courts if the FCC did not reopen its hearings. Horner said the department "had issued a statement saying that it would not go to court." The *Times* reporter asked him to read her that statement which she testified only said that "the Department had not decided what it would do if the Commission refused to reopen the hearing." When she said that he had "improperly characterized" the statement, Horner again told her her reporting was unfair, a remark that angered her. According to her colleagues, she yelled at Horner [71] that he had insulted not only her but also her editors and she hung up the phone.[72] Miss Shanahan then called the Justice Department and inquired about the statement Horner had read to her over the phone. As it turned out, such a "statement" had never been released—the information was a private communication to the company from the department.

Continuing her testimony, Miss Shanahan said that during one of the commission's earlier hearings she had missed a brief portion of the testimony. Upon her return Horner informed her of what she had missed. He supposedly told her, in an "insistent and nasty" tone, that "I expect to see headlines just as big on this one as on what happened the other day," [73] presumably referring to an article that Horner considered unfavorable.[74] Miss Shanahan said a similar incident had only happened once in her five years with the *Times*.[75] Her editor, she said, also told her that this was uncharacteristic of the paper's previous contacts with the company.[76]

[67] *The ABC-ITT Merger Case Reconsideration,* June 22, 1967, Sec. 2.
[68] Ridgeway, "The Voice of ITT," pp. 17–19.
[69] *Ibid.,* p. 31.
[70] *The Wall Street Journal,* April 21, 1967, p. 10.
[71] *The ABC-ITT Merger Case Reconsideration,* June 22, 1967, Sec. 2.
[72] *The Wall Street Journal,* April 21, 1967, p. 10.
[73] *The ABC-ITT Merger Case Reconsideration,* June 22, 1967, Sec. 2.
[74] Graham, "3 Reporters Allege Pressures by ITT," p. 45.
[75] *The ABC-ITT Merger Case Reconsideration,* June 22, 1967, Sec. 2.
[76] Graham, "3 Reporters Allege Pressures by ITT," p. 45.

PRELUDE TO DECISION

During the April 20 hearings, ITT counsel attempted to question the reporters about their sources within the Justice Department,[77] on the grounds that the company was "entitled to show that the Department of Justice has had conversations with the press [also]. This bears directly on ITT's efforts to get two-sided coverage." However, the hearing examiner sustained a Justice Department objection of immateriality.[78] The ITT lawyer himself then objected on the grounds that ITT and ABC were being denied their right of free speech in getting their side of the merger to the public while secret government sources were allowed to present their own side.

In general, ITT spokesmen would not comment about the testimony after the hearings were over, but James Hagerty of ABC said he accepted Aug's statement that someone from the network had asked him to change a story before it was finished but that the company was unable to determine who made the call.[79]

On April 21 the president of ABC News, Elmer Lower, testified before the commission. In reference to Hagerty's reported statement that he would resign if ITT attempted to influence the network's news policies, Lower said, "I think I would hear about it before Mr. Hagerty did and I would be out the door ahead of him." According to Lower, no one of his superiors in the ABC hierarchy had ever exercised any control over the network's news programming, and he did not expect any change in this policy in the future.[80]

Arguments of both sides in the merger case continued until June 2 when ITT concluded its oral arguments with assurances that "the independence of ABC programming from any other ITT commercial or similar interest shall be inviolate."

According to the attorneys for the two companies, the "built in guarantees of independence for ABC news"—sections of the merger agreement and internal policy documents signed by ITT President Harold Geneen— answered "the major issue the Justice Department relies on" in attempting to prevent the merger. Accordingly, any changes in this policy would be communicated to the commission.[81]

The Justice Department maintained, however, that the commission

77 *Ibid.*
78 *The Wall Street Journal,* April 21, 1967, p. 10.
79 Graham, "3 Reporters Allege Pressures by ITT," p. 45.
80 "A.B.C. Station Aid on Merger Urged," *The New York Times,* April 22, 1967, p. 36.
81 "ITT Gives Pledge on News Policy," *The New York Times,* June 3, 1967, p. 63.

would not "find it possible to monitor . . . on a day to day basis," ITT's pledge of a hands-off policy.

In answer to questions from the commission, ITT attorneys said that the company's actions regarding attempts to influence the news coverage of the merger hearings "were more than the normal kind of public relations [in] one or two instances" and did not represent company policy.

Commissioner Johnson asked if the FCC could believe that ITT "will follow higher principles with ABC," with whom it had economic influence, than with reporters such as those covering the FCC hearings, over whom it had no control. ITT counsel replied that the company now had "a greater sensitivity and a greater awareness" of the need for a free press.[82]

FCC'S "RECONSIDERED" OPINION

On June 22 the FCC announced its decision to allow the merger.[83] The commission agreed with ABC News President Elmer Lower that the greater financial resources available to ABC if the merger took place "would increase, rather than decrease, the independence of the news gathering organization." Without ITT's finances, the commission stated, the network would not be able to equal the "cultural programming innovation, news and public affairs expansion" necessary to compete with the other two TV networks, CBS and NBC.

The commission added that "news and public affairs programs are not profitable and that the ability of a television network to produce and present such programs depends in large part on its financial prosperity and resources." The majority opinion cited Fred Friendly, former head of CBS News, as saying that NBC, with the financial strength of RCA behind it, was in a more advantageous position regarding the type of nonprofit public service programming it could present and initiate.

Thus since ABC was not as highly profitable as NBC and CBS, "it is obvious that ABC is at a tremendous disadvantage."

Finally, that the heightening of competition between the networks will serve the public interest needs no exposition. Therefore, based on our knowledge of the industry and the present network situation, we find on the supplemental record that there will be a significant benefit to the public interest in this respect.

[82] *Ibid.*

[83] All quotations in this section will be found in Federal Communications Commission, "Opinion and Order on Petition for Reconsideration," *The ABC-ITT Merger Case Reconsideration,* June 22, 1967, Sec. 1, pp. 30, 31, 34.

In regard to ITT's and ABC's alleged pressuring of news reporters, the commission cited only one instance of improper conduct. In general,

> there is no evidence that either ITT or ABC did any more than ask reporters covering the proceeding to be factually accurate in their reporting. It is clear that there was some difference of viewpoint as to what the significant facts were, and this difference persists among the parties, counsel, reporters, and others concerned with the case. There is no impropriety in approaching the press to inform or to attempt to correct supposed inaccuracies. All of the reporters testified that this is a common, even daily, occurrence for reporters. The Commission's own "fairness doctrine" is premised on the right to do just this with respect to broadcast reports of news and commentary concerning controversial matters.

Only Gerrity's relating of false information to Miss Shanahan was cited as "improper" and only an "isolated incident."

The majority dismissed Justice's fears of ITT pressure on numerous grounds, including (1) "the Commission's experience with similarly situated enterprises in the industry," (2) "the past performance of both applicants as long time licensees of the Commission," and (3) the fact that "the area of broadcast reporting of news and public affairs is a field in which the Commission has experience and special competence and in which the Department has no special qualifications."

DISSENTING OPINION

Commissioners Bartley, Cox, and Johnson dissented from the FCC majority opinion in the reconsideration.[84] The actions of the two companies with regard to alleged pressuring of news reporters and other incidents

> show the disdain in which ITT holds the Commission, and other persons and institutions in our society, seen as bothersome obstacles in the way of their merger or other ITT design. Such conduct is relevant to the credibility of ITT's self-serving statements generally, and especially its assurances to this Commission of its regard for the integrity and independence of ABC programming decisions and of its

[84] All quotations in this section will be found in Federal Communications Commission, "Dissenting Opinion of Commissioners Robert T. Bartley, Kenneth A. Cox, and Nicholas Johnson," *The ABC-ITT Merger Case Reconsideration,* June 22, 1967, Sec. 2, pp. 27–29, 31, 33, 34–37, 40.

sense of responsibility in making commitments to this Commission as a broadcast licensee.

The minority opinion characterized ITT's "treatment and attitude towards the working press reporting these proceedings [as] shocking."

During reporters' testimony before the FCC, it was brought out that ITT public relations men had at various times called reporters at their homes: "Such repeated remonstrances and requests, and the willingness to contact the reporters at home indicate a zealousness which we believe, at least, an unusual evidencing of extraordinary sensitivity to press treatment."

The incident involving Gerrity and Shanahan

evidences (1) overbearing behavior generally, (2) an insensitivity to the independence of the press, (3) a contempt for the proper functioning of government, (4) either a willingness to engage in deliberate misrepresentations of fact, or incredible naïveté in accepting and spreading unsubstantiated rumor, and (5) an attitude completely accepting the propriety, indeed the inevitability, of news reports reflecting the extraneous economic interests of a reporter's friends or employers.

The conduct of John Horner, ITT's head of PR in Washington, and other officials in pressuring Miss Shanahan regarding the Justice Department "statement"

demonstrates an abrasive self-righteousness in dealing with the press, a shocking insensitivity to its independence and integrity, a willingness to spread false stories in furtherance of self-interest, contempt for government officials as well as the press, and an assumption that even as prestigious a news medium as The New York Times would, as a matter of course, want to present the news so as to best serve its own economic interests (as well as the economic interest of other large business corporations). Despite this, ITT offered no rebuttal of any of the testimony of Miss Shanahan.

The minority opinion went on to say that it was not clear if the ITT public relations department had acted on its own or "was ordered, encouraged, or merely condoned by the top management of ITT. The least that can be said is that the officials involved presumably thought they were acting in accord with the wishes or policies of top management, or in the interests of the corporation." Indeed, ITT merely characterized the Public Relations Department's behavior as "overzealous," and no apologies or reprimands were made public. Even if public relations was acting outside of company policy (and ITT did not make this clear), "ITT would then be left with the fact that it cannot guarantee ABC's autonomy. If it cannot control its own senior vice president's conduct it has little hope of controlling lesser officials and employees."

The minority opinion also cited previous instances in which ITT allegedly had behaved illegally or improperly. In one, the company acquired an international carrier and transferred control of it from one subsidiary to another, before the required FCC approval, *then* sought the commission's permission to perform an act already accomplished. Another instance was cited in which ITT, even though it had not yet been merged with ABC, used the economic pressure of its advertising accounts to influence other corporations to benefit the network. The behavior of ITT lawyers during the supplementary hearings was also characterized as "high-handed," and reference was made to a company lawyer's telephoning a Justice Department witness

and, in a two-hour conversation, tried to get him to change three sentences in the testimony which he was proposing to give. On cross examination, when asked if he felt he had been pressured, his first reaction was: "It depends, I am fairly tough, but two hours on a telephone, you know. I don't know. You can interpret that in your own way."

The opinion cited the chief hearing examiner's characterization of ITT lawyers' behavior as "improper" when they were delivering notes to witnesses who had not yet testified and who were excluded from the hearing room by order of the examiner himself. ABC lawyers were also accused of proffering witnesses with "positively misleading information" and making no attempt to set the record straight.

In regard to ITT's behavior with respect to the news media and FCC witnesses, the three commissioners said:

ITT officials performed these acts and displayed these attitudes in a period which should have been filled with incentive for the most exemplary behavior because of the company's assurances about ABC's freedom from news management and pressure. Certainly it is likely that never again will there be such a depth and immediacy of public scrutiny of ITT's posture in this regard. Yet, with full knowledge of this public attention, ITT not only failed to match its assurances about the future with its deeds of the present, but actually conducted itself in a deliberate manner that gives these assurances a distinctly hollow ring. If ITT behaved this way with the spotlight on it, how much credibility can be given to assurances that ITT would not be led to similar conduct when the pressures, subtle and overt, can be transmitted with a minimum of visibility and accountability? It is not unreasonable, therefore, to believe that ITT would evidence similar disdain for ABC as a press medium, whether arising from such misguided managerial élan or conflicting business goals inherent in its conglomerate and international operations.

In our view, this recurrent conduct on the part of ABC and ITT officials and attorneys has gone far beyond the bounds of natural prejudice and advocacy. The examples are far more numerous than we have recited. . . . We cite this deeply disturbing pattern of behavior because we believe it makes it impossible to approach the self-serving testimony of applicants' officials with anything but skepticism. And it is that testimony which constitutes a major part of the majority's "justification" for this merger.

SHADES OF RALPH NADER

On July 8 *The New York Times* and the *New Republic* reported Eileen Shanahan as saying that John V. Horner had been making inquiries about her "professional and personal life."

> She said that three different persons, two of them her former employers, had told her of the inquiries and that in one of the cases she had been told that Mr. Horner had made a telephone call whose sole purpose was to inquire about her.[85]

After hearing from the second person approached, Miss Shanahan contacted ITT's counsel for the FCC hearing and "demanded that the investigation be stopped." The attorney called her the next day and said that he did not think there had ever been a "systematic investigation" and that no further inquiries would be made anyway. According to Horner, there was, and there had been, no investigation. He admitted that Miss Shanahan's name might have come up in "normal chitchat" with people, but no inquiries were made that were not "entirely normal, clean and above board." Horner said he "couldn't say" if he had contacted her former employers as "I don't know who her former employers were." [86]

[85] "Reporter on Times Says ITT Made Inquiries about Her," *The New York Times*, July 8, 1967, p. 22.
[86] *Ibid.*

On September 7 the *New Republic* said that ITT had been investigating, through third parties, the personal life of James Ridgeway whose articles in that magazine had been critical of the proposed merger.[87] One of the third parties was James Mackey, a researcher for *Army Times* of Washington, D.C. According to the *New Republic,* Mackey called the magazine's office and asked

> what sort of articles did [Ridgeway] write, how often did they appear, how long had he worked there. . . . What was his height and weight, what restaurants did he frequent, did he drink, was he married, . . . was his wife a reporter. Did she help out with his work, was he friendly with the other employees (Does he say good morning), did the editor care much for him and so on.

Later on, Mackey said that one of ITT's advertising agencies had asked him to "find out anything, everything I could about a guy named James Ridgeway." Mackey had never done this before, but his newspaper depended heavily on its advertisers and wanted to please their ad agencies.

Ridgeway questioned Mackey who replied, "This is all above board as far as I know. Gee, don't think your name is Ralph Nader or anything like that." An ITT representative told Ridgeway, "We're not conducting any investigation of you, and we have no reason to . . . I don't know anything about the *Army Times.* It seems to me that if you have an argument with somebody, it's them not us." [88]

In a letter in the September 30, 1967, issue of the *New Republic, Army Times* Vice-President William F. Donally said that Mackey "undertook the investigation . . . entirely on his own and without authorization from *Army Times* or anyone connected with *Army Times"* and was dismissed for his "incredible behavior."

Donally said it was his opinion that neither ITT "nor anyone else" authorized the investigation. Mackey, according to the vice-president, refused to discuss the matter with his former employer, though the *Times* continued to try to get an explanation from him.

According to Donally, the newspaper was "totally unaware" of Mackey's investigation and had "never done any investigation of any individual for anyone: not for advertisers, not for editors, not for anybody." [89]

---

[87] Eileen Shanahan, "Justice Department Disputes Faith Shown by FCC in Its Approval of ITT-ABC Merger Proposal," *The New York Times,* September 8, 1967, p. 30.
[88] "ITT's Press Relations," *New Republic,* September 16, 1967, p. 6–7.
[89] "The Ridgeway Caper," *New Republic,* September 30, 1967, p. 36.

JUSTICE RETURNS

Also on September 8, the Justice Department brought the FCC decision to the court of appeals on the grounds that the commission could not insure that ITT would maintain a hands-off policy regarding ABC News if the merger were to take effect. According to the department, any attempt to "enforce" ITT's promise not to influence ABC public affairs and news programs for its own interest was an "impossibility" and "would come dangerously close to the kind of program censorship which is barred by the First Amendment and the Communications Act." [90]

The company also came under fire. "It is plainly absurd to think that the FCC will receive advance written notice [as ITT promised] before ITT tries to kill an ABC documentary or before ABC officials on their own, shelve subjects which would be embarrassing or detrimental to ITT." The Justice Department also challenged the commission's contention that ITT did not differ from RCA as a television network parent company, although RCA had extensive business with foreign countries. Unlike RCA and CBS:

> ITT is, in origin, a foreign operating company and its predominant source of profit overseas is in the sale of telecommunications equipment.
>
> Since the postal, telephone and telegraph functions in other countries are almost invariably performed by governmental entities, ITT's position in these markets is largely dependent upon its success in dealing with the officials of governmental or quasigovernmental bodies.
>
> [Thus] ITT could have strong motivation to use a news medium affirmatively to promote certain of its investments, by showing officials or programs of a foreign government in a favorable light.

Dangers exist in that "internal corporate pressures" and "subtle influences" may result "in avoidance of subject matter, blunting of criticism, the treatment of controversy in a noncontroversial manner, because of the economic interest of the company."

The Justice Department attacked the FCC majority opinion's statement that there was only one "isolated" instance of improper conduct in regard to ITT's pressuring reporters covering the hearings. Indeed, certain activities of ITT officials were "outrageous conduct" and were central to "the

---

[90] All quotations in this section will be found in Shanahan, "Justice Department Disputes Faith Shown by FCC," p. 30.

very matter" of the Justice Department's worry over "ITT's assuming responsibility for ABC's news and public affairs activities."

The FCC filed its brief with the court of appeals during the first part of October and said the Justice Department erred in its contention that the commission could not enforce ITT's promise that it would not interfere with the network's news and public affairs programming.[91]

The merger was canceled by ITT on January 1, 1968, before the court of appeals had made its decision.

91 "ITT Scores Suit to Block Merger," *The New York Times,* October 3, 1967, p. 28.

Eastman Kodak Company (B), Rochester, New York

Conflict with a Minority Group—FIGHT: The Role of the News Media

The media report and write from the standpoint of a white man's world. The ills of the ghetto, the difficulties of life there, the Negro's burning sense of grievance are seldom conveyed. Slights and indignities are part of the Negro's daily life, and many of them come from what he now calls the "white press"—a press that repeatedly, if unconsciously, reflects the biases, the paternalism, the indifference of white America. This may be understandable, but it is not excusable in an institution that has the mission to inform and educate the whole of our society.

—Report of the National Advisory
Commission on Civil Disorders (1968)

From the very beginning the news media played an important part in the Kodak–FIGHT controversy. Both protagonists were aware of the role mass media could play in informing and influencing public opinion. The news media were therefore an important variable for Kodak and FIGHT,

This case material has been adapted from S. Prakash Sethi, *Business Corporations and the Black Man* (Scranton, Pennsylvania: Chandler Publishing Company, 1970). Copyright © 1970 by Chandler Publishing Company. Used by permission.

and the strategies of the two parties were carefully designed to *manipulate* and *use* the media to their best advantage.

Would the Kodak–FIGHT altercation have received national attention had not radio and television, wire services, national newspapers, and magazines covered Stokely Carmichael's visit to Rochester, Minister Florence's press conferences, and the demonstrations at Kodak's annual stockholders' meeting? The news media apparently played an important role in bringing the issue before the public. Furthermore, it is becoming apparent that the media's role in molding public opinion is increasingly critical in similar situations and that all parties to a conflict must consider the media before deciding on a course of action.

The news media are of interest in this case because to some extent they helped to create the news they reported. FIGHT's attempts to make its disagreements with Kodak a nationwide controversy were aided by the media. Several times throughout late 1966 and the first half of 1967, Florence was able to win support among various segments of the American public because he kept the issue at a controversial level. This strategy, to a large degree, accounts for the often bizarre manner in which FIGHT's spokesmen and supporters acted before television cameras to attract public attention. By focusing solely on its sensational aspects, the news media chose to elevate the controversy to a national level and at the same time distorted and exaggerated its impact.

The conflict between Kodak and FIGHT was covered nationwide by the major news services and by national magazines and journals of all types and political persuasions. Although events were reported throughout the controversy, national coverage was heaviest immediately after Kodak repudiated its agreement with FIGHT and at the time of the stockholders' meeting in Flemington, New Jersey.

THE LOCAL NEWS MEDIA [1]

The only English language daily newspapers in Rochester—the *Democrat & Chronicle* and the *Times-Union*—were both part of the Rochester-headquartered Gannett newspaper chain and were both published by Paul Miller, president of the chain.[2] Before the FIGHT–Kodak controversy

---

[1] The accounts of coverage by local television and radio stations reported in this section were indirectly obtained through newspaper reports and magazine articles.

[2] Gannett Co., Inc., is a chain of newspapers and radio and television stations located in small and medium-size cities primarily in the northeastern states. In 1967 it had 30 newspapers (29 owned and one affiliated) with circulation ranging from 6,500 to 218,600. In addition, Gannett owned AM radio and VHF television outlets in Rochester and Birmingham, New York; AM-FM radio outlets in Danville, Illinois,

erupted, the Gannett chain had a reputation for progressive thinking and constructive work in the area of civil rights. In 1962 the *Times-Union* published an updated version of a 1960 series under the title "Winds of Revolt," which showed "how badly the Negroes were housed in a city famous for its homes, its trees and lilacs, its culture, its generosity, and its depression proof economy." [3]

In 1963 Paul Miller assigned Gannett's executive director, Vincent Jones, to investigate the different ways Northern cities were coping with racial unrest and urban crisis. More than forty editors and reporters contributed to the investigation, and more than one hundred articles were prepared and distributed within a year, starting in July 1963 under the general title of "The Road to Integration." This series won journalism's highest award, the Pulitzer Prize, the first ever awarded to a group or chain.[4] The same series won a Brotherhood Award from the National Conference of Christians and Jews.

However, when the Board for Urban Ministry invited Saul Alinsky to Rochester, Gannett raised a strong protest. The reaction probably reflected the views of publisher Paul Miller who, since 1966, had led a one-man crusade against FIGHT, church organizations supporting FIGHT, Saul Alinsky, and all other persons sympathetic to FIGHT.

The *Times-Union* and its radio and television affiliate WHEC dispatched a three-man team to Chicago to study the operations of Alinsky's Industrial Areas Foundation in the Woodlawn section of Chicago. The outcome was a three-part series in the paper and two one-hour television documentaries during prime time. According to Vincent Jones, "both sides praised these presentations as objective and informative." [5]

However, neither this series of articles nor the opinions expressed by local clergy changed any minds at Gannett. As Jones put it:

> We have tried to keep our feet on the ground and to pursue a moderate, practical policy. . . . The invitation [to Saul Alinsky] was issued by the Council of Churches without first consulting the community. Because of the way it was handled, and a belief that Alin-

---

and Cocoa, Florida; and a VHF television outlet in Rockford, Illinois. Of the two Rochester newspapers, the *Democrat & Chronicle* was published mornings and Sundays (circulation 142,794 and 218,586 respectively), and the *Times-Union* was an evening paper (circulation 143,855). See *Ayer Directory of Newspapers and Periodicals, 1967* (Philadelphia: N. W. Ayer and Son, 1968); *Broadcasting Year Book, 1968* (Washington, D.C.: Broadcasting Publications, 1968), p. A-112; *Editor and Publisher Year Book, 1968* (New York: Editor & Publisher Co., 1968), p. 312.

[3] Vincent S. Jones, "How Rochester Reacted," *Nieman Reports,* June 1965, pp. 16–17.

[4] *Ibid.*

[5] *Ibid.*

sky's controversial methods would do more harm than good, the *Times-Union* questioned the whole project. It was a moderate editorial stand, but left no doubt of the newspaper's belief that the move was risky at best.[6]

Miller's wrath was directed as much, if not more, against the Rochester Area Council of Churches (RACC) as it was against FIGHT and Saul Alinsky. According to an article in the *New Republic:*

At the church breakfast in late 1966, Miller was once more belaboring the ministers for "sneaking" the organization past responsible citizens, and bringing into their midst this "ill-mannered tiger" [Alinsky] to preach "his hate."

"Rochester, New York, is not Rochester, Alabama," said Miller, who sounds like an undertaker. "We have primarily a refugee problem, not a racial problem." How inappropriate it was, he went on, for church people to cultivate in Negroes the idea that in Rochester as in the South, they must take something away from somebody to make progress. Miller recommended to the ministers an article in the December *Reader's Digest* entitled "Are We a Nation of Hoods?" It provided a valuable perspective on the teachings of Jesus.

"If the organization you finance be continued," he said, "why not see that it gets a name somewhat less offensive to the total community. How about W-O-R-K instead of F-I-G-H-T, how about L-O-V-E, how about T-R-Y, how about D-E-E-D-S?"[7]

Again in January, Miller made an editorial attack in the *Times-Union* on those of the clergy who had supported FIGHT. The editorial, entitled "The Gulf between Pulpit and Pew—One Layman's View," drew a large number of letters to the editors of both papers, and most of the letters were critical of FIGHT and its supporters. However, it was not so much the letters as how they were headlined that reflected the bias of the editorial staff and management.

The two papers gave extensive coverage to Kodak and generally accorded front-page space to its press releases. Again the titles were invariably pro-Kodak or anti-FIGHT. The newspapers' coverage on FIGHT's activities and its position was small compared to that on Kodak or to that accorded FIGHT by the national news media. This bias was carried further into 1967 when an editorial in the *Democrat & Chronicle* of June 16, 1967,

[6] *Ibid.*
[7] James Ridgeway, "Attack on Kodak," *New Republic,* January 21, 1967, pp. 11–13.

entitled "Council's Defense," derided the attempt of the Rochester Area Council of Churches to defend their support of FIGHT.[8]

Gannett newspapers were not the only media that did not like Alinsky and FIGHT. As noted in part C of the Kodak study (page 467), radio WHAM canceled a free hour it had been giving to the RACC. In an editorial attack on the council, reported in the *New Republic,* WHAM said:

> Thinking members of Rochester area churches have admitted many times over that the solution to the plight of any minority cannot be solved overnight—that demands are one thing, but that people do not become economically equal just because the various members of the Christian faith would have it that way. More realistically, members of the human race must prove their capacity to compete and to want to be part of the community.[9]

FIGHT's only local outlet was WBBF, which Kodak people called "the Voice of FIGHT." This station presented FIGHT's publicity releases as news copy and made no attempt to give Kodak's viewpoint to listeners.

Coverage by the wire services and the nationally prominent newspapers was quite extensive, and most leading metropolitan dailies reported the conflict at its various high points, many relying on the wire services for their information. The biggest coverage by the press, radio, and television was accorded the stockholders' meeting. The proceedings of the meeting, the demonstrations outside the auditorium where the meeting was held, and the pronouncements of the spokesmen for Kodak and FIGHT were reported by all of the national television networks, radio stations, and newspapers across the country. The only other occasion when network television cameras visited the scene was to record Stokely Carmichael's visit to Rochester in January 1967.[10] The role of television seems to have been crucial to Minister Florence's strategy. To some extent he was able to use television networks to escalate the issue to national prominence, and he believed that only in this way could he pressure Kodak into conceding FIGHT's demands.

To get a better idea of the emphasis given to the Kodak–FIGHT con-

---

[8] "Alinsky Defends Black Power" and "Kodak Reviews Record on Job Talks with FIGHT," *Rochester Times-Union,* October 24, 1966, and September 21, 1966; "FIGHT Vows New Push for Kodak Jobs," "Kodak Questions FIGHT Job Demands," and "Council's Defense," *Rochester Democrat & Chronicle,* October 26, 1966, September 8, 1966, and June 16, 1967.

[9] James Ridgeway, "Saul Alinsky in Smugtown," *New Republic,* June 26, 1965, pp. 15–17.

[10] The account of coverage by network radio and television described here was gathered only indirectly through a study of the press reports.

troversy, it is necessary that we make a detailed analysis of the nature and extent of coverage accorded the incidents by various news media.

The New York Times, perhaps the most influential newspaper in the country, was constantly on the scene. Starting with the first FIGHT convention in June 1966, the paper continuously reported the story as it developed. Immediately after Kodak's repudiation of the agreement of December 20, the Times published a long article, followed by four more related articles in January 1967 (three in the first week alone), two in February, nine in April, and three in May. The coverage thereafter declined in quantity but was adequate for reporting all the relevant news.

A close reading of the Times coverage reveals certain interesting points. First, the reporting was carefully balanced and "objective." John Kifner, who did most of the reporting, as well as Edward Fiske and M. J. Rossaut, presented opposing views in every story. The captions for different articles were either neutral or balanced to give equal billing. Nevertheless, the complete lack of the interpretive articles or in-depth analyses generally associated with this paper is striking. Not a single editorial was written on the controversy which had vast social implications and had received so much national attention. Moreover, the reporting appeared to be somewhat indifferent, in that it was confined to merely quoting the spokesmen for Kodak and FIGHT. (As will be shown in the following section, The Wall Street Journal did the best investigative job of reporting, although it printed fewer stories than the Times.)

The Washington Post presented the other extreme. Nicholas Van Hoffman made no secret of where his sympathies lay. In a long article on January 9, 1967, entitled "Picture's Fuzzy as Kodak Fights FIGHT," he blamed Kodak for a large part of the conflict. In colorful language he suggested that the Kodak management was "out of focus" and hinted darkly that if the situation did not improve soon, "Negroes may again be out on the streets shooting, and not with Brownie Instamatics!" [11]

Among the national news magazines and general periodicals that covered the story at various times were Time, Newsweek, and U.S. News and World Report. Of the three, Newsweek's coverage was more extensive, with sufficient interpretive material to enable readers to see the conflict in its proper perspective. However, there was no expressed opinion by any of the magazines.

In contrast, the national magazines with liberal leanings were full of interpretive articles by well-known writers. The New Republic carried two articles by James Ridgeway, "Attack on Kodak" and "Saul Alinsky in Smugtown." The Reporter had two articles, one by Barbara Carter entitled "The FIGHT against Kodak" and the other by Jules Witcover entitled

11 "Picture's Fuzzy as Kodak Fights FIGHT," Washington Post, January 9, 1967.

"Rochester Braces for Another July." The *Atlantic* had an article by William C. Martin entitled "Shepherds vs. Flocks, Ministers vs. Negro Militancy." While most of these articles listed the contributions made by Kodak to Rochester's civic causes, they minimized their real value in the light of changing social conditions. These authors also faithfully reported Kodak's position but berated its rationale and were generally pro-FIGHT in their writings.

The conservative magazine *National Review,* in an article entitled "The FIGHT–Kodak Fight" by Dorothy Livadas, took a strong pro-Kodak position and largely blamed "the starry-eyed churchmen," Saul Alinsky and Florence, for aggravating racial tension in Rochester. The article implied that most Rochester blacks wanted "no part of FIGHT" and suggested that Saul Alinsky was a man who "capitalized on the plight of the down-trodden and made a hero of himself while exploiting their misery." [12]

In a personal interview, a Kodak public relations executive expressed the conviction that the company's position in the controversy was not being fairly reported in the national press:

It always makes good copy for David to be throwing a stone at Goliath. If Minister Florence were anywhere in the vicinity, the reporters would go after him to say something and he would take full advantage of this opportunity. . . .

The problem was primarily local in nature until the stockholders' meeting when, despite the 116 newspaper people present, the national press reported the thing so poorly that most people who read the account that appeared in a local paper hadn't the slightest idea what it was all about except that Kodak was having some trouble with Negroes.

According to an article by Raymond A. Schroth in the magazine *America,* "Kodak officials are still smarting from stories by James Ridgeway in the *New Republic* (January 21, 1967) and by Nicholas Van Hoffman in the *Washington Post* (January 9, 1967), in which Kodak claims to be misquoted." [13] In an interview with Schroth, Kodak spokesmen again repeated this charge.

THE BUSINESS NEWS MEDIA

The Kodak–FIGHT controversy was of special interest to the business community as businessmen all over the country were asking themselves,

[12] "The FIGHT–Kodak Fight," *National Review,* June 27, 1967, p. 683.
[13] "Self-Doubt and Black Pride," *America,* April 1, 1967, p. 502.

"Will this happen to my corporation?" Alinsky himself saw Kodak as just the beginning of a pattern of attacks by racial minorities against outmoded corporate behavior.

The business news media covered the controversy extensively as news, provided their readers with in-depth analyses and interpretive articles, and also wrote policy editorials. The opinions of most business magazines ran from sympathy for Kodak to extreme hostility toward FIGHT in terms of both its objectives and its tactics.

The news coverage by *The Wall Street Journal* was perhaps the best of any newspaper in the country. For example, it was the *only* newspaper to report that after the Kodak repudiation, Mr. Florence offered to amend the agreement in any manner acceptable to Kodak or even to scrap it if Kodak officials would jointly announce with him on television their willingness to cooperate with FIGHT "to get more jobs for Negroes." [14] This was indeed an important concession by FIGHT, asking to do only what the company had said all along that it was willing to do. Yet Kodak officials turned down FIGHT's offer.

Why did FIGHT not choose to publicize Kodak's refusal? Florence was desperate after Kodak's repudiation and was probably willing to go to great lengths to salvage at least something from the situation. He might also have realized FIGHT's lack of staying power in a long contest. However, after his turndown Florence kept this incident quiet for fear it would appear to his followers as a "sellout" and would show lack of courage and militancy on his part. Kodak was not interested in publicizing the event because it would make the company look stubborn and unreasonable and would refute all the pro-cooperation propaganda it had been making in public.

The kind of coverage given the Kodak-FIGHT controversy by the business news media is exemplified in some of the story titles and excerpts from these stories:

The Wall Street Journal: "Eastman Kodak Accuses Rochester Rights Groups of Pushing for Power," "Kodak Refuses to Restore Negro Job Pact; Rights Group Vows 'War' against Concern," "Eastman Kodak and Negro Group Reach Compact to Work in Harmony," "Kodak's Ordeal: How a Firm That Meant Well Won a Bad Name for Its Race Relations," "Kodak Announces Plan to Help Slum Dwellers Start Own Business." [15]

Business Week: "The Fight That Swirls around Eastman Kodak," "Kodak and FIGHT Agree to Agree," "What the Kodak Fracas Means." [16]

---

[14] Earl C. Gottschalk, Jr., "Kodak's Ordeal: How a Firm That Meant Well Won a Bad Name for Its Race Relations," *The Wall Street Journal,* June 30, 1967, pp. 1ff.

[15] *The Wall Street Journal,* January 9, 1967; April 26, 1967, p. 7; June 26, 1967, p. 9; June 20, 1967, pp. 1ff.; November 20, 1967, p. 15.

[16] *Business Week,* April 29, 1967, pp. 38–41; July 1, 1967, p. 22; May 6, 1967, p. 192.

Fortune: "And Kodak Will Ask, 'How High?' " (a reference to Stokely Carmichael's inflammatory statement in his Rochester press conference on January 19, 1967).[17]

Factory: "There's a FIGHT in Kodak's Future." [18]

Barron's National Business and Financial Weekly: "Who's Out of Focus? A Note on the Harassment of Eastman Kodak" (an attack on FIGHT and the church organizations supporting FIGHT).[19]

Reviewing Kodak's handling of the situation, *Business Weekly* [20] commented that after the second meeting, "Kodak was admittedly sidestepping FIGHT's demands. . . . [No] major company could remain union free in New York State, as has Kodak, without considerable skill at evasive tactics." On Kodak's repudiation of the agreement, *Business Week* said: "While the agreement clearly ran counter to what Kodak had insisted all along, disavowing it weakened the company's position." Quoting an executive, the same periodical stated: "At least one executive thinks Kodak's lack of labor negotiating experience explains some of its clumsiness. 'Union negotiating teaches you when your name is on something, you have got an agreement.' "

Fortune, on the other hand, confined itself to quoting Kodak spokesmen and wrote:

> Two days later, Kodak declared that the agreement was "unauthorized" and unacceptable. Chairman William S. Vaughn subsequently issued a statement saying that Mulder . . . had acted "through an overzealous desire to resolve the controversy." [21]

Barron's presented the extreme end of the continuum on anti-FIGHT opinion. In an article on May 1, 1967, it stated: "Legally and morally, however, the company could not make the commitment demanded by FIGHT." *Barron's* thought Kodak had a lot to learn about labor relations: "If anything, it has taken not too hard a line, as its radical critics aver, but too soft. The presence on the pay roll of an executive who failed to grasp the elementary principles cited above suggests as much." [22]

Although some of the business magazines recognized the need for change in corporate behavior and suggested more positive action in the area of assistance to minorities, most of them were editorially critical of FIGHT and its supporters.

[17] *Fortune,* June 1, 1968, p. 78.
[18] *Factory,* June 1967, p. 69.
[19] *Barron's,* May 1, 1967, p. 1.
[20] *Business Week,* April 29, 1967, pp. 38–41.
[21] *Fortune,* June 1, 1968, p. 78.
[22] *Barron's,* May 1, 1967, p. 1.

In an editorial entitled "What the Kodak Fracas Means," *Business Week* called the Kodak–FIGHT conflict the forerunner of similar conflicts. The editorial further stated:

The demand that Kodak simply put to work whatever Negroes FIGHT produces is preposterous. . . . It is not the business of any corporate management to run a public welfare establishment. Efficient production of goods and services is the name of the business game. Personnel policies that are violently inconsistent with profitability violate one of the private corporation's cardinal rules. Management must retain its rights to hire, fire, promote, and assign work in ways that serve business objectives.[23]

The editorial urged business to understand and appreciate the objectives of civil rights groups in Rochester—the main objective being blacks—but said that "hiring unskilled Negroes cuts into profits, at least in the short run," and argued that "business must be paid for undertaking what is in the end a public responsibility." It exhorted civil rights groups to abandon their militancy and warned them that like the Wobblies and the Knights of Labor, "they will get nowhere unless they avoid inflicting serious injury on the effective operation of private business in this country. . . . Black Power won't work any better than did labor power, when directed at radical objectives."

In another article *Business Week* commented:

Alinsky—and FIGHT—are intent on using Kodak to press their conviction that corporations must assume more responsibility for the poor in their communities than business customarily takes on. Says Alinsky: "American industry had better recognize—and some do— that they have a special obligation. . . . [The] Kodak situation dramatically reveals that today's ghettobound, militant urban Negro may generate even more problems for business than the civil rights struggle in the South created."

No business would find it easy to keep pace with Alinsky's fast-moving, bare-knuckles style of civil rights campaign. . . .[24]

Kodak's dealings with FIGHT, in fact, starkly dramatize the clash of modern radical black tactics with well-meaning but traditionalist business attitudes.

An editorial in *Fortune* described FIGHT's action at the stockholders'

[23] *Business Week,* May 6, 1967.
[24] *Business Week,* April 29, 1967, pp. 38–41.

meeting as a harassment and described the Kodak–FIGHT situation so that businessmen would understand "what the battle is really about." The editorial agreed that

> many U.S. industrial corporations are failing to move fast enough to help Negro applicants qualify for employment. No company can be expected to "create instamatic jobs," as Minister Florence has said Kodak should. But in one way or another, industry should try to help unskilled and uneducated Negroes who want jobs to qualify for jobs. What makes FIGHT's "war" against Kodak appalling is that Kodak has recognized its obligations here. It is hard to imagine a worse way for Negro organizations to try to beat down employers.[25]

The clergy's desire to support better job opportunities was good, but *Fortune* questioned their use of stock-voting proxies to achieve these objectives. However, in the Kodak case, a proxy for FIGHT was not a vote for blacks but a vote for giving FIGHT power. "And that cause imposes no moral claim upon churchmen or businessmen or anybody else."

Barron's rebuked Kodak for its softheadedness in dealing with FIGHT and questioned the logic of the concept of social responsibility for corporations:

> The time has also come to do a little soul-searching with respect to corporate responsibility. Companies want to be good citizens, and, by providing jobs, paying taxes and the like, they generally succeed. However, management is the steward of other people's property. It can never afford to forget where its primary obligations lie.
>
> [The] company policy as outlined in a 1966 Management Letter . . . speaks of going beyond selection of the best qualified person, to seeking "to help the individual who lacks the necessary qualifications to become qualified."
>
> More suited to a sociology text than a corporate manual, the Letter adds: "Industry must look less critically at the individual's school record and work experience and more at his potential." Throughout the protracted dispute with FIGHT, Kodak's executives have chosen to ignore repeated provocations, insults and lies, an excessive forbearance which has merely incited their tormentors. In the corporate realm, as in any other, appeasement is a losing game. For Kodak and the rest of U.S. industry, it's time to stop turning the other cheek.
>
> The clergy is in bad company. In taking issue with the employment policies of Eastman Kodak, moreover, the churchmen stand on very shaky ground.[26]

[25] *Fortune*, June 1, 1968, p. 78.
[26] *Barron's*, May 1, 1967, p. 1.

THE RELIGIOUS PRESS

The religious press not only actively participated in informing its audience about the Kodak–FIGHT conflict but also contributed to molding the opinion of the nationwide clergy. Generally speaking, it supported the stand taken by national church organizations in assisting FIGHT and also supported FIGHT's demands against Kodak.

In an editorial entitled "Economic Leverage of the Churches," *America,* the national Catholic weekly, supported the stand taken by Protestant groups in withholding their proxies from the management of Eastman Kodak and further asserted:

> Anyone who believes that it is morally reprehensible to buy the products of a firm that discriminates against colored workers must hold that passive, uncritical ownership of the firm's securities is also wrong.
>
> It must be admitted, however, that in many cases it simply has not occurred to managers of church funds or purchasing agents to use their economic power for moral goals. Like other investors, they have single-mindedly sought security and a satisfactory rate of return. Similarly, purchasing agents have felt that they discharged their duties when they obtained goods and services at a favorable price.
>
> All this leads one to wonder why a theology of consumption and investment for modern market societies has not been more intensively cultivated. The humbling fact is that before the civil rights movement challenged God-fearing people to practice what they preach, most of us in transacting business performed as economic men. Or, which is nearly as bad, we absentmindedly followed the rule attributed to the late Henry Ford: "Whatever is good business is also good morals." [27]

The *Episcopalian* echoed similar views [28] as did the *United Church Herald,* which commented on the involvement of the churches in the Kodak–FIGHT conflict:

> Nor will the role of the churches in these developments go unnoticed. The Christian community often has been called the conscience of America but seldom has its voice been heard so clearly. Such a role is bound to be controversial—especially when the church

[27] "Economic Leverage of the Churches," *America,* May 13, 1967, p. 714.
[28] "Church vs. Kodak: The Big Picture," *Episcopalian,* June 1967, pp. 43–44.

challenges the intentions of its own members. But in a nation where the structures of power are increasing rapidly in size and influence, the corporate body of Christ must speak its convictions and may occasionally need to flex its muscles.[29]

The Belgian *Chronicles and Documents* commented in an editorial on the economic wealth of the church and its possible uses:

But, have the Church administrators always been aware of the duties imposed by the possession of this wealth? In countries where the economy rests greatly on private initiative, shouldn't it be necessary that the Church herself show some initiative, and set an example wherever the possession of certain resources gives her the right to be present? The Kodak case shows very clearly the positive role that the ecclesiastic structures could play in a business concern.[30]

The religious press, however, did not unanimously support church involvement in racial problems, issues of job discrimination in general, and FIGHT in particular.

The *Christian Century* for one did not agree with either FIGHT or its church supporters and editorialized:

But one wing of the clergy—greatly and properly concerned and determined to do something, even if it is the wrong time—gulp and swallow what in the opinion of many of us is a highly dubious nostrum. Moreover, this minority is enraged by those of us who, having studied the Alinsky method closely and for a long time, resolutely refuse to gulp and swallow. What amazes and puzzles us is not Alinsky—he declares himself most forthrightly—but the hypnotic effect he has on some members of the clergy.[31]

In another editorial entitled "Episcopal Editor Denounces Saul Alinsky," the *Christian Century* concurred with the opinion of another Alinsky critic, Carroll E. Simcox, editor of the *Living Church,* by saying:

And Simcox, with whom we are not always in agreement, said a great deal more to which we found ourselves tapping our feet, including his statement: "I don't want one nickel of my church offering

[29] "Rare Days in Any Month," *United Church Herald,* August 1967, p. 23.
[30] "The Church and Capitalism," *Chronicles and Documents,* Brussels: Auxiliaire de la Presse, S. A. Bureau voor Persknipsels, N. V., 1967.
[31] "Alinsky Denounces Reconciliation," *Christian Century,* July 5, 1967, p. 861.

ever to find its way to anything that this man Alinsky administers or even comes near, and if I learn in advance that it has an Alinsky-related destination I won't offer it." [32]

The editorial policy of *Christianity Today* also did not support FIGHT. In "Church Leaders Put the Squeeze on Kodak," the paper cautioned:

> Members of denominations backing FIGHT must consider whether their churches should be so deeply involved in big business, and whether their stock voting power should be used to harass responsible private enterprise. . . .
> Every Christian must be committed to equal-employment opportunities for men of all races. But race is not the only issue in the Rochester controversy. The basic issue in all agitation aroused by the Saul Alinsky forces centers on changing the economic structure of our nation. Church members should repudiate and withhold financial support from leaders who back such rabble-rousing causes. All Christians should become involved in the Church's foremost enterprise, sharing with men poor in spirit the unsearchable riches of Christ.[33]

In another editorial, "A Fight Church Officials May Regret," [34] *Christianity Today* said:

> Denominational officials are rendering a great disservice to the cause of Christ and the betterment of the Negro's status in American life by supporting the Saul Alinsky FIGHT organization in its calculated controversy with the Eastman Kodak company. . . . In its zeal to aid the Negro, the Church must exercise care that it does not promote organizations that sow disruption and seek political power while professing to help the less fortunate.

The *Presbyterian Journal* was perhaps the most vocal and vociferous in its attack against those clergy who sympathized with FIGHT or supported their churches' involvement in seeking economic justice for the poor. In a strange indictment of FIGHT supporters, it said:

> *Notice that the people on whose behalf the Church was called to picket were not necessarily Christians. No. The Church merely con-*

[32] "Episcopal Editor Denounces Saul Alinsky," *Christian Century*, November 15, 1967, p. 1452.

[33] "Church Leaders Put the Squeeze on Kodak," *Christianity Today*, April 28, 1967, p. 1.

[34] "A Fight Church Officials May Regret," *Christianity Today*, May 12, 1967.

sidered that its mission was to decide between two contending factions in a business dispute, and join the picket lines across the nation against one faction. [Emphasis added] [35]

Dr. L. Nelson Bell, in an article in the *Presbyterian Journal*, stated his views on the blacks. They sounded like an echo of the apologetics of the segregationists of a (hopefully) bygone era. Among other things, he stated:

Perhaps Eastman Kodak Co. has been too slow in making use of all available labor. On the other hand, some may be demanding "rights" for which they are not equipped. We do believe the Church in its eagerness to promote civil rights may have omitted an even greater duty—the promotion of a sense of responsibility which can only be attained by hard work.[36]

THE BLACK PRESS

The Kodak–FIGHT conflict was covered for the black press by the Negro Press International. Its reporting—quite sparse compared with other special-purpose media—was confined to the statements made by the spokesmen for FIGHT and Kodak on different occasions during the dispute. The only black paper of national repute, the *Chicago Daily Defender* (national edition), carried a total of eight stories on the dispute, only three of which related the background in any detail. The paper also carried an editorial entitled "Economic Justice." [37] However, this editorial was devoid of any statement of position or philosophy by the editors or publisher of the newspaper and was just a brief summary of events.

Crisis, the official organ of the NAACP, published only one article on the problems of Rochester, Arthur L. Whitaker's "Anatomy of a Riot," [38] and carried two short news items ("NAACP Hits Rioters" and "Rochester NAACP Aids in Bringing Peace to Riot-Torn City") in the news section under the heading "Along the NAACP Battlefront." [39] The news items appeared in the August–September 1964 issue. Mr. Whitaker's article appeared in the January 1965 issue and preceded the Kodak–FIGHT conflict by at least six months.

[35] "Re: Church Strikes and Boycotts," editorial, *Presbyterian Journal*, March 8, 1967.

[36] L. Nelson Bell, "Church Activities Have Gone Wild," *Presbyterian Journal*, March 8, 1967.

[37] "Economic Justice," editorial, *Chicago Daily Defender*, nat. ed., May 20–26, 1967, p. 10.

[38] "Anatomy of a Riot," *Crisis*, January 1965, pp. 20–25.

[39] "Along the NAACP Battlefront," *Crisis*, August–September 1964, p. 470.

D.

CORPORATIONS AND THE CHURCH

Eastman Kodak Company (C), Rochester, New York

Conflict with a Minority Group—FIGHT: The Role of the Church

The church is not an impersonal edifice, although all too often it seems that way. The church is what we have made it. The dilemma is that while its mission should be the righting of wrongs and the active pursuit of the great Judeo-Christian values, we have instead made it for the most part a force for the status quo.

—John D. Rockefeller, Jr.

The activities of the church [1] played a very important role in the Kodak–FIGHT controversy. It was an agency of the church that was instrumental in bringing Saul Alinsky to Rochester and thus creating FIGHT. Moreover, it was the local clergy who provided FIGHT with its initial momentum and sustained it in the early stages. Even after FIGHT was a going concern, the church was one of its strongest supporters at both local and

This case material has been adapted from S. Prakash Sethi, *Business Corporations and the Black Man* (Scranton, Pennsylvania: Chandler Publishing Company, 1970). Copyright © 1970 by Chandler Publishing Company. Used by permission.

[1] *Church* is defined here as all organized Christian religious organizations in the United States.

national levels. Protestant and Catholic church organizations consistently supported FIGHT, although their membership was predominantly white. These groups were under constant pressure, especially at the local level, to disengage themselves from this controversy. Obviously, it was not the most usual activity for the church to engage in. Although members of the clergy had been involved in civil rights actions in the South and had participated in sit-in demonstrations and peace marches, their action in Rochester was unprecedented in many ways. It involved a deliberate attempt at organizing local minorities through techniques that were unorthodox and unacceptable even to some of the most liberal groups in the United States. These techniques carried with them the potential for violence. In a city like Rochester, which had been the scene of race riots, this action seemed particularly foolhardy. It was sure to incur the displeasure of a majority of the town's citizens who were, after all, church members and had the right to ensure that the churches satisfy their spiritual needs rather than become rabble-rousers.

Why then did the church become involved in the controversy? To understand this, we must realize that in Rochester the various elements of the church, ranging from the Rochester Area Council of Churches to the individual ministers and priests, had somewhat different, at least short-run, objectives and more often than not were subject to different pressures or allegiances.

The Board for Urban Ministry was the organization originally responsible for inviting Saul Alinsky and his Industrial Areas Organization to Rochester with a view to encouraging organization among the local minorities and giving them a new voice in representing their views to the city and its establishment. The board realized that this action might not be acceptable to the city's other powerful and equally well-meaning groups because of Alinsky's reputation as a radical. To understand the board's action it is necessary to consider the circumstances and the source of the board's authority.

The Board for Urban Ministry was a semiautonomous offshoot of the Rochester Area Council of Churches (RACC). Although the RACC endorsed the board's action, it was the board and not the council that was actually responsible for bringing Alinsky to Rochester. The distinction between the two, often overlooked, is strategically important. As William C. Martin, writing in the *Atlantic,* put it:

> The Council is composed of more than 200 member congregations and is ultimately answerable to them. The Board for Urban Ministry is composed of representatives from eight denominations and is thus not directly answerable to individual churches. According to the policy of the two organizations, the Board could have invited Alinsky

without the Council's approval, but the Council was not obligated to poll its member churches as to their desires in the matter.

The Board for Urban Ministry issued the invitation to Alinsky and led in providing his fee. Over half the fee came from church agencies such as the Presbyterian Board of National Missions. Much of FIGHT's most articulate support at Flemington came from similar denominational offices. These agencies and their staffs are ultimately responsible to a constituency, but even if that constituency opposes a policy decision strongly enough to try to countermand it, it is likely to move too late or hit the wrong target.[2]

THE ATTITUDE OF THE NATIONAL CHURCH ORGANIZATIONS

Only during the past twenty years or so have American churches become conspicuous in causes against race prejudice and economic inequality. Thus the National Council of Churches went on record in 1954 as working against those forms of economic injustice that are expressed through racial discrimination.[3] It is also on record in support of equal employment opportunity for all,[4] the use of nonviolent demonstrations to secure social justice,[5] the elimination of segregation in education,[6] and the prevention of discrimination in housing.[7]

The use of economic pressure in racial issues was specifically proposed and approved in a background paper prepared for the National Council of Churches:

We believe it is of primary importance that Christian people everywhere recognize that what may be called bread-and-butter injustice can be equally as devastating to human life and well-being as civil injustice, if not more so, largely because bread-and-butter pur-

[2] William C. Martin, "Shepherds vs. Flocks, Ministers vs. Negro Militancy," *Atlantic,* December 1967, pp. 55–59.

[3] National Council of Churches of Christ in the United States of America (NCCCUSA), "Christian Principles and Assumptions for Economic Life." Resolution adopted by General Board, September 15, 1954.

[4] NCCCUSA, "Christian Influence toward the Development and Use of All Labor Resources without Regard to Race, Color and Religion or National Origin." Resolution adopted by General Assembly, December 9, 1960.

[5] NCCCUSA, "The Church and Segregation." Resolution adopted by General Board, June 11, 1952. Also see "Resolution on the Sit-In Demonstrations." Adopted by General Board, June 2, 1960.

[6] NCCCUSA, "Statement on the Decision of the U.S. Supreme Court on Segregation in the Public Schools." Adopted by General Board, May 19, 1954.

[7] NCCCUSA, "The Churches' Concern for Housing." Resolution adopted by General Board, November 18, 1953.

suits are so necessary to the maintenance of life. Because these forms of injustice are so closely related to habit, local mores, and man-to-man relationships, they can only partially be opposed or regulated by law or civil authority.[8]

The General Board, therefore, resolved on June 8, 1963:

> When other efforts to secure these rights do not avail, to support and participate in economic pressures where used in a responsible and disciplined manner to eliminate economic injustice and to end discrimination against any of God's people based on race, creed, or national origin.[9]

The National Council of Churches has gone even further by recognizing that the churches' own purchases must be based on other than strictly economic criteria. The basic philosophy of the council was very well articulated in the policy statement adopted by the General Board on September 12, 1968:

> The institutional church enters into the economic life of society in a variety of ways. . . . The economic activities and financial transactions of the church total many billions of dollars annually. As a result, the church is inevitably involved in the exercise of substantial economic power. . . . We reaffirm that all economic institutions and practices are human structures conceived and designed by men; that they affect the conditions and quality of life of persons, many of whom cannot exercise any control over their functioning. . . . The market system which characterizes the American economy is one such institution. When the church approaches the marketplace in its role of purchaser of goods and services, it inevitably becomes a participant in an intricate network of economic forces involving ethical issues, policies and decisions. . . .
>
> Most purchasing decisions by the church involve a selection among competing vendors. Such factors as quality, performance, convenience and price—conventional determinants of most purchasing decisions—although relevant to the economic activity of the church, are not sufficient criteria for its selection among vendors. The nature of the church requires that as an economic institution it also consider

---

[8] NCCCUSA, "Background Paper of Information Relating to Resolution on the Use of Economic Pressures in Racial Tensions." Prepared by Department of Church and Economic Life in consultation with Department of Cultural Relations of Division of Christian Life and Work, June 9, 1963, p. 5.

[9] NCCCUSA, "The Use of Economic Pressure in Racial Tensions." Resolution adopted by General Board, June 8, 1963.

the social impact of its purchasing decisions in terms of justice and equality. . . .

In cases where injustice is found to exist, the church should make vigorous efforts through moral persuasion to secure correction of the abuses. . . . Where such measures prove to be inappropriate in securing justice, or where past experience demonstrates that these means alone are ineffective, the church is not only justified, but in faithfulness to its nature, is required to give its patronage to sources of goods and services which it finds to have policies and practices that better serve social justice. . . .

When such action is taken, the church is free and indeed may be impelled, as a form of witness, not only to inform the vendors involved but also to announce publicly the nature of its action and the reasons for it.[10]

The problem of the church's concern for economic issues and its involvement in conflicts where it is not a direct party has another dimension which is equally explosive: the choice of strategies. The National Council of Churches has supported the use of nonviolent methods in securing economic justice for minorities.[11]

However, what should the church do if nonviolent and peaceful means do not succeed? When is a violation of man-made laws justified if there is a superior law of conscience? Economic pressures can be used not only by the church but also by other groups that the church is opposing. If these measures by the church can be justified because of the righteousness of the cause, how can they be condemned when used by other groups if the latter are equally honest in their belief of the justness of their cause and are not motivated by bigotry, selfishness, or prejudice? The mere existence of power, be it legal or implied, is not enough justification for its use. However, if ends are to be used as criteria for legitimizing means, the church as a party to the conflict has no more right to proclaim that its values are the "justifiable" ends than have the other parties to the conflict.

The National Council of Churches, recognizing some of these issues, justified its approach thus:

Use of economic pressures also involves the possibility of violence. Though violence may sometimes result from an action, this possibility does not necessarily call for opposition to such action, particularly on the part of those who seek to use non-violent economic means to eliminate or decrease discrimination.[12]

[10] NCCCUSA, "The Church as Purchaser of Goods and Services." Policy statement adopted by General Board, September 12, 1968.
[11] "The Use of Economic Pressure in Racial Tensions," NCCCUSA, June 8, 1963.
[12] "Background Paper of Information," NCCCUSA, June 9, 1963.

The council also recognized that there might be occasions when a company might lose its regular clientele if it were to cater to the special needs of a particular group. It thus argued that such a company was only an innocent bystander, not the offending party, and should therefore not be subjected to economic pressures by the church. These measures might involve yet another party—those people who give tacit support to discriminatory practices of some businesses by not actively opposing those companies and their activities and by continuing to patronize them. Notwithstanding, the council maintained:

> These factors make more difficult, but no less necessary, the understanding of and resistance to the use of economic pressures as a means to enforce racial discriminations or oppression. They serve to highlight the importance of looking with broad historical perspective at the full sweep of economic injustice which the victims of economic injustice now seek to remove, or at least alleviate through the use of economic pressures being made against them.
>
> It is, therefore, no wonder that the board was more in tune than the council with the trends of national church organizations and more willing to use less conventional approaches to solving the problems of Rochester's minorities. The board was assured of the support of the National Council of Churches in view of the latter's public statements and official resolutions favoring the use of economic pressures and other direct action to promote the cause of the minorities. Moreover, financial independence and only indirect representation of the local churches insulated the board from local pressures and in a sense made it insensitive to the feelings and desires of the local clergy and citizens.[13]

In inviting Alinsky, the board knew that it was creating "an atmosphere of controversy," [14] but the ferocity and, to some extent, the direction of opposition were unexpected. The RACC and its member congregations came under immediate attack from media and laymen alike. The local newspapers accused the council of bringing in "outsiders" and troublemakers and of supporting militants who were intent on creating unrest among the people of Rochester. As reported in the *New Republic,* the city's most powerful radio station, WHAM, an ABC affiliate, in an editorial warned that

> if the clergy persisted in bringing Alinsky into town then the ministers must start paying $275 for the hour-long Sunday morning church

[13] *Ibid.*
[14] "The Fight That Swirls around Eastman Kodak," *Business Week,* April 29, 1967, pp. 38–41.

service the station had been broadcasting free. WHAM said Alinsky was a "troublemaker." . . . The Council held its ground against WHAM and the Sunday morning radio program was cancelled.[15]

Commenting on the intensity of local hostility to the council's action, the same observer stated:

In the face of this intensive barrage, many laymen found themselves in a quandary over the role their pastors and denominational leaders were playing. For weeks, representatives of the Board for Urban Ministry and the Council of Churches spent their evenings interpreting the realities of life in the ghettos and the dynamics of the Alinsky approach to groups of troubled laymen.[16]

It was easy and perhaps spiritually comfortable for most of the educated, suburban, affluent laymen to support their clergy's involvement in social action, as long as it did not go beyond the discussion stage and as long as any action was confined to peaceful methods of protest. However, these parishioners could not reconcile themselves to the idea of their clergy being involved in an open struggle for power between different groups in the community. The lack of precedent, the absence of a clear-cut philosophy, and the feeling of uncertainty about possible achievements further added to the laymen's confusion and frustration, as reflected in the nature and intensity of their response. There was a widespread cancellation of pledges—sometimes running into thousands of dollars. William C. Martin reported: "Resentment of church involvement ran so high in some congregations that church leaders would not pass out brochures presenting FIGHT's request for third-year funding until after the annual pledge drive." [17]

There was a serious question as to how long clergymen could function under strain and still maintain their sanity. One minister, tormented by threats and telephone calls, took his own life; the calls were then made to his wife.[18] Others were victims of anonymous letters circulated among the congregations and of telephoned threats against their families. A minister who had been attacked for supporting FIGHT found that the lug bolts had been taken off the wheels of his car.[19] In a large number of cases

---

[15] James Ridgeway, "Saul Alinsky in Smugtown," *New Republic*, June 26, 1965, pp. 15–17.

[16] *Ibid.*

[17] Martin, "Shepherds vs. Flocks," pp. 55–59.

[18] Jules Loh, Associated Press Feature Story for Sunday A.M. papers, April 23, 1967.

[19] James Ridgeway, "Attack on Kodak," *New Republic*, January 21, 1967, pp. 11–13.

parishioners simply stopped talking or being friendly to their clergymen. William Martin, writing in the *Atlantic,* commented:

> The loss of members and money affects a minister because they are tangible signs of his professional "success," however much he may wish they were not. But the confusion, bitterness, and hostility that he sees in his people cause him the greatest pain. In [one] case, members made a point of telling the minister's children that the church could never make progress until their father left. In some churches dissident laymen organized attempts to get rid of the offending minister. In others, leaders withheld salary increments or warned the pastor not to spend too much of his time in activities related to FIGHT.[20]

The resentment of the local citizenry against the Rochester Area Council of Churches was even more vocal and violent. According to William Martin:

> Letters and telephone calls—some reasonable, others obscene and threatening—poured into the council office. Numerous churches and individuals decided to "teach the council a lesson" by lowering or canceling contributions for the coming fiscal year. One church, recognizing that FIGHT was only one part of the council's activity, raised its contribution $500, but accompanied its pledge with a letter strongly critical of the council's stance. Others were not so charitable. At the final tally, the council's annual fund drive for the coming year missed its goal by $20,000. Ironically, the attempt to punish the council has had no effect whatever on FIGHT, which has in fact been guaranteed third-year funding by the various denominational bodies and church agencies, nor on the Board for Urban Ministry, which is also funded denominationally and has never been more secure financially.[21]

CHURCH ACTIVITIES AFTER THE AGREEMENT
OF DECEMBER 20

When the executive committee of Kodak's board of directors repudiated the agreement signed by John Mulder, the RACC found itself in a worse dilemma than ever before. The community was already hostile to RACC's earlier actions, and any support of FIGHT would further intensify the

[20] Martin, "Shepherds vs. Flocks," pp. 55–59.
[21] *Ibid.*

conflict. FIGHT's actions immediately following the repudiation did not help. On January 19, 1967, against the advice of many of his supporters, Minister Florence invited Stokely Carmichael to Rochester. In his speech Carmichael made inflammatory statements against Kodak, Rochester, and every other organization that did not agree with FIGHT.

The council was really concerned about the danger of the situation getting out of hand; yet it could do nothing but support FIGHT's cause since it felt that Kodak had indeed broken a promise which the other party had accepted in good faith. The council's hand was further forced when Kodak took full-page ads in the local newspapers to publicize its reasons for rejecting the agreement. The council wanted to avoid a further deterioration of the situation, but it could not desert FIGHT's cause without losing all the work done so far and perhaps permanently discouraging the minorities from putting any faith in the white man's promises. The council took double-page ads in the papers urging Kodak to honor the agreement and at the same time asking FIGHT to support Kodak's training programs. However, with supporters of both factions having raised community passions to a high pitch, the council's appeal to patience and reason was lost in the hysteria, while its support for FIGHT was overblown. The reactions were predictable though unfortunate.

DENOMINATIONAL DIVISION OF OPINION OF FIGHT

The controversy caused division among individual denominations in the Council of Churches. Stokely Carmichael's visit prompted six of Rochester's eighty Presbyterian churches (FIGHT's largest church supporters) to consider withdrawing their support of FIGHT while their parent body's Health and Welfare Association condemned Kodak.[22] The Episcopalians were reportedly the second-largest church supporters of FIGHT. In response to criticism of FIGHT by the Gannett newspapers, the bishop of the Episcopal diocese of Rochester appointed a committee to "assess FIGHT and to determine," by April 1967, "whether the diocese which has already contributed $19,000 should continue its support." [23] The third-largest church group, the Baptists, decided to continue their contributions, but a third of the delegates voted against the proposal.[24]

The Reverend Elmer G. Schaertal, pastor of the Lutheran Church of the Redeemer, openly dissented with the council's stand in a letter to the

[22] Barbara Carter, "The Fight against Kodak," *Reporter*, January 21, 1967, pp. 28–31.

[23] Raymond A. Schroth, "Self-Doubt and Black Pride," *America*, April 1, 1967, p. 502.

[24] "And Kodak Will Ask, 'How High?' " *Fortune*, June 1, 1967, p. 78.

Rochester Democrat & Chronicle. Schaertal equated the disrespect for authority that was sweeping the country with that of FIGHT for Kodak:

> . . . the disrespect sweeping our country of youth, of college students, of ministers, and leaders like Adam Powell and James Hoffa for the law and courts and of FIGHT for Kodak which is the most community minded company that I know. . . . The demands of FIGHT call for a special privilege because of color. . . . This seems crazy to me and would do great harm to both company and all the workers who would resent the man coming in by paternalistic power rather than qualifications for the job. If one asks why Florence and FIGHT are so insistent in this, one can only answer that it is for power and would be used in that way rather than for benefit of workers, or company or Rochester. . . . As to the Council of Churches and the denominations supporting FIGHT, I do not believe the majority of either their ministers or their people are in sympathy with the stand their leaders have taken or the support they have given.[25]

Several other ministers used their pulpits to advocate reason and even some rethinking on the part of the church. However, none took as harsh a stand as Mr. Schaertal. One minister said that many church people were "facing the future with some misgivings" and that "we must find our way back to the true image of the church and lessen the gap between clergy and laity." Another minister commented that "part of the reason why we have this controversy and the strong difference of opinion within the church is that we are in new times and the church is facing new and greater issues for which we have no sharp guidelines from the past." Another minister asked that Kodak and FIGHT "call it a draw," saying that the struggle was "like that between the elephant and the whale, which are different animals living in different environments and moving in different worlds." [26] Some ministers, even had they wanted to, could not support FIGHT because of individual circumstances, such as age, health, or special situations in their churches.[27]

There followed a spate of letters to the newspapers by irate citizens opposing the church's stand on the controversy. Many strongly supported Mr. Schaertal's views. Few, if any, sympathized with the position taken by the Rochester Area Council of Churches. Here is a representative sample of the comments made by some of the readers:

[25] Elmer G. Schaertal, "A Pastor Speaks Up for Kodak," *Rochester Democrat & Chronicle,* January 15, 1967.
[26] "Pastors Refer to FIGHT Case," *Rochester Times-Union,* January 23, 1967.
[27] Martin, "Shepherds vs. Flocks," pp. 55–59.

I commend Pastor Elmer Schaertal for expressing his opinion so clearly in his letter to the D. & C.

In the long run more could be accomplished if everyone were allowed to devote full time and attention to his own problems. Eastman Kodak to the business of manufacturing and selling its products, FIGHT to sending its people to the proper place—the school—for education, the Rochester Area Council to preaching the Gospel.

The local crusading knights of the cloth, johnny-come-latelys in the civil rights bandwagon, cloaked in their spiritual aura of infallibility, are quite ready to order others to place their houses in order according to their views, integratively speaking, but have woeful shortcomings in their own houses of worship.

Every day we read that more and more people believe that religion is becoming less meaningful. Therefore, why don't preachers either return to the pulpit and extol an almighty and just God, or leave the church to campaign for Minister Franklin Florence, Saul Alinsky and other radical dissidents under their own names. Let those disenchanted clergy look about them. Hardly an area in or about Rochester has not benefited from the Eastman Kodak Company. There isn't a major company in the United States with a more liberal and higher standard of employment ethics.[28]

The expression of resentment and dissent also took other forms. The president of the Council of Churches (a Kodak employee) and two directors of its board (one of whom was a Kodak employee) resigned from the council in protest.

Fundamentalist and Evangelical churches kept out of the Kodak–FIGHT controversy, perhaps because of theological conviction. These groups believed the primary function of the church was to prepare individuals for life after death and saw no relationship between socioeconomic and religious issues. The deed of one church specifically prohibited the discussion of social or political issues anywhere on church property. According to William Martin:

Some are simply not aware of what is going on in their city. One insisted that Negroes "are basically a happy, satisfied people who like to work as servants and live in a haphazard way." He doubted many in his church would object if Negroes tried to become members, "but, of course, if too many came, then we'd start a colored work." Another admitted he was not too well informed about FIGHT, but

28 "The Ordeal of the Black Businessman," *Newsweek,* March 4, 1968, p. 34.

he hoped Hoagy Carmichael would not get to be its president. Most, however, are as concerned as their more liberal colleagues but cannot reconcile conflict tactics with their understanding of the gospel. "We feel," one evangelical minister said, "that you will never get rid of slums until you get rid of the slum in men. You have to start with the individual man, and you don't start by teaching him to hate." [29]

THE POSITION OF THE CATHOLIC CHURCH

For the most part, the Catholics (not represented in the Protestant Council of Churches, of course) steered clear of the Kodak–FIGHT dispute. However, on January 3, 1967, when the turmoil in Rochester was at its peak because of Kodak's December 20 repudiation, Bishop Fulton J. Sheen asked the Reverend P. David Finks—a FIGHT sympathizer—to advise him on the problems of the poor by appointing him an episcopal vicor of urban ministry. Finks was a member of FIGHT's advisory council and was on the execitive board of Friends of FIGHT at the time of his appointment. Bishop Sheen admitted that the appointment was "a very unusual step" but said, "I do not follow traditional methods, except in the faith." He also raised the possibility of strong cooperation with other faiths "even to the sharing of houses of worship . . . in poor neighborhoods." According to *The New York Times:*

> Spokesmen for the Roman Catholic diocese declined to say whether the priest's appointment was connected with the current controversy between the Negro group and the Eastman Kodak Company. They commented that the letter naming Father Finks to the post speaks for itself.[30]

Speaking before the city's Chamber of Commerce on January 23, 1967, Bishop Sheen said:

> As the Church had to learn that the world was the stage on which the gospel was preached, so the world has to learn that the inner city is the area where the secular city will find God. Could not all the industries of the secular city begin to give a proportion of their blessing to the inner city—not just "tokens" but something more substantial? The whole world looks at Rochester, . . . but it does not see the city's beauty: it sees the blemish on its face.[31]

[29] Martin, "Shepherds vs. Flocks," pp. 55–59.
[30] "Sheen Appoints a Vicar for Poor," *The New York Times,* January 4, 1967, p. 4.
[31] Schroth, "Self-Doubt and Black Pride," p. 502.

Father Finks expressed his views on FIGHT and his philosophy on religion and church in an address to the Pittsford-Perinton Council on Human Relations:

Those seeking social justice for the have nots of this world should support a viable community organization of minority groups dedicated to bring about the necessary social change. The most viable group here is FIGHT. . . . Christianity is not a mere belief or ritual, but is basically living like Christ did. We will be judged on whether we respond to the urgent call for social justice. . . . Tensions are necessary and can be used creatively in making the democratic process work. . . . Members of the clergy have been chaplains of the establishment too long.[32]

THE PART PLAYED
BY NATIONAL CHURCH ORGANIZATIONS

Florence was quite successful in his appeal to various organizations to withhold their proxies from the management and also to boycott Kodak's products and demonstrate against its plants in all parts of the country. At the Kodak stockholders' meeting in April 1967, seven of the eight dissenting groups, which represented forty thousand of the 80.7 million outstanding shares, were religious organizations. Although the stock represented by these groups was but a small fraction of the total, it would be misleading to measure the impact only in terms of the number of shares. Unlike FIGHT, these organizations were well-established institutions representing a large number of churches. They had access to the public forum which, though not equal to that of business institutions, was quite important. Kodak—or for that matter any other business corporation— could not afford to treat the voice of this group as representing merely one-half of one percent of their stock.[33]

Bishop Dewitt, who represented the Episcopal Church at the annual stockholders' meeting, read a statement prepared by the church's executive council for the press. This statement perhaps sums up the feelings of many other churchmen who were also present at that meeting.

Possession of power conveys the obligation to use that power reasonably. Corporations—and indeed investing churches—must measure

[32] Chuck Boller, "Priest Backs FIGHT," *Rochester Democrat & Chronicle*, February 2, 1967.

[33] For example, the Episcopal Church had 3,340,759 members in 7,547 churches and the United Church of Christ had 2,067,233 members in 6,957 churches. John Kifner, "2 Churches Withhold Proxies to Fight Kodak Rights Policies," *The New York Times*, April 7, 1967, p. 1.

the responsible use of their resources by social as well as financial yardsticks. . . . We stand with Negro communities in their real grievances and their urgent need for organizational power to participate in an open society. And we stand with the management of corporate enterprises which seek to manage their affairs for the well-being of the total community.[34]

FIGHT's request for national demonstrations against Kodak's plants was not enthusiastically received by some of the church organizations. In an editorial entitled "Re: Church Strikes and Boycotts," the *Presbyterian Journal* rejected that church's activities in the area of community organization:

> For those who see the church as an organization existing for the purpose of helping achieve certain needed social, economic and political objectives (in much the same way Kiwanis Clubs work for the betterment of boys generally) these developments are a logical outgrowth of their concern. But for those who still hold to the Scriptural mission of the church, to win men to salvation in the Lord Jesus Christ, these developments must be viewed as radical departures from the assignment given the church by her Lord.[35]

The same editorial reported that the Nashville Presbytery, when asked to support Project Equality, which involved sponsoring official boycotts of businesses that did not practice fair employment, turned it down by a vote of two to one.

FIGHT's popularity waned somewhat among the clergy when Florence escalated his demands to Kodak and threatened to start a nationwide demonstration that summer. The Rochester Area Council of Churches, in its first official criticism of FIGHT, passed a resolution criticizing the organization's intemperance and urging a cancellation of a candlelight demonstration.[36] Church pressure, as well as lack of interest in Florence's planned demonstrations, may well have speeded the "reconciliation" between FIGHT and Kodak on June 23, 1967.

Kodak officials were also not happy with the stand taken by the RACC in the Kodak–FIGHT controversy. During an interview with the author, some Kodak spokesmen expressed the opinion that the RACC's involvement in originally hiring Alinsky kept it from objectively assessing the company's side of the dispute. This bias spread to other churches locally

---

[34] "Church vs. Kodak: The Big Picture," *Episcopalian*, June 1967, pp. 43–44.

[35] "Re: Church Strikes and Boycotts," editorial, *Presbyterian Journal*, March 8, 1967.

[36] Martin, "Shepherds vs. Flocks," pp. 55–59.

and to the communication the RACC had with the National Council of Churches. As evidence of this bias, the Kodak men stated that in only a handful of instances across the country did clergymen attempt to look into the Kodak side of the story. Even when Kodak officials tried to present the facts as they saw them, their efforts were rebuffed by the clergy.[37] Kodak spokesmen gave the impression that the RACC was not only primarily responsible for creating FIGHT and for the resulting tension in the community but also largely instrumental in engaging the National Council of Churches in the conflict and in generating adverse national publicity and reaction against Kodak.

THE RAMIFICATIONS OF CHURCH INVOLVEMENT

Where has the involvement between Kodak and FIGHT left the church? The Rochester Area Council of Churches certainly has not won any kudos for its efforts from any group in the community. In fact, as the Reverend Paul R. Hoover pointed out, "the loudest condemnation of the RACC's actions has come from inner-city citizens of all races." [38] The dissatisfaction of the community's affluent is reflected in the financial problems of the RACC. Referring to the slump in the council's financial support, the *Rochester Democrat & Chronicle* said that it indicated disillusionment with sponsorship of FIGHT and disappointment in an approach to helping blacks based on acrimony and upheaval rather than on goodwill and orderly processes. The newspaper further said that it would be more in keeping with reality "if the Council just admitted a misjudgment and went on from there." [39]

[37] Kenneth Howard of the Industrial Relations Department, Eastman Kodak Company, said in an interview with the author that a "member of the Presbyterian clergy in Missouri was urged to send us a telegram by a clergyman in New Orleans. The clergyman in Missouri called Kodak to hear our side of the story. I had a long talk with him and sent him some information. He never sent the telegram to Kodak.

"The amusing sideline to this is that I am also a graduate of a divinity school. In the middle of this network of communications, we discovered that a former very close friend of mine in the divinity school was sending out his literature to clergymen all over the country. So I called him and said that I had heard he was interested in the Rochester situation and asked him whether he had ever visited Rochester and he said 'yes, oh yes.' So I told him that since I was also involved in this issue from the other side, it might be worthwhile if we got together sometime and talked about it. I pointed out to him that I believed there were certain inaccuracies and half-truths that were being circulated about Kodak and that I was sure he wouldn't want to be a party to them. But he never called me, he never came to see me, he wouldn't send me a copy of what he sent out around the country. This was typical of the whole problem. He wasn't in the least bit interested in knowing the facts."

[38] Paul R. Hoover, "Social Pressures and Church Policy," *Christianity Today,* July 21, 1967, pp. 12–14.

[39] "Council's Defense," *Rochester Democrat & Chronicle,* June 16, 1967.

According to one observer, one of the key factors in the Rochester situation was the presence of a closely knit group of activists in the Board for Urban Ministry who were instrumental in inviting Alinsky and also in attracting like-minded ministers from the local clergy. This group did not share the apprehensions of the local people nor did it identify with their objectives. Those in the group believed themselves to be working for a great cause and had a different and more radical outlook as to what ailed society and how it could be cured. Equally important in their indifference to the local pressures was the fact that their personal advancement and goal achievement depended on satisfying a peer group that was national in character and was not likely to be influenced by the opinions of the Rochester power elite.

Reviewing the situation in Rochester, the Reverend Paul R. Hoover wrote in *Christianity Today:*

The frightening events in Rochester have left behind two tragic consequences: (1) a growing lack of confidence in churches and church leaders, not excluding inner-city ministers whose motivation and actions over the years were hardly open to question; and (2) a growing fear of what the future may hold in view of the reckless threats of members of the FIGHT organization at the Kodak annual meeting in Flemington, New Jersey. . . . Part of the soul-searching on the part of ministers, particularly those working within the city, centers on how long they can physically and mentally stand the pressures that stem from the difference in attitudes and professional experiences between the suburban congregation and the mission-oriented inner-city congregation.[40]

[40] Hoover, "Social Pressures and Church Policy," pp. 12–14.

SELECTED BIBLIOGRAPHY

The following selected bibliography deals with various subject areas covered in the book. The author found these sources interesting and useful in his teaching and research in the field of business and society. The references included in this list were selected because of their philosophical content, theoretical nature, or wide applicability, rather than limited relationship to a specific case study.

ACKERMAN, ROBERT W., "How Companies Respond to Social Demands," *Harvard Business Review,* July–August 1973, pp. 88–98.

ADAM, JOHN, JR., "Put Profit in Its Place," *Harvard Business Review,* March–April 1973, pp. 150–60.

ADELL, B. L., "Labour Law-Collective Agreement—Right of Individual Employee to Sue Employer," *Canadian Bar Review,* 45 (May 1967), 354.

ALBERT, ETHEL M., "Conflict and Change in American Values—A Cultural-Historical Approach," *Ethics,* October, 1963, pp. 19–33.

ALBERTS, DAVID S., and JOHN MARSHALL DAVIS, "Decision-Making Criteria for Environmental Protection and Control." A paper for the 12th American Meeting of the Institute of Management Sciences, Detroit, October 1971.

ALDRIDGE, JOHN W., *In the Country of the Young.* New York: Harper & Row, Publishers, 1970.

ALEXANDER, TOM, "The Big Blowup over Nuclear Blowdowns," *Fortune,* May 1973, p. 216.

————, "The Social Engineers Retreat under Fire," *Fortune,* October 1972, p. 132.

ALLEN, LOUIS L., "Making Capitalism Work in the Ghettos," *Harvard Business Review,* May–June 1969, pp. 83–92.

ALLVINE, FRED C. "Black Business Development," *Journal of Marketing,* 34 (April 1970), 1–7.

AMERICA, RICHARD F., JR., "What Do You People Want?" *Harvard Business Review,* March–April 1969, pp. 103–12.

American Bar Association, *Report of the ABA Commission to Study the Federal Trade Commission.* Chicago, Ill.: 1969.

ANDREWS, KENNETH R., "Can the Best Corporations Be Made Moral?" *Harvard Business Review,* May–June 1973, pp. 57–64.

————, "Application of the Sherman Act to Attempts to Influence Government Action," *Harvard Law Review,* 81 (February 1968), 847–58.

ARENDT, HANNAH, *On Violence.* New York: Harcourt, Brace & World, Inc., 1970.

ARMSTRONG, ROBERT W., "Why Management Won't Talk," *Public Relations Journal,* November 1970, pp. 6–8.

ARON, RAYMOND, "Student Rebellion: Vision of the Future or Echo from the Past," *Political Science Quarterly,* 84 (June 1969), 289–310.

ATHOS, A., "Is the Corporation Next to Fall?" *Harvard Business Review,* January–February 1970, pp. 49–61.

ATLESON, JAMES B., "A Union Member's Right of Free Speech and Assembly: Institutional Interests and Individual Rights," *Minnesota Law Review,* 51 (1967), 403–90.

AUSTIN, ROBERT W., "Responsibility for Social Change," *Harvard Business Review,* July–August 1965, pp. 45–52.

AVNER, C., "Evolution of the Corporation as a Social Institution," *Commercial Law Journal,* 75 (August 1970), 241–47.

BACHRACH, PETER, "Corporate Authority and Democratic Theory," in

Political Theory and Social Change, ed. David Spitz, pp. 257–73. New York: Atherton Press, 1967.

BAHR, HOWARD M., and JACK P. GIBBS, "Racial Differentiation in American Metropolitan Areas," *Social Forces,* 45 (June 1967), 521–32.

BAKER, LEONARD, *The Guaranteed Society.* New York: The Macmillan Company, 1970. Section on SST.

BALDWIN, WILLIAM, "The Motives of Managers, Environmental Restraints, and the Theory of Managerial Enterprise," *Quarterly Journal of Economics,* 78 (May 1964), 238–56.

BARAM, M., "Trade Secrets: What Price Loyalty," *Harvard Business Review,* November–December 1968, pp. 66–74.

BARBER, R. J., *The American Corporation.* New York: E. P. Dutton & Co., Inc., 1970.

BAUER, RAYMOND A., ed., *Social Indicators.* Cambridge: The M.I.T. Press, 1966.

BAUER, RAYMOND A., and DAN H. FENN, "What *Is* a Corporate Social Audit?" *Harvard Business Review,* January–February 1973.

BAUER, RAYMOND A., and STEPHEN E. GREYSER, "The Dialogue That Never Happens," *Harvard Business Review,* November–December 1967.

BAUER, RAYMOND A., ITHIEL POOLE, and LEWIS DEXTER, *American Business and Public Policy.* New York: Atherton Press, 1963.

BEAM, FLOYD A., and PAUL E. FERTIG, "Pollution Control through Social Cost Conversion," in *The Accounting Sampler,* ed. Thomas J. Burns and Harvey S. Hendrickson. New York: McGraw-Hill, 1972.

BEARDWOOD, ROGER, "The Southern Roots of the Urban Crisis," *Fortune,* August 1968, p. 84.

BELL, DANIEL, *The Coming of Post-Industrial Society.* New York: Basic Books, Inc., Publishers, 1973.

———, "The Corporation and Society in the 1970's," *Public Interest,* Summer 1971, pp. 5–32.

BERGER, FRED R., " 'Law and Order' and Civil Disobedience," *Inquiry,* 13, No. 3 (1970), 254–73.

BERLE, ADOLF, "Second Edition/Corporate Power," *Center Magazine,* January 1969, pp. 76–84.

———, *The Three Faces of Power.* New York: Harcourt, Brace & World, Inc., 1967.

BERMEN, JEFFREY A., "The Birth of a Black Business," *Harvard Business Review,* September–October 1970, pp. 4–6ff.

BERNSTEIN, MARVER, *Regulating Business by Independent Commission.* Princeton, N.J.: Princeton University Press, 1955.

BIRCH, DAVID L., *The Businessman and the City.* Boston: Harvard Graduate School of Business Administration, 1967.

BLADES, LAWRENCE E., "Employment at Will vs. Individual Freedom: On Limiting the Abusive Exercise of Employer Power," *Columbia Law Review,* 67, No. 140 (1967), 1404–35.

BLAUNER, ROBERT, *Alienation and Freedom.* Chicago: University of Chicago Press, 1964.

BLUMBERG, PHILLIP I., "Corporate Responsibility and the Employee's Duty of Loyalty and Obedience: A Preliminary Inquiry," *Oklahoma Law Review,* August 1971, pp. 270–318.

———, "Corporate Responsibility and the Social Crisis," *Boston University Law Review,* 50, No. 2 (Spring 1970), 157–210.

———, "The Politicalization of the Corporation," *Business Lawyer,* July 1971, pp. 1551–87.

———, "Selected Materials on Corporate Social Responsibility," *Business Lawyer,* July 1972, pp. 1275–99.

BONAPARTE, T. H., "Influence of Culture on Business in a Pluralistic Society," *American Journal of Economics and Society,* 28, No. 3 (July 1969), 285–300.

BORK, ROBERT H., "The Supreme Court vs. Corporate Efficiency," *Fortune,* August 1967, pp. 92–93ff.

BOROD, R. S., "Lobbying for the Public Interest—Federal Tax Policy and Administration," *New York University Law Review,* 42 (December 1967), 1087–117.

BOWERMAN, FRANK R., "Managing Solid Waste Disposal," *California Management Review,* 14, No. 3 (Spring 1972), 104–6.

BRADLEY, GENE E., "What Businessmen Need to Know about the Student Left," *Harvard Business Review,* September–October 1968, pp. 49–60.

BRADT, WILLIAM R., *Organizing for Effective Public Affairs,* Public Affairs Study No. 5. New York: The Conference Board, 1969.

BRADY, ROBERT A., *Business as a System of Power.* New York: Columbia University Press, 1951.

BRAUER, J. C., "The Student Revolution Today," *Dialogue,* 6, No. 2 (1967), 131–41.

BRAYMAN, HAROLD, *Corporate Management in a World of Politics.* New York: McGraw-Hill Book Company, 1967.

BREMER, OTTO A., "Is Business the Source of New Social Values?" *Harvard Business Review,* November–December 1971, pp. 121–26.

BRIMMER, ANDREW F., "The Negro in the National Economy," in *The American Negro Reference Book,* ed. John P. Davis, Chap. 5. Englewood Cliffs, N.J.: Prentice-Hall, Inc., 1966.

BRONOWSKI, J., *Science and Human Values.* New York: Harper & Row Publishers, 1965.

BROWER, MICHAEL, and DOYLE LITTLE, "White Help for Black Business," *Harvard Business Review,* May–June 1970, pp. 4–6ff.

BROWN, CLAUDE, *Manchild in the Promised Land.* New York: The Macmillan Company, 1967.

BROZEN, Y., "Rule by Markets and Rule by Men," *Freeman,* September 1967, pp. 515–27.

BRUFF, HAROLD H., "Unconstitutional Conditions upon Public Employment: New Departures in the Protection of First Amendment," *Hastings Law Journal,* 21 (November 1969), 129–73.

BUCHANAN, JAMES M., "Student Revolts, Academic Liberalism, and Constitutional Attitudes," *Social Research,* 35, No. 4 (Winter 1968), 666–80.

BUCKLEY, DONALD H., "Political Rights of Government Employees," *Cleveland State Law Review,* 19 (September 1970), 568–78.

BUNKE, HARVEY, "Negro Must Be Full Partner in Market," *Business and Society,* 5, No. 2 (Spring 1965), 3–9.

———, "Priests without Cassocks," *Harvard Business Review,* May–June 1965, 103–9.

BURCK, GILBERT, "The Hazards of 'Corporate Responsibility,'" *Fortune,* June 1973, pp. 114ff.

BUSKIRK, RICHARD H., and JAMES T. ROLFE, "Consumerism—An Interpretation," *Journal of Marketing,* 34 (October 1970), 61–65.

CAIN, STANLEY A., "Environment—An All-Encompassing Phenomenon." Remarks at the 12th American Meeting of the Institute of Management Sciences, Detroit, October 2, 1971.

CALLAHAN, DANIEL, "The Quest for Social Relevance," *Daedalus,* 96, No. 1 (Winter 1967), 151–79.

CAMPBELL, ANGUS, *White Attitudes toward Black People.* Ann Arbor: Institute for Social Research, 1971.

CANNON, JAMES, and JEAN HALLORAN, "Steel and the Environment: A Long Way to Go," *Business and Society Review/Innovation,* Winter 1972–73, pp. 56–61.

————, "Capitalism Today," *Public Interest,* Fall 1970. Special issue.

CARR, ALBERT Z., "Can an Executive Afford a Conscience?" *Harvard Business Review,* July–August 1970, pp. 58–64.

————,"Is Business Bluffing Ethical?" *Harvard Business Review,* January–February 1968, pp. 143–53.

CARY, WILLIAM L., *Politics and the Regulatory Agencies.* New York: McGraw-Hill Book Company, 1967.

CASSELL, ERIC L., "The Health Effects of Air Pollution and Their Implications for Control," *Law and Contemporary Problems,* 33, No. 2 (Spring 1968), 197–216.

CATER, DOUGLASS, *Power in Washington: A Critical Look at Today's Struggle to Govern in the Nation's Capital.* New York: Random House, Inc., 1964.

CERVANTES, ALFONSO T., "To Prevent a Chain of Super-Watts," *Harvard Business Review,* September–October 1967, pp. 55–65.

CHAMBERLAIN, NEIL W., *Business and Environment: The Firm in Time and Place.* New York: McGraw-Hill Book Company, 1968.

CHASS, ROBERT L., "Air Pollution Control: The Case of Los Angeles County," *California Management Review,* 14, No. 3 (Spring 1972), 92–103.

CHATHAM, GEORGE N., and FRANKLIN P. HUDDLE, *The Supersonic Transport,* pp. 71–78. Washington, D.C.: Library of Congress, February 26, 1971.

CHEIT, EARL F., ed., *The Business Establishment.* New York: John Wiley & Sons, Inc., 1964.

CHERINGTON, PAUL W., and RALPH L. GILLEN, "The Company Representative in Washington," *Harvard Business Review,* May–June 1961, pp. 109–15.

CHURCHMAN, C. WEST, *Challenge to Reason.* New York: McGraw-Hill Book Company, 1968.

————, *The Systems Approach.* New York: Dell Publishing Co., 1968.

"Cigarette Advertising: Deceptive and Against the Public Interest," *Kansas Law Review,* 17 (June 1969), 684.

CLOWARD, RICHARD A. and FRANCES FOX PIVEN, "Corporate Imperialism for the Poor," *Nation,* October 16, 1967, pp. 365–67.

COHEN, DOROTHY, "The Federal Trade Commission and the Regulation of Advertising in the Consumer Interest," *Journal of Marketing,* 33 (January 1969), 40–44.

COHEN, OSCAR, "The Responsibility of American Business," in *The Negro*

Challenge to the Business Community, ed. Eli Ginzberg, pp. 100–103. New York: McGraw-Hill Book Company, 1964.

COHN, JULES, "Is Business Meeting the Challenge of Urban Affairs?" *Harvard Business Review,* March–April 1970, pp. 68–82.

COLITT, LESLIE R., "The Mask of Objectivity," *Nation,* June 17, 1968, pp. 789–91.

Committee for Economic Development, *Budgeting for National Objectives.* New York: Committee for Economic Development, 1966.

Committee for Economic Development, *Social Responsibilities of Business Corporations.* New York: Committee for Economic Development, June 1971.

The Conference Board, *Business Amid Urban Crisis: Private-Sector Approaches to City Problems,* Studies in Public Affairs, No. 3. New York: The Conference Board, Inc., 1968.

The Conference Board, *Corporate Organization for Pollution Control.* New York: The Conference Board, Inc., 1970.

The Conference Board, *Organizing for Effective Public Affairs: How Companies Structure the Corporate Unit,* Studies in Public Affairs, No. 5. New York: The Conference Board, Inc., 1969.

"Constitutional Law—Freedom of Speech—Statute Prohibiting Political Activity by Public Employees Held Unconstitutional for Overbreadth," *New York University Law Review,* 42 (October 1967), 750–55.

"Constitutional Law—Public Employees—'Freedom of Association' Guarantees the Right to Unionize but Not the Right to Bargain Collectively," *Tulane Law Review,* 44 (April 1970), 568–75.

COOPER, G., "Tax Treatment of Business Grassroots Lobbying; Defining and Attaining the Public Policy Objectives," *Columbia Law Review,* 68 (May 1968), 801–59.

R. COPPOCK, M. DIERKES, H. SNOWBALL, and J. THOMAS, "Social Pressure and Business Actions." A paper presented to the Seminar on Corporate Social Accounts, Battelle Seattle Research Center, November 10–11, 1972.

"Corporate Assaults on the Privacy of Outside Critics," *Georgetown Law Journal,* 59 (1970), 190–208.

"Corporations—Liability of Employees—Corporations May Seek Indemnity for Civil or for Criminal Liability Incurred by Employee's Violation of Antitrust Law without Corporation's Knowledge or Consent," *Harvard Law Review,* 83 (February 1970), 943–50.

CORSON, JOHN J., "More Government in Business," *Harvard Business Review,* May–June 1961, pp. 81–88.

Council on Economic Priorities, "Minding the Corporate Conscience 1973," *Economic Priorities Report,* January–February–March 1973.

Council on Economic Priorities, "Minding the Corporate Conscience: The 1972 Movement for Corporate Responsibility," *Economic Priorities Report,* March–April 1972.

Council on Economic Priorities, "Paper Profits: Pollution Audit 1972," *Economic Priorities Report,* July–August 1971.

COX, EDWARD F., ROBERT C. FELLMETH, and JOHN E. SCHULZ, *The Nader Report on the FTC.* New York: Richard W. Baron Publishing Co., 1969.

COX, HARVEY G., "The 'New Breed' in American Churches: Sources of Social Activism in American Religion," *Daedalus,* Winter 1967, pp. 135–50.

CRAMER, JOE J., *"Acceptance* of Social Responsibility and *Delivery* by Business." A paper presented at the American Association of Collegiate Schools of Business Assembly, May 5, 1972.

CRANDALL, ROBERT W., "FCC Regulation, Monopsony, and Network Television Program Costs," *The Bell Journal of Economics and Management Science,* Autumn 1972, pp. 483–508.

CRAVENS, DAVID W., and GERALD E. HILLS, "Consumerism: A Perspective for Business," *Business Horizons,* 13 (August 1970), 21–28.

CREECH, W. A., "Privacy of Public Employees," *Law and Contemporary Problems,* 31, No. 2 (Spring 1966), 413–35.

CROSS, THEODORE L., *Black Capitalism.* New York: Atheneum Publishers, 1969.

DAHL, R., "Alternative Ways of Controlling Corporate Power." Address given at the Nader Conference on Corporate Accountability, 1971.

DALE, ERNEST, "The Social and Moral Responsibilities of the Executive in the Large Corporation," *American Economic Association,* May 1961, pp. 540–63.

DANIEL, CALDWELL, III. "The Regulation of Private Enterprises as Public Utilities," *Social Research,* 34, No. 2 (Summer 1967), 347–54.

DAVIES, J. CLARENCE, III, *The Politics of Pollution.* New York: Pegasus, 1971.

DAVIS, JOHN P., ed., *The American Negro Reference Book.* Englewood Cliffs, N.J.: Prentice-Hall, Inc., 1966.

DAVIS, KEITH, "Understanding the Social Responsibility Puzzle," *Business Horizons,* 10, No. 4 (Winter 1967), 45–50.

DAY, GEORGE S., and DAVID A. AAKER, "A Guide to Consumerism," *Journal of Marketing,* 34 (July 1970), 12–19.

DEMERATH, N. J., III, and RICHARD A. PETERSON, eds., *System, Change and Conflict.* New York: The Free Press, 1967.

DIRECTOR, STEVEN, and SAMUEL DOCTORS, "Do Business School Students Really Care about Social Responsibility?" *Business and Society Review/Innovation,* Spring 1973, pp. 91–95.

"Discharge from Private Employment on Ground of Political Views or Conduct," *American Law Reports, Annotated,* 51 (1957) ALR 2d, 742–62.

"Dismissals of Public Employees for Petitioning Congress: Administrative Discipline and 5 U.S.C. Section 652 (d)," *Yale Law Journal,* 74 (May 1965), 1156.

"Dissenter and Government," *Journal of Urban Law,* 47, No. 2 (1969–70), 475–89.

DIXON, DONALD F., and DANIEL F. MCLAUGHLIN, Jr., "Do the Poor Really Pay More for Food?" *Business and Society,* 9, No. 1 (Autumn 1968), 7–12.

DOMHOFF, G. WILLIAM, *Who Rules America?* Englewood Cliffs, N.J.: Prentice-Hall, Inc. 1967.

DOMM, DONALD R., and JAMES E. STAFFORD, "Assimilating Blacks into the Organization," *California Management Review,* 15, No. 1 (Fall 1972), 46–51.

DOUGLAS, WILLIAM O., *Points of Rebellion.* New York: Random House, Inc., 1970.

DOWNS, ANTHONY, "Alternative Futures for the American Ghetto," *Daedalus,* 94, No. 4 (Fall 1965), 1331–78.

———, "Up and Down with Ecology—the 'Issue-Attention Cycle,'" *Public Interest,* Summer 1972, pp. 38–50.

DOWNS, ANTHONY, and R. JOSEPH MONSEN, "Public Goods and Private Status," *Public Interest,* Spring 1971, pp. 64–77.

DOWNS, ANTHONY, et al., *The Political Economy of Environmental Control.* Berkeley, Calif.: Institute of Business and Economic Research, University of California, 1972.

DRAKE, C. D. "Wage-slave or Entrepreneur," *Modern Law Review,* 31 (July 1968), 408–23.

DRAKE, ST. CLAIR, "The Social and Economic Status of the Negro in the United States," *Daedalus,* 94, No. 4 (Fall 1965), 771–814.

DROTNING, PHILIP, "Why Nobody Takes Corporate Social Responsibility

Seriously," *Business and Society Review,* Autumn 1972, pp. 68–72.

DRUCKER, PETER F., *The Age of Discontinuity.* New York: Harper & Row, Publishers, 1969.

———, "The New Markets and the New Capitalism," *Public Interest,* Fall 1970, 44–79.

———, "The Sickness of Government," *Public Interest,* Winter 1969, 3–23.

———, *Technology, Management and Society.* New York: Harper & Row, Publishers, 1970.

DUPRE, T. STEFAN, and W. ERIC GUSTAFSON, "Contracting for Defense: Private Firms and the Public Interest," *Political Science Quarterly,* 57 (June 1962), 161–77.

EHRLICH, PAUL R., ANNE H. EHRLICH, and JOHN P. HOLDREN, *Human Ecology: Problems and Solutions.* San Francisco: W. H. Freeman & Co., Publishers, 1973.

EISENBERG, MELVIN ARON, "The Legal Roles of Shareholder and Management in Modern Corporate Decision-Making," *California Law Review,* 57, No. 1 (January 1969), 1–60.

"Emerging Law of Students' Rights," *Arkansas Law Review,* 23, No. 4 (Winter 1970), 619–33.

EPSTEIN, EDWIN M., *The Corporation in American Politics.* Englewood Cliffs, N.J.: Prentice-Hall, Inc., 1969.

———, *Corporations, Contributions, and Political Campaigns: Federal Regulation in Perspective.* Berkeley: Institute of Governmental Studies, May 1968.

———, "The Historical Enigma of Corporate Legitimacy," *California Law Review,* 60, No. 6 (November 1972), 1701–17.

ESPOSITO, JOHN C., *Vanishing Air, The Nader Report.* New York: Grossman Publishers, 1970.

"Extrajudicial Consumer Pressure: An Effective Impediment to Unethical Business Practices," *Duke Law Journal,* October 1969, p. 1011.

"The Fallout from the I.T.T. Affair," editorial, *Fortune,* May 1972, p. 151.

FALTERMAYER, EDMUND K., "The Energy 'Joyride' Is Over," *Fortune,* September 1972, p. 99.

———, "More Dollars and More Diplomas," *Fortune,* January 1968, pp. 140ff.

———, "We Can Afford Clean Air," *Fortune,* May 1972, pp. 159–63.

FELLMETH, ROBERT, *The Interstate Commerce Omission.* New York: Grossman Publishers, 1970.

FENN, DAN H., JR., "The Case of Latent Lobby," *Harvard Business Review,* January–February 1967, pp. 22–29.

————, "Executives as Community Volunteers," *Harvard Business Review,* March–April 1971, pp. 4–16, 156–57.

FICHTER, JOSEPH H., "American Religion and the Negro," *Daedalus,* Fall 1965, pp. 1085–106.

FINLEY, GRACE J., *Mayors Evaluate Business Action on Urban Problems.* New York: The Conference Board, 1968.

FINN, DAVID, *The Corporate Oligarch.* New York: Simon and Schuster, Inc., 1969.

"The First Amendment and Public Employees," *Georgetown Law Journal,* 57 (1968), 134–61.

FLEISCHER, ARTHUR, JR., "Corporate Disclosure/Insider Trading," *Harvard Business Review,* January–February 1967, pp. 129–35.

FLETCHER, ARTHUR, "Whatever Happened to the Philadelphia Plan?" *Business and Society Review/Innovation,* Spring 1973, pp. 24–28.

FLOWER, BARBARA J., *Business Amid Urban Crisis,* Public Affairs Study No. 3. New York: The Conference Board, 1968.

FOGELSON, ROBERT M., "From Resentment to Confrontation: The Police, the Negroes, and the Outbreak of the Nineteen-Sixties Riots," *Political Science Quarterly,* 83 (June 1968), 217–47.

————, "White on Black: A Critique of the McCone Commission Report on the Los Angeles Riots," *Political Science Quarterly,* 83 (September 1968), 337–67.

FOLEY, EUGENE P., "The Negro Businessman: In Search of a Tradition," *Daedalus,* Winter 1966, pp. 107–44.

FRANKLIN, RAYMOND S., "The Political Economy of Black Power," *Social Problems,* 16, No. 3 (Winter 1969), 286–301.

FREEMAN, A. MYRICK, III, and ROBERT H. HAVEMAN, "Clean Rhetoric and Dirty Water," *Public Interest,* Summer 1972, pp. 51–65.

FRIEDMAN, MILTON, *Capitalism and Freedom.* Chicago: University of Chicago Press, 1962.

FRIEDMANN, WOLFGANG G., "Corporate Power, Government by Private Groups, and the Law," *Columbia Law Review,* 57 (February 1957), 155–86.

GASSLER, LEE S., "How Companies Are Helping the Undereducated Worker," *Personnel,* July–August 1967, pp. 47–55.

GINZBERG, ELI, ed., *The Negro Challenge to the Business Community.* New York: McGraw-Hill Book Company, 1964.

GOLDMAN, MARSHALL, ed., *Controlling Pollution. The Economics of a Cleaner America.* Englewood Cliffs, N.J.: Pentice-Hall, Inc., 1967.

———, *Ecology and Economics.* Englewood Cliffs, N.J.: Prentice-Hall, Inc., 1972.

GOODE, KENNETH G., "Query: Can the Afro-American Be an Effective Executive," *California Management Review,* 13, No. 1 (Fall 1970), 22–26.

GOULD, JOHN W., NORMAN B. SIGBAND, and CYRIL E. ZOERNER, JR., "Black Consumer Reactions to 'Integrated Advertising': An Exploratory Study," *Journal of Marketing,* 34 (July 1970), 20–26.

GRAHAM, GENE S., "History in the (Deliberate) Making: A Challenge to Modern Journalism," *Nieman Reports,* September 1966, pp. 3–7.

———, "The Responsibilities of the Doubly Damned," *Quill,* February 1968, pp. 8–12.

GREEN, MARK J., BEVERLEY C. MOORE, JR., and BRUCE WASSERSTEIN. *The Closed Enterprise System.* New York: Grossman Publishers, 1972.

GRETHER, E. T., "Business Responsibility toward the Market," *California Management Review,* 12, No. 1 (Fall 1969), 33–42.

GRETHER, E. T., and ROBERT J. HOLLOWAY, "Impact of Government upon the Market System," *Journal of Marketing,* 31 (April 1967), 1–5.

GRIER, GEORGE C., "The Negro Ghettos and Federal Housing Policy," *Law and Contemporary Problems,* 32 No. 3 (Summer 1967), 550–60.

GROSS, BERTRAM M., ed., "Social Goals and Indicators for American Society," *Annals of the American Academy of Political and Social Sciences,* 371 (May 1967). Entire issue.

GROSS, EDWIN J., "Needed: Consumer Ombudsmen," *Business and Society,* 9, No. 1 (Autumn 1968), 22–27.

HAIRE, MASON, "The Concept of Power and the Concept of Man," in *Social Science Approaches to Business Behaviors,* ed. George B. Strother. Homewood, Ill.: Dorsey Press, 1962.

HAMILTON, JAMES L., "The Demand for Cigarettes: Advertising, the Health Scare, and the Cigarette Advertising Ban," *Review of Economics and Statistics,* November 1972, pp. 401–11.

HANDLIN, OSCAR, *Race and Nationality in American Life.* Boston: Little Brown and Company, 1957.

HANRAHAN, GEORGE D., "Why Social Programs Fail," *Economic and Business Bulletin,* Spring–Summer 1972, pp. 51–59.

HARL, N. E., "Selected Aspects of Employee Status in Small Corporations," *Kansas Law Review,* 13 (October 1964), 23–58.

HARRINGTON, MICHAEL, *The Other America.* New York: The Macmillan Company, 1962.

———, "The Other America Revisited," *Center Magazine,* January 1969, pp. 36–42.

———, "The Urgent Case for Social Investment," *Saturday Review,* November 23, 1968, pp. 32–38.

HARWOOD, EDWIN, "Youth Unemployment—A Tale of Two Ghettos," *Public Interest,* Fall 1969, pp. 78–87.

HAYDEN, KARL, "The Business Corporation as a Creator of Values," in *Human Values and Economic Policy,* ed. Sidney Hook. New York: New York University Press, 1967.

HAYNES, ROBERT, "The Environmental Scene: Just How Bad Is the View?" *Business and Society Review/Innovation,* Winter 1972–73, pp. 73–80.

HAZARD, LELAND, "Business Must Put Up," *Harvard Business Review,* January–February 1968, pp. 2–13.

HEILBRONER, ROBERT L., *The Future of Capitalism.* New York: The Macmillan Company, 1967.

———, "On the Limited 'Relevance' of Economics," *Public Interest,* Fall 1970, 80–93.

———, "Rhetoric and Reality in the Struggle between Business and the State," *Social Research,* 35, No. 3 (Autumn 1968), 401–425.

———, ed., *Economic Means and Social Ends: Essays in Political Economics.* Englewood Cliffs, N.J.: Prentice-Hall, Inc., 1969.

HENDERSON, HAZEL, "Ecologists versus Economists," *Harvard Business Review,* July–August 1973, pp. 28–40.

———, "Should Business Tackle Society's Problems?" *Harvard Business Review,* July–August 1968, pp. 77–85.

HENNER, SIONAG M., "California's Controls on Employer Abuse of Employee Political Rights," *Stanford Law Review,* 22 (May 1970), 1015–58.

HERFINDAHL, ORRIS C., and ALLEN V. KNEESE, *Quality of the Environment: An Economic Approach to Some Problems in Using Land, Water, and Air.* Washington, D.C.: Resources for the Future, Inc., 1965.

HERRMANN, ROBERT O., "Consumerism: Its Goals, Organizations and Future," *Journal of Marketing,* 34 (October 1970), 55–60.

HICKEL, WALTER J., *Who Owns America?* Englewood Cliffs, N.J.: Prentice-Hall, Inc., 1971.

HILL, F. G., "Veblen, Berle and the Modern Corporation," *American Journal of Economics,* 26 (July 1967), 279–95.

HILLS, GERALD E., and DAVID W. CRAVENS, "A Conceptual Approach for Analyzing Environmental Systems," March 27, 1972. Portions presented at XIX International Meeting, Institute for Management Sciences, Houston, Texas, April 5, 1972.

HILTON, GEORGE W., "Federal Participation in the Supersonic Transport Program," *Business Horizons,* 10, No. 2 (Summer 1967), 21–26.

HOBBING, ENNO, "Business Must Explain Itself," *Business and Society Review,* Autumn 1972, pp. 85–86.

HODGSON, JAMES, and MARSHALL H. BRENNER, "Successful Experience: Training Hard-Core Unemployed," *Harvard Business Review,* September–October 1968, pp. 148–56.

HOLTON, RICHARD H., "Business and Government," *Daedalus,* Winter 1969, pp. 41–59.

HOOK, SYDNEY, ed., *Human Values and Economic Policy.* New York: New York University Press, 1967.

House Committee on Appropriations, *Department of Transportation and Related Agencies Appropriations for 1970: Hearings before Subcommittee,* 91st Cong., 1st sess., Part III, pp. 216–348. Washington, D.C.: Government Printing Office, 1969.

House Committee on Banking and Currency, Subcommittee on Domestic Finances, *Commercial Banks and Their Trust Activities: Emerging Influence on the American Economy,* Staff Report, 90th Cong., 1st sess. Washington, D.C.: Government Printing Office, 1968.

House Committee on Science and Astronautics, *Technology: Processes of Assessment and Choice,* Report of the National Academy of Sciences. Washington, D.C.: Government Printing Office, July 1969.

HUGHES, EMMET JOHN, "The Negro's New Economic Life," *Fortune,* September 1956, pp. 254ff.

HUTCHINSON, G. SCOTT, "Reactions to the Latent Lobby," *Harvard Business Review,* July–August 1967, 166–68.

INGRAM, TIMOTHY, "On Muckrakers and Whistle Blowers," *Business and Society Review,* Autumn 1972, pp. 21–30.

"Is Black Capitalism the Answer?" *Business Week,* August 3, 1968, p. 60.

"Is Business Meeting the Challenge of Urban Affairs?" *Harvard Business Review,* March–April 1970, p. 68.

"Is the Press Biased?" *Newsweek,* September 16, 1968, pp. 66–67.

JACOBY, NEIL H., "The Conglomerate Corporation," *Center Magazine,* July 1969, pp. 40–53.

————, *Corporate Power and Responsibility.* New York: The Macmillan Company, 1973.

————, "Organization for Environmental Management—National and Transnational," *Management Science,* June 1973, pp. 1138–50.

JANGER, ALLEN R., and RUTH G. SHAEFFER, *Managing Programs for the Disadvantaged.* New York: Conference Board, 1970.

JENNINGS, RICHARD W., "The Role of the States in Corporation Regulation and Investor Protection," *Law and Contemporary Problems,* 23, No. 2 (Spring 1958).

JENNINGS, EUGENE EMERSON, *The Executive in Crisis.* New York: Mc-Graw-Hill Book Company, 1965.

JENSEN, W., Jr., "Public Officials: Fair Game for Fair Comment?" *American Business Law Journal,* 3, No. 3 (Winter 1965), 267–86.

JESSUP, JOHN K., and IRVING KRISTOL, "On 'Capitalism' and the 'Free Society,'" *Public Interest,* Winter 1971, pp. 101–5.

JOHNSON, GRACE, "Corporate Philanthropy: An Analysis of Corporate Contributions," *Journal of Business,* 39 (October 1966), 489–504.

JOHNSON, HAROLD L., "Socially Responsible Firms: An Empty Box or a Universal Set?" *Journal of Business,* 39 (July 1966), 394–99.

JORDAN, G. I., "Three Models of Political and Social Change," *Administrative Law Review,* 22 (June 1970), 529–78.

KAIN, JOHN H., and JOSEPH J. PERSKY, "Alternative to Guilded Ghetto," *Public Interest,* Winter 1969, pp. 74–87.

KANGUN, NORMAN, "Environmental Problems and Marketing: Saint or Sinner?" Prepared for presentation and discussion at the National Conference on Social Marketing, University of Illinois, Champaign-Urbana, December 2–5, 1972, p. 31.

KARIEL, H., "The Corporation and the Public Interest," *The Annals of the American Academy,* 343 (September 1962), 39–47.

KATY, WILBUR G., and HAROLD P. SOUTHERLAND, "Religious Pluralism and the Supreme Court," *Daedalus,* Winter 1967, pp. 180–92.

KATZ, W. G., "Responsibility and the Modern Corporation," *Journal of Law and Economics,* 3 (October 1969), 75–85.

KAYSEN, CARL, "Another View of Corporate Capitalism," *Quarterly Journal of Economics,* February 1965, pp. 41–51.

KEEZER, DEXTER M., "The Score against Capitalism," *Harvard Business Review,* September–October 1968, pp. 158–75.

KEFALAS, ASTERIOS G., "The Management of Environmental Information: A Machine for Adapting a System to Its Environment." Presented at the 12th American Meeting of The Institute for Management Science, Detroit, September 29–October 2, 1971.

KELLY, FRANK K., "Second Edition/Who Owns the Air," *Center Magazine,* March–April 1970, pp. 27–33.

KEMPIN, FREDERICK G., JR., "The Public Interest in the Corporation," *Dickinson Law Review,* 64 (1960), 357–81.

KENISTON, KENNETH, "Social Change and Youth in America," *Daedalus,* Winter 1962, pp. 145–71.

KERNER COMMISSION, *Report of the National Advisory Commission on Civil Disorders.* New York: Bantam Books, Inc. 1968.

KEY, V. O., JR., *Politics, Parties and Pressure Groups* (5th ed.). New York: Thomas Y. Crowell Company, 1967.

KNEESE, ALLEN V., "Management Science, Economics and Environmental Science," *Management Science,* June 1973, pp. 1122–37.

———, "Protecting Our Environment and Natural Resources in the 1970's." Testimony before the Subcommittee on Conservation and Natural Resources, Committee on Government Operations, U.S. House of Representatives, February 6, 1970.

———, "Why Water Pollution Is Economically Unavoidable," *Transaction,* April 1968, pp. 31–36.

KOHLMEIER, LOUIS M., JR., *The Regulators.* New York: Harper & Row, Publishers, 1970.

KRAFT, ERWIN O., "The Political Role of Bankers." A research project presented at the meeting of the Research Committee of the Financial Public Relations Association.

KREPS, THEODORE J., "Measurement of the Social Performance of Business," *Annals of the American Academy of Political and Social Sciences,* 343 (September 1962), 20–31.

KRISTOL, IRVING, " 'When Virtue Loses All Her Loveliness'—Some Reflections on Capitalism and 'The Free Society,' " *Public Interest,* Fall 1970, 3–15.

"Labor Law: Duty of Employer to Arbitrate with Union Representing Employees of Purchased Company," *Columbia Law Review,* 66 (May 1966), 967–73.

LAMONT, CORLISS, *Freedom of Choice Reaffirmed.* Boston: Beacon Press, 1970.

LARSON, JOHN A., ed., *The Regulated Businessman: Business and Government.* New York: Holt, Rinehart & Winston, Inc., 1966.

LAVE, LESTER B., "Safety in Transportation: The Role of Government," *Law and Contemporary Problems,* 33, No. 3 (Summer 1968), 512–35.

LAWSON, R., "Blame and Contractual Liability," *Northern Ireland Legal Quarterly,* 20 (March 1969), 43.

LAZARUS, SIMON, "Halfway up from Liberalism: A Critical Look at the Regulatory State as a Response to Corporate Power." Address given at the Nader Conference on Corporate Accountability, 1971.

LEAVITT, HAROLD, "The Corporation President Is a Berkeley Student," *Harvard Business Review,* November–December 1967.

LEONARD, RICHARD, "Role of the Press in the Urban Crisis," *Quill,* May 1968, pp. 8–11.

LESSING, LAWRENCE, "The Revolt against the Internal Combustion Engine," *Fortune,* July 1967, 78–83.

LEVITT, THEODORE, "The Johnson Treatment," *Harvard Business Review,* January–February 1967, pp. 114–28.

LEWIN, KURT, *Resolving Social Conflicts.* New York: Harper & Row, Publishers, 1948.

LIEBHAFSKY, H. H. *American Government and Business.* New York: John Wiley & Sons, Inc., 1971.

LINDBLOM, CHARLES E., "The Rediscovery of the Market," *Public Interest,* Summer 1966, pp. 89–101.

LINOWES, DAVID, "Let's Get on with the Social Audit: A Specific Proposal," *Business and Society Review/Innovation,* Winter 1972–73, pp. 39–49.

LIPSET, SEYMOUR, "Students and Politics in Comparative Perspective," *Daedalus,* Winter 1968, 1–20.

LOOMIS, CAROL J., "Harold Geneen's Moneymaking Machine Is Still Humming," *Fortune,* September 1972, p. 88.

LUNDBORG, LOUIS B. (Chairman of the Board, Bank of America NT&SA). Testimony before the Senate Committee on Foreign Relations, Washington D.C., April 15, 1970.

LYFORD, JOSEPH P., "Business and the Negro Community," in *The Negro Challenge to the Business Community,* ed. Eli Ginzberg, pp. 96–100. New York: McGraw-Hill Book Company, 1964.

MCCALL, DAVID B., "Profit: Spur for Solving Social Ills," *Harvard Business Review,* May–June 1973, pp. 46–56.

MCCONNELL, GRANT, *Private Power and American Democracy.* New York: Alfred A. Knopf, Inc., 1966.

———, "The Spirit of Private Government," *American Political Science Review,* September 1968, pp. 754–70.

MCDONALD, D., "The Church and Society," *Center Magazine,* July 1968, pp. 28–35.

MCDONALD, JOHN, "Oil and the Environment: The Views from Maine," *Fortune,* April 1971, p. 84.

MCELRATH, DENNIS C., "Urban Differentiation: Problems and Prospects," *Law and Contemporary Problems,* 30 (Winter 1965), 103–10.

MCFARLANE, ALEXANDER N., "Leaping the Ghetto Gap," *Vital Speeches,* December 15, 1968, pp. 157–60.

MCGAFFIN, WILLIAM, and ERWIN KNOLL, *Scandal in the Pentagon.* New York: Fawcett, 1970.

MACIVER, ROBERT M., *Politics and Society.* New York: Atherton Press, 1969.

MACK, RAYMOND W., "Riot, Revolt or Responsible Revolution or Reference Groups and Racism," *Sociological Quarterly,* 10, No. 2 (Spring 1969), 147–56.

MCKEE, JACK EDWARD, "Water Pollution Control: A Task for Technology," *California Management Review,* 14, No. 3 (Spring 1972), 88–91.

MCKERSIE, ROBERT B., "Vitalize Black Enterprise," *Harvard Business Review,* September–October 1968, pp. 88–99.

MCKIE, JAMES W. "Regulation and the Free Market: The Problem of Boundaries," *The Bell Journal of Economics and Management Science,* Spring 1970, pp. 6–26.

"Making Capitalism Work in the Ghetto," *Harvard Business Review,* May–June 1969, p. 83.

MALKIEL, B. G., and R. E. QUANDT, "Moral Issues in Investment Policy," *Harvard Business Review,* March–April 1971, pp. 37–47.

MANCKE, RICHARD B., "An Alternative Approach to Auto Emission Control," *California Management Review,* 14, No. 4 (Summer 1972), 82–86.

MANNE, HENRY G., "Corporate Responsibility, Business Motivation and Reality," *Annals of the American Academy of Political and Social Sciences,* 343 (September 1962), 55–64.

———, "The Myth of Corporate Responsibility—Or Will the Real Ralph

Nader Please Stand Up?" *Business Lawyer,* 26 (November 1970), 533–39.

MANNE, HENRY G., and HENRY C. WALLICH, *The Modern Corporation and Social Responsibility.* Washington, D.C.: American Enterprise Institute, 1972.

MASON, EDWARD, ed., *The Corporation in Modern Society.* Cambridge: Harvard University Press, 1959.

MASON, PHILIP. "The Revolt against Western Values," *Daedalus,* 96, No. 2 (Spring 1967), 328–52.

"Master's Defamation of His Servant," *Cleveland-Marshall Law Review,* 18 (May 1969), 332.

MAYER, CHARLES S., "Requiem for the Truth-in-Packaging Bill?" *Journal of Marketing,* 30 (April 1966), 1–5.

MAYER, LAWRANCE A. "A Large Question about Large Corporations," *Fortune,* May 1972, p. 185.

MEADOWS, DONELLA H., and JORGEN RANDERS, "The Carrying Capacity of the Globe," *Sloan Management Review,* 13, No. 2 (Winter 1972), 11–27.

MEYERSON, MARTIN, "The Ethos of the American College Student: Beyond the Protests," *Daedalus,* Summer 1966, pp. 713–39.

MILIBAND, RALPH, *The State in a Capitalist Society.* London: Weidenfeld and Nicolson, 1969.

MILLER, ARTHUR S., "Corporate Gigantism and 'Technological Imperatives,'" *Journal of Public Law,* 18 (1969), 256–310.

———, "Foreword: Public Interest Undefined," *Journal of Public Law,* 10 (1961), 184–202.

———, "Toward the 'Techno-corporate' State? An Essay in American Constitutionalism," *Villanova Law Review,* 14, No. 1 (Fall 1968), 1–73.

MILLER, IRWIN, "Business Has a War to Win," *Harvard Business Review,* March–April 1969, pp. 4–13.

MILLER, ROGER LEROY, "The Nader Files: An Economic Critique." A paper presented at the Conference on Government Policy and the Consumer, Center for Research in Government Policy and Business, October 27–28, 1972.

MINTZ, MORTON, and JERRY S. COHEN, *America, Inc.* New York: The Dial Press, 1971.

MITCHELL, ROBERT E., "Class-Linked Conflict between Two Dimensions of Liberalism-Conservatism," *Social Problems,* 13 (Spring 1966), 418–27.

"Model N.Y. Lobbying Statute," *Columbia Journal of Law and Social Problems,* 4 (March 1968), 69–86.

MOSKOWITZ, MILTON, "The Social Audit: Redemption through Mathematics," *Business and Society,* October 31, 1972.

MOSS, FRANK E., *Initiatives in Corporate Responsibility.* Washington, D.C.: Government Printing Office, 1973.

MOWRY, CHARLES E., *The Church and the New Generation.* Nashville: Abingdon Press, 1969.

MOYNIHAN, D. P., "Toward a National Urban Policy," *Public Interest,* Fall 1969, pp. 3–20.

MUELLER, WILLARD F., "The Rising Economic Concentration in America: Reciprocity, Conglomeration, and the New American 'Zaibatsu' System," *Antitrust and Economics Review,* Spring 1971, pp. 15–50.

MURDOCH, WILLIAM, and JOSEPH CONNELL, "All about Ecology," *Center Magazine,* 3 (January–February 1970), 56–63.

MYERS, JOHN G., "Social Issues in Advertising." Working Paper #65, Institute for Business and Economic Research, University of California at Berkeley, October 1970.

NADER, RALPH, ed., *The Consumer and Corporate Accountability.* New York: Harcourt Brace Jovanovich, 1973.

NADER, RALPH, and MARK J. GREEN, eds., *Corporate Powers in America.* New York: Grossman Publishers, 1973.

NADER, RALPH, and DONALD ROSS, *Action for a Change: A Student's Manual for Public Interest Organizing.* New York: Grossman Publishers, 1971.

NADLER, LEONARD, "Helping the Hard-Core Adjust to the World of Work," *Harvard Business Review,* March–April 1970, pp. 117–26.

NARVER, JOHN C., "Rational Management Responses to External Effects," *Academy of Management Journal,* March 1971, pp. 99–115.

National Industrial Conference Board, *Company Experiences with Negro Employment,* No. 201 (1966), 1–55.

NIEBUHR, R. H., *Christian Realism and Political Problems,* pp. 149–96. New York: Charles Scribner's Sons, 1953.

NIMMER, MELVILLE B., "Does Copyright Abridge the First Amendment Guarantees of Free Speech and Press?" *UCLA Law Review,* 17 (1970), 1180–204.

NISBET, ROBERT A., *The Quest for Community.* New York: Oxford University Press, 1953. Reproduced in Clarence Walton and

Richard Eells, eds., *The Business System* II, pp. 1149–54. New York: The Macmillan Company, 1967.

NOLL, ROGER C., "The Behavior of Regulatory Agencies," *Review of Social Economy,* March 1971, pp. 15–19.

NONET, PHILIPPE, *Administrative Justice: Advocacy and Change in a Government Agency.* New York: Russell Sage Foundation, 1969.

O'DEA, THOMAS F., "The Crisis of the Contemporary Religious Consciousness," *Daedalus,* 96, No. 1 (Winter 1967), 116–34.

ODEGARD, PETER H., "A Group Basis of Politics: A New Name for an Ancient Myth," *Western Political Quarterly,* 11 (September 1958), 689–702.

O'HANLON, THOMAS, "The Case against the Unions," *Fortune,* January 1968, pp. 170–73.

OLECK, HOWARD L., "Non-profit Organizations: Impact on U.S. Society," *Cleveland State Law Review,* 19 (May 1970), 207–38.

OLSEN, MARVIN E., "Perceived Legitimacy of Social Protest Actions," *Social Problems,* 15 (Winter 1968), 297–309.

PALMERI, RICHARD A., "Business and the Black Revolt," *California Management Review,* 11, No. 4 (Summer 1969), 31–36.

PARENTI, MICHAEL, "Ethnic Politics and the Persistence of Ethnic Identification," *American Political Science Review,* 61 (September 1967), 717–26.

PARK, JOHN NELSON, "Freedom, Value and the Law: Three Paradoxes," *Ethics,* October 1951, pp. 41–47.

PARSONS, J. E., "Locke's Doctrine of Property," *Social Research,* 36, No. 3 (Autumn 1969), 389–411.

PASCAL, ANTHONY H., "Black Gold and Black Capitalism," *Public Interest,* Spring 1970, 111–19.

PATTERSON, JAMES M., "Corporate Behavior and Balance of Power," *Business Horizons,* 12, No. 3 (June 1969), 39–52.

PECKHAM, JAMES O., "The Consumer Speaks," *Journal of Marketing,* 27 (October 1963), 21–26.

PELES, Y., "Economics of Scale in Advertising Beer and Cigarettes," *Journal of Business,* January 1971, 32–37.

PERLOFF, HARVEY S., ed., *The Quality of the Urban Environment.* Baltimore: Johns Hopkins Press, 1969.

PETERS, CHARLES, and TAYLOR BRANCH, *Blowing the Whistle: Dissent in the Public Interest.* New York: Frederick A. Praeger, Inc., 1972.

PETERS, LYNN H., "The Paradoxical Fate of Business Ideology," *Business and Society,* 7 (Spring 1967), 33–40.

PETERSON, RICHARD E., "The Student Left in American Higher Education," *Daedalus,* Winter 1968, 293–317.

PETERSON, SHOREY, "Corporate Control and Capitalism," *Quarterly Journal of Economics,* February 1965, pp. 1–24.

———, "Corporate Control and Capitalism: Reply," *Quarterly Journal of Economics,* August 1965, pp. 492–99.

PETERSON, WILLIAM J., "J. Irwin Miller: The Revolutionary Role of Business," *Saturday Review,* January 13, 1968, pp. 62–72.

PETTIGREW, THOMAS, *A Profile of the Negro American.* Princeton, N.J.: D. Van Nostrand Co., Inc., 1964.

———, "White-Negro Confrontations," in *The Negro Challenge to the Business Community,* ed. Eli Ginzberg, pp. 39–55. New York: McGraw-Hill Book Company, 1964.

POIRIER, RICHARD, "The War against the Young," *Atlantic,* October 1968, pp. 55–64.

"Political Activity and the Public Employee: A Sufficient Cause for Dismissal?" *Northwestern University Law Review,* November–December 1969, pp. 636–49.

"The Politics of Environmental Disruption," editorial, *Fortune,* January 1971, p. 69.

"Poor and the Political Process: Equal Access to Lobbying," *Harvard Journal of Legislation,* 6 (March 1969), 369–92.

POSNER, RICHARD A., "National Monopoly and Its Regulation," *Stanford Law Review,* 21 (February 1969), 548–643.

POTTER, FRANK M., JR., "Everyone Wants to Save the Environment but No One Knows Quite What to Do," *Center Magazine,* March–April 1970, 34–40.

———, "Pollution and the Public," *Center Magazine,* May–June 1970, pp. 18–24.

President's Advisory Council on Executive Organization, A New Regulatory Framework: Report on Selected Independent Regulatory Agencies, January 1971.

"Professional Associations and the Right to Free Expression: Constitutional Limitations on Control of Members," *Firestone* v. *District Dental Society* (New York 1969), *Georgetown Law Journal,* 58 (1970), 646–56.

"Protest in the Sixties," *Annals of the American Academy of Political and Social Sciences,* 382 (March 1969). Entire issue.

PROXMIRE, WILLIAM, *Report from the Wasteland: America's Military-Industrial Complex.* New York: Frederick A. Praeger, Inc., 1970.

"Public Disclosure of Lobbyists' Activities," *Fordham Law Review,* 38 (March 1970), 524.

PURCELL, THEODORE V., "Break Down Your Employment Barriers," *Harvard Business Review,* July–August 1968, pp. 65–76.

————, "The Case of the Borderline Black," *Harvard Business Review,* November–December 1971, pp. 128–33, 142–50.

PURCELL, THEODORE V., and GERALD F. CAVANAGH, *Blacks in the Industrial World.* New York: The Free Press, 1972.

PURCELL, THEODORE V., and ROSALIND WEBSTER, "Window on the Hard-Core World," *Harvard Business Review,* July–August 1969, pp. 118–29.

RAHNER, KARL, ed., "Christians in the Modern World," in *Mission and Grace,* Part I. London: Sheed & Ward, Stag Books, 1963.

RAND, AYN, *The Virtue of Selfishness: A New Concept of Egoism.* New York: New American Library, 1964.

RATNER, D. L., "The Government of Business Corporations: Critical Reflections on the Rule of 'One Share, One Vote,' " *Cornell Law Review,* 56, No. 1 (November 1970).

RAYMOND, JACK, "Growing Threat of Our Military-Industrial Complex," *Harvard Business Review,* May–June 1968, pp. 53–64.

REAGAN, MICHAEL D., *The Managed Economy.* New York: Oxford University Press, Inc., 1967.

REDDING, SAUNDERS, "The Methods," in *The Negro in America,* ed. John Hope Franklin and Isidore Starr, pp. 113–16. New York: Vintage Books, 1967.

REICH, CHARLES A., "Individual Rights and Social Welfare: The Emerging Social Issues," *Yale Law Journal,* 74 (June 1965), 1245–57.

————, "The Law of the Planned Society," *Yale Law Journal,* 75 (July 1966), 1227–70.

————, "The New Property," *Yale Law Journal,* 73 (April 1964), 733–87.

————, "Social Welfare in the Public-Private State," *Pennsylvania Law Review,* 114 (February 1966), 487–93.

"Restraint of Individual Liberty in Contracts of Employment," *McGill Law Journal,* 13 (1967), 521.

REUSCHLING, THOMAS L., "The Business Institution—A Redefinition of Social Role," *Business and Society,* 9, No. 1 (Autumn 1968), 28–32.

RICHARDSON, M. E., "Lobbying and Public Relations—Sensitive, Suspect or Worse?" *Antitrust Bulletin,* 10 (July–August 1965), 507–18.

RICHMAN, BARRY, "New Paths to Corporate Social Responsibility," *California Management Review,* 15, No. 3 (Spring 1973), 20–36.

RIDGEWAY, JAMES, *The Last Play.* New York: E. P. Dutton & Co., Inc., 1973.

RITCHIE-CALDER, LORD, "Polluting the Environment," *Center Magazine,* May 1969, pp. 7–12.

RITTER, LAWRENCE S., "A Capital Market Plan for the Urban Areas," *California Management Review,* 11, No. 4 (Summer 1969), 37–46.

ROCKEFELLER, JOHN D., 3D., *The Second American Revolution: Some Personal Observations.* New York: Harper & Row, Publishers, 1973.

ROCKEFELLER, RODMAN C., "Turn Public Problems to Private Account," *Harvard Business Review,* January–February 1971, pp. 131–38.

ROSE, ARNOLD M., "The Negro Protest," *Annals of the American Academy of Political and Social Sciences,* 357 (January 1965), 1–126.

ROSE, G., "Do the Requirements of Due Process Protect the Rights of Employees under Arbitration Procedures?" *Labor Law Journal,* 16 (January 1965), 44–58.

ROSZAK, THEODORE, *The Making of a Counter Culture: Reflections on the Technocratic Society and Its Youthful Opposition.* Garden City, N.Y.: Doubleday & Company, Inc., 1969.

RUFF, LARRY E., "The Economic Common Sense of Pollution," *Public Interest,* n.d., pp. 69–85.

RUML, B., "Corporate Management as a Locus of Power in Social Meaning of Legal Concepts No. 3: The Powers and Duties of Corporate Management," *Kent Law Review,* 29, No. 3 (June 1951), 228–46.

RUSSETT, BRUCE M., "Who Pays for Defense?" *American Political Science Review,* 63 (June 1969), 412–26.

SAMPSON, ANTHONY, *The Sovereign State of ITT.* New York: Stein & Day, 1973.

SAYLES, LEONARD R., *Individualism and Big Business.* New York: McGraw-Hill Book Company, 1963.

SCANLON, JOHN J., "How Much Should a Corporation Earn?" *Harvard Business Review,* January–February 1967, pp. 4–20, 186–88.

SCHEIBLA, SHIRLEY, "Fairness by Fiat: Some Employees These Days Are More Equal Than Others," *Barron's,* January 20, 1969, pp. 5–27.

———, "Gentleman's Agreement? Government Is Making Business Its

Unwilling Partner in Bias," *Barron's,* December 23, 1968, pp. 9–17.

SCHELLING, THOMAS C., "On the Ecology of Micromotives," *Public Interest,* Fall 1971, pp. 59–98.

SCHLUSBERG, MALCOLM D., "Corporate Legitimacy and Social Responsibility: The Role of Law," *California Management Review,* 12, No. 1 (Fall 1969), 65–76.

SCHRAG, PHILIP C., *Counsel for the Deceived.* New York: Pantheon Books, Inc., 1972.

SCHULZE, ROBERT J., "The Role of Economic Dominants in Community Power Structure," *American Sociological Review,* 23 (February 1958), 3–9.

SCHWARTZ, DONALD E., "Towards New Corporate Goals: Co-Existence with Society," *Georgetown Law Journal,* 60, No. 1 (October 1971), 57–109.

SCHWARTZ, LOUIS B., "Institutional Size and Individual Liberty: Authoritarian Aspects of Business," *Northwestern University Law Review,* March–April 1960, pp. 4–20.

SCOTT, ROBERT A., "Seeking Clients for Welfare Agencies," *Social Problems,* 14, No. 3 (Winter 1967), 248–57.

SELEKMAN, SYLVIA K., and BENJAMIN M. SELEKMAN, *Power and Morality in a Business Society.* New York: McGraw-Hill Book Company, 1956.

SELZNICK, PHILIP, "Institutional Vulnerability in Mass Society," *American Journal of Sociology,* January 1951, pp. 320–31.

Senate Committe on Judiciary, Subcommittee on Antitrust and Monopoly, *Economic Concentration,* Part 8A, Appendix to Staff Report of the Federal Trade Commission's *Economic Report on Corporate Mergers,* Part 8, 91st Cong., 1st sess. Washington, D.C.: Government Printing Office, 1969.

SETHI, S. PRAKASH, *Business Corporations and the Black Man.* Scranton, Pa.: Chandler, 1970.

———, "The Corporation and the Church: Institutional Conflict and Social Responsibility," *California Management Review,* 15, No. 1 (Fall 1972), 63–74.

———, "Getting a Handle on the Social Audit," *Business and Society Review/Innovation,* No. 4 (Winter 1972–73), 31–38.

———, ed., *The Unstable Ground: Corporate Social Policy in a Dynamic Society.* Los Angeles: Melville Publishers, Inc., 1974.

SHERMAN, HOWARD, and E. K. HUNT, "Pollution in Radical Perspective," *Business and Society Review,* Autumn 1972, pp. 48–53.

SHONFIELD, ANDREW, "Business in the Twenty-First Century," *Daedalus,* 98, No. 1 (Winter 1969), 191–207.

SIGAL, B. C., "Freedom of Speech and Union Discipline: The 'Right' of Defamation and Disloyalty," *New York University Conference on Labor,* 17 (1969), 367.

SILK, LEONARD S., "Business Power Today and Tomorrow," *Daedalus,* Winter 1969, pp. 174–90.

SILVERMAN, CHARLES E., *Crisis in Black and White.* New York: Random House, Inc., 1964.

SIMON, HERBERT A., "Technology and the Environment," *Management Science,* June 1973, pp. 1110–21.

SIMON, JOHN G., CHARLES W. POWERS, and JON P. GUNNEMAN, *The Ethical Investor.* New Haven: Yale University Press, 1972.

SLEEPER, C. FREEMAN, *Black Power and Christian Responsibility.* Nashville: Abingdon Press, 1969.

"Society and Its Physical Environment," *Annals of the American Political and Social Sciences,* 389 (May 1970). Entire issue.

SPENCER, HOLLISTER, "The Dangers of Social Responsibility—Another Perspective," *The Conference Board Record,* November 1972, pp. 54–57.

SPITZ, DAVID, ed., *Political Theory and Social Change.* New York: Atherton Press, 1967.

SPITZER, HUGH, "Business and Students," *California Management Review,* 13, No. 2 (Winter 1970), 83–88.

SPRATLEN, THADDEUS H., "A Black Perspective on 'Black Business Development,' " *Journal of Marketing,* 34 (October 1970), 72–73.

STEINER, GEORGE A., "Social Policies for Business," *California Management Review,* 15, No. 2 (Winter 1972), 17–24.

STERN, LOUIS L., "Consumer Protection via Increased Information," *Journal of Marketing,* 31 (April 1967), 48–52.

STERN, PHILIP M., *The Rape of the Tax Payer.* New York: Random House, Inc., 1973.

STERNLIEB, GEORGE, "Is Business Abandoning the Big City?" *Harvard Business Review,* January–February 1961, pp. 6–12, 152–64.

STOCKFISH, J. A., and EDWARDS, D. J., "The Blending of Public and Private Enterprise—The SST as a Case in Point," *Public Interest,* n.d., pp. 108–17.

"Student Power in the Universities," *American Journal of Comparative Law*, 17, No. 3 (1969).

STURDIVANT, FREDERICK D., "Better Deal for Ghetto Shoppers," *Harvard Business Review*, March–April 1968, pp. 130–39.

———, "The Limits of Black Capitalism," *Harvard Business Review*, January–February 1969, pp. 122–28.

SULLIVAN, D. P., "Court Arbitration of Public Employee Labor Relations Disputes," *New Hampshire Bar Journal* 10, No. 2 (Winter 1968), 84–93.

SUNDQUIST, JAMES L., "Jobs, Training, and Welfare for the Underclass," in *Agenda for the Nation*, ed. Gordon Kermit, pp. 49–76. Washington, D.C.: Brookings Institution, 1968.

"Symposium: Student Rights and Campus Rules," *California Law Review*, 54 (March 1966), 1–178.

TANNENBAUM, FRANK, *The Balance of Power in Society and Other Essays*. New York: The Macmillan Company, 1969.

———, "Institutional Rivalry in Society," *Political Science Quarterly*, 61 (December 1946), 481–504.

TAVISS, IRENE, "The Technological Society: Some Challenges for Social Science," *Social Research*, 35, No. 3 (Autumn 1968), 521–39.

TAYLOR, JOHN F. A., "Is the Corporation Above the Law?" *Harvard Business Review*, March–April 1965, pp. 119–30.

THEIBOLD, ROBERT, ed., *Social Policies for America in the Seventies*. New York: Doubleday & Company, Inc., 1967.

THUROW, LESTER C., "The Causes of Poverty," *Quarterly Journal of Economics*, 81 (February 1967), 39–57.

TOBIN, JAMES, "On Improving the Economic Status of the Negro," *Daedalus*, Fall 1965, pp. 878–98.

TRAINOR, JAMES L., "Government Use of Nonprofit Companies," *Harvard Business Review*, May–June 1966, pp. 38–56.

TROBINER, MATTHEW O., and JOSEPH R. GRODIN, "The Individual and the Public Service Enterprise in the New Industrial State," *California Law Review*, 55 (November 1967), 1247–83.

TUGWELL, REXFORD G., "Galbraith Discovers the Corporation," *Center Magazine*, October–November 1967, pp. 44–47.

TURNER, JAMES C., *The Chemical Feast, The Nader Report*. New York: Grossman Publishers, 1970.

TURNER, RALPH H., "The Public Perception of Protest," *American Sociological Review*, 34 (December 1969), 815–30.

U.S., Departments of Labor and Commerce, *The Social and Economic Status of Negroes in the United States, 1969,* BLS Report No. 375, Current Population Reports, Series P-23, No. 29.

VANDERWICKEN, PETER, "G.M.: The Price of Being 'Responsible,'" *Fortune,* January 1972, p. 99.

VON HOFFMAN, NICHOLAS, *We Are the People Our Parents Warned Us Against.* Chicago: Quadrangle Books, 1968.

VOTAW, DOW, "Genius Becomes Rare: A Comment on the Doctrine of Social Responsibility," Part I, *California Management Review,* 15, No. 2 (Winter 1972), 25–32.

———, "Genius Becomes Rare: A Comment on the Doctrine of Social Responsibility," Part II, *California Management Review,* 15, No. 3 (Spring 1973), 5–19.

———, *Modern Corporations.* Englewood Cliffs, N.J.: Prentice-Hall, Inc., 1965.

———, "What Do We Believe about Power?" *California Management Review,* 9, No. 4 (Summer 1966), 71–88.

VOTAW, DOW, and S. PRAKASH SETHI, *The Corporate Dilemma: Traditional Values versus Contemporary Problems.* Englewood Cliffs, N.J.: Prentice-Hall, Inc., 1973.

———, "Do We Need a New Corporate Response to a Changing Social Environment?" Parts I and II, *California Management Review,* 12, No. 1 (Fall 1969), 3–32.

WAGNER, SUSAN, *Cigarette Country.* New York: Frederick A. Praeger, Inc., 1972.

WALTERS, KENNETH DALE, "Freedom of Speech in Modern Corporations." Doctoral Dissertation, University of California, Berkeley, 1972.

WALTON, CLARENCE C., *Corporate Social Responsibilities.* Belmont, Calif.: Wadsworth, 1967.

———, *Ethos and the Executive.* Englewood Cliffs, N.J.: Prentice-Hall, Inc., 1969.

———, ed., *Business and Social Progress.* New York: Frederick A. Praeger, Inc., 1970.

WAYS, MAX, "Business Needs to Do a Better Job of Explaining," *Fortune,* September 1972, p. 85.

———, "'Creative Federalism' and the Great Society," *Fortune,* January 1966, pp. 121–24.

———, "Don't We Know Enough to Make Better Public Policies," *Fortune,* April 1971, p. 64.

————, "How to Think about the Environment," *Fortune,* February 1970, pp. 98–101.

WEINWURM, G., "The Creative Challenge of Individualism," *California Management,* Winter 1970, pp. 83–88.

WEISS, NANCY J., "The Negro and the New Freedom: Fighting Wilsonian Segregation," *Political Science Quarterly,* 84 (March 1969), 61–79.

WESTIN, ALAN, *Privacy and Freedom.* New York: Atheneum Publishers, 1967.

"What Business Can Do for the Cities," editorial, *Fortune,* January 1968, pp. 127–28.

WHEELER, JOHN H., "Civil Rights Groups—Their Impact upon the War on Poverty," *Law and Contemporary Problems,* 31, No. 1 (Winter 1966), 152–58.

WHITE HOUSE CONFERENCE ON THE INDUSTRIAL WORLD AHEAD, *A Look at Business in 1990.* Washington, D.C.: Government Printing Office, 1972.

"Who Runs the University?" *Saturday Review,* January 10, 1970, pp. 53–58.

WILKINSON, JOHN, "The Quantitative Society," *Center Magazine,* July 1969, pp. 64–71.

WILSON, JAMES Q., "The Dead Hand of Regulation," *Public Interest,* Fall 1971, pp. 39–58.

WRIGHT, J. S., "Defamation, Privacy, and the Public's Right to Know: A National Problem and a New Approach," *Texas Law Review,* 46 (April 1968), 630–49.

YOUNG, WHITNEY M., *To Be Equal.* New York: McGraw-Hill Book Company, 1964.

ZEIGLER, HARMON, *Interest Groups in American Society.* Englewood Cliffs, N.J.: Prentice-Hall, Inc., 1964.